The Handbook of Psychological Testing

The Handbook of Psychological Testing provides a comprehensive and modern guide to all aspects of psychological testing. It covers psychometric theory and its application in the construction of tests, applied psychometrics in the educational, vocational, occupational and clinical fields, and an evaluative list of the best psychological tests.

The theoretical section includes detailed accounts of classical test theory, including factor analysis and item characteristic curve theories. The descriptions of the different types of tests reveal their strengths and weaknesses for test users, and their applications in the various practical fields of psychology are fully discussed. Finally there is a description and evaluation of the best tests so far produced. Appendices of formulae and definitions of technical terms are included to aid understanding of the text.

Handling the sometimes complex mathematics with great clarity, *The Handbook of Psychological Testing* combines academic precision with practical and comprehensible application. The only clear, modern account of psychometrics to be found in one volume, it will be required reading for all psychologists and students of psychology who are concerned with testing in any form.

Paul Kline is Professor of Psychometrics at the University of Exeter, and has worked extensively as a consultant in test construction.

Also available from ROUTLEDGE

Intelligence
The Psychometric View
Paul Kline

Handbook of Test Construction
Introduction to Psychometric Design
Paul Kline

Fact and Fantasy in Freudian Theory
Second Edition
Paul Kline

Psychology and Freudian Theory
Introduction
Paul Kline

Modern Psychometrics
The Science of Psychological Assessment
John Rust and Susan Golombok

The Handbook of
Psychological Testing

Paul Kline

London and New York

First published 1993
by Routledge
11 New Fetter Lane, London EC4P 4EE

Simultaneously published in the USA and Canada
by Routledge
29 West 35th Street, New York, NY 10001

Reprinted 1994, 1995, 1998

© 1993 Paul Kline

Typeset in Garamond by
LaserScript Limited, Mitcham, Surrey
Printed and bound in Great Britain by
Mackays of Chatham PLC, Chatham, Kent

British Library Cataloguing in Publication Data
A catalogue record for this book is available from the British Library

Library of Congress Cataloguing in Publication Data
A catalogue record for this book is available from the Library of Congress

ISBN 0-415-05480-X (hbk)   ISBN 0-415-05481-8 (pbk)

Contents

Section IV Psychological Tests: Lists, Descriptions and Evaluations

Appendices

 2 Glossary   575

    References   581
    Name index   608
    Subject index   615

Figures and Tables

FIGURES

TABLES

Introduction

In *The Handbook of Psychological Testing* I aim to provide a book that will be useful for anyone who has to deal with psychological tests: professional psychologists in the applied fields of occupational, educational or clinical psychology; research psychologists who need to measure with as much precision as modern psychometric methods allow; psychometrists who are developing new tests and methods; and students in all these aspects of psychology. In addition there are many professionals – social workers, doctors and nurses, just for example – for whom a knowledge of testing, both its weaknesses and strengths, can be useful and this book could be valuable for these purposes as well as for more specialised users.

The handbook is a comprehensive account of modern psychometric theory and practice although every effort has been made to avoid jargon and to explain as clearly as possible all statistical methods and procedures. The first section is devoted to psychometric theory and methods. This is included because a proper understanding of the theoretical and statistical basis of psychometrics is vital for evaluating tests to be used in the applied setting. It also answers many of the naive objections to psychological tests as well as making psychologists aware of the genuine problems in their use.

In this first section can be found chapters on reliability, validity, the classical model of test variance, standardisation and norms, Rasch, Guttman, Thurstone and Likert scaling, computerised testing, tailored testing and item banking. Then come discussions of special psychometric methods in which I include discussions of factor analysis, factor analytic and item analytic test construction, criterion-keyed test construction, and finally other methods of constructing tests.

The second section is concerned with the different types of psychological tests. The rationale and the items of these tests are described and discussed. Intelligence tests, ability tests, tests of motor skills, aptitude tests, personality questionnaires, projective and objective personality tests, motivation and interest tests, mood and state scales and other special types of test are scrutinised.

The third section is concerned with the use and interpretation of tests. I should like to point out in connection with this part of the book that although most of my research has been concerned with theoretical aspects of psychometrics, as a former schoolteacher I have always retained an interest in the real-life application of tests. Furthermore I have been concerned with the development of a battery of tests for use in occupational psychology. In this section I discuss the practical and ethical problems in using tests in educational psychology, clinical psychology, counselling and guidance, and occupational psychology.

In the final section of the handbook I list what I consider to be the best tests in the various categories which were discussed in Section II. These tests are described and subjected to a critical review of their reliability, validity and standardisation. Their suitability for various applications is also indicated. This section of the handbook will be ideal for practitioners who need a test for any particular purpose.

From this description it is clear that the handbook contains chapters on every aspect of psychological testing, both theoretical and applied. It is my hope that this book will improve the quality of psychological testing which in many cases falls far short not only of what is desirable but what is currently attainable.

Section I

PsychometricTheory and Method

Chapter 1

Reliability of Tests
Practical Issues

Reliability, as it is applied to tests, has two distinct meanings. One refers to stability over time, the second to internal consistency. The reliability of a test over time is known as *test-retest reliability*. This test-retest reliability (r_{tt}) must now be discussed.

TEST-RETEST RELIABILTY

Measurement of test-retest reliability

This is measured by correlating the scores from a set of subjects who take the test on two occasions. The correlation coefficient measures the degree of agreement between two sets of scores. The more similar they are the higher the correlation coefficient, which runs from + 1 to − 1. A correlation of + 1 indicates perfect agreement, while − 1 shows complete disagreement, i.e. the top person on the one test would be the bottom on the other, the whole order being thus inverted. Both these eventualities are extremely rare. A correlation of 0 indicates that there is absolutely no relationship between the two sets of scores. Naturally most correlations fall between these points and squaring the correlation coefficient indicates the extent of the agreement between the sets of scores. For example a correlation of .7 shows an agreement between the sets of scores of 49 per cent.

From this it is clear that the closer to 1 the test-retest reliability of a test is, the better the test. If we had to weigh a set of objects on two occasions we would be disappointed in our scales if there was not a virtually perfect agreement between the resulting two lists of weights. Indeed if the test-retest reliability were not 1 we would regard the scales as worthless or else suspect that there was human error in recording the results.

This example though simple is instructive. Firstly we make the quite reasonable assumption that, between the weightings, the weight of these objects has not changed. Secondly we assume that there is no problem in using the scales, that the results can be accurately recorded. In the case of many psychological tests from the nature both of the test itself and the variable being measured, neither of these assumptions is necessarily true and this may disturb our measurement of test-retest reliability.

Factors influencing the measurement of test-retest reliability

In fact the test-retest reliability of most psychological tests is less than one, often far less, and the reasons for this must be examined.

1. Changes in subjects

If we were to give an intelligence test to a group of subjects and, immediately they had finished it, we were to ask them to do it again we would, undoubtedly, obtain a very high test-retest reliability, provided that the subjects were not too bored or fatigued. However this would be false in that most subjects would remember their answers and so the reliability would appear to be extremely high.

To avoid this difficulty it is normal to leave at least a three-month gap between the two testing sessions. However, if children had been tested it is quite possible that within the three-month gap before retesting there would be real changes and since children develop at different rates the correlation between the sets of scores would fall well below unity and the test-retest reliability of the test would appear to be low. Note the word appear. This word reflects the fact that the changes in scores which contribute to lowered reliability are assumed to be errors of measurement, not real changes in the variables. An example will clarify this point. If we were to attempt to measure a transient state or mood, such as anger or fear, test-retest reliability, as measured by the correlation, would be bound to be low. This is because real changes would be present on the two occasions. Thus to measure the test-retest reliability of a test of a transient variable such as this we would have to attempt to arouse fear or anger on both occasions.

From this it is clear that although we want the test-retest reliability of a test to be as high as possible since if scores are different on two occasions there is no reason to trust either of them, in practice the reliability of a test may be lower than 1 because real changes may have occurred. Thus in assessing the reliability of a test we have to take account of the sample from which it was obtained and the nature of the variable itself.

2. Factors contributing to measurement error

We must now discuss those factors which contribute to poor test-retest reliability and thus measurement error. Some are obvious and require little discussion. Some subjects will not feel at their best when they are tested and this will reduce their performance. Typical reasons for this are physical ailments such as colds or headache; domestic or emotional problems obviously also affect scores. Simple fatigue from a late night . . . the list is endless. Other factors of a similar nature can also reduce scores – an uncomfortable seat, a poor pencil or biro, the accident of turning over two pages at once. All these are capable of lowering the test-retest reliability of any test. It will be realised that such factors are an integral part of life, of being human, and that is why the reliability of even the best test is never unity.

So far the factors which we have discussed relate to the subjects rather than the tests themselves. However there are certain characteristics of the tests which can lead to poor test-retest reliability. In an ideal world these would be eliminated during test construction, as will be described fully in our later chapters. Nevertheless in some tests it is not possible to remove entirely these sources of error and these must be mentioned.

a. Poor test instructions. One common source of error is poor test instructions so that the subjects do not grasp easily what they are supposed to do. This can result is subjects doing markedly better on one occasion than the other. Another similar source of error occurs when the test demands a complicated form of response from the subject. For example if a subject has to tick off either a or b on a response sheet there is little room for error. However sometimes test responses are so complex that this is the source of the difficulty.

b. Subjective scoring. Another source of error can be found in subjective scoring which allows differences to arise between scorers, either different scorers or the same scorer on different occasions. Obviously this is deleterious to high reliability and most psychological tests use objectively scored items for this reason.

c. Guessing. Guessing is another source of unreliability. Clearly it mainly affects ability tests. However if multiple-choice items are used, and there is a large number of items, the effects are small.

3. Factors boosting or otherwise distorting test-retest reliability

As has been discussed, test-retest reliability is measured by the correlation coefficient. This correlation may be boosted by various factors so that it does not represent true test-retest reliability in the sense of stable error-free measurement.

a. Time gap. One source of such distortion has been mentioned. This is to leave a very small lapse of time between the two testings. In this case the correlation is boosted because subjects remember some of their responses. At least a three-month period is recommended for a reliable estimate of test-retest reliability.

b. Difficulty level of items. Another source of distortion is particularly important in tests of ability, where items have a difficulty level. If items are much too easy for the subjects then this leads to very high test-retest reliability, because they will always get them right. An example of such an item which would be unaffected by most of the factors which we have discussed as causing unreliability would be: 2+2 =?. Very difficult items have the same effect on test-retest reliability, since they will always be impossible for subjects.

c. Subjects: sampling. Another source of distortion of the correlation coefficient arises from the samples from whom it was obtained. A few examples will clarify this point. If we have a test that is designed for clinical groups then it is essential that the test-retest reliability coefficient be obtained from these groups. Thus schizophrenics are notoriously difficult to test. With such a sample it is inevitable that reliability would be low. The clinical psychologist must be aware of this problem in interpreting test results from such subjects, as is fully discussed in our chapter on the use and interpretation of psychological tests in the clinical setting. Thus a reliability coefficient derived from a normal sample for a test designed for use with abnormal samples would be misleading.

d. Sample size. Correlations, along with most other statistical indices, have standard errors, indicating how trustworthy the results are. The formula and the explanation of this standard error can be found in the statistical glossary at the end of this handbook. However, it can be said that the larger the number of subjects the smaller the standard error of the statistic. Now this means that it is essential that the test-retest reliability coefficients are derived from a sample sufficiently large to minimise this statistical error. In practice this means that the samples should contain at least 100 subjects.

At this stage in our discussion a more general point needs to be made about sampling, because this affects many methods and results in psychometrics. A distinction needs to be drawn between populations and samples. If we are interested in the differential intelligence (if any) of boys and girls aged 12, then two populations are involved: boys, aged 12, and girls, aged 12. Clearly it would be impossible to measure these populations in their entirety and thus samples have to be chosen.

Now, as I have indicated, with reference to the standard error of the reliability coefficient, samples must be sufficiently large to minimise standard errors. However size alone is not enough to ensure that a sample is good. Size simply minimises the standard error. However if the sample is not representative of the population any statistics derived from it will be distorted. To take our example of intelligence again, if I obtained my sample of boys from Manchester Grammar School, which selects its pupils by intelligence, then however small the standard error of the statistics, the sample would be totally unrepresentative of boys of that age and thus would be useless. Thus samples must be large and representative of their populations. How good samples are drawn is discussed in a later chapter of this handbook.

4. Conclusions concerning test-retest reliability

Test-retest reliability, if a test is to be of any value, either in practice or in establishing theory, must be high. A correlation of .8 is a minimum figure. To be trustworthy the two testings should be separated by at least a three-month gap and the subjects should be a large and representative sample of the population for whom the test is intended. Samples should comprise at least 100 subjects.

INTERNAL CONSISTENCY RELIABILITY

We must now discuss the second meaning of reliability – internal consistency. Most psychometric test constructors aim to make their psychological tests as internally consistent as possible. There is a sensible rationale for this demand for internal consistency since if one part of a test is measuring one variable, then the other parts, if internal consistency is low, cannot be measuring that variable. Thus if a test is to be valid, i.e. measure what it is intended to measure, then internal consistency must be high. This is the argument used by the vast majority of test constructors (e.g. Guilford, 1956; Nunnally, 1978) who write that high internal consistency is a prerequisite of high validity. This is further supported by classical psychometric theory, which is fully discussed in Chapter 3 of this handbook, and many test constructors use increasing internal consistency as a criterion for retaining items in a test, as will also be fully described in the requisite chapter of the handbook.

There is only one significant dissenting voice to these apparently power-ful arguments that internal consistency must be high. Cattell (e.g. Cattell and Kline, 1977), who is one of the great figures in psychometrics, has always argued that very high internal consistency is actually antithetical to validity. Most tests measure variables of some breadth, for example extraversion, anxiety or intelligence. Any one item in any of these tests must be narrower or more specific than these variables. Thus, if all items are highly consistent they must be highly correlated and the test will be necessarily narrow and specific and thus not valid. There is considerable force in this argument. There are, without doubt, many tests whose items are little more than paraphrases of each other. Not surprisingly these tests have high internal consistency but they are highly specific (Cattell, 1973, calls them bloated specifics) and of low validity. However we must not fall into the logical error of assuming that, because in some instances high reliability precludes validity, this is so in all cases. Not all reliable tests are bloated specifics.

Cattell's claims are supported on a number of grounds. First, as we shall show below, indices of internal consistency reliability do increase as the correlations among the items increase. Furthermore in any multivariate study where we want to maximise the correlation or prediction of a criterion from a set of tests, this is best done when the correlation between the tests is zero. A moment's reflection will show why this must be so. Suppose we had two tests that were perfectly correlated. It would be pointless to use both of these because the second of them would add no new information. Clearly, then, maximum prediction must occur when the correlations between the tests are zero. Now a test can be seen as a set of items with which we intend to predict the criterion test score. This, similarly, is best done when each item correlates positively with the total score and zero with each of the other items. Such a test would have, inevitably, a low internal consistency.

It seems that Cattell is theoretically correct and his arguments are difficult to refute. Nevertheless, to my knowledge, no test constructor has been able to construct a test in which the items correlate with the criterion score but not with each other. Cattell has always argued that his own tests, particularly the 16PF personality test (Cattell *et al.*, 1970), followed these principles. Nevertheless a careful investigation of the test by Barrett and Kline (1982) showed that it was not entirely successful. There is little doubt that this test would be improved if its scales were more internally consistent.

In general, therefore, despite these caveats, it can be concluded that, as most psychometrists have argued, high internal consistency reliability is necessary, but not sufficient, for good tests.

Measurement of internal consistency reliability

As was the case with measurement of test-retest reliability all indices must be computed on samples of subjects which are representative of the population for whom the test is designed and of sufficient size to minimise statistical error. A minimum size sample would be 100 subjects.

The measurement of the internal consistency reliability cannot be properly understood without reference to the classical psychometric test theory (Nunnally, 1978) which is described in Chapter 3. Consequently we shall discuss its measurement in that chapter. Coefficient alpha (of which the formula may be found at the end of this chapter and in the Statistical Appendix) is the best index of internal consistency but we can briefly describe here a simple approximation to alpha which was used by test constructors before the age of rapid computation. This gives a good indication of the nature of internal consistency reliability. This is the split-half reliability.

Split-half reliability

Here a test is split in half and the two halves are correlated. It is possible to split the test using the first half of the test and the second half, or, more commonly, using the scores on the even and odd items. This is particularly important with a test of ability where items are often arranged in order of difficulty. Clearly where this is the case there might be a poor correlation between the first and second halves of the test.

There are a number of problems with the split-half reliability estimate which mean that it is only a rough approximation of the true reliability of the test.

1. Only one split is used. Clearly a set of items can be split in half in a number of ways. All these splits will give different estimates of test reliability and the odd-even and first and second-half splits are quite arbitrary choices, selected only for their convenience. This is an obvious defect with split-half reliability. However it has to be said that in my experience of actual test construction, split-half reliability and the alpha coefficient have differed only at the third decimal place, a discrepancy of no practical or theoretical interest.

2. Reliability is related to test length. The longer a test is the more reliable it is. This means that split-half reliability is always an underestimate of the true reliability. A correcting formula has been introduced to compensate for this, the Spearman-Brown formula, which may be found in the Statistical Appendix. A full discussion of the relation of test length to reliability may be found in Chapter 3. It is sufficient to note, at this point, that tests of fewer than ten items are unlikely to be highly reliable. This is certainly the minimum number of items for a reliable test.

Importance of internal consistency reliability

1. Test correlations are limited by reliability. A test cannot correlate with anything more highly than itself. Thus, the internal consistency reliability of a test limits its validity, since essentially the validity of a test is measured by its correlation with a criterion of some kind. Despite the dangers of boosting the reliability of a test by making the items highly similar to each other, in which case validity is reduced, reliabilities should ideally be high, around .9, especially for ability tests. Certainly alphas should never drop below .7, a value stressed by both Guilford (1956) and Nunnally (1978). The rationale and proof of these claims are bound up in psychometric theory and are given in Chapter 3.

2. Correction for low reliability. Since correlations between tests are limited by their reliabilities, it is possible to correct the correlation for this attenuation. The argument for so doing is that if we are investigating, for example, the correlation between reading ability and intelligence we want to know the true relationship rather than the obtained one limited

by the low reliability of the measures. Although this is so, such figures are estimates and cautious investigators may prefer to stay more closely with the data. The real answer to this problem is to develop highly reliable tests so that there is little point in applying the correction.

The rationale for this correction for attenuation due to unreliability is given in Chapter 3 and the formula may be found in the Statistical Appendix and at the end of this chapter.

3. Standard error of measurement. The standard error of measurement is used to establish confidence zones around a score obtained from a test. If we were to give a large number of tests of the same variable to a subject we would obtain a distribution of scores and the mean of this distribution would be the best estimate of her status on the variable. This standard error of measurement is the estimated standard deviation of scores if a person were to be given a large number of tests. The standard deviation, S.D. or sigma, is a measure of the variance of a set of scores, their deviation from their mean. The formula for the standard deviation may be found in the Statistical Appendix. In a normal distribution, 68 per cent of scores fall between the mean and one standard deviation, 95 per cent between the mean and two standard deviations. Thus the standard error of measurement allows us to set up confidence limits for an obtained score, 68 per cent of scores falling between the obtained score and one standard error. If this range is small we can be confident that the score is accurate. However, it should be noted that, as Nunnally (1978) points out, this use of the standard error of measurement, to set confidence zones, although widely used in practice, is not strictly correct theoretically, a matter which will be examined further in Chapter 3.

This standard error of measurement is derived from the reliability of the test. The higher the reliability the lower the standard error. Its statistical rationale is discussed in Chapter 3 and the formula may be found in the Statistical Appendix and at the end of this chapter. Obviously where decisions have to be made about individuals on the basis of their test scores then this standard error of measurement must be as low as possible. Hence the argument that reliability must be as high as possible.

Parallel-form reliability

It is often useful, especially in the applied setting, to have different versions of the same test. For example if we were monitoring psychotherapy, a test of anxiety or depression might be useful, given at regular intervals. To administer the same test repeatedly is obviously difficult and parallel forms are the solution to this problem. However to make comparisons of scores viable the correlations between the various forms should be high (as well as the means, standard deviations and distributions of scores). This correlation is the parallel-form reliability. When it falls below .9 it is difficult to assume comparability of scores. Few tests give parallel form reliabilities as high as this, although with the huge progress in computing, the construction of genuinely parallel forms is much easier than it was, as will be discussed in our chapters on test construction.

RELATION OF THE THREE KINDS OF RELIABILITY

From this discussion I hope that it is clear that although the three kinds of reliability are normally dealt with separately in fact they are closely related. Thus internal consistency reliability involves the relationship of the items in a test. These items are considered to be a random sample of a universe or domain of items. Thus parallel-form reliability is essentially similar but the items have been put into two rather than one test. Test-retest reliability is, like internal consistency, a correlation of the items within a test but, in this instance, of the items administered on two occasions. Here there is the added complication of sources of distortion, mentioned in the section on test-retest reliability, that occur between the tests. Nevertheless all these estimates of reliability should be similar, with the test-retest reliability being the lowest.

SUMMARY AND CONCLUSIONS

It has been shown that the internal consistency reliability of a test must be as high as possible, although high reliability can be achieved at the expense of validity. As was the case with test-retest reliability, the samples from which the reliability coefficients are derived must be representative of the populations for whom the test is designed and sufficiently large to be statistically reliable. A reliability of .7 is a minimum for a good test. This is simply because the standard error of measurement of a score increases as the reliability decreases, and thus tests of low reliability are useless for practical application, where decisions concerning individuals have to be made. Where repeated measurement is required high parallel form reliability is useful.

High reliability, both test-retest and internal consistency, is essential for the validity of tests. In Chapter 2 test validity will be discussed and in Chapter 3 the statistical basis of both reliability and validity will be set out.

FORMULAE

Coefficient Alpha

$$r_{kk} = k/k - 1 \,(1 - \Sigma\sigma^2_i/\sigma^2_t)$$

where r_{kk} = the alpha coefficient of a test of k items, k = the number of items, σ^2_i = the item variance and σ^2_t = the test variance.

Correction for attenuation due to unreliability

$$r \text{ (corrected)} = \frac{r_{12}}{\sqrt{r_{11}} \sqrt{r_{22}}}$$

where r_{12} is the obtained correlation between tests 1 and 2, r_{11} is the reliability of test 1 and r_{22} is the reliability of test 2.

Standard error of measurement

$$\sigma_{meas} = \sigma_x \sqrt{1 - r_{xx}}$$

where σ_x = the standard deviation of test x and r_{xx} = the reliability of the test.

Chapter 2

The Validity of Psychological Tests

In the previous chapter we showed that reliability, in both its senses, was essential if a test was to be valid, even though under special circumstances very high internal consistency reliability can lead to lowered validity. In this chapter the notion of validity will be scrutinised and described. First its meaning will be elucidated and its relationship to test reliability will be explicated. How validity is assessed will be discussed and its importance will be examined.

MEANING OF VALIDITY

A test is said to be valid if it measures what it claims to measure. This is not as banal as it might first appear since, as shall be seen throughout this book, many psychological tests are of surprisingly low validity. Indeed the construction of valid tests, procedures which are fully described in later chapters of this handbook, is not a simple matter.

The first point which needs to be discussed concerns measurement. How can we tell whether a test is valid or not? An example will illustrate some of the problems involved. Suppose that we have constructed a test of conscientiousness, a variable which has been shown to be highly important in understanding personality (Norman, 1963). It is not obvious how such a test might be shown to be valid. What would make the task easier would be some independent measure of conscientiousness, but if this itself were easy to obtain, a test would hardly be required. However it is not meaningless to speak of people as more or less conscientious, and most of us make such judgements in everyday life so some form of assessment of this variable is possible. Ratings of conscientiousness by people who know subjects well is one solution to solving the problem: we could correlate test scores and ratings. This however assumes that the ratings are valid, an assumption that cannnot usually be made.

This example has been cited simply to show that demonstrating a psychological test to be valid, i.e. measuring its validity, is not a straightforward procedure, unlike the case of reliability, where assessing the reliability of a test is essentially a technical matter.

There are various methods of showing whether a test is valid and their use will now be discussed. At this juncture it should be pointed out that, again unlike reliability, there is no one validity coefficient for a test. This is because, as Vernon (1960) argued, a test is always valid for some purpose and thus is more valid in some circumstances than in others. It should be noted that these different approaches to indicating or measuring the validity of tests are essentially different types of validity.

Face validity

A test is said to be face valid if it appears to be measuring what it claims to measure. In fact there is no logical relationship between face validity and real validity although in some conditions there may be a positive correlation between them, whereas in other circumstances, such as selection, face validity may be a real disadvantage (Cattell and Warburton, 1967).

The advantage which face validity bestows on a test is that it can increase the motivation of the subjects; and high motivation, where all subjects are trying to complete the tests as well and as accurately as possible, is essential for valid testing. For example, if we are trying to select pilots from highly trained personnel, face-valid tests of tracking ability or rapid reaction time will ensure full cooperation because subjects believe them to be valid indicators of flying skill. If, however, a test required them to make animal noises or add up numbers while distracted by jokes (genuine objective tests in the Compendium of such tests by Cattell and Warburton, 1967) many would refuse, thinking them to be absurd even if they were valid. In general most adults are loath to complete tests which seem to be ridiculous and time-wasting. Even if they are forced so to do, as in selection procedures, their attitude towards them is antithetical to high validity. The only exceptions to this are students and children. Children are used to having to do incomprehensible tasks and students, especially in America, are required to fill in tests and take part in other psychological experiments as part of their course work. These students are grimly inured to anything.

From all these arguments it might be thought that face validity is a highly desirable feature of tests, if they are to be valid. However, this is not so. This is simply because, by definition, subjects can guess what a face-valid test is measuring. Hence it is likely to induce faking or deliberate distortion, especially in selection. Now to what extent such distortion affects the test scores depends to a large extent upon what is being measured. In the field of abilities it makes little difference since the fact that one knows that an item is measuring intelligence does not affect one's ability to get it right. In the field of personality, however, this is by no means the case. For example a face-valid test of anxiety in civil pilot selection, where we will assume for the sake of the argument that pilots low on anxiety are required, would never work. What subject would admit to 'feeling anxious, if things get difficult', 'disliking working under pressure', 'going weak at the knees at the thought of danger' and so on, all these being typical anxiety test items?

In conclusion it can be said that face validity is not related to true validity and brings with it the disadvantage that it encourages deliberate distortion, especially in selection. In the case of ability tests this is unimportant but in other types of test face validity is best avoided for this reason, provided that valid items can be written. In constructing non-face-valid tests care must be taken that they appear sensible and engage the interests of the subjects. Non-face-valid items, it must be realised, are not necessarily ridiculous. Item writing and test construction are fully described in later chapters of this handbook.

Concurrent validity

A test is said to possess concurrent validity if it can be shown to correlate highly with another test of the same variable which was administered at the same time. There are a number of problems with concurrent validity which require careful examination. However, before these are discussed I must point out that all discussions of validity studies assume, as was the case with reliability, that large and representative samples have been used.

The first of these concerns the meaning of 'correlate highly'. As was shown in the last chapter the reliability of a test limits the extent to which it can correlate with another test. However if we assume that all tests in the concurrent validity study are of reasonably high reliability, this is not too important a factor. Theoretically correlations beyond .9 would be the upper limit for most tests. However if these coefficients were corrected for attenuation due to unreliability, then these correlations would approach unity, i.e. the tests would be identical and perfect validity would be demonstrated. The rationale for this correction is to be found in the chapter on reliability and the formulae are given in the Statistical Appendix to this handbook. However, in practice, a validity coefficient of 1 is extremely rare. Thus we have to consider how high a correlation must be before it indicates that a test is valid.

This question has no simple answer since it depends, to some extent, on the quality of the criterion test with which the new test is to be correlated. This difficulty of the criterion test is a further, yet related, problem. If the criterion test is a benchmark test for the variable to be measured, as it should be if concurrent validity is to be a good index of validity, then the correlation should be as high as possible, i.e. around .9, which indicates, as was shown above, virtual identity. In practice correlations beyond .75 would be regarded as good support for the concurrent validity of a test where there were benchmark criterion tests. However in most fields of psychology there are no such tests and even where there are, matters are not as simple as might be expected.

Problems where there are benchmark tests

Almost the only field where accepted tests exist such that high correlations with them indicate validity is intelligence. Here two individual intelligence tests, the Wechsler Scales (Wechsler, 1975) and the Stanford-Binet (Terman and Merrill, 1960), are generally accepted as measuring what psychologists mean by intelligence. However even here there are difficulties. Both these tests, excellent as they are, have roots going back more than half a century and modern concepts of intelligence, both factorial and cognitive, are not well matched to them, although they are still widely used. Thus those who adopt the most modern and well supported view of intelligence, namely that there are two factors, fluid and crystallised ability (Cattell, 1971), or Undheim's more recent claim (Undheim, 1981) that this fluid ability is really the old g factor of intelligence, described by Spearman (1927), would not be so happy with these tests as criteria.

In most other fields confusion reigns, although in the area of personality measurement, there is a growing consensus that two variables, neuroticism or anxiety and extraversion, are of particular importance (Kline and Barrett, 1983). Since the Eysenck Personality Questionnaire (EPQ) (Eysenck and Eysenck, 1975) is widely accepted as a highly valid measure of these two personality dimensions it is possible to use it as a criterion test. Benchmark tests can also be used in construct validity studies, as will be described in a later section of this chapter.

However, even if we accept the argument that there are a small number of tests so well established as valid measures that concurrent validity studies are meaningful, there are still problems. First, if there is a test so good that it can be taken as a standard, what is the point of a new test? Clearly any different tests must have some special qualities that differentiate them from the criterion test. In the case of our intelligence tests this is a genuine possibility. Thus both these tests have to be administered individually which is time-consuming. A group test of high validity would, therefore, be valuable. Furthermore both these tests are lengthy, taking from forty-five minutes to an hour. A brief five-minute group test with high validity would be a real addition to the library of good tests.

The EPQ, on the other hand, is a short group test. Improvements here would necessitate a test which was less obvious and less face valid, thus making it, in fact, more suitable for use in selection, just for example.

Thus it may be concluded that where criterion tests of accepted validity exist, concurrent validity is a useful form of test validity. Correlations must be high (.75 is a minimum) and the test must have some other advantage compared with the criterion test.

Problems where there are no accepted benchmark tests

As has been made clear, in the vast majority of cases a test will be measuring a variable in which there is no criterion test of acceptable validity. Here, therefore, to establish concurrent validity requires a different line of reasoning. Buros's *Mental Measurement Yearbooks*, which are published every five years (e.g. Buros, 1978), and contain descriptions and reviews of tests published in Great Britain and the USA, make clear that tests exist of almost any variable that could be thought of, thus reflecting Thorndike's well known dictum, beloved of true psychometrists: If anything exists, it must exist in some quantity and thus be susceptible to measurement. It is also made clear, in these yearbooks, that the majority of these tests are of moderate reliability and of even lower validity. Hence in attempting to establish the concurrent validity of a test, in most normal practice we have to correlate the experimental tests with one or more measures of dubious validity, a situation far different from that envisaged in most theoretical accounts of validity.

The best that can be done is to correlate the new test with whatever tests can be assembled, which imperfectly measure the variable, and to be content with moderate correlations, around .4 or .5. This, however, is manifestly unsatisfactory as an index of validity. On their own, moderate correlations of this size could not attest to the validity of the instrument. They would have to be considered alongside other evidence of validity. However if this is done the correlations become part of the construct validity of the test, an approach to validity which we examine below.

In brief, concurrent validity is only useful where good criterion tests exist. Where they do not concurrent validity studies are best regarded as aspects of construct validity.

Predictive validity

A test may be said to have predictive validity if it will predict some criterion or other. Since prediction is always regarded as an important part of the scientific method, prediction often being considered as indicative of understanding (despite the fact that the rise of the sun can be predicted empirically, without such understanding) predictive validity is good support for the efficacy of a test. However, as was the case with concurrent validity, to establish predictive validity is not as simple as it first appears.

The difficulties stem from one problem – that of finding a clear criterion for prediction. I shall first take the case of intelligence tests which exemplify many of the difficulties and their solutions. The predictive validity of an intelligence test might be demonstrated by correlating the intelligence test scores of a group of children, at age 5, with their subsequent academic success. This presumes that academic success depends, in part at least, on intelligence. Measurement of academic success could be in terms of degree class, or number of subjects passed in school examinations. Since, obviously, intelligence is only one factor in academic success, a correlation, significant but moderate in size, around .3 or .4, would be expected. Such a result could be regarded as evidence for the predictive validity of the test.

There are several points to be noted about this example.

1. Criterion measurement. Measuring academic success is not clear cut. For example, it must be the case that, even if we use degree classes as the criterion score, there are considerable problems. There are differences between subjects. It is highly likely that a degree in theoretical physics is more intellectually demanding than a degree in tourist studies, for example. This can certainly confound results. Similarly even within the same subjects there may be differences between institutions. Even if this is denied in Great Britain it is true of the USA. A Harvard and a Liberal College degree are not comparable. Thus even in a field such as educational success where criteria exist, there is plainly a problem of measurement. This difficulty is magnified many times in fields of activity where there is no such obvious measure in the first instance.

2. Homogeneity restricts or attenuates the correlations. In our discussions of reliability the effects on correlations due to restriction of range were pointed out (and a correcting factor was mentioned). This is often a difficulty where advanced educational criteria are used. Thus, in the case of university qualifications, since only the more intelligent go on to university, a large part of the range on intelligence is excluded from the correlation. Inevitably this reduces the validity coefficient. Although this may be boosted by the correcting formula, this is only an estimate and great care has to be taken in its interpretation.

3. Claims that the correlation of the IQ test and academic success does not support the validity of the test. Some authors (e.g. Howe, 1988) have attempted to argue that such correlations do not support the predictive validity of the test. Rather the correlations are better explained in terms of some other common influence, affecting both test and academic success. Although this is a possible argument it is contrary to the factorial evidence concerning academic success where motivational and personality variables are separate from IQ (Cattell and Butcher, 1968), and the variance cannot be explained away by social class (e.g. Vernon, 1961). However the truth or falsity of these counterclaims is not strictly relevant to this section. They indicate that even in a relatively clear-cut case, such as educational success, predictive validity is by no means equivocal. They also indicate that careful statistical analysis, factoring the variables, or holding social class constant in the correlation, can answer such points empirically. A full discussion of factor analysis is to be found in Chapters 7 and 8 of this handbook.

To attempt to establish the predictive validity of an intelligence test is not a difficult problem in comparison with the demands of most variables. I shall examine how the predictive validity of the EPQ (Eysenck and Eysenck, 1975) might be established. Neuroticism is the least difficult of the variables which this test measures. Thus a good measure of its predictive validity would be its correlation, after one or two years, with the criterion of admission to a psychiatric department for treatment (inpatients or outpatients) including, in addition, treatment for psychiatric problems by general practitioners. Psychotic patients would have to be excluded since they are supposedly high on psychotism rather than neuroticism. This suggests that a criterion for the psychotism scale might be diagnosis of psychosis of whatever kind. This is certainly not correct, for the P scale is a measure of tough-mindedness. Psychotic patients would be expected to be high on this variable but so would many others, who were not psychiatrically ill. Perhaps, for the P scale, it would be possible to use the criterion of psychiatric diagnosis in a predictive validity study, but a high correlation could not be expected. The results would be, at best, equivocal.

If a psychotism scale is a variable for which predictive validity is difficult to establish, then the case of extraversion must be regarded as virtually impossible. The extravert is usually defined as outgoing, sociable, noisy, adventurous and cheerful. Given this collection of traits, which is one of the best-established personality variables, it is hard to see how a predictive validity study could be set up. Clearly for a variable such as this, this approach to validity is not useful. As it happens many psychological variables are of this type such that to establish convincing predictive validity is impossible.

Since, as we have seen, for many psychological tests a similar difficulty arises with concurrent validity, it is clear that alternative measures of validity are required and these will now be discussed.

Content validity

Content validity is applicable only to a small range of tests where the domain of items is particularly clear cut. Tests of attainment and ability are of this kind. A musical ability test is a type of measure where to establish content validity is valuable although, even when this is done, some further index of validity is necessary.

To demonstrate the content validity of a musical test (perhaps for students who had studied the subject for three years) we would give the test to a number of musicians and ask them to say whether the test covered all the important aspects of musical ability that could reasonably be expected of a student with this length of experience. They could indicate where they thought the test might be lacking or where there was material tested which was not important or suitable for the population. In this way we might guarantee that the content of the test was pertinent and relevant for its purpose. The reason that a test of musical ability is a suitable candidate for content validity is that there is a good measure of agreement concerning the basic skills and knowledge, as is the case in language and mathematical ability.

In a sense it might be thought that content validity is little more than an elaborate form of face validity. However, this is not so. If the item in the music test required the subject to recognise a particular chord, it is an actual example of the skill 'chord recognition'. If the item, and others like it (a one-item test is never reliable, as was shown in Chapter 1), are answered correctly, then it follows that the subject can recognise chords. In the case of content validity it so happens that face and content validity overlap. This is very different from a personality test item such as 'Do you sometimes feel anxious, for no particular reason?' This is a face-valid item for the measurement of anxiety. However it has to be demonstrated empirically that it is, in fact, valid. This is because, as will be fully discussed in the chapters on test construction in this handbook, such items can be distorted by deliberate lying, by imperfect self-awareness, by response sets to put the socially desirable response or to agree with items, regardless of content, or by ignorance: a fearful subject might think a level of anxiety that others would regard as intolerable as quite normal and thus put a negative response. Of course, none of these things might occur and the item might be valid. That is why empirical demonstration is necessary.

However even when a test has clear content validity it is advisable to demonstrate that it is valid by some other means. With tests of attainment and ability this is not usually difficult: predictive validity against the criterion of public exams or teachers' ratings is usually possible. One further point needs brief discussion. If with these tests predictive validity is a viable procedure it is pertinent to ask why content validity needs to be established. The answer to this is that predictive validity is only required because it could be that a content-valid test was rendered invalid by poor instructions or poor modes of responding. In fact content validity is the validity to aim for, where it is relevant, and it should be backed up with evidence of predictive or concurrent validity.

Incremental and differential validity

These are two rather specialised forms of validity (well explicated by Vernon, 1961), of particular importance in selection procedures for reasons which will become obvious. If we have given a battery of tests in a selection procedure it might be thought that a test which correlated only moderately with the criterion was not useful. However if this test were correlated zero with all the other tests in the battery, this low correlation would add in new information and would thus be valuable. Where this occurs the test is said to have incremental validity.

There is one important point to note about this example. The first illustrates the claim that there is no one validity coefficient but that a test is always valid for some purpose. Thus the incremental validity of this test applies only to selection for this particular job. Indeed it is more specific than that. It applies to selection for this job with this battery. If some of the tests in the battery were changed the new ones might correlate with the test and thus its incremental validity would disappear. The statistical method used to demonstrate incremental validity is multiple regression. The formula for this may be found in the Statistical Appendix and the whole procedure is discussed in Chapter 22.

It is worth pointing out that the argument for attaching importance to the incremental validity of a test, even when the correlation with the criterion is low, is identical to that concerning the ideal items discussed in the first chapter. Here it was argued that despite the demand for high homogeneity, ideally items should correlate with the total test score but correlate zero with each other. In other words each item has incremental validity.

Differential validity is a not dissimilar concept and is best exemplified by interest tests. These correlate only moderately with university success but they do so differentially for different subjects. Thus they may be said to possess differential validity for academic performance. Intelligence tests, on the other hand, have higher correlations with academic success at university but cannot differentiate between subjects. This is hardly surprising given the nature of intelligence and interest. Thus intelligence is regarded as a factor involved in virtually all intellectual performance, hence its ubiquity (Kline, 1990). Interest in science, just for example, is hardly likely to be correlated with performance at music or history, although we would expect correlations with success in science.

Construct validity

It should be clear from what has been said so far about different kinds of validity that there is still a wide variety of tests for which none of these methods is appropriate. To overcome this important difficulty, Cronbach and Meehl (1955) introduced the notion of construct validity. First the meaning of 'construct' must be explained. The term 'construct' is virtually synonymous with 'concept'. In the sciences constructs are frequently the object of investigation or study but are only useful where they can be precisely defined. A good example of a construct is the notion of species. It makes good sense to investigate this construct and to see how it may be defined such that different animals are properly classified. However there is no such thing as a species: it cannot be directly studied or observed. It is a category, constructed by the mind, which is useful in understanding the relationships of different types of living organisms. Members of any species are, however, open to observation and experiment.

In establishing the construct validity of a test we carry out a number of studies with it and demonstrate that the results are consonant with the definition, i.e. the psychological nature, of the construct. A few examples will clarify the notion of construct validity.

I shall take a simple example first – an intelligence test. From the nature of intelligence, which, of course, is a construct, we can set up a number of hypotheses about the results from a valid intelligence test. After each hypothesis I indicate in parentheses the type of validity (if any) entailed by it. This illustrates the fact that construct validity embraces validity of every type.

1. Scores on the test will correlate with scores on other intelligence tests administered now and in the future (concurrent and predictive validity).
2. Scores on the test will not correlate with tests that are not supposed to be intelligence tests. This is a form of definition by exclusion. This hypothesis belongs only to construct validity, although I suppose it might be seen as a form of concurrent validity.
3. Scores on the test will correlate with academic performance now and in the future. This hypothesis springs directly from the nature of intelligence, as it is described in the psychometric research (e.g. Cattell, 1971) (predictive validity, at least the second hypothesis).
4. Scores on the test will discriminate at a high level of significance among different occupational groups. This hypothesis stems from the nature of intelligence and the study of work. Some jobs, such as that of theoretical physicist or administrative civil servant, demand a high level of intelligence, whereas others do not. This is not simply a matter of high social class or prestige since many well-paid jobs are relatively routine and require little more than average intelligence, as is well demonstrated in job analysis, which has been fully discussed in Kline (1975) and in Chapter 22 of this handbook.
5. In a factor analytic study of ability factors the test will load highly on the first general factor. This hypothesis is based on the notion of psychometric g as a pervasive general factor, as described initially by Spearman (1904) and fully supported by modern research (Kline, 1990).
6. With social class partialed out, there will still be a significant correlation between the test and academic performance. This hypothesis has been set up in order to answer the criticism that hypotheses 3, 4 and 5 simply reflect social class differences. There is a relationship between IQ and social class simply because there is a tendency for the intelligent to be upwardly mobile while the less intelligent descend the order. However this migration is smaller than might seem desirable (at least to those at the bottom), the social class system not being easily destroyed.

The partial correlation (of which the formula may be found in the Statistical Appendix) allows the correlation between two variables to be computed while the effects of a third variable (in this case social class) is taken out. It should be noted that the same result could be achieved by putting social class into a factor analysis, as in hypothesis 5. If the effects of social class are distinct from those of intelligence, as is argued, then there should be two factors on which academic success loads – one a factor of general ability and a second including the social and environmental influences, such as type of school, parental income and education, just for example.

These six hypotheses give a good idea of how the construct validity of an intelligence test might be established. If they were all supported there could be little argument concerning its validity. If only some of them were supported, then careful consideration of the failures would have to be undertaken. Actually, as should be obvious, these hypotheses are so coherent that it is unlikely, if the test is valid, that only partial support would be received.

One possible reason for failure is that the construct validity studies had some technical fault – poor samples or bad criterion tests or, in the case of factor analyses, inefficient factorial methods (see Chapter 8 of this handbook for a discussion of technically adequate factor analytic methods). It goes without saying that all construct validity studies must be properly executed. If some of these hypotheses were not supported in sound studies then the validity of the intelligence test would have to be called into question. I would certainly be unhappy to use an intelligence test where the construct validity, as assessed by these hypotheses, could not be confirmed.

One further point should be noted. These hypotheses are not the only ones that might be investigated in order to establish the validity of an intelligence test. Readers may be able to think of others that are equally satisfactory if not more so. Nevertheless if the six hypotheses were supported it would be sufficient to establish test validity.

As was argued in the beginning of this section, to establish the construct validity of an intelligence test is relatively easy, on account of the clarity with which intelligence has been defined and from the nature of intelligence itself, a variable of pervasive influence in many aspects of human life. However, many psychological tests are not so amenable and I now intend to discuss how the construct validity of a test of obsessional traits might be established.

I have picked this variable simply because I have struggled, over the years, to validate my own test, Ai3Q (Kline, 1971a) but have never done so completely to my satisfaction. There were a few tests of obsessional traits already constructed but none of these had been shown to be valid or was generally accepted as a good test of obsessionality. Thus a concurrent validity study, on its own, was not feasible. However, moderate positive correlations with these tests could be hypothesised. I was also keen to demonstrate that the test did not measure the two most pervasive personality variables, extraversion and neuroticism, as measured by Eysenck in the EPI (Eysenck and Eysenck, 1965) or the main primary factors, as measured by Cattell (Cattell *et al.*, 1970) in the 16PF test. This could be established by factor analyses with these tests.

This factor analysis was designed to do more than indicate that Ai3Q did not overlap these well established personality factors. It was intended also to locate the obsessional factor in factor space. For example it was expected to be related to both factor G, conscientiousness and to Q4, id pressure.

Another more clinical approach was also adopted. The Minnesota Multiphasic Personality Inventory (MMPI) (Hathaway and McKinley, 1951) measures obsessional symptoms, which are differentiated from obsessional personality (Pichot and Perse, 1967) and the Dynamic Personality Inventory (Grygier, 1975) measures thirty-three Freudian personality scales, of which one, the anal character (Freud, 1908), is highly similar to the obsessional personality. Ai3Q was, therefore, correlated and factored with these scales.

Finally, in the original validation study of this scale, the scores on this test were compared with rating scales of students by teachers. It is not necessary to describe the results of this research, which, fortunately, came out in support of the validity of Ai3Q and which is fully reported in the manual to the test (Kline, 1971). What is important is to see how the construct validity of the test could be established. What is also important is the fact that even if all these hypotheses were supported the evidence for validity is still inferential. A sophisticated opponent might well manage to argue against its validity. Construct validity, in cases such as these, cannot be proven. At best it can be said to have strong support. Actually a more recent research (Kline and Cooper, 1984a) in which this test was included in a factor analytic study of the authoritarian personality, did support its validity in that it loaded strongly on an authoritarian factor which was shown to be one of the largest personality factors among normal subjects (Kline and Barrett, 1983).

Conclusions concerning construct validity

From these two examples the nature of construct validity becomes clear. In general construct validity is established by setting up a number of hypotheses, derived from the nature of the variable, and putting them to the test. It is important to demonstrate what the test does not measure, as part of the construct validity exercise. The problem with this approach is (unlike reliability) that there is a subjective, inferential element in the judgement. Nevertheless if the rationale for the derivation of the hypotheses is made clear construct validity can be very strong evidence that the test does measure what it claims.

RELATION OF VALIDITY AND RELIABILITY

If a test is regarded as valid when it measures what it claims to measure then the relationship of validity to reliability becomes clear. First it is difficult to see how a test can be valid if it is not reliable, although, as we have seen, under certain conditions, a reliable test is not necessarily valid. In brief reliability is necessary but not sufficient for validity.

The variance of a test can be broken down into two parts: error variance and reliable variance. If the reliability coefficient is squared we can see how much reliable variance and thus how much error variance is in the particular test. This alone demonstrates the importance of high reliability for validity, since a perfectly valid test would contain no error. However this should not lead one to suppose that reliability is identical to validity. A highly reliable test can be invalid. For example a test that contains many of the same questions, in essentially paraphrases, will be reliable, that is with little random error in the variance, but it will not be valid because the reliable variance will be specific to the test. In the next chapter of this handbook, the psychometric theory underlying this statement will be set out. Similarly some personality tests will contain reliable variance but be invalid since part of the reliable variance will be concerned with response sets such as social desirability, the tendency to endorse the socially desirable response, or acquiescence, the tendency to agree with an item, regardless of content.

The conclusion from this argument is that it is never sufficient to demonstrate that a test is reliable and then assume that it must be valid, because there is little error variance. It is always necessary to show, using the methods and arguments which I have described, that the reliable variance is what was intended, i.e. that the test measures what it is claimed to measure. How this is achieved in practice can be found in the chapters on test construction.

CONCLUSIONS CONCERNING VALIDITY

I have described and discussed several methods of demonstrating the validity of tests. Construct validity is closely tied to our definition of a valid test as one which measures what it purports to measure. It is perhaps the most important approach to validity especially where tests are to be used to extend psychological knowledge. Differential validity, however, is some-what different. This is aimed at demonstrating the validity of a test for a specific purpose and is almost an operational definition of the utility of a test. Indeed, in occupational psychology, for example, this is an important aspect of validity.

From this discussion it is clear that it makes no sense to quote one figure as a validity coefficient for a test. Rather we have to take into account a set of findings if we wish properly to assess the validity of a test. As we have seen it is no easy matter to show that a test is valid. Consequently it is hardly surprising that relatively few tests have good evidence for their validity. Indeed perhaps the opposite is true: the fact that any tests have been shown to be valid is surprising.

DISCRIMINATORY POWER

I shall conclude this chapter on validity by a brief discussion of an allied topic – the discriminatory power of tests. If a test failed to discriminate between individuals it would be unlikely to be valid (unless by some rare chance all the subjects had the same status on the variable). Thus discriminatory power, defined as the ability of a test to produce a spread of scores, is necessary but not sufficient for validity. It is possible, by good test construction, to ensure that tests are discriminating (see the relevant chapters in this handbook) and this is where tests have the advantage over other forms of assessment such as ratings, for example, where it has been found that about nine categories are the maximum that can be held in mind by a rater (Vernon, 1961). Such rating scales would have low discriminating power compared with a psychological test with a large number of items.

Discriminatory power is related to the variance and spread of scores, and is at its maximum when the spread of scores is maximised. This occurs when we have a rectangular distribution. Thus if we had a twenty-item test and the same number of subjects obtained each score on the test, from 0 to 20, i.e. the distribution was rectangular, maximum discrimination would be obtained. Minimum (nil) discrimination is obtained when all subjects have the same score. Both these extremes are unlikely to occur but the more the distribution approaches the rectangular the more discriminating the test.

The measure of test discrimination is Ferguson's Delta (Ferguson, 1949). This runs from I (rectangular distribution) to 0. The normal distribution yields a delta of .93 and generally a good test should have a delta beyond .9. The formula for delta may be found in the Statistical Appendix.

This concludes our chapter on the validity of tests. Almost by definition, good tests must be valid. How validity may be built into tests is described in the chapters on test construction, while in the next chapter the underlying psychometric theory (actually error theory) is set out. This will clarify the nature of both reliability and validity.

Chapter 3

The Classical Model of Test Error

In the first two chapters of this handbook I discussed the meaning of reliability and validity and showed how these were measured. As was made clear in these discussions, underlying many of the methods, especially those concerned with reliability, was a psychometric theory of test error. This will now be described and scrutinised. This discussion has been put into a separate chapter because experience of explicating this theory (e.g. Kline, 1986) has shown that it is difficult to grasp until readers are relatively familiar with the meaning and measurement of reliability and validity. In addition by so separating the theory from the practice readers who want simply to understand sufficient to construct a reliable and valid test or choose the best test for their needs off the shelf, and this applies to many practitioners, can avoid this chapter. Nevertheless it must be stated at the outset that to follow the precepts of the preceding chapters without understanding their psychometric rationale, is to accept dogma, the antithesis of a scientific approach to psychological testing, a cast of mind which in earlier times led inevitably to the dark ages.

ERROR

First it is necessary to discuss the nature of error in measurement. All measurements, in whatever field, are subject to error, of varying magnitude. Even in the physical sciences, measurement is not error free, despite its precision. Most psychological tests are confounded by error. Errors can be of two kinds, random or systematic. A watch calibrated such that it loses two minutes every twenty-four hours would be measuring time with systematic error. Systematic errors are often of relatively little importance in psychology, especially where the interest is in individual differences, as is the case with psychometrics. This is because these systematic errors affect all measurements equally. Notice that even where mean scores, i.e. norms, for groups are set up, such systematic errors would in no way affect interpretations. Indeed systematic errors would only prove troublesome where comparisons were made with a test free from such error.

Random error is more serious in its effects on the accuracy of measurement. Unfortunately in psychological tests, as we discussed in Chapter 1, there are many possible sources of random error: how the subject feels when tested, tired, upset, ill; guessing; poor test instructions; unclear format for the test response; subjective marking; or too few items, especially in ability tests. Schuerger *et al.* (1989) examined more than 100 studies of test-retest reliability to see if they could predict it using multiple regression. They discovered that age and status of the subjects, the number of items, the intercorrelation of items and thus the internal consistency reliability were all significant predictors. This is by no means a full list of all possible determinants of random error but it is sufficient to indicate that it is hardly surprising that the proportion of valid psychological tests is not large (e.g. Buros, 1978).

The classical theory of test error is concerned with random error. Systematic sources of error are dealt with, where appropriate, in the chapters on test construction. Thus in the rest of this chapter wherever error is mentioned it refers to random error.

RELIABILITY AND TEST ERROR

As was discussed in Chapter 1, the less the error in a test the more reliable it is, i.e. repeatable. Since replicability is the essence of science it is regarded as axiomatic that tests should be as reliable as possible, although not at the expense of validity as can happen in the case of bloated specifics. As was argued in Chapter 1, reliability is necessary but not sufficient for test validity, a conclusion reached by Nunnally (1978). Nunnally makes a brilliant exposition of this classical theory of test error and for a full mathematical treatment of this subject readers will find his text an excellent addition to the discussion here, where I have attempted to keep the mathematical aspects as simple as possible.

Nunnally (1978) and Guilford (1956) point out that although more complex models of test error have been developed, the principles and conclusions which may be derived from them are little different from those derived from the classical model which is discussed in this chapter. Furthermore the vast majority of psychological tests of any repute are underpinned by this model which is easily applicable to a wide range of tests. In any case the more complex models of test error cannot be understood unless the classical model is fully understood. Where relevant to particular tests or methods some of these other models will be mentioned.

First I shall define some important terms and discuss some assumptions of the theory.

Terms and assumptions

The true score

It is assumed that for any trait (intelligence, anxiety, musical ability, just for example) each individual has a true score. The score on a test which an individual may obtain on any occasion – *the obtained score* – differs from his or her true score on account of random error. If we were to test an individual on many occasions, on the same test, a distribution of scores would be obtained. It is assumed that the mean of this distribution, which is assumed to be normal, approximates the true score.

From this it can be seen that if we want to obtain the most accurate measurement possible we should test subjects on many occasions. In general, however, this is simply impossible and we make the best of one obtained score. It should be pointed out that the assumption of the normal distribution of these obtained scores around the true score is derived from the fact that random errors are expected to be normally distributed.

The standard error of measurement

The standard error of measurement which was briefly described in Chapter 1 has its basis in the true score. If it is found that, for an individual, there is a large variance of obtained scores it is obvious that there is a considerable error of measurement. The standard deviation (the square root of the variance, see formula in the Statistical Appendix) of this distribution of obtained scores can be regarded as an index of error. Thus if the standard deviation were zero, as would be the case if every score were the same, there would be no error. The larger the standard deviation, the larger the error. Indeed since it is reasonable to assume that the error is the same for all individuals this standard deviation of obtained scores, or errors, becomes the standard error of measurement.

Of course, in general, we do not have a sufficient number of observations to calculate the standard error of measurement from the distribution of obtained scores. However the test-retest reliability of a test is obtained from two administrations, as was seen in Chapter 1, and the higher this correlation is the smaller must be the standard error of measurement, according to this classical model. This is indicated by the formula for the standard error of measurement (S.E.$_{meas}$):

3.1 S.E.$_{meas}$ = S.D.$_{.t}/\sqrt{1 - r_{tt}}$

where S.D.$_{.t}$ = the standard deviation of the test and r_{tt} = test-retest reliability.

The universe, population or domain of items

In our discussion of the standard error of measurement we used the concept of the true score: the larger this standard error the greater the imprecision of the obtained score as an estimate of the true score. It is now necessary to define the true score in more detail since it is intrinsic to the classical model of error.

This theory assumes that any test consists of a random selection of items from the universe, population or domain of items (which I shall refer to, from now on, as the universe) relevant to the trait being tested. Thus a test of tough-mindedness is assumed to consist of a set of items from the universe of tough-minded items. For almost all traits this universe of items is hypothetical, although I suppose for a test of vocabulary or spelling there is a finite universe of items from which to sample.

Although, as Nunnally (1978) points out, items are rarely a random sample of the universe, this does not render the model inappropriate since most test constructors seek to produce as diverse a set of items as possible which produces much the same effect as a random selection. To the extent that items in the test do not reflect the universe of items the test will be errorful.

The true score and the universe of items

In the classical model of error, as I hope is clear from the preceding discussion, the true score is hypothetical, being the score an individual would obtain if he or she were tested on the universe of items. Hence the error of tests reflects the failure of the test items accurately to sample the universe of items. It is obvious that this model is too simple, as Nunnally (1978) points out, since, as our discussion of the causes of errors of measurement showed, it neglects many important factors: the adequacy of the tester, the health of the subjects and the circumstances of the testing, just for example. However it is not difficult to expand the basic model, once it has been fully understood, to embrace these other factors.

Statistical assumptions of the model

The true score is the score on the hypothetical universe of items. This universe of items is assumed to possess certain statistical properties, and these will now be set out and discussed. The universe of items produces an infinitely large matrix of inter-item correlations. The average inter-item correlation of this matrix, $r(average)_{ij}$, indicates the extent of a common core among the items. If for example, we were to construct a set of test items by taking one item from as diverse a range of tests as we could find the average inter-item correlation would be 0.00, because, deliberately, there was no common core among the items. The dispersion of correlations around this average inter-item correlation is also meaningful: it indicates the extent to which items vary in sharing this common core. In this classical model it is assumed that all items have an equal amount of the common core, meaning that the average correlation of each item with all the others is the same for all items. Thus the average of each column of the hypothetical matrix would be the same and this would be the same as the average correlation of the whole matrix. This, then, is the basic assumption of the model: that the average correlation of each item with all the others is the same.

Correlation of an item with the true score

With this basic assumption it can be proved that the correlation of an item with the true score equals the square root of its average correlation with all other items.

3.2 $r_{it} = \sqrt{r(\text{average})_{ij}}$

where r_{it} = the correlation of an item with the true score, and $r(\text{average})_{ij}$ = the average correlation of of an item with all other items.

Nunnally (1978) shows how this simple formula is derived from the basic statistical assumption of the model. In principle this formula holds only when the number of items is infinite. However when this figure is reduced to 100, the results differ little. This fundamental equation 3.2 is the basis of many of the other statistical techniques of test construction, which we shall discuss in this chapter.

Significance of formula 3.2 for test construction

It should be clear that for practical test construction formula 3.2 is highly important. Thus, if a large pool of items has been developed it provides a rationale for item selection: those items whose average correlation with the other items is high. This means the items correlate highly with the true score. From such items a reliable and error-free test must result. Formula 3.2, therefore, is the statistical basis for item selection. It should be pointed out that these arguments do not apply to speeded tests since there are artificially high correlations among some items if these are generally not completed. Speeded tests should be constructed from items administered without a time limit. This can then be applied after the items have been selected by the usual methods.

These same arguments which apply to items, indicating that they measure the true score, are precisely applicable to parallel forms of the same test, each test being regarded as a random sample of items from the universe of items. On this assumption it follows that the means and variances of the parallel forms of the test must differ from the true means and variances only by chance. Thus, if in all the equations from which formula 3.2 was derived, standard scores for items are replaced by standard scores for tests, which, as we have seen, are only random groups of items, then formula 3.2 can be rewritten such that r_{it} becomes the correlation of the test score with the true score and $r(\text{average})_{ij}$ becomes the average correlation of the test with all tests in the universe.

RELIABILITY

It is a convention, as Nunnally (1978) points out, that this average correlation of one test, or one item, with all the tests or items in the universe is called the reliability coefficient, r_{11}. As can be seen from formula 3.2, the square root of the reliability is the correlation of the test, or item, with the true score. This is the reason why such importance is attached to the reliability coefficient, in the classical theory of error.

Estimates of reliability

It is not possible to compute the average correlation of a test or item with all tests or items in the universe, because the infinity of the universe can never be generated. Since tests are not random assortments of items from the universe, any actual reliability coefficients are only estimates of the reliability as conceptualised in the formula 3.2.

It is obvious that the estimates of reliability of a test (and I shall restrict my discussion to tests from now on, although everything is equally applicable to individual items) will be more accurate if they are based on the correlations with a large number of parallel form tests rather than just one other test, as is usually the case. The question arises as to whether one correlation can be a good estimate of an infinite number of possible correlations.

We will assume in the arguments that follow that our obtained reliability for a test, r_{11}, is a good estimate of the average correlation of the test with all tests in the universe, r(average)$_{11}$.

Fallible or obtained scores

Fallible scores are the scores that are actually obtained from the administration of a test. Fallible scores consist of true scores plus measurement error. Formula 3.2 showed that the correlation of a test with the true score equalled the square root of its reliability. This means, of course, that this correlation can be computed. Given this it is possible to estimate true standard scores from fallible scores by the following formula:

3.3 $Z'_t = r_{1t}Z_1 = \sqrt{r_{11}}Z_1$

where Z'_t = estimates of true standard scores, Z_1 = standard fallible scores, r_{1t} = correlation of true and and fallible scores and r_{11} = the reliability of the test.

There is another important corollary of formula 3.2. Since the square of a correlation equals the variance in one variable explainable by variance in another variable, r^2_{1t} equals the percentage of true score variance explainable by a fallible measure and vice versa. Then it can be said that r_{11} equals the same percentage of true score variance in the fallible measure. Indeed, as Nunnally (1978) shows, if the test scores are not expressed as standard scores but as deviation or raw scores, the reliability can be expressed in the following equation:

3.4 $r_{11} = \sigma^2_t / \sigma^2_1$

where σ^2_t = variance of variable 1 explainable by true scores and σ^2_1 = variance of test 1.

Formula 3.4 indicates that the reliability of a test can be seen as the amount of true score variance in a test divided by the actual variance.

In the theory of test error which we have discussed in this chapter it is assumed that the tests are randomly parallel tests of items from the universe which may differ in means, standard deviations and correlations on account of sampling errors. It was also argued that the reliability of a test is best assessed by correlating it with other tests from the universe of items. In practice, however, this is rarely done. The correlation with one test usually suffices for the reliability and an obvious problem arises from the fact that this is a limited sample.

However if it is assumed that that the two tests are truly parallel (defined by an identity of standard deviations, correlations with the true score and error variance) then reliability coefficients can be derived without having to consider the precision of the estimates, as is necessary in the randomly parallel model.

Nunnally (1978) shows, however, with this model that the essential equations concerning measurement error are identical to those which are derived with the random model, despite the differences in assumptions. I do not intend to work through these arguments for three reasons. First because the equations are identical it cannot be claimed that the models are different in any important respect from the viewpoint of understanding reliability, test error and their implications for test construction. Second, it is demonstrated by Nunnally (1978) that the truly parallel test model is but a special case of the more general model which we have described. Third, and most important of all, Nunnally (1978) convincingly argues that the parallel test model is not a good one for test development since the true score is defined in terms of only two tests. This gives me little confidence concerning the psychological meaning of this true score. This is a severe problem with the random model to which I shall return later in this chapter. Suffice it to say here that it can still be argued that the true score measured by the test is not the true score intended by its constructor.

For all these reasons, I am fully persuaded by Nunnally's arguments that the theory or model of error which has been elucidated in this handbook is far more useful than the limited, if simpler, version which assumes that tests are truly parallel.

Homogeneity of items and reliability

From all that has been discussed so far in this chapter, it is obvious that reliability is closely related to the intercorrelations of the items. A universe of items in which the average correlations were zero would be of no interest from the viewpoint of the psychological tester because it would indicate that these items had no common core, i.e. they measured no variable. What is required in a good universe of items is a relatively high average correlation, not too high, however or the variable may be little more than a specific.

The reliability of a test is related to this average intercorrelation among the items, or their homogeneity. However since item intercorrelations are obviously not identical, there must be a distribution of these around their mean. In the classical model of measurement error it is assumed that this distribution is normal. With this assumption, Nunnally (1978) shows that it is possible to estimate the precision of the reliability coefficient by computing the standard error of the estimate of the average item intercorrelations in the universe of items. This is clearly important since, as we have argued, there is the difficulty that reliability is usually computed from one set of correlations, a poor sample of all the possible correlations. The formula is set out thus:

3.5 $\sigma_{r\,(average)\ est\ ij} = \sigma_{rij}/\sqrt{\tfrac{1}{2}k(k-1)-1}$

where $\sigma_{r\,(average)\ est\ ij}$ = standard error of estimating the average item inter-correlations in the universe of items; σ_{rij} = standard deviation of distribution of actual intercorrelations of items within a test; and k = number of items in the test.

Formula 3.5 indicates that the standard error of the estimate of the average item intercorrelations in the universe of items is obtained by dividing the standard deviation of the item correlations by the square root of the number of possible correlations among k items. The minus one gives the correct degrees of freedom for the estimate.

Examination of formula 3.5 reveals two important points for test construction. The more item intercorrelations differ among themselves (i.e. the greater their standard deviation), the greater is the standard error of this estimate. As the number of items (k) increases the smaller the standard error of the estimate must be. Thus this formula 3.5 shows that increases in test homogeneity and length increase the precision of estimating the reliability of tests (and their reliability, as will be shown later).

Indeed I shall discuss in more detail the inferences that can be made from this formula 3.5. First I want to reiterate the meaning of the standard error of the estimate of the average item intercorrelation in the universe of items. It means that 68 per cent of all sample average correlations fall between the mean plus or minus one standard error and that 95 per cent fall between plus or minus two standard errors. If it is assumed that the standard deviation of correlations in a set of test items is .15, which is a typical value, then the application of formula 3.5 reveals the following results:

In a 10-item test the standard error is .02;
in a 20-item test it drops to .01;
in a 30-item test it is .007.

From these examples it is clear that even with as few as 10 items the precision of the estimate of the mean item intercorrelation is high. With more items it is almost negligible. From the viewpoint of the test constructor this precision is extremely valuable. In practice it is clear that even with a brief test there is little error in the estimation of reliability due to random error in item selection. Furthermore, as Nunnally (1978) points out, when purportedly parallel tests have low correlations between them, as parallel versions frequently do, this cannot be attributed to random errors in item selection. Either the items must represent different universes of items, which means, in fact, that they are measuring different variables, which is the usual cause, or else there is sampling error due to subjects. In brief the error is systematic not random.

From formula 3.5 it is clear that random error is not likely to ruin the statistical analyses of test construction. Estimates of reliability can be precise even with few items, although as shall be seen, the more items the better.

Nunnally (1978) derives from this classical model of test error a considerable number of principles of great value in test construction, the reason indeed that I am subjecting this model to so careful an examination. I shall concentrate upon three topics: the relation of test length to reliability; the reliability of samples of items; and the estimation of true scores from obtained or fallible scores, the standard error of scores. When these arguments are understood, the evaluation of psychological tests can be rational and effective.

Reliability and test length

Before I examine this topic I shall point out briefly its importance in applied psychology. The shorter a test the more useful it is. A psychological test which requires ten hours to complete, no matter its reliability and validity, is essentially useless. Subjects would not complete it and no testers would be given time to use it. Thus, in the applied setting there is a trade-off between brevity and reliability. If we understand the relationship between test reliability and length we shall not make fatal errors, as indeed many test constructors do, as will be demonstrated in the final section of this handbook where a large number of psychological tests are reviewed.

It is obvious that reliability increases with test length. Since we have defined true scores as the scores on the universe of items, it must be the case that the longer the test, the higher its correlation with the true score. The extreme (and hypothetical) example, where a test consists of all the items in the universe except one, clarifies this point.

The important practical question concerns, however, the rate of increase in reliability as the number of items increases. It is often difficult to construct large numbers of good test items and as we have seen, brief tests are preferable, all other things being equal.

3.6 $r_{kk} = kr(average)_{ij}/1+(k-1)r(average)_{ij}$

where r_{kk} = the reliability of the test, k = the number of items and $r(average)_{ij}$ = the average intercorrelation of items.

This formula 3.6 is known as the Spearman-Brown Prophecy formula and is used in calculating the split-half reliability of tests. I shall apply formula 3.6 to three hypothetical examples. Suppose that we have three sets of items, each with average correlations between items of .2. Set A has 10 items; set B has 20 items and set C has 30 items. The application of formula 3.6 yields the following reliabilities.

    set A r_{kk} = .714
    set B r_{kk} = .833
    set C r_{kk} = .882

From this it is clear that even a 10-item test can give a tolerable reliability if the items are measuring a common core, and the 20-item test yields a highly satisfactory reliability. Since the square root of the reliability gives us an estimate of the correlation of the set of items with the true score it can be seen that the 30-item test is impressive: .939. These reliabilities were calculated from sets of items in which the average correlation was .2. In some fields of psychological testing it is realistic to hope for more homogeneous items and for a final illustration I shall take a 30-item test where the average item intercorrelation is .4. Applying formula 3.6 a reliability of .952 emerges. This is a very high figure and few tests exceed this.

From this discussion it is quite clear that a reliable test can be made from as few as 10 homogeneous items but this is probably a minimum figure for a good test. This is simply because a smaller number of highly homogeneous items would be likely to be far too specific to be a valid measure even if it were reliable, as it could be if the item intercorrelations were substantially beyond .2.

It is also obvious that if a reliable 30-item test is split into two parallel 15-item tests, each will be itself reliable, although less so than the composite. Indeed r_{kk} is the estimate of the correlation of a test of k items with another set of k items from the same universe. Finally, as is clear from formula 3.6, it should be noted that the reliability thus calculated, r_{kk}, of a k item test, is determined from the intercorrelations of the items in the set.

This Spearman-Brown Prophecy formula (3.6) is used in the calculation of the split-half reliability of a test where the correlation between the two halves is corrected for length, the original correlation being an underestimate because the test is twice as long. The formula 3.6 applies because each half of the test may be regarded as a sample from the universe of items. This enables the formula to be simplified for the special case (k=2). It is true that k now refers to groups of items rather than items but it can be shown that formula 3.6 applies regardless of the size of units, items or tests.

3.7   (special case of 3.6) $r_{kk} = 2r_{12}/1+r_{12}$

where r_{12} = the correlation between the two halves of the test.

Reliability and samples of items

Formula 3.6 could be used to calculate the reliability of a test which depends entirely on the number of items and the correlations between them. However it is tedious and costly, even with modern computing facilities, to compute all the correlations between items and there are more simple methods of achieving the same result. In the practice of test construction these simpler methods are more frequently used and it is their results which are usually found in the manuals to handbooks and tests. Thus it is necessary to describe and discuss them.

Coefficient alpha

Nunnally (1978) and Cronbach (1976) both consider coefficient alpha to be the most important index of test reliability. Cronbach (1951) developed the statistical rationale of alpha and although the formula for the alpha co-efficient looks different from formula 3.6, in fact it can be derived directly from it. In place of the average intercorrelation among items the average covariance among items is used and the average of the item variances is substituted for 1 in the denominator. Virtually identical formulae are derivable from other models of measurement error. It is for all these reasons that coefficient alpha is regarded as the fundamental index of reliability. As was the case with the Spearman-Brown Prophecy formula, coefficient alpha indicates the expected correlation of a test of k items with an alternative form with k items. Its square root is the estimate of the correlation of the test with the true score. The formula for the alpha coefficient is set out in 3.8.

3.8 $r_{kk} = \dfrac{k}{k-1} [1 - \Sigma\sigma^2_i/\sigma^2_y]$

where r_{kk} = coefficient alpha, k = the number of items in the test, $\Sigma\sigma^2_i$ = the sum of the item variances and σ^2_y = the variance of the test.

Many tests, especially personality tests, have dichotomous items. In this case formula 3.8 can be further simplified into a form which can be easily calculated with a hand calculator. This special variant of coefficient alpha is known as the Kuder-Richardson Formula 20 (KR20). The formula for KR20 is set out in 3.9.

3.9 $r_{kk} = \dfrac{k}{k-1}\,(1 - \Sigma pq/\sigma^2_y)$

where r_{kk} = KR20, k = the number of items in the test, p = proportion passing each item and q = 1-p and σ^2_y = the variance of the test. The equivalence of formulae 3.8 and 3.9 comes about from the fact that in the dichotomous case $1-\Sigma pq = \Sigma\sigma^2_i$.

As has been argued throughout this chapter, coefficient alpha is implicated in the classical theory of measurement in a wide variety of ways, the most important of which for understanding tests have been set out. Nunnally (1978) contains many more esoteric derivations which are beyond the scope of this handbook to go through in detail. Two further points, however, require further discussion. The first can be brief. It can be shown from the formula for coefficient alpha that reliable tests have greater variance than unreliable measures. Thus, for example, the more reliable of two tests of the same length will have greater variance and thus be more discriminating and more valuable as a test. These arguments have been set out in Chapter 1. The second point concerns standard error of measurement.

Standard error of measurement

At the beginning of this chapter we introduced the concept of the standard error of measurement, which is the expected standard deviation of scores of an individual taking a large number of tests comprised of items from the same universe. This standard error is used to set confidence limits around any obtained score (although, strictly, these limits lie around the true score, a fact that is conveniently ignored in practice). As formula 3.1 indicates, the lower the reliability the larger is this error. This is why for practical testing with individuals high reliability is essential. The derivation of this formula is closely tied to the classical model and to the alpha coefficient.

Other models

From the discussion in this chapter, I think that the rationale of the psycho-metric emphasis on reliability as a prerequisite for valid tests has been made clear. It is evident that that there is a sound logical and mathematical basis for psychometrics in this classical test theory. Nevertheless there are other models of test variance, as Nunnally (1978) makes clear. With one exception these will not be discussed since their derivations are highly similar to those of the classical theory which is quite adequate for understanding tests. This exception is the factor analytic model. This is highly important since many of the most famous tests have been constructed by factor analysis.

Factor analysis and its rationale for test construction is fully described in Chapter 7 of this handbook. It is argued there that it is fundamental to good testing that each test measure only one factor. If this is so scores on the test are genuinely comparable in psychological meaning. A score of 10, for example, on a test measuring two factors may be composed of a variety of combinations of the two factors. Thus two scores of 10 are not necessarily equal.

In principle, as Nunnally (1978) argues, the classical model of test error does not have to assume that the universe of items is unifactorial. If two factors, x and y, ran through the items true scores would consist of combined ability on x and y and random samples of items from the universe would tend to correlate the same with each other. However even if this is the case, there is no doubt that from the viewpoint of psychological meaning it makes little sense to work with universes of items that are not unifactorial. Thus in practice it is sensible to think of the factor analytic approach to test construction as being underpinned by the classical model. It ensures that the universe of items is unifactorial and thus makes the resulting test variables psychologically meaningful and interpretable.

CONCLUSIONS

In this chapter I have set out the statistical and psychometric rationale of reliability and validity, as it may be derived from the classical model of error measurement, and we have seen how it applies even to factor analytic tests. This completes the account of reliability and validity, two of the attributes of good tests. In the next chapter I shall turn to the third of the important characteristics of good psychological tests – standardisation.

Chapter 4

Standardising the Test

MEANING OF STANDARDISATION

To standardise a test is to set up norms. Norms are sets of scores from clearly defined samples and the importance of standardisation is that it gives test scores psychological meaning and thus makes interpretation possible. An example will illustrate this point. Suppose a subject obtains a score of 10 on an intelligence test. If 10 is a score attained by only the top 2 per cent of the general population it is obvious that this person is highly intelligent. If, on the other hand, it turns out that 10 is attained by 98 per cent of the population, the converse is true. Without any norms at all the meaning of the score is impossible to gauge. Clearly, therefore, standardisation of tests is essential, where tests are to be used to make decisions about individuals, as in vocational guidance or personnel selection. Norms are also valuable where tests are to be used for screening purposes, as in times of war or in initial selection procedures from a huge pool of applicants. Indeed, in summary, standardisation is essential for the practical test user.

There is one application of tests where standardisation is not so important. This is in the psychometric analysis of individual differences – the scientific study of human attributes, ability, personality, motivation and mood, just for example, aspects of psychological measurement which are each discussed in later chapters of this handbook. For this purpose, the application of psychometrics to psychological theory (fully discussed by Kline, 1979), direct, raw scores are perfectly satisfactory, and transformation to norms could even lose information, as will be seen in our discussion of norms and standardisation later in this chapter.

PROBLEMS AND DANGERS IN STANDARDISATION

If norms are to be used for the interpretation of the meaning of test scores it is obvious that they must be accurate. If, according to the norms, a score of y is obtained by the top 20 per cent of the general population, this must really be so and not a quirk of the normative sample. If the norms are inaccurate they can be completely misleading. This is particularly dangerous in clinical and psychiatric work where tests may be used for diagnosis. Thus if a child were to be consigned to a particular form of education on the basis of test scores, it is essential, in the interests of justice, that the norms are accurate. For this reason, in this chapter we set out the demands of good standardisation.

Before describing the techniques of standardisation and the varieties of norms which can be used, there is a more general point which needs to be made. The fact that psychological tests can be so easily standardised, thus allowing accurate comparisons with normative groups, makes them particularly effective forms of assessment, with great advantages over other methods which cannot be so standardised, such as interviews or repertory grids (Kelly, 1955) which deliberately exclude comparison and are fully described in Chapter 18 of this handbook.

Of course norms are necessary for psychological tests because there is no true zero in their scale of measurement. Many forms of measurement have a true zero; length and weight can be measured on such scales, for example. However it should not be imagined that the absence of true zero implies that measurement cannot be precise or is therefore unscientific. Temperature can be accurately measured but the different scales have a different and arbitrary zero, in one case the freezing point of water, under atmospheric pressure, being chosen.

SAMPLING IN STANDARDISATION

This is the crucial factor in the standardisation of a test. The quality of the norms depends upon the adequacy of the samples on which they are based. In sampling there are two important variables: size and representativeness. The normative sample must be a good reflection of the population which it represents and it must be sufficiently large to render the standard errors of its descriptive statistics, such as mean, standard deviation and distribution, to negligible proportions.

To reduce standard errors a sample size of 500 is more than adequate. However, the representativeness of a sample is largely independent of size although a small sample cannot be truly representative of a large population. Norms for the general population would have to be very large to represent it accurately (in the region of 10,000 subjects) but for smaller specialised populations, or for homogeneous groups, they could be far smaller. For example there are approximately 5000 university professors in the United Kingdom and a sample of 500 could be representative.

There are two points worthy of further note in the previous paragraph. Firstly it is clear that the size of an adequate normative sample is no absolute matter. Much depends upon the population, both its size and its homogeneity. Thus professors of chemistry are more homogeneous than professors in general and could be represented by a smaller sample. Secondly it is clear that a small but representative sample is superior to a large but biased sample. A small standard error is of no value if the observed value is inaccurate.

METHODS OF SAMPLING

The most heterogeneous population must be the general population of which all others are subsets, although it is logically possible for such a subset to be as heterogeneous as the whole. Thus to obtain a sample of the general population is the most difficult sampling problem, in terms of making the sample representative. Actually there is a further sampling problem in working with smaller specialised populations and this concerns their definition. This is clearly illustrated in the study of criminality. Thus in an investigation of thieves it might be thought adequate to define the population by conviction for theft. This, however, will not do since there are large numbers of uncaught thieves. Such a definition would ensure only a sample of convicted thieves. This problem of definition will be examined later in this section.

1. Random sampling

A sample is said to be random if there is an equal chance that any individual in the population can be a member of the sample. If a random sample is sufficiently large it can be thoroughly representative of the population from which it was drawn. If we do not know the important categories within the population which we are trying to sample a random sample is the best method of ensuring representativeness. For example when I was required to sample 11-year-old children in Ghana to set up an efficient assessment procedure it became necessary to standardise our tests on a sample of such children. Since as a newcomer to that country I had no knowledge of the important variables likely to affect achievement in school, a random sample was the most sensible approach to obtain a representative sample. In this instance a list of primary schools in the relevant area of the country was obtained. These were numbered and numbers were drawn from a table of random numbers to select schools. All 11-year-olds in these schools were then tested. In this case I had resources to test only a fixed number of children and the sample was drawn until that size was reached, in all about 1000 children. In fact this procedure was vitiated in practice because accurate records of ages were not kept. What was obtained was a random sample of children purporting to be 11 years of age, usually so designated by their teachers.

This example illustrates one important aspect of random sampling, namely the provision of an equal chance for any individual in the population to be selected in the sample. It was impossible to obtain a list of pupils of 11 years of age and this is a general difficulty in random sampling: how to obtain a preliminary list from which to sample, or in the language of sampling how to define the population.

Defining the population

It is not sufficient to define the population theoretically. This may be easy, for example, with the general population of Great Britain, which includes every person residing in the country. It is necessary to have some operational or concrete definition. In this case a list would be necessary but where could one be found? Certainly if we restrict our discussion, for the moment, to adults, there is no obvious list. Censuses are rapidly out of date; voting lists are usually incomplete, especially with the advent of Poll Tax; telephone directories over-represent the middle classes, as do lists of buyers of cars even if these could be available. As can be seen, an operational definition of the general population is by no means easy.

In many cases, we may wish to establish special norms for tests and then it is necessary to sample special populations. Here again definition may be difficult, both theoretical and operational. I have mentioned the case of offenders. It is possible to obtain lists of all the inmates of prisons, to exclude remand prisoners, and thus sample offenders. From this it should be possible to draw up a random sample of offenders. Here a clear definition of the universe or population of offenders who have been sent to prison is possible. However if we were required to establish schizophrenic norms, not only would such a list be impossible to draw up, but in addition, as is clear from psychiatric textbooks (e.g. Mayer-Gross, Slater and Roth, 1961, and there is little reason to believe that there has been improvement in recent years) there is poor agreement in diagnosis. An adequate sample of schizophrenics is exceedingly difficult to draw.

A further point requires discussion. The basis of the definition of the population can vary. My Ghanaian example illustrated this point. We needed to define the population of schoolchildren. This could be done either by listing children or schools. A random sample of schools is far easier to obtain. However if these units are too gross this will not necessarily provide a random sample of the members of the units. Schools, however, are sufficiently small units to be a reasonable basis for a random sample of children.

Drawing the sample from the population

In addition to the problem of defining the universe, in the first place, the procedure of actually obtaining the sample must be discussed.

The standard procedure for ensuring that any member of the list can enter the sample is to use random number tables. Each individual in the population should be given a number and then numbers can be read off from the tables of random numbers. This is laborious and an easier procedure is to have a computer produce random numbers for selecting the sample.

It is also possible to select the sample by interval, every ith subject, i being fixed by the proportion of the population in the sample. This is only viable where position in the list is itself random.

In conclusion it is clear that random sampling is possible only where the universe or population can be adequately listed. To ensure that a sample from it is representative it must usually be large because a fairly high proportion of the population is necessary. This means that random sampling for the establishment of norms for tests is time-consuming and expensive and for this reason stratified sampling is preferred by most test constructors. Indeed Cattell, Eber and Tatsuoka (1970) argue that, size for size, stratified sampling is more effective than random sampling. Of course, just as the value of a random sample depends upon its being genuinely random so a stratified sample must be properly stratified. What this entails will be discussed below.

2. Stratified sampling

Stratified sampling, as the name suggests, involves dividing a heterogeneous population into a number of more homogeneous populations such that samples of the homogeneous populations can be combined to form a representative sample of the whole population. Since homogeneous populations require smaller samples to be representative, stratified samples can be more representative size for size than random samples, as has been argued in the previous paragraph. It is obvious that smaller samples are needed adequately to reflect homogeneous compared to heterogeneous populations. Thus to sample a mixture of ten chemicals would require a small proportion of the total but to sample adequately a collection of ten differently coloured balls would require a far larger sample.

Selection of stratifying variables

Critical to the representativeness of a stratified sample are the variables used in the stratification. If too many are used the sample becomes enormous, larger than an adequate random sample. If the wrong variables are used the sample will not be representative. There is a simple rule for the selection of stratifying variables: they must be correlated with the variable being studied, i.e. the standardised test, and in addition, as has been pointed out, we must minimise the number of stratifications. Some examples will clarify these rules.

The Lorge-Thorndike Intelligence Test

To illustrate the problems of obtaining a good stratified sample of the general population I shall scrutinise the norms for the Lorge-Thorndike Intelligence Test (1957) for children which is generally accepted as having excellent norms, as has been argued by Jackson and Messick (1967).

Intelligence test scores must be related to age and for the moment I shall consider how Lorge and Thorndike sampled each age group.

Definition of population   Communities formed the basis of the sampling. To obtain a representative sample of these communities, a stratified sample was used.

Stratifying variables   The basis of the stratification were the factors most highly correlated with intelligence test scores, in communities. These were: (1) percentage of adult literacy; (2) proportion of professional workers; (3) percentage of home ownership and (4) median home rental value.

Each community was then classified on these four variables into five categories running from very high to very low. Stratified sampling on this basis resulted in forty-four communities and every child in each age group in the sample communities was tested to establish the norms.

This resulted in an N of 11,000 for each age group, from 6 to 17 years of age, yielding a total of 136,000.

Comments   It can be seen that this method of sampling must have yielded a representative sample of communities and thus a representative sample of children, given that all in each community were chosen. However, it illustrates the point that to sample the general population adequately requires an extremely large sample and is expensive in both money and time. Such standardisation is certainly beyond the individual test constructor.

I pointed out that the stratification was based upon the variables most highly correlated with intelligence. If we were establishing norms for a test of anxiety, it might be appropriate to stratify on other criteria. It should be noted that Thorndike and Lorge supplied norms for the subgroups on these social class variables and these are useful for comparative purposes. Indeed, in working with individuals these subgroup norms can be more useful than the general norms. However to be accurate the Ns in these subgroups must be large, as they were in this test. In brief the norms for the Thorndike-Lorge Intelligence Test are a good example of stratified sampling in the establishment of general population norms.

I mentioned that the stratification criteria would not necessarily be the same for a test of anxiety and I shall now examine the general population sample of a personality test.

The Cattell 16PF Test (Cattell, Eber and Tatsuoka, 1970)

As was discussed above these authors, in reference to their standardisation of the 16PF test, have claimed that that a small, well stratified sample is superior to a larger random sample so that it is interesting to examine how they standardised this test. They report in detail on the standardisation of the test on females and this is what will be scrutinised.

Basis of stratification   The USA was divided into eight geographical areas and eight population densities. The population was divided into five age groups and seven family income groups. The percentages in the population of each of these categories was reflected as accurately as possible in the sample of women which was approximately 1000.

Comments   There seems little doubt that the stratification in this sample was well planned. However when we look at the numbers in some of the individual categories it becomes clear that there are difficulties. For example, there were only 30 women in the mountain area and 239 in the two categories of cities with populations greater than two million. I do not see how so small a sample could be truly representative. This stratified sample of females, despite the soundness of its stratification, is simply not large enough. As was pointed out in the case of the Thorndike-Lorge test, about 10,000 cases seems to be required for a reasonable stratified sample. Furthermore the numbers in this 16PF sample are far too small to make meaningful comparison between the subgroups.

It may be concluded from this discussion that 1000 subjects, however well stratified, is not really a satisfactory basis for general norms. For these reasons the norms for this test have to be treated with some caution.

Rules for general norms

1. A stratified sample is more efficient, size for size, than a random sample and is best used for standardising tests.
2. Four classifications are usually sufficient, and care has to be taken lest too many criteria increase, inordinately, the size of the sample.
3. The variables to use in the stratification are those that are most highly correlated with the test. For many psychological variables sex, age and social class are important.
4. In each subgroup there should be sufficient subjects to form an adequate sample. If we took 300 at a minimum, and if we have, for example, five social classes, two sexes and five age groups there are already fifty categories which gives a sample size of 15,000.
5. From this it is clear that to sample adequately a general population inevitably requires a huge number of subjects, as was used in the

Thorndike-Lorge Test. However, to establish such norms requires resources that are usually beyond most test constructors.

Special group norms

Because of the logistic and financial problems in standardising a test for the general population many test constructors prefer to use norms for the specific groups for whom the test was designed. Of course, for these special groups all the principles of sampling still apply. However because they are more homogeneous adequate samples can be smaller. To clarify the problems of standardising tests in special groups I shall examine the published norms of some other tests.

The Conservatism Scale (Wilson and Patterson, 1970)

This scale claims to measure dogmatism or rigidity, as described by Rokeach (1960), an attitude which has a profound effect in many important spheres of life and is clearly to be seen in the conflicts current in Beirut and Belfast. A large number of different norms are provided in the manual to the test, although no rationale for their selection is given. These include university students from four countries, college of education students (a useful reminder that norms go out of date, since this is a category of educational institution which no longer exists), New Zealand professionals, skilled workers, schoolgirls and heterogeneous males.

Comments   Examination of the numbers in each of these groups suggests that these norms must be treated with considerable caution. The largest N is to be found in the New Zealand occupational sample – 340 subjects. Yet, on the grounds which we have discussed above, such a sample size could hardly be representative of so heterogeneous a sample as professionals. There are fifty university students from the United Kingdom and given that there are more than forty universities in the country, most of them with more than 5000 students, this sample cannot be used as a basis for norms. Many of their other samples are similarly far too small to be used for norms: 22 lab-technicians, 22 clerical workers and 30 businessmen.

Conclusions   It must be concluded that these norms are of little value and could not be used in the interpretation of test scores. The choice of groups is quite interesting but larger samples of these are required. It is to be noted that it would not be possible to sum all these results to form a general population norm. Specific group norms have to be based upon larger and more representative samples than those for this test.

Ai3Q (Kline, 1971a)

In 1971 I developed Ai3Q, a test of the obsessional personality. I established norms for English sixth-formers and I shall briefly describe how this was done because at the time I was fortunate enough to be working with a large team of researchers and had considerable resources.

Obtaining the sample of sixth-formers   To obtain a good sample of sixth-formers it was necessary to ensure that we had an adequate sample of sixth forms. Thus the basis of the sample was to take all the sixth-formers in a stratified sample of sixth forms. This is highly important. A large sample of sixth-formers from schools with huge sixth forms and high academic standards such as Manchester Grammar School, St. Pauls and Cheltenham Ladies would be worthless and completely misleading as a basis for norms.

Stratifying variables for schools   Four stratifying variables for schools were used. Although some of these are now no longer applicable it is not important since this is an illustration of how a stratified sample may be built up.

1. Source of finance: public school, direct grant, aided or state.
2. Sex: boys, girls, mixed.
3. Geographic location; inner city, town, rural.
4. State school system: grammar schools, comprehensive schools and sixth-form colleges.

It was difficult to draw up a precisely balanced sample on all variables simply because there are few inner-city public schools, at least outside London. Nevertheless a sample reflecting the proportions of such schools in the population, even if there were only two schools per category, would yield adequate norms and such a sample was drawn up. All the schools in each category were listed and two from each were chosen by random number.

This procedure yielded a sample of approximately 1000 males and 1000 females and, it must be stressed, this covered just the north of England. Again it shows how, even with a homogeneous category of subjects from a geographically restricted area of the country, huge samples are required if they are to be at all representative. Even for this sample large resources of time and money were required and, since I left that team, I have never been able to establish such reliable norms.

Myers-Briggs Type Indicator (Briggs and Myers, 1962)

This test which classifies subjects into Jungian categories (thinking extraverts, intuiting intraverts, and so on) exemplifies how excellent specific norms should be set up. However it illustrates clearly some of the problems. For example they have norms for 11th and 12th grade children based upon more than 3500 boys and 2500 girls from twenty-seven Pennsylvania schools. This must be an excellent sample of children from that state but it is possible that these norms are inappropriate for other states. Similarly their sample of more than 4500 liberal arts and engineering students derived from eight universities which demand high entrance qualifications from their students must be representative of such colleges but, it must be asked, what about the other colleges which are not so demanding, colleges which form a huge majority in the USA?

While these norms are sound for the possibly limited populations which they reflect, some of the other normative groups are clearly unsatisfactory: gifted children (34 males, 25 females) and 40 creative architects can hardly be considered adequate.

In brief this test exemplifies the problem in establishing good norms. Even when the investigators know how to do this they often make do with far less, usually because the resources to improve the norms cannot be obtained.

Rules for sampling special groups

1. Stratify the groups by the variables most highly correlated with the test.
2. The minimum number for samples is 300. It is often necessary to build up the sample over a period of time.
3. A small sample, as in the Conservatism Scale, is better than nothing. However if small numbers have been used, test users should be warned. Norms based upon small samples are only tentative and suggestive. They can be completely misleading.

Conclusions

The conclusions from this section on sampling in the establishment of norms can be short. I make no apology for examining this topic in detail because inadequate norms can be entirely misleading.

In the main the difficulty in sampling is not theoretical or intellectual. It is the practical problem of sufficient resources. If a test is to be used to make decisions about individuals it is essential that the norms are set up to the standards which have been discussed. In brief, large and properly stratified samples are essential for good norms.

EXPRESSING THE RESULTS

If good normative groups have been tested the results have to be expressed and there are various ways to do this which must now be examined and scrutinised. Almost all these methods compare an individual's score with the relevant normative group by means of some transformation of the raw score which reveals her or his status relative to the group.

Some different norms

In this section I shall describe some of the more commonly used norms and point out their various advantages and disadvantages.

1. Percentiles

A percentile is the score below which a given percentage of the normative group falls. Thus the 30th percentile is the score below which 30 per cent of the sample falls. Percentiles have one advantageous feature which is of some relevance in applied psychology, namely that they can be understood by subjects who have taken a test. Most adults understand percentages.

However, as norms percentiles suffer from two important defects.

  a. Percentiles are ordinal scores which means that they cannot be subjected to parametric statistical analysis.
  b. The second problem with percentiles is probably more serious. The distribution of percentiles is rectangular whereas the distribution of test scores generally approaches the normal. This means that there are two kinds of distortion inherent in percentiles: small differences around the mean become exaggerated while relatively large differences at the tails of the distributions become compressed.

Because percentiles are not suitable for statistical analysis and because they tend to distort raw scores these norms are not recommended, except for simple explanations of the results.

2. Standard scores

The most useful norms are standard scores. There are many varieties of these and the most commonly used will be discussed.

Z scores

The z score is calculated by dividing the deviation of each score from the mean by the standard deviation of the scores. Formula 4.1 sets out the formula.

4.1 $z = (X - M)/\sigma$

where z = the standard z score, X = the obtained score on a test, M = the mean of the distribution of scores and σ = the standard deviation of scores.

The standard deviation of a test (the formula for which may be found in the Statistical Appendix) is a measure of the variability of the test, how much the scores vary round the mean, which is the average of the test.

Properties of the z score The great advantage of z scores compared with raw scores is that, unlike raw scores, the same z scores are always equivalent. Thus a z score of 2 is always two standard deviations above the mean. This, of course, allows meaningful comparison of scores on different tests.

Let us suppose that we have a set of test scores with a mean of 50 and a standard deviation of 5. For illustration Table 4.1 sets out some raw scores converted to z scores, using the formula 4.1.

Table 4.1 Raw scores and z scores

Raw score	z score
50	0
55	1
60	2
45	−1
43	−1.4

From Table 4.1 it is clear that z scores have a mean of 0, a standard deviation of 1 and take positive or negative values. The larger the z score the further away it is from the mean, positive scores being above and negative scores below the mean. The transformation of raw scores to z scores is linear so that the distribution of the raw scores is maintained in the z scores. If the raw scores are normally distributed then the z scores will range from +3 to -3. Because the area under the normal curve is known, normally distributed z scores are particularly informative. For example approximately 95 per cent of the normal distribution lies between the mean and two standard deviations. Thus a z score of 2 can immediately be interpreted in percentage terms: i.e. 2 per cent have done better, the other 2 per cent being at the other tail of the distribution. Any z score can be so translated by reading off the value of the z score from tables setting out the area under the normal curve.

Despite the advantages of z scores, particularly their comparability, there are two major problems with them such that, although they are the simplest form of standard score, they are not often used as test norms. These problems are discussed below.

a. A scale that appears to have so narrow a range as a z score (approximately +3 to −3) and a mean of 0 has little meaning for those who are not used to such scores, e.g. psychologists. Since the main use of norms is in applied psychology where the results usually have to be discussed with subjects, this is a severe disadvantage.

b. Although many tests yield more or less normal distributions, equally many do not. Where distributions are not normal neither are the distributions of the z scores with the result that the ready translation to percentiles is not possible.

To overcome these difficulties many test constructors transform the z scores into other standard scales and these must be described. In fact there is an infinity of transformations that might be made but I shall discuss only those which are commonly used. The others are equivalent and they have no advantages over the common transformations.

Z score transformations into other standard scores

Formula 4.2 shows how z scores may be transformed into standard scores with a given mean and standard deviation. These scores are, like z scores, always comparable with other standard scores transformed with the same mean and standard deviation.

4.2 $z_t = a + bz$

where z_t = the transformed z score, a = the mean of the transformed distribution, b = the standard deviation of the transformed distribution and z = the z score.

As Cronbach (1976) argued, the most common transformation of z scores is to standard scores with means of 50 and standard deviations of 10. In Table 4.2 we use formula 4.2 to convert the z scores of Table 4.1 to transformed z scores, with a mean of 50 and standard deviation of 10.

Table 4.2 Z score transformation

Raw score	z	z_t score
55	1	60
60	2	70
45	−1	40
43	−1.4	36

Although this z score transformation, mean of 50 and standard deviation of 10, is the most common it is obvious from formula 4.2 that a transformation to any mean and standard deviation could be made.

Conclusions concerning standard scores   Given that all standard scores are equivalent, in the opinion of this writer there is little point in using any other scale than the one with a mean of 50 and a standard deviation of 10, unless normalised scales are desired. These are discussed below.

Normalised standard scores

Some test constructors prefer normalised standardised scores. Intelligence is always claimed to be normally distributed (Vernon, 1961), for example, so that it makes sense to produce normally distributed standard scores. In addition, as was discussed above, it is simple to translate normalised standard scores into percentiles.

To normalise a set of z scores the following steps have to be computed. These are given because it is the best explanation of what normalised z scores are and what is entailed in the process of normalisation.

a. The cumulative proportion of the sample at each raw score has to be computed.
b. This entails computing the cumulative frequency (cf) at each score. Thus the cumulative frequency for score x is the number of subjects scoring below x.
c. This cf has to be calculated for the mid-point of each score interval which is computed by adding to the cf for each score half the number of subjects at that score. Thus if the cf for x was 10 and 6 subjects scored x the mid-point cf would be 13.
d. Each mid-point cf is converted to a proportion by dividing by N.
e. In statistical tables which show the area under the normal curve these mid-point cfs can be translated into z scores.
f. These z scores are however normally distributed and may be referred to as z_n scores.
g. These normalised z scores may be transformed into any type of standard score using the formula 4.2.

T scores In the *VIIth Mental Measurements Yearbook* (Buros, 1972) can be found the American Psychological Association's guide for test constructors. They suggest that if normalised standardised test scores are required they should be scaled to means of 50 and standard deviations of 10. Such normalised standard scores are known as T scores.

Other normalised standard scores

a. Stanine scores. These have means of 5 and standard deviations of 2. They divide the normal curve into nine scores.
b. Stens. These have means of 5.5 and standard deviations of 1.5. These are favoured by Cattell, especially for personality tests, and divide the normal curve into ten scores.
c. The Wechsler Intelligence tests (Wechsler, 1958) use a scale with a mean of 100 and a standard deviation of 15 (occasionally 16), as do many intelligence tests.

Use of normalised standard scores

Normalised standard scores, despite their ready translation into percentiles, should only be used in special circumstances.

a. They should be used only where the original distribution is approximately normal. If this is not the case, the normalisation will result in a distortion – especially at the tails of the distribution.
b. In addition they should only be used where there is some theoretical expectation of a normal distribution.
c. Finally it is essential that we are confident that the standardisation group is sufficiently large and representative that the distribution is an accurate reflection of the population especially at the tails. If this is not the case the distortions could be misleading.

Conclusions and summary

From this discussion of standardisation and norms the following conclusions can be drawn.

a. Psychological test raw scores are only meaningful in relation to the scores of normative groups.
b. The value of norms depends entirely upon the adequacy of the sample or samples on which they are based. Only where these samples can be shown to be adequate can norms be used with any confidence.
c. It was shown that normative samples were inevitably large, sometimes in the order of 10,000.
d. It was shown that stratified samples were more efficient than random samples and that the variables by which samples should be stratified were those most highly correlated with the test variable.
e. There are many different methods of expressing normative scores.
f. Percentiles were not recommended because they were unsuited to statistical analysis.
g. Standard scores are recommended, the most useful being the standard score with a mean of 50 and a standard deviation of 10.
h. Normalised standard scores are only recommended under special circumstances. If required the T score is the most useful.
i. From this it follows that if we are using any test in applied psychology it is essential that all the details of the standardisation procedures are given. A set of standard scores can be quite misleading if the sampling is poor. Hence all details of the provenance and the number in the normative sample must be supplied.

Alternative methods of interpreting test scores

There are some further methods of interpreting scores which are different from norms but which are valuable only in somewhat restricted circumstances. These must now be discussed.

1. The content criterion

In our discussion of content validity in Chapter 2 it was pointed out that if a test demanded certain skills to complete or if to pass it certain behaviours had to be evinced then that test was *ipso facto* a valid measure of those skills or behaviours. For example if a music test demands that subjects recognise the dominant in a series of major chords, then if they get the items right they possess that skill. It is quite clear that content validity is relevant only where there is some clear content to specify. This is relatively easy at the elementary level in the sciences and for music and mathematics although it becomes progressively more difficult at the higher levels of attainment. Content validity is most applicable to tests of attainment and to ability tests.

I have introduced the notion of content validity because the content criterion is applicable where tests have been designed to be content valid. For example to test musical notation a music test could be designed with every variety of musical notation, although it should be noted that the problem of musical notation is having to respond quickly as in actual playing. In this test a score of 100 per cent would indicate complete mastery and x per cent would show x per cent mastery. With tests of this sort it is necessary to have clear evidence of where the cut-off point should be if a student is to continue her or his course, for example that a high proportion of those below a certain score fail to complete their course. In many educational establishments such empirical evidence is usually lacking, being replaced by the somewhat arbitrary views of the teachers, the product of experience.

Difficulties with the criterion method

Apart from the restriction of the criterion method to subjects where the content can be clearly stated, there is another problem. This concerns the sampling of the subject matter. The test items must be a sample from the universe of items. This makes it difficult to argue that any score in fact represents mastery of that percentage of the subject. This means that the content criterion can only be used to interpret test scores where there is a narrow and tightly specified content to the test.

Conclusions

It is clear that the content criterion is suitable only for achievement tests and only for those where the content can be strictly defined. At the lowest and most basic educational levels of the primary schools, however, such tests can be valuable. Schonell (1951) for example, developed a set of diagnostic tests for reading where the results indicated the exact problems, such as reversal of particular letters, or confusions of particular letters.

2. *Criterion prediction*

Another method of interpreting test scores which makes no use of norms is to set out the probability of subjects at each score reaching a particular criterion. This requires expectancy tables to be constructed. There are several points here worthy of note.

a. Expectancy tables can be constructed only where clear criterion scores are possible. This is usually only possible in certain educational and industrial applications of tests. Examination scores and grades make good criteria for expectancy tables, although it has to be said that in practice many public examinations both at school and university do not release marks. For occupational selection similar scores are also obtainable – examination scores for police promotion and supervisors' ratings are obvious examples, although the latter may be of dubious reliability.

b. These expectancies are not theoretical but empirical. This means that large scale studies of the relevant populations have to be carried out. This, of course, involves all the sampling problems which I have discussed in relation to the establishment of norms. Indeed, in this sense, the probabilities of expectancy tables are normative data. However there is a problem over and above the sampling – obtaining adequate criterion data. Although, as I have indicated, it may be difficult to use actual scores more crude criteria, such as pass/fail or promoted/not promoted are obtainable.

c. Expectancy tables illustrate with an uncompromising clarity an important dilemma of applied psychology and of psychometrics: the use of actuarial predictions in the individual case. If a particular score on a test indicates a .45 probability of passing an examination, it means that 45 per cent of individuals (in the normative sample) with such a score passed the examination. The implication of the expectancy tables is that 45 per cent of subjects with this score will pass the examination. However it does not say which 45 per cent and this is a highly important question in applied psychology. Rationally, therefore, a selector would reject all candidates with such a score and in the long run he or she would be more right than wrong. But for any one individual this may be the wrong decision. This is the dilemma of actuarial psychology, and, as should now be obvious, most psychometrics is actuarial. However the problem is particularly acute in respect of expectancy tables and for this reason I think that they should be used with considerable caution.

To construct expectancy tables the sample must be divided into criterion groups – pass/fail is a common and useful criterion. The test scores are then divided so that there are equal numbers in each group, except at the extremes, and the proportion of these groups passing and failing the exam are computed. These proportions represent the probability of individuals with these scores on the test passing the examination.

I have described how expectancy tables are constructed because it highlights the absolute necessity for numbers in each of the test score categories to be both large and representative. If sampling is poor the expectancy tables are likely to be highly misleading. Indeed, it can be argued that since large and representative samples are required for expectancy tables, there is little difference in this approach from normal test standardisation. Instead of locating a subject's score relative to the normative group, as in the establishment of norms, with expectancy tables his or her score is located relative to performance on some criterion. Essentially, therefore, it could be argued that expectancy tables are a rather different form of norms rather than some essentially different approach, as suggested by Brown (1976).

3. The regression method

Another method of constructing expectancy tables is to use a regression equation to predict the criterion scores from the test scores. This can be done by the following regression equation:

4.3 $Y_{pred} = a + b_y \times X$

where Y_{pred} = the predicted criterion score; a = the intercept constant; b = the regression or slope constant; X = the score on the predictor test.

Of course this formula can only be used when a and b are known. The formula for these is set out in 4.4 and 4.5.

4.4 $a = Y - b_y \overline{X}$

4.5 $b_y = r_{xy} \times \sigma_y / \sigma_x$

where Y = the mean of the criterion score; $\overline{X}$ = the mean of the test score; r = the correlation of x and y; σ_y = the standard deviation of Y and σ_x = the standard deviation of X.

With this formula we can set up a table of predicted scores from each test score. However Y_{pred} is the predicted average score on the criterion of subjects with a given test score and is thus subject to error unless there is a perfect correlation between the test and the criterion score. Thus it is necessary to compute the standard error of the estimated scores. As with all standard errors 68 per cent of all estimated scores will fall between the estimate and one standard error and 95 per cent will fall within two standard errors. Formula 4.5 computes the standard error of estimated scores.

4.6 $S_{est} = \sigma_y \sqrt{1 - r^2_{xy}}$

where σ_y is the standard deviation of the obtained test score and r_{xy} is the correlation of the test and the criterion.

The predicted scores together with their standard errors can be displayed graphically thus allowing the predicted criterion scores to be read off together with their standard errors.

If the standard error of the estimates is low these regression-based expectancy tables can be useful. However since to be accurate large samples and very high correlations between test and criterion scores are required, considerable resources are necessary to establish good expectancy tables. Again this method is not essentially different from the establishment of norms.

Conclusion

From this chapter one clear conclusion can be drawn. There is no escape, in the establishment of norms, from setting up large and representative samples.

IPSATIVE SCORES

To conclude this chapter mention must be made of ipsative scores. These may be found in any test where there are forced choices, for example, and where each choice is scored. Thus in the Defence Mechanism Test (Gleser and Ihelevich, 1969) subjects have to choose, for each item, the most and least liked of five responses, each representing one of five defences. This means that at the end of the test the scores can represent only the relative strength of the defences in that individual. There must be negative correlations between some of the scores simply as an artefact of the scoring system, in that if one chooses one response as the best that excludes the four others. This scoring system fails to measure the absolute strength of the defences. An alcoholic example makes the point. A social drinker might rate whisky as his favourite drink, followed by gin and rum, a combination also selected by a dipsomaniac. Clearly these choices are hardly comparable.

Where forced-choice responses produce ipsative scores, and many tests do use this format, two consequences follow. First, the correlation matrix is not meaningful since the scales are artefactually negatively correlated. Factor analysis of the correlations defies interpretation. Second, it makes no sense to collect norms for these scales, since, as has been argued, scores are not comparable across individuals. Thus norms are entirely innocent of psychological meaning.

The only norms that might be collected could be of rank orders. Thus it is meaningful to argue that 60 per cent of males rank outdoor interests first and interest in embroidery last. However, even this is of dubious worth because the differences in distance between ranks are unknown, as well as the differences in strength such that, ultimately, the psychological meaning of rank-order norms is dubious.

This means that essentially ipsatively scored tests are only useful as a basis of discussion with the subject who has completed them. Then the meaning of the score's ranks can be explicated. This means that the use of such tests is restricted to contexts where test scores are used as a basis of discussion and where the quantification is relatively unimportant. This means that these tests can be useful in clinical psychology and in vocational guidance and counselling, both settings for testing where the rapport and trust between the subject and tester is important. Applied testing is the subject of Section 3 of this handbook and the use of tests in vocational guidance is discussed in Chapter 21. Testing in clinical psychology is scrutinised in Chapter 20.

Conclusions

From this it is clear that normative tests are far superior to ipsative tests as precise measures of psychological characteristics. Ipsative scores are only suitable as a basis of discussion. Since, however, it is perfectly possible to use normative tests as a basis of discussion and have, in addition, scores suitable for statistical analysis, there seems no reason to use ipsatively scored tests and they are not recommended.

Chapter 5

Rasch Scaling and other Scales

In Chapter 3 of this handbook I discussed the classical model of test error, a model which subsumes the vast majority of psychological tests in regular use. Nevertheless there are other models of test response which lead to different types of scales and I shall discuss these in this chapter. In addition I shall discuss certain other scales, which are somewhat different from conventional psychological tests, although their statistical basis resides in the classical model.

OTHER TYPES OF SCALING

Although most of the work on other types of scales, particularly that based upon the computation of item characteristic curves (discussed in the next section) is modern, in fact similar scales were developed alongside traditional scales by a number of important psychometrists. Thus both Thorndike and Thurstone developed scaling procedures which I shall mention briefly because, as has been shown by Engelhard (1984), these yield results virtually identical to the Rasch model, which is the most widely applied of the new methods and which is described later in this chapter.

The aim of the Thorndike, Thurstone and Rasch procedures is to minimise item variance. Thus objective measurement demands that the calibration of the test be independent of the sample that is used in the calibration and that the measurement of the object should be independent of the items which happen to be used in the measurement. This is the object of all these scaling methods. As Engelhard (1984) points out, Thorndike (1919) transmuted scores on items into measurements on the basis of an assumed distribution. Once the general form of the distribution is specified an item's position on the latent trait based on an index of variability can be computed. Thorndike overcame the problem of item invariance in different groups by adjusting for differences of means in different groups.

Thurstone (1925) attacked the problem by developing his method of absolute scaling, which should not be confused with the Thurstone scaling described later in this chapter in the construction of attitude tests. It was called absolute scaling because it is independent of the scoring unit of the raw scores. The unit of measurement is the standard deviation of test ability in any given age group. Thurstone assumed a normal distribution of ability for any given group on the latent trait. He further assumed that items would define points on this scale which would itself define the latent trait. The location of the item on the latent trait was defined by the proportion of correct responses for a specified group. Then a numerical value for each group was defined with the standard deviation as the unit of measurement and the proportion of correct responses for an item expressed as standard normal deviates – the sigma values.

Having assigned the item a numerical value Thurstone made adjustments so that each group could be properly located on the latent trait.

Engelhard (1984) then takes a data set and demonstrates a high degree of similarity between the Thurstone and Thorndike methods, both of which were designed to overcome the problem of item variance. He demonstrates also that they yield similar results to Rasch scaling, one of the new approaches to test construction, based upon item characteristic curves, which are described below.

ITEM RESPONSE MODELS

The modern approach to scaling items and obtaining item and population-free scores involves the calculation of item characteristic curves and latent traits which the items are supposed to measure. Before these models can be understood it will be useful to define some of the essential terms.

Latent traits

In latent space theory, as Hattie (1985) argues, it is assumed that responses to an item can be accounted for by a number of latent traits within each subject. The latent traits can be represented by a vector. This vector is an n-tuple which can be represented geometrically as a point in n-dimensional space. The dimensionality of the latent space in a unidimensional test is one, this being a special case. The regression of the item score on the latent trait vector is called the item characteristic function. For a dichotomous item this item characteristic function is the P, the probability of a correct response to the item. This probability, as shall be seen below, is a function of the discriminating power of the item – the degree to which the response varies depending on the level of the latent trait; the item difficulty, indicated by the location of the item characteristic curve on the latent trait scale; and a guessing parameter, the probability with which a person, infinitely low on the latent trait, can get the item right. The latent trait provides a scale for the item characteristic curves.

The fundamental assumption of the latent trait model is local independence, namely that if the latent trait, theta, is fixed any two items should be uncorrelated although they could be correlated within a group since here theta will vary. In other words the latent trait must account entirely for the item response. Thus the latent trait can be interpreted as a quantity which the items measure in common since it serves to explain all mutual statistical dependence among items. Although this is a more rigorous definition than the factor analytic account of item intercorrelations, since items may be uncorrelated yet not statistically independent, it is clear that in practice there may be little difference in the notion of a latent trait or a factor accounting for item variance.

Item characteristic curves

Item characteristic curves delineate, in general, the probability of response to an item plotted against an index of status on a particular trait or ability. A highly technical and sophisticated research literature has developed in this field (e.g. Lord, 1974, 1980), the most important aspect of which I shall summarise in this chapter.

Based upon these item characteristic curves a variety of different models of item response have been generated. However I shall not describe all these models for two reasons. Few of them have led to psychological tests of any note and, more important, it has been shown by Levy (1973) that there is considerable agreement between all these models. Rather I shall discuss two models which have been used to construct psychological tests – those of Rasch (1960) and Guttman (1950).

Before I do this, however, I want to scrutinise item characteristic curves because without some understanding of these curves the models based upon them will be incomprehensible. Two typical item characteristic curves are set out in Figure 5.1.

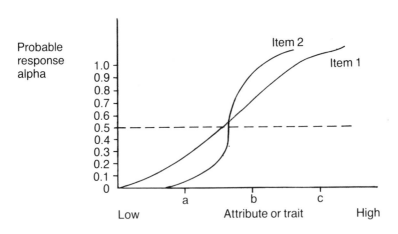

Figure 5.1 Two typical item characteristic curves

The first point to notice, as Nunnally (1978) emphasises, is that the latent trait or attribute is notional or hypothetical and has to be inferred from the nature of the items. This, however, does not render scales derived from these models different from those developed by factor analysis since the meaning of the factor which accounts for the item variance is inferred from the nature of the items.

To illustrate the meaning of Figure 5.1 let us suppose that the latent trait is verbal ability. This is a continuum, running from low to high along which subjects are distributed. In Figure 5.1 a, b and c represent three points on this continuum of verbal ability. Subjects at point a have a probability of .015 of putting the correct response to item 2 and .15 of putting the correct response to item 1. Those at point c, on the other hand, have a probability of 1 of getting item 2 correct and .95 for item 1.

The shape of these curves is not accidental but typifies responses to items in the ability sphere. Models of item response based upon item characteristic curves assume that these are normal ogives, i.e. cumulative normal distributions, or because it has computational advantages that they are logistic curves. This assumption is supported by the fact that psychophysical judgements approximate logistic curves, as Nunnally (1978) argues.

The use of item characteristic curves in test construction

It is not assumed that the item characteristic curves for all the items in a test should be identical. Indeed, if they were, as shall be seen, it would not lead to a good test since all the items would have identical psychometric characteristics. Rather it is assumed that the items tend to fit the logistic curve. Figure 5.1 illustrates some of the psychometric qualities of items which may be obtained from their item characteristic curves:

1. Difficulty level (d). This is reflected in the position of the curve – how far to the left or right it is displaced. It is defined as the point on the attribute or latent trait continuum where the curve crosses the .5 probability value. Thus the difficulty levels of the items in Figure 5.1 are virtually identical.
2. Discriminability (r). This is reflected in the steepness of the curve. The higher the value of r the more sharply the item discriminates among people who are in the zone, on the latent trait, corresponding to a p value of .5.

Subsets of items

Figure 5.1 demonstrates that it is possible to estimate the scores of subjects on items which they have not taken, provided that their position on the latent trait is known. Of course the item characteristic curve of the item must also be known. This means that scores from subsets of items allow estimates of scores on the full test to be made. Furthermore it is possible to construct subsets of items which are equivalent. These indices of difficulty calculated from item characteristic curves tend to be more stable than does the more simple index of difficulty given by the proportion getting the item correct.

Item information curves

In classical test theory, precision of measurement is assessed through an index of reliability, which is of course applicable to the whole test. In item response theory measurement, precision is indexed by a conditional standard error of measurement which can differ for each value of the latent trait (Waller and Reise, 1989). Item information in a two-parameter model, where item discriminability and item information are allowed to vary, can be stated thus:

Item information = a^2PQ where a = the discrimination of an item and P = the conditional probability of responding in the keyed direction and Q = 1-P.

Test information curves

Just as the item information curve can be plotted across the latent trait so can item information curves. These curves can be summed to produce a test information curve and this indicates the level of precision of a test at any given level of the latent trait. The conditional standard error of test = the inverse square root of the test information. Thus plotting the test information curve enables the conditional standard error to be computed.

There are insufficient tests which have been constructed by these methods to be confident about how effectively they might work in practice. Nunnally (1978) has argued that the correlation between a test constructed according to the classical item analytic and factor analytic methods and by item characteristic curve models is high, so high, indeed, that he does not advise their use. Nevertheless one particular model, that of Rasch (1960, 1966), has been powerfully advocated by many testers (e.g. Elliot, 1983) and been strongly criticised (e.g. Mellenbergh, 1983) so that it will be necessary to examine it in a little more detail. It typifies, it should be said, the models of test response based upon item characteristic curves.

Before I do this, however, it will be useful to consider the relationship between classical test theory, which was described in Chapter 3 of this handbook, and item characteristic curve theory, since, as we have seen, there is a high correlation between tests constructed by the two methods.

CLASSICAL TEST THEORY AND ITEM RESPONSE CURVES

As Roskam (1985) argues, and as I hope is already clear to readers, classical test theory rests upon the assumption of a general linear model which is basic to correlational analysis, linear analysis and factor analysis. It is concerned, therefore, with additive errors of measurement and score components. Item response theory, on the other hand, is couched in stochastic terms, with a probabilistic response model of which the parameters express certain item characteristics.

Yet the normal ogive model is in fact little different from the classical model, as can be seen from the Guttman model which I shall describe in more detail later in this chapter, since it has been used in the construction of certain attitude tests. If we have 10 items in a Guttman scale, arranged in order of difficulty, then if a subject endorses item 8 we can be certain that she or he will endorse all the previous 7 and so on. In other words each item has a perfect biserial correlation with the total score. Now if we assume that a subject's latent trait score fluctuates according to a normal distribution then the normal ogive model may be derived from the Guttman model. Thus the normal ogive model is a probabilistic form of the deterministic Guttman model.

Indeed, as Roskam (1985) shows, if the true latent trait score is normally distributed then the factor analysis of the item correlations (tetrachoric) is a good test of the unidimensionality of the items under the normal ogive model and the item loadings of the first factor are good estimates of the slopes of the item characteristic curves. Indeed, de Gruijter (1986) demonstrates that from p, the proportion putting the keyed response to an item, and r, the correlation of the item with the total test score (the standard indices of classical item analysis, as discussed in Chapter 10 of this handbook), the difficulty, discriminability and pseudo-guessing parameters of item response models can be calculated – extremely useful for the construction of item banks which is discussed in the next chapter.

From this it may be claimed, as Roskam argues, that the distinctive feature of the normal ogive model compared with the classical model is that the former takes differences in item difficulties into account. Indeed Roskam (1985) cites evidence that it is indeed the case that the principal factor analysis of the tetrachoric correlations between items yields essentially the same results as a proper Rasch analysis (the Rasch model being virtually identical to the normal ogive model). Such analyses, of course, are similar to work of de Gruijter (1986), discussed above.

Despite these essential similarities between models Rasch analysis has certain other features which mean that those who want to exploit its characteristics are not content to factor matrices of tetrachoric correlations but prefer to use the model as it was described by Rasch (1960).

In fact I myself am dubious as to whether in the context of practical test construction, as distinct from experimental statistical studies, factoring tetrachoric correlations could ever give rise to accurate Rasch indices. This is because tetrachoric correlations between items are strongly affected by the proportions of the sample responding to each item. In addition the standard error of tetrachoric coefficients is double that of the product moment correlation (Guilford, 1956). This leads to considerable instability of factor loadings unless huge samples are used.

RASCH SIMPLE LOGISTIC RESPONSE MODEL

The logistic model, developed by Rasch (1960), can be expressed in several equivalent forms but I shall concentrate upon the most simple and basic one. The Rasch model is an example of a one-parameter latent trait model which involves only the estimation of the difficulty parameters. As Waller and Reise (1989) point out, this is the least complex of a family of models. There is a two-parameter model, in which estimates are made of item difficulty and item discrimination, and a three-parameter model where pseudo-guessing is also included. The Rasch model has two purposes:

1. It provides a procedure to reveal whether a scale is internally consistent irrespective of the trait variance in populations.
2. It identifies any item–population interactions (where within population item variance differs from between population variance) which would render of dubious psychological significance any comparisons between populations. This is a severe problem in test interpretation as may be seen in the heated discussions of the meaning of the intelligence test score differences between American Negros and other ethnic groups (e.g. Jensen, 1980).

When subject z encounters item i and responds Yes or No to it a response variable x_{zi} is scored 0 or 1 depending on whether the response points to a low or high status on the trait being measured. The response is taken to depend on two variables: (1) the facility item i has for eliciting the trait among all subjects (corresponding to the difficulty level of the item in classical theory); (2) The status of the subject on the latent trait, a status which governs her or his responses to all the items. This corresponds, in normal language, to the ability of the subject, if the latent trait is, say, intelligence.

5.1 The Rasch Equation $P\{x_{zi}/a_i, T_z\} = \dfrac{\exp((T_z - a_i)\, X_{zi})}{1 + \exp(T_z - a_i)}$

T_z is the parameter representing the status of subject z on the latent trait; a_i is the parameter representing the facility item i has for eliciting this status; P is the probability of the response of the subject to the item.

From the Rasch equation it is clear that the larger the value of T the greater the probability that the subject will have 1 for his or her response and the lower the value of a the higher the probability that the subject will score 1. This is nothing more than formalising the somewhat obvious point that the higher the status of the subject on the latent trait and the easier the item the more likely it is the subject will get the item correct. It is also implicit in the model that the subject and item paameters are unidimensional. If the responses of subjects to a set of items conform to this Rasch model the items form a unidimensional scale or in the terminology of the traditional classical model the items are homogeneous and internally consistent.

The critical quality of the Rasch model in Formula 5.1, as Rasch (1960, 1961) and Wright (1968) stress, is that the estimates of a_i are independent of the values of T_z and are, therefore, independent of the distribution of the trait in any sample of subjects whose responses are analyses. That is estimates of a_i can be obtained from any subjects, regardless of the variance of the latent trait within the sample. This also means that evidence regarding the internal consistency of a scale can be obtained without it being distorted by the lack of variance in the sample. Furthermore a check on the scale consistency within different populations can be made. Thus Rasch scale item parameters are population free, and it follows that subject parameters are item free, i.e. obtainable from any subset of items.

A number of different algebraic procedures have been developed for estimating a_i and T_z and for identifying items which do not fit the model. The estimation of the parameters involves maximising the likelihood of the response matrix with respect to the item and subject parameters simultaneously. The test of fit entails checking whether the observed data can be recovered by the model from the estimates of the subject and item parameters. However, as Hattie (1985) points out, one of the problems is the precision of the goodness of fit tests. Rogers (1984), cited by Hattie (1985), concluded that the tests were so insensitive that it was necessary to know that the items were unidimensional before Rasch scaling was begun. This means that in any but the simplest achievement tests items should be first factored. This considerably lowers the value of Rasch scaling as an approach to psychological test construction. However the more complex two- and three-parameter models do allow infringements of unidimensionality to be detected.

The check of the internal consistency of items in a single population is called the within-population item-fit. The check as to whether the items fit the model relative to a number of populations is called the among-populations item-fit. The procedure for carrying out this check depends upon the property of the Rasch model that the estimates of the item parameters are independent of the samples who have completed the test. For each item the parameter values obtained from a sample of each population of subjects are compared statistically. These equations, the maximum likelihood estimates, are highly complex and readers are referred to Wright (1968) or Rasch (1961) for the computational, algebraic details. In a test of any length a computer program is essential.

As we have seen, the advantages which have been claimed for the Rasch model as a method of test construction are that the items may be used to obtain accurate scores for subjects regardless of their level of ability simply because the model can distinguish between level of ability and item difficulty. From this it follows that subsets of items can be given to subjects, each subset being exactly equivalent, a valuable characteristic where repeated testing is required, as in the study of ongoing processes such as education or psychotherapy, and in developmental psychology generally.

Problems with the Rasch model

As was discussed above, Roskam (1985) had argued that the Rasch model was really a special case of the latent trait model and was a probabilistic form of Guttman scaling. As Levy (1973) has demonstrated this may well mean that it is basically unsuited to many areas of psychological measurement. In addition to this there are various other difficulties with the Rasch model which must now be discussed.

1. Some of the assumptions of the model are quite simply wrong

  a. It assumes that items are equally discriminating. In fact no test would be so constructed since it makes sense to vary the discriminatory power of items in a test of ability, even though, of course, Rasch measurement is population free. In addition it is difficult to construct a set of items which are equally discriminating even if it were so desired, except in certain narrow areas of ability and achievement. Of course two-parameter item response models have been developed, and Waller and Reise (1989) have argued that such two-parameter models are suited to the construction of personality tests.

  b. It assumes that there is no guessing. It is clearly difficult to stop guessing, especially where tests are used in the applied setting and the results are important to subjects. It is possible to insert an extra parameter into the model to accommodate guessing, as, indeed, Birnbaum (1968) has done, but, in this case, as Wood (1976) has argued, the dimensionality of the model is destroyed.

2. There is a serious problem with the calibration in Rasch scaling

Lord (1974) has shown that huge samples have to be tested if reliable, population-free scaling is to be established. Indeed samples quite as large as those required for adequate standardisation are required, as was discussed in Chapter 4 of this handbook. In addition experience with the construction of item banks for attainment testing convinced Chopin (1976) that virtually no items fit the model if enough calibration is carried out. Indeed there is even disagreement among specialists in item characteristic curve theory over just what is the best method of measuring fit. Perhaps an even more serious finding was that of Wood (1978) who showed that random data could be made to fit the Rasch model. Nunnally (1978) has also argued that there is a very high correlation between Rasch scales and those constructed by normal classical methods.

3. As has been mentioned in connection with tests of goodness of fit there is a problem with the dimensionality of Rasch scales

Barrett and Kline (1981a) showed in a study of the EPQ (Eysenck and Eysenck, 1975) that Rasch scaling of this test produced a meaningless scale, a composite of items from all the four scales.

Conclusions

From this it is quite clear that Rasch scaling is not the psychometric panacea that its initial description might suggest. Nevertheless where, in relatively simple fields of ability testing, there is little reason to doubt the notion of a clear latent trait, where the ability is cumulative, where large calibration samples have been used and where there is a need for equivalent subsets of items, as in developmental studies, for example, then Rasch scaling may be useful. In most circumstances, however, it has no worthwhile advantages over a well standardised test constructed on the classical model and I think that it should be used only in the special circumstances mentioned above.

Two-parameter models where item discriminability is allowed to vary and three-parameter models to accommodate guessing overcome some of these problems. However, with all the item response theory models the problem lies in the rigour of the definition of latent trait. For many psychological tests where, unlike achievement tests or tests of simple cognitive function, it is difficult to specify what the items may be measuring, these item response models are inappropriate and the classical model seems better. Certainly the best known and validated tests in the field of ability, personality and motivation have not been constructed using these models. Their field would seem to be achievement, where the notion of comparable sets of items makes good sense and perhaps in tailored testing, which is discussed in Chapter 6 of this handbook. However, it should be mentioned that Thyssen and Steinberg (1988) have argued that these models fit data in role-conflict, personality, politics and life satisfaction. I should like to see valid tests constructed according to these models before I could accept such claims.

ATTITUDE SCALES

There are three kinds of scale which have been commonly used in the construction of attitude tests each with a number of purported advantages. These will be described and evaluated in the following sections.

Guttman scaling

In my discussion of Rasch scaling it has been pointed out that Rasch scales are probabilistic versions of Guttman scales. These will now be described and evaluated and this relationship will become clear.

Guttman scales are members of a family of models, known as deterministic models, where it is assumed that the item characteristic curves are without error. This can be seen from the following description of a Guttman scale. Suppose that we have a 20-item Guttman scale, with the items in order of difficulty. Then if a subject gets item 9 correct, he or she is bound to get items 1–8 correct. If he or she fails on item 10, items 11–20 will also be failed. Such ordering will be true for all subjects on a Guttman scale.

In terms of item characteristic curves this Guttman model assumes that up to a point on the latent trait or attribute, the probability of response alpha is 0 and beyond this point it is 1. This implies that each item has a biserial correlation with the total scale score of 1 and that it discriminates perfectly at some point on the latent trait continuum. All these points are obvious if one thinks carefully of the Guttman scale described in the previous paragraph.

Construction of Guttman scales

I shall not describe in detail how Guttman scales may be constructed but it is sufficient to say that the aim is to select items with a level of difficulty such that, as described above, to fail an item means that all easier items will be passed and harder items failed. This is a massive sorting task, where large numbers of items and subjects are used and this latter is essential if the Guttman scaling is to hold up on further administration of the items. Fortunately computer programs are now available for scaling items, a task for which, previously, there were a number of tedious algorithms, known collectively as scalogram analysis.

From the discussion so far it should be apparent that Guttman scales are most appropriate where a clear ordering along the attribute is possible. In the field of abilities and attainments, for example, hierarchical, structured subjects such as mathematics and music would appear better suited to a Guttman scale than would, say, history or sociology.

Intuitive appeal of Guttman scales

As Nunnally (1978) argues, there is a definite intuitive appeal to Guttman scales. Their perfect ordering of items seems consistent with common-sense knowledge of measurement. Thus if we were to think of the measurement of length, we see there is a Guttman scale as there is for weight or volume. A series of items: are you 100 kg; are you 99 kg; are you 98 kg; and so on, would form a perfect Guttman scale.

There is a further obvious advantage with a Guttman scale, namely that if we know how many items a subject got right we know his or her performance on the whole test. The reproducibility of the score patterns is, indeed, an index of the efficacy of a Guttman scale. It should be noticed that this reproducibility is more than knowing the score a person would have obtained. It also indicates the actual items the subject got correct and wrong.

Problems with Guttman scales

We have already discussed the objection of Levy (1973) to Rasch scaling, namely that its underlying model is not in accord with most psychological theory. This same objection applies to Guttman scaling. It seems unlikely that the item characteristic curves of items in a Guttman scale would fit any data in the real world. It is unlikely that items would correlate perfectly with total scores on the attribute. Thus the model, which as we have seen assumes such a correlation, is a bad fit.

A further objection to Guttman scaling stems from the fact that scales can be constructed by choosing items widely spaced out in level of difficulty, or endorsement rate in the case of attitude scales. Such wide dispersion of items creates a Guttman scale but it is necessarily short and not highly discriminating. With such a scale the item characteristic curves no longer fit the model.

In fact this objection has been developed by Nunnally (1978) into a more severe point. He argues that the fact that a Guttman scale has been constructed does not ensure that the scale is unidimensional. Thus an easy, a medium, a hard and a severe item, although each were measuring different things, might well form a Guttman scale. However the item characteristic curves would refer to no attribute or latent trait. This is the same objection as the one which was raised to Rasch scaling in the study of the EPQ by Barrett and Kline (1981a) where E, N, P and L were inextricably compounded. The basic problem is that the Guttman scale is scaled in terms of item difficulties.

The final difficulty with Guttman scales is that they allow only ordinal measurement. As Nunnally (1978) argues, ordinal measurement precludes any but the most simple statistical analyses and it is impossible to conceive of a science based upon ordinal measurement.

Conclusions

For all these reasons Guttman scales cannot be recommended and I am highly dubious of the validity of any such scales unless there is clear empirical evidence in their favour.

Thurstone scales

In the Guttman model the item characteristic curves are assumed to have perpendicular ascents and descents, i.e. they are deterministic models. Where this is not assumed the model is some kind of probability model and one of the best known such models in the field of attitude measurement is Thurstone scaling. This is a non-monotone probability model in which the item characteristic curves are assumed to be be normal and the attribute is continuous.

This somewhat formal introduction will be clarified by example. The basic approach to the development of a Thurstone attitude scale involves three steps: (1) A large number of statements relevant to the attitude is collected together; (2) these are rated by a large number of judges on an 11-point scale ranging from 'strongly favourable' to 'strongly unfavourable'; (3) 10 to 20 items are selected where there is good agreement among judges (as measured by a small standard deviation of ratings). In addition to this, care must be taken that the statements embrace the whole range of the attitude, i.e. some obtain extreme ratings. A subject's score can be either the mean rating of the items with which she or he agrees or the highest scale rating of any of the items which she or he endorses.

Problems with Thurstone scales

There are sufficient problems with this model of attitude scaling as to render its use dubious, which is why I have been content to describe it briefly. These difficulties are set out below.

1. Edwards (1957) has argued convincingly that if the scaling is to be reliable 100 judges are necessary. To obtain such a large number is clearly not easy. Furthermore these judges must be representative of the population for whom the the test is intended or, again, the scaling will not be accurate. This is a practical difficulty.
2. Nunnally (1978) considers that an even more severe objection to Thurstone scaling can be made on theoretical grounds. He argues that, as with all non-monotone probability models, items rarely fit the Thurstone model. Thus the essence of this model is that each item should tend to receive the keyed response only at one segment of the attribute dimension. Thus if we have an item 'sexism is unfair' this might be endorsed by those at the middle point of the Sexist Attitude scale but

it would also be endorsed by those at the high end. This is true of many items and the fact is the model does not fit the structure of attitudes or indeed of anything else. It would be entirely dissonant to the structure of abilities or attainments. The fact is that attitude items are monotonic but the Thurstone scaling model is not.

These two objections, practical and theoretical, are sufficient to ensure that the use of Thurstone scales is not recommended.

Likert scales

In fact many modern attitude scales use Likert scales and these will now be described. First a small but important theoretical point needs to be made. Likert scales, developed by Likert (1932), are described by Nunnally (1978) as belonging to the category of monotone models with unspecified distribution forms which he regards as ideal for the measurement of attitudes. These models make three main assumptions which do not run counter to the nature of attitudes.

1. It is assumed that each item has a monotonic trace line but this need not be the same for each item.
2. It is assumed the sum of the trace lines for all the items (i.e. the trace line for total test scores) is approximately linear. Thus the departures from linearity of trace lines by each individual item are expected to cancel each other out. Notice that, as was pointed out in Chapter 3 on classical test theory, all the arguments that apply to items apply equally to sums of items, i.e. tests.
3. It is assumed that the items measure only the attribute in question. This is assumed in almost all methods of test construction and is the basis of the item analytic and factor analytic methods of test construction, which are fully described in later chapters of this book. Indeed, not unnaturally most tests make this assumption since it would be odd to have a test which yielded a composite score. Its psychological meaning would be indecipherable.

These assumptions constitute the linear model, so called because it assumes that the sum of the item scores has a linear relationship with the attribute. Furthermore the model leads to a linear combination of items. This of course is the model of almost all psychological tests and the model in the classical theory of error which was discussed in Chapter 3.

From this it is clear that, on strict psychometric grounds, Likert scales should be considered alongside tests constructed on the basis of the classical model of error, but we have dealt with them here because they are attitude scales and thus provide a neat contrast with the less orthodox Guttman and Thurstone scales.

Likert scales consist essentially of statements followed by 5- or 7-point rating scales which indicate the extent of a subject's agreement with the item. As was argued above, no unwarrantable assumptions are made by this model and the sum of endorsed items should represent a subject's status on the attribute.

Since the model underlying Likert scales is that underlying most tests, the classical model of error variance, I shall not describe how these are constructed in this chapter for this is fully dealt with in the chapters on test construction.

CONCLUSIONS

The conclusions that may be drawn from this chapter are simple and clear. On analysis it is difficult to justify the models of test response that underlie Rasch scaling, except perhaps in certain well structured fields of attainment. Similarly the models of attitude testing implicit in Thurstone and Guttman scales are unrealistic. Likert scales based on the classical model of error variance (which, conveniently, are far more simple to construct) are more consonant with the structure of attitudes. For all these reasons the classical model of error variance is still seen as the most valuable for understanding and constructing psychological tests and most of the remainder of this handbook will be concerned with tests and methods derived from this model.

Chapter 6

Computerised and Tailored Testing

In this chapter I shall discuss the principles of computerised testing and evaluate and compare the use of this method with traditional testing procedures. In addition I shall discuss one special application of computers to psychometric testing – tailored testing. However I shall not discuss specific computerised or tailored tests; descriptions of these may be found in the final section of this handbook.

IMPORTANT ASPECTS OF COMPUTERISED TESTING

1. Items There is no magic about computer testing. A computerised test is no more or no less than the sum of its items, as is the case with traditional psychometric tests. However it is possible, in principle, to use items that could not be presented other than by computer. An obvious example arises in the sphere of tests of reaction time and tracking tasks, such as are found in arcade computer games. However, a computer test, even if it consists of what might be called computer-bound items, must still be judged against the standard psychometric criteria of reliability, discriminatory power, validity and the quality of normative data, where these are applicable.

2. Comparability between a paper and pencil test and a computer-administered test It is possible to computerise virtually any traditional psychometric test. It is far easier to present on the computer screen verbal and numerical items than visual items where there is always the possibility that the screen image will be different from the printed test, even with modern graphics and light-sensitive pens. Nevertheless, no matter how identical the two tests appear to be it is essential that the reliability, validity and standardisation of the computer version be checked. Furthermore it is essential to show that the correlation between the two versions is high. Indeed, if the computer version is to be regarded as identical with the traditional test this correlation should be at least .9. Thus the computer test should be considered to be a parallel form. Generally, it must be said, as

Bartram and Bayliss (1984) point out, computer-administered tests and their traditional counterparts have turned out to be highly equivalent.

There is obviously a severe problem here. If, due perhaps to the low reliability of the original test, this correlation is only around .5, then it is impossible to regard the two tests as measuring the same variable. Clearly only tests with high reliability should be transmuted for computer. In any case, as has been said, new reliability, validity and standardisation data should be collected. Comparability has to be demonstrated rather than assumed.

3. Computer test instructions In a traditional psychometric test, as was made clear in our discussion of reliability, it is essential that the instructions are comprehensible to all subjects. In a computer-presented test it is similarly absolutely essential that the procedure for answering the questions, for obtaining the next question, for altering responses and for looking back (if that is allowed) are clear and easily worked by subjects. Computerised tests must be computer friendly in the simplest sense. If subjects are anxious about working the machine or are making errors as they proceed, or are unable to operate the computer, the test will fail. The British Psychological Society (Bartram *et al.*, 1987) has drawn up sensible guidelines as to how this should be done and their points will be discussed later in this chapter.

4. Indices of item difficulty These, or other similar indices, can be stored in the computer. This allows the tester to present a sample of the items in the test and yet arrive at an accurate score. This is known as tailored testing and as this technique is so important a special section will be devoted to it.

These first four points concern the presentation of tests via computer, but after the test has been administered there are other important aspects of computer testing which must be discussed. These concern the presentation and analysis of results, psychometric issues which have been revolutionised by the computer.

5. Analysis of data An enormous advantage of computerised tests is that data analysis, both for individuals and for groups, is made absurdly easy. I shall deal first with the analysis of an individual's test data.

a. Individual data. The computer can automatically store the results of the test item by item, as well as any other relevant information. Before starting the test all subjects should be required to insert the following information, as a minimum: age, sex and level of education (in numerical form: for example, 1 for no qualifications up to 5 for a higher degree).

This means that the computer can immediately produce the subject's score and its standard error (see Chapter 1), and the most appropriate standard score, if norms are established for the computer test. In addition it can show items which are wrong, or in the case of personality and attitude tests, items not endorsed in the keyed direction, all of which may be useful information for the tester, in various applied settings. In vocational guidance, for example, it is often valuable to discuss actual responses to individual items with the subject. Thus the computer can immediately, on completion of the test, provide the raw and standardised test score and any appropriate standard errors.

b. Analysis of group data. The computer stores the results of each subject's data. Thus, after a substantial number of subjects has been tested, it is simple to analyse the data. Item analysis, factor analysis, group norms, comparisons across categories of subjects by analysis of variance, are all possible with commercially available programs. Almost all the psychometric methods and techniques discussed in this handbook can be applied to the data which automatically build up with computer-presented tests.

6. Presentation of results to subjects   Immediately the test is finished the computer can present the results to the subject, either on screen or as a printed document. Although I shall discuss, in the relevant sections of this handbook, how these results are best used in various applied settings, at this point I shall simply discuss what can be presented.

In addition to the numerical score of the subject, it is possible to produce an interpretation of the score. Based upon the norms a description of the typical individual at each point on the scale can be produced and printed out.

Incidentally it should be pointed out that some of these facilities are possible with paper and pencil tests which are computer scored. Here the test is administered to subjects in the usual way, but the responses are punched into the computer. This allows the printed report for the subjects and comparisons with norm groups to be produced. It also allows a data base to be built up for the development of special norms. What of course is not possible is the presentation of items appropriate to the subject, as determined by the subject's responses.

ADVANTAGES OF COMPUTER TESTING OVER TRADITIONAL METHODS

As I indicated in the relevant section, tailored testing will be discussed separately in this chapter so that its advantages *vis-à-vis* traditional testing will be discussed there.

1. The first and greatest advantage in computer-administered testing is the capability it provides for almost immediate feedback of results. In the applied setting this is of considerable value. For example, in all counselling and therapeutic applications of tests immediate access to results is an enormous advantage. The test can be discussed while the whole thing is fresh in the subject's mind. In selection where the number of candidates is small and there is personal contact between the selector and candidates again immediate results are valuable. Where a huge number of subjects is tested, as in selection procedures for the armed services or civil service, this facility is not so important. In general, however, there can be no doubt that immediate feedback is a valuable characteristic of computer testing.

2.   A second advantage of the computer-administered test is that the administration is always the same. Variance due to testers is, therefore, eliminated. It should be pointed out that there is a possibility that a different computer screen from that on which the test was standardised might produce a different result so that strictly identical computers should be used to those for which the test was specified. Of course, traditional tests can be administered by tape recorder to ensure identity of administration, but this always seems, in my experience, somewhat artificial, when the human tester is present, whereas the impersonal computer is more acceptable.

3.   Where there is a shortage of skilled personnel, the prewritten interpretations can be valuable. These are used by many personnel managers in commercial organisations where the psychological and psychometric knowledge of the test users is low, or even non-existent.

4.   Obviously where valid items are used which can only be presented on computer, the computer is simply irreplaceable. However, except in certain specialised applications, computer items have not yet replaced those used in traditional tests.

It is possible to develop computer programs that will produce items of a given difficulty level where the item parameters are simple. This can be done for elementary cognitive tasks, as defined by Carroll (1983). These, as the title suggests, measure the simple cognitive processes which constitute general intelligence (according to cognitive theorists such as Carroll, 1983, and Hunt, 1978). Semantic encoding and spatial orientation are typical examples.

Irvine *et al.* (1990) and Dan *et al.* (in press) have produced a set of tests in which items of given difficulty level are generated by the computer, and have discussed some of their underlying rationale. Their arguments and claims will now be scrutinised.

Irvine and Dan (in press) press the point that the computerisation of tests has made possible the application and advance of item response theory, which allows more precise and concise estimates of human ability than does classical psychometric theory which is still the basis of the vast majority of psychological tests. This is partly because it enables equivalent forms to be produced with great ease, and that, as Mellenbergh (1983) has shown, is useful for removing test bias (although, as was pointed out in the previous chapter, differences in item response theory and the classical theory of error are not as great as has often been claimed). However, the most important point is that computerised testing permits new applications of item response theory and performance modelling, resulting not only in new tests but in improved understanding of abilities. This is exemplified in the work of Irvine *et al.* (1990). Drawing on cognitive theories, whose veracity and accuracy are uncontested, together with previous empirical research, they hypothesise the causes of difficulty of several types of test item: letter checking, symbol rotation, transitive inference, alphabet forward and backward test and the number distance test. Using algorithms to produce items of given difficulty levels they were able to produce four sets of items with virtually identical means and standard deviations. Factor analysis of these tests indicates that they load one factor, distinct from but correlated with the factor loading the general entrance test for army recruits, which is surely crystallised intelligence. This factor they claim is one of working memory.

However, their conclusion that these tests, measuring differences in encoding, comparison and reconstructive memory processes, explain parsimoniously IQ performance does not stand careful scrutiny. In the first place the correlations with the army entry test are small – around .3 and .4. In addition we do not have the correlations of the general factor running through these tests with the g factor. Furthermore the identification of these tests as measures of these processes is based on cognitive theory, but this is simply theory. It is identification by authority. To validate these tests other measures also claimed to tap these processes would have to be included, as well as measures which clearly did not.

What this work does show is that careful analysis of the items enables difficulties to be predicted with great accuracy. This is fine, but deals only with the last of the parameters of the item response model. The critical parameter from the psychological rather than the technological view is the first parameter, theta, the subject's ability, and about this these algorithms have nothing to say.

In conclusion we would agree with Irvine and his colleagues that computerised testing of this kind allows accurate specification of difficulty levels and is ideal for the application of item response theory. However it is uncertain whether much has been added to our knowledge of abilities.

One final point remains. Although this work is cited by Irvine and colleagues as exemplifying the importance of the computer in testing, these tests were actually paper and pencil tests although clearly they could have been computerised. Still, the items were generated by computer and in this sense they deserve to be called computer tests.

5. The fact that, in computer-administered tests, the data for each item are automatically stored makes the statistical analysis of the test effortless. It saves the necessity, and the possible errors, of punching in all the data.

Indeed Krug (1986) has shown more precisely with special reference to the 16PF test just what can be done with the computer, although in this instance the results have to be punched in or read by light-sensitive cell. At a recent conference on the industrial use of the 16PF test Krug (e.g. 1986) argued that computer analysis of tests was going to be the next big advance in the application of psychometrics.

A few examples will clarify this point. In the Executive Profile Survey (Lang and Krug, 1978) every item is given a fractional weight in estimating each scale. In fact this means that the 94-item response vector has to be multiplied (because there are 11 scales) by a 94 x 11 matrix. Clearly scoring this scale by hand is essentially impossible. Similarly age corrections for the 16PF test are far too complex, it is asserted, to be carried out by hand since a quadratic function seems best to fit the data. Krug advocates similar complex corrections for distortions due to faking. Nevertheless, it should be pointed out in connection with this last point that many distinguished psychometrists, such as Cronbach (1976) do not advocate these complex corrections for faking or other distortions on the grounds that the test responses, distorted or not, are the only data available and nothing warrants their alteration. This topic is fully discussed in Chapter 15 of this handbook.

In the 16PF Handbook (Cattell *et al.*, 1970) there may be found, based upon empirical research, linear regression equations, behavioural equations for the 16PF scales and some criteria, for example leadership effectiveness, creativity and a number of other occupations. These equations give the regression weights for the scales. While these can be computed by hand, with the computer it is possible to provide instant correlations of a subject's scores with the criteria.

Another approach is to compare an obtained profile (on the sixteen scores and the second orders, if required) with the profiles of different occupational groups. In the 16PF Handbook a pattern similarity coefficient may be found for this purpose which, again, can be instantly computed.

Needless to say all these techniques can be used with other tests, and in other fields, where the criterion data have been collected. There can be no doubt that these are valuable capabilities which only computer analysis can provide. Thus, for example, in clinical psychology if a test has good multiple correlations with some clinical diagnostic category exactly the same technique can be used, and as Krug (1986) argues there is some evidence that this type of clinical work is more efficient than the unaided clinician working with the test scores, a point that was convincingly argued, before such computer facilities became available, by Meehl (1954). The use of this kind of computer analysis in the clinical setting is fully discussed in the section of this handbook devoted to the practical application of tests.

This illustration by Krug (1986) of the use of the 16PF test is really an example of the use of tests as part of an expert system, defined by Beaumont (in press) as a system which can solve problems normally solved by experts and consisting of a knowledge base, an inference engine and a user interface. Thus the knowledge base might consist of norms for test scores, difficulty levels or scaling values for items, just for example. The inference engine is a logical system which can interpret rules with respect to the contents of the knowledge base in order to find valid conclusions. The user interface allows the system to communicate with the user.

In this sense every computer test which refers the scores to a data base and produces some print-out of results is an expert system, although if it merely does what a reader of the test manual would do, but faster and with greater accuracy, it is little more than a convenience. However in principle such an expert system could combine test scores and regress them to various criteria in ways which would be time consuming and perhaps in practice impossible for a test user, as indeed the work of Krug (1986) illustrates. Thus expert systems have a useful place in applied psychology and we shall discuss some of these applications in Section 3 of this handbook.

6. One impressive application of computerised tests, which will be fully discussed in the section on clinical testing in this handbook, is in testing the severely handicapped. If, for, example, subjects have very poor motor control, special keyboards with large keys can be used. Wilson *et al.* (1982) discuss some useful input devices for this purpose. For those whose vision is poor large script can be used on the computer screen. Of course, such tests are special tests and they could not be used for comparison with normal subjects. Nevertheless valuable clinical information can be obtained from such special computer testing.

In summary it is clear from the examples cited by Krug (1986) that there are many advantages of the computer for rapid and complex data analysis. These are the main advantages of computer testing in comparison with traditional psychometrics. It is quite clear from this general discussion that computer testing has sufficient advantages to make it a useful part of psychometrics where it is appropriate. Where this is, however, will be obvious when I have discussed the disadvantages of computer-administered tests.

DISADVANTAGES OF COMPUTER-ADMINISTERED TESTS

1. The need for individual computer terminals for each person limits the number of subjects who can be tested at any one time – given that in any commercial organisation psychological testing has to show cost benefits. Without going into details this means that for the organisation the costs of testing subjects for selection must be paid back in increased efficiency of those selected. Where the cost of failure is very high, as in pilot selection, an organisation may think it worthwhile to invest heavily in selection. However, where mass testing is required computer-administered tests cannot be advised.

Nevertheless it must be pointed out that some of the advantages can be gained by computer marking of the traditional tests. This can be aided by direct scoring of the response sets through light-sensitive readers.

2. It may not be easy to establish that a traditional test administered on a computer is equivalent to the original one, particularly if this was not highly reliable.

3. Some subjects, particularly older subjects and those of low intelligence, may have difficulties using computer-administered tests. Even though, as was pointed out in the discussion of the advantages of such testing, it is possible to develop special testing procedures for individuals who are so handicapped that other forms of testing would be almost impossible, these could not be used by normal subjects.

4. Some psychologists feel that an essential of good testing is to establish rapport with subjects. Heim *et al.* (1970), in their series of intelligence tests, have an introductory series of example items for subjects to solve and to find out whether they have answered them correctly. This is partly to acquaint subjects with the type of items in the test. However, the more important function of these trial items is to establish good rapport between the subjects and the tester without which, in the view of the authors of these tests, good testing is impossible because subjects will be too anxious to perform at their best in tests of ability and not be prepared to be self-revealing, as is required in tests of personality and interest. For such testers the impersonality of the computer is anathema.

Hedl *et al.* (1973) found that computer-administered intelligence tests produced higher levels of anxiety and poorer attitudes to the testing than did traditional testing, a study supporting the objections raised by those who feel that computer-administered tests destroy test rapport. However as regards honesty of response in questionnaires concerning personal or intimate information there is some evidence that the computer-administered test, presumably because it avoids embarrassment, yields more honest responses (Evan and Miller, 1969; O'Brien and Dugdale, 1968).

Bartram and Bayliss (1984) on the basis of this evidence and, more important, that of the work with computer programs that respond to clients' answers in psychotherapeutic sessions, argue that the establishment of rapport for testing is not a problem. However, their argument will not do. These computer-administered therapy sessions, where the computer was programmed to reflect back, in the Rogerian style, without understanding, what the client said, were claimed by Weizenbaum (1965) to show great rapport between client and program. However, this is quite different from the test session, where there is none of the reflecting back of what the client says. Nor are the subjects, as in psychotherapy, seeking reassurance. Often the contrary is true. Thus the situations are not analogous and no inferences could be drawn from computer-administered psychotherapy and computer-administered testing. Furthermore I am not convinced by the findings of the Rogerian computer. This approach to psychotherapy is simply too crude to be credible.

Indeed individual tests rather than group tests of intelligence always provide the benchmark, criterion intelligence test score, partly because of the rapport established between the tester and subject. This, it must be noticed, is despite the subjectivity that can affect this approach to testing. The very objectivity of a testing technique where interaction is impossible, such as computer-administered testing, detracts from rather than increases the validity of testing. These are the arguments of psychologists in the clinical and educational spheres, as represented by Heim.

Brierley (1971), indeed, pointed out that automated testing destroyed another aspect of individual testing that was always regarded as important. In computerised testing the tester missed out the incidental observations of the subject as she or he completed the test, observations which could be highly valuable. This of course is true, but, as was pointed out by Bartram and Bayliss (1984), such automated testing gives the human tester more not less time to interact with her or his subject. This may be so in theory but in practice, when testing time is short, Brierley (1971) is more likely to be correct.

In my practical experience of testing I have always found that it is useful to establish good rapport and that results are apparently more valid. Certainly there are less spoiled responses. Furthermore, all these arguments ignore the human aspect of testing, what it feels like to be a subject, to be tested, to be in the hands of a psychologist. This is an aspect of the ethics of testing and will be discussed in the section of this handbook devoted to the application of tests. Nevertheless this impersonal quality of computer-administered tests, where subjects are objects, seems only justifiable if the improvements in validity are enormous – much as painful but effective surgery is acceptable. Only where this is demonstrated do I think computer-administered tests are acceptable ethically.

5. We have seen the arguments presented by Krug (1986) for computer interpretation of tests. However, I am unhappy about this computer interpretation. This works by writing descriptions of each score on each variable and on certain combinations of variables. Given that the reliability of most personality tests is far lower than is desirable – hardly any reach .9 – then these interpretations must be to some extent spurious. Given the standard error of measurement the most that can be reliably done with scores is to divide them into three groups: high, average and low. Descriptions of these broad categories by computer would be adequate but most users require more specific information than this because by definition most scores will be around the mean. With broad descriptions many candidates might find themselves virtually identical.

In addition to this if subjects are, just for example, low on intelligence and high on anxiety, fascistic tendencies and schizophrenia, a computer print-out informing them of these results is not a pleasant thing. Clearly there are different ways of conveying information without causing offence or deflating egos. Since this can be done only with respect to an individual even the most careful, written computer interpretation may fail. Even more than with the presentation of results the ethics of testing make the use of computer interpretations dubious.

The ideal way in which computer interpretations should be used is where the tester goes through the print-out with each subject individually, explaining the meaning of the results and discussing legitimate worries and concerns about any findings, whether, objectively, flattering or denigratory. However, if this is done there is little point in having a computer interpretation.

A full discussion of how computer-administered tests should be used in practice will be found in a later section of this handbook.

CONCLUSIONS

There are certain advantages to computer-administered and computer-scored tests – especially the rapid calculation of a subject's results and the immediate presentation of her or his scores in terms of normative groups or other criteria. In addition there are advantages in the ability to present subsets of items (a matter which will be discussed below under the heading 'tailored testing'). There are further advantages including the ability to store all results and develop new or local norms, and the opportunity they allow the tester to examine the statistical qualities of the test, right down to the item level. Finally, types of item can be used which are impossible in the traditional test.

All this is good and provided that the ethical problems (of presenting results to subjects without their being able to discuss their implications and their own reactions to them) are dealt with, computer-administered tests can be useful. Indeed this problem of computer testing exemplifies a wider difficulty with the whole of psychometrics: treating subjects as objects. In fact as psychometrics becomes more scientific, i.e. the subjectivity of the test is reduced, this difficulty tends to become more acute. Much, in the end, depends upon the humanity and awareness of the particular psychometrist. There is little doubt, however, that computer-administered testing can lead to ethical abuse.

TAILORED TESTING

I shall now discuss tailored testing, one of the clear advantages that computer-administered tests have over traditional psychometric measures.

Meaning of tailored testing

In tailored testing, as the name suggests, a subset of items is administered to each subject, this subset being selected exactly for that subject: bespoke rather than off-the-peg testing. Before describing how this is done two points need to be made. First, computerised tailored testing does with precision what many experienced testers do intuitively. Thus in giving the WISC (Wechsler, 1974), a test fully described in Chapter 23, one does not administer all the items (which are arranged in order of difficulty) in each scale to every subject. Rather one makes an estimate of her or his level and begins there. If she or he gets it wrong, an easier item is tried. A confident and immediate correct response is usually sufficient to make the tester skip on to yet more difficult items. All untested items before the starting level are, of course, assumed to be answered correctly. It might be noticed that strictly· such a procedure would only be accurate in a Guttman scale, which was described in the previous chapter, but practical testers have found that in experienced hands, this procedure is quite satisfactory. This is what the tailored test does precisely.

The second point concerns Rasch scaling or tests devised according to item response theory, which were described in the previous chapter. Here, it will be remembered, when items had been Rasch scaled, exactly equivalent subsets of items could be given to subjects, thus allowing re-testing and the development of truly parallel tests. This is done in part by tailored testing although it should be realised that with Rasch scaling tailored testing would not be necessary since item indices are supposedly population free and any subset of items is as good as any other for any subjects.

However, tailored testing often utilises the two- and three-parameter models. Here items are chosen on the basis of their item characteristics relevant to the individual being tested. Thus it will be remembered that item characteristic curves show the efficiency of items at different points on the latent trait thus increasing the possible precision of measurement in comparison with the p value of the classical model. This means that the best items (defined by responses to the previous items) for any individual can be rapidly discovered and administered. This is the most effective form of tailored testing.

The essentials of tailored testing

These can be easily described.

1. Item difficulties, the p values from the item analyses (the proportion of the trial sample who got the item right) are stored together with each item.
2. If the test has good norms different p values for different samples can be used. Thus subjects would be asked to put into the computer, before the beginning of the test, personal details and from these the appropriate p values could be selected.
3. Instead of using the raw p values, Rasch scale item difficulty indices could be used which would be population free. Only one such set would be required. Alternatively the item difficulty and discriminability parameters from other item response models could be used. For these good sampling would be important. As already mentioned, this is the most efficient approach to tailored testing.
4. In the simplest tailored testing a subject is presented with an item at the 50 per cent level of difficulty for her or his relevant norm group.
5. If she or he responds correctly a more difficult item is given; if she or he gets it wrong, an easier item. It should be realised that with well normed tests these moves up and down the continuum of difficulty can be both precise and small.
6. By this procedure an accurate difficulty level for each candidate can be established quickly.
7. In so doing, a brief, tailored test has been created, using a subset of items.
8. As has been indicated a sophisticated tailored test can be constructed making use of the personal data which was discussed in (2).
9. Alternatively, a random and small subset of items which had been Rasch scaled could be presented to a subject. Of course, this would not really be tailored testing, for the item statistics, being population free, require no such fitting to subjects. If the two- or three-parameter models were used the most powerful items in terms of the position of the subject on the latent trait, as determined by the first item or group of items, would be used.

These basic procedures for tailored testing have been elaborated although the principles are identical. Vale (1981), for example, distinguishes three types of algorithm. In inter-item branching each test item (depending on the response) leads to a pre-specified set of questions. In inter-subtest branching the branching point consists of several items. In some forms after a set of items and depending on the results, one of several sets of items is administered. In another form even after the initial set of items, the subject's performance is monitored, and appropriate items given.

Advantages of tailored testing

There are some obvious advantages to tailored testing and these can be quickly listed.

1. A brief test is sufficient for most subjects.
2. If a large pool of items has been developed, tailored testing, in which only a subset is used, is ideal for repeated testing, as in developmental studies or the study of therapeutic efficiency. It is also useful in selection procedures, for the fact that each subject has a different set of items means that subjects cannot tell other candidates about the items and, perhaps more important, the whole process is brief. In most occupational work time is at a premium.

Disadvantages of tailored testing

Despite these genuine advantages there are some problems with the method and these are discussed below

As has been made clear in this description of tailored testing, much turns upon the p values, the difficulty level of the items, or the equivalent item difficulty parameter. In certain fields of psychological testing the notion of a difficulty level makes sense. Thus in ability and attainment tests the meaning is clear, because there is a dimension of difficulty, underlying the items. If I argue than calculus is more difficult that addition, few would disagree. However in the field of personality and motivation the meaning of the p values is by no means so clear. For example, few subjects answer the item 'I enjoy killing cats' positively. It means simply that this is a rare behaviour in our culture and an even rarer admitted behaviour. Of equivalent rarity might be an item such as 'I enjoy eating snakes.' However in what sense they could be used as equivalent items in item subsets is by no means clear. In brief, because the p value does not represent a difficulty continuum in tests other than ability and attainment it is not a sensible basis on which to rest item equivalence.

All this seems to indicate that even if tailored personality or motivation tests (subsets of items) could be constructed, based upon the p values of their items, it is by no means obvious that the tests would be equivalent. Indeed I would argue, a priori, that such brief tests would be likely to be invalid. This is because, to simplify the issue, the universe of items (fully discussed in Chapter 3 of this handbook) for most personality tests is too large for brief tests, equivalent only by their p values, to be valid. Without question, before tailored personality tests could be used there would have to be strong evidence that they were valid and that item subsets were equivalent.

In addition it must again be stressed that in tailored testing it is essential that the p values and the item parameters be derived from large and representative samples or there will be considerable inaccuracy.

Semi-tailored testing

At this point mention must be made of what might be called semi-tailored testing. Because of the problems of the meaning of difficulty level for personality tests true tailored testing has not been extensively tried out, although Sapinkopf (1978) attempted to computerise the Californian Psychological Inventory (but with little success). Waller and Reise (1989), however, working with extraversion items, did produce a tailored version which required only about half the items of the original. This is work which needs replication before it can be fully accepted, given all the problems which have been discussed.

Johnson *et al.* (1979) have produced the Psychological Systems Questionnaire. This contains branching and true–false questions, and measures, for example, extraversion and social desirability. The branching questions are response contingent so that a subject has to answer only relevant questions. This is only like a modern tax form so that if the category does not apply, e.g. married, or widowed, certain questions can be skipped. However although it is adaptive in respect of demographic and personal information, this is not the case for the actual personality test items. Nevertheless this test is a beginning in this field.

Conclusions

Tailored testing is a useful technique in those fields of testing where the p value (or item difficulty parameter) reflects a real difficulty level in the items. Where this is the case, then tailored testing can be useful provided that the p values are derived from large and representative samples.

ITEM BANKING

In our discussion of tailored testing we have made mention of a pool of items from which subsets can be drawn. These pools of items are referred to as item banks and a little needs to be said about the development of item banks before I draw this chapter to a close, because great improvements have been recently made in methodology due to the application of item response theory.

As van der Linden (1986) points out, the item bank consists at the outset of a set of items measuring the same domain of knowledge or ability. The test is first composed of the items judged best on a priori grounds. After the first trial the item responses are fed back into it to score the test and to estimate the item parameters, depending on the response model chosen, and thus the quality of the items. As the items are used again response parameters may be updated and made more accurate. Eventually with the item parameters accurate it is possible to choose tests which are long, short, easy, difficult, or discriminating at a particular level, or equivalent. If the Rasch model has been used any subset should be equally valuable. Furthermore once the bank is functioning new items can be inserted and their parameters and comparability can be estimated. Thus an item bank can be constantly made larger.

Such is the general case for an item bank as made by one of the experts in this area. However, I should like to make two comments. First it is odd that such emphasis is placed on tailoring the test so precisely in terms of item parameters, when the Rasch model allows equivalence amongst any subset of items. In practice, as was suggested in the previous chapter, the Rasch model may be difficult to instantiate. The second point is that it is assumed that the test is valid because the item parameters indicate that the item is measuring the latent trait. However, that it measures a latent trait is one thing, and what the latent trait is, is another. In terms of the classical test theory these item banks are homogeneous but not necessarily valid. This failure to consider the nature of the latent traits springs from the fact that these response models were developed mainly with achievement and ability tests where item content is a reasonable guide to validity.

However it is true that an item bank allows the construction of a test of great precision since the item characteristics and the information characteristics of each item at each point of the latent trait are known. In brief the item bank consists of a set of items in which the item parameters have been calibrated. There are various problems in setting up item banks and these must be briefly mentioned.

1. Linking item parameters onto a common scale. Ideally it is best if all items are administered to a common sample. However with a large item bank this may be impractical. Usually subsets of items have been administered to different samples, yet item parameters should be linked to a common scale. Vale (1986) compared a number of methods. In summary it appears best that great efforts are made, in the first instance, to use random groups who do not differ on the latent trait; and that the longer the tests the better the calibration. The number of overlapping items in the samples of items did not seem to be important – as few as two apparently being sufficient. Details of the specialised methods required to carry out the linkages can be found in Vale (1986).

2. Selecting the optimal items from the item bank in adaptive (tailored) testing. In my discussion of tailored testing I underlined the principle of selecting items based upon difficulty levels or on item parameters at the specified level of the latent trait. Actually, of course, the possible combination of items that might be chosen from an item pool is huge and since one combination is presumably best it is necessary for maximum efficiency (i.e. the shortest possible test) to have an optimal selection procedure, or algorithm. Theunissen (1986) has developed such an algorithm. However, I remain unconvinced by such complex selection processes. I should like to see if there were any substantive or even statistically significant differences between subjects' scores on tests selected by simple criteria derived from the item response models and these highly complex approaches. I believe that such differences are likely to be minimal as has been found in the comparison of scores on items weighted according to their factor loadings and with unit weights.

Conclusions

Item response theory, like factor analysis, is complex mathematically and it is easy to allow these mathematical problems to become the focus of interest rather than the items themselves. It must be reiterated that a test is no better than the original items no matter how elegant the item response model used to describe the responses, nor how ingenious the extraction of items from the bank. Thus it is essential in tests developed from item banks that the validity of these tests be demonstrated. In theory item response models should allow, at least for tests of achievement and ability, more precise tests than the classical model. Whether these advantages in the real case, as distinct from simulations, are borne out still remains to be seen, since the best validated tests are still those constructed on the classical model.

Chapter 7

Factor Analysis

In this chapter and Chapter 8 I shall describe and discuss factor analysis, the statistical method which was developed by Spearman at the beginning of the century for the analysis of psychometric data, in the field of abilities. It lies at the heart of psychometrics. Many of the disagreements between different psychometrists have turned out to be due to differences in their use of factor analysis so that it is important to understand the technique. As Cattell (e.g. 1978) has stressed, many factor analyses are so technically deficient that their results are misleading.

Consequently, in this chapter, I shall set out with their rationale the best methods of factor analysis, as far as there is agreement between the experts in the field. I do not intend to treat this subject in detail algebraically since all computations are now done by computer. Furthermore the working through of the matrix algebra by hand still does not give insight, other than to gifted mathematicians, into what is actually happening to the data. Nevertheless for readers who want to delve into the mathematics Cattell (1978) is a highly useful book as is Harman (1976). However I shall discuss some of the essential underlying mathematics because without this the notions become insubstantial and vague.

FACTOR ANALYSIS: A GENERAL DESCRIPTION

Factor analysis is a statistical method in which variations in scores on a number of variables are expressed in a smaller number of dimensions or constructs. These are the factors. In the vast majority of factor analytic studies, especially in psychometrics, factor analysis is applied to the correlations between variables. The resultant factors are defined by their correlations (factor loadings) with the original variables. An artificial example from the field of human abilities will illustrate the nature of factor analysis.

Suppose that we had measured the attainments of a large sample of school children in a wide range of school subjects. We would find that there were intercorrelations among all these scores although of varying size. If we were to ask what accounted for these correlations, factor analysis could be used to answer the question. Thus a three-factor solution would account for most of the variance in this correlation matrix (see Vernon, 1961 or Kline, 1990, Chapter 5 for example, for the psychological reasoning for this claim). One factor would be general with factor loadings on all subjects. The highest loadings would be on 'hard' or complex subjects such as Latin or Greek, mathematics or physics. The loadings on domestic studies, ecological problems in urban life, and physical education would be far smaller. From this pattern of loadings the factor could be identified as g or general ability or intelligence. A second factor would load on all the subjects where language skills play an important part. This from such a pattern is the verbal factor. Finally there would be a factor of numerical reasoning loading on all subjects where this ability is important, such as mathematics, physics, chemistry and statistics. This example has been chosen because the factor analysis of abilities yields a clear structure of the kind that has been described above and because it illustrates the nature of factor analysis with great clarity.

Thus it is possible to see how factors may be identified from their loadings. After all it takes no great powers of inference to see that a construct which correlates positively with English, Spanish, Classics, and those subjects where language plays a part but is unconnected to the sciences and mathematics, is verbal ability. Similarly its obverse with loadings only on mathematical subjects is mathematical reasoning or something similar.

In the best quality factor analytic research, it should be said, factor identification does not depend only on the factor loadings. It is always necessary to identify the factor by some different method. Thus if we thought that a factor was a mathematical factor we would administer its scale to, say, a group of Wranglers at Cambridge and their Arts faculty controls. We could do a similar thing with a verbal factor. If both hypotheses were supported, namely that the Wranglers were better at the former than the latter test, with the results reversed for the Arts graduates, we could consider that the factors had been correctly identified.

Furthermore this example illustrates the powerful simplification of complex data that factor analysis makes possible. To consider the scores on all subjects and all the intercorrelations requires far more information processing than the human mind can manage. However it can consider the scores on and correlations between three factors, and the scores on these three factors would be virtually as good an indication of the ability of the subjects who had taken all the tests as would the original scores. Thus where a huge mass of data requires simplification factor analysis is a useful technique.

DEFINITIONS

As Nunnally (1978) points out many discussions of factor analysis are vitiated by inadequate definitions not only of factors but of some of the other necessary technical terms. At the outset of this discussion of factor analysis I want to ensure that all these ambiguities are removed. For the fact is that factor analysis, although a complex technique, is not so difficult as to defy understanding and produce the regular misuse that is commonly found even in reputable journals, as has been shown by Cattell (1978). This discussion owes much to Nunnally (1978), whose explication of the mathematical basis of factor analysis is hard to improve upon.

Exploratory factor analysis   In the example of factor analysis that was described above, factor analysis was used to simplify a large set of data, to map out the most important variables. This is called, for obvious reasons, exploratory factor analysis. It is still, by far, the most common use of the technique. However factor analysis can be used to confirm hypotheses.

Confirmatory factor analysis   As the name suggests confirmatory analysis is used to confirm or support hypotheses. Thus, for example, if, on theoretical grounds, we were to expect three personality factors, perhaps ego, id and superego, we could use confirmatory factor analysis to investigate whether the data fitted such a hypothesis. This could be a powerful technique, but, as shall be seen later in these chapters, there are considerable technical, statistical difficulties with confirmatory analysis.

Components and factors   There is a distinction between components and factors. Components are real factors because they can be directly derived from the data of a study. Common factors are hypothetical because they are estimated from the data. There is a further important distinction: in component analysis there are only a few viable solutions, whereas in factor analysis there is an infinity of solutions and the choice of the best one is a matter of controversy, although as we shall see in our later discussion, there at last seems to be some agreement as to how this controversy should be resolved.

This discussion implies that component analysis is superior to factor analysis and since it is mathematically far simpler it might be argued that factor analysis is not worthy of further consideration. However, as shall be seen as the discussion develops, this is not entirely the case, although as Harman (1976) argues, with large matrices of variables there is little difference between the results of component and factor analysis.

Image analysis   At this point image analysis which is a special technique of obtaining common factors which are not estimates but directly derivable from the data must be mentioned.

Data matrix   Component-factor analysis (from now on I shall refer to this as component analysis) and factor analysis operate upon a data matrix. This consists of the scores, on a set of variables, of a sample of subjects.

Definition of a factor   Any linear combination of variables in a data matrix is a factor or component of that matrix.

THE NATURE OF FACTOR ANALYSIS

With these definitions of the most important concepts in factor analysis we are now ready to examine the nature of factor analysis in some detail. As further definitions are required these will be given in the text. In my discussion of the basic mathematical and logical rationale of factor analysis I shall concentrate upon component analysis because this is far more simple and because, as Nunnally (1978) points out, common factor analysis is a modification of this basic model.

Definition of a factor: further comments   A linear combination of variables, any combination, is a factor. Combinations may involve differential weightings of each variable, or weights can be the same. Weightings can be positive or negative for any variable. The factor score of a subject is the combination of her or his scores on the variables in the combination, each weighted as in the combination, and usually expressed as a standard score. Different methods of computing these weights for the linear combination are used in different methods of component analysis. In principle non-linear factor analysis is a possibility, for example where combinations include the products of variables. These, however, will not be discussed in this handbook because, to the best of my knowledge, no psychometric tests have used such abstruse techniques.

Factor loadings   We have already mentioned factor loadings in our preliminary description of an exploratory factor analysis of abilities. Factor loadings are the correlations of each variable with the factor or component. Since a factor score is a score on a given linear combination of variables for each subject it is clear that this score can be correlated with the score on each variable in the data matrix. These correlations are the factor loadings. These correlations can be positive or negative and of any size. Readers must note that this is the meaning of factor loading in component analysis. When we discuss factor analysis a further meaning will become clear.

Factor iteration   It is highly unlikely that the variance in a large data matrix could be explained by one factor. Thus after the first factor has been extracted it is usually necessary to extract a number of other factors. How many are required depends upon the factor loadings on the first and subsequent factors. Very high loadings imply that only one factor is necessary. A first factor with virtually zero loadings implies that there is no common factor. In practice the first factor usually has moderate loadings, ranging from around .3 – .7 (the sign is irrelevant to the size). Where this is the case, further factors can be extracted.

Extracting the second factor

1. Factor 1 must be partialed out from each variable. Take variable x, as an example. The factor loading of x on factor 1 is multiplied by each standard score on factor 1. This is then subtracted from each score on x. This is done for every variable in the matrix. This produces a new partialed data matrix (matrix 1, to show that factor 1 is partialed out of it). Because each variable in this new partialed data matrix must correlate zero with factor 1, any combination of variables in the new matrix must also correlate zero with factor 1. Hence this method of iterative factoring must yield a set of uncorrelated or orthogonal factors.
2. Factor 2 is then extracted as was factor 1, from any linear combination of variables. It must be pointed out here that not all linear combinations of variables are equally useful in factor analysis and this will be discussed below.
3. The loadings on factor 2 are obtained by correlating the original variables with scores on factor 2.

Extracting further factors After the extraction of two factors further iterations can be carried out to produce more factors. To produce the third factor, factors 1 and 2 must be partialed out of the matrix. This can be done by partialing 2 from the partial matrix from which 2 was obtained. From this new matrix a third factor is extracted and so on.

The number of factors to be extracted How many factors should be extracted? The limit to the number of factors is the number of variables. If there were X variables, the scores in matrix X would be zero. If a smaller number of factors, Y, can explain the variance in the data matrix then the scores in matrix Y would be zero. As was explained in our introductory example in the field of abilities, factor analysis is useful because, usually, the variance can be explained by a smaller number of factors.

This description of the procedures of component analysis shows the mathematical principles underlying the extraction of factors. It demonstrates the clear and elegant mathematical basis of the claim that factors can account for the variance in a matrix, with great simplicity, if the number of factors is small.

With this basic account of the nature of components in mind it is now possible to explicate some further properties of both components and factors.

Factor loadings As previously defined the factor loadings are the correlations of the variables with the factors.

a. Factor loadings squared. The squared factor loading of a variable indicates how much of the variance of that variable is explained by the factor. Thus if variable a loads .8 on factor 1 it means that 64 per cent of the variance of a is explained by the factor.

b. Average squared loadings on a factor (columns of a factor matrix). The average squared loadings of a factor shows the percentage of variance in the data matrix explained by the factor.

c. Sum of the averaged squared loadings. This indicates the proportion of variance in the matrix explained by the factors. The larger this is the better the factors are in explaining the original variables.

d. Sum of squared loadings of a variable on the factors (rows of the factor matrix). This indicates the proportion of variance in each variable which the factors can explain. This is known as h^2 or the communality. The more a variable shares common factors with other variables the larger the communality will be. The larger the communality, the better the factors account for the variance of the particular variable.

e. Estimating variables from factor scores. If as many components as variables are extracted the variables can be exactly reproduced from the factors. Where, as is usual, only a few components, the large ones, have been extracted, the scores have to be estimated from the multiple regression of the variable on those factors.

In a three-factor solution the best estimate of variable a is obtained from the sum of the standard scores on the three factors, each standard score being multiplied by the regression weights, the beta weights, of the variable a on each factor.

When the predictor variables are uncorrelated (as in the case of components, as has been shown) the squared multiple correlation equals the sum of the squared predictor–criterion correlations. Since components are uncorrelated, it follows that the factor loadings are the beta weights of the variable for the factor. This enables us to redefine factor loadings.

f. Factor loadings. Factor loadings are the correlations of the variable with the factor. They are also the beta weights for predicting the variable from the factor, where all variables are expressed as standard scores and where the factors are uncorrelated.

Reproducing the correlations among variables from the factor loadings   One of the tests of the adequacy of a factor analysis is how closely it is possible to estimate the correlations between the variables from the factor loadings of the variables. Indeed it is this ability of factors to reproduce the correlations between the variables that enables us to argue that factors explain the correlations or the common variance between variables. If as many components as variables are extracted from the matrix then the correlations between variables can be reproduced perfectly. However, in reality, when only a few factors are extracted, if these explain a good proportion of the variance, the correlations can be reproduced partially. Thus if three factors had been extracted, the correlation between variables x and y would be partially explained by the sum of the cross products of their loadings, as set out in Formula 7.1.

7.1 $r_{xy} = r_{x1y1} + r_{x2y2} + r_{x3y3}$

Residual matrix   Using Formula 7.1 it is possible to attempt to reproduce all the correlations in the original data from the factors which have been extracted. These correlations can then be subtracted from the original correlations and the resulting matrix is the residual matrix. The size of this matrix indicates how well the factors account for the correlations.

Factors as linear combinations   Throughout this discussion of the mathematical basis of factor analysis we have talked of factors as being linear combinations of variables. This is all very well but in a data matrix of any size there is a very large number of possible linear combinations and the question arises as to how the most efficient (at accounting for the correlations) are to be obtained. In fact the correlations between the variables, and their size, are important in determining these linear combinations.

Factoring the correlation matrix   For example if there is a positive manifold, that is all the correlations are positive, it implies that there is something in common between all variables and it makes sense to give positive weights to all variables. Variables with predominantly negative correlations would be negatively weighted. Similarly a variable that correlated highly with many of the other variables could be given a larger weighting in the linear combination.

Furthermore, the computation of the correlations of variables and factors (the factor loadings) is far more easily done from the correlation matrix than from the original data matrix, and this is set out in Formula 7.2 (where it is assumed that all variables are expressed as standard scores).

7.2 $r_{aX} = \dfrac{\Sigma r_{aX}}{\sqrt{R}}$

where a = the variable correlated with the factor; X = the linear combination or factor; Σr_{aX} = sum of all correlations between variable a and each variable in X, and R = sum of all elements in the correlation matrix of variables in X.

It should be pointed out that the formula applies whether or not a is part of the factor. If it is, its correlation is assumed to be 1.

Similarly, extracting the second and further factors from the matrix by partialing out the effects is easy to compute from the correlation matrix using the formulae for partial correlations.

Thus in practice, because all the computations for factoring are done on the correlation matrix, it is usual to speak of factoring correlations. This however, while true, is really a matter of convenience. Factors are nothing more than linear combinations of variables.

THE FACTOR ANALYTIC MODEL OF VARIANCE

In the factor analytic model there are three uncorrelated components of variance.

1. Common variance. This is the proportion of the variance that can be explained by common factors.
2. Specific variance. This is the variance that is particular to a test – for example that arising from the form of the items in the test (in as much as they are different from others) and from the particular content of the items.
3. Error variance. In Chapter 3 of this handbook, it was shown that the reliability of a test was an estimate of its true variance; the rest was error.

Unique variance

In general, error and specific variance are not separated out and are known as unique variance. Thus unique variance can be calculated from the sum of the squared factor loadings, the communality, h^2.

7.3.   U (Unique variance) = $h^2 - 1$

One possibile way to separate the error variance from specific variance is to insert into the diagonals of the correlation matrix not 1 but the reliabilities of the tests. Any variance not explained by common factors, the unique variance, must then be specific variance.

Actually, as Nunnally (1978) argues, there is no perfect method of separating unique from common variance although, as will be discussed, there are various attempts to achieve this. Nevertheless, Formula 7.3 can be approached with reasonable precision.

Factors as linear combinations: condensing the variables

So far in this discussion of the basis of factor analysis, we have avoided the vital question of exactly how these linear combinations of variables are obtained. It has already been argued that the correlation matrix is useful, in comparison with the data matrix, because it suggests how variables might be combined into factors. However, we need more than suggestions.

This condensation of the variables into a relatively small number of factors, which yet explain a large proportion of the total variance, is what factor analytic methods set out to achieve. After this has been done with the maximum possible statistical efficiency (maximum variance explained) factors are generally rotated to make them more simple to understand.

Rotated factors

Rotated factors are simply linear combinations of the linear combinations. They explain the same variance as the original set of factors and the h² for each variable remains the same even though the pattern of loadings changes. Here, in rotation, statistical efficiency having been obtained in the previous condensation, the criterion becomes simplicity. More will be said about rotation in Chapter 8.

Methods of condensation

The best method of condensation extracts as much variance as possible with each factor. Various methods have been developed and readers must be referred to the specialist texts for details. Cattell (1978) and Harman (1976) are excellent for this purpose.

However it is generally agreed that one method, principal components factor analysis, is particularly efficient at condensing variables prior to rotation. It does so by maximising the sum of squared loadings for each factor as it is extracted and thus it confirms to the criterion of ideal condensation. It is, indeed, widely used and it must now be discussed.

Principal components factor analysis (PC)

Principal components analysis as it is worked on modern computers is algebraically complex, but its mathematical basis, as developed by Hotelling (1933) illustrates the method with great clarity. My description owes much to Nunnally (1978) and readers must be referred to that text for more detail.

First a few terms need to be defined.

The characteristic equation Weights for the variables to obtain each principal component are required. The problem is to estimate a target matrix – correlations with unities in the diagonals (the correlation matrix of variables). The solution is the characteristic equation of a matrix. This solution requires two sets of values:

1. The characteristic vectors of the matrix. These are also called the latent vectors or the eigen vectors of the matrix. They will be symbolised by the term V_i. A vector is simply a column or row of numbers in a matrix.
2. The characteristic roots. These are also called latent roots or eigen values. These will be symbolised by the term l_i.

Definition of characteristic vectors When a correlation matrix is subjected to a principal components analysis the characteristic vector is simply a column of weights each applicable to one of the variables in the matrix. Thus if twenty tests, A,B,C, . . . n are factored then there would be twenty weights in the first characteristic vector, corresponding to the first factor. This characteristic vector will be symbolised as V_a, V_b, V_c, etc. The corresponding factor loadings will be symbolised as F_a, F_b, F_c, etc. It can be shown that each characteristic vector is proportional to its corresponding column of factor loadings. Thus F_a is obtained by multiplying each element of V_a by the square root of l_a, the characteristic root or eigen value. That is why to solve the characteristic equation the eigen values must be known.

Normalising a vector For mathematical simplicity each characteristic vector is derived so that it has unit length. Unit length is defined as follows: The sum of squares of its weights equals 1.00. This is computed by dividing each element in a set of weights at any step by the square root of the sum of the squares of the raw weights. This is normalising the vectors. Thus the sum of squares of the weights of any characteristic vector is 1.00. To convert a characteristic vector to a factor, therefore, the characteristic roots or eigen values are required.

Definition of the characteristic root Although the sum of squares of each characteristic vector is 1.00, the sum of squares of the corresponding column of factor loadings is not 1.00 but reflects the proportion of variance explained by the factor. This total amount of variance is the characteristic root, l_i, for the factor. The larger the characteristic root of a factor, the more variance in the original variables and in the correlation matrix is explained by the factor. Thus the factor with the largest root explains the most variance, the one with the second largest the most remaining variance and so on.

The computation of eigen vectors, roots and principal components As has been stated above, the approach of Hotelling (1933) will be described. As Nunnally (1978) points out, these methods are particularly clear whereas more modern and computationally efficient methods yield little insight as to what the mathematics are doing. The principle of the method is that the characteristic vectors and roots are derived by an iterative solution. First a vector is tried out (one weight for each variable) and tested against a criterion set of values. To the extent to which it differs from the criterion, the first trial vector is modified (by a set procedure), to produce a second vector, and so on until the solution converges, i.e. until additional iterations produce virtually identical results.

Iteration In the iterative approach characteristic vectors are derived one at a time, and the corresponding characteristic root or eigen value is obtained at the same time from the computations. As was described in the previous paragraph, trial vectors for the first characteristic vector are obtained until a goodness of fit criterion is reached. When the trial vectors are so similar that they are identical up to several decimal points the iterative solution has converged and Hotelling (1933) proved that convergence must occur. When it does one may accept that the characteristic vector is identical. The eigen value may then be calculated for the vector. The same iterative approach can be used to search for succeeding vectors.

Calculating the characteristic vectors: the first trial characteristic vector The derivation of the first trial characteristic vector begins with the correlation matrix of the original variables. To simplify the discussion we shall assume that the majority of these correlations are positive, such that the sums of coefficients in all columns and rows are positive. (If they are not, reflections can be made, where the signs of some of the variables are changed such that the column and row totals are maximised).

Step 1. Sum the coefficients in each column including the 1 (the correlation of a test with itself) in the diagonal. The column sums can be thought of as a vector of such sums and it is symbolised as U_{a1}.

Step 2. Normalise U_{a1}. This is done by squaring and adding the column sums in U_{a1} and then dividing each element in U_{a1} by the square root of the sum of squares. This is V_{a1}. Thus the first trial characteristic vector is the normalised U_{a1}.

Step 3. The second trial vector, V_{a2}. Elements in V_{a1} are accumulatively multiplied by the first row of R, the correlation matrix, to obtain the first element in a new vector, U_{a2}. A similar procedure is carried out for the second row of R to obtain the second element in U_{a2}. An example will clarify successive multiplication. To multiply V_{a1} by the first row of R, the first element in V_{a1} would be multiplied by the first element in the first row of R (always 1.00); this would be added to the product of the second element of V_{a1} multiplied by the second element in the first row of R, R_{12}, which would be added to the third element in V_{a1} multiplied by R_{13} and so on for all corresponding elements in V_{a1} and the first row of R.

The second element of U_{a2} is obtained in a similar fashion by accumulatively multiplying V_{a1} into the second row of R. The same is done for every row of R to produce all the elements of U_{a2}.

Step 4. Normalise U_{a2}. This is done by dividing each element by the square root of the sum of the squared elements which would yield V_{a2}.

Step 5. The two trial vectors, V_{a1} and V_{a2}, are compared. If they are not the same, V_{a2} is used as was described above to produce V_{a3} and so on until the solutions converge, i.e. until the new vector is virtually identical with the last one. If, for example, V_{a15} and V_{a16} were identical V_{a15} would be V_a, the first characteristic vector. The square root of the sum of squares in U_{a16} would equal the first characteristic root, or eigen value, 1_a. The factor loadings are obtained by multiplying the elements in the vector, V_a, by the square root of the eigen value (NB Nunnally (1978) is misleading on this point).

Obtaining the second factor The second factor is obtained in the same way as factor one, that is the characteristic vector, the characteristic root and the factor loadings are computed as above, trial characteristic vectors being computed until convergence occurs. However these vectors and roots have to be extracted, not from the original matrix of correlations but from a residual matrix after the factor has been partialed out.

Obtaining the residual matrix (R_1) The residual coefficient which corresponds to the original correlation is obtained thus: the loadings for the two variables on the first component are multiplied. This is done for all possible pairs of variables. This produces a matrix of cross products. In each diagonal space is the square of each factor loading. This matrix of cross products is then subtracted element by element from the original correlation matrix and the result is the residual matrix with the first component partialed out.

The nature of the residual matrix Each diagonal element is a partial variance, i.e. the variance remaining after the first component is partialed out. Each off diagonal element is a partial covariance, being the covariance between two variables after the influence of the first factor has been removed. These elements are not partial correlations although it is simple to compute these from the matrix (see Nunnally, 1978 for details).

Reflecting the residual matrix As was mentioned before, it is usual to change the signs of some rows and columns of the matrix to maximise the sum of coefficients in the residual matrix as a whole. When the factor loadings have been obtained, the variables that were reflected simply have their signs changed.

Extracting the second and subsequent components The second component is then extracted from the reflected residual matrix, exactly as the first component from the correlation matrix. A new residual matrix is then computed and reflected, partialing out the second component; a third component can be extracted, and so on.

The number of components to extract How many factors to extract will be discussed later in this section. In fact, there are various criteria. If the elements in the residual matrix are close to zero there is little point in extracting further factors as these will, obviously, be small. Some workers continue on to the bitter end, extracting as many components as there are variables, while others may stop arbitrarily, or in accord with some presupposition.

As Nunnally (1978) argues, this description of the computation of principal components makes it clear how the claim can be made that factors account for the variance and correlations within correlation matrices. As more factors are extracted and the residual coefficients become smaller and smaller until they approach zero, the meaning of the components is transparent. It is particularly striking, as can often happen, in the field of abilities, when three or four factors remove most of the variance from the correlation matrix.

Nevertheless it must be realised that modern computing methods for principal components do not follow precisely this routine but use powered matrices to increase the rapidity of convergence. Nevertheless the logic and the results are identical. A principal component is a principal component. Harman (1976) and Tatsuoka (1971) contain details of these more advanced methods.

Mathematical properties of principal components

Principal components have a number of mathematical characteristics which are of great value for the analysis of psychological data and these must be briefly discussed. All these follow directly from the logic of their computation which was described in the previous section.

1. The principal components are ordered by the proportion of variance in the original matrix for which they account. No other linear combination of variables could explain more variance, at any stage of extraction, than do the components at least for the sample in the study.
2. A given number of principal components (provided that it is less than the number of variables in the matrix) will account for more or as much variance in the matrix as the same number of factors derived by any other method.
3. Thus from 1 and 2 it can be argued that the principal components method maximises the variance explained for any number of factors.
4. The amount of variance explained by each principal component (the sum of the squared loadings) equals the corresponding characteristic root, latent root or eigen value of the component. When the latent roots are divided by the number of variables they show the roots as proportions of the total variance explained. These proportions when multiplied by 100 can be expressed as percentages of variance explained.
5. All eigen values should be either zero or positive. If they are not there is mathematical inconsistency in the results either due to error in the data or because the correlation coefficients contain rounding errors but large negative eigen values can never thus arise. Such eigen values indicate that the factor analysis is not trustworthy.
6. The number of positive roots (eigen values) represents the number of principal component factors required to explain all the variance in a positive correlation matrix. However, in principal components analysis, as has been stated, to explain all the variance, as many components as variables have to be taken out. Generally the last components are very

small, so that they can be disregarded. However the criterion for deciding upon how many components are important has been a matter of controversy and will be discussed in the next chapter. It is, as Cattell (1978) has argued, a critical matter for the proper interpretation of factor analytic results.

7. The sum of eigen values or latent roots equals the sum of the diagonal elements in the correlation matrix. Since, in principal components analysis, 1.00 is inserted in the diagonal spaces, the sum of the eigen values equals the number of variables in the analysis. The proportion of variance accounted for by factors can be thus calculated. In a ten-variable principal components analysis, if the first three eigen values added up to 4.9, we could say that these three factors accounted for 49 per cent of the variance.

8. Principal components are linear combinations of actual scores. Furthermore these components are orthogonal or uncorrelated. The factor loadings are used with the correlations to obtain the linear combinations that constitute the factors.

9. The orthogonality of the factors as linear combinations does not guarantee that the columns of factor loadings in the factor matrix are uncorrelated. However in the case of principal components both the columns of factor loadings and the linear combinations are orthogonal or uncorrelated. Nevertheless, even with principal components the rotated factor loadings may be correlated. However, as Nunnally (1978) points out, this orthogonality of the original factors in principal components is highly useful for further mathematical analysis.

10. The product of all eigen values in a matrix equals the determinant of the matrix. This is useful in the matrix algebra required when working with fewer factors than variables, where some of the eigen values will be zero, and thus their product will be zero and the determinant is necessarily zero.

Other characteristics of principal components

In addition to these ten mathematical properties of principal components, there are certain other characteristics which are important for interpreting the results of principal components analysis and these will now be discussed.

1. In most cases the first component explains far more variance than do the other components and the size of the eigen values of the factors falls off rapidly.

2. If the vast majority of the correlations in the matrix are positive, the first principal component usually has large positive loadings on most of the variables. This is then labelled a general factor.

3. Subsequent factors are usually bipolar, i.e. they have both negative and positive loadings.

From these three characteristics a number of important points follow. First it is somewhat absurd, if one is searching for a general factor in exploratory analysis, to claim support from the first factor of a principal components analysis. This is simply because, as has been seen, a general factor is an artefact of the algebra. A second important point concerns the interpretation of the factors. Where there are factors with a large number of loadings both negative and positive interpretation is difficult. Hence some method of simplifying the factors is required. In fact this is done by factor rotation. However, this important topic is dealt with in the next chapter.

Other methods of condensation

Before going on to discuss rotation in Chapter 8 I want to say something about some other methods of condensation. As was mentioned at the beginning of the section on principal components, this is only one approach, although a particularly effective one in terms of maximising the variance explained in the correlation matrix. We chose to explicate its computation because its calculating procedures lay bare the essential nature of factor analysis. Nevertheless one other method, maximum likelihood factor analysis, has become particularly popular in recent years partly because several powerful statistical programs have now become generally available of which this forms a part. Much of this new approach stems from the work of Joreskog (e.g. Joreskog, 1973).

Characteristics of maximum likelihood factor analysis

1. Maximum likelihood factor analysis is described as a statistical method because it obtains, by successive factoring, a set of factors which each in turn explains as much variance as possible in the population correlation matrix, as estimated from the sample correlation matrix. Principal components, in contradistinction, explains as much variance as possible in the observed data. Maximum likelihood analysis is labelled a statistical method because, as do all inferential statistics, it seeks to extrapolate from sample to population. Naturally such extrapolation depends upon the adequacy of the sampling and the number of subjects.
2. Although maximum likelihood factor analysis can be used in exploratory analysis, in which case it must be followed by rotation, to give meaning to the factors, it is a technique better suited to confirmatory analysis, which was described briefly earlier in the introduction to factor analysis. The use and value of confirmatory factor analysis is described later in Chapter 8.
3. The distinction between components and hypothetical common factors has already been made. Maximum likelihood analysis is usually used to search for factors although, when communalities are high and test

reliabilities are high the difference between principal components and maximum likelihood analysis is negligible. Indeed, in the development of a personality test, the PPQ (Kline and Lapham, 1990a), we found that principal components and maximum likelihood analysis yielded factors that were psychologically virtually identical, i.e. regardless of which method was used, the same items loaded the factors. The only differences affected a small number of items with low loadings on the factors, whichever method was used.

Nunnally (1978) summarises the case most succinctly when he argues that maximum likelihood analysis seldom has any advantages over principal components as a method of condensation when all or nearly all the total variance is to be explained. This occurs when values of .9 or larger are inserted into the diagonal spaces of the matrix.

4. Those who advocate maximum likelihood analysis do so mainly for the reason that there is a significance test for the extraction of each successive factor whereas other factoring methods are essentially convenient algorithms. It is, of course, an efficient method of extracting common factors (as distinct from components) and more will be said of these methods later in this chapter.

5. It must be pointed out that the mathematics of maximum likelihood analysis is far more complex than that of principal components and it can be understood only by well trained mathematicians. Indeed, its complexity is such that computing time with large matrices even with modern computers can be a problem. I shall not describe the computational procedures and readers who wish to pursue these further are referred to Gorsuch (1974) who also discusses the computing programs.

Conclusions This discussion of maximum likelihood factor analysis has been concerned with it as a method of condensation, not in its use in confirmatory analysis. As a method of condensation, I think that it is difficult to justify its use. It generally gives results little different from principal components and these, as Harman (1976) points out, are themselves little different, in matrices of any size, from common factor methods. Its statistical and computing complexity, therefore, can be justified only by the fact that there is a statistical basis to the factor extraction, even though the results are highly similar to those of less complex methods. Thus for initial factoring there seems little reason to use maximum likelihood methods.

Common factor analysis

The distinction between components and common factors has been mentioned. Some researchers, e.g. Cattell (1978) prefer to work with common factors, even though in most cases the difference between factors and principal components is negligible. Nevertheless there are some important differences between the two methods, particularly in respect of the underlying factor model, and these must be discussed.

Meaning of a factor   In the computation of principal components unities were placed in the diagonal spaces of the correlation matrix. In a real correlation matrix this must be so since by definition a variable correlates 1.00 with itself. Furthermore given the definition of a factor loading as the correlation of a standardised variable with a standardised linear combination of a set of variables, the algebra necessitates that unities are placed in the diagonals of the correlation matrix. As Nunnally (1978) argues, if any other values are placed in these diagonals then one is not correlating an actual variable with a linear combination of actual variables.

Variance   We have seen how the factor analytic model of variance identifies three independent sources of variance: common variance, specific variance and error variance. In most factor analytic models specific and error variance are not split but are treated as the unique variance, the goal of the analysis being to separate common factor variance from the unique variance. When, as is the case with principal components, unities are placed in the diagonal, this separation is imperfect. This is so because the variables themselves, including their uniqueness, determine the factors. This must be so if factors are linear combinations of scores because this must mix specific characteristics of each test in the combination with what they have in common.

Comparison of principal components and common factors
Nunnally (1978) succinctly summarises the difference between these two approaches. Principal components deals with real or actual factors since the factors are actual combinations of variables and the factor loadings are real correlations of the variables with those factors. However, common factors are hypothetical because they have to be estimated from actual variables. To obtain common factors mathematical procedures have to be used which specify factors entirely in terms of common variance. This almost always involves using communalities, numbers in the diagonal spaces, of less than 1.00.

Principal factor analysis   One approach to common factor analysis is to estimate communalities in the diagonal spaces of the correlation matrix and then submit it to principal factor analysis. This is identical to principal components analysis except that the diagonals are less than 1.00. There are, in addition, other factor analytic methods for extracting common factors of which maximum likelihood analysis is an example.

Compared with principal components there are certain attractive features of common factor analysis. If unique variance could be separated out from common variance this would be an excellent thing because the unique variance, whether error or specific, is of no scientific interest. There is another important aspect to common factors in that the hypothetical factors accounting for correlations are of some theoretical interest. Thus a common general factor may account for the correlations among variables but is not completely defined by them. The multiple correlation of the variables with the factor could be less than 1.00. This is what makes it theoretically interesting because if we posit a factor such as intelligence, for example, as accounting for much of the variance in a matrix, it is odd if the factor is perfectly defined by the variables loading on it.

There are a number of problems with common factor analysis which must be discussed so that a proper understanding of its results becomes possible.

The definition of common and unique variance   The meaning of both these terms is not unambiguous. If common variance is defined as what can be explained by component factors which are real combinations of variables in the score matrix, then there is no problem in extracting the common variance. Indeed common factor analysis is not required. As we have seen principal components analysis extracts common variance thus defined.

If common variance is defined as all the reliable variance in a data matrix, thus getting rid of error variance, then by putting the reliability coefficients in the diagonal spaces, a principal factor analysis will extract the common variance.

However, as Nunnally (1978) argues common variance is frequently given a far wider, and psychologically more important meaning, although the definition is vague in the extreme. For example common variance is conceptualised as the variance a variable would have in common with a domain or universe of variables. This universe, however, is rarely defined. Thus attempts have been made to map the ability sphere through factor analysis; see Kline (1990) for a description of the most recent findings. There, however, I was forced to point out that this map was, inevitably, unbounded because the domain of abilities was undefined. All that could be said was that it was not completely measured. Thus there are no tests of the ability to tell if cheeses are ripe, of persuading horses to race and not race (a skill that pays the best jockeys far more than those similarly high on g) and this list is endless. A common factor thus defined, e.g. verbal ability, is necessarily vague.

Thus Nunnally (1978) concludes that common variance cannot be precisely defined if the common factors are not completely specified by the variables. This, of course, only occurs in principal components. However such variable bound factors are of less scientific interest than common factors because obviously they are likely to vary from study to study. Nevertheless it must be emphasised this is a conceptual problem that may be overlooked in practical research because, as shall be seen later, fortunately most factor analytic solutions show remarkable agreement.

METHODS OF FACTOR ANALYSIS

As can be seen from the discussion in the previous paragraph, the major problem in defining common variance turns around, in computational terms, what is put into the diagonal spaces of the correlation matrix. The unities of principal components mean that factors are totally defined by their variables while inserting reliabilities means that error variance is excluded from the matrix. Many different factor analytic methods are essentially concerned with what should be put in the diagonals, because this, of course, affects the concept of the emerging factors.

I do not intend to go into any detail concerning the computations of these different methods. For this, readers must be referred to Cattell (1978), Harman (1976) or Gorsuch (1974). The description of the procedures of principal components is certainly sufficient to understand the nature of factor analysis and, as has been stated, principal factor analysis is identical except that values less than 1.00 are placed in the diagonal spaces. What I want to do here is simply to mention some of the most important methods and point out their particular defining characteristics. This will then complete this chapter on the extraction of factors in exploratory factor analysis.

1. Estimating communalities by Thurstone's iterative method   In this method some value, perhaps the reliabilities of the variables, is placed in the diagonal spaces of the matrix and principal factorisation is carried out, until the matrix of residual coefficients is tiny. The number of factors to achieve this is regarded as the rank of the matrix, i.e. the number of factors required to explain its variance.

Then h^2 is computed for each variable and compared with the estimated communality in the principal factor analysis. Unless this difference is tiny these h^2 values are put into the diagonal spaces of the matrix, in place of the original estimates and the principal factor analysis is performed again, the same number of factors being extracted. The new h^2 values are again compared with the communality estimates and the whole process is repeated until the differences between those inserted and the new communalities are negligible. The factor loadings which result from the final factoring are then used as the correct factors.

Although this iterative procedure is used in a number of factor analytic methods it has certain difficulties, notably that an assumption has to be made initially about the rank of the matrix, and although the iteration will find communalities to fit this rank there can be no certainty that this rank is correct. Furthermore the first estimate that is put into the first factor analysis to determine the rank of the matrix in fact affects the final solution so that there can be no great confidence in the final result. In addition, as Nunnally (1978) points out, these iterative procedures can lead to communalities greater than 1.00 which make no sense.

2. The squared multiple correlation (SMC) as an estimate of the communalities The SMC for estimating each variable from all the others in the matrix is obtained and the value is placed in the diagonal spaces of the matrix. Guttman (1956) showed that this was the lower bound for the communality. However as Nunnally (1978) points out there are problems with this method of estimation. The common variance determined by the SMC is what is in common between the particular set of variables in the matrix. However, communality is usually taken to indicate how much a variable has in common with a hypothetical set of factors (see p.98). This is certainly the more interesting meaning psychologically. There are two other severe difficulties with the use of SMCs. First, in artificial matrices where the factors are known, using them as communalities fails to reproduce the factors. Second, in large matrices with large numbers of variables, the SMCs rapidly approach unity. Nunnally (1978) suggests that the SMCs are a good starting point for the iterative approach that has been discussed above.

3. Statistically significant factors One way of looking at factor analysis, first developed by Thurstone (1947), is as a method of reducing the rank of a matrix. The smaller the rank (the fewer factors) to which it may be reduced the more elegant the solution. With this approach the problem turns around how to choose the correct number of factors.

One solution is to test if the original correlation matrix is due to sampling error. If it is not a first factor or component is extracted and the residual matrix is then tested. This goes on until the residual matrix is no longer statistically significant. The number of factors extracted up to that point is then declared the rank of the matrix. These factors are regarded as significant.

However, as Nunnally (1978) points out, although these statistical tests are mathematically and logically sound they are so lenient that they fail to describe the matrix as economically as possible, i.e. they allow too many factors to be extracted. These elegant statistical solutions are not useful for practical factor analysis. However, workers in this field (especially Cattell, 1978) have developed some empirically based algorithms and these will be described in the next chapter, on effective technical solutions to the various difficulties in factor analysis.

4. Factor analyses which avoid using the diagonal elements in the matrix One way of overcoming the problems associated with the diagonal elements of the correlation matrix is to develop methods of factor analysis which do not use them in the computations. Two factor analysts have developed methods which do this – Comrey (1962) and Harman (1976): methods known as minimum residual factor analysis.

I do not intend to describe in any detail these methods, which differ essentially only in that Comrey extracts one factor at a time until a satisfactory solution is achieved while Harman extracts a specified number of factors before the residual matrix is examined. This is because these methods have not been widely used in factor analysis. This may be because, on occasion, as Nunnally (1978) points out, misleading solutions are produced or communalities greater than 1.00 occur. A further reason for not going into detail about these ingenious methods is that both Cattell (1978) and Harman (1976) agree that Harman's Minres (as it is known) is excellent for establishing communalities. If these communalities are then inserted into the original correlation matrix and principal factors are extracted, the result is virtually identical to the original Minres solution.

Specialised workers in the development of factor analytic methods have developed a number of other factor analytic methods which deserve mention.

1. Image analysis   In image analysis, which was developed by Guttman, the common core of the variables is what can be predicted by multiple regression from the other variables in the matrix. What is done, therefore, is to predict variable 1 from all the others and variable 2 from all the others and so on. The predicted variable scores are placed into an image matrix. From this image matrix, a covariance rather than a correlation matrix is computed and this is subjected to any of the methods of condensation or initial factor analysis which we have discussed. Thus the factor loadings in image analysis are not correlations but covariances of the image variables with a linear combination of the image variables.

Nunnally (1978) claims that there are several advantages to image analysis, namely that it provides a unique solution to the common variance between variables and that the image factors are actual combinations of scores in the image matrix.

However there are also problems with the method especially as regards the meaning of the factors which, as has been said, are covariances of image variables with actual combinations of these variables. Given the way the image was derived, I have always found it difficult to interpret the meaning of the image factors, although Nunnally (1978) suggests that they can be interpreted as if they were normal factors. A further difficulty concerns the meaning of 'common' in the concept of 'image'. As with principal components it explains the common variance in a particular set of variables but as was discussed above in respect of common factors, this is a somewhat limited meaning of factors. A final problem with image analysis, according to Nunnally (1978), is that in artificial matrices where the underlying factors are known image analysis does not always reproduce the factors.

Cattell (1978) is not greatly in favour of image analysis on the grounds that specific factors in all the variables have entered into the estimation of the images so that the factoring is no longer in the old factor space but in an 'ersatz space built up with an admixture of the specifics'. Furthermore he claims that the results are only trivially different from those of iterative factoring. For all these reasons, clever as it is, there seems little justification for using image analysis.

2. Alpha factor analysis The aim of alpha factor analysis is to produce factor score estimates of the highest possible reliability – hence its name. However, Cattell (1978) makes cogent criticism of the rationale of the technique – namely that there is little sense in thus boosting the common factor contribution. The gain in reliability is essentially illusory. Furthermore, and this seems to me to vitiate the whole procedure, the results of such alpha factoring are little different from those of more conventional methods.

I have mentioned some of the main approaches to extracting factors from the correlation matrix. In general there is remarkably little difference in the results between principal factor analysis when the communalities have been well estimated and other methods. Although maximum likelihood factor analysis is more sophisticated statistically than the other methods, with large matrices Cattell (1978) claims that it gives results so similar to those of principal components analysis that its increased computing complexity is simply not worthwhile. This is certainly what I recently found in the development of the PPQ (Kline and Lapham, 1990a). Maximum likelihood analysis is at its best in confirmatory analysis rather than exploratory factor analysis, which has been the subject of this chapter.

Chapter 8

Factor Analysis: Rotation of Factors and other Topics

ROTATION OF FACTORS

When factors have been extracted by any of the methods which have been discussed in Chapter 7, it is possible to interpret them (although this is usually difficult). The first general factor, for example, from a principal factor analysis is usually not interpretable unless it so happens that in the particular psychological domain a general factor makes sense.

Although I have not discussed the geometric approach to factor analysis, it is possible to represent factors in a Euclidean factor space.

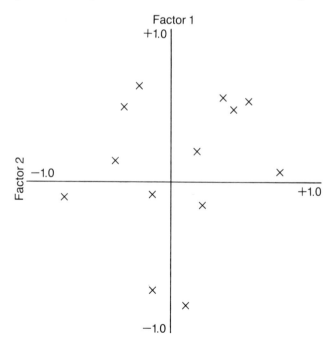

Figure 8.1 Two factors with their factor loadings

As Cattell (1978) points out this depiction of factors in factor space allows us to see a real problem with factor analysis and one that makes rotation of factors one of the most critical issues in the scientific study of psychology using the factor analytic method.

As was evident from the algebra of factor analysis the factor loadings were determined by the correlations of the variables, the resulting factors explaining the variance in the correlation matrix. However the position of these axes is not fixed. It is possible to spin these axes into any position and, as we do so, the loadings of the variables on the factors will change, but the amount of variance explained remains the same. That is why there is a virtual infinity of equivalent mathematical solutions to a factor analysis. In a large study, with perhaps ten factors, all these ten could take up any position in factor space. This spinning of factors is known as rotation. Since there is no particular merit in any position, mathematically, since all are equivalent there is no reason to interpret the set of factors as they emerge from the analysis rather than any other set which rotation of the axes might produce.

This, then, is the problem. Which of this infinite set of factors do we choose? This is no minor statistical difficulty, as in a sense, was the choice between the different methods of initial factor extraction which all tend to give, especially where there is a clear structure to the data, remarkably similar results. This is not the case with rotation. Rotating factors to different positions produces factors sufficiently different to produce drastically different psychological interpretations. Indeed Kline and Barrett (1983) were able to show that many of the apparent differences in the results of the factor analysis of personality tests were due to these rotational differences, as Cattell (Cattell and Kline, 1977) has always argued.

As can be seen from Figure 8.2, rotating factors changes the factor loadings but not, as has been said, the variance explained.

Choosing the best position: rotation to simple structure

All the different positions of the axes in the factor analysis account equally well, mathematically, for the variance in the original matrix. If we consider any set of factor loadings as an hypothesis to account for the observed correlations, then following the law of parsimony, Lloyd Morgan's canon or Occam's razor, the principle that entities should not be multiplied beyond necessity, we should pick the simplest explanation of those that fit the facts. This principle of simplicity has served the natural sciences well, and it is the rationale for rotating to simple structure.

Definition of simple structure   Thurstone (1947) was the first proponent of simple structure as the solution to the problem of the indeterminacy of factor analysis. Simple structure is essentially defined as the attainment of factors with mainly zero or near zero loadings and a few high loadings.

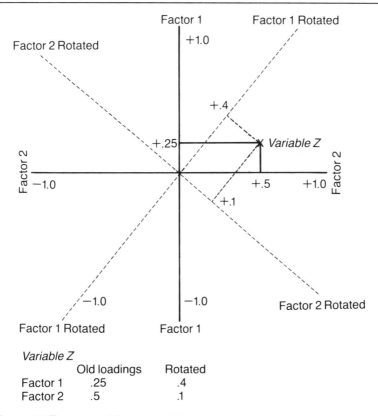

Variable Z		
	Old loadings	Rotated
Factor 1	.25	.4
Factor 2	.5	.1

Figure 8.2 Two rotated factors and their loadings

Such a structure not only has the advantage that it is the simplest explanation of the correlations but also such factors are easily interpretable. Cattell (1978) has shown that simple structure has two other features which make its attainment an essential of good factor analysis.

1. In studies of matrices where the determinants are known it can be shown that simple structure rotations yield factors closely approximating to them.
2. Simple structure factors are replicable. It should be easy to see that reproducibility of factor structures is no simple thing given the infinity of equivalent solutions. However rotation to simple structure does yield replicable factors from study to study, even when some of the variables are different. This is highly important if factor analysis is to be used in any but a descriptive mode. For example if we have an intelligence factor we should expect it to load on a variety of intelligence tests. However if a factor were entirely restricted to a particular data set, it could not be given any scientific or psychological generality.

Thus I agree with Cattell (1978), as do most serious workers in factor analysis, that the attainment of simple structure is an essential of adequate factor analysis and that where simple structure has not been reached there is no reason to take the results seriously.

The attainment of simple structure

How simple structure can be obtained was until relatively recently a matter of some dispute, which to some extent accounts for the disparity of factor analytic findings. However, the approaches adopted by Harman (1976) and Cattell (1978) are now generally accepted.

I have shown graphically how rotation of the factor axes changes the loadings. This procedure is carried out in modern computer programs by matrix algebra. I do not intend to describe this in any detail (readers are referred to Cattell, 1978 or Nunnally, 1978) but I shall describe the basic principles of how simple structure is reached. Before I can do this, a few further terms require explanation.

1. Orthogonal rotation   In orthogonal rotation the factor axes are kept at 90 degrees to each other. This means that the factors are uncorrelated. The cosine of the angle between the factor axes indicates the correlation between the factors.

Cattell (e.g. Cattell and Kline, 1977) has always argued that orthogonal solutions are unlikely to be the simplest, in terms of maximising the number of zero loadings and yet having a few high loadings on each factor, simply because the positions that the factor axes can take up are constrained. In addition, since Cattell regards factors as determiners, or highly important sources of variance, he argues that such determinants would be unlikely to be uncorrelated. In the field of personality, for example, it would be surprising if the main determining factors were uncorrelated, given their genetic and environmental basis.

2. Oblique rotation   In oblique rotation the factor axes can take up any position relative to each other, hence the name. These factors are correlated. This is the solution that Cattell favours since the factors can be rotated to their simplest position and, as has been argued, oblique factors fit psychological theory better than do orthogonal factors.

One further point needs to be noted concerning the question of whether oblique or orthogonal rotations are best. Guilford (1967), in the development of his structure of intellect model of intelligence, has always favoured orthogonal solutions. He argues that although each individual factor in an oblique rotation may be more simple by Thurstone's criteria than those in the orthogonal set, the oblique set, because it is correlated, is more complex than the orthogonal. This argument is ingenious and it must be settled empirically. In fact, as we shall see later in this chapter, Guilford's (1967) approach cannot be supported.

Of course, there are still a huge number of oblique rotations and how the simplest is chosen will be described after some more terms have been defined.

3. Factor structure   These are the correlations of the original variables with the rotated factors. The factor structure loadings in a rotated factor analysis are the equivalent of the factor loadings in the unrotated factor matrix.

4. Factor pattern   These are weights which are mainly useful for determining the factor scores. Unfortunately because the pattern matrix usually closely resembles the structure matrix it is often used in research reports as if it were a matrix of correlations of variables.

In the case of orthogonal rotation, the factor pattern and the structure matrix are identical but in oblique rotation this is not so. It is important in factor analysis that after oblique rotation the factor structure is interpreted and not the pattern.

5. Reference vector structure   As an aid to computation a reference vector structure matrix is used which consists of the loadings on axes which are 90 degrees from the oblique factors. Some factor analysts report the reference vector structure as if it were the oblique structure matrix, although its meaning is not the same. Nunnally (1978) regards this practice as one of the many easy ways to fool yourself and others with factor analysis.

6. Higher order factors   When test scores are subjected to factor analysis the resulting factors or components, rotated or unrotated, are known as primary or first order factors. These account for the variance and correlations among the variables. Second order factors, on the other hand, arise from factoring the correlations among oblique factors. They thus account for the correlations among the primaries. Of course second order factors can only be extracted after oblique rotation. It is possible to compute the loadings of the original variables on the second order factors. If there are a number of second order factors, yet higher order factors can be extracted. Clearly the higher order a factor the broader it is and the more variance it accounts for. Modern work in intelligence by Undheim (1981) suggests that the old general intelligence factor, g, is, in fact, a third order factor.

Technical rules for obtaining good simple structure analyses

I hope that readers are now in a position to understand factor analysis and rotation of factors. It is now necessary to discuss how simple structure is to be obtained. I shall combine this explanation with some more general rules that have been agreed upon by most factorists as to how adequate factor analyses, in exploratory analysis, should be conducted. These rules were developed first by Cattell (1973).

1. Sampling variables If we are attempting to map a whole field, such as ability, by exploratory factor analysis, then it is essential that the whole range of ability variables is sampled. Actually, as has been shown by Cattell (1971), it is almost impossible to test for all abilities. The majority of abilities which are important in education and which can be readily assessed by traditional psychometric methods, present no problem: there are valid and reliable measures of these variables. However there are skills which have never been measured, and whose factorial structure is quite unknown (in the previous chapter we used the examples of the skills of a jockey or cheese-tester).

The point is that, in a factor analytic study, no matter how brilliant the rotation and how elegant a simple structure has been reached, if no measures for certain factors are put into the analysis these factors cannot emerge. Thus in exploratory factor analysis a good method of sampling variables is essential.

2. Sampling subjects The factors emerging from factor analyses are affected by the samples. Guilford (1956) has argued that samples must be homogeneous and that scores from different groups must not be added together. There is some truth in this statement since for example if we rated skin colour 1–5 and then studied 100 truly black negroes and 100 Scandinavians of the fairest hue, the mean skin colour of this total group would reflect not a single individual in the sample.

However, high homogeneity lowers correlations and reduces the variance of factors. The way around this problem is to ensure that samples reflect populations. If it is considered that the factor structure may differ in subgroups then separate analyses of those groups should be carried out.

Furthermore Guilford's (1956) suggestion can lead to error. For example, if one were to investigate the determinants of academic success at university by using a sample of scholarship holders at Oxford and Cambridge, then it is highly likely that intelligence, g, would not be an important factor. However, this is not because intelligence is not important in the determination of academic success but because the sample would be restricted in range, i.e. be too homogeneous. All the subjects would be highly and sufficiently intelligent to do well. Hence other variables come to the fore. If we were to extend the study to all colleges, universities and polytechnics, where the range of intelligence is much greater, then intelligence would again become salient.

One further example will clarify this point. Cattell and Child (1975) in their survey of motivational factors did not find that hunger was an important drive. However this is simply because in most of the industrial West the range of hunger as a drive is too small. Factor analyses of the inmates of German concentration camps could well have told another story.

In summary it is important to sample widely and representatively when carrying out exploratory factor analyses. Factors from general samples should be checked out in more homogeneous subgroups.

3. Sample size The size of the sample (as distinct from its representativeness) is also important if reliable factors are to be obtained. Guilford (1956) argues that 200 subjects is the minimum for a good analysis. However Barrett and Kline (1981b) carried out an empirical study of this problem with 1200 subjects who had taken the EPQ (Eysenck and Eysenck, 1975). The full sample yielded factors of almost perfect clarity, especially the extraversion and neuroticism scales. Then random subsamples of various sizes were taken and the factor structure was examined. It was found that the main factors remained clear and unequivocal until the sample dropped below 100. Guilford's figure would seem to be unduly pessimistic, at least where clear factors can be extracted. Below 100 subjects any factors require replication.

4. Variable to subject ratio Here the leading authorities in the field vary considerably in their advice. On one point there is complete agreement. For reasons of matrix algebra it is essential that there are more subjects than variables. In a square or less than square matrix, the results, although computable, are bound to yield apparently big factors. As regards the ratio of subjects to variables, claims run from the conservative Nunnally (1978) at 10 to 1 down to Guilford at 2 to 1. Barrett and Kline (1981b) in the study referred to in the previous paragraph also examined this question. They found that at a ratio of 2 to 1 the main factors were clear and from 3 to 1 there was no improvement if the ratio were increased. On these grounds, I am happy to trust factors derived from samples where the ratio is 2 to 1 or greater. Actually Arrindel and van der Ende (1985) claimed that this ratio was not important compared with the ratio of sample size to factors. Stable factors required the sample to be twenty times larger than the number of factors.

From the discussion so far it is clear that in exploratory analyses representative samples of at least 100 subjects and with a variable to subject ratio of at least 2 to 1 are essential for good factor analyses. It is also important to note that the sampling of variables must be carefully done. This would generally ensure the requisite sample to factor ratio. These recommendations are aimed at ensuring that the emerging factors are reliable and not affected by direct statistical sampling problems.

5. Choice of factoring method For exploratory factor analyses, as our discussion of the different methods made clear, there was usually little difference in the final result. Principal components, with unities in the diagonals, makes use of the all the variance, general and unique, in the matrix, and this may lead to problems in certain special cases although with large matrices the difference between principal components and principal factors is negligible. In my view principal factors should be used. It is efficient and has no disadvantages. The statistical elegance of maximum likelihood methods seems to add nothing useful for exploratory factor analysis although for confirmatory analysis it is valuable, as will be discussed later in this chapter.

6. Number of factors to be rotated When the principal factor analysis has been conducted, perhaps ideally with communalities derived from the Minres method, which has been discussed (see p. 113), an absolutely critical aspect for obtaining simple structure turns on the number of factors to be rotated.

Cattell (1978) has shown that rotation of too few factors tends to produce second orders at the first order. Rotation of too many factors causes factors to split. A common solution to this problem and the default solution on many computer packages is to rotate all factors with eigen values or latent roots greater than one. However Cattell (1978) has shown that with large matrices this is an overestimate of the number of significant factors and Cliff (1988) has suggested that this criterion should be abandoned. Barrett and Kline (1982a) examined a number of methods of selecting the correct number of factors and showed that two methods appeared to reach the best solution in terms of the known number of factors and in allowing subsequent simple structure. These were the Scree Test (Cattell, 1966) and the Velicer method (Velicer, 1976). The Scree test requires some subjective judgement as to how many factors There are but with practice it is a procedure with high reliability. It should be noted that the Scree test works on principal components and it is useful to compute these, select the number of factors and then compute principal factors before rotating.

As Cattell (1978) argues, there is no hard and fast best method of selecting the number of factors to rotate. It seems best to use both the Scree and Velicer tests and if these disagree rotate the number of factors each suggests.

7. Type of rotation There are now a huge number of different rotational methods both for orthogonal and oblique rotation. These are fully described by Gorsuch (1974) and I shall not discuss them here. Suffice it to say here that they are algebraic methods of rotating the factors, as depicted earlier in this chapter. All aim at simple structure. Cattell (1978) and Hakstian (1971) have compared the efficiency of many of these methods and there is now surprising agreement as to the most efficient rotation at obtaining simple structure.

a. Orthogonal rotation. If, for some reason, an orthogonal solution is desired, few would dispute that the Varimax rotation (Kaiser, 1958) is the one to choose.

b. Oblique rotation. Here again there is little doubt that in most circumstances Direct Oblimin (Jennrich and Sampson, 1966) gets very close to ideal simple structure. The criterion used is the hyperplane count, the number of zeros or near zeros in the hyperplanes round the factors. The only challenge to this comes from Cattell (1978) who favours his own topological approach, Maxplane, followed by delicate hand adjustment using his Rotoplot method. This is a highly skilled procedure and in most circumstances adds little to simple structure, as indeed Hakstian (1971) has shown.

Both Varimax and Direct Oblimin are available on the commonly used computer factor analytic procedures. With these rotations simple structure is likely to be closely approached.

By utilising all these methods, sampling properly the universe of variables and subjects, and rotating to simple structure the correct number of principal factors by Varimax or Direct Oblimin, the factor analyst should emerge with a reliable set of factors, which economically explain the variance in the original data matrix.

Two more checks remain to be done. The first is to replicate the factors in other studies, and measures of factor similarity may be found in Cattell (1978). Finally it is useful to examine the second order structure of the factors. If two sets of factors in two studies really are similar their second order factors should also be similar. If both these checks are positive, then the factors may be interpreted with some confidence that they are important psychologically as determiners of the original variables.

CONFIRMATORY FACTOR ANALYSIS

So far in our discussion of factor analysis we have outlined the technique and shown how it is useful for mapping out the most important determinants of variance within a field. This is the main use of factor analysis – exploratory analysis.

However, as was mentioned when the maximum likelihood method of condensation was described, factor analysis can be used to support or refute hypotheses and I want to scrutinise briefly this use of factor analysis. It should be pointed out here that many psychologists, trained in the experimental tradition, prefer confirmatory analysis because it is a form of hypothesis testing. They condemn normal exploratory analysis as blind empiricism.

1. Multiple group method of confirmatory analysis

In this approach variables are first grouped by the investigator and then any of the methods of condensation is applied to the groups of variables. If by so doing the residual matrices consist virtually of zeros, then clearly the grouping has been confirmed by the analysis. If the residual matrix still contains variance further factors can be extracted, a method which combines exploratory and confirmatory analysis. Again this method can refute hypotheses if, for example, a variable hypothesised to load on a particular group factor in fact loads on a factor from another group.

I shall not go into the detailed computation of these group factors but the principle is clear. The factor analysis is no different from that of the exploratory methods which have been described. The confirmatory aspect arises from the fact that the variables have been grouped by the investigator before the analysis begins. Full computational details may be found in Harman (1976) or Mulaik (1972).

2. Procrustes solutions

In Procrustes solutions a target factor matrix is specified and a factor analysis is rotated to fit this target matrix as closely as possible.

I do not intend to say much about this approach because, in my view, work by Horn and Knapp (1973) has shown the Procrustes method to be flawed. Indeed, I would not have mentioned it at all had it not been for the fact that the important work on the nature of intelligence by Guilford and his colleagues (Guilford and Hoepfner, 1971) is supported by Procrustes rotations. Thus it is important to understand its flaws.

The problem with the Procrustes method, as was shown by Horn and Knapp (1973), is that it is so powerful a technique that it can fit target matrices of random data where no factors exist. Even worse it can fit target matrices in which the hypothesised factors are actually antithetical to those in the data. Thus the fact that Guilford (e.g. 1967) could find tests (factors) which fitted his structure of intellect model by using Procrustes solutions cannot be regarded as confirming the model.

One of the major difficulties with Procrustes solutions is that unless the target matrix is specified with high precision, and that is rarely possible, very high positive and negative loadings and zeros are inserted and the least squares method of estimating the factor structure is simply too efficient.

Thus it is not possible to recommend the use of Procrustes solutions in confirmatory analysis.

3. Maximum likelihood confirmatory analysis

Maximum likelihood confirmatory analysis, as was the case with the multiple group approach, described above, operates directly on the correlation matrix, rather than using the targeted rotations of true Procrustes methods. Nunnally (1978) argues that to avoid chance effects with this method a large sample of subjects should be used with at least ten times, better twenty, subjects to variables. Its great advantage over Procrustean methods is that there is a test for the statistical significance of factors and for confidence limits for the loadings.

However, I have two objections to maximum likelihood factor analysis. The first and most important is that the chi-square test of fit of the target matrix to the maximum likelihood solution is so powerful that it is difficult to reject hypotheses, even where these are psychologically different (and this is particularly so with large samples). The second problem is that, to my knowledge, no substantive major psychological findings have ever been made with this method. This is partly due to the formidable computing time and capacity required by the method but I have the feeling that this is an approach to confirmatory analysis that is liked for its statistical elegance rather than its ability to answer psychological questions.

Nunnally (1978) makes it clear that of these methods (1–3) of confirmatory analysis, unless the hypothesised factor structure is highly complex, he prefers the simple and direct multiple group method. Nevertheless in modern journal articles almost all researchers use maximum likelihood analysis. In view of this this is probably the technique to recommend but it must be used with caution.

4. Simple structure analysis as confirmatory analysis

There is one further approach to confirmatory analysis which I have used in various studies of Freudian theory (e.g. Kline and Storey, 1978b). Here the psychoanalytic theory was tested (Freud, 1905) that certain items alleged to reflect fixation at the oral level would load on two factors. However, a simple structure rotation was performed, on the grounds that if simple structure did reflect the basic underlying dimensions and was the most parsimonious explanation of the data, then if it was different from the hypothesised factor structure this would refute it. In a more general form there is a problem if the simple structure solution is different from the one supported by confirmatory analysis. Thus I argue that congruence between simple structure analysis and hypothesised structure is a useful form of confirmatory analysis which has the advantage of making no use of chance.

This brings an end to the description and discussion of exploratory and confirmatory factor analysis. However before leaving this topic, I want briefly to mention what Cattell (1957) calls other factor analytic designs because some of these can be useful in applied psychometrics.

1. R analysis. R analysis is regular analysis, of the kind discussed in these chapters on factor analysis. In this, correlations between variables are factored and the resulting factors account for individual differences between people. This is by far the most widely used form of factor analysis and from it have arisen some of the major findings of psychometrics, factors such as extraversion, neuroticism and intelligence.

2. P analysis. In P analysis the traits within one individual are correlated and subjected to factor analysis. P factors are, therefore, unique to the individual. P analysis has been little used because repeated measurements on all variables are necessary to compute the correlations, and it is no easy matter to obtain sufficient data.

3. Q analysis. In Q analysis correlations between people rather than variables are factored. The data matrix of R analysis is turned on its side. For algebraically sound Q analysis at least two times the number of tests to subjects is required. Hence if large samples are used a considerable amount of testing is required. The resulting factors load on individuals who are thus classified into groups. Q analysis can be useful in the applied field where classification of people rather than tests is the objective.

4. O analysis. Here the scores of the same subject on different occasions are factored. If measures of ongoing processes such as education or psychotherapy or a list of environmental events were also included in the analysis some determinants of change might be discovered.

5. T analysis. Here the test-retest reliability coefficients are factored.

6. S analysis. In this the responses of two people on several occasions are factored. Neither T nor S analysis has been much used although such data are obtainable.

CONCLUSIONS

In these two chapters I have discussed factor analysis in some detail because it is one of the most important statistical methods in psychological testing and without some understanding of factor analysis it is not possible to understand either the problems or their solutions in psychological testing.

I have shown how it can be claimed that factors explain the variance of a data matrix and can account for correlations. I have discussed various methods of initial factoring and demonstrated that rotation to simple structure is an answer to the indeterminacy problem of factor analysis. I have also set out what are generally regarded as the best set of rules for carrying out technically sound analyses which are replicable.

All this referred to exploratory factor analysis aimed at mapping out a complex field. Methods of confirmatory analysis were discussed but some reservations about them all, especially Procrustes rotations, were expressed. Finally some different modes of factor analysis were described.

In sum I hope that readers can now see that factor analysis is a powerful technique for answering the questions which are raised in psychological testing, and in the study of individual differences.

Chapter 9

Test Construction: The Criterion-keyed Method

In test construction items are written and then administered to trial samples of subjects. These data are then subjected to a variety of statistical procedures with the aim of producing a valid and reliable test, preferably measuring one factor. The selected items will be tried out again to ensure that the statistical criteria of a good test are met. Finally the test is standardised.

In this chapter one of the statistical methods for producing a test from a set of items, the criterion-keyed method, will be described and scrutinised. In the next chapter of this handbook some different statistical procedures will be discussed. How the original items are written will be discussed in later chapters of this handbook, when the different types of test, e.g. intelligence or ability tests, are described.

In criterion-keyed test construction items are selected from the pool if they can discriminate one or more criterion groups from controls, hence the name. Some of the most widely used tests in clinical and medical psychology, e.g. the Minnesota Multiphasic Personality Inventory, known as the MMPI (Hathaway and McKinley, 1951), and the Strong Vocational Interest Blank, usually referred to as the SVIB (Campbell, 1971), and much used in vocational selection and guidance, were developed by this method.

In the case of the MMPI the items were written from a knowledge of the typical symptomatology of patients seeking psychiatric help. Thus the items, of the true–false variety, refer to behaviour and feelings that abnormal subjects often exhibit. Consequently the scales which finally discriminated the groups have an obvious face validity.

However, there is no need, when using the criterion-keyed method, even to try to write items which would appear to be relevant to the discrimination of the criterion groups. Instead an entirely empirical approach may be adopted. An item is selected if it will discriminate the criterion group whether it is apparent why this should be so or not. Many of the items in the SVIB are of this kind. Thus the rationale of the criterion-keyed item is pragmatic, not theoretical or intuitive. If it discriminates include it.

THE MAIN USE OF CRITERION-KEYED TESTS

These tests are used where the purpose of testing is the discrimination of certain groups. This is why they are popular in applied psychology, where there is a clear purpose to the testing, as in diagnosis, selection or guidance, where, indeed, what matters is the ability to discriminate, not an understanding of why the test does discriminate. A few examples will clarify this point.

Criterion-keyed tests in selection In many selection procedures, at some stage it is useful to screen out certain subjects. Thus in recent years in selecting soldiers to man the bunkers of nuclear weapons it was considered essential to screen out, as a first step, all who might be at all unstable or psychopathic. For such a purpose a well validated criterion-keyed measure, which would reliably discriminate the unstable, would be excellent. Clearly many selection procedures involve screening and this is one use of the criterion-keyed test.

Criterion-keyed tests in diagnosis If, for example, there were clearly different treatments for different categories of mental disorder, then any test which could reliably discriminate one clinical group from another would be valuable and this was the basic rationale behind the development of the MMPI.

Criterion-keyed tests in guidance This was one of the main uses of the SVIB. Here the practitioner would tell the subject that her or his pattern of scores resembled that of a certain occupational group and would then discuss what she or he felt about the possibility of training for or attempting to obtain a position of that type. Again, so the advocates of the criterion-keyed method of test construction would argue, it is a matter of indifference why these items discriminate or why the subject endorsed them as she or he did. All that matters is the fact that her or his score resembled that of the criterion group.

In brief it can be seen that the criterion-keyed test is a product of true, or some might say blind, empiricism. Even where such tests are effective this empirical, atheoretical bias does have certain disadvantages and these, together with other problems with the criterion-keyed method, must now be discussed.

PROBLEMS WITH THE CRITERION-KEYED METHOD

1. Selection of criterion groups

In many fields of psychology there are difficulties in the selection of criterion groups. This is particularly so in clinical psychology and psychiatry, where classification into diagnostic groups is highly unreliable (Beck, 1962). Where this is the case, as should be obvious, items that discriminated well in the test trial will be far less discriminating on subsequent occasions. As Vernon (1950) showed many years ago, classifications in general tend to be of somewhat low reliability and all this adds in error to the criterion-keyed test.

There is a more specific problem with the MMPI, namely that in addition to the unreliability of classification in psychiatric diagnosis there is poor agreement as to what categories should be used. Thus the MMPI uses categories which are of interest only to those trained in the Kraepelin system of classification (and some might add by psychiatrists at Minnesota).

To some extent these classification problems occur in all spheres. Thus occupational categories are often very broad: financial advisers, executives and managers exemplify the argument. Such problems simply increase the error variance.

2. Lack of psychological meaning

Let us ignore for the moment these problems of classification or assume that they have been overcome. There is a far more serious objection to criterion-keyed tests. This concerns their lack of psychological meaning. The MMPI illustrates this point.

The MMPI has nine standard clinical scales, based on their ability to discriminate clinical groups (a full description may be found in Chapter 25 of this handbook). The items in the manic scale were selected because they could discriminate the manics from normals and the other clinical groups. However it is not unlikely that manics differ from these groups not just on one variable but on a variety of variables. Such a scale, therefore, would be unifactorial, measuring one variable, only by chance. This has two consequences. First, if two subjects have the same score on the scale, the scores are not necessarily psychologically equivalent. Second, there is no way of knowing what the scale measures since we do not know what variables distinguish these groups one from another. Thus if a subject scores x on the manic scale there is no meaning that can be attributed to the score except that to a greater or lesser extent her or his score resembles that of the criterion manic group.

From this it is clear that a problem with criterion-keyed tests is this lack of psychological meaning. Some readers might well wonder why this should be important. This can be easily explained. If we build up over the years a good data base about various clinical or occupational groups and if the test variables are meaningful we have acquired a considerable body of psychological knowledge. With criterion-keyed tests, however, this is not the case. All we know is the extent to which the test scales will or will not discriminate the groups. Thus, the lack of meaning of criterion-keyed scales is an important defect, except for simple basic screening.

3. Specificity of criterion-keyed tests

A difficulty with criterion-keyed tests is that the results are difficult to generalise. An example from the use of such tests in occupational psychology will clarify this point. If we had a scale which would discriminate accountants, it could well prove useful in the selection of accountants. However if the job should change, as it has recently with the advent of computing, such scales would be useless. This is particularly important with the SVIB, which is an American test. Some jobs, lawyers are the obvious example, are quite different in different countries. Clearly cross-cultural comparisons are fraught with problems if the tests are criterion keyed.

Indeed I believe that all these problems are sufficiently serious to contraindicate their use. I much prefer to use tests which have been constructed by the methods to be described later. Nevertheless I shall set out briefly the steps in constructing tests of this type. In so doing I think that it will become evident in what circumstances criterion-keyed tests are worthy of use.

THE CONSTRUCTION OF CRITERION-KEYED TESTS

I shall describe the basic steps in the construction of criterion-keyed tests. I shall not deal with more elaborate refinements of the methods on account of the problems which I have discussed.

1. Set up (a) the criterion group or groups; or (b) a criterion score

Suppose that we were trying to devise a test for helicopter pilots. Two criterion groups might be composed – of the best passes and the worst failures. If there are, as is often the case where there has been rigorous selection, relatively few failures all would have to be included in the fail group.

A criterion score might be constructed by following up all the pilots who had passed and obtaining from their supervisors a rating of their flying ability. Similar methods could be used for any profession, although it should be noted that only in large organisations, such as the armed services or the civil service, would failures remain within the organisation, and thus allow the establishment of the criterion groups.

2. Sample size

In the construction of criterion-keyed tests the sample consists of the criterion groups. Thus the larger the number in these the more reliable the resulting statistics.

3. Item trial

The pool of items from which we hope to derive the final test is then administered to the criterion groups or to the subjects from whom we have obtained a criterion score. There should be at least 200 in the sample as a whole and if there are men and women in the sample these should be analysed separately. Ideally there should be at least 200 of each sex.

4. Statistical analysis

a. Criterion groups In a criterion-keyed test we want items which will discriminate the two groups. There are various methods of item selection. One is to compare the mean score of the two groups for each item. Items are selected if they show a significant difference between the groups. This can be done using a simple Student's t test; or, more sophisticated, and taking account of the correlations between the items, a discriminant function could be computed between the groups. Those items with the biggest weights in the function would be selected for the test. A third possibility, and the one that is probably the most widely used, is to correlate each item with membership of the groups. This is a correlation between dichotomous variables and, although there are some problems with the choice of coefficient (a difficulty discussed later in our section on the construction of factor analytic tests where it is crucial) the most favoured is the phi (see the statistical appendix for the formula). Thus the phi between each item and group membership is computed. All significant items are selected, or if there is a large number of such items the twenty or thirty best, depending on the desired length of the test. It should be noted that, in the construction of criterion-keyed tests, we need never look at item content in this selection of items. All that matters is that the item discriminates.

There should be separate analyses for males and females. If possible it is easiest to select items which are equivalent for both males and females. This involves selecting items for which the statistics are identical or highly similar for males and females.

b. Using the criterion score In this method the test is given to all those subjects from whom a criterion score has been obtained. Then each item is correlated with the total criterion score. For this purpose the point biserial correlation is used, r_{pbis} (see the statistical appendix for the formula). Again the items with the highest correlations or all the significant items are selected. As previously if males and females are tested these same correlations are done for each of the sexes and if possible items which have identical or highly similar correlations among males and females are selected. Again, since this is a criterion-keyed test, the content of the items is unimportant.

Should there be insufficient items to form a test, it is worth looking at the successful items and the failures and then writing new items in the light of this comparison. These should then be tried out as before and the best selected.

The items discriminating the criterion groups or correlating with the criterion score should be collected together to form the test and the reliability coefficient should be calculated, as described in Chapter 1.

However it should be noted that there is no reason to expect that the items in a criterion-keyed scale will be homogeneous particularly if the groups differ on a variety of variables. The reliability of such tests is often low because they are multifactorial. This, of course, brings into question what they are measuring since reliability is intimately related to the true score, as was shown in Chapter 3.

These test items should be cross-validated on new criterion groups or with a criterion score derived from a new group. Unless this is done it is impossible to use the test with any confidence, even for practical screening. This is because any two groups will differ on variables particular to those two groups and the criterion-keyed method utilises this chance aspect in its discrimination.

Should some of the test items fail to discriminate the new groups new items must be written and the same analyses carried out until a test of sufficient length and of cross-validated items has been developed.

CONCLUSIONS

From this description of the method of constructing criterion-keyed tests and from our discussion of some of the difficulties and problems associated with tests of this kind, a number of conclusions may be drawn.

1. Criterion-keyed tests are best in the practical context where classification into groups is desired. Even here there are disadvantages and where possible other tests should be used.
2. All criterion-keyed tests should be cross-validated and the advantage of well established measures such as the MMPI is that, whatever their theoretical shortcomings, the vast mass of evidence as to their discriminatory power makes them valuable. Indeed the MMPI is still the most widely used personality questionnaire in the world. This work will be discussed in Chapter 25 of this handbook.
3. Nevertheless the fact that the scales have no necessary psychological meaning is serious because, as has been argued, it limits the generalisability of the findings and fails to add to psychological knowledge.

However, this last difficulty may be overcome by careful validation of the scales, as, to some extent, has been done with the MMPI, as can be seen, for example, in Dahlstrom and Welsh (1960). To complete this chapter I want to discuss this general approach to improving the psychological utility of criterion-keyed tests.

Validating the criterion-keyed test through factor analysis

The standard approach to validating a criterion-keyed test is to demonstrate that it will discriminate between the groups, as intended by the test constructor. There is nothing wrong with this form of validation but it does nothing to answer the objection that these tests have no psychological meaning.

However, in Chapter 2 on test validity, under the heading 'construct validity', the notion of locating factors in factor space was discussed. Now if the criterion-keyed scale were to be located in factor space its psychological meaning would be explicated, and this objection would be removed.

There are two points about this procedure which should be noted.

1. Factoring the scale. It is possible to locate the scale in factor space. This involves factoring the scale score together with the most important and best established personality factors. This is a viable procedure only if it so happens, and it will be good fortune if this is indeed the case, that the scale measures one, or at the most two factors. Where this is so the scale will load substantially on one or two factors and its psychological meaning will become plain.

   However, if, as is more likely, the scale is a mixture of factors, then its psychological meaning will not be clarified by scale factor analysis for it will have moderate or small loadings on a variety of factors. All that can be said, in that case, is that the scale is not homogeneous.

2. Factoring the items. Here the items in the scale would be factored along with the items in other scales. Then the factor analysis would show what the items were measuring, the extent of their similarity to other scales and so on. This is by far the best approach but it has to be said that it is no different, essentially, from constructing tests by the factor analytic method which will be discussed in the next chapter.

   This approach would indicate what factors were important in discriminating the criterion group. However, it would be far better and more efficient to use individual tests of these factors and weight them optimally to produce the discrimination by discriminant function analysis.

In summary it can be seen that it is possible to explicate the psychological meaning of criterion-keyed tests through factor analysis either of scales or items, but if this is done it usually leads to the conclusion that factored scales might have been used in the first instance. Thus the ineluctable conclusion has to be drawn that criterion-keyed tests should not be used even for practical selection. Factored scales are far superior.

Chapter 10

Test Construction: Factor Analytic and Item Analytic Methods

In this chapter I shall describe and discuss two methods of test construction, the item analytic and the factor analytic, which are widely used and which have, as their basic rationale, the classical model of test error which I scrutinised in some detail in Chapter 3 of this handbook. There, it will be recalled, test variance was conceptualised as true score and error variance, or in factor analytic terms common and unique variance. The higher the reliability of the test the lower the error or unique variance. Thus a homogeneous and highly reliable test is the aim of methods based on the classical model of error and this is the rationale of the two methods to be described in this chapter.

FACTOR ANALYSIS

In constructing tests using factor analysis the aim is to produce tests which load on only one factor – unifactorial tests. Such a test is inevitably reliable and valid in that it measures a factor. Of course it is necessary to demonstrate, in studies of validity, what that factor is.

From the viewpoint of establishing psychological knowledge the great advantage of a unifactorial test is that scores always mean the same thing. Two scores of 10 reflect the same status on the factor measured by the test. If a test measures more than one factor this is not necessarily so. Obviously a score of 10 could represent 5 and 5, 4 and 6 and so on, on the two factors. Thus a unifactorial test is the psychometric ideal.

Some tests, such as achievement motivation scales (McClelland, 1961), are not unifactorial yet appear to measures useful syndromes or variables. While this is so it must be pointed out that measurement would be improved if separate measure of the factors involved in achievement motivation were used. These scores would be more revealing than the pooled score obtained from the multifactorial measure, for the reasons already discussed.

However, it is not as easy as it might first appear to produce a unifactorial test that measures a factor of any importance, for reasons which can be best understood from a detailed examination of the method. I shall set out the main steps in the construction of a test using factor analysis but I shall say nothing of the factor analytic computations which have been fully discussed in Chapters 7 and 8 of this handbook. Some of the procedures which are suggested, to avoid errors, are based upon the arguments about factor analysis which were discussed in those chapters.

The procedures and their rationale of factor analytic test construction

1. Items

As was the case in the previous chapter on criterion-keyed tests the provenance of the items will not be discussed. I shall simply assume that we have a sufficient pool of items from which to derive a test.

In factor analytic test construction it is actually easier to construct several tests at once, than a single scale. This is because, as will be remembered from Chapters 7 and 8, the initial factoring procedures tend to produce a general factor plus several smaller bipolars. Rotation to simple structure to obtain the replicable and most elegant solution simply reduces the variance of this general factor. However in test construction a general factor is what we want. This problem is removed if we construct several different scales at once. Here rotation will break up the first factor, as desired. Thus the statistical analysis suits the objectives of the work.

Number of items

Thus ideally we establish a pool of items to measure several different factors. These are then administered to a trial sample. It is important to note that the number of items must not be so great that subjects get bored or fatigued in completing them. About an hour is the maximum that can be expected from adult subjects and much less with children. Small children could not be expected to stand more than, at most, half an hour's testing. Of course these figures vary with the type of test; personality and motivation tests are less tiring than tests of ability.

The other factor affecting the number of items to be tried out is that, generally in test construction, it is sensible to write twice as many items as will be used in the final test. This allows for items failing to load or turning out unsatisfactory for a variety of reasons that will be discussed later in this section. As will be remembered from the chapter on reliability, ten items is the absolute minimum for a reliable scale and the more items the higher the reliability. I aim for twenty items per scale except where time is highly important, as in occupational selection where I will use shorter scales provided that they are still reliable and valid.

2. Sampling

As has been made clear in previous chapters of this handbook, there are two aspects to sampling – size and representativeness.

Size: statistical considerations

The size of the sample must be large enough to reduce the standard error of the correlations to negligible proportions and this would generally be regarded as about 200. The absolute minimum would be 100.

With factor analysis there is also the problem of the subject to variable ratio. As was previously shown, a ratio of 2 to 1 when the factors are clear can be tolerated but ideally a ratio of at least 3 to 1 should be aimed for. This means, if we are testing out items for several scales, as was suggested above, that large samples are required simply for statistical reasons. Thus, for example if we are constructing five scales of twenty items each we will be trying out 200 items. At a ratio of 3 to 1 this means that 600 subjects will have to be used.

Sex difference must be taken into account in test construction. This means that analyses must be separate for the sexes. Thus in the example above 600 males and 600 females would be necessary.

Size: representativeness

The sample on whom the items are tried out must reflect the population for whom the test is intended. How this can be ensured has been fully discussed in Chapter 4 on standardising tests. Suffice it to say here that at this stage of test construction the sample need not be as carefully chosen as in standardisation because the relationship between items rather than mean scores are important. However the nature of the sample cannot be ignored in the quest for numbers. Remember, too, that if there is insufficient variance in a sample, no factor can emerge. Too great homogeneity is not desirable.

3. Correlations between the items

As should be clear it is necessary to correlate the items before carrying out the factor analysis. With items there is always the problem of what correlation to choose. This must be discussed and depends, to some extent, on the responses to each item.

If the items are dichotomous we have to choose a correlation coefficient designed for that purpose. If the items have a response scale, e.g a five-point scale, there is the difficulty that Pearson product moment correlations work most efficiently with variables with a greater range (Guilford, 1956).

a. Dichotomous items

Many personality tests have items of this type, fully discussed in Chapter 15 of this handbook. In addition many ability and intelligence test items are dichotomous because they are either right or wrong. There are three correlation coefficients that might be used with dichotomous items and since there are problems with all of them, these must be scrutinised carefully.

The phi coefficient The formula for the phi coefficient may be found in the statistical appendix to this handbook. Phi is effectively a short form of the Pearson product moment correlation (the standard correlation coefficient). It yields the same value as would be obtained if standard item scores were entered into the formula for the Pearson correlation. This mathematical equivalence is important because, as Vegelius (1973) has shown, only eta coefficients, of which the product moment correlation is one, are suitable for factor analysis. This is an important point in favour of using phi for inter-item correlations.

Unfortunately there are certain problems with this coefficient. First, as the rate of item endorsement departs from the 50 per cent level, so phi cannot reach 1, the size of the restriction of value reflecting the difference in endorsement rates for each item. These rates are known as the p values for each item, the proportion passing or putting the keyed response to each item and will be referred to thus in all discussions.

Furthermore, the phi correlation is affected by the polarity of the item (whether it happens to be keyed 'Yes' or 'No', which could be changed without loss of test validity).

Thus there are sources of fluctuation in the values of phi coefficients which mean that they do not always reflect well the true correlation between the items. Since factor analysis attempts to account for the variance in the correlation matrix, resulting factors are necessarily compounded by statistical error.

The tetrachoric correlation, r_{tet} The tetrachoric correlation was used in the early days of factored tests because its computation can be extremely rapid. However it should not be used as a basis of factor analysis. It is not an eta coefficient, its standard error is twice that of a Pearson product moment correlation, and like phi it is affected by the p values of the items. Where modern computing facilities are available there is no reason to use this coefficient.

There is a further difference between phi and r_{tet} which should be mentioned. Strictly the latter should be used with continuous variables which have been dichotomised, at some point on the continuum, whereas phi is designed for genuine categories. As Nunnally (1978) argues, however, it is not difficult to regard test responses as categorical although the 'Yes/No' response to a personality test item could be regarded as the break on a continuum running from 'always' to 'never'. Certainly this point is not sufficient reason to use the tetrachoric correlation rather than phi for the correlation matrix.

The G index (Holley and Guilford, 1964) This is a little known statistic developed by Holley who has used it in an extensive series of studies with the Rorschach test (Holley, 1973). Vegelius (1974) has also provided a good account of its statistical basis and shown how it may be extended beyond simple dichotomous variables. Hampson and Kline (1977) also found it to be a useful statistic in a projective test study of adult criminals.

The G index has the advantage that it is not affected by item polarity or by the p values of items. This would be, therefore, the perfect inter-item correlation coefficient, were it not for the fact that in such factor analyses it tends to produce factors of item difficulty, that is to say each factor loads up on items of similar difficulty level, as shown by Levy (1966). Holley (1973) recommends that the G index should be used only in Q factor analysis where people rather than items or tests are intercorrelated.

In the light of all these difficulties with all the coefficients phi is the best correlation coefficient to choose, when factoring items.

Low variance in the phi matrix When the phi matrix has been computed for all the items there remains a further problem. As Nunnally (1978) points out, inter-item correlations tend to be low. The average is often around .2. Furthermore there is little variance. These conditions are such that it is difficult for a clear factor structure to emerge. The ideal is a matrix with some high correlations and large variance.

Parcelling items In an attempt to overcome this problem Cattell (1973) has proposed a method, which is used virtually only by Cattell and his colleagues – item parcelling. With this technique groups of items, which are homogeneous but not factor homogeneous (exactly how these are selected is described in Cattell, 1973), form the basis of the correlation matrix. The resulting correlations thus show more variance and yield a better structure.

However there are difficulties in the formation of these parcels. If the parcels are long, no matter how they have been formed, they are no different from scales or factors (defined as the linear sum of variables). Thus resulting factors, although more reliable than those stemming directly from items, would tend to be second order factors. Furthermore there is no information on the items within the parcels so full factor analyses of the items would have to be carried out at some later point. Despite its statistical ingenuity item parcelling does not overcome the difficulties with item factoring.

Factored homogeneous item dimensions (FHIDs)   In the construction of the Comrey Personality Inventory (Comrey, 1970) Comrey factored not the item intercorrelations but the correlations between the FHIDs. Despite the label 'factored', FHIDS are composed of items selected because they appear to be homogeneous. They are, therefore, simply small groups of similar item. The scores on these FHIDs form the basis of the correlation matrix which is more reliable and of greater variance than the comparable matrix of item correlations.

However, the problem with FHIDs is that they are effectively brief scales, factored, as it were, by eye. Resulting factors tend to be second orders, as was shown by Kline and Barrett (1983). Although they increase the variance of the matrix FHIDs are not the answer to the problems of low variance.

b. Items with a response scale

A method of avoiding these difficulties with dichotomous items is not to use them. Instead some test constructors include after each item a five-, seven- or even nine-point response scale. Likert scales (discussed in Chapter 5 of this handbook) use a five-point scale representing the degree of agreement and disagreement.

The non-statistical problems with these response scales are fully discussed in Chapter 15 and will be but mentioned here. Thus the claimed advantage, over dichotomous items, that more variance is introduced into the correlation matrix is more than offset by the disadvantages that some subjects choose extremes while others avoid them. Furthermore even nine-point scales are of small range for a product moment correlation and nine-points are the maximum that can be held in mind (Vernon, 1963). Most tests use only five-point scales. For these reasons there is little justification for using items with response scales simply because they may increase the variance in the correlation matrix.

However, if these items are used because they make more sense than dichotomous items which can appear crude with some item content, then the Pearson product moment correlation is the one to choose.

Thus a matrix of inter-item product moment correlations or phi coefficients, derived from at least 200 subjects to reach a ratio of twice the number of subjects to items, is prepared for factoring.

4. Factor analysing the correlation matrix

a. The initial factoring   As was made clear in Chapters 7 and 8, the initial factoring is best done with a principal factors or axes analysis. Any slight advantage from the maximum likelihood method is more than offset by the computing time involved.

b. Choosing the significant factors to rotate With a large matrix of items it is usual to obtain a factor analysis with a large number of small factors. In these circumstances, as Cattell (1978) has shown, the criterion of rotating all factors with latent roots greater than one overestimates the number of factors. The best solution is first to analyse the matrix by principal components analysis and take out the factors deemed significant by the Scree test (Cattell, 1966). That number of principal factors can then go into the rotation. Since the precise number of factors to be rotated is not crucial in test development since there are certain to be more factors than scales it is not normally worth checking the Scree test by any other method.

c. Choosing the type of rotation I am assuming for this discussion that we are developing a number of scales at once, since this is the most sensible use of the factor analytic method. Suffice it to say that if only one scale is being developed it makes little difference whether an oblique or an orthogonal rotation is used.

In the case of more than one scale the choice must depend on the nature of the scales. The rule is simple. An orthogonal rotation (yielding un-correlated factors) should be used only where this is a strong theoretical reason for assuming that the scales will be orthogonal. Without this, or where there are reasons for thinking that the scales might be correlated, an oblique factor analysis (yielding correlated factors) should be chosen.

As was made clear in our chapters on factor analysis, for orthogonal rotations Varimax analysis (Kaiser, 1958) should be used. For oblique rotations Direct Oblimin (Jennrich and Sampson, 1966) appears to be the best.

d. Obtaining the p value Although the p value, the proportion of the sample getting the item correct or putting the keyed response is not part of the actual factor analysis of items, it is a useful statistic to obtain in test development. It is usual in most tests to select items with p values between .2 and .8. This is not simply an arbitrary figure. The rationale is that items which have p values beyond these bounds are not discriminating. An item to which everyone responded identically might as well not be included in a test. The only exception to this rule is where the p value is low but those endorsing the item are all the highest scorers on the test. Such an item would load well on its factor whereas items with a low p value which are not of this kind would not.

5. Selecting the items after the factor analysis

Since we want as far as possible unifactorial tests, items are selected for scales which load significantly on only one factor. Thus if we are trying to develop five scales we take items which load only one of the first five factors.

For most purposes loadings greater than .3 can be regarded as significant. When items loading .3 or more on only one factor have been selected the p values are examined to ensure that they are within the limits mentioned in the previous section. If, for example, the majority of items have p values beyond .8 we can see that, in the case of an ability or intelligence test, the test is too easy even though the items load a common factor. Similarly if the majority of items have p values below .2 then the test is too difficult.

Generally, however, if our initial item writing was carefully considered (as discussed in the later chapters of this handbook), this is unlikely to occur.

In principle, then, factoring an inter-item correlation matrix, as described above, will result in a set of unifactorial scales. However there are a number of largely practical difficulties which can interfere with this basically simple procedure, and these must now be described.

6. Practical problems in factor analytic test construction

a. Sex differences

The analyses described above should be carried out separately for each sex. Since it is easiest to have tests which are identical for each sex items should be selected for the final test only if they reach the criteria of factor loadings and p values in both cases. Only where this turns out to be impossible, after trying out new items and new factor analyses, should different versions be developed.

Although there are tests of factor similarity (see Cattell, 1978) I do not consider that in the development of tests without sex differences, it makes sense to use them, given the inevitably large standard error of loadings on items. If the rank order of items on the factors is essentially the same and if the interpretation of the factor would not differ between the sexes then I think the items may be considered sufficiently similar to use. Certainly in my experience of test construction small differences in p values and factor loadings of items between the sexes have not led to different mean scores or variances for males or females on the test.

It should be noted that there is a logical problem with this approach to the problem of sex differences in items. Some examples will clarify this point. In general up to the age of about 16 girls are superior on verbal tests to boys who tend to be better in mathematical abilities. Verbal and mathematical items will be bound to show sex differences, especially of p values.

Many personality and attitude test items are similarly likely to show sex differences in response: items concerned with sport, clothes, appearance, cars, relationships and interest in people, just for example. Thus to summarise the point, in a variety of tests it is not unreasonable to expect that sex differences will occur.

Our solution to this difficulty – to sample the sexes separately and to choose items that pass the criterion in both groups and show no important differences in factor loadings or p values – is somewhat illogical. For by so doing sex differences are virtually excluded.

This exemplifies a fundamental problem in psychometric testing which is not properly understood by most test users and psychologists. This is that differences between groups on tests are functions of the items chosen for the test. Thus if I select items with identical p values and factor loadings for males and females, sex differences on the test are ruled out by virtue of that procedure of item selection. Similarly if I use items where the p value for females is higher than it is for males females will score more highly on the test, as a function of selecting such items.

From these examples it is clear that the means and variances of groups are functions of the items in the test. Thus it is not meaningful to argue from test scores alone that one group is different from another. The same is true of the shape of distributions. As Lewis (1966) pointed out it is nonsense to argue that intelligence is normally distributed on the grounds that test scores are thus distributed because all distributions on tests are a function of the p values of the items in the test. Very difficult items would produce a different distribution, certainly not normal, from very easy items, just for example.

Given this problem, the best approach seems to be to assume the null hypothesis, that there are no sex differences between the sexes unless there are strong theoretical or empirical grounds for not so doing. Thus verbal ability tests would be expected to show sex differences, not on theoretical grounds but simply because in school performance girls are generally superior to boys (Vernon, 1961). With the null hypothesis we would select items with similar indices for males and females, as has been suggested. It must be noted that if there are real differences between the sexes no matter how many items are tried out the item statistics will always be different. If this is the case there are two possibilities.

The difference can be accepted as true, and not an artefact of the items. In this case the test is the same for males and females but one of the sexes will score higher than the other on the test. The other approach is to use items with different indices but to correct the difference by providing different norms for males and females in the standardisation procedure.

In summary, therefore, it is argued that it is best to select items which do not show sex differences in the item analysis, except where on theoretical grounds such differences are expected. If sufficient items which show no differences cannot be written, the imbalance can be corrected at the stage of standardisation (described in Chapter 4 of this handbook) with different norms.

Whichever solution is chosen, what is important to realise is that sex differences, as are all other differences, are functions of the items in the test, and are not *necessarily* reflections of some absolute truth.

b. Factors of small variance and low loadings

As has been pointed out, it is often the case that item factors account for rather low proportions of variance and few items load much more than .3 or .4 on the factors. Despite this, it should still be possible to select items loading only on one factor above .3.

If this is not possible, new items must be written and the whole set must be tried out again. The reason for the low loadings in item factoring is essentially that, as one-item tests, items are unreliable.

The reason that some authorities, such as Nunnally (1978), dislike the low variance accounted for in item factoring is that in a five-factor solution the factors may account for only about 40 per cent of the variance. One may well ask about the rest of the variance. An item which loads .31 on a factor has about 90 per cent of its variance unexplained.

c. Items with substantial loadings on two or more factors

It is not unusual to have items that load on more than one factor, especially when the tests are correlated. However, because if scales are not unifactorial the meaning of scores is unclear the temptation to use such items must be avoided.

This point illustrates the advantages of factoring sets of items together. In the development of the PPQ (Kline and Lapham, 1990a), some of the scales were developed separately to save computer time. Factor analysis, as described above, enabled us to select a set of high loading items. However in subsequent analyses some of these had to be abandoned because they loaded also on the other scales.

d. Rotational difficulties

Although I have advocated the use of Varimax or Direct Oblimin rotations in the factor analysis of items it should be noted that if one test is being developed, the rotation, which distributes the variance from the first general factor, is strictly illogical in that we are looking for a general factor. Of course, if more than one scale is being developed this problem disappears.

Conclusions

Despite all these problems a set of tests developed by factor analysis of the phi matrix of item intercorrelations and the selection of items loading on only one factor, after a simple structure rotation, should yield reliable unifactorial measures.

7. Replicating the factors

After a set of factored tests has been developed, as described above, it is necessary to ensure that the factor structure can be replicated on a new sample before finalising the items in the test.

Generally, in my experience of factor analytic test construction, at the stage of replication a few items will have to be thrown away, because they fail to load, or they load on more than one factor, or there are sex differences.

8. Validating the final set of test items

So far the results of the test construction have yielded tests which each measure one factor. However it is still necessary to demonstrate what that factor is. Such a demonstration is, effectively, validating the test.

This last and essential aspect of test construction is often ignored by psychologists who, while not psychometrists, develop their own tests for use in their research. It is essential because it is by no means obvious why items should load their factors. To regard a factored test as measuring a variable simply from the appearance of its items is no more than face validity, which we showed in Chapter 2 of this handbook was not a reliable guide to true validity.

In Chapter 2 the meaning and the measurement of test validity was fully discussed so I do not intend to repeat the arguments here. It is sufficient to point out in this chapter that in the case of ability tests it is always necessary in the demonstration of validity that it be shown that they do not measure the g factors of intelligence (Cattell, 1971), a phenomenon which renders dubious the use of many aptitude tests, as will be discussed in Chapter 14 of this handbook. A simple way to do this if we have been constructing ability tests is to factor the new scales with the best known ability factors which are described in Chapters 12 and 13 of this handbook. Locating them in factor space explicates precisely what they measure.

In the case of personality tests and other questionnaires it is even more important to validate the factor. This is because a factor can be little more than a bloated specific or a tautologous factor. A set of items which are little other than paraphrases of each other will load a factor. However, factoring the scale with the major personality factors will make its specificity clear. Similarly if a test is measuring the response sets of acquiescence or social desirability (fully discussed in Chapter 15 of this handbook), it will load a factor but it will not be valid, and, again, factoring with other selected scales will make this clear.

Of course a factored test can be validated by other means than factoring as described in Chapter 2. The specificity of a test, for example, becomes obvious when it fails to correlate with anything.

9. Establishing the reliability of the test

From the validity data it is possible to compute the reliability of the test. Ideally, as was fully described in Chapter 1, for a test that is to be used with individuals the reliability should be greater than .7. The alpha coefficient is the best index of reliability in the sense of internal consistency and this should be calculated (see Chapter 3).

The test-retest reliability should also be computed after a three-month gap, and again this should be as high as possible and certainly above .7.

10. Standardising the test

Finally the test should be standardised with appropriate and relevant norms as was described in Chapter 4 of this handbook.

If all these procedures are carried through on adequate samples, if all the statistical criteria are met and if the validating process indicates that the factor is not a specific or some unwanted variable, such factor analytic tests are close to the psychometric ideal. Nevertheless, as should be clear from our discussion, there are sufficient problems and difficulties with the method to ensure that other alternative methods are used. One of these, item analysis, will now be described.

ITEM ANALYSIS IN TEST CONSTRUCTION

Rationale

In item analysis a pool of items is administered to a trial sample and each item is correlated with the total score. Since the aim of the analysis is to produce a homogeneous and unifactorial test, the rationale is simple. By definition, each item should be measuring what the test measures, hence the criterion of the correlation of item and total. The other criterion for item selection is the p value. As was discussed in the section on factor analytic test construction, items with p values between .2 and .8, i.e. discriminating items are selected. Thus the dual criterion is a satisfactory p value and a correlation of the item with the total score, beyond .3.

Problems with the item analytic method

1. The circularity problem

There is an immediate objection to the rationale of item analysis. If all the items were wide of the mark in respect of measuring what was intended, the very procedure of selecting items which correlate with the total score would compound the original error. This is the circularity in the assumptions underlying the procedure.

This objection is sound. Its answer has to be empirical. All that item analysis provides is a homogeneous test which must be measuring a variable. As was the case with factor analytic tests it is essential to demonstrate what the variable is. It is indeed possible, by either method, to construct a reliable but invalid test.

2. Homogeneity is not the same as factor purity

A more severe objection to item analysis can be made, namely that the procedure ensures the homogeneity of tests but not their factor purity, that they measure one factor. Thus if our test items were tapping two correlated factors, say verbal ability and intelligence, an item analysis would pick both types of item, since both would be correlated with the total score. Thus the test would be homogeneous but multifactorial. In this respect, therefore, item analysis is inferior to factor analysis if unifactorial tests, as distinct from homogeneous tests, are desired (and they should be desired).

It is possible to counter this objection to the item analytic method by further investigation of the tests so constructed. Thus if an item analytic test is factored with a large number of other tests it will become obvious whether it is unifactorial or not. If it is not then the items in the test will have to be factor analysed, as described in the previous section of this chapter. When this is done separate factor scores may be derived from the test, provided that there are enough items to make the scales reliable.

Advantages of item analysis

Given that homogeneous tests are not necessarily unifactorial and that in the final paragraph of the section on factor analytic tests it was argued that they came close to the psychometric ideal, an obvious question arises as to why it is worth bothering with item analysis.

The advantages of item analysis over factor analysis as a method of test construction are largely practical. In a perfect world the latter would be the choice. First it is not necessary to have so large a sample. There are only two constraints: one that it be representative of the population for whom the test is designed, so that the p values will be accurate, and the other that it be large enough to reduce the standard errors of the correlations to negligible proportions. For this 100 subjects is enough.

Understandably, given the fact that Nunnally (1978) argues that for factor analysis ten times the number of subjects to variables is essential, he regards this economy on the use of subjects as an important advantage for item analysis. Certainly if resources of time and money are strained, item analysis can be used in the first trial stages. This is because although it may include items that may have to be removed later from the test on factoring, it is unlikely to exclude any that would have turned out to be useful.

Indeed this is what Nunnally advocates as a sensible practical procedure: that the first item trial is by item analysis and that factor analysis of items be carried out on the refined and briefer item set. This argument is further supported by the fact that, where the tests are unifactorial, there is a very high correlation between item analysis and factor loadings. Indeed Barrett and Kline (1982b) in their study of the EPQ items (Eysenck and Eysenck, 1975) found correlations of 1.

In the construction of the PPQ (Kline and Lapham, 1990a) we found little difference between item and factor analysis where the factor structure was clear. However, in the initial studies some items loaded on scales different from those which we had intended and these items were completely excluded by item analysis, as they were correlated with a total score on a variable which they did not deliberately measure.

In summary I would argue that where possible factor analysis should be used in test construction. However item analysis is a simple alternative and if one can be confident, within reason, in writing homogeneous and unifactorial items as is often possible in the field of abilities and with some personality factors, item analysis in the initial stages is useful. It should always be followed by a factor analysis to confirm that homogeneity does not hide a multifactorial or bifactorial structure.

When trying, however, to develop a set of scales where the structure is not clear item analysis is probably not a sensible approach. My own procedure is to use factor and item analysis on the same data. Usually these yield the same set of items. Where they differ is often informative.

The procedures of item analysis

Much that was said about factor analytic test construction applies to item analytic methods and will not be repeated here. We shall describe only those aspects of the method which are particular to it.

1. Items

As with the factor analytic method I am assuming that we have written a set of items which, prima facie, are suitable for the test. With item analysis it is possible to try out one or a number of tests at once. Twice the number of items than are required should be tried out. The same constraints as to time and the fatigue and concentration of subjects, especially children, apply to item analytic item trials as they did to factor analytic trials.

2. Samples

All that was said about sampling in relation to factor analytic tests applies here with the exception of the number in the sample. Samples must be representative and the larger the better because this cuts down on statistical error. However there is no constraint on size from the number of items being tried out. Statistically, samples of 100 are large enough to be reliable. Thus the real criterion as to sample size in item analytic test construction concerns its representativeness.

3. Sex differences

Separate item analyses should be carried out for males and females. Items should be selected which show no differences. This will produce tests which are equally suitable for both sexes. All the arguments concerning this approach which were fully discussed in the section on factor analytic test construction apply here.

4. Statistical indices in item analysis

In item analysis two indices are used – the p value for each item and the correlation of the item with the total score.

P values have already been mentioned. The p value is the proportion passing the item or putting the keyed response. As was previously stated, items are rejected if they fall outside the .2 to .8 values, since they are then poor discriminators.

There are a number of different indices available for correlating items with the total score in item analysis and these will be discussed.

- a. Pearson product moment correlation. Nunnally (1978) regards this as the best correlation coefficient for items with multi-point response modes. However, as has been pointed out, it requires a larger range than the commonly used five-point scale.
- b. Point-biserial correlation. This is the most suitable coefficient for dichotomous responses. Some test constructors reduce other response formats to dichotomies, right/wrong, or keyed/not keyed, and then use the point-biserial correlation. Numerically it is exactly equivalent to the Pearson product moment correlation.
- c. Biserial correlation. This is similar to the point-biserial but is an estimate of the Pearson product moment correlation. In many cases especially where the total test score is not normally distributed these estimates can be inaccurate (Nunnally, 1978). Although used, mainly in the past, it is not recommended.
- d. Phi coefficient. This can be used if the total score is dichotomised into

pass/fail or above and below the mean. As has been mentioned it assumes that these are non-continuous categories.
e. Tetrachoric correlation. This can be used in place of phi without the categorical assumption. However, as was mentioned in connection with the best coefficient for the correlation matrix prior to factor analysis, it suffers from having a large standard error.

Neither phi or the tetrachoric correlation is recommended for item analysis since to reduce the total score to a dichotomy is to lose much valuable information.

Anstey (1966) discusses twenty-one further indices for the correlation of items in item analysis. However the advent of computing has rendered most of these ingenious coefficients redundant and there is little point in discussing them here. These were essentially short-cut methods. Furthermore as Nunnally (1978) points out, correlations between the results of item analyses where different item total correlation indices have been used are very high. No material difference to item selection would be made.

In item analysis there is little doubt that the best coefficient to use is the point-biserial correlation. This item total correlation is particularly valuable because, as was discussed in Chapter 3 of this handbook, on the classical model of test error, this correlation equals the average correlation of the item with all other items in the pool. Its mathematical equivalence to the Pearson product moment correlation means that, in practice, the latter is computed.

5. Selecting the items

Items are selected which correlate with the total score beyond .3 and have a p value between .8 and .2. If insufficient items pass these criteria more items must be written, having regard to those which passed the criteria and those which were rejected. All items including the old ones must be tried out again.

I have assumed that all these computations were done on a sample of one sex. As described previously, the same analyses must be conducted for each sex and items must be chosen which reach the criteria in the two groups, if a test with no sex differences is required.

In this way a test which clearly measures some variable, is discriminating and shows no sex differences will be produced.

6. Replicating the findings

Since items are unreliable, the selected items should be administered to two new samples (males and females) and the items which pass both criteria on both occasions should be selected for the final test.

7. Validating and standardising the test

As was the case with factored tests it is necessary to show what the variable is that the test is measuring and the test needs also to be standardised with the appropriate norms.

All that was said about factored tests applies here except that it is also useful to factor analyse the items to ensure that they are unifactorial and not bifactorial or worse. Nunnally (1978), who advocates item analysis as a preliminary first step in test construction, argues that before factor analysis, there will generally be good agreement between the factor analysis and the item analysis. In the rare instances where factor purity has not been obtained more item writing and factor analysis will be necessary to increase the pool of factor pure items.

In the course of these computations it is sensible to calculate the internal consistency reliability, coefficient alpha being the index to use. Alphas of beyond .7 are necessary for tests to be used with individuals, as has been pointed out.

If all these procedures are carefully executed a univariate, reliable and valid test can be constructed using these item analytic methods. However before I leave this topic I want briefly to discuss a number of practical problems which can arise, problems which have some interesting and more theoretical implications.

Practical problems with item analysis

1. Constructing more than one test at the same time

The problem here is that in constructing tests simultaneously by item analysis scales have to be scored as intended. If as sometimes happens in constructing personality tests it turns out that items intended for one scale fit better into another scale (which factor analysis of items reveals) as exemplified by the Cattell 16PF test (Cattell, Eber and Tatsuoka, 1970), item analytic methods simply exclude the items. Item analysis depends on the test constructor being correct in his or her intuitions concerning what items measure.

Thus in some field of psychometric testing, such as abilities, where it is not difficult to distinguish items in different tests, item analysis is fine for constructing several tests at once.

2. The reliability coefficient in item analytic test construction

It was shown in Chapter 3 of this handbook on the classical model of error that the higher the reliability of a test the less the obtained scores were contaminated with error. Thus one approach to test construction is to seek, in the first instance, to maximise the alpha coefficient in the pool of items.

This is done as follows. First the normal item analysis is computed with the p values, the item total correlations for each item and the alpha coefficient for the whole pool of items. Then the item with the lowest correlation is removed and the alpha is recalculated. This procedure is repeated until alpha reaches its highest point and begins to fall. The set of items which yields the highest alpha then constitutes the final test. Alpha, of course, increases as the bad items are removed and the test becomes more homogeneous. It begins to fall as the test becomes shorter. Thus there is, in practice, usually a plateau of items where alpha remains approximately the same. The first point on the plateau would be chosen for the longer a test the better, given that is within a length suitable for its intended subjects.

In practice this approach to test construction yields virtually identical item sets to the standard item analytic procedure and there is little to choose between them. Although it appears to make no use of p values it does so implicitly since, except in rare circumstances, items with extreme p values also correlate low with the total score.

3. Item total correlation corrections

It is obvious that the correlation between an item and the total score is biased by the fact that the total score includes the contribution of the item. An ideal index would be the correlation of the item with the total score on all the other items.

As Nunnally (1978) demonstrates, in a five-item scale where the correlations between items were zero, each item would correlate substantially with the total scores, even though its correlation with the other four items would be zero. Thus the item total correlation is inflated.

However in an item analysis with a large number of items (eighty or more) this inflation is trivial. Thus it can be said that where a large number of items are used and where there is a large sample of subjects to reduce the standard error of the correlation coefficients, there is no need for any correcting factor.

Nevertheless if we are attempting to construct relatively brief tests a correcting factor may be required, although it should be pointed out that the corrected item total correlations have the same rank order as the originals so that any differences in item selection affect only the last and weakest items in the pool, with the lowest correlations.

There are two approaches to correcting this item total correlation. One is to build into the item analysis program the facility actually to correlate each item with the total score on all other items.The second is to apply a correcting factor. This is given in Formula 10.1.

10.1   Formula for correcting item total correlations for influence of the item

$$r_{1(T-1)} = \frac{r_{T1}\sigma_T - \sigma_1}{\sqrt{(\sigma^2_1 + \sigma^2_T - 2\sigma_1\sigma_T\, r_{T1})}}$$

where r_{T1} = correlation of item 1 with total score T; σ_T = standard deviation of total scores; σ_1 = standard deviation of item 1; $r_{1(T-1)}$ = correlation of item 1 with sum of scores on all items except 1.

4. Weighting items

In most tests items are equally weighted. Each contributes to the score if it is answered correctly. There is no theoretical reason why this should be so and it ought to be possible to weight items to maximise the effectiveness of the score, just as in a multiple correlation weights are given to the variables to maximise the correlation with some criterion.

One simple approach would be to weight items according to their correlation with the total score, or, in the factor analytic approach, according to their factor loadings. However I shall not go into details concerning how such weighting might be done because it can be shown that most weighting procedures produce results so highly correlated with the simple unit weighting of all items that it is simply not worth the effort.

5. Producing tests that discriminate at a special point of a distribution

Sometimes a test is required which will discriminate at a special point in the distribution of scores. An obvious example can be found in selection procedures for particular schools. Thus in Gateshead, many years ago, about 9 per cent of an age group went to grammar school so selection procedures had to be aimed at that point of the distribution. In other areas such as rural Wales about 40 per cent had places. Clearly different tests would have to be constructed for these purposes since tests are not equally discriminating at all points of the distribution. Tests developed as described above, both factor analytic, and item analytic, are most discriminating around the mean.

There are essentially two approaches for dealing with this specialised problem. One is to concentrate on items with the requisite p values. Thus to take the Gateshead example, we would conduct item analyses and then select items with p values relevant to this group. Research has shown that contrary to intuition to obtain maximum discrimination at the .09 level items should be chosen which are less extreme than this, around the .2 to .3 mark (Lord, 1952).

A second method is to select items, after the usual item analytic procedures, on their ability to make the split at the required point. Thus the top 9 per cent on the test would be scored 1 and the rest 0. Then phis would be calculated for each item and the dichotomous groups. Items with the highest phis would be selected. In this way a test that was most discriminating at the desired point of the distribution could be produced. Such a method could, of course, be used after items had been selected by factor analysis.

CONCLUSIONS

From this discussion I hope it is clear that both the item analytic and the factor analytic approaches to test construction are powerful methods for obtaining homogeneous tests. Given unlimited resources of time and money the factor analytic method is the one to choose. If resources are not so great, item analysis, followed by factor analysis, is effective.

Chapter 11

Other Methods of Test Construction

In Chapters 9 and 10 we have described and discussed the three most common methods of test construction. However, as we saw in Chapter 5, there are other forms of scaling such as Rasch scales, Thurstone and Likert scales, used mainly in attitude tests, and Guttman scales. In this brief chapter I shall describe how these tests are constructed. I can be brief since the construction of such tests follows naturally from the nature of the scales, which has been described in Chapter 5. In addition, as I argued in that chapter, there is some doubt as to the value of these methods in psychological testing, except for certain special purposes. Nevertheless it is useful for understanding the problems with these scales and for seeing when they might be valuable, to grasp the basic principles of their construction.

CONSTRUCTING A RASCH SCALE

The theoretical basis of Rasch scaling has been fully discussed in Chapter 5 and it will not be repeated here. It will be remembered that the aim of Rasch scaling is to produce a set of items which can be used with any sample regardless of their position on the trait being measured. Rasch scaling is said to be population free and the scores are said to be item free. The Rasch model involves two parameters: t, a subject's status on the trait and a, the facility the item has for eliciting the trait. The Rasch scale formula for calculating the probability of a subject's response to an item was set out in Chapter 5 – Formula 5.1.

The method which I shall describe is the simplest form of the Rasch model which has been extensively elaborated by specialists in item characteristic curves (e.g. Lord, 1980). However it indicates clearly the strengths and weaknesses of the Rasch model.

Since, as was argued, the model works best where there is little doubt concerning the dimensionality of the items I shall assume here that we are constructing a relatively straightforward, unidimensional test of ability such as a mathematical ability test.

a. Items These are administered to a trial sample of subjects.

b. Sample As was discussed in Chapter 5, despite the claims that the model is population free Lord (1980) has shown that the the first item calibration must be carried out on a large and representative sample. Furthermore since the parameters of the model are calculated using maximum likelihood estimates, for statistical reasons a large sample is required. For this reason 1000 subjects is the minimum sample size for adequate Rasch scaling.

c. Sex differences Although it might be argued that, being population free, sex differences would not be important, separate samples of males and females are suggested for the purposes of calibration.

d. The sample must be split into two groups – high and low scorers. All in the former group should score higher than any in the latter.

e. Compute the Rasch parameters It will be remembered that the maximum likelihood estimates of the two Rasch parameters, t, the subject's status on the trait and a, the facility of the item for eliciting the trait, are independent of each other. This is, essentially, what distinguishes the model from the conventional psychometric approach where a subject's score is certainly not independent of the difficulty level of items.

Indeed, it is precisely this independence of these two Rasch parameters which renders the model attractive, from the viewpoint of measurement, and completely contra-intuitive.

As was mentioned in Chapter 7 in our discussion of maximum-likelihood factor analysis the algebra is so complex that it is best left to the computer program, its explication adding little to understanding unless one is already a good mathematician. For this reason I shall not set out the algebra of Rasch scaling. For most purposes it is sufficient to compute the estimates of the Rasch parameters.

f. Select items If a, the facility of the item for eliciting the trait, is the same (within the limits of the standard errors) for both groups items are held to conform to the Rasch model, and are, therefore, selected for the scale.

To put this criterion of identity of a in context, it must be remembered that the conventional p value of the items would be quite different in these groups.

g. If insufficient items reach this criterion new items should be rewritten in the light of this first analysis. All these together with the successful items would have to be tried out again and the results scaled as described above.

So far this procedure has yielded a set of items which show the same facility level in the two groups and thus conform to the Rasch model. However the point of the Rasch model is to produce item-free measurement of subjects, and this is the second aspect of constructing Rasch scales.

The test of item-free measurement, of course, is whether subsets of items will yield the same scores for subjects.

Item-free measurement

h. Split the items into two tests – one test containing the easiest items, the other the hardest. Clearly on two such sets of items, scored as in a conventional test, subjects would get different scores.

i. Compute t, the subject's status on the trait, and its standard error, for each subject on the two tests. If the items fit the model, each subject will receive the same score on both tests within the boundaries of the standard errors. If they do not items must be removed or rewritten.

j. Cross-validation of items When two sets of population-free items have been obtained which yield the same scores for subjects and thus fit the Rasch model, it is necessary to cross-validate the items on a new sample of subjects, which need not be so large. Rasch scaling can be regarded as complete only when the item sets continue to work on new samples.

k. Sex differences Here we would proceed as above to produce a set of items, from the same pool, that would work as a Rasch scale with females. The final selection of items for a joint scale would include those that scaled equally well in both sexes.

Another approach would be to Rasch scale the items using males and females as the two groups. This would produce a set of items equally good for both sexes. These could then be used in a joint sample of high and low scorers. All items which also scaled in this study could constitute the final scale.

l. Guessing As was discussed in Chapter 5, guessing is a major problem with the Rasch model. This is because the probability of response to some items at least depends not only on the parameters a and t of the model but is also influenced by guessing. Where guessing has occurred it is highly likely that items will not fit the model. One solution to this is to write such good distractors for the items that it is largely eliminated, although this item writing is by no means easy.

Birnbaum (1968) has developed the Rasch model into a three-parameter model, including guessing, but this destroys the dimensionality of the model and loses as much as it gains.

m. Converting Rasch scales to conventional scores Chopin (1976) developed a conversion procedure which is useful for explaining the scores to the users of the test, who find it hard to understand Rasch scaling which runs from +4 to -4. After all what, precisely, constitutes negative ability is a fair question.

From the Rasch equation it can be shown that when the trait ability estimate of an individual exceeds the facility level of an item by one unit, the probability of a correct response increases by 2.178. As Wilmott and Fowles (1974) point out, one of the advantages of the scale developed by Chopin (1976) is that there is a clear link between the scale score, item difficulty and the probability of a correct response. Thus for every five points difference between a subject's trait score and item difficulty, the probability of success increases or decreases three times. This is a useful index, therefore, for tailored testing and developing sets of comparable items.

I shall not detail the computations involved in this scaling procedure which is only one of many that might be adopted. I have brought it into this discussion simply to point out that conversion scales for Rasch scaled tests are possible, where these are required.

In Chapter 5 the statistical rationale of Rasch scaling together with its advantages and disadvantages were thoroughly scrutinised. These arguments will not be repeated here. Nevertheless from this description of the computations involved in Rasch scaling it is quite clear that the critical issue is the maximum likelihood estimation of the indices a and t. Their independence depends upon these estimates but these require large samples if they are to be accurate.

In conclusion, as was pointed out in Chapter 5, this is a useful technique for certain ability tests if large calibration samples can be used. It is unlikely that it will replace the classical item analytic and factor analytic techniques discussed in the previous chapter.

THE CONSTRUCTION OF ATTITUDE SCALES

Guttman scales

In Chapter 5, it was shown that Rasch scales were probabilistic versions of Guttman scales. It was also pointed out that there were many severe disadvantages with these scales, of which the most serious were the fact that Guttman scaling does not ensure unidimensionality and that it is only an ordinal scale. For these reasons my description of how such scales may be constructed will be brief.

1. Items A large number of trial items must be used, for the sorting process involved in Guttman scaling will cause a large number to be rejected.

2. Subjects Administer the items to a large and representative sample of subjects – 500 of each sex would be sufficient.

3. First analysis To ensure unidimensionality the items should first be factored and only items loading on the first common factor should be selected. This overcomes one of the problems of Guttman scaling.

However, it should be noted that, strictly, this procedure may be challenged on the logical grounds that Guttman scaling is based upon latent traits rather than factors. However, without this preliminary analysis, the lack of dimensionality in Guttman scaling is a serious defect.

4. Guttman scaling analysis Guttman scaled items show perfect ordering. Hence if a subject gets item 6 correct, for example, we know that items 1 to 5 are also correct. Similarly if item 10 is wrong we know that all subsequent items are wrong.

Thus what is required for Guttman scaling is a massive ordering program such that a set of items can be produced which show these characteristics. Usually, as was argued in Chapter 5, if there are large differences in p values between the items, it is easier to produce a Guttman scale.

The unidimensional set of items is put through a Guttman scaling program which simply sorts items into a scale based upon their response pattern.

5. Sex differences This is repeated for the other sex and items which scale in the same order are incorporated into the final test.

Conclusions

From this description of the construction of Guttman scales it is clear that despite the advantages of the method, the reproducibility of the scale and the ability to give brief sets of items to estimate the whole scale score, there are obvious losses. Thus if the preliminary factor analysis of the items had yielded a good first factor (and if it had not the Guttman scale would not have been useful), many good items would necessarily have been rejected through the sorting process of the scaling. Essentially, therefore, it can be seen that a Guttman scale is little different from a factored scale except that it is ordinal and its use could be advocated only in the special circumstances of wanting variables with very brief scales.

Thurstone scales

In Chapter 5 the objections to Thurstone scaling were set out, the most serious being that the scaling model simply did not fit the real world of item responses and attitudes. Nevertheless, I shall briefly describe how such scales can be constructed, and in so doing some severe practical problems become evident.

1. Items   These are statements taken from books or articles relevant to the attitude. It is important that, as far as is possible, the whole range of the attitude is reflected in the pool of statements.

2. Judges   These statements are given to judges to rate on an eleven-point scale as strongly favourable to strongly unfavourable.

3. Selection of judges   This is a critical aspect of Thurstone scaling. No matter its statistical and theoretical problems, if the selection of judges is poor the scaling is bound to fail. Edwards (1957) has argued that 100 judges are required to ensure that the whole range of opinions is sampled. This is especially important, as is the necessity that the judges reflect the population for whom the test is intended.

It is obvious, from this brief description, that there are considerable practical problems in recruiting so many judges who are prepared to and capable of rating a large number of attitudinal statements. It must be stressed that while a large number of judges is essential the size of sample alone is quite insufficient. It is also essential that all shades of opinion be represented. Thus a sample of *Guardian* readers would rate the statement 'The integration of education for Asian and White pupils must proceed as quickly as possible' quite differently from a sample of *Telegraph* readers.

4. Selecting the items   In Thurstone scaling items are selected against two criteria: (a) items must cover the whole range of attitude. Thus there must be items rated at all the eleven points of the scale; (b) items are selected with the smallest possible standard deviation of judges' ratings. The smaller this standard deviation the greater the agreement among the judges as to its place on the scale. On these two criteria, range and homogeneity of rating, from fifteen to twenty items are selected.

A subject's score on the scale can be the highest scale rating of the items which she or he endorsed or the average rating of those items.

Conclusions

There are practical problems involved in obtaining good samples of judges and these combined with the statistical difficulties which have been discussed in Chapter 5 mean that there would have to be special reasons for developing a Thurstone scale rather than a Likert scale, the construction of which will now be described.

The construction of Likert scales

The theoretical, statistical rationale of Likert scales was fully discussed in Chapter 5, where it was shown that they were in accord with the classical model of test error and were linear scales. For this reason and because they are more simple to construct than either Thurstone or Guttman scales these scales are widely used in the study of attitudes.

Although their construction is essentially either item analytic or factor analytic, since it follows the classical model, I shall set out the steps briefly since there are some problems which are particular to Likert scales.

1. Items Relevant and direct attitude statements should be collected or written. These should not be too extreme since in a normal sample they would show little variance and would be affected by the response set of social desirability, the tendency to endorse items because it is socially desirable so to do (Edwards, 1957). Similarly neutral bland items will show little variance and these should be avoided. Best, therefore, are items which are mildly positive or negative, half keyed positive, half negative in respect of the attitude. This makes the test less obvious and eliminates, to some extent, the other ubiquitous response set – acquiescence, agreeing with items regardless of content (Cronbach, 1946).

2. Response scale Likert scales have a characteristic response mode of a rating scale, five or seven points, indicating a subject's extent of agreement or disagreement. There has been considerable research into the psychometric aspects of rating scales and I shall summarise the most important findings.

a. Graphic scales In a graphic scale the seven points are set out with the ends marked as shown below.

Completely agree 1 2 3 4 5 6 7 completely disagree

b. Numerical scales Here the numbers are defined and written in spaces opposite the items to be rated.

It is generally agreed that graphic scales are superior to numerical scales (e.g. Nunnally, 1978) as they are easier for the subject to use and are less liable to error.

c. Reliability and number of steps in the scale Guilford (1956) showed that the more steps there are in a rating scale, the more reliable it is. It has also been demonstrated that this reliability quickly increases up to the point of seven steps and then gradually levels off. After eleven steps there is little advantage to be gained. Since other studies (e.g. Vernon, 1961) show that nine categories are about as many as most subjects can hold in their heads, it is obvious that Likert scales should have either seven or nine steps.

d. Odd or even numbers of steps Generally it is preferable to have an odd number of steps (hence seven or nine above) because this allows a neutral or uncertain category. It is annoying for subjects to have no such category in a field such as attitudes. This outweighs the problem of subjects choosing neutral responses as a response set. If items are really salient this chance is much reduced.

e. Response sets   Guilford (1956) discussed a number of response sets which are important with personality test items. We have mentioned acquiescence and social desirability, the latter of which can, of course, affect Likert scale items. However the other response sets such as leniency towards people and lack of information are not considered to be important sources of difficulty in attitude scales, especially because these are actual aspects of attitudes.

The tendency to endorse extremes and the tendency to use the middle response are factors which might affect the Likert scale. However if the items are salient to the lives of the individuals concerned and if they do endorse extremes it may well be that this endorsement is genuine in the same way as those putting the neutral response are in reality tentative and uncertain. That is why if items show themselves to be effective in statistical analyses, I am loath to attempt to correct for these response sets. In brief these response sets may not be sets at all or, if they are, the sets may indicate genuine aspects of attitudes.

f. Anchors   Anchors are the definitions of the scale steps and, obviously, without these rating scales cannot be used. Usually, to facilitate ease of response, numerical anchors are combined with other types, of which the most common is the scale 'completely disagree' to 'completely agree'. Where this is applicable to the items this is the simplest to write and use. Another possibility which allows more steps is the percentage scale. Divided into twenty steps this can, with the right items, be a useful anchor. The percentage of support for various institutions could be a good index of political attitudes.

Thus seven- or nine-step graphic scales with anchors indicating the degree of agreement would appear to be useful for Likert scale construction.

3. Subjects   As with the construction of tests by either factor analysis or item analysis, a large representative sample should be used for item trials. For factor analysis at least 200 subjects is advisable or more if that is not at least twice the number of variables. For item analysis a minimum of 100 subjects is required statistically, but a larger sample is likely to be more representative.

4. Sex differences   A similar sized sample to that described above should be drawn up for both males and females.

5. Analysis of data   The trial data should be analysed either by item analysis or factor analysis, as described in the previous chapter. Since attitudes may not be factorially simple it may be sensible to use item analysis first to select the items. Factor analysis can then be employed on the subset.

6. Selection of items   Items should be selected which fit the criteria of item analysis, p values between .2 and .8, and a correlation with the total of beyond .3. In the case of factor analysis items would be selected which loaded on the first factor beyond .3.

To create a test which was equally suitable for both sexes items would be selected which performed similarly in both female and male samples.

7. Cross-validation of items   The selected items would be given to a new sample to ensure that the item and/or factor analysis held up.

8. The test would then be validated and standardised   if appropriate, as described in the previous chapter.

Conclusions

From this description of the three common types of attitude scale, it is quite clear that there is no reason to use either Guttman or Thurstone scales. In addition to posing theoretical problems, which were discussed in Chapter 5 of this handbook, they are more difficult to construct than Likert scales which have all the psychometric advantages of being based on the classical model of error.

COMPUTER AND TAILORED TESTS

I shall not discuss the construction of computer and tailored tests in this chapter because their special problems and difficulties have been fully discussed in Chapter 6. Similarly tailored testing turns on the presentation of items depending upon their difficulty level and the response of the subject. This is a matter of computer programming; its rationale has been minutely examined in Chapter 6 and no further comment is required.

THE CONSTRUCTION OF SPEED TESTS

Almost all that has been written so far in this first section of the handbook on psychometric theory and methods has concerned unspeeded tests where subjects are given as long as they like to complete the test. Such tests are known, especially in the field of abilities, as power tests.

However, most ability and intelligence tests are not untimed. Nevertheless this does not mean that they are speed tests, in the true sense of the term. This is because putting a time limit on intelligence and ability power tests, as is usually done, has little effect on the results. There is a high correlation between speeded and unspeeded forms of ability tests, little short of the reliability of both of them (Vernon, 1961). This is because having more time, in a well constructed power test, unless the limit is exceedingly short, is not useful. The problems are usually such that either one can solve them or not.

The true speed test, the subject of this section, is far different. This consists of items which, if given unspeeded, would be correctly answered by virtually everybody. Thus speed items have a p value of greater than .95 when unspeeded. Examples of such items are computational speed, the addition and subtraction of simple sets of digits, letter cancellation or recognition. In tests such as these the only way to obtain variance is to speed them such that the average individual has time to complete about half the items.

Speed tests are important in a number of aptitudes, such as clerical skill, where number checking, letter cancellation and perceptual speed tasks form part of clerical aptitude tests such as the Differential Aptitude Test (Bennet *et al.*, 1962).

However, the principles underlying the construction of conventional tests do not hold in the case of speed tests for reasons which will become obvious as the rationale of the construction of speed tests is scrutinised.

The classical model of test error

This model, which was discussed in detail in Chapter 3 of this handbook, forms the basis of most of the methods of test construction and psychometric methods. Critical to test construction is the correlation of items and this is closely related to the reliability of tests, and the true score.

However, in speeded tests, as defined here, tests with items with p values of .95 or more if given unspeeded, the correlation of items is an artefact of the timing and of the order of items. Thus if the time is generous, and the p values are .95 or greater, the correlation between items will be close to zero. If time is very short items will similarly correlate near zero. Somewhere between these timings a time could be found where the average item p value was .5 in which case the average item correlation would also be high. Thus the correlation of items is an artefact of the time for the test.

In addition the order of items affects the pattern of correlation between the items and this order of items is arbitrary. In a speeded test the p values of the first items are always very high, and their correlations with the other items will, therefore, be close to zero. The last items in the test will have very low p values and their correlations with the other items will be close to zero. The middle items, on the other hand, would have substantial correlations with each other and the total score. However since the order of items is arbitrary so is this pattern of correlations. Clearly these can be no basis for inclusion or exclusion in a test.

Principles of speeded test construction

1. Items A pool of items should be constructed. This is normally simple since all items in speeded tests (letter cancellations and additions, for example), are easy to write. All items are essentially highly similar and the only difficulty is to know how large the pool should be. In speed tests the reliability of the test is related not to the number of items but to the length of the test.

2. Subjects As with the construction of factor analytic and item analytic tests a large and representative pool of subjects is necessary. Since these will be divided into groups, as set out below, about 500 subjects are required. Separate pools for males and females should be used for the elimination of sex differences.

3. Timing the test The best time for a speed test is that which yields the most reliable distribution of total scores. To discover this the items should be administered to, say, five groups, selected at random from the subject pool, each group being given a different time. The actual times involved should be worked out from the time taken to solve an item and the overall time requirement of the test in the practical situation, taking account of the possible boredom and fatigue of subjects which always lowers the reliability of tests.

4. Measuring the reliability of the distribution of scores The only reliability measure which is not infirmed by the artefacts inherent in the speed test is the alternate form reliability. This can be calculated simply by giving two forms of the test and trying them both out. The correlation between their scores under each of the timings would be computed and the timing which showed the best correlation would be the one selected to form the final test.

Another approach to this is to correlate the first half of the test with the second half, scoring the odd items against the even (split-half reliability). To do this in each of the five groups half the items would be administered for half the set time. When this was reached the other half would be given. This split-half reliability would then be corrected by the Spearman-Brown formula, as set out in Chapter 1 of this handbook.

There is a short-cut method, suggested by Nunnally (1978), for calculating the most reliable timing. In fact the reliability of the distribution is related to its standard deviation. Thus the timing which produces the largest standard deviation can be selected and the reliability of this timing can be computed.

5. Validating the test The speed test can be validated by any of the methods which have been discussed in the chapters on test construction and in Chapter 2 on test validity. However it should be noted that it is not useful to factor the items of speed tests. This is because, as has been argued, the item correlations are artefacts of timing and order. Item factor analyses, therefore, produce factors of item order, closely grouped items loading each factor. Factor analysis of the scale scores, however, is permissible and is useful in the construct validation of speed tests.

TEST BIAS

Before concluding this section on the theoretical rationale of psychometric tests and test construction methods I want briefly to discuss test bias, since this is an accusation which is regularly launched at most psychological tests, especially tests of intelligence. It is claimed that these are biased against minority groups, especially Blacks and women. I have left this topic until the end of this section because I can briefly refer to methods and concepts which have now been described and discussed.

Meaning of test bias

As Jensen (1980) has pointed out in a huge book devoted to the topic of test bias, there are certain fallacies concerning the definition of test bias which must be immediately dismissed.

1. The egalitarian fallacy This assumes that if any mean difference occurs between groups on a test, the test is de facto biased. The absurdity of this argument needs no further discussion. While no psychologist would openly argue this case, for all tests and all groups, it lies at the heart of much criticism of intelligence tests which reveal that Blacks score less highly than other groups. I am not arguing that Blacks are less intelligent but simply that it is a false assumption to use such data as evidence of test bias. Other data than group differences are necessary to make the point.

2. The culture bound fallacy This assumes that group differences on a test are due to the culture bound nature of items. Thus an intelligence test item which was concerned with some aspect of knowledge which was common ground in one group but rare in another would be assumed to be a source of bias. The point stressed by Jensen is not that such items are not a source of bias. Clearly they are. Rather that it is impossible, without empirical investigation, to know which items are thus biased. It is necessary to determine on psychometric and statistical criteria whether an item is biased and, if it is, then it can be removed.

3. The standardisation fallacy It is often assumed that if a test is stand-ardised on one population, it is necessarily biased if it is used on another.

Again this is not necessarily so. Other evidence would be needed to decide if the test was biased in a different population.

Given that we cannot assume test bias on any of the three grounds discussed above, I shall now examine the data which would constitute test bias in any groups.

1. Predictive test bias As Jensen (1980) argues the most important indicator of bias is the regression equation between a test and its criterion. If for any group there is a significant difference in the slopes or the intercepts, or in the standard errors of the estimates of the regression lines, then the test is biased. This is the statistical definition of test bias. It is obvious that if this is not the case, an individual's group membership makes no difference as to the predictive power of the test. Thus there can be no bias. This definition assumes perfect reliability (which never occurs) and constitutes an ideal definition. However, even in the real case, where the reliabilities are less than unity, the arguments still hold. It is obvious that, as has been stressed throughout this section, high reliability is vital no less for unbiased tests than for other purposes.

2. Internal evidence of test bias It is possible to examine the characteristics of the tests themselves to investigate test bias.

    a. The construct validity of the test should be the same for both groups. Construct validity, defined by the patterns of correlations of a test with other variables, should not differ in the groups. The variable can hardly be said to be the same if the correlations with other variables are different, i.e. the test is biased.

    b. Test-retest reliability should be the same for both groups in an unbiased test, for obvious reasons.

    c. Internal consistency reliability should be the same for both groups. If it is not this may be due to differences in item difficulty. If after this has been allowed for the average correlation between the items is different in the two groups this is evidence of item bias – the items must be measuring different variables.

    d. If we carry out an analysis of variance of item scores there should be no group x item interactions. If there is then this is evidence of item bias, and the relevant items can be changed or removed. Notice that there can be mean differences between the groups without such interactions. Thus unbiased tests can yield group differences.

    e. In standard item analyses correlations between items and total score should be the same for the two groups although p values may vary. However large differences in p values should be investigated, i.e. the nature of the item should be carefully examined.

f. In factor analyses of the items the factor loadings of the items should be the same for both groups, within the limits of the standard errors. Biased items will differ.

g. The item characteristic curves of the items will be the same for the two groups. Details of the detection of bias by these methods can be found in Mellenbergh (1983).

FINALE TO SECTION 1

This discussion of test bias ends Section 1 of this handbook which has been concerned with the theory and methods of psychometrics. We have dealt with the measurement of reliability and validity and its basis in psychometric theory. We have discussed norms and the standardisation of tests together with types of tests, Rasch scales, Thurstone scales and Guttman scales which have a different rationale. We have explicated factor analysis because, without an understanding of this statistical method, much of psychometrics must remain a mystery; and finally we have outlined the methods of test construction which illustrate the application of psychometric theory to the production of tests.

Section II

Types of Psychological Tests
Rationale and Problems

In Section II I shall discuss psychological tests, the results of applying the theories and methods which were discussed in Section I to various fields of psychology.

I shall not discuss, in this section, particular tests which may be used in applied or research psychology. The best and most useful tests will be described in Section IV. Here I shall scrutinise all the different types of test: intelligence tests, ability tests, tests of motor skills, aptitude tests, personality tests, questionnaires, projective tests and objective tests, motivation and interest tests, attitude scales, clinical tests for brain damage and malfunction and other special tests which do not fall into any of these categories.

This scrutiny will involve discussions of the types of items used in the tests and their rationale, the validity of the tests and comparisons of the various approaches to measurement within each of the fields. The various difficulties and problems in measurement in different areas of psychology will then become apparent. To understand these is particularly important for the last two sections of this handbook – Section III on the use and interpretation of test results and Section IV, listing and evaluating the best tests.

Chapter 12

Intelligence Tests

HISTORICAL CONTEXT OF INTELLIGENCE TESTS

Intelligence tests are among the oldest psychological tests. Binet and Simon (1905) developed tests in Paris, at the turn of the century, with the aim of discovering who might benefit from education. These tests, indeed, were developed into what was to become one of the most widely used individual intelligence tests – the Terman Merrill Test (Terman and Merrill, 1960, for the latest edition) also known as the Stanford Binet Scale.

At about the same time, in an even more more significant study, Spearman (1904) reported the first factor analysis of human abilities. This claimed that all human abilities were explicable in terms of g, a general ability factor and a factor specific to that ability. Spearman, the founder of the London School of psychology, which includes some of the great figures in psychometrics (Burt, Cattell and Eysenck to name the most famous or notorious), developed this notion of intelligence as a general factor (Spearman, 1927) and it is this factor (or factors, as shall be seen) which most modern intelligence tests attempt to measure.

Although Spearman's tetrad method of factor analysis was by modern standards crude, in respect of parsimoniously explaining the variance in a correlation matrix, and although, as was discussed in Chapters 7 and 8 on factor analysis, the technique has become highly sophisticated, yet the factors extracted from matrices of correlations between measures of ability still include a recognisable general factor. That is why modern intelligence tests still aim to measure g.

DEFINITION OF INTELLIGENCE AND THE DEFINITION OF G

Jensen (1980) has pointed out that there are a huge number of different definitions of intelligence both among psychologists and among non-specialists. Sharp, acute, quick are often terms used in the definitions and their opposites: dim, sluggish, slow. However such verbal definitions or descriptions are too vague to be scientifically useful.

Boring (1923) attempted to get round this difficulty by defining intelligence as what intelligence tests measure. At first this seems to be a perfectly circular and thus useless definition, unless it is possible to define with precision and clarity what tests do measure. Indeed it has led some critics of intelligence tests to claim that they measure ability at intelligence tests and nothing else.

However, the factor measured by intelligence tests can be defined and the claim that it is specific to intelligence tests can be shown to be wrong, utterly and completely. Intelligence tests measure a factor usually called g_f, or fluid ability. Now as was seen in Chapter 7, a factor can be defined precisely by its loadings. Thus far from becoming a vague term, intelligence, if equated with fluid ability, can be objectively defined by its factor loadings. When this is done it can be seen that intelligence is a broad, basic reasoning ability that is useful in the solution of a wide variety of problems.

That this problem solving ability is not specific to intelligence tests is demonstrated by the fact that intelligence test scores correlate with many external criteria such as academic success and performance in jobs, as has been fully documented by Jensen (1980) and Kline (1990).

In summary we can define the intelligence of intelligence tests as the basic reasoning ability of an individual which she or he can employ in problem solving of many kinds. Its importance is attested by the fact that it is always the largest factor in any factor analysis of abilities. However intelligence, in the real world, is usually evinced in particular skills which are valued in the culture, and this aspect of intelligence is defined by a factor, g_c, crystallised ability – fluid ability as it is expressed in the culture.

To understand clearly what intelligence tests are trying to measure, and also the other tests of ability and aptitude, which will be discussed in later chapters of this section of the handbook, it will be necessary to set out the factor structure of abilities.

THE FACTOR STRUCTURE OF HUMAN ABILITIES

We have seen in our discussion of factor analysis how there is an infinity of solutions. This has led, until recently, to severe problems in attempting to set out the structure of abilities. Heim (1975), indeed, went so far as to regard the use of factor analysis as deleterious to the study of abilities, although, ironically, her own tests of intelligence, the AH series (Heim *et al.*, 1970) load highly on the two g factors and will be described in Section IV of this handbook.

However, there is now agreement as to how factor analyses should be conducted – rotation to simple structure being the key, as was described in Chapter 8. When this is done, there emerges a list of factors upon which there is a fair consensus, as has been discussed in considerable detail by Kline (1990).

Table 12.1 Primary ability factors, as found by Hakstian and Cattell (1974)

V   *Verbal ability* – understanding words and ideas. Loading on synonyms, meaning of proverbs, analogies. Probably the best indicator of g_c – crystallised intelligence.

N   *Numerical factor* – this is facility in manipulating numbers which is factorially distinct from arithmetic reasoning.

S   *Spatial factor* – the ability to visualise two- or three-dimensional figures when their orientation is altered.

P   *Perceptual speed and accuracy factor* – which involves assessing whether pairs of stimuli are similar or different.

Cs   *Speed of closure of factor* – this taps the ability to complete a gestalt when parts of the stimulus are missing. Speed of verbal closure correlated 0.61 with word fluency suggesting that familiarity with words plays a part in the results.

I   *Inductive reasoning* – this involves induction, reasoning from the specific to the general.

Ma   *Associative or rote memory* – memory for pair for which no mediating link exists. There are substantial correlations between the word-number pairs test and figure-number pairs test although according to the Guilford model these should be orthogonal.

Mk   *Mechanical ability or knowledge.*

Cf   *Flexibility of closure* – this involves disregarding irrelevant stimuli in a field to find stimulus figures. According to Hakstian and Cattell (1974) this factor is a manifestation of Witkin's field independence (Witkin, 1962) and is related to the personality factor independence.

Ms   *Span memory* – this is the short-term recall of digits or letters as has long been used in the WISC and WAIS tests (Wechsler, 1958). It is noteworthy that the mean correlation of the Ms tests with the Ma tests (factor 7) is only 0.18.

Sp   *Spelling* – recognition of misspelled words. Hakstian and Cattell (1974) point out that spelling has not appeared as a factor in previous researches because usually there was only one test, thus making the emergence of a factor impossible. Since there are good correlations with V and W whether spelling is a narrow primary or dependent on these two factors is not yet clear.

E   *Aesthetic judgement* – the ability to detect the basic principles of good art. Like Mk, this would appear to depend much on previous experience.

Mm   *Meaningful memory* – this involves the learning of links between pairs in which there is a meaningful link. The mean correlation of Mm with Ma tests is only 0.35, suggesting that Ma and Mm are behaviourally distinct.

O1   *Originality of ideational flexibility* – this loaded on the multiple grouping tests of Guilford and Hoepfner (1971) which fall into the divergent production of semantic classes cell of the Guilford model. There are substantial correlations between this O1 factor and O2 and F1.

Fl   *Ideational fluency* – the ability to reproduce ideas rapidly on a given topic. This is distinct from Wl word fluency and associational and expressional fluency which were not included in this study, although discussed by Guilford and Hoepfner (1971).

W   *Word fluency* – the rapid production of words, conforming to a letter requirement, but without meaning. This factor was found as early as 1933 by Cattell and has regularly occurred ever since.

O2   *Originality* – as with O1 this is a relatively new factor loading on the Guilford tests where subjects have to combine two objects into a functional object. Originally the test was designed to mark the convergent production of semantic transformations but it actually loaded on a divergent production factor (Guilford and Hoepfner, 1971).

A   *Aiming* – involving hand–eye coordination at speed.

Rd   *Representational drawing ability* – drawings of stimulus objects scored for precision of lines and curves.

Source: Kline (1979)

Table 12.2 Further primary factors, found in Cattell (1971)

D	*Deductive reasoning*
Mc	*General motor coordination* – this is tested by the pursuit meter, among other tests.
Amu	*Musical pitch and total sensitivity* – found in the Seashore (musical aptitude) test.
Fe	*Expressional fluency* – found in Guilford (1967), verbal expression for assigned ideas.
ams	*Motor speed* – found in Guilford (1967).
asd	*Speed of symbol discrimination* – found in Guilford (1967).
—	*Musical rhythm and timing.*
J	*Judgement* – ability to solve problems where judgement and estimation play a part. Again found in Guilford (1967).

Source: Kline (1979)

Discussion of tables 12.1–12.3

From the viewpoint of this chapter Table 12.3 is critical, since this is where the two intelligence factors, g_f, (fluid ability) and g_c (crystallised ability) are to be found.

It will be remembered from Chapter 8 of this handbook that second order factors result from the correlations among the primary factors. Thus these two intelligence factors are the two largest second orders and they account for much of the variance in tests of ability.

Fluid and crystallised ability

The nature of fluid and crystallised ability has been extensively studied by

Table 12.3 The five second order factors underlying primary factors, found by Horn and Cattell (1966)

g_f	*Fluid intelligence* – loading on the Culture Fair Test, inference, induction, memory span and flexibility of closure. Also it loads on intellectual speed and level tests.
g_c	*Crystallised intelligence* – this is the factor of traditional intelligence tests. Loading on verbal, mechanical, numerical and social skills factors.
g_v	*(now Pv) Visualisation* – loads all skills where visualisation is helpful, spatial orientation, formboards. This factor loads some of the tests of the Culture-Fair Test thus demonstrating that even here visualisation can be useful. Cattell (1971) points out that in some earlier research, visualisation had appeared as a primary but this work by Horn and Cattell clearly shows this not to be the case.
g_r	*Retrieval capacity or general fluency* – loading on ideational fluency, association fluency and irrelevant association test, it is the general retrieval power which accounts for a variety of skills.
g_s	*Cognitive speed factor* – this affects speed in a wide range of tasks although it is a minor factor in solving gf problems. This factor is speed in mechanical performance, e.g. writing or numerical computation.

Source: Kline (1979)

Cattell (1967a and b, 1971). In his investment theory of ability, fluid intelligence, which is a largely heritable basic reasoning ability, reflecting the efficiency of the flow of information through the brain, is invested in the skills valued in a culture (differing, of course, from culture to culture). Thus is crystallised ability produced.

From the viewpoint of the test constructor this is a highly important distinction. It means that crystallised ability can be tested by items which demand the knowledge and skills that may be reasonably expected of individuals of the relevant age in a culture. Fluid ability, however, has to be measured by tasks, either that demand virtually no knowledge or knowledge that is so overlearned as to become virtually automatic, or by tasks so novel that all subjects have to work at them afresh.

The majority of intelligence tests, especially those which were constructed before the factorisation of tests was clarified by good simple structure rotations, measure a mixture of fluid and crystallised ability.

Spearman's g, g_f and g_c

I do not want to go into the history of the factor analysis of abilities, which I have discussed in my book *Intelligence: The Psychometric View* (Kline, 1990), for there has been a huge variety of factor structures claimed to account for the correlations of variables in the sphere of abilities – a phenomenon referred to as the positive manifold. Nevertheless it is worth noting that Spearman's g factor, which turns out to be a second order factor, and which many intelligence tests attempted to measure, has split into crystallised and fluid ability. These are correlated, highly at a young age, but as individuals learn or do not learn (depending on their school and family) the cultural skills, these gradually diverge.

It must not be thought that it is only Cattell and his colleagues who hold to this notion of two g factors. In fact Carroll (1983) has independently replicated this structure and the primary factors listed by Ekstrom *et al.* (1976) are highly similar to those of Cattell.

Indeed the only factor analyst of any note who postulates a structure of abilities so different that no tests of intelligence would be constructed is Guilford (1967). However as was discussed in Chapter 8, his factor analyses, being based upon Procrustes rotations, are not to be trusted, a problem compounded by the fact that he uses orthogonal rotations which automatically exclude second order factors and thus the g factors.

Finally it must be pointed out that some investigators have tried to equate fluid ability with Spearman's g factor, notably Undheim (1981) and Cronbach (1984). However there are technical difficulties associated with this identification which, as Gustaffson (1988) argues, could be settled by the appropriate maximum likelihood analyses. If this were true, that fluid ability were Spearman's g, this would leave crystallised ability as equivalent to an educational attainment factor which was extracted by Vernon (1960) and labelled as V.Ed. However from the viewpoint of the intelligence test constructor and user, this labelling is somewhat academic. Tests are required which measure both factors, and V.Ed., or g_c, still represents the expression of fluid ability in the culture.

I feel that it is more sensible to regard Spearman's g as a mix of two factors, fluid and crystallised ability, basic reasoning ability, the ability to perceive relations and educe correlates, which can be applied to any task, rather than to see it as equivalent to fluid ability (although a large confirmatory factor analysis might lead me to change this view). In any case, regardless of their interpretation, modern intelligence tests are aimed at these g factors. This is their factor analytic base.

INTELLIGENCE TEST ITEMS

Thus with definition of intelligence as the basic reasoning ability, the ability to educe correlates and perceive relationships, we must now consider the types of item which can be used to measure this ability. Fluid ability is likely to be measured, as has been argued, by unfamiliar tasks or with materials so well known that individual differences in learning and acculturation are unlikely to affect results. Crystallised intelligence, on the other hand, can be tested with materials which reflect the skills acquired and valued in a culture. Here we might well find differences due, in part, to education or social class.

I shall not deal with every type of item which may be found in intelligence tests. However I shall describe and discuss the types of items which are most widely used and which are known to load highly on their respective factors. In scrutinising these items and their rationale it becomes easier to understand the nature of the g factors which they measure.

Before describing the different types of item, a few further points need to be made. In intelligence tests it is useful if the difficulty level of items can be easily varied. Thus for comparative purposes it is useful if the same types of item can be used with different age groups. This, as we shall see, is a difficulty in the study of infant intelligence, where of necessity, the test items are so different from those in other intelligence tests that it is by no means clear whether the same factor is being measured as in intelligence tests for older children and adults.

Another valuable characteristic for a type of item is what might be called its flexibility. It is useful if the item form is applicable to a variety of materials. Where this is the case the item type can be used for both tests of fluid and crystallised ability. This will become clear as we discuss the different item types.

Analogies

The analogy is a type of item which is found in most intelligence tests. The difficulty level is simple to manipulate, both in respect of the actual relationship which has to be educed and (of less importance) as regards the obscurity of the objects to be related. Furthermore it is a highly flexible type of item, it being possible to construct analogies in a wide range of materials. This makes it a popular item. Indeed it so typifies the factor analytic meaning of intelligence that analogies were extensively and minutely studied by Sternberg (1977) in an attempt to elucidate the cognitive processes which were involved in solving problems requiring intelligence.

Examples of analogies

Before setting out my examples of analogies I must point out that these items, except where stated, are not taken from actual tests in order that the integrity of published intelligence tests may be maintained. These examples have been chosen to explicate the nature of the g factors they are trying to measure. As I hope is clear from the chapters in this handbook on test construction, the quality of items has to be judged empirically. If they load on the right factor and discriminate they are good. Thus I am not claiming that these examples are good items, and their validity is necessarily face validity.

Analogies are used in testing for the g factors because their solution involves educing the relevant relationship in the first part of the analogy and applying it to the rest of it.

Item 1   Wagtail is to bird as viper is to . . .
            a. animal, b. ant, c. fish, d. bird, e. reptile.

This item is easy and is a measure of g_c, crystallised ability, because elementary biological knowledge, of the kind required to solve this item, is a cultural expectation in the West. It is also an easy item because the relationship of class membership is simple and the solution of putting 'viper' into an analogous class should not tax the average 9-year-old. However, if the item were to be used in cross-cultural studies it would fail where these species were not present.

Multiple-choice distractors

A word needs to be said about the distractors in this item. It is important that distractors do distract. Thus in item trials it is essential to note what proportion of the samples completed each distractor. If, for example, three of the distractors are so obviously wrong that nobody chooses them the item becomes easier to guess. It is also important that one of the distractors is not so enticing that the best subjects choose it. However, if this happens the item fails the item analysis, since its correlation with the total score would be considerably reduced.

Sometimes it is difficult to write good distractors. A useful way of obtaining them is to give the items to a sample with a free response, i.e. with no alternatives. Then the four most common wrong answers provide the distractors. The position of the correct answer, a, b, etc. should always be randomised so that correct answers cannot be inferred from their position.

Item 2   Parrot is to bird as koala is to . . .
a. animal, b. ant, c. mammal, d. bird, e. reptile.

This item represents a possible cross-cultural equivalent for Item 1, obviously for use in Australia. Item analyses to compare the p values, item-total correlations and factor loadings would have to be carried out to see whether, in fact, these items were equivalent. Item characteristic curves might also be compared.

Item 3   *Samson Agonistes* is to *Comus* as *The Bacchae* are to . . .
a. *Oedipus Rex*, b. *Medaea*, c. *The Cyclops*, d. *Prometheus Bound*, e. *The Tempest.*

I have used this and the next item before (Kline, 1990) to illustrate certain aspects of the analogy as an item, but I cannot think of better examples for this purpose. The first point to note is that this item obviously requires literary knowledge. It is a difficult item unless one knows who wrote these texts and the nature of the works. However this difficulty stems from the content involved rather than the relationship and thus this item must measure crystallised ability if it measures anything. However it is likely to be a poor item because the relationship is not difficult to educe. *Comus* is a light work (by Milton's standards) contrasted with a tragedy. *The Bacchae* is a Euripidean tragedy so clearly we have to look for a non-tragedy by Euripides. This is c., *The Cyclops.*

This item illustrates how a difficult analogies item may well not measure either fluid or crystallised ability where the difficulty stems from the obscurity of the content. My reason for including it is that it resembles the items in a test which is widely used in graduate selection in America – Miller Analogies (Miller, 1970). In this test the information required to solve the items is high. However, good crystallised ability items at this high level need to have difficult relationships embedded within the rarefied content of the analogy. This may well have been achieved in Item 4.

Item 4   Television is to microscope as telephone is to . . .
a. amplifier, b. microprocessor, c. microdot, d. microphone, e. loudspeaker.

This item certainly demands knowledge. Thus again it must measure crystallised ability, if it works at all. However even if subjects know about modern electronic gadgets, the relationship to be educed is not so simple as in the previous examples. The relationship is one of distance to size magnification in the visual field. Thus the correct answer in the aural field is a.

The distractors in this item have been carefully chosen, although in reality they would be demonstrated in item trials to be efficient before they were adopted. Thus subjects who have not worked out the precise relationship would probably choose microphone, and all the distractors are concerned with sound or micros to trap those who are guessing.

The examples which have been discussed so far have used class membership and opposition as the basis of the analogies but the great advantage of these items is that many types of relationship can be built into them. For example, size can be manipulated in analogies:

Item 5   Hawk is to eagle as van is to . . . correct answer lorry.

Clearly this a simple item measuring crystallised ability and suitable for children at a primary school.

Example 6 illustrates how abstraction can be used in analogies:

Item 6   Huge is to enormity as weary is to . . . correct answer lassitude.

This is an interesting measure of g_c, because it depends on having a good vocabulary. The relationship of noun to adjective is probably not difficult to educe. However it has been shown (e.g. Vernon, 1961) that vocabulary is about the best single predictor of crystallised ability and verbal reasoning also loads highly on this second order factor.

All the six examples of analogies are measures of crystallised rather than fluid ability (assuming that they were successful items) simply because they test reasoning as it is expressed in our culture. However, it should not be thought that analogies cannot be used to test fluid ability.

Cattell (1971) argued, it will be recalled, that fluid ability is best tested by items that all subjects in a culture have overlearned or by items which are equally unfamiliar to all subjects regardless of education and social background. Relationships between letters in the alphabet and numerical relationships that do not require any complex mathematics can all be tested within analogies. Furthermore, non-verbal visual items, based on spatial configurations, can be used.

The examples of visual, numerical and alphabetic items are all simple and may be too trivial or obscure to be adequate tests of fluid intelligence. They have been included because they illustrate how analogies can be used to tap fluid ability. As with all these examples their quality must be determined empirically by their factor and item analyses.

Item 7

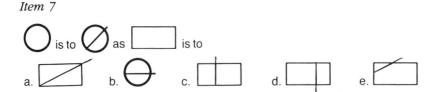

This is a typical, non-verbal, g_c item, measuring spatial ability. Notice that no knowledge is required to solve this admittedly simple item. However it is clear how items of this type but of considerable difficulty could be constructed. Indeed similar, non-verbal items are used in the cross-cultural testing of intelligence although care must be taken that members of the culture are familiar with two-dimensional drawings, or the items may be invalid (see Deregowski, 1980).

Item 8   E is to H as G is to . . .
            a. P, b. J, c. K, d. O, e. E.

This example is a straightforward, easy item based on alphabetic sequence. The type of reasoning required to solve this item is identical to that required to solve the verbal items which we have discussed in earlier examples.

Item 9   D is to W as L is to . . .
            a. O, b. N, c. T, d. R, e. H.

This is a less obvious item; the relationship of D and W is that they are symmetrical with respect to their position at the end of the alphabet. A similar symmetry has to be worked out for L.

Item 10   25 is to 10 as 53 is to . . .
            a. 2, b. 8. c., 31, d. 15, e. 24.

Here the relationship is not obvious but is certainly not one requiring great mathematical or computational skill to work out: 10 is a multiple of 2 and 5.

As was mentioned in the introductory paragraph to these non-verbal analogies it may well be that these items are not good measures of fluid ability. That would have to be determined in the item trials and in validating the subsequent test.

These ten examples of analogies show how this form of item can test the ability to educe relationships of various kinds, at various levels of difficulty and with a variety of materials, verbal and non-verbal. Level of difficulty, it should be noted, refers to the complexity of the relationship to be educed rather than to the obscurity of the necessary information. Heim (Heim *et al.*, 1970) has some brilliant examples of difficult analogies in her intelligence tests devised for discriminating among undergraduates, tests which are described and discussed in Section 4 of this handbook. If one considers carefully the reasoning required to solve analogies it is possible to see why they load so highly on the g factors because they require subjects to educe relationships to solve them, the essence of intelligence as conceptualised by Spearman, a notion still viable today.

There is no doubt that a good test of intelligence could be constructed from analogies of different types. However as was discussed in Chapter 3 on the classical model of error and in Chapters 7 and 8 on factor analysis, test variance can be broken down into common and unique variance. This latter consists of error and specific variance. Now scores on a test constructed from one kind of item would be compounded by variance specific to that item. Thus it is not good psychometric practice to use only one kind of item in a test. This is a weakness of the otherwise excellent tests of fluid ability, Raven's matrices (Raven, 1965a) and one reason why the matrices are usually administered together with a vocabulary test, the Crichton or the Mill-Hill (Raven, 1965b, 1965c). The other reason for administering both tests is that vocabulary measures crystallised ability while the matrices tap fluid ability. All these tests are discussed and described in Section 4 of this handbook.

Before leaving this topic of variance specific to analogous items it should be pointed out that Cattell and Cattell (1959) deliberately included matrices and other item types in the Culture-Fair Test in order to minimise the effects of specific variance. This is also described and discussed in Section 4.

Other types of item used in intelligence tests

1. Odd-man-out items

Odd-man-out items consist of sets of, for example, nouns or verbs, or objects, or numbers, or shapes, of which all but one fall into a category. The subject has to pick out the one which does not fit. This entails, again, the subject's having to educe the relationship between the items to establish the similarities and differences and the basis of class membership. As was the case with analogies this form of item can be easily manipulated in terms of difficulty level, both of relationship and information required. To test g_f, items with low informational demands should be written. To test g_c, this is not important although it must be remembered that where arcane knowledge is necessary for solution social class and educational level may swamp the effects of intelligence unless the reasoning required by the item is also difficult.

Examples of odd-man-out items

1. Sparrow, starling, gull, bat, swallow. This is a simple item measuring crystallised ability and based upon the ability to classify into birds and non-birds (mammals or implements).

2. Gull, swallow, swift, duck, starling. This example illustrates how items can be made more subtle and difficult with much the same material as easy items. Here the correct response is starling because this is the only one which does not have a meaning other than avian. If lark had been substituted for duck the item would have become ambiguous for then gull would have been the only bird that swims.

3. Concrete, abstract, furry, lovely, swiftly. This is a very simple g_c item, in which the correct response is the only adverb among the adjectives. Notice that the correct response could not be concrete, as the only noun, because that would leave nothing in common among the others in the list. This is what distinguishes the intelligence test item from a test of attainment (grammar), that it also demands the eduction of relationships.

4. 24, 63, 10, 48, 35. This item exemplifies how odd-man-out items may be numerical, although as is the case with all these items one cannot be sure that they measure crystallised ability and all depends upon the empirical evidence. Here the relationship between four of the numbers is that they are squares –1. Thus given a mathematical knowledge to this simple level the problem becomes one of crystallised ability, to discover this relationship.

5.

This is a simple non-verbal odd-man-out item, inserted only to exemplify how such items may be constructed. Although easy, only one item has no straight lines, it requires no knowledge and it could well be a good fluid ability item for young children, although even among these subjects it might prove too easy. It would be no problem to increase its difficulty. For example shapes could be made with two straight lines, the odd-man-out having one or three.

Thus it is clear that a wide variety of items suitable for testing both fluid and crystallised ability can be written using this item form.

2. Sequences

This is an item form which again is suited to verbal, numerical and non-verbal items, thus making it useful for testing both the g factors. However it is particularly suited to non-verbal and numerical items. With numerical items care has to be taken that the solution to the items does not involve too much mathematical knowledge or reasoning, which are both distinct from the g factors. Non-verbal sequences are the sole form of item in a test to which I have previously referred – Raven's Matrices (Raven, 1965a). Despite the fact that it must be compounded to some extent, as has been argued, by variance specific to this type of item, this test is one of the best markers on the fluid ability factor (Carroll, 1983).

Examples of sequence items

1. 9, 13, 15, 19, 21 . . .

This is an example of how numerical sequences can be constructed which require a minimum of mathematical knowledge, in this case addition, since the items increase by 4 and 2 in turn.

2. 0.4, 2.4, 14.4., 86.4 . . .

This item demonstrates the danger of numerical items. Here the relationship is simple to determine but it requires a knowledge of decimals and some of even the most intelligent children may not have been so taught, thus rendering the item useless. In any case the relationship is probably far too simple to allow it to work.

3.

This is about the simplest non-verbal sequence possible. However it clearly illustrates how such materials may be used for the construction of items. In the Culture-Fair Test and the Raven's Matrices items of considerable difficulty have been devised.

4.

This sequence is slightly more difficult and subjects would be asked to complete it by having to select the correct response from five choices. It should be pointed out that sequences need not be completed. Often subjects are given the beginning and end and have to fill in the missing middle item.

5. Minute, tiny, small, . . . large, enormous. Subjects have to fill the gap from minuscule, big, enormous, prodigious, heavy.

This item illustrates verbal sequences. Of course these items are suitable only for tests of crystallised ability but, given the high loading of vocabulary on g_c, verbal sequences could be useful items.

These are the three forms of item that are widely used in tests of intelligence. As has been seen, they are particularly useful because they can be used with a variety of materials, and can embrace all levels of difficulty. They are equally useful for tests of both g factors.

In order to reduce the monotony of taking tests (boredom always reduces the reliability and hence the validity of tests), variants of these basic types of item have been developed and these will now be listed.

1. Variant of analogy. Alice Heim uses an interesting variant of the standard analogy in the AH series of tests (Heim *et al.*, 1975). Two words are given to subjects. From a further list subjects are required to select one which bears a similar relationship to both words. These items can be made fiendishly difficult, although they need a good vocabulary for their solution and thus are simply tests of g_c for highly educated subjects.
2. Variant of odd-man-out. A list of words with some common feature is shown. Subjects have to select from a further list a word or words that lack these features.
3. Variants of sequences. a. Subjects are required to find the mid-term of a series, a variant which has been briefly mentioned above. b. Subjects are required to complete not the next term but some later term. c. Subjects have to rearrange terms in sequences.

Summary

These three categories of item and their variants are the building blocks of intelligence tests. From this discussion it is clear how tests at any level of difficulty can be constructed. It is also clear that difficulty level should be manipulated in terms of the complexity of the relationship which has to be educed rather than in the obscurity of the materials. At the same time it is also clear how items measuring g_c can draw on knowledge whereas items measuring g_f must avoid information as far as possible and rely, in consequence, on non-verbal and numerical items.

Most important of all, it is clear from this examination and scrutiny of the types of item in intelligence tests that they have a common core: their solution depends upon the ability to educe the relationships between the terms of the item. It is this basic reasoning ability which is the essence of intelligence and hence intelligence tests as defined in factor analysis. It is also, as the correlations between intelligence tests and external criteria show, a reasoning ability which is useful in the wider context of society.

OTHER ITEM TYPES

However, especially in tests of crystallised ability, other types of item are used and these must now be discussed.

1. Vocabulary As has been mentioned, vocabulary is the highest loading test on the crystallised intelligence factor and features in the best known individual intelligence tests – those by Wechsler (1958) and the Stanford-Binet (Terman and Merrill, 1960).

2. General information This is also commonly used as a measure of crystallised intelligence. As Jensen (1980) argues it is the fact that the highly educated both know more and are more intelligent than the less educated which gives rise to the loading of information on crystallised intelligence. However, there is a little more to it than this. The highly intelligent person can see more connections between new material and what she or he knows than the less intelligent, and this makes retention much easier.

3. Miscellaneous items Jensen (1980) contains a catalogue of item types which he has culled from actual tests. Most of these are highly similar to the basic types of item which have been described. These include: verbal similarities where the two most similar words in a set are selected; similar opposites – pairs of words have to be labelled; sentence completion where the blanks have to be inferred; scrambled sentences which have to be understood; proverbs – their meaning has to be elucidated; logical reasoning problems; verbal classification where words of a similar category to a list have to be chosen; syllogisms; synonyms; drawing inferences from material presented; syntactic inference where the form of a meaningless word has to be inferred; pedigrees where relationships between individuals have to be worked out; and numerical reasoning problems.

All these are verbal items and, as is clear, they exemplify the basic reasoning ability which intelligence tests attempt to measure. Jensen (1980) also lists a variety of non-verbal items which may be found in tests and these will be briefly set out. Again they exemplify the basic reasoning measured in these tests.

Non-verbal items include: pictorial odd-man-out; pictures with errors which have to be recognised; figure classification in which the two figures of a series which go together have to be selected; embedded figures where a shape embedded in other shapes has to be discovered; gestalt completion where familiar shapes and figures have to be completed; reversed figures where subjects have mentally to manipulate geometric shapes; block counting where pictures of blocks are presented which have to be counted (both these last two tests also measure spatial ability); block comparison, in which pictures of blocks have to be judged the same or different; spatial visualisation in which subjects have to imagine how a piece of paper will fold into an object.

Performance test items include: making patterns from beads; form boards where shaped objects have to be fitted to their corresponding holes; block building to patterns; assembling objects; finding ways through mazes; and drawing people.

Again, with the possible exception of the last two performance items, which comprise special tests, the Porteus Maze Test (Porteus, 1965) and the Draw a Man Test (Goodenough, 1926), all these types of item demand a basic ability to reason, to educe relationships.

INDIVIDUAL AND GROUP TESTS OF INTELLIGENCE

Intelligence tests can be divided into two categories – individual and group tests. As the names suggest individual tests require that subjects be tested one at a time, while group tests allow large numbers to be tested together.

Advantages of individual tests

There are several advantages to individual intelligence testing compared with en masse administration. The first is that it eliminates sources of error such as subjects turning over two pages at once, or breaking their pen or pencil. This is a minor point but where decisions are taken on the basis of test scores these sources of error are best eliminated.

Individual tests allow the tester to see how subjects go about solving the items. This can be revealing about any difficulties that the subject may be having. For example, one subject may find an item difficult but refuse to go on until she or he has got the correct answer even though it is obvious that she or he will never be able to do it. This approach to problem solving can lead to difficulties at school, university and work. Another subject, on the other hand, may work at great speed and when confronted by a difficult item may simply give the first answer that comes to mind rather than attempt to solve it. Thus individual tests yield more information to the psychologist than the intelligence test score.

The other great advantage of individual intelligence tests over group tests is that it is possible to ensure that the subject is really trying, or if that proves impossible, at least to know that she or he was not fully engaged in trying to solve the test items. Thus poor scores on group tests may be due to the fact that subjects were not motivated, or were actively attempting to do badly.

For all these reasons if the most accurate assessment of intelligence is required an individual intelligence test should be given. Two such tests, the test developed by Wechsler (e.g. Wechsler, 1944, 1974) and the

Stanford-Binet Scale (Terman and Merrill, 1960) are widely used for this purpose and these tests are fully described and evaluated in Chapter 23 of this handbook.

Advantages of group tests

The obvious advantage of group tests especially in applied psychology is that it is possible to test large numbers of subjects at once, an essential for any large scale testing in selection, for example. Furthermore the tester does not require the same level of skill and training as does the psychologist administering an individual intelligence test. Thus on simple practical and financial criteria group tests are superior to individual tests.

In addition to this the group test is truly objective, whereas the individual test is subjective to the extent that the tester must gain good rapport with the subject and this inevitably varies from subject to subject. Furthermore there is a subjective element in deciding whether a response is correct, although it is clear from the manuals to the best individual tests that inter-tester reliability is high.

Nevertheless, as is clear from Vernon (1961) and Jensen (1980), the correlation between the best group tests and individual tests is high and one can be confident that a good group test gives a valid measure of intelligence. Of course, this is hardly surprising since a commonly used method of validating a new group test of intelligence is to correlate it with an individual test. The best group intelligence tests will also be described and evaluated in Chapter 23 of this handbook.

Conclusions

The conclusions from this comparison of group and individual intelligence tests may be easily summarised. For most purposes group intelligence tests are satisfactory. Where there is some specific problem with a person, then an individual test is to be preferred for it must be remembered that the high correlations between the two types of test do not preclude any one subject's score on one of the tests being way out for some of the reasons discussed above. The proper use of group and individual intelligence tests is discussed in Section 3 of this handbook on the use of tests in applied psychology.

THE IQ

To conclude this chapter on the nature of intelligence tests a brief mention should be made of the intelligence quotient, the IQ, once described by Pedley (1955) as those mystic figures before which the psychologist bowed his head in awe. In fact the IQ is simply a standardised and normalised score (see Chapter 4) with a mean of 100 and a standard deviation of 15. Such a standardisation makes comparison between scores and with the general population easy and meaningful.

It should be pointed out that, in the early days of intelligence testing, the 1Q was derived by dividing a child's mental age, based upon her or his test score, by chronological age and multiplying the result by 100. Thus if a 10-year-old child had a mental age of 12 this gave an IQ of 120. A similarly aged child with a mental age of 8 would have an IQ of 80. However this method was dropped because it implies that a difference of, say, two years between MA and CA is equivalent at all ages, which is clearly wrong. Furthermore if used with adults, since mental age begins to slow in growth around the age of 15, there are serious problems. For all these reasons this method of calculating IQ was replaced by standardised, normalised scores.

Chapter 13

Ability Tests

RATIONALE OF ABILITY TESTS

From Tables 12.1, 12.2 and 12.3 (pp. 173–4) two points are evident. On the one hand the two g factors account for a good proportion of the variance in measures of ability – hence the importance of intelligence tests. On the other hand there are clearly some big factors which intelligence tests do not completely measure. Some of these (such as W – word fluency, the ability to produce words conforming to a letter requirement) seem somewhat narrow and specialised, while others (such as V – verbal ability) appear to be of broader, more general interest. At the second order (Table 12.3) the retrieval and the visualisation factors also appear to be of some real-life significance.

In this chapter I shall discuss tests aimed at measuring the most important of the ability factors other than intelligence. In the main, as might be expected, tests have been constructed to measure the abilities most useful in education, for selection and guidance, and in industrial psychology where the emphasis is on selecting people for the right jobs.

To argue that ability tests, such as verbal or spatial ability, are valuable for predicting educational or occupational success does not run counter to the claim, in Chapter 12, that the g factors are general to all problem solving. The point is that the g factors are important but so also are these other factors. For example, high g is necessary to be a good engineer and to be a good journalist. However for the former high spatial ability is also required, a factor which confers little advantage on a journalist. For her or him, however, high verbal ability is obviously useful.

TYPES OF ABILITY TEST

As was done in the previous chapter, I shall scrutinise the items in the main ability tests so that the essence of what they measure becomes clear. The value and advantages of using tests of ability will also be discussed.

1. Tests of verbal ability

The essence of verbal ability is understanding words and ideas. It loads on synonyms, meaning of proverbs, vocabulary and verbal analogies. Verbal ability is probably the best single indicator of crystallised intelligence almost certainly because, in Western culture, education is essentially verbal. From this it can be seen that the verbal factor mirrors closely how verbal ability is generally understood by non-psychologists.

Items

In this discussion of items for the various tests of abilities I shall describe the items in terms of what they are attempting to measure.

In one of the best tests of verbal reasoning – the Verbal Reasoning Scale of the Differential Aptitude test (Bennet *et al.*, 1962) the items are all of only one form: verbal analogies. As was mentioned above, verbal ability loads highly on crystallised intelligence, which is hardly surprising given the similarity of items. However it must be pointed out that verbal ability tests are well validated. They measure verbal ability but this is correlated with g_c. This problem of the correlation of ability factors with the g factors and how it affects the use of tests will be discussed later in this chapter.

The analogies used in this test are of particular interest because both the first term and the last are missing and each has to be completed from two lists. This enables extremely difficult items to be constructed without having to resort to obscure content or words.

Other verbal ability tests, especially for adults, contain passages of English, with multiple-choice comprehension questions to test understanding. Such tests however, tend to load crystallised ability, and are often used as intelligence tests rather than as measures of verbal ability *per se.*

It should be noted, in considering items, that tests of ability should not be confused with attainment tests. Attainment in English is expressed by knowledge of grammar, vocabulary and syntax, just for example. It is dependent on and correlated with verbal ability but it is not identical with it. Thus an individual with high verbal ability who had only recently moved into a country with a language different from his own would show poor attainment in that language. Thus in writing verbal reasoning items it is important not to confuse the issue by including items which demand considerable knowledge. Thus difficult grammatical items would never be satisfactory.

Other items used in verbal reasoning scales test comprehension and understanding by asking subjects to explicate the meaning of proverbs, usually in multiple-choice form, and by vocabulary tests. All these tests load highly on crystallised ability.

Discussion and description of the best tests of verbal reasoning and, indeed, of all the ability factors can be found in Section IV of this handbook.

2. Numerical ability

Numerical ability is the facility to manipulate numbers rapidly and accurately. It is not closely related to mathematical ability which is much more highly correlated with inductive reasoning, spatial ability and the two intelligence factors. Of course numbers cannot be manipulated except by the rules of mathematics so that items require a certain minimal level of arithmetic attainment.

Items

In a test designed for adults multi-choice items would be used of no great mathematical difficulty but testing speed and accuracy. In the Differential Aptitude Test, for example, items test the following processes: addition, subtraction, division, square roots, percentages, cube roots, fractions, and decimals.

From this it is clear that numerical ability is concerned with the speed and accuracy of handling numbers. It does not require any great reasoning abilities which accounts for its modest correlation with high mathematical attainment.

3. Spatial ability

This is the ability to visualise two or three dimensional figures when their orientation is changed. This is an important ability in some forms of mathematics, such as geometry and topology, in engineering and in certain aspects of chemistry, where structures are important, just for example.

Items

As might be expected from the description, items usually consist of a shape followed by a further set of shapes. Subjects are required to say which in the set of shapes is the same as the exemplar turned round. Another item asks subjects to identify from the set of shapes the one which is the same as the first one seen in a mirror or turned over. Another variant requires the subject to identify the original turned over and around.

It should be pointed out that spatial items of this kind in which geometrical shapes are reoriented in space and have to to be recognised are ideal for presentation on computer, where orientation can be infinitely varied and controlled.

Another type of spatial ability item shows piles of blocks in which the heights of the columns vary. Here subjects are asked to work out the total number of bricks in the pile, including those which cannot be seen. A variant of this question is to ask subjects how many blocks touch at least x blocks full face.

Yet another type of spatial ability item shows, flattened out, a design for paper folding with the folds indicated. Below this is a series of folded paper constructions and subjects have to indicate which of these the flat design would have made.

4. Perceptual speed and accuracy factor

This factor involves rapid recognition of perceptual details and the ability to perceive similarities and differences in visual patterns. It would appear to be important in certain occupations such as pilot or radar operator and it emerges clearly as an important perceptual factor (Cattell, 1971; Nunnally, 1978).

Items

As the name suggests, speed is important in measuring this factor. Thus items are not hard given unlimited time. To measure perceptual speed, which is often used in tests of clerical aptitude, as in the Differential Aptitude Test (Bennet *et al.*, 1962), items consist of a shape which has to be compared with another shape and marked as the same or different, or letter or number combinations which have to be compared with other similar combinations. Large numbers of these items have to be completed in a brief time.

5. Perceptual speed of closure

This is the other perceptual factor which appears in factor analyses of tests. This involves the ability to complete a shape when parts of it are missing. As was pointed out in Table 12.1 this factor correlates .61 with word fluency.

Items

Degraded words is a particular type of item which loads highly on this factor. Words are presented with bits missing from the letters and subjects have to identify them. Again the essence of this is speed although the actual recognition can be made difficult if the degradation is considerable. Similar items can require subjects to identify degraded letters or numbers.

May *et al.* (1987) used such a test in a study of flexible thinking. In some studies it was presented on a computer, the degradation being achieved by switching off certain numbers of relevant pixels.

6. Inductive reasoning

This factor (not surprisingly) involves induction, reasoning from the specific to the general. This factor, as would be expected from the definition of intelligence in Chapter 12, is a salient variable on the fluid ability factor.

Items

Letter grouping is a typical test of inductive reasoning. Five sets of four letters each are presented. Subjects have to find the rule which relates four of the sets and to select the set which does not fit.

Figure classification is another test which loads highly in induction. Each item presents two or three groups each of which contains three geometrical figures which are similar according to some rule. The second row of each item presents eight figures. Subjects have to discover the rules and classify these eight figures into the appropriate groups.

7. Ideational fluency

This is a factor which has been much stressed by Guilford and his colleagues (e.g. Guilford and Hoepfner, 1971). It is the ability to produce large numbers of ideas on any topic. The emphasis is on the speed and fluency of production rather than quality.

Items

Unusual-uses is a typical item to measure this factor. Here a number of objects is listed and subjects have to suggest as many different uses as possible for them. In some tests in place of an object a theme, such as foreign travel, is used. Yet another test is to list all the objects which are alike in some specified way.

8. Word fluency

This is a factor which has also been emphasised in the work of Guilford on creativity or divergent thinking (as compared to the convergent thinking required by the standard tests of intelligence, measuring the g factors). This factor is correlated with ideational fluency but is distinct. It involves the ability to produce a flood of words conforming to some letter requirement but unrelated semantically except by chance. This is the factor underlying skill at the well known game 'Scrabble'.

Items

These are obvious: write as many words as possible with a given ending or with a given beginning or with both ends fixed.

9. Originality of ideational flexibility

This is a measure of originality of ideas and has been studied mainly by Guilford.

Items

The items are similar to those used to measure ideational fluency. However, the measure is a judgement of the originality of the ideas produced in response to the items. This originality can be a subjective judgement or it can be original in the sense of rare, i.e. it is compared with norms. Although this latter form of scoring is more reliable than subjective judgement it is likely to be less valid because the rarity of a response does not mean that it is original in the creative sense of the word. Schizophrenic and psychotic as well as plainly stupid responses will be scored on this factor. For example, if for uses for a feather a subject wrote: scalpel, microscope and nuclear trigger, these would be normatively original, although totally ridiculous.

10. Originality 2

As was made clear in Table 12.1 this factor is relatively new, having split off in the work by Hakstian and Cattell (1974) from the first originality factor. It differs in the sense that the originality here has to be utilised in a constrained situation, as is made clear from the typical items which measure this factor.

Items

Subjects are asked to combine two objects into a functional object. Measures of ideational fluency can be obtained from these items as well as measures of this originality factor.

This covers the types of item used to measure the ten most important of the primary factors. As can be seen from the second order factors of ability in Table 12.3 if we were to measure subjects on these ten primaries we would effectively be able to measure them on these higher order factors. Some of these items, indeed, have been discussed in our list of miscellaneous intelligence test items, in the previous chapter. The retrieval factor, g_r, is the most educationally important of these second orders, apart from the two intelligence factors, since it it embraces originality and fluency which are correlated with creativity at least to a limited extent (Butcher, 1973).

Advantages of measuring the primary factors

Since most of these primaries load on the second order ability factors it may well be asked what the point is of having tests of these primaries at all. Although the application of psychometric tests in educational, clinical and occupational settings is discussed in Section 3 of this handbook, it is sufficient to point out here that on some occasions we may desire a measure of one of these more specific abilities. For example if we had to select subjects for training for flying civil helicopters we would want subjects high on spatial ability, and would concentrate on this. Now the factor of visualisation is important here but it would certainly be a more reliable testing procedure to give separate tests of the primaries loading this factor. Thus it could be that two scores were identical on the second order factor but were composed of different scores on the first orders.

This argument, it must be emphasised, does not run counter to the claims made in Chapter 12 concerning the importance of the intelligence factors which are second orders. For most testing situations intelligence tests are the most useful measures. Indeed one of the problems of testing a large number of primaries is that they all tend to be correlated, their variance being explained by the g factors. This is a major difficulty with the use of aptitude tests as will be discussed in Chapter 14 of this handbook. They are not properly differential on account of the primacy of the g factors.

TESTS OF SPECIAL ABILITIES AND OTHER TESTS

I hope that it is obvious that, from the nature of factor analysis, there can be no definitive list of human abilities. The primary factors of Table 12.1 are those that account for most of the variance when a large number of tests of ability are given. However, as Cattell (1971) has argued, most of the tests which have been developed are of the pencil and paper variety (and modern computer tests, as shall be seen, do not change the position) measuring the kinds of ability that are useful in conventional academic education. Clearly if no tests of a factor have been included in batteries no factor can emerge, no matter how elaborate the analysis. However there are many abilities which can be observed in everyday life for which no tests as yet exist, as exemplified in the skills practised by craftsmen and women all over the world. Clearly, if tests of such skills and abilities were factored, some new factors would emerge.

There is a converse to this argument which prevents any list of factors from being definitive. This concerns the problem of the difference between a general factor and a bloated specific, which was discussed in our chapters on factor analysis. However in all test construction there is a danger of constructing bloated specific factors by writing a large number of similar items. These form a factor which, however, correlates with nothing else except other similar items. This is, in part, what has occurred with the Guilford model of human abilities (Guilford, 1967) which postulates more than 100 such abilities.

Yet despite these problems there is some agreement, in psychometry, that there are certain other special abilities and tests have been devised to measure them. I shall discuss these special ability tests together with certain other tests which, although not strictly in this category, can be dealt with conveniently, from the viewpoint of logic and sense, at this point in the handbook. It should be noted that these tests will be dealt with briefly in this chapter which is concerned with types of tests. Actual tests will be described in the final section of this handbook.

Music ability

Shuter (1968) in her study of musical ability makes it clear that these abilities can be measured with a variety of tests. This is hardly unexpected since it is clear that musical ability is distinct from intelligence and other abilities since, even if these are necessary, they are clearly not sufficient for musical expertise. It could be argued that musical proficiency is simply an attainment which anyone could reach. However this is belied by the study of musicians. It is true that with effort a certain mastery of music can be attained by a large number of people. However, the speed with which gifted musicians learn the art suggests that there must be special abilities. A number of musical ability tests exist of which the most famous is one of the oldest developed by Seashore (1919) in his research into musical ability.

Items

Most musical ability tests contain items which tap the skills which any musician should possess. Pitch change, chord analysis, memory, rhythm, harmony, intensity and phrasing are all measured. Some tests use the piano, others pure tones. The Seashore test attempts to measure basic musical abilities which, Shuter (1968) argues, are sense of tonality (measured by pitch discrimination), sense of rhythm and an inner ear for music. These are correlated and, in Shuter's view, there is probably a general musicality factor. Apart from the Seashore test, a good practical measure is the test developed by Wing (1962) in England, and the American test developed by Gordon (1965).

Artistic ability

It is highly probable that the notion of artistic ability makes sense in explaining individual differences in the ability to draw and paint and in the appreciation of great art, although there is no doubt that hard work and good teaching can do much to increase a subject's artistic skills. However just what factor or factors constitute artistic ability remains unknown.

Partly as a result of this and because selection for art school is usually based upon performance no highly valid tests of artistic ability have been produced. The best known test is the Art Judgement test by Meier (1963) which requires subjects to judge which is the better of two drawings, one being a good work of art and the other an altered version. However, as has been indicated, there is no evidence that this is a valid test and it would be difficult to put reliance on such a measure.

Infant abilities

Developmental psychologists have developed a number of measures which are hoped to measure intelligence or intellectual development from a very early age, as soon as the child is capable of responding. The Bayley scales of infant development (Bayley, 1969), for example, are suitable for children from 2–30 months. I shall briefly describe this test because it typifies measures of infant ability and is regarded by specialists in this field as one of the best (Damarin, 1978). Furthermore it draws on items with a well established pedigree – her own extensive studies and the Gesell Developmental Schedules (Gesell and Amatruda, 1947).

It measures mental development, motor development as well as aspects of the infant's social behaviour, through rating scales. The notion of item is hardly applicable since infants are given a ring or a bell, for example, and their responses are noted. Sustained inspection of the ring adds to the developmental score, as does turning to observe a moving object. These are very early tests apparently measuring attentiveness and responsiveness, whereas at 1 year the items are concentrated on the ability to communicate and on conceptual development. Following instructions and imitations are important indices of development in the Bayley scale, the children being required to handle dolls, cups and toys, and to scribble both spontaneously and in imitation. As can be seen, it is a hotch-potch of items, which, incidentally, are well standardised and reliable.

The problem with the Bayley scales, as with all similar measures of infant development, is that they do not correlate well with later measures of intelligence. Consequently, as Damarin (1978) argues it is difficult to know what to make of the results, either clinically or in terms of research and theory. I have described some of the items in this test (which I must stress is typical of other infant scales) because the fact that scores do not correlate well with later IQ scores should not be surprising since the item content is totally different.

I think these scales do measure infant development but the rate of this development (which is essentially the basis of the scores) is not related to later intelligence. Cattell (1971) has argued that this is not surprising given that speed of development among different species even of mammals is negatively correlated with their position on the phylogenetic scale.

Such scales may prove useful in the diagnosis of severe cases of mental retardation with an organic basis but as indices of intelligence, for normal, non-medical subjects, it is difficult to recommend them.

Psychomotor and physical abilities

It is obvious that in many tasks and skills motor and physical abilities play their part, intertwined with cognitive and personality factors. These are particularly important in sport or perhaps surgery or woodturning but they play some part even in tasks such as writing or typing.

These motor abilities have been subjected to research over many years by Fleishman and his colleagues (e.g. Fleishman, 1964, 1975; Fleishman and Quaintance, 1984). In fact nineteen main factors have been isolated. I set out these factors with a brief description and an indication of the marker test for each factor, as summarised by Peterson and Bownas (1982). Together these give a good indication of the nature of these psychomotor abilities.

1. Static strength: degree of muscular force exerted to move continuously a heavy object. Test – Weight lifting, dynamometer.
2. Explosive strength: the ability to mobilise energy for a burst of effort, as in throwing. Test – Ten yard sprint, jump.
3. Dynamic strength: the power of arms and trunk to move body's own weight continuously. Test – Pull-ups.
4. Stamina: ability to maintain physical activity over a long period. Test – 600-yard run-walk.
5. Extent flexibility: the ability to flex muscle groups. Test – Twist and touch test.
6. Dynamic flexibility: the ability to make repeated trunk or limb movements where both speed and flexibility are required. Test – Floor touch.
7. Gross body equilibrium: the ability to maintain body balance. Test – Rail walk test.
8. Choice reaction time: speed of reaction to a stimulus where more than one stimulus is present. Test – Choice reaction.
9. Reaction time: speed of reaction to a single stimulus. Test – Simple reaction.
10. Speed of limb movement: the speed with which limb movements can be executed. Test – Plate tapping, two foot tapping.
11. Wrist–finger speed: obvious from label of factor. Test – Tapping.
12. Gross body coordination: ability to coordinate trunk and limbs. Test – Cable jump.
13. Multilimb coordination: obvious from label of factor. Test – Complex coordination test.
14. Finger dexterity: ability in skilfully coordinated finger movements. However it does not refer to the ability to manipulate machines or control mechanisms. Test – Purdue Pegboard.
15. Manual dexterity: similar to the above but refers to the hand. Test – Minnesota rate of manipulation test.
16. Arm–hand steadiness: ability to make precise, steady, arm–hand positioning movements. Test – Track tracing test.
17. Rate control: ability to make timed motor adjustments relative to changes in speed of a moving target. Test – Single dimension pursuit test.

18. Control precision: the ability to make controlled muscular movements necessary to operate a machine or control mechanisms. Test – Rotary pursuit.

Several points should be noted about this list of factors. As was the case with the list of cognitive factors which constitute the most important variables to be measured in the field of cognitive abilities, so this list suggests the important variables in the psychomotor field.

Some of these factors are hardly psychological such as speed of limbs or stamina (although there is a psychological component determining when a person actually abandons the task) while others such as reaction time and choice reaction time are highly related to intelligence (variability of reaction time has been suggested as a possible objective measure of IQ variability) as has been shown by Jensen (1980) and is fully discussed in Kline (1990).

In any attempt to predict behaviour it is clear that tests of these psychomotor abilities should be included along with tests of the main cognitive, personality and motivational factors (see Chapters 15 and 17).

Psychomotor tests

Many of the tests of these factors are simple physical tests, as can be seen from our description above, and need no further elaboration. The Purdue Pegboard consists of a wooden board with holes into which subjects have to insert pegs. Pursuit rotor tests consist of turntables with a spot on which subjects have to keep a stylus. Electrical contacts register whether contact is maintained or not. Reaction timers have sets of lights and corresponding buttons which have to be pressed when the light comes on. With the subject's hand on a home button reaction time as distinct from movement time to reach the response key can be measured. Variability in these reaction times correlates with g about .4.

One of the interests of Fleishman and colleagues has been in the prediction of job success and in occupational selection. Corresponding to all these psychomotor factors Fleishman has developed rating scales for jobs so that job and person may be matched (Fleishman, 1975), although description of these is beyond the scope of this chapter. I shall not say more about these factors, because many of them are physical rather than psychological and because the correlations with real life performance are rather low and vary at different stages of of training (Fleishman, 1966). Thus as a subject learns a skill certain of these factors are important but as the skill progresses others become more salient. All this complicates the use of these tests in occupational selection in general, although for specific tasks they may be important.

CONCLUSIONS

In this chapter I have described the large number of ability factors and their tests which contribute to the description of human abilities, beyond the intelligence factors which were discussed in the previous chapter. If we were to measure subjects on all these factors we would have a reasonably complete picture of their cognitive and motor abilities. In the next chapter I shall describe the personality and dynamic factors and their tests which go to complete the description of human characteristics.

Chapter 14

Aptitude and Attainment Tests

In the previous two chapters we have discussed the main factors in the sphere of ability, the all-pervasive intelligence factors and the most important primary ability factors. It was shown there how general intelligence, g_f, underlies many human abilities. These factors are highly useful in personnel selection, for example. Thus we might expect engineers to be high on intelligence and spatial ability while journalists would be likely to be equally intelligent but high on verbal ability.

MEANING OF APTITUDE

In ordinary, non-technical English, the term aptitude is frequently used, defined by the Penguin English Dictionary (Garmonsway, 1979) as a natural capacity, suitability and even intelligence. Certainly it is common usage to describe a person as having an aptitude for cricket (often qualified as natural) or computing, or for mathematics. Aptitude is also part of psychological terminology and there are a variety of aptitude tests, some widely used, such as the Differential Aptitude Test, the DAT (Bennet *et al.*, 1962). Clearly aptitude is a word of such broad meaning that it is important to define precisely what is meant by aptitudes or, at least, clarify the ambiguities of the concept. Indeed, if we hope to measure aptitudes such clarity is essential since, as should be evident from this handbook, tests are essentially operational definitions of variables.

In psychology aptitude is used in as confused a manner as it is in the English language. It is thus a highly unsatisfactory scientific concept unless its meaning is deliberately restricted. Aptitude usually refers to a collection of abilities which happen to be of value in a particular culture. Thus in the DAT, referred to in the previous paragraph, we can find, *inter alia*, tests of verbal and clerical aptitude. These two tests reveal the confusion in the concept which embraces both factors and collections of quite disparate abilities and skills.

Thus verbal ability is a well established primary ability factor, V, loading on synonyms, the meaning of proverbs and analogies (see Table 12.1).

Clerical aptitude, however, nowhere emerges as a factor. Instead it is a collection of abilities which happen to be useful in a modern bureaucratic society. It involves, for example, speed and accuracy in copying and writing and in simple calculations, conscientiousness in checking lists and the ability to resist boredom in repetitive tasks. Now this is not only multifactorial, as has been argued, but some of these necessary characteristics are more in the temperamental than the ability sphere. Psychometrically, therefore, verbal and clerical aptitude are quite distinct, the former being a primary ability factor, the latter a convenient collection of traits.

APTITUDE TESTS

This distinction, as should be obvious from earlier chapters of this handbook, is crucial to aptitude testing. Thus the verbal aptitude test is nothing more than a test of the verbal ability factor. The clerical aptitude test will be a mixture of items, tapping several factors. Indeed this latter type of aptitude test could be constructed empirically by selecting items which discriminated those who were adjudged to possess the aptitude from controls who did not. Examination of aptitude test batteries confirms this analysis since most of them contain tests of these two types, unifactorial and multifactorial.

Problems with aptitude tests

One of the most widely used aptitude tests, especially in America, where it was developed for vocational guidance and selection, is the DAT (Bennet *et al.*, 1962). This test is fully described and evaluated in Chapter 24, but I want to set out here the variables which it measures because this is necessary to understand the general difficulties involved in the use of aptitude tests. They are: Verbal reasoning, numerical ability, abstract reasoning, clerical speed and aptitude, mechanical reasoning, space relations, spelling and grammar.

1. Tests should be unifactorial

In Chapter 3 of this handbook, I set out the classical theory of test error which underlies the methods of test construction used by psychometrists and described in this book, in Chapters 9 and 10. It became clear that it is essential, for good testing, that tests be unifactorial. Only when this is the case do two identical scores have identical psychological meaning. Multifactorial tests are best replaced by separate tests measuring each factor. If this is done it might also be possible to improve the predictive power by differential weighting of the factors, the weights having been determined by multiple regression to the criterion. Thus to use the clerical aptitude test as an example, a multiple correlation between separate tests of the various factors and success in clerical positions would be computed and the beta weights would be used to weight the test scores.

Examination of the DAT variables illustrates this problem of multifactorial tests. The clerical aptitude test has been mentioned and spelling and grammar are clearly aspects of attainment. It should be noted that the spelling factor of 12.1 is not quite the same as the ability to spell (it was based on the perception of incorrect words) and, in any case, was correlated with V, verbal ability and W, word fluency. This spelling factor is probably narrow and the spelling test of the DAT would certainly load on this factor, together with V and W. Thus the DAT spelling test is a fine illustration of a multifactorial variable, although no doubt it is useful in applied work to know whether a a person can spell or not.

There is no contradiction in allowing that a spelling test could be useful in vocational guidance and selection and arguing that unifactorial tests should always be chosen where possible. This is because spelling is, in truth, not an aptitude at all but an attainment. There is no reason why an attainment, defined as knowledge, should be unifactorial. Thus spelling may depend for its acquisition on two ability factors, verbal ability and verbal fluency. However if we are interested in a subject's attainment in spelling, as distinct from understanding its psychological determinants, this is quite irrelevant. All we want to know is whether that subject can spell. The nature of attainment testing is described in a later section of this chapter.

It should be noted that clerical aptitude is not an attainment. It is rather a set of abilities required for a particular set of skills. Perhaps, since spelling is an attainment, it might be argued, aptitude should be regarded as embracing three components – pure factors, disparate collections of abilities and attainments. However this is not really so. It simply happens that spelling is a highly useful attainment for a number of jobs. It is not an aptitude as such but it is quite sensible to include it in a test which will be used for vocational guidance and selection. The same arguments apply to the grammar test although here this attainment is much more a function of V alone.

Conclusions

No more needs to be said. It is quite clear that the DAT contains multifactorial scales and, for this reason, falls short of what is desirable for a test of abilities, although the attainment aspects of the test are satisfactory as are the tests of primary factors. However if they are tests of primary ability factors there is no reason to call them aptitude tests, a term which is simply confusing.

2. The g factors and aptitude tests

The second problem with aptitude tests concerns the fact that, despite their multiplicity of variables, they are rarely differential. This is due to the pervasiveness of the g factors, as Quereshi (1972) has convincingly argued in his review of the DAT. The test manual (Bennet *et al.*, 1962) reveals this difficulty which is common to all aptitude tests. Thus the engineers, in the occupational samples, scored highest of all the groups on all the tests, not just the mechanical aptitude. If, therefore, we were to attempt to use the DAT for guidance or selection, this is not a helpful result. They were far higher than the clerks, for example, on the clerical aptitude scale. Indeed, the sum of scores on the DAT is probably the best predictor of job success, being the best measure of g.

This of course is not unexpected, as should be obvious to readers of Chapters 12 and 13. It indicates that the engineers had the highest g of all the groups tested and that the DAT scales load the g factors. Essentially these scales are measuring g. However it will be a measure of g made inefficient by the specific content of the particular aptitude test. If g is to be measured it is better to do it with scales uncontaminated by other factors. Thus this information from the DAT could have been obtained more efficiently from an intelligence test.

A possible counter-argument is that the influence of the g factors will show in the overall level of scores but that the profile of scores on aptitude tests may still be revealing. Unfortunately this is not so. Thus the highest score of the clerks was not on the clerical aptitude test. This is partly due to the fact that not all scales are equally saturated with the g factors.

In brief it is argued that the apparent differential power of aptitude tests is illusory because the scales load to varying extents on the g factors. Quereshi (1972) went to the trouble of factoring some of the data in the DAT test manual. His Varimax, orthogonal solution (which was far from ideal; an oblique rotation would have been more meaningful) revealed that four factors accounted for most of the DAT variance. It would be interesting to see how much predictive power was left in any aptitude tests after the g factors had been partialed out. It will be noticed, I hope, by vigilant readers that an oblique factor analysis is essential to investigate the influence of the g factors because these factors are correlated.

The final nail in the coffin of the DAT as a differential test, and the argument must apply to any aptitude test, is found in the manual to the DAT, which has certainly made no attempt to hide the problems with the test. The correlations between the DAT scales and the Otis Intelligence Test, a well respected and validated group test of intelligence, are significant in every case, but not only significant. Many are high: .81 with verbal reasoning, .69 with numerical ability, .65 with abstract reasoning, .58 with space relations, .61 with mechanical reasoning, .31 with clerical speed and accuracy, .48 with spelling and .48 with sentences. Given the reliability of the scales, these correlations demonstrate the truth of what has been argued in the previous paragraphs, that the DAT test is essentially an inefficient intelligence test.

These arguments appear to be so powerful that the question inevitably arises as to why anybody should bother with aptitude tests. In America, for example, not only is the Differential Aptitude Test widely used but there is another even more popular aptitude test, the General Aptitude Test Battery (USA Government Printing Office, 1970) used by their Department of Employment.

There is no doubt that for personnel selection or vocational guidance, we need more information than g alone can provide, important though this is. However this can arise from measures of the other important group factors such as verbal or spatial ability. Yet, ideally, we should still like further information. This is what the aptitude test appears to provide but, as we have shown, fails. Essentially an aptitude test, as was argued in the first section, consists of tests of group factors and somewhat arbitrary collections of skills.

This last phrase illustrates a further practical problem with aptitude tests which must now be discussed. On its resolution the justification for aptitude tests will depend.

3. Abilities and attainments

When we talk of abilities and skills there is often a somewhat loose use of words. Two terms are confused, capacity or potential, and attainment. Attainment refers to the possession of skills which have been acquired, through experience or deliberate training. Capacity or ability refers to the potential for acquiring such skills.

If we are selecting individuals for courses of training, or for jobs which they have not done, as in the selection of soldiers, the measurement of ability is essential. Here we need to measure the major ability factors which are implicated in the occupation. However, in general, personnel selection is not of this kind. In many instances we are dealing with individuals who already have the necessary skills and training. Thus for these an attainment test is of far more significance. If we want a surgeon, far better to have one who has mastered the techniques than one who has the capacity. As Tacitus said of a rather poor Emperor: *capax ingenium, nisi imperasset* – a man thought to be ideal for ruling the empire until he did so.

In brief, therefore, if individuals have acquired the skills and training it is far better to use their attainments as a selection measure than their capacities or abilities. Thus for these people aptitude tests are not valuable. For young people wanting to enter training courses, aptitude tests would be useful were they differential. However, as has been shown, they tend to measure only general ability which is better assessed by an intelligence test. If group or more specific factors are important for the occupation then tests of these factors should be used. It is therefore difficult to justify the use of aptitude tests.

Aptitude tests, consequently, are not as valuable as their name suggests. What value the DAT (and other aptitude tests) has resides in its capacity to measure general intelligence and the main group factors. For most jobs attainment at the job or in the necessary skills is the most sensible index of likely performance, with one proviso. Given the same level of skill it makes sense to select the person with the highest g scores because it is likely that she or he will be superior at applying the knowledge and acquiring new knowledge as the field progresses. Thus I think it sensible always to administer in selection procedures intelligence tests to eliminate the dull slogger and the person who has benefited from superb tuition.

Conclusions: the concept of aptitude

As a psychometric or scientific concept the term aptitude should be abandoned. It embraces both abilities and attainments, which are quite different. In addition, aptitude tests are barely differential on account of the nature of general intelligence. What they measure is better achieved with intelligence tests, group factor tests and measures of attainments.

ATTAINMENT TESTING

We argued above that, in many cases, where subjects had reached good standards of attainment, it was better to use these attainments as an index of their suitability for a job rather than give aptitude tests whose main value was for those about to enter training courses. This leads us on to a discussion of how attainments are best measured. I do not intend to say much about attainment testing because this is really only tangential to psychological testing but since attainment tests may be part of a psychometric testing procedure some discussion is necessary.

All tests which seek to assess how much subjects have learned in any field are attainment tests. Thus the public examinations which most of us have sat at school, O level, A level, GCSE, CSE, Scottish highers, degree examinations in university and polytechnic, are all attainment tests. However, and this is the critical point, they are attainment tests of highly variable quality and few of them match the psychometric criteria of good tests.

Criteria for good attainment tests

1. They must cover the content of the courses or field of knowledge
A fault of many attainment tests is that they fail to do this and candidates can pass them although knowing only a small portion of the course.

2. They must be reliable   As was discussed in Chapter 1 of this handbook, this means that they should have a large number of items and be objectively scored. It is interesting to contemplate the typical British degree examination

– four essays. Actually it is ironic that in my own psychology department we have a one-item general paper.

3. They should be valid Many attainment tests are not valid, although curiously enough they may be more useful for selection purposes for this reason. Thus where essays are required candidates high on verbal ability are favoured, and if the examiners like to see arguments rather than facts high g comes into the picture perhaps more than attainment. Thus a good British honours degree examination tests a mixture of attainment, g and verbal ability. All these are no doubt valuable characteristics but it is better, as has been stressed throughout this handbook, to measure separate variables separately.

Actually the British degree illustrates this problem to perfection, if we are attempting to select graduates for a job. Thus a good second-class degree can represent a huge effort of learning by a not highly intelligent or verbal candidate. On the other hand, it may be achieved by a highly intelligent but somewhat idle person with only a slight knowledge of her or his subject. Which we might choose would depend on the nature of the post to be filled.

Thus the question of the validity of a degree examination depends upon how the degree is conceived. Some educators might be pleased that it tested both verbal ability and intelligence, believing that the award of a degree should imply the possession of both these characteristics. If there are any such educators left they must be bitter and cynical in the extreme or deluded. Others would regard this as a serious flaw. For example medical examinations are regarded as pure attainment tests and subjects have to achieve close to 100 per cent to pass. Of course the fact of being a doctor, in the medical view, confers unusual intellectual status, so they are free to test attainment.

Psychometrically, the best solution to this difficulty is achieved by the most prestigious American universities. They select their postgraduates on intelligence and verbal and numerical ability so that they are satisfied that their students are sufficiently able. The degree examinations are thus primarily measures of attainment.

The characteristics of good attainment tests

In the light of this discussion it is possible to characterise a good attainment test.

1. Many items, chosen to cover the whole field Experts should be consulted to check this out. This involves consultations with panels of specialists in the various subjects who specify what should be known, at various stages, in their specialities. For testing children they should be able to specify what should be known at each age. These experts should be able to rank in importance the various, different aspects of the subject matter. It is absurd, for example, to have a large number of questions on a trivial part of the subject.

2. Selection of items in relation to objectively defined criteria To carry this out properly it is first necessary that the objectives of the course be stated as clearly as possible so that the relevance of items can be assessed. Bloom's *Taxonomy of Educational Objectives Handbook* (Bloom, 1956) is a useful guide to formulating objectives in such a way that they are amenable to testing.

Precisely how these decisions concerning test content are made is not really the province of psychometrics (in fact this field is now called edumetrics) and I shall not go into further details here. Thorndike and Hagen (1977) contains a useful summary of these procedures.

Diagnostic tests At this point brief mention should be made of diagnostic tests such as those of Schonell and Schonell (1950) for arithmetic and spelling problems. These are attainment tests so devised that the exact problem may be discovered, for example, the carrying of 0s in long division or the confusion of b and d. These are highly useful in the diagnosis of learning difficulties and are a special form of attainment test.

Attainment tests in which the content has been precisely selected, by the methods which we have discussed, can yield scores which are referred to as criterion referenced scores. Thus if a subject scored 85 on a particular mathematics test a criterion referenced score would indicate that she or he was likely to solve correctly 85 per cent of algebra problems involving matrix inversion.

3. Items with the full range of difficulty level, ensuring a normal or symmetrical distribution, as discussed in Chapter 9 of this handbook.

4. Objectively scored items Examples of these will be given below.

5. Good norms Standardisation is valuable, as described in Chapter 4 of this handbook.

6. Attainment tests suited to Rasch scaling or fitting other models derived from item response theory (see Chapter 5) could be used as an alternative to 3.

Of course, to obtain standardised, reliable attainment tests for all subjects, for a commercial organisation, is impossible in practice on the grounds of cost. Thus we have to make do with the public examinations at school and university level. Nevertheless this list of desirable characteristics of attainment tests does highlight the inadequacies of the British public examination system. This is immensely costly and could be replaced by psychometrically efficient tests.

Item forms in attainment testing

There is an obvious objection to the attainment testing of the type advocated above, which as Vernon (1960) points out, is always raised by traditional educationalists, namely that such tests merely test facts and that there is more to a good knowledge of a subject than facts. This objection is not without force. As will be seen below, it is easy to put factual material into objective test items but it is also possible to test more subtle aspects of a subject, as the best American attainment tests indicate.

1. Multiple-choice items

These are the most commonly used items in tests of attainments, being suited to a wide variety of subject matter. Each item has two parts: (a) the stem which contains the question or problem and (b) the options which constitute a set of possible answers, one of which the subject has to select. Most test constructors supply four or five options.

I shall briefly set out some well-accepted rules for writing good multiple-choice items, because this will illustrate their advantages compared with traditional attainment tests.

- a. Items should be as simple as possible. This is to avoid, or at least reduce, contamination of attainment scores by V, verbal ability and g_c, crystallised intelligence.
- b. All distractors (incorrect options) should be equally plausible. If the distractors are obviously incorrect the item is worthless, since it will have about a 100 per cent pass rate. Distractors are best chosen by selecting wrong answers to the item in a trial with open-ended answers to the items.
- c. There must be only one correct option. Sometimes a different way of looking at the question gives another possible answer. If it does abandon the item or change the distractor.
- d. Ensure that the distractors to items do not answer or make obvious the correct answers to other items.
- e. Avoid writing items just because they are easy to write. This is the way trivial items come into being.
- f. Avoid the distractor 'none of these' except where the item is unequivocally correct – as in a spelling test.
- g. Avoid the distractor 'all of these' which leads to sloppy item writing which is rarely taxing.

These are the most important rules for writing multiple-choice items and some, as will be seen, apply to writing other types of item. For more information on the construction of multiple-choice tests readers must be referred to the excellent guide published by the Educational Testing Service (1963), whose attainment tests show that objective tests can be intellectually taxing.

Advantages of multiple-choice items

a. Each item is perfectly reliable, in the sense of reliability between markers and if the item is scored on more than one occasion.
b. The items are easily scored. This is important for attainment tests where a large amount of material may have to be covered. In addition it allows tests to be as long as desired which improves reliability and validity. Ease of scoring also reduces clerical error.

   It should be pointed out that multiple-choice answer sheets, which can be hand scored by cut-out marking keys, are ideal for computer scoring. Indeed a multiple-choice set of items is easy to present on computer, as is discussed in Chapter 6 on computerised testing.
c. Guessing. This can be a problem but a multiple-choice test reduces the possibility of correct guessing to one in five, provided that the distractors are equally attractive. The problem of guessing will be discussed later in this chapter.
d. Test content. With a set of multiple-choice items a precise account of the test content is possible which thus allows the tester to assess the suitability of the test for her or his purposes.

2. True-false items

These items consist of statements which subjects have to mark as true or false. There are problems with this type of test which are discussed below.

a. Guessing. This is a real difficulty since there is a 50 per cent chance of getting the answer correct by chance. Indeed if a test were balanced for true and false correct answers, the subject who replied either true or false to all items would obtain a 50 per cent score.
b. It is difficult to write items that are unequivocally true or false and the cleverest students are those who may see the disconfirming case.
c. Triviality. The need for precision may lead to an emphasis on trivial items.

These last two objections are most relevant to arts and social science tests. In the sciences more absolute truth (in the item sense) is possible. In general true-false items, consisting of statements, can usually be replaced by multiple-choice items which are preferable since they reduce the effects of guessing.

However there is one class of true-false items where the format is useful. This is where information is presented to the subject in the test and her or his ability to understand it is measured. For example, in Kline (1986) I set out a graph showing two distributions of intelligence, one for men and one for women. To this were appended a large selection of true-false items:

a. There are more men than women with very low IQ – <45
b. There are more men than women with very high IQ – >140.
c. The distribution of intelligence among women is approximately bimodal.
d. The distribution of intelligence among men is approximately normal.
e. The mean IQ of men and women is approximately the same.
f. There are more women than men of IQs between 120 and 140.
g. There are more men than women of IQs between 50 and 60.

This method of testing understanding of material is highly effective and gives the lie to those who claim that objective test items can only measure rote-learned material. In this example if the subject could not interpret and understand frequency graphs the items could only be guessed. Furthermore an item of information, whether bimodal distributions were known, was slipped into the test.

There is a further use for the true-false item in attainment testing and this concerns its application in testing detailed knowledge. For example:

The following correlation coefficients are eta coefficients:
a. tetrachoric correlation; b. biserial correlation; c. point-biserial correlation; d. tau; e. rho; f. phi; h. G index.

Conclusions concerning true-false items

In brief the true-false item can be useful in testing the understanding of presented material and of examining knowledge in great detail, where multiple-choice items would be clumsy. However it must be realised that its effectiveness is dimmed by guessing. However, for this reason, for most item writing the multiple-choice item is to be preferred.

3. Matching items

In matching items subjects are required to match items in two lists. These items are best suited to the elicitation of factual material. Authors and books and classes of mammals are obvious examples. Thus we might have four named authors, A,B,C,D, and eight titles of books. Subjects indicate by letter who wrote which book, leaving a blank if none of them did so.

It is clear that this is a neat form of testing detailed knowledge. Thus, although a multiple-choice item could have been constructed we would have needed eight items and thirty-two distractors, far more clumsy and difficult to write.

True-false items could have dealt with this subject matter but again they would have been less neat than the matching items. First, four items would be necessary, one for each of the authors. However the same examples could not be used in each of the four items because answers to the earlier items would rule out answers to the later ones. Obviously if author A wrote book 1 authors B, C and D did not do so.

The second statistical true-false item concerning eta coefficients could be reformulated as a matching item with some additional information. Thus we could have a list of three types: eta coefficients, non-parametric techniques and rank-order methods. We would then add in a few extra examples to fit these categories. This would be a better item than the true-false, in this instance, because more information is obtained – from those items which are answered false in the true-false method. However, on occasions it is difficult to find good lists which fit the categories and this makes the true-false format better. Thus for detailed knowledge both methods are useful, and the choice of item type depends upon the particular knowledge to be tested.

However it must be noted that for the first true-false example, where information was presented to the subjects and the items tested understanding, it would be exceedingly difficult if not impossible to use the matching items in their place. Indeed it is a rough rule that true-false items are best when testing information presented in the test. Other item formats are much more clumsy.

To reduce the effects of guessing and to ensure that, as the subjects proceed through the choices in each item, the answer does not become obvious, the lists to be matched should be of unequal length and it is sensible to indicate that some items in the lists cannot be matched.

In both matching and true-false items one point must be noted. Although, as has been shown, true-false items are useful in testing understanding, both these item formats are ideal for eliciting detailed knowledge. This means that there is always the risk of testing trivia. Thus, for example, to know that the G index is an eta coefficient means little if the notion of an eta coefficient is not understood. Similarly to know that Scott wrote *Waverley* is unimportant compared with the ability to enjoy and criticise the novel.

Conclusions: comparison of the three item types

In the next section I shall attempt to summarise a rationale for using each of these types of item. A number of issues have to be considered.

a. Specific factors   In Chapter 3 on classical test theory and in Chapters 7 and 8 on factor analysis, specific factor variance was discussed. Thus it is always advisable to use as many types of item as possible to minimise specific variance due to a particular type of item. In a battery of tests such item type specific variance could load a factor that would resemble a genuine group factor although it would be a bloated specific – ability at answering a particular type of item. A variety of item types is therefore advantageous.

b. Boredom   A variety of items is likely to reduce the boredom experienced by subjects in completing attainment tests, as Cronbach (1976) argues, and this will improve the reliability of the testing procedure.

c. Item efficiency   In attainment tests we want maximum efficiency of items. As has been shown, how good each item is depends to some extent on the material to be tested. Nevertheless, some rules are possible as regards the best type of item.

1. Most material is best tested by the multiple-choice item and this is the basic attainment test item.
2. For detailed factual information, matching and true-false items are useful.
3. For testing material presented in the test the true-false item is valuable.
4. For reasons presented in (1) and (2) a mixture of items is the best, although too many true-false items increases the difficulties due to guessing.

Writing items

The best approach is to begin with a multiple-choice item. If this seems neat and satisfactory there is little point in attempting to produce the other two types of item. However, if it seems impossible to test it with a multiple-choice item, or if the item seems clumsy, or there is a problem with distractors then the true-false and matching items should be written.

Criteria for choosing items

1. Clarity. Choose the form of item which is likely to be the clearest for subjects.
2. Guessing. Choose the form which reduces the effects of guessing to a minimum.
3. Precision. Choose the form which is the most neat and precise.
4. Relation of items. Check that the options to items or even the items themselves do not answer or give clues to other items in the test.
5. Balance. Where all choices are possible, choose the type of item which is rarest, while bearing in mind point 2.

Other types of item

The three types of items which have been discussed above are the most common and useful in attainment testing. Nevertheless there are others and these will be briefly mentioned since they are useful if the material remains intransigent to testing by the above three methods.

a. Limited-response item   These items require subjects to make their own responses which are, however, constrained or restricted, thus ensuring objective marking provided that the items have been properly worked out.

b. Free-response item   Here subjects can put anything. However with correct wording of the question there is only one possible response.

The free-response item has to be most carefully worded if it is to be fair to the candidates and objectively scorable. Let us suppose that we are testing knowledge of oblique factors. The question 'What are oblique factors?' is so broad that it would require an essay rather than a short answer to do it justice. Clearly we must be more specific. Let us suppose that we wish to find out whether subjects know that oblique factors are correlated. Obviously a true-false item would do the trick as would a multiple-choice. However in free-response form we might use the item: 'In what way do oblique factors differ from orthogonal factors?' Again this is too vague since subjects could rightly point out that oblique factors are at less than right angles. So we ask 'What information of psychological significance can be obtained from the angles between oblique factors?' This truly restricts correct answers and such a free-response item ought to work.

The advantage of the free-response item is that, as can be seen, it is less a test of rote learning, for there are no prompts from distractors, and it is more interesting for subjects to complete than a comparable multiple-choice item.

Limited choice items   These are attractive and they can be written to provide perfect reliability. The comparable example to our free item would be 'From the angles between oblique factors their . . . . can be worked out.'

Conclusions

I do not want to spend too much time on these item forms because they are essentially only of limited use where the answers can be made so precise that they are of value. The free items are difficult to write such that one can be sure that candidates do themselves justice. To this extent the limited-response form is superior.

However their main attraction lies in the fact that they are a relief for the candidate from objective questions and for this reason, provided that they are precise, a few of them are useful. It should be noted that they are not suitable for machine scoring and this may be a severe disadvantage. For more information on writing such items readers must be referred to Kline (1986).

Guessing

Finally I want to deal with the problem of guessing. It is clear that in multiple-choice items and even limited-response items, guessing must be a distorting feature which introduces error into the variance and lowers validity. As I pointed out earlier the shrewd subject should be able to get half of any true-false items right by chance.

Furthermore if these tests are used in matters which are important to the subjects such as job selection or promotion or admission to courses, then guessing is inevitable. How can its influence be minimised?

1. Instruct subjects to guess. In the test instructions there should be a requirement to guess. 'Do not leave blanks. If you do not know the answer, or are uncertain, guess the correct solution.'
2. Fill in all blanks at random before scoring the test. This is the equivalent of guessing. A computer scoring system can be programmed to do this.

With these methods all scores will be distorted, hence the importance of such distortion is minimised.

Guessing-correction formula

Some testers use a formula to correct for guessing. The common formula is:

14.1 $X \text{ correct} = X - \dfrac{W}{n-1}$

where X correct = score corrected for guessing; X = number of correct items; W = number of wrong items; n = number of options in the items.

There are at least four problems with this guessing correction:

1. It assumes that all wrong answers are due to guessing but this is not necessarily so. Subjects may be misinformed. The guessing formula treats such subjects harshly.
2. It assumes that, where guessing has occurred, there is an equal chance for each option to be chosen. However this is not so since in some items subjects may have eliminated some of the distractors but still guess the answer. For these subjects the correction formula is an under-estimate.
3. Items with different numbers of options require different guessing corrections, as is clear from Formula 14.1. This is no problem with computer programs but it must not be overlooked.
4. This guessing correction applies to subjects on average. In any individual case it may well be wrong.

For all these reasons the guessing-correction factor is only rough. I agree with Vernon (1960) that guessing is best ignored in multiple-choice tests with a large number of items. It is obviously a problem with true-false items and only small numbers of these should be used. Guessing is also encouraged in highly speeded tests but these are poor tests unless speed is the variable being tested. Thus guessing correction is not recommended.

Conclusions

From this discussion of attainment tests it is clear that with their wide selection of items which can be reliably scored and which can cover the whole field of attainment, properly constructed attainment tests must be superior to traditional kinds of tests. The varieties of item that are available ensure that almost all content can be put into item form and that items need not be restricted to the trivial. Finally it is clear that guessing need not be a serious form of distortion in a long test of mainly multiple-choice items.

Chapter 15

Personality Questionnaires

In this chapter I shall describe and scrutinise personality questionnaires. I shall examine the different types of items used in these tests, and discuss their relative advantages and disadvantages in the study of personality and in their use in applied psychology. Although I shall illustrate these points with reference to specific tests these will not be described in any detail in this chapter. The description and critical evaluation of specific personality tests may be found in Section IV of this handbook (Chapter 25).

A personality questionnaire consists of a set of items, usually questions or statements about feelings or behaviour, to which subjects have to respond, by answering the question or agreeing or disagreeing with the statements.

ADVANTAGES

Personality questionnaires are much favoured by psychometrists as instruments for measuring personality because it is relatively simple to construct reliable tests and to establish norms. In brief it is possible to make questionnaires psychometrically efficient. However, it will be noticed that no mention is made of validity. The demonstration of the validity of any personality test is difficult from the nature of the variables involved and, as will be seen, there are psychometrically powerful personality tests with little evidence of validity. Some psychometricians, indeed, ignore the problems of validation. They resort, in fact, to classical test theory: a reliable test must be measuring something.

PROBLEMS

There are certain problems with personality questionnaires which it is useful to list at the beginning of this chapter so that readers can be aware of them as the various features of these tests are discussed. Some of them will be examined in detail later in this chapter, and will be little more than mentioned at this point. However there is one problem which outweighs all others and must be discussed first.

1. The problem of the variables to be measured

In Chapter 12 of this handbook, it was shown that, by the use of exploratory factor analysis in the field of human abilities, a relatively small number of factors was agreed to subsume the variance in human ability. From the nature of factor analysis (see Chapters 7 and 8) it is obvious that the most efficient ability tests should be measuring these factors. Theoretically, from their statistical nature, we would expect factors to be psychologically meaningful and so it has proved in the field of ability where the factors are important concepts, not simply test variables, in understanding human abilities, as is discussed in Kline (1990).

Factor analysis of the personality sphere

In the field of personality the application of factor analysis to discover the fundamental variables began much later than in the field of abilities, and proved more difficult because it was by no means clear what variables should go into the analysis to start with and, as has been demonstrated, in exploratory factor analysis it is essential to sample the population of variables.

This difficulty was overcome by Cattell and his colleagues (Cattell, 1957) who essentially produced sixteen factors from ratings of all trait terms – factors embracing the semantic personality sphere. Cattell (e.g. 1981) still argues that these factors account for much of the normal personality variance. In respect of abnormal behaviour he has isolated a further twelve factors (Cattell, 1973).

The problem here is that, as Kline and Barrett (1983) have pointed out, there are almost as many factor analytic solutions as factorists, all claiming that their solution is the best. Thus only recently has it been possible to draw up a list of personality factors, at least among normal subjects, about which there is any agreement. This agreement comes about because, following on the work of Cattell (1978) on simple structure factor analysis, and the development of efficient computer programs for oblique rotation, replicable factor analyses can be computed. These methods were discussed in Chapters 7 and 8 of this handbook.

Kline and Barrett (1983) carried out their own studies of the Cattell 16PF Test (Cattell, Eber and Tatsuoka, 1970), the EPQ (Eysenck and Eysenck, 1975) and the Dynamic Personality Inventory (Grygier and Grygier, 1976), all tests discussed in Chapter 25 of this handbook, and demonstrated that four factors could be found in these questionnaires. Furthermore, from a careful study of the factor analyses of other personality questionnaires, having regard to sometimes inefficient rotational procedures or orthogonal rotations, it was argued that these four factors could be found in those questionnaires such as the Comrey (Comrey, 1970) and the Guilford-Zimmerman test (Guilford *et al.*, 1976). These four factors were:

(1) extraversion; (2) anxiety; (3) tough-mindedness; and (4) obsessionality.

There is no doubt that personality questionnaires should measure these factors. Support for this assertion comes from the fact that the most recent studies of the ratings of personality (e.g. McCrae and Costa, 1987) argue for five factors which bear a striking resemblance to those above. Indeed three are the same: extraversion, anxiety and tough-mindedness. Obsessionality is split into two – conscientiousness and conformity. Indeed Digman (1990) has argued that these five factors, the big five, underlie the variance in most personality inventories, evidence which is fully discussed in Chapter 25 when the validity of the best personality inventories is examined.

Thus factor analysis suggests, as was the case with the field of abilities, the variables which personality questionnaires should measure. It appears that there are further factors important in the abnormal personality sphere which tests should measure but there is little agreement about these abnormal factors.

Other methods of test construction

However, as was discussed in Chapters 9 and 10 of this handbook there are methods of test construction other than factor analysis – criterion-keyed tests being an important non-factor analytic approach. Clearly it would be possible to develop a personality test by developing sets of items which discriminated individuals of different personality. In fact two well known personality questionnaires, the MMPI (Hathaway and McKinley, 1951) and the Californian Psychological Inventory (Gough, 1975) have been created by this method. Both of these tests are discussed in Chapter 25 of this handbook.

The only other rational method of selecting variables to measure is to adopt a personality theory and put the variables within it to the test. The problem here is that, as Allport (1937) argued, there are many theories and no agreement as to which is correct, an even more severe problem, as will be seen, in the development of tests of motivation. Nevertheless a number of well known tests have decided to rely on theory as their basis, Jackson's Personality Research Form (Jackson, 1974), using Murray's (1938) theory of needs and presses and the Myers–Briggs Inventory (Briggs and Myers, 1962) which tests Jungian notions of personality types, being cases in point.

Clearly, therefore, the theoretical bases of personality tests are complex. As should be clear I favour the empirical factor analytic approach because personality theory is not well enough developed for purposes of test development, most theories being highly speculative. Furthermore, as was pointed out in Chapter 9 of this handbook, the blind empiricism inherent in criterion-keyed tests renders such tests of dubious psychological meaning.

Conclusions

Thus to conclude this section on the selection of variables which should be included in personality questionnaires, as was the case with the field of ability, psychometrists are best guided by the factor structure in the personality sphere. This, however, still leaves a host of problems with personality questionnaires which must now be discussed.

2. Items

The difficulty with items is that, no matter how skilled the item-writer the items are inevitably simplistic. It is impossible to catch the rich subtlety of human feelings in brief statements. As Heim (1975) argued, to ask subjects to agree or disagree with some simple statement or answer a question 'Yes' or 'No' affronts their intelligence and sensibilities and creates poor co-operation in the testing process. I shall take a few examples from a variety of personality tests and the point will become clear. I must assure readers that I am not selecting particularly bad items.

'I find it hard to keep my mind on a task or job.' Subjects have to respond 'True' or 'False' to this statement. This is an excellent illustration of the point. It all depends on what job. As one subject told me after filling in a long and tedious set of items which included one of similar meaning, normally he had no difficulties but for psychological tests . . . . Furthermore it also depends to some extent on how one feels. In brief the item does not seem sensible, given the answering format.

'I have very few quarrels with members of my family.' Here we have a number of difficulties, compounded into one item. First what is the meaning of 'very few'? One a year, one a week, who knows the mean frequency of family quarrels? Even more difficult, what constitutes a quarrel, as distinct from an argument, tiff or row? Just for example those who are used to a disharmonious marriage might accept as normal what would appear frightful to someone more fortunate.

'Drafting new rules for society.' To this item subjects have to respond 'Like' or 'Dislike'. Surely here is an item which fits Heim's objection. This is an activity which to many people is so irrelevant as to merit neither answer.

'Keeping a large stock of canned goods in your cupboard.' Again little more needs to be said. Even if it were the case that those who felt strongly about this item, negatively or positively, had distinct personality characteristics, without a middle category this item could not be successful.

'It would be more interesting to be: a. a guidance worker helping young people find jobs, b. uncertain, c. a manager in charge of efficiency engineering.' This item has a middle category but it does not cater for those who have no desire to be either (a) or (c) or who would actively hate both.

'In constructing something I would rather work: a. with a committee, b. uncertain, c. on my own.' Once again this item illustrates the problem of what is meant by constructing something. For many people whether they would prefer to work on their own or not would much depend on what had to be done.

These six examples illustrate the problems inherent in personality test items. Yet these are all taken from good tests and are by no means bizarre or extreme. These latter are easy to find: I could live in a pig pen without letting it bother me; If I were asked to lift a ten-ton weight I could do it; When I wake up in the morning my heart is beating; I could and would drink blood if I had nothing else available.

Although item writing is difficult some of these problems can be minimised by selecting the item form which is most suited to the content of the items and to the population and purposes for which the test is intended. The most commonly used types of item will discussed later in this chapter. I shall, at this point, discuss some of the other problems with personality questionnaires.

3. Other problems

a. The response set of acquiescence This is the tendency to agree with items regardless of content. It is most likely to occur, according to Guilford (1959), where items are somewhat vague. For example it is easier to agree with the item 'I like sport' when, in fact, one has little interest in it than it would be to the item 'I play cricket three times a week' when one does not. Of course, it could be that acquiescence is a genuine personality variable, in its own right. However, if this is so it must be measured separately and not be allowed to distort the measurement of other variables.

b. The response set of social desirability This is the tendency to endorse items depending upon how socially desirable it is to do so. Edwards (1957) in his original investigation of this response set showed that, with the MMPI items (Hathaway and McKinley (1951), there was a high correlation between social desirability, as estimated by judges, and the endorsement rate of items. This response set sometimes can be thought of as faking good but it is not necessarily entirely conscious and deliberate.

c. Response set of using the middle or 'uncertain' category Where there is a middle category, denoting uncertainty of response, this proves for certain subjects fatally attractive. As a result it is difficult to learn anything about a subject's behaviour other than she or he likes to use the middle category.

d. The response set of using the extreme response If subjects are required to respond to items on a rating scale, running, perhaps, from 'always' to 'never' on a 5- or 7-point scale, then a proportion of them endorse the extreme responses, simply because they are extreme. It is the obverse of those who prefer the neutral category.

e. Face validity of items In tests of ability an item is largely self-evident provided that the instructions are clear. Thus if items require subjects to work out fractions then that ability or knowledge is *ipso facto* tested. However the face validity of personality test items is a different matter. As Cattell and Kline (1977) have argued, it is not necessarily the case that responses to personality questionnaire items can be taken as true, or even that they need be so. They refer to item responses as Q and Q^1 data. The former are treated as if they reflect subjects' behaviour, the latter simply as responses which load particular factors or discriminate criterion groups, without any implication that subjects actually behave as the items suggest.

f. Sampling the universe of items In Chapter 3 we discussed the classical theory of test error in which it became evident that a good test was one which consisted of an adequate sample from the hypothetical and infinite universe of items. In tests of ability and aptitude, as has been seen, it is relatively easy to define and thus to sample the universe of items. For example, at the crudest level of analysis, it is possible to classify items as belonging to linguistic, scientific or mathematical universes without much risk of error. However, in the field of personality and temperament, this is not the case.

Sometimes, indeed, even the most experienced and skilled item writers (see for example Cattell, 1957 and his description of the construction of the 16PF Test) are surprised by items loading on factors different from those which they were designed to tap and by items which fail to load at all. Kline and Lapham (1990a) in the development of the PPQ test, fully described in Chapter 25 of this handbook, found that items which appeared to be identical except that one contained a negative and was thus scored the opposite way loaded on different factors or that one loaded and the other did not. Furthermore the response set of acquiescence (see above) could not explain these anomalies. These difficulties simply reflect the problem of defining the universe of items. This means that it is difficult to sample the universe and to define the true score – all serious problems in developing valid tests.

g. Sampling subjects   In Chapter 4 we discussed the problems of sampling subjects in connection with the standardisation of tests. There it was concluded that a stratified sample was more efficient than a random sample and that the strata should be chosen which were the most highly correlated with the test variable. With personality tests this constitutes a problem since it is by no means agreed what variables are correlated with personality. Thus both for test development and standardisation large samples are required, if bias is not to be introduced, and this requirement is not always met because of the large resources required.

h. Problems in establishing the validity of personality tests   As was fully discussed in Chapter 2, there are severe difficulties in establishing the validity of personality tests simply because, in most instances, it is not possible to establish clear external criteria. In practice this means that predictive and concurrent validity studies are ruled out, except for those rare variables, such as extraversion and anxiety, where there are clear marker factors. This, of course, is quite different from the field of abilities where it is relatively easy to establish external criteria. Some test constructors including me with Ai3Q (Kline, 1971a) have attempted to demonstrate validity by correlating the test scores with ratings. However ratings are themselves highly dubious, as has been shown by Vernon (1963).

In general the only effective means of demonstrating the validity of personality inventories is in construct validity studies. Here factor analyses of batteries of tests allow hypotheses concerning the location of the personality factors in factor space to be put to the test. Furthermore hypotheses concerning high and low scorers on the variables can be checked. However such studies are usually far from definitive and often the claims for validity pay tribute to the subtlety and ingenuity of the claimants rather than to the validity of the tests themselves.

From this discussion it is clear that there are many difficulties with personality questionnaires. These have been mentioned at the beginning of this chapter so that readers can bear them in mind as we examine and scrutinise in more detail the nature of personality questionnaires.

TYPES OF ITEM

Personality test constructors are well aware of all the difficulties which I have discussed in the introductory paragraphs. They attempt to write items, therefore, which minimise these problems, and in the main these items tend to take the following forms, which I shall now describe. Certainly the types of items which are set out below are those found in the majority of reputable personality tests.

1. The yes–no item Eysenck and Eysenck (1975) use this type of item in their EPQ. A typical item of this kind would be: I am afraid of mice. It has the advantage that it is simple to write and, even more important, it is easy to understand and quick to fill in. In general, as Guilford (1959) argues, the more simple and straightforward an item, the less likely it is that subjects will fall prey to the response sets which have been described above. Furthermore the briefer a test the less likely it is that subjects will not bother to complete it properly, although as was shown in Chapter 1, brevity must not be at the expense of reliability. For all these reasons the yes–no item is a good choice.

The emphasis on the simplicity of items must include the instructions for subjects. It is essential that subjects understand exactly what they have to do and that they are asked to complete the items as quickly as they can. The example in the previous paragraph 'I am afraid of mice' precisely exemplifies this point. What I would be searching for with this item would be the immediate reaction that some people have to mice, a mixture of repugnance and fear which is quite irrational. If one reads this item quickly there is an immediate response of 'Yes' or 'No'. However a careful analysis of the item may make it impossible to answer. A subject's ruminations might be: 'What is meant by afraid? I don't like mice much and I wouldn't like one inside my shirt, but I don't think that means that I am afraid of them. Anyway it's not all mice I don't like . . . and so on.'

The major disadvantage with the yes–no item is that its welcome simplicity can verge on the simplistic, as has already been discussed. Subjects complain that the item just cannot be answered by a 'Yes' or 'No'. If offending items cannot be re-written they should be cast in another form or abandoned. True empiricists, sometimes called blind empiricists, may well ignore all complaints and simply include items if they load up on their factors. However, in my experience such items are usually failures and never get beyond the item or factor analysis of the test development.

2. The yes–?–no item This is a variant of the yes–no item, with the middle category inserted to overcome the problems of having to force subjects to choose extremes when, in fact, they are indifferent. However the problem with the trichotomous item is that its middle category is attractive and yet uninformative. Many years ago Bendig (1959) showed that with items in the Maudsley Personality Inventory (Eysenck, 1947), essentially an early version of the EPQ, there were virtually no differences between forms with dichotomous or trichotomous items. They plumped for the original item form on the grounds that it forces subjects to choose.

In my view there is so little difference between the two forms that it is simply a matter of personal preference which form a test constructor chooses. Cattell, Eber and Tatsuoka (1970), in the 16PF Test, use trichotomous items in some cases.

3. The true–false item   This is the item form used by Hathaway and McKinley (1951) for the MMPI, one of the most widely used personality questionnaires. These items consist of statements which subjects have to indicate as either true or false for them. These items are usually cast in the first person and a typical example is: 'I really enjoy the thrill of dangerous sports.' As is obvious it is a form of item highly similar to the yes–no item and the same comments apply to both. The only point worth noting is that the choice of one rather than the other of these items does affect the English style of the item.

4. The like–dislike item   This item, usually a single word or phrase, to which subjects have to indicate 'like' or 'dislike' is used by a number of test constructors, notably Grygier (1975) in the Dynamic Personality Inventory and by Wilson and Patterson (1970) in the Conservatism Scale. These items are inevitably both clear and simple and the skill of writing them lies only in choosing salient words or phrases. This choice usually has a theoretical basis and will be discussed in a later section of this chapter when the content of items is examined.

It should be noted that Grygier and Grygier (1976) in the *Manual to the Dynamic Personality Inventory* claim that their items are projective in nature and that this test should be regarded as a projective inventory. I doubt whether this claim can be maintained and is meaningful, but regardless of this point, this is a useful item form provided that there is a clear rationale for the selection of items. For example, by definition obsessionals are clean and have a pathological fear of germs and dirt. The following items might, therefore, be viable: (a) The smell of disinfectant; (b) an unswept bedroom; (c) unwashed crockery; (d) neat piles of ironing.

5. Items with rating scales   With this item form rating scales, often with five or seven points and running from 'never' to 'always' or 'definitely' to 'definitely not', depending on English usage, are appended to statements, as set out below: I enjoy gardening: always, very frequently, frequently, occasionally, rarely, very rarely, never. Comrey (1970), in the Comrey Personality Inventory, utilises these items for two reasons. First they overcome the statistical problems of attempting to correlate dichotomous items, namely lack of variance (problems which have been fully discussed in Chapter 10 of this handbook) and, in addition, subjects tend to prefer them because they allow more flexibility of response than dichotomous items. However, as I have argued in the opening section of this chapter, there is an added complication of this item form being open to the response set of putting the extreme response. There is a further source of possible error in these items – that different individuals may interpret the frequency scales differently, one person's 'rarely' being another's 'fairly frequently'.

6. Trichotomous items These items are no more than variations on the items described under (2). In the 16PF test Cattell uses these items because they make more sense than 'Yes', 'Uncertain', 'True' in many cases. Examples of these are: true, uncertain, false; generally, sometimes, never; agree, uncertain, disagree. Which of these variants is used depends simply upon the content of the item.

7. Trichotomous items with choice These are further variants of the items discussed in category (6). They are forms of item which allow almost any idea to be encapsulated into item form. These items involve subjects in choosing usually one of three categories. An example item might read: 'If I were really worried: (a) I would talk it over with my parents; (b) have a few drinks to make me feel better; or (c) carry on as usual until the worries had gone away.' The Myers–Briggs Type Indicator (Briggs and Myers, 1962) uses this form of item with two, three and four choices. These items are, as is clear from the example, forced-choice items, which have been claimed by Edwards (1957) to have special advantages.

In the Edwards Personal Preference Schedule (Edwards, 1959) Edwards used forced-choice items which had been matched for social desirability. By this technique he hoped to eliminate this response set, which he had shown (1957) to vitiate the MMPI. Ironically, however, it was shown by McKee (1972) that when matched items were thus paired together slight differences in social desirability became magnified so that the response set was not altogether eliminated.

8. Other item forms The items which have been described above include the vast majority of items in personality tests of any repute. This is because they are relatively easy to write and are capable of dealing with a wide range of content. In addition they are items which are easy and simple for subjects to complete. Nevertheless there are some other useful formats and these will be mentioned briefly.

    a. Preference items. In the Myers–Briggs Type Indicator an item form is found where subjects have to indicate which of a pair of words appeals to them. This resembles the like–dislike item which we have discussed in (4) above, and like those items it resembles a projective test although it is objectively scored. Perhaps it is no more than a variant of the like–dislike item.

    b. The 'ideal' item. Kline and Lapham (1990a) in their development of the Professional Personality Questionnaire used the following item form. A statement 'Ideally I would like a job where . . .' was followed by items to which the subject had to respond 'Yes' or 'No', for example 'workers were treated with respect'. The advantage of this item form was that it made the test seem relevant to the personnel selection for which the test was to be used. Clearly a different stem could be used to render tests appropriate for different applied contexts.

c. Items other than self-report items. All the items which we have examined up to this point require the subject to report upon her or his own feelings and behaviour even though, as was argued by Cattell (1957), it is not strictly necessary that subjects report accurately. It is possible to write items, in any format, with instructions such that subjects answer them as they believe other people see them. Such items are used by Edwards (1967) in the Edwards Personality Inventory, in yet another of this author's valiant attempts to reduce the response set of social desirability.

The types of item which have been described have all been found to be successful in testing personality. As has been made clear they can deal with almost any content, they can be made brief yet comprehensible and subjects find them tolerable.

ITEM CONTENT

So far we have discussed the various forms which personality items may take. However I shall now turn to the problem of content. What is the content of personality test items? How are the constructs chosen? How can we attempt to establish, other than empirically, that the items relate to the constructs? The solution to all these problems has been greatly eased by a study aimed directly at them by Angleitner *et al.* (1986) and I shall summarise their remarkably full account and discuss their arguments.

Jackson (1967) exemplifies one approach to the development of items for questionnaires in his Personality Research Form, which is generally considered to be one of the most carefully constructed personality measures. In this test he attempted to measure the most important presses and needs, described by Murray (1938). First he defined the constructs, ensuring that there was no overlap between the definitions and that they were mutually exclusive. These definitions were based on a review of the literature. I do not wish to decry this work but it seems an obvious thing to do. The initial item pool for each construct was written after a grid had been constructed of behaviours and situations. This, of course, is a systematic method of ensuring that nothing in the trait or construct descriptions is left out. Finally for a sample of the items judges were asked to rate their applicability to the constructs, having been given a portrait of subjects who exemplified the traits. In addition they estimated the endorsement rate for each item by these prototypical subjects. All this is fully described by Jackson (1970).

This method, which can be summarised as careful definition and subjecting the items to the judgement of experts before item trials is a sound and sensible approach to the problem of obtaining the best possible item content. The only problem is that it requires considerable resources to obtain a good sample of judges.

A second approach makes use of what might be called the natural knowledge of personality which is entailed in the language of a culture. Buss and Craik (1983) utilised this approach. Having isolated a number of traits which they wished to measure they asked a large sample of subjects to define these traits in terms of behaviours. A further sample then rated the prototypicality of these behaviours for the traits. Support for this notion that psychological knowledge is encoded into the language comes from the fact that in this study there was little difference in the judgements of prototypicality between experts in personality and lay judges.

This approach seems as likely as any to result in trait-relevant items although there are two difficulties with it. The first is that it can only be applied to traits that are generally recognised in the culture. Abnormal behaviour or traits that have no name (if this is a logical possibility, but see the discussion of Cattell's 16PF test, in Section IV of this handbook) are not suited to this method of item writing. The second problem concerns the samples of expert and non-expert judges. These are not easy to obtain without considerable resources, a difficulty which is also relevant to the work of Jackson.

Angleitner *et al.* (1986) point out, however, that the majority of personality questionnaires were not constructed on this rational basis. They argue that three strategies are used, often together. One strategy is to construct new items without indicating their rationale. They argue that this is essentially the method used by Cattell in the construction of the 16PF test (fully discussed in Section IV; I shall not examine this question at length here, except to say that the items were written having regard to the L factors that had been isolated by analysis of ratings).

While it is true that Cattell never made explicit how each item related to the factors, one has to be wary of such explication. To take Jackson's work on the PRF as an example, although a grid was drawn up of situations and behaviours it is still a subjective judgement that an item relates to these. Test constructors, such as Cattell, simply do not externalise these operations.

The second strategy, according to Angleitner *et al.* (1986) is to ask experts to supply what are regarded as typical trait manifestations. Again I cannot see how this differs much from the procedures of Jackson (1970) who carefully reviewed the literature – presumably the descriptions of experts.

The third strategy is to copy items from other questionnaires. Goldberg (1971) has shown that among American personality inventories there is considerable copying with items surviving from the turn of the century right up to modern times and even being revived in translated guise. Angleitner *et al.* (1986) conclude that item content is selected idiosyncratically with the result that it is difficult to replicate the process. More succinctly item writing may be seen as an art rather than a science.

I largely agree with these conclusions of Angleitner, although I am less impressed by the procedures which they regard as reproducible. Thus the fact that judges agree that acts are prototypical of traits only externalises what the individual test constructor does implicitly and ensures that these judgements are not idiosyncratic. However, it is by no means obvious that such agreement is the best way to construct items. I would much prefer to trust the judgement of an insightful person than a madman and I do not believe that all individuals are equally good at item writing, without very good evidence that this is so. Such evidence would not include results that showed naive item writers could generate successful items (Jackson, 1975). It could well be that good item writers were rare.

There is one further method of generating trait-relevant items which I have used, for example in the construction of my obsessionality questionnaire, Ai3Q (Kline, 1971a). For this test items were generated from descriptions of the obsessional or anal character (Freud, 1908) in the literature. These descriptions were written down and the phrases or sentences were converted into items with the minimum possible change. With this method it was difficult to argue that the items did not reflect the trait as it was described.

The nature of items

Angleitner *et al.* (1986) carried out systematic investigations of the content of items in some well known personality questionnaires. These authors classified content in a number of ways:

1. description of reactions which could be overt, covert or bodily reactions;
2. trait attributions which might be unmodified or modified by situational constraints;
3. wishes and interests;
4. biographical facts;
5. attitudes and beliefs;
6. reactions of other persons;
7. bizarre items.

These questionnaires were given to a large number of judges so that the items might be classified as objectively as possible. The vast majority of items were judged to be direct reactions but as might be expected the kinds of items used varied with the constructs being measured and to some extent with method of scale construction. Thus the MMPI which was constructed, as has been discussed, by the method of criterion-keying, contained more heterogeneous items than the other tests.

Despite the huge research effort that was put into this work, some of the conclusions of Angleitner *et al.* (1986) are banal. They argue that the writing and selection of items should be preceded by reflection about the trait construct and about the characteristics of relevant items. It would be hard to go against this point. They have four other conclusions.

1. Researchers should have a strong rationale for measuring one trait rather than another.
2. Items should not be borrowed from other questionnaires but should be based on an explicit definition of the trait construct which should discriminate it clearly from other constructs and which should include behaviour, wishes and interests relevant to the trait.
3. To avoid idiosyncratic scales items should be generated by a sizeable sample of people and the selection of items should be based upon agreements of judges as to their relevance.
4. The item set should embrace as wide a variety of situations and contexts as possible.

These conclusions seem sensible although it is not always easy to obtain samples for item writing and judgements. In Great Britain, at least, I would not be confident that student samples, as used by Angleitner *et al.* (1986) would take the work seriously. Furthermore, despite all the rules of item writing that might be drawn up, I still believe, in the psychometric tradition, that there are large individual differences in the ability to write good items. For this reason I prefer items to be generated by one good item writer although scrutiny by judges is probably useful.

Content can be classified in a variety of ways very different from categories such as actions, attitudes and wishes. For example, Angleitner *et al.* (1986) report on studies of the surface characteristics of questionnaire items which they carried out. They found that items were frequently neither short, as is generally recommended, nor simple, in that there were negations and more than one clause. However I shall not comment further on this aspect of their research which seems more concerned with item form than content.

These authors report their empirical studies of these items, classified and rated for comprehensibility, ambiguity, self-reference and evaluation (whether the response invokes standards and norms). More than half the items were rated as not immediately comprehensible, more than 80 per cent in the 16PF form B, and substantial numbers were evaluative, thus increasing the likelihood of social desirability distorting responses; and around half were abstract.

It is obvious that these characteristics are likely to lead to error. Ambiguity means that different subjects may be responding to different aspects of the item; difficulty of comprehension means that differences in verbal ability and intelligence will confound the results. Abstract and non-self-referent items are also likely to increase error and subject variability.

Relation of item characteristics to item stability and validity

Perhaps the most interesting part of this detailed investigation of personality items was the study of the relationship between all these variables to item stability and item validity as measured by the item total correlation. The average correlations between the item characteristics and both stability and validity were about .3 and the multiple correlations were about .5. This means that responses to items can be predicted by these formal characteristics of items. This being the case it is important to stress that items should be comprehensible, brief and unambiguous. The content of the item, and from the personality tester's point of view, the unimportant content of the item, does affect item responses.

Conclusions from the work of Angleitner et al. (1986)

This work shows without doubt that the wording of items, no matter what their form, their reference, their ambiguity, their comprehensibility and their length differ considerably among all the best-known personality questionnaires and that these variables together determine significantly the stability and the internal validity of items. Furthermore, their studies show that most of these items bear little more than a subjective relationship to the constructs or factors which they were trying to measure.

GOOD PERSONALITY QUESTIONNAIRE ITEMS

I shall now discuss how good personality items may be constructed. I do this not simply so that readers can construct good tests of their own but, perhaps more important, in order that readers can judge the probable efficiency and quality of a personality test which is new to them.

These recommendations are set out in the context of the problems with personality test items, the different item types, the empirical research of Angleitner *et al.* (1986) and my experience, over the years, of attempting to construct a variety of personality tests.

These guidelines, in some cases, may appear obvious, yet inspection of large numbers of tests shows that this is not the case.

1. Reduce the insight which subjects may have into the items If subjects believe that an item measures a particular trait, then the response may well reflect their view of their status on the trait rather than their actual status. Thus the validity of the item will be confounded if a subject's self-view is false. As Guilford (1959) argues an ideal for personality tests is to tap traits unknown to the subjects, with items which she or he does know. This point is well supported by the findings of Angleitner *et al.* (1986) concerning the importance of self-reference of items.

2. Items should be clear and unambiguous This is so obvious as to be apparently pointless. However as we have seen above, many items are not unambiguous and such ambiguity affects the reliability of items.

3. The items should refer to specific rather than general behaviour
An item such as 'Do you enjoy sport?' is far too general. The term 'sport' is vague, as is 'enjoy'. It is far better to be quite specific if this is the behaviour that we want to tap and ask a number of absolutely specific items. For example: 'Do you regularly play a game?' or 'Do you regularly watch horse-racing on the course?' are so specific that only deliberate falsification or real change could lead to poor replicability. Effectively this is a method of reducing ambiguity.

4. Each item must ask only one question or make one statement This point is best illustrated by example: 'Dogs and children should be banned from certain parts of parks.' This item is hopeless. Some people will think that dogs only should be banned and others that children are the nuisance. Both of these will answer 'No' although they are clearly different from those who want neither of them banned. Similarly an item designed to tap racism that mentioned Blacks and other races would be equally flawed.

5. Avoid, as far as possible, terms of frequency This point was discussed by Angleitner *et al.* (1986) and I agree with Buss and Craik (1983) that it is better to make items reflect specific acts. An example will clarify this point. Take the item 'Do you dream a lot?' The problem turns on the meaning of 'a lot'. Some subjects might feel that dreaming once a week constitutes the positive response. Another, knowing that research indicates that we dream four or five times a night, might think that his dream rate of twice a week constitutes a negative answer. Such an item is thus totally misleading. However it can easily be improved by making it specific: 'Do you dream twice a week or more?'

I shall take one more example. 'Do you sometimes feel miserable for no obvious reason?' Here the difficulty lies in the meaning of 'sometimes'. Since it actually means 'more than once' truthful subjects are bound to put 'Yes'. However since people do vary in the frequency of experiencing causeless misery this is potentially a good item. Again a change to the more specific would improve it: 'Have you felt miserable for no obvious reason within the last two weeks?'

It is interesting to note that Werner and Pervin (1986) who studied the items in six well known personality inventories found that approximately 40 per cent of the items contained frequency terms.

6. Avoid terms of feelings, as far as is possible To avoid such subjective terms, where this is possible without ridiculous contortions of sense, is an excellent aid in reducing ambiguity. Again, some examples will illustrate this point. As was the case with my previous example of enjoying sport, the aim is to make the item behavioural. There 'enjoy' was replaced by 'play'. A subject either plays or he does not. Enjoy is a far different case. A highly educated, pedantic and verbally articulate subject may well long ponder the meaning of 'enjoy'. She likes it, yes, but enjoy is going a bit far . . . .

The same objection might be launched at the use of the term 'miserable'. However a behavioural translation is absurd other than to an experimental psychologist: 'Do tears spring to your eyes and your lips quiver for no obvious reason?'

Thus where feelings can be replaced by more precise behaviour then it is probably best to do so. Otherwise the items should be tried out and if there is too much ambiguity in the items the item analyses and factor analyses should weed them out. Again it is interesting to note that Werner and Pervin (1986) found that around 25 per cent of items referred to feelings in their study of personality items.

7. Write items that are pertinent for the designated subjects of the test and which provoke powerful responses   Some examples will make this point.

'Do you like potatoes?'   In Great Britain where potatoes are a staple diet, this item will provoke few strong responses. Any that there are will simply reflect particular food fads. It would be most unlikely to be a successful item.

'Do you enjoy watching eels?'   This item is again useless. Most people are completely uninterested except, possibly, a few anglers or biologists. It is also somewhat bizarre, a characteristic of test items which can alienate subjects and thus render responses suspect because subjects no longer take the test seriously.

'Do you let your dog lick your face?'   This is an item which was tried out in the development of my obsessional test, Ai3Q (Kline, 1971a). As should be obvious this item was intended to tap cleanliness since it was argued that those without dogs would obviously respond in the negative and that hygiene was often a reason for not keeping pets. Although items which provoke strong responses are to be desired this item turned out to be far too powerful. Some individuals, on reaching this item in the test, refused to continue further, saying that the whole thing was disgusting. One subject claimed that he had never been so insulted, and that the act was filthy and obscene. This item failed the item analysis.

'Are your efforts usually in vain?'   This is an item which I used in a test of oral pessimism, OPQ (Kline and Storey, 1980). In discussion with subjects,

while the test was under development, some said it was exactly what they felt but they had never articulated it before, while others said that they had never felt it. Thus this item seemed to invoke the strong responses that are important in the construction of good tests.

8. Ensure that the instructions insist that subjects give the first answer that comes to mind and do not mull over the meanings of the items. As many of the examples in the previous sections have shown, much of the ambiguity of items stems from the ultimate imprecision of language other than mathematics. An item such as 'Do you approve of fox-hunting?' provokes in most people an instantaneous response. It is these first, as it were uncensored, responses that are of interest to the personality tester. However if subjects do not answer immediately then problems arise. What is meant by 'approve'? It depends upon how the fox is hunted and where. If it is in an area where they are vermin perhaps it is not so bad, provided that they are rapidly dispatched when they are caught. With too much time items become difficult to answer, and considerable unreliability is introduced into the test.

The item 'Do you have vivid dreams?' is a further illustration of the difficulty of answering questionnaire items if too long a time is spent over them. How vivid must a dream be to call it vivid? To me my dreams are vivid but I don't know how vivid are the dreams of other people. In any case I have some vivid dreams but some are simply dull and boring. 'Uncertain' is the likely response to this item and to many others, if time is allowed.

Even a simple item mentioning friends, for example, as in many extra-version scales, can cause difficulty. Thus if required to say whether one has many friends or not there is an immediate gut response. However deliberation, as usual, yields all kinds of difficulties. What is the meaning of 'many' as applied to friends (as distinct from microbes)? What is a friend? Is X a friend or an acquaintance? I know her well but I can't depend on her. There is no end to these possibilities and it is conscientious subjects who run into these difficulties.

It is obvious from these examples that it is important to require subjects to answer questionnaire items as quickly as possible. However it is one thing to put the instruction at the top of the test. It is another that subjects comply. Inevitably some do not and in a study of obsessionality, carried out in the validation of Ai3Q (Kline, 1971a), there was a particularly clear instance of this problem. One item asked whether subjects made up their minds quickly and stuck to their decisions. However on several questionnaires this item showed evidence of several changed answers although it was eventually endorsed 'Yes'.

Alice Heim (1975) has objected to personality and interest test items on the grounds that they are so simplistic that they insult subjects' intelligence and, in many cases, are essentially meaningless, on careful analysis. This last example where the way in which the item was completed contradicted the meaning of the test item illustrates the point. To put it crudely how could such items measure anything?

Powerful though this objection appears it is answered empirically. In Chapters 9 and 10 of this handbook I described the statistical procedures used in test construction. These ensure that a test is produced which is homogeneous and reliable, and measures some variable. Studies of the validity of the test show what this variable is, as was described in Chapter 2. Hence a test that meets the normal psychometric criteria of validity and reliability cannot be worthless and objections to the items on rational grounds cannot be sustained.

Conclusions

The most important aspects of writing good items have now been discussed. In my experience these have proved useful in writing items that, at least, loaded on factors. However, there are still severe difficulties with items, as was described earlier in this chapter, which we have not yet scrutinised and it is to these which we now turn.

REDUCING THE EFFECTS OF RESPONSE SETS

Response sets can destroy the validity of personality tests. In the following section I shall discuss how the effects of response sets can be diminished, if not eliminated, by careful item writing.

1. Acquiescence

Response sets were defined by Cronbach (1946) as stylistic consistencies arising from the form of response which was required by items in personality tests. In the opening section of this chapter on the problems of personality tests, I singled out as the two most pervasive response sets social desirability and acquiescence. This latter, the tendency to agree with items regardless of content, is obviously a problem that must be dealt with.

The use of balanced scales

Messick (1962) argued that balanced scales minimised the influence of acquiescence on test scores, a balanced scale being one in which the number of items keyed 'Yes' and 'No' is approximately equal.

However it should be noted that balanced scales do not in fact eliminate the influence of acquiescence. What happens is that the acquiescent individual is not confused with the high scorer on the test, as Knowles (1963) has argued. In research designs where high scorers are compared with others balanced scales are satisfactory. However, in theory, it is possible that the positive items on the scale are answered, influenced by acquiescence, so that scores are still inaccurate. Furthermore acquiescent high scorers on such scales may also be missed.

The answer to these objections to balanced scales lies in the empirical study of the variables measured by them. If they are shown to be valid these objections come to naught.

There is a further point which should be remembered. Balanced scales are only successful if equally meaningful, unambiguous and compelling items can be written, keyed negatively. If the negative items are inferior in quality (judged against the criteria which were discussed above) the scales will be made far worse. This point may sound strange to those who have never attempted to write test items. However, in my experience both as an item writer and a teacher of item writing, negatively keyed items are more difficult to write. Some examples will clarify the reasons for this difficulty.

a. 'Do you enjoy parties?' This is a positively keyed item to measure extraversion. Its reversed form, in a balanced scale, would be 'Do you dislike parties?'. In this instance there is no problem with idiom or sense. It is quite usual to talk of disliking and enjoying parties. Furthermore, and this is of greater importance, the high extravert enjoys parties and the intravert dislikes them. The item polarity, therefore, makes psychological sense. Often, however, this is not the case and the reversed item is not satisfactory.

b. My next example is from my test of obsessional traits, Ai3Q (Kline, 1971a). This item failed because the reversed item did not tap the trait. The obsessional delights in statistic. The reversed item, therefore, was: 'Are you one of those people who find tables of statistics and figures a complete bore?' Needless to say, this item was a complete failure. Reflection shows that it is possible to answer this item 'No' without necessarily really enjoying them, which is the obsessional trait. In more general terms, reversing items may fail, especially where the item refers to some extreme of behaviour, because underlying most items is some continuum of behaviour. Reversing items implies, often, a dichotomy of response, so that where the relevant responses are dichotomous, item reversal is possible. Some further examples will clarify this point.

c. An authoritarian item is a useful example: 'Do you like giving orders?' The reversed item will not be successful for it is possible not to dislike giving orders without exhibiting the authoritarian trait of actually enjoying them. There is a middle category of indifference. It is not dichotomous as was the enjoyment and hatred of parties which characterises the extravert and the intravert.

d. 'Schools greatly over-emphasise neatness.' This item was supposed to tap the obsessional trait of orderliness. It was argued that the obsessional character would consider that neatness was so important that it could not be over-emphasised. In this case the negative response truly taps the trait involved. Although from the viewpoint of item reversal this is a good item, it must be pointed out that it has a fatal flaw, namely that it could be the case that schools so devalue neatness that the statement that they over-emphasise it is factually untrue, regardless of the value, virtually, that one might give to the trait.

These examples illustrate two most important points in writing negatively keyed items. They work well where the negative response is the relevant behaviour or where there is a clear dichotomy in the responses without a somewhat uncertain middle ground.

Ambiguity and acquiescence

Guilford (1959) has argued that acquiescence is far more likely to occur where the items are vague, ambiguous and general. We have mentioned, in the list of desirable characteristics of items, the need for items which refer to specific behaviours. This is important in the elimination of acquiescence. I shall take an example which I used previously in my book on test construction (Kline, 1986) because it illustrates, better than any other I can think of, the folly of items which are too general, and not only for eliciting acquiescence.

The item 'Do you play a musical instrument from music?' illustrates the influence of unambiguity on acquiescence. If a subject did not do so he or she would have to be remarkably acquiescent to respond positively to it. Indeed I do not believe that acquiescence could affect this result.

The item, on the other hand, 'Do you enjoy music?' is precisely the opposite. The term 'enjoy', applied to music, is so vague that acquiescence is highly likely to be a factor in endorsing this item positively. Readers must not think that the use of the term 'enjoy' is necessarily bad. In our previous example it was used with reference to parties and there it is satisfactory because its meaning is clear.

It is worth considering in a little more detail exactly what might be embraced by the phrase 'enjoy music'. It includes the feelings of great composers when listening to, playing, remembering, writing or simply thinking about music. It also must include those people who enjoy Musak while sipping a pre-flight cocktail at Heathrow. Similarly there are so many kinds of music, that a genuine claim to enjoy it can vary, behaviourally, from singing counter-tenor in Venetian polyphony, to listening to Mantovani while eating milk chocolate. This is not cultural snobbery, asserting that one is better than the other, it is simply that they are different. Any item in which such different behaviour is encapsulated in the same response is bad.

As can be seen, the influence of acquiescence can be reduced although it is virtually impossible to eliminate it entirely. Even with clear items and balanced scales acquiescence may distort the variance. For these reasons it is useful to check the extent of the influence of acquiescence on item responses. Factor analysis can be useful for this purpose.

2. The response set of social desirability

As has been stated earlier in this chapter, Edwards (1957) demonstrated that there was a strong social desirability effect with the items in the MMPI in that there was a correlation between the endorsement rate of each item and its social desirability as rated by judges. Edwards claimed, on this evidence, that social desirability must be a determinant of response to items and should be eliminated. Although it is probably a vain hope entirely to obviate the effects of this response set, there are methods of reducing them and these will be discussed below.

In the Edwards Personal Preference Schedule, the EPPS (Edwards, 1959) Edwards developed pairs of forced-choice items of matched social desirability. Thus, choice could not be dependent on social desirability. However there are a number of objections to this technique which must be discussed.

First, as Edwards (1957) admits it is no easy matter to write items that are matched in terms of item content and social desirability. Indeed as was argued by Kline (1979) there is little evidence that the EPPS measures the variables it intends to measure. It resembles, rather, a clever exercise in test construction.

Second, as was mentioned in the introductory section of this chapter, small differences in social desirability between items become magnified when presented in the forced-choice format, thus nullifying the point of using this item format (Corah *et al.*, 1958; Edwards, Wright and Lunneborg, 1959).

Third, the method of having judges rate statements for social desirability makes the assumption (which is a priori unlikely) that social desirability is unidimensional. Thus what would seem to be necessary would be a multidimensional scaling of social desirability among items and a rating of items for the different dimensions. Related to this is the point raised by Messick (1962), namely that there are considerable individual differences in social desirability. What is socially desirable to readers of the *Telegraph* is likely to be negative for those who favour the *Guardian*, to take somewhat extreme groups.

For all these reasons the forced-choice matching item method is not recommended as a method of reducing social desirability.

There are, however, a number of simple and obvious devices which can reduce social desirability in tests but which are still ignored even by modern test constructors.

Despite the difficulties over the dimensionality of social desirability some items will be bound to be thus categorised for they are concerned with human characteristics which many individuals would prefer to deny. I shall give first some examples which are so obvious as to appear ludicrous:

I am a bad loser.
I have a good sense of humour.
I will cheat, if necessary.
I am a sexual pervert.
I am basically dishonest.
I am mean.
I am trustworthy.
I am vicious.

I am certain that if these were used as items they would be worthless because so few individuals would endorse the undesirable response. Of course, as far as I know, none of these have been used as items in a test. However I shall quote some items from a new test which would appear to suffer from similar problems:

I get anxious when I have to work to tight deadlines.
I feel a little nervous when I am asked to take responsibility.
I have a reputation for being thick skinned.

Since this is a test which is specifically designed for occupational selection this problem of social desirability would appear to be particularly salient.

In brief it is possible to avoid items which are obviously socially desirable or undesirable, simply by thinking carefully before writing the item. However, although this eliminates a certain amount of social desirability this is no guarantee. If it were that easy to eliminate there would be no problem.

Furthermore, on occasions it may be necessary to measure traits that are in fact socially undesirable. Thus anxiety, tough-mindedness and, in some cases, obsessionality, have definite undesirable aspects. To eliminate socially undesirable items would, with these variables, render measurement impossible, and these are some of the best-established personality factors as was discussed at the beginning of this chapter (and see also Chapter 25 of this handbook).

To attempt to overcome this problem a more indirect approach to item writing has to be adopted. Some examples are set out below.

1. As one of our bad items above we had: I am mean. However parsimony is one aspect of the obsessional character and it would be a serious defect in personality questionnaires if we were to conclude that such a trait could not be measured. However when I was developing Ai3Q (Kline, 1971a), a measure of obsessional personality, I argued that a mean person might consider that old saws and proverbs about thrift were sensible whereas the generous would hold opposite opinions. On this hypothesis the following yes–no item was tried out: 'Waste not want not: every child should have this imprinted on his mind.' To endorse either response to this item would seem to have little social desirability and the positive response would seem to reflect a certain parsimony. In fact this item worked in all the item analyses although it has to be said it could be that it was not the parsimonious aspect of the item to which the obsessional responded but the coercive aspect, controlling children.

2. In the description of the anal character the trait of vindictiveness was mentioned by a number of writers. Now it is obvious that an item 'Are you vindictive?' is tainted by social desirability. However in an attempt to measure this trait, the following argument was used: in Freudian theory undesirable traits are projected onto others, hence the vindictive person who employs this defence is likely to judge them to be vindictive. This resulted in the item: 'Vindictive savagery is the motivation of most revolutionaries.' I hoped in constructing this item that so few subjects would have actually met revolutionaries that their opinions would reflect defences rather than facts. Notice that I am not concerned whether revolutionaries are or are not revolutionary. This item passed all item analyses and factor analyses and appears to tap the trait, as was intended.

This item exemplifies the indirect approach which is required for testing socially undesirable aspects of personality. Using projection is a method which, at least, provides items that are worth trying out. Nevertheless, if projection is used, it is necessary to be careful not to choose examples on which people hold opinions determined by factors other than projection. Thus if an item concerned the laziness of workers, it would be unlikely to work because for political reasons some people would endorse the item while others denied it and yet others would be convinced (both ways) by their personal experiences. Of course such an item, to which the responses are multi-determined, could never pass an item analysis or factor analysis.

Use of a lie scale to combat social desirability

One approach to dealing with social desirability is to insert a special set of items – the lie scale – to catch out those putting the socially desirable response. These items refer to small and trivial peccadillos which almost everybody has at some time committed. Although it is possible that an individual will genuinely have never offended in perhaps one of these instances the likelihood of her or his having failed to transgress in two or more becomes increasingly small. Thus these scales usually have a cut-off point: thus far and no further. The scores on the personality scales of those beyond this threshold score are simply discounted. Thus the use of these social desirability scales does not obviate the problem but rather eliminates those subjects who thus distort their responses.

Social desirability is a response set which appears at its strongest for obvious reasons in applied psychology, especially selection. In research, where responses are anonymous and do not matter to the subjects, it is perhaps less important and Eysenck and Eysenck (1976) argue that in such a setting the L scale is an interesting personality variable in its own right. Typical L scale items are: I have never lied; I have never kept money that I have found, however little; I am never irritable; I would never claim credit for something I had not done; I would never try to cheat the customs; and so on.

Conclusions concerning social desirability

As may be seen from this discussion social desirability is a response tendency which can cause distortion of scores, particularly in selection. Nevertheless I think that many specialists in this field exaggerate its influence because if the original test construction and validation were properly carried out, as described in the relevant chapters of this handbook, its effects are necessarily small.

FINALE

I have described the essential characteristics of personality questionnaires and examined the problems of constructing items for them, both as regards form and content. In addition the main problems of distortion have been discussed.

It should be clear from this discussion that the production of a reliable personality test is not difficult, although to develop a valid test is far more so.

Chapter 16

Projective and Objective Tests of Personality

In this chapter I shall discuss two other types of personality tests, projective tests and objective tests, which attempt to overcome some of the defects of personality questionnaires, although, as shall be seen, they have considerable problems of a different nature.

As was evident from the last chapter, personality questionnaires are, inevitably, somewhat superficial, are usually transparent and thus easy to fake, and, ultimately, seem too crude to encapsulate the subtlety and the richness of personality. Projective and objective tests together overcome these difficulties and despite the objections to them from Eysenck (1957) and other academic psychologists on the grounds of unreliability and invalidity (important points, by any standards, which will be scrutinised in detail in this chapter), it would be wrong to dismiss as worthless tests which, properly used, can still be useful both in research and in practical applications.

Before defining these categories of tests I want to discuss briefly a distinction in personality tests which is often made – that between nomothetic and idiographic measures.

Nomothetic tests are concerned with the development of rules for understanding personality. They are concerned, therefore, with measuring the common traits or dimensions, on which people differ in their status. Personality questionnaires are typical nomothetic measures and factor analysis is the statistical technique best suited for the analysis of nomothetic tests. Psychometrics, as a branch of psychology, is essentially concerned with the study of individual differences and hence with nomothetic tests.

Idiographic tests are, in contradistinction to nomothetic tests, concerned with measuring what is unique and individual to a person – all those aspects of personality which are not shared with anyone else. It is these unique and individual aspects of personality which projective tests aim to measure.

With this distinction in mind it is easy to see why clinical psychologists, for example, who work with individuals and not groups, which, after all, are somewhat arbitrary, have always favoured projective tests despite the objections of academic and scientific psychologists, typified by Eysenck (1959) who described projective tests as vehicles for the riotous imagination of clinicians. Furthermore it can be seen that there could be some truth in the argument of Allport (1937) who claimed that nomothetic personality questionnaires failed to measure what was interesting about personality which was precisely what was not common to individuals.

It is in the context of these arguments that the sustained interest in projective tests and to a lesser extent in objective tests has to be seen. This is why, in the face of the statistical and other objections, psychologists have continued to work with them.

PROJECTIVE TESTS

A simplified definition of a projective test, yet one which does not do violence to the concept, is a stimulus, to which subjects have to respond, so designed that it encourages subjects to project onto it their own feelings, desires and emotions. Some discussion of these points and a few examples of typical projective test materials will clarify the nature of projective tests and allow finally a meaningful and more formal definition.

1. The meaning of projection   One of the objections raised by Eysenck (1959) to projective testing is that it lacks a coherent theory. That is there is no theoretical account as to how or why or in what conditions an individual would project anything about her or himself onto a projective test stimulus. Apropos of this point it must be made clear that the Freudian defence mechanism of projection is not necessarily involved in projective testing, although in some circumstances and with some subjects, it might occur. Freud (1911) claimed that there was a defence mechanism of projection in which subjects attributed to others aspects of themselves which were unacceptable to them, and hence repressed into the unconscious.

Projective testing has never made these claims. It asserts that subjects simply project their innermost thoughts and feelings onto the stimulus (Murstein, 1963, for example).

2. The projective stimulus   Some of the best-known and widely used projective techniques, for example, the Rorschach (Rorschach, 1921) and the Thematic Apperception Test (Murray, 1938), use ambiguous visual stimuli which subjects have to describe. The Rorschach, a test known to non-psychologists and symbolising to many people psychological assessment, consists of symmetrical inkblots, the TAT, ambiguous human figures.

The essence here is ambiguity. Many projective tests, but not all, use ambiguous stimuli on the ground that it is ambiguity which causes subjects to project. Thus if a life size, accurate picture of an apple were to be shown, at least to Western subjects, there would be little projection. All except psychotics and subjects wishing to sabotage the test would be bound – stimulus bound – to say that it was an apple and most would not be able to add much to this.

However, so the projective argument goes, asked to describe a stimulus with little form or obvious content, subjects' descriptions must reflect something about themselves. It is interesting to note, in this respect, that if subjects describe any of the Rorschach inkblots as an inkblot this is regarded as a defensive response.

From these arguments it is obvious why many projective test constructors have opted for ambiguous stimuli: responses not being stimulus bound must have arisen from something within the subjects.

3. Identification Many projective test workers assume that subjects will identify with the individual portrayed in the picture. Thus Murray (1938) assumed that subjects would identify with what he referred to as the hero in the TAT. For this reason, to aid identification, there are often different cards for males and females.

Some projective testers consider that it is easier, especially for children, to identify with animals, although some animal figure projective tests are used with adults (e.g. Blum's Blacky Pictures, Blum, 1949). Bellak (Bellak *et al.*, 1974) with the Children's Apperception Test (CAT) offers two versions, one with human, the other with animal figures. Such identification with the hero, it is hoped, will aid projection.

4. Projective test stimuli (non-visual) The reason that it is not correct to define projective tests as ambiguous stimuli to which subjects have to respond is that even if this fits the best-known projective tests there are numerous other projective tests which are not of this type and which the definition fails to include.

Types of test

Here I shall mention some of the types of test although, as was the case with the other chapters in this section of the handbook, I shall leave description and comment on particular projective tests until Chapter 26.

1. Sentence completion Here, as the name suggests, subjects are required to complete sentences. How they complete them is held to indicate something about their idiodynamics. Thus a person who completes all mothers are . . . by 'evil' is presumably different from one who writes 'long-suffering'.

Goldberg (1965), surveying sentence completion methods, argues that it is by no means obvious how sentence completion involves projection, although much depends upon the stem of the sentence. Presumably, in the example above, differences in response should reflect something about views of mother which, to some psychologists, would be regarded as important data relevant to personality.

It should be noted that sentence completion is not unlike what might be considered to be the earliest form of projective test – word association – used by Jung (1910) to indicate complexes or unconscious conflicts and by Kent and Rosanoff (1910). Association has been used in a recent test, devised to assess vocational interests rather than personality, the Brook Reaction Test (Heim and Watts, 1966).

2. Free drawing   Some projective tests require subjects to draw certain objects. These drawings are then interpreted. The best known of such tests is the House Tree Person Test (Buck, 1970), in which subjects are required to draw these three things and are asked questions about them.

3. Solid objects   A number of projective techniques have utilised solid objects – of which the best known are those of Lowenfeld who has used dolls and sand and other miniature objects, people and trees, for example. As Bowyer (1970) has pointed out such doll play should be considered as a means of observing certain aspects of a child's personality rather than a test. Lowenfeld's (1954) Mosaic Test consists of wooden shapes which have to be made into an object, and various objective and subjective scores can be obtained from it.

4. Auditory projective tests   A number of testers have produced auditory projective tests of which a typical one is the Sound Apperception Test (Bean, 1965). Here sounds have to be interpreted by the subject.

This covers most of the types of material used in projective tests. It is not intended to be a full list of tests and I have not discussed the validity and reliability of most of them because in general there is a dearth of research to report and generally, where there is good research it is not favourable to any kind of projective test let alone the more outlandish varieties in (3) and (4). The best projective tests will be described and evaluated in Section IV of this handbook. The list here is to enable us to see what projective tests are like, so that a discussion of their advantages and disadvantages *vis-à-vis* personality inventories will be meaningful.

Problems with projective tests

The problems with projective tests have been examined in considerable detail by Vernon (1963) so that I shall summarise here his main conclusions about which there is little disagreement. Eysenck (1959) has also subjected projective tests to similar powerful criticisms which will also be discussed.

1. Poor reliability   It is generally the case that if projective test protocols are scored blind, i.e. the scorer has no knowledge of who completed them, there is poor inter-scorer reliability concerning interpretations, even in some cases extending to the sex of the subject.

2. Low validity   Most projective techniques have poor evidence in support of their validity. Eysenck (1959) argued that the more rigorous the study the lower the validity coefficient. Certainly the majority of test manuals cite only clinical evidence in support of their claims. This, of course, will not do. Hypotheses must be refuted to claim scientific support.

3. Contextual influences on scores   Vernon (1963) cites studies to show that projective test scores are influenced by a number of contextual factors. For example the race of the tester, the sex of the tester, the manner of administering the test, whether relaxed or severe, the view of the subject as to what the test measures, have all been shown to affect protocols.

This is hardly surprising but it runs somewhat counter to the projective testers' claim to be measuring the idiodynamics of the subjects, the deepest layers of the personality. If projective tests do measure these things their scores are certainly distorted by the contextual factors which we have discussed.

4. Poor rationale for scoring system   It has already been mentioned that Eysenck (1959) has argued that there is a poor rationale for the scoring system of many projective tests. As he writes, it is curious that a test such as the Rorschach, if the manuals are examined, appears to be able to measure virtually any aspect of the subject – temperament, motivation, defences, abilities and attitudes. This is very different from the measures used in most sciences which are strictly univariate, the aim of the factored psychometric test, as we have seen in Chapter 3 of this handbook.

In addition there are two further problems with the scoring of projective tests. These concern the implicit theories behind such scoring. In some tests, for example the Blacky Pictures (Blum, 1949) and the PN Test (Corman, 1969) there is a definite psychoanalytic, psychosexual, developmental theory underlying the choice of stimulus and the interpretation and scoring of the responses. However, obviously, if this theory is not considered viable, the test cannot be used. Similarly, but less explicitly, psychoanalytic ideas underlie many other projective tests, especially those for children. Thus the CAT (Bellak *et al.*, 1974) shows pictures with clear psychoanalytic connotations: two figures in bed, and a monkey in danger of losing its tail, oedipal and castration pictures.

The Thematic Apperception Test, on the other hand, is linked to Murray's theory of personality, measuring the needs and presses in the environment (Murray, 1938). Although this test can be scored in a more eclectic fashion, as Murstein (1963) illustrates, it must be interpreted, as must all projective tests, on the basis of some theory. This then raises the question, where the theory is not explicit, as to what theory it is.

Generally in interpreting most projective tests, where there is no explicit theory, implicit is a psychodynamic theory of some kind with notions of depth of personality and unconscious drives and feelings. In this sense the whole projective testing approach assumes a psychoanalytic view of personality. Clearly, for opponents of psychodynamic theory, projective tests are anathema. However, even for those who espouse this theoretical approach, the lack of clear evidence for validity and reliability is alarming.

Reasons for the continued use of projective tests

It may be asked, therefore, in the light of all these criticisms of projective tests, why they continue to be used. Eysenck (1957) by implication at least would attribute their continued use by clinicians to their scientific naivety. While, in some cases, this may be correct, there are other good reasons why, despite these admitted problems, some psychologists are prepared to countenance their use, although results should be treated with considerable caution and not accepted as substantive findings without further and different supporting evidence.

1. They are unique sources of data   Most projective tests, especially from the well known tests such as the Rorschach and TAT, provide data of a quality different from that which can be obtained by any other means. Thus in the study of personality we might gather data from observations at home or at work, personality test inventories, as discussed in the previous chapter, interviews or the application of special techniques such as repertory grids (see Chapter 18). All these, however, yield information and data quite different from that of projective tests, the responses to strange and ambiguous stimuli, which, in all probability, subjects find completely novel, never having encountered anything resembling them.

Thus data which are unique and cannot be gathered in any other way, are valuable in principle: it would be senseless to abandon them. All this suggests, of course, that some more objective scoring methods and more careful interpretation based upon them could be highly useful.

2. Some results from projective tests suggest that they are powerful techniques   One of the essentials of any good measurement technique is that, given adequate training, anybody can use it. This is certainly one of the clear advantages of personality inventories. The fact that there is poor inter-scorer reliability for projective tests shows that is not the case with these tests. However scrutiny of some of the research carried out with the Rorschach and the TAT, tests which have been used in many thousands of research projects, indicates that in the hands of highly skilled practitioners (whatever skilled may mean) some insightful and impressive findings have been made, which, furthermore, could not have arisen from any other test.

One outstanding example of this genre, which convinces me that it would be madness to consign projective testing to the category of phlogiston or ley lines is the work of Carstairs (1957). He studied a community of the Rajput in India and investigated their belief systems, attitudes and personality using a variety of techniques including the Rorschach. The way in which the Rorschach protocols were incorporated into the delineation of the psychology of this community was clear evidence of the value of projective testing – in the right hands.

3. The richness of projective test data This point might, perhaps, have been included in the first argument on behalf of projective tests. However, and this is undoubtedly what keeps the projective test user convinced of the value of the tests despite the academic evidence, they yield rich and fascinating data which appear insightful and important in understanding personality. In comparison with this, personality inventory items seem colourless and crude. It is surprising, on simple intuitive grounds, that inventories are superior to projective tests.

4. The success of some objective scoring methods A number of objective scoring schemes have been attempted for the Rorschach and the TAT tests especially. Murstein (1963) describes some of these for the TAT and Holtzman (Holtzman *et al.*, 1968) has produced a psychometrically improved version of the Rorschach Test. Holley (e.g. 1973), in a number of studies, has used a specially scored Rorschach together with a multivariate analysis of the data with some considerable success and all this suggests that new, objective scoring for projective tests coupled with powerful statistical analysis of the data could be valuable in personality assessment.

Conclusions

From this discussion some simple conclusions may be drawn. Rigorous investigation of projective tests shows that they can offer little evidence of validity and that they are certainly not reliable. On the other hand, they yield rich and unique data and in some hands appear to be useful tests. Furthermore there is some evidence that objectively scored and well analysed projective test data can be powerful.

Thus if some improvements could be made to the reliability of the tests, without losing the special quality of the data, it is likely that they might become useful methods of personality assessment which could complement, not replace, personality inventories.

For all these reasons in the next section of this chapter I shall briefly describe the methods used by Holley and his colleagues and show how they are applicable to projective tests in general, not just to the Rorschach, and that treated in this way projective tests have a part to play in the measurement of personality.

G analysis

G analysis has been described in considerable detail by Holley (1973) and since that date it has been extended and developed by Holley and his Scandinavian colleagues, notably Vegelius (1973). G analysis is a set of statistical techniques, based upon a statistic, the G index (Holley and Guilford, 1964), which is ideal for the discrimination of groups. The data on which G analysis works make it peculiarly suited to the objective analysis of projective tests.

In this description of G analysis I shall restrict myself, in the main, to its basic formulation as described by Holley (1973) rather than detail the elaborations of the method by Vegelius (1974) which are largely of statistical interest, extending the use of the method beyond the dichotomous variables for which it was designed. However these will be discussed where it is appropriate.

Description of G analysis

In G analysis dichotomous variables are scored and *subjects* are correlated, using the G index. This correlation matrix between subjects is then factored, an example of Q analysis, and, based upon the factor loadings, groups are formed. D estimates are then calculated which give a discrimination index between each item and membership of the groups. Thus one can see which items (in this instance aspects of the projective test responses) discriminate the groups.

This description of the basic G analysis I shall clarify with some examples from the research of the Scandinavian group and from research with the method which I have conducted with colleagues in Exeter over a number of years. I shall then discuss the advantages and undoubted problems of G analysis. First, however, it is necessary, for a proper appreciation of G analysis, to set out the formulae, which, fortunately are not complicated.

16.1 The G index

$$G = 2Pc - 1$$

Where Pc = the sum of a + d in a typical contingency table, as set out below, in Table 16.1.

Table 16.1 A typical contingency table

		Variable 1	
		+	−
Variable 2	+	a	b
	−	c	d

16.2   The D estimate

$$D = \frac{a}{a+b} - \frac{c}{c-d}$$

where a, b, c and d are the proportions in a typical contingency table as portrayed in Table 16.1.

Comments on G analysis

1. Although the G index was developed by Holley and Guilford (1964) Holley does not claim that it is his invention. A number of other statisticians have cited it under different names, for example Sandler (1948), and various generalisations have been offered of which the best known is that of Cohen (1969).

2. The G index is designed to deal with dichotomous data. From the viewpoint of the analysis of projective tests this is particularly important. It means that projective tests must be scored for dichotomous variables – usually the presence or absence of variables in the protocols. This scoring is as much part of G analysis as are the statistics which have been described.

How this dichotomous scoring is carried out will be exemplified below. It should be pointed out that such dichotomous scoring can be applied to items in personality questionnaires or interview data, for example, and can be included in the G analysis alongside the projective test variables, a technique which is exceedingly useful for identifying the factors emerging from the G analysis.

3. Unlike other indices used for correlating dichotomous variables, the G index is unaffected by item polarity (whether an item is scored 1 or 0 which is quite arbitrary) and by the evenness of the dichotomy. This is highly important where the stability of the correlations is essential, as it is in factor analysis. This resistance to item polarity makes it superior to either phi or the tetrachoric correlation.

4. Vegelius (1973), in an important paper, demonstrated that the G index belongs to a family of correlation coefficients – E coefficients – which satisfy the assumptions necessary for component analysis, which, for example, the tetrachoric coefficient fails to do. Thus the G index is suitable for factor analysis.

5. Holley (1973) showed that Q factor based upon G indices have R factor equivalents among the variables. This is an example of Burt's reciprocity principle and is important in interpreting the meaning of the factors in G analysis, as will be shown in our examples of the technique.

6. Finally it should be noted that the G index is not suited to the analysis of variables, R analysis as distinct from subjects, Q analysis, hence the importance of the reciprocity principle, mentioned above. This is because, as has been pointed out by Levy (1966), if the G index is used with variables it yields factors loading on items of a given difficulty level which are thus of little psychological interest.

Scoring the projective test protocols preparatory to G analysis

As was mentioned above an essential part of G analysis is the dichotomous scoring of the projective tests. Indeed, there is an arguable case, which will be discussed later, that it is this dichotomous scoring which is the most important part of G analysis rather than the statistics. Thus other forms of multivariate analysis, such as discriminant functions, could well be just as effective once they have been scored.

I shall illustrate the method of scoring projective tests from the House Tree Person Test, which I have used in G analysis (Hampson and Kline, 1977), although it must be stressed that the method can be applied to any projective test.

Essentially the projective test responses of each individual are subjected to a minutely detailed content analysis. Suppose subject 1 has drawn a tree with leaves, flowers and fruit together with a split trunk, right in the centre of the page and running from margin to margin. For subject 1 we set up the following variables: leaves present; fruit present; flowers present; split trunk present; centre page; full width of page. This exemplifies the scoring system and the whole protocol would be reduced to a set of variables in this manner. On all these variables subject 1 scores 1.

Let us suppose subject 2 drew a bare tree, without leaves, fruit or flowers, and with a single trunk. This tree had large roots showing at the base, and bark with a carved heart. It was also drawn right in the centre of the page and went its full width. This subject would score 0 on: leaves present; fruit present; flowers present; split trunk. He would score 1 on: large roots; centre page and full width of page. Note that for this subject 2 we have had to formulate a new variable – large roots. Subject 1 would be scored 0 on this.

In this way it is possible to score dichotomously projective test protocols from a group of subjects. As each new subject has to be scored on new variables all the previous subjects are scored 0 on these. The outcome of this process is a vast matrix of 0s and 1s. For large samples detailed scoring of this type is a daunting task.

Reliability of the objective scoring

Holley (1973) claims extremely high reliability of scoring can be achieved by this method – beyond 90 per cent agreement, a figure which was obtained by Hampson and Kline (1977). We found that where there were disagreements these were usually simple errors. Occasionally there was a genuine difference but this could always be resolved on discussion.

It may be safely asserted that this objective scoring system is highly reliable and this may well be an important contributory factor to the effectiveness of G analysis with projective tests. It certainly overcomes the problem of low reliability which has dogged the projective test from the outset.

Problems with the scoring system

There are really two problems with the scoring system which need to be taken into account. First, although it is possible to score all projective tests using this method, Hampson and Kline (1977) formed the impression that it was difficult to capture all the richness of the responses, especially to the TAT. Certainly some data were easier to score than others.

Second, with this scoring system, with a large sample, one ends up with a huge number of variables. On many of these variables – all those peculiar to one subject – all the rest of the sample score 0. Thus if all variables are put into the factor analysis there emerges a huge common factor, discriminated by these unique variables. This is, of course, psychologically meaningless, an artefact of the method and it must be removed. To do this it is necessary to remove all variables with low p values. If there are common variables with high p values, these must be retained since these are meaningful, although they may turn out to be of little interest.

All this results in an edited matrix of 0s and 1s. This is then subjected to G analysis, as has been described. Thus correlations between subjects are computed, using the G index and the resulting correlation matrix is then subjected to factor analysis, in this case Q analysis.

Problems with the factor analysis in G analysis

1. The first problem has been dealt with – the removal of non-discriminating variables which produce a general factor.

2. With Q analysis as was described in Chapter 8, it is individuals who load on the factors and thus the factors delineate groups. However what it means to say that a group is correlated with another group is not clear. This means that the status of simple structure oblique rotation is more dubious than in R analysis. For this reason I think it is likely to yield better results if orthogonal, Varimax, rotation is used. Direct Oblimin rotation could be tried but it would only be worth considering the groups delineated by it if they were different from the orthogonal case.

3. Selecting the groups Figure 16.1 sets out a typical orthogonal rotated Q factor analysis, after G analysis. The individuals enclosed by the lines appear to show clear groups.

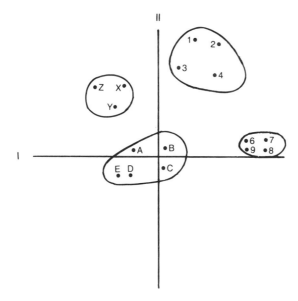

Figure 16.1 Orthogonal rotated Q factor analysis, after G analysis

However the rationale for grouping them in this way is not strong. It appears convincing and in this particular figure it probably does represent genuinely different groups. However it is to be noted that subjects Z, X and Y could have been grouped with A, E and D (all with negative loadings on factor 1) and B and C could have been included with 6, 7, 8 and 9.

Where the factor loadings are more spread out than in this example selecting the groups does become a problem. In practice G analysis is often used in an attempt to discriminate designated groups. If this is at all possible in terms of factor loadings, then this removes the problem. However, given that the grouping is to some extent arbitrary, replication is essential.

4. Discriminating the groups   D estimates are used, as set out in Formula 16.2, to compute which variables discriminate the groups. This is a highly important aspect of G analysis. Thus the factor analysis demonstrates that there are separate groups. The D estimates indicate what variables have brought this about and thus they effectively describe the nature of the groups. Thus Hampson and Kline found, in their study of young offenders, that certain House, Tree, Person variables discriminated between two groups of offenders. On looking at the interpretation of these variables in the handbook to the test (Buck, 1970) we found that one group appeared to be immature. On the other hand, some of the discriminating variables made no apparent sense.

5. Problems with replication A difficulty which regularly arises in G analysis concerns these discriminating variables. Thus to use the example with abnormal offenders again, which was beset with problems, on replicating the results with another group of offenders we obtained excellent separation of groups but the D estimates showed that this was achieved with an entirely different set of variables. In this case we were forced to conclude that the differences between the two samples were genuine, i.e. the two studies had drawn samples from different populations of criminals.

6. Conclusions I have made no attempt to hide any of the difficulties which can arise in G analysis. Nevertheless this description shows clearly how it enables projective tests to be used in the quantitative study of personality. Essentially it reveals which of the dichotomised variables discriminate groups. What is generally found and what makes the approach so interesting is that projective tests, used in this way, can discriminate where personality inventories cannot. This was shown by Holley (1973) using the Rorschach with schizophrenics and depressives and by Fallstrom and Vegelius (1976) with diabetic children, just for example. Kline (1979) contains a full discussion of this empirical evidence in favour of the method. This type of analysis and the results obtained from it strongly suggest that there is something valuable in the best projective tests.

Developments of G analysis

As was made clear at the beginning of this section, the basic G analysis has been described because this illustrates clearly, without statistical complexity, how objectively scored projective tests can be used in the discrimination of groups. However there are some developments, aimed largely at overcoming some of the difficulties which have been discussed, which extend the scope of the method. The most important of these will now be scrutinised.

Holley and Kline (1976a) developed a new form of G, G_o, for use with ordinal data. Meyer and Kline (1977) developed a method by which delegate scores (Sandler, 1958) could be used as marker variables, which helps to overcome the problem of replication, delegate scores indicating group membership. Holley and Kline (1976b) suggested the symmetrical square root method of factor analysis to align factors with markers, in yet another attempt to overcome the rotational and replicative difficulties.

None of these developments is at all radical. They all extend the basic methods but are recognisable as G analysis. However careful consideration of what G analysis does has suggested to some researchers perhaps even more efficient techniques which achieve the same end but do not actually use the G index. These will be briefly mentioned, although as yet there is little research to support the claims of their efficacy with projective tests.

WHIDD analysis (Vegelius, 1974) This is not strictly G analysis. Instead of the G index it uses the weighted H index, the initials standing for the weighted H index delegate discriminant analysis. This H index is an extension of the G index for interval scales and is an E coefficient, making it suitable for factor analysis and other analogous multivariate techniques. In this method factor analysis is not used but discriminant functions are computed between groups.

Discriminant functions This is a standard multivariate approach to the problem of attempting to discriminate between two groups on a number of variables, exactly the purpose of G analysis. Discriminant functions are closely related mathematically to component analysis. Indeed since the discriminant function is a linear combination of variables (which maximally discriminates the groups) in a sense it is a factor. Indeed to obtain the functions a principal components analysis is performed on a matrix of discrimination indices. It remains to be seen whether discriminant function analysis of objectively scored projective tests would be as effective as G analysis.

Replacing D estimates The D estimate is a highly idiosyncratic aspect of G analysis. After the groups have been defined by Q analysis, the variables which discriminate the groups might be computed by other more orthodox means.

One approach would be to use discriminant functions, as suggested above, on the groups emerging from the Q analysis. This is distinct from using discriminant functions on pre-designated groups.

A second approach is to calculate factor scores (using the reciprocity principle) for all subjects in the study and to see whether there are significant differences between the groups. This is similar to calculating the discriminant functions but these optimally weight variables for maximum discrimination. Cooper and Kline (1989) used this approach with a study of pilots and controls using percept genetic tests (described in Chapter 18 of this handbook). These seemed to be effective.

Conclusions

All these new developments need far more research using projective test data before any firm judgements can be made concerning their effectiveness. However it can be concluded that projective test data, objectively scored, as described above, and subjected to G analysis or one of its variants, can be powerful in the study of groups.

It is apparent that this method shows that projective tests are not worthless as their opponents have claimed. A large factor in the success of G analysis must reside in the reliable scoring, which removes considerable error. The statistical analyses make the most of the data, multivariate analyses being, in this situation, far more effective than simple univariate analyses.

In brief a study of G analysis indicates that it would be folly to abandon the use of projective tests.

OBJECTIVE TESTS

Cattell (e.g. 1973, 1957) in his extensive work on personality refers to three sources of data: L, Q and T data. L data, life data, refer to observations of actual behaviour; Q data are derived from questionnaires and T data refer to measurement from objective tests, defined, essentially, as tests whose purpose is hidden from subjects. It is noteworthy that Cattell regards L data as the criteria on which to base tests of all types. Thus for Cattell objective tests are the third main source of quantitative data in the field of personality. These tests, however, are far less widely used than either questionnaires or projective tests and tend to be the province of specialists.

Cattell (1957) and Cattell and Warburton (1967) define objective tests as tests whose purport is hidden from subjects, thus making deliberate distortion (but not sabotage) difficult, and whose scoring is objective. Such tests are sometimes referred to (e.g. Cronbach, 1976) as performance tests, although I shall use the Cattellian term 'objective tests' because Cattell and his colleagues have worked extensively in this field.

Acute readers may notice that, strictly according to his definition of objective tests, projective tests, objectively scored, should be regarded as objective tests. Indeed the Rorschach test, thus scored, is included in the compendium of objective tests (Cattell and Warburton, 1967). However I prefer to include objectively scored projective tests as projective tests because this is how they were thought of by their authors and the category of projective tests is well established in personality measurement.

Advantages of objective tests

The reason we are discussing objective tests in this handbook is that, if they could be shown to be valid, they have clear advantages over questionnaires and some projective tests.

1. The fact that they are impervious to guessing, because their purpose is unclear, makes them far more suited than other personality tests to use in selection and applied psychology.
2. It is also likely that most of these tests will not be subject to response sets, which distort questionnaires.
3. It is also possible that some objective tests, especially the physiological measures, may be useful in the cross-cultural study of personality, a field where questionnaires are of dubious value (Kline, 1977).

For all these reasons the development of valid objective personality tests constitutes an important aim of psychometrics although there is little evidence at present of much progress in this direction.

Types of objective tests

Cattell and Warburton (1967) in their compendium of objective tests (which I shall refer to throughout this section as the compendium) list 688 tests from which are derived more than 2300 variables and these are only a fraction of the objective tests that might be constructed. As is obvious from the definition of objective tests all that is required is some task which shows variance, which can be objectively scored, and of which subjects cannot guess the purpose.

To exemplify this problem I could ask subjects to clean their shoes, providing brushes and polish for them. The following variables might be extracted from this test.

1. Number of questions asked before beginning cleaning.
2. Time taken before beginning.
3. Time taken to complete the task.
4. Number of brush strokes used in the process.
5. Did subject remove shoes?
6. Did subject match the brush and polish?
7. Did subject use soft cloth?
8. Did subject remove laces?
9. Did subject clean the tongue of the shoes?

It is clear from these nine tests that there is a virtual infinity of objective tests which can be made and that the only limit is the ingenuity of the test constructor. However these nine tests indicate a further serious difficulty with objective tests – their validity. How do we even guess at what any of these tests may measure? This is especially difficult in the case of objective tests because if we can guess, it is likely that subjects are able to do so and, by definition, they cease to be objective.

The problem of the validity of objective tests

Both these problems ultimately are concerned with the validity of objective tests. Since these are not face valid it is essential that their validity be empirically demonstrated. No objective test should be used unless there is sound empirical evidence that it is a valid and reliable test.

Rationale of objective tests   As my nine examples indicated it is clear that there must be some rationale to the construction of objective tests. One approach possible in principle but in practice far too time consuming would be to invent objective measures and put them to the empirical test. However, as the compendium indicates, this is impossible. The vast majority of tests which are listed there have no evidence of validity. Some rationale for objective test construction, even if it were only a guideline, is a necessity. Alternatively a taxonomy of objective tests would be valuable.

Cattell and Warburton (1967) present both a taxonomy of objective tests and a set of principles for the construction of such tests and both must be discussed so that objective tests can be understood. I shall summarise these as succinctly as possible and for further details readers are referred to the compendium and to Kline (1986).

A taxonomy of objective tests

There are three sources of variation in psychological tests.

1. Test instructions. These affect how subjects view the test.
2. Test materials.
3. Scoring the responses.

Since the first two categories are not independent because the instructions refer to the test materials, these two sources of variation are collapsed into a broader category – the stimulus-instruction situation.

Stimulus-instruction situation This varies along the following parameters.

1. To react or not react. Usually reaction to the stimulus is required but this is not always so, as, for example, in tests of pain sensitivity.
2. Restricted vs. unrestricted variety of response. Completely unrestricted responses are unknown but they can be relatively free, as in the Rorschach, or restricted as in reaction time measures, to take two extremes.
3. Inventive vs. selective responses. The TAT requires inventive responses, the personality questionnaire item the selective.
4. Single vs. repetitive responses.
5. Ordered vs. unordered sequence of responses.
6. Homogeneous vs. patterned responses. Some tests require responses of the same kind, others a variety of responses.
7. Natural vs. limited responses. 'Work at your own speed' compared with 'work as fast as possible' exemplifies this parameter.
8. Concluding reaction vs. reaction to reaction. The subject either reacts to the test material or to his or her own reaction, as in evaluation or associating to it.

Cattell and Warburton (1967) add to these eight most important parameters five other dimensions of which the first three are subjective and are particularly important for objective tests.

9. Immediate meaning vs. referent meaning. In reaction time tests there is no meaning beyond the test itself. In other tests, for example where opinions are examined, there are external and symbolic referents and it is these which are involved in all the typical test distortions with problems of the subjective meaning of words and concepts.

10. Itemised vs. global presentation. Some tests consist of a single task, others of a set of items.

11. Psychological decision of the test. Some tests require cognition for their responses (e.g. a correct judgement), others judgement of feelings, and others judgement of familiarity or recognition.

12. Variation in motives for accepting the test situation.

13. Variation in freedom to end the test situation.

This taxonomy indicates the huge variety of possible objective tests – there are here 2^{13} types of stimulus-instruction situation.

However this does not complete the taxonomy for, so far, we have ignored the third source of variation in tests – scoring the response. Although the response-score parameters are not entirely independent of the parameters which have been described, they are sufficiently so for the total number of possible tests to be the product of the stimulus-instruction and response parameter. These latter are set out below.

Response-scoring parameters

1. Objective vs. self-evaluative. This is a highly important parameter which has to be properly understood before the nature of objective tests, which often resemble personality inventories, can be grasped. I shall exemplify the parameter from an actual objective test, the Critical Evaluations Test (T8 in the compendium). In this test subjects are required to state whether a particular performance, e.g. a waitress bringing six meals to a table in ten minutes, is very good, good, poor or very poor. The subject matter of the items is irrelevant, the score being the number of poor or very poor responses, i.e. the number of critical evaluations. This is entirely objective and impossible for subjects to guess. Thus although this test resembles a personality inventory it is, in fact, quite different. All objective tests are objective in terms of this first parameter.

   Finally, it should be noted that a standard personality inventory, as described in the previous chapter, could be scored on the objective pole of this parameter and it would thus become an objective test. For example, one could count all the 'Yes' or 'True' responses and all the 'False' responses.

2. Overt behaviour vs. physiological response. Overt behaviour involves the total organism whereas physiological responses involve part, as exemplified in pupil dilation, blushing or perspiring.

3. Parametric vs. non-parametric response-scores. Parametric response-

scores involve dimensions of the response such as time, errors or repetitions. The non-parametric reveals the number and variety of classes of response, as in many creativity tests (see Chapter 13 of this handbook).

4. Total quantity or number of responses vs. fraction of responses which meet a criterion. This parameter cuts across (3) since some scores (e.g. a variety score) could be classified into either of the categories here.

5. Single homogeneous score vs. patterned relational score. The former is possible only when the test is scored as a whole, as is the case with a personality inventory. The latter can take many forms. One example would be the difference in time to complete the first and second halves of the test.

6. Normative vs. ipsative scoring. Normative scores have been fully described in Chapter 4 of this handbook, and will not be further discussed. Ipsative scoring (in this Cattellian sense) is brought about when the score of a subject on an item is the deviation of that item from her or his mean score.

Such are the parameters which are held by Cattell and Warburton (1967) to underlie objective tests. Although not every combination is viable, it is clear that there are a huge number of possible types of objective tests: 2^{13} x 2^6 which is well in excess of 50,000.

Even if it were possible to complete a wide variety of tests in all these categories there is still, in this taxonomy, no guide as to content, as to how we might make tests for any particular variable. However, even if there were further principles for objective test construction, it is clear that these 50,000 categories could not be used. Cattell and Warburton shorten the list down to sixty-four varieties drawn from the three most important stimulus and scoring parameters, allowing eight varieties of each. Even so there is no shortage of possible objective tests.

It is clear that this taxonomy, useful though it is, especially in a more brief and practical guise, is not sufficient to understand objective tests. It is important in understanding their form but as regards content it is worthless. For this further principles are required and these must now be discussed.

The first difficulty concerns what class of variable objective tests might measure – ability, temperament or motivation. There is no a priori reason why objective tests should not measure variables in all these spheres and it is necessary now to scrutinise the distinction between them.

Distinguishing objective tests of ability, temperament and dynamics

It is simple enough through factor analysis with marker variables to discover what objective tests measure but this, of course, is after they have been constructed. What is required is some guide for constructing a test of a given variety, even though empirical evidence as to its validity is still necessary.

Cattell and Warburton (1967) provide a detailed discussion of this problem, which can be briefly summarised.

1. Two situations – incentives and complexities – are defined.
2. Definition of incentive: an incentive provokes a striving for a goal and is a symbol of the goal or the goal satisfaction. This can be discovered through process analysis – the statistical pattern analysis of a sequence of behaviour over time. The relevant sequence is the path of activities leading to goal satisfaction. An incentive situation can be recognised, therefore, from its relationship to the goal (i.e. by common fluctuations in strength and constant precedence). In a diary study of one subject over a period of a month, using the objective test, the Motivation Analysis Test (Cattell, Horn and Sweney, 1970), Kline and Grindley (1974) showed just such a relationship between the dynamic variables, measured by this test, and real-life events.
3. Definition of complexity. All that which is not incentive. Thus it is dependent on an accurate assessment of incentive.
4. As incentives change, so do the scores on objective tests. As complexities change, so do the scores on cognitive tests. All other tests are tests of temperament.
5. It follows from this that the measurement of dynamics and ability is considerably intertwined. However it is relatively easy to obtain pure measures by ensuring that one of these class of variables is held constant. For example, if we have measures of ability which are absurdly easy, differences in scores are not reflections of differences in ability but dynamic differences such as how hard subjects are trying. Similarly in a real selection procedure, where all subjects are trying, ability tests are purely cognitive.
6. As has been indicated, having been constructed tests must be factored, to demonstrate that they do measure the variables, as intended. Thus if factored without marker variables each test of a given class should load together. With marker variables the correct markers should load the factors.

With these guidelines the objective test constructor has some sort of rationale for constructing objective tests. However, as was admitted by Cattell and Warburton (1967), these taxonomies and analyses are highly abstract to such an extent that for the detail of actual test construction they may be found somewhat tenuous. For this reason they present a series of practical hints, based upon their considerable experience of objective test construction and on their own intuitions. The most important of these I shall now scrutinise.

Practical guidelines for the construction of objective tests of personality and motivation

These will be discussed not from the viewpoint of constructing such tests, although that would certainly be possible, but for the insight they give into the nature of objective personality tests. First Cattell and Warburton (1967) list five points to be avoided, the usual recourse of amateur test constructors.

1. Avoid face-valid questionnaire items (which, by definition, could not be objective tests). However, as discussed previously, questionnaire items can be used as a basis for objective tests to define certain relevant behaviour.
2. Avoid puzzles and problems. These, from the distinctions discussed above, are likely to measure cognitive variables.
3. Avoid placing too much reliance on the 'stress situation'. At best these tests will tap fear or aggression but there are many other emotions which these tests leave untapped.
4. Avoid tests of aesthetic and stylistic preference. It is quite true that these tests may well tap some aspect of personality. However it is quite absurd to think that they could measure all aspects of personality, even if we were to ignore the obvious fact that responses to these tests must be influenced by education and culture.
5. Avoid the simple use of projective tests – the responses to which are usually factorially complex, as was shown by Wenig (1952).

In addition to these five features to be avoided in objective tests there are certain other characteristics of objective tests which are designed to overcome certain awkward problems. These are again discussed in great detail in the compendium and I can only discuss here the most salient among them.

1. Differential motivation of different subjects   This is a difficulty with all tests but is particularly acute with objective tests since the subject has no idea what the test may be measuring and hence it may seem like a total waste of time. However, since there are some individuals who have to be best at everything and always try there are bound to be unintended motivational factors influencing the results.

Cattell and Warburton (1967) discuss five possible ways to reduce this distortion.

a. The test is divided into two parts for which motivation is assumed to be the same. The score is the difference between the two parts or the ratio, one part being deliberately designed to affect motivation. An example will clarify this point. There is an objective test, for ego strength, known as memory under distraction. Here the score is the comparison of memory for digits, on their own, and dispersed among jokes.
b. A different approach is to motivate subjects such that it is reasonable to assume that individual differences have been removed. This is done, as Cattell and Warburton (1967) argue, by utilising basic drives such as fear, sex and hunger, rather than drives which are of lesser significance, such as the culturally moulded sentiments, e.g. feelings towards family or

religious sentiments, which have greater variance. However, in practice, due to ethical problems such stimulation is not easily administered (starvation would be impossible) although pictures of nude figures and electric shocks (of a mild kind) are frequently used.

c. Scoring should be restricted to stylistic or formal aspects of performance because, Cattell and Warburton argue, these vary less with motivation than do most other variables. Handwriting, for example, remains recognisable for individuals across a wide variety of situations.

These three methods apply to temperamental tests rather than dynamic objective tests. The last two points apply to dynamic tests which will be described in Chapter 17. However it is convenient to discuss these problems here rather than repeat the arguments in that chapter.

d. It is possible that a subject's motivational level over the whole battery of tests could be factored out. If this is so then all the variables with substantial loadings on this factor could be removed.

e. Finally the test constructor can seek to motivate the subjects so as to produce complete involvement with the procedure. How this can actually be done in practice is not easy to work out.

2. The test as a situation The test itself may be regarded as a situation involving, to some extent, social behaviour which is an important aspect of personality. Indeed Mischel (e.g. 1968) has attacked personality testing in general as invalid on the grounds that scores are situationally determined.

Cattell and Warburton (1967) have faced up to the fact that taking a test is a specific situation and created a set of objective tests which clearly involve social interaction. These miniature situations, as they are called, are, however, difficult to devise and complex to administer in practical testing. Furthermore, the few which are listed in the compendium have no evidence for validity and this type of test is mentioned simply as one worth research but not yet ready for application in psychology.

3. The influence, on objective test scores, of ability and attainment
If we are trying to measure personality (or motivation) by objective tests the influence of ability and attainment on the scores from such tests is a major source of distortion. This should be no surprise given our earlier discussion of the differences between cognitive and personality tests in the objective test realm. These are intertwined.

Obviously this influence must be minimised or removed if we are to measure personality with any validity. Let us take the objective measure of interest as an example. It is known that a measure of the amount of information relevant to a particular subject is a good measure of how interested in it she or he is (Cattell and Child, 1975). Thus children interested in cricket or football are usually hugely knowledgeable about every detail of players' lives and careers. However it is obvious that this measure must be distorted by ability variables. It is likely that a highly intelligent subject with a mild interest might know more than, or as much as, a less intelligent subject with a greater interest. Thus the simple measure of information will not do as a measure of interest. One way round this difficulty is to ipsatise the scores for each subject. This involves using the deviations on a test from a subject's mean as the score.

Cattell and Warburton (1967) suggest five methods of disentangling the effects of ability on objective personality tests.

a. In devising the tests reduce the demands on ability and knowledge as far as is possible.
b. As was the case in overcoming the problem of differential motivation, differential ability can be dealt with by using ratio or difference scores from a test divided into two parts.
c. All tests should be factored and those loading on ability factors should be removed from the battery.
d. Use a wide variety of content in the objective test, embracing the whole gamut of human interests. The more varied the tests the more likely it is that they will measure the whole spectrum of personality.

I have now discussed most of the problems involved in the construction of objective tests of personality and motivation, and the formal guidelines which may be used to help in their development. However in addition to all these parameters and taxonomies, Cattell and Warburton admit that certain much more vague intuitions and ideas are important in their construction. These include:

1. clinical intuition;
2. observations in everyday life of critical incidents which appear to reflect personality differences;
3. folklore, proverbs and saws;
4. emotional situations in games and sport;
5. observed conversations; and
6. literary sources.

In addition, it should be pointed out that objective personality tests can be either group or individually administered and that where possible it is sensible to aim at the former, which makes testing more cost effective.

Conclusions

This concludes my discussion on the nature of and the problems with objective tests of personality. As with all tests it is essential to demonstrate their validity and this can only really be done by the factor analysis of the tests with marker variables in the field of personality, ability and motivation.

As might be inferred from the complexity of the rationale of these tests there are few if any such tests with high validity. The majority of objective tests listed in the compendium are simply of unknown validity. Few are even in published form. To complete this chapter I shall simply give a few examples of objective personality tests. Further information can be found on objective tests in Chapter 17 and in the final section of this handbook, where the few published examples are evaluated.

Examples of objective tests

1. Fidgeting as measured by the fidgetometer The fidgetometer is a swivel chair with electrical contacts at various points which are closed by movements. the score is the amount of movement recorded over a fixed time. The rationale of the test is that fidgeting is a sign of anxiety. Thus it was expected that the test would load on the anxiety factor. However, it does not thus load, illustrating to the full the difficulty of attempting to construct valid objective tests.

Notice that with this test even if subjects realised that the chair measured movement (and few subjects do) it would be difficult to fake. Should one remain rigid, natural or what?

2. Slow line drawing Subjects are required to draw a line as slowly as possible across a page. Various scores can be derived from this test: the length of line, or whether the subject cheated, e.g. by lifting the pencil so as to make no mark or by stopping. These last scores would be expected to load on the psychotism factor of Eysenck, as measured by the EPQ and to load negatively on Cattell's factor G. It was expected, further, that the length of line would load on inhibition but none of these loadings was supported by the evidence.

3. Willingness to play practical jokes This test is a questionnaire in which the subject expresses his or her willingness to play various practical jokes. The rationale of the test was that timid subjects should enjoy the jokes, seeing them as an opportunity to get their own back. This was supported in factor analytic studies. However, an unexpected loading for this test was on the anxiety factor – stable subjects enjoyed such jokes.

4. Basal metabolic rate This test exemplifies a physiological objective test. Subjects' smallest oxygen consumption for six minutes is converted to calories per hour per square metre of body area. It was thought that this test would load on extraversion and exuberance, which was the case. However it loaded on a number of other personality factors and illustrates the problems of attempting to devise physiological measures of personality. These must always have clear evidence of validity.

These four examples show the rationale of some typical objective tests. However from the huge number of tests in the compendium it is not a good sample. To conclude I shall simply list a few other tests which, according to Hundleby (1973) show some evidence of validity.

Greater number of admissions of minor wrongdoings or frailties.

Greater acquiescence in the answering of questionnaires.

Higher score on a checklist of annoyances.

Little confidence that a good performance could be reached in a wide range of novel skills.

All the above loaded the anxiety factor. The following tests loaded the assertiveness factor.

Preference for socially acceptable book titles compared to questionable titles.

Faster tapping speed.

Faster tempo of arm and leg circling.

Faster speed of reading when asked to read at normal rate.

Higher speed at reading poetry and copying stick figures.

Greater preference for sophisticated or highbrow activities.

I think that this is a sufficient indication of the vast variety of objective tests and readers should refer to the compendium to see the huge ingenuity that has gone into their development. All that remains (and this is an essential and difficult task) is to investigate and establish which, if any, are valid and reliable measures of important personality factors.

Chapter 17

Interest and Motivation Tests

In Chapters 15 and 16 we discussed three types of personality test. Personality questionnaires are concerned with temperament and it is customary to label projective tests as personality tests, although, as was obvious in Chapter 16, projective tests claim to measure all aspects of personality including, in some cases, dynamics, i.e. motivations and interests. Some objective tests, too, as we shall see, claim to measure motivation. Thus, to some extent, the distinction between personality and motivation tests is somewhat arbitrary. Nevertheless there are some essential differences sufficient to make it convenient and not grossly in violation of psychology and logic to discuss motivation and interest tests in a separate chapter.

Distinction between dynamics and temperament Temperamental dimensions or traits, the variables measured by personality questionnaires, account for the differences in how we do things. I sit typing this chapter at my word processor. I type slowly and with errors banging the keys with great force. In the next room, my wife sits at her word processor. Her fingers race errorless and light over the keys. Having written a first draft, she revises, maybe many times, while I prefer to get a correct first draft. These differences reflect differences on temperamental factors such as obsessionality, conscientiousness and introversion.

Motivational traits, on the other hand, reflect the dynamics of behaviour, accounting for why we do things. Why are we both writing away? What variables lead us to spend our time thus engaged in a pursuit which brings little reward either of money or fame yet is difficult and tiring? These and similar questions are the province of the study of human dynamics and the psychometric approach is to attempt to discover and to measure the main dimensions of the field, the factors which account for the dynamic variance.

Defining the field of dynamics As we have seen in earlier chapters of this handbook, the psychometric contribution to the psychology of ability and personality has been to establish, through factor analysis, the main dimensions of these fields and to develop efficient psychological tests loading these factors. In so doing, variables have emerged, such as fluid and crystallised ability, extraversion and neuroticism, which are psychologically of great importance in understanding ability and personality.

Clearly, therefore, a basis for motivational and interest tests ought to be the factor analysis of human dynamics and this is, indeed, as shall be seen, the approach of Cattell (e.g. Cattell and Child, 1975). In addition, of course, just as in the field of personality, we may expect to see motivational tests developed by other methods, such as criterion keying, just as was the MMPI (Hathaway and McKinley, 1951), and again this is the case.

Problems in establishing dynamic factor structure Before setting out the dynamic factor structure as a basis for motivational and interest tests, a few problems must be discussed. This is because compared with the fields of ability and personality, it is a far more difficult problem to factor analyse the dynamic sphere. There are many reasons for these difficulties but the main problem can be encapsulated as the difficulty of defining dynamic variables.

Defining dynamic variables In the field of abilities it is not difficult to define and thus sample from the population of abilities. Observation of human behaviour reveals countless such skills, as has been fully discussed in Chapters 12 and 13 of this handbook. Similarly, it has proved possible to sample traits, in the field of personality, using ratings of behaviour as a basis, as has been described in Chapter 15 of this handbook.

In the dynamic field it has not proven so easy and only Cattell and his colleagues have even attempted the task. Generally, as shall be seen, interest tests have no factorial basis and their psychological meaning is highly dubious.

Reasons for the difficulty of factoring the dynamic field A major difficulty in the dynamic field is that in psychology there is almost no agreement as to what the main dynamic variables are, thus offering a poor basis for measurement, without which no factors can emerge. A few examples will clarify this point.

Freud (1940) proposed a two-variable dynamic theory, in which behaviour was driven by Eros and Thanatos, the Life and Death instincts. These are by no means simple to test, either psychometrically or with projective tests. In an earlier formulation, Freud (1933) had argued that sex and aggression were the major determinants of human behaviour. In any case much of motivation was unconscious. Murray (1938), on the other hand, was far less parsimonious, claiming that were at least twenty-two needs and their associated environmental presses. He did at least provide a test of these drives, the Thematic Apperception Test (Murray, 1938) which is discussed in Chapter 26 of this handbook. McDougall (1932) listed fifteen propensities which are certainly equivalent to drives, while Adler (1927) saw human behaviour as dynamically unifactorial, the factor being 'the upward striving for superiority'. This last has been taken up, in altered form, by McClelland (1961) in his work in achievement motivation which is claimed to be paramount among entrepreneurs.

This is bad enough for a psychometrist seeking to factor the field but there is worse to be found in experimental psychology. Thus Skinner (1953), along with most behaviourists, rejects the term motivation as being redundant and vacuous, claiming that it arises from a scientifically naive and primitive tendency to create abstract concepts from descriptive terms. Intelligence is one such example, being a reification to account for intelligent behaviour, aggression for aggressive behaviour and so on. Motivation in the psychology of operant conditioning has, therefore, no place. We do what we do because we have been thus reinforced. Our introspected motives are epiphenomena of our past patterns of conditioning. The psychometrist who seeks the dimensions of motivation is wasting her or his time. Psychometrics and multivariate analysis are doomed to failure. Fortunately, although the logic of these arguments is sound, they are empirically false, as the abstract notion of intelligence demonstrates (see Chapter 12).

Nor is this all. Further complexity is added to understanding motivation if the effects of classical conditioning are taken into account, as propounded by Dollard and Miller (1950), whereby almost anything may become a drive and drive reducing. Classical conditioning leads us on, by a natural transition, to the consideration of animal behaviour. Animal psychologists, notably ethologists such as Lorenz (1966) and Tinbergen (1951) have argued that in animals critical learning periods and sign stimuli are important determiners of their behaviour and that vestiges of these may still be important in understanding humans. This view has received even more powerful expression in the work of the sociobiologists, especially Wilson (1978), who have regressed to a unitary notion of motivation, the furtherance of an individual's genes.

This discussion of differing psychological views of the nature of motivation illustrates that there is no obvious, straightforward approach to the psychometric study of motivation, as there was with personality and ability. It will be instructive to compare the position for motivation with that of personality discussed in the opening pages of Chapter 15. There we found that three approaches had been used. One was to factor analyse the universe of personality traits, the method adopted by Cattell (1957). However in the study of motivation, as we have seen, what variables should be factored is difficult to state. This is particularly so because of the disparate nature of the different theories and because of problems in quantifying motivational variables, in the first place. The second approach to develop tests by criterion-keying is again more complex than with personality because the criterion groups are less obvious in the field of motivation. Finally, given the morass of theorising about motivation it would be a foolhardy psychometrist who attempted to utilise one theory and base her or his test on that. Given the number of theories such a test would be bound to satisfy fewer psychologists than it pleased.

The work of Cattell (Cattell and Child, 1975; Cattell and Kline, 1977; Cattell, 1985)

Cattell is virtually the only factor analyst who has attempted to apply factor analysis to the dynamic field and thus elucidate its structure and hence develop effective tests in the factor analytic, psychometric tradition. Because of the difficulties inherent in this work, for the reasons which have been outlined in the previous section, before setting out motivational structure, I shall be forced to discuss briefly the rationale of the analyses, paying particular attention to the variables from which the factors were derived. This is particularly important because it is not simple to ensure that any resulting factors are dynamic. For example, Jackson (1974) developed the Personality Research Form (see Chapter 25) from Murray's (1938) personological theory. Now this is a dynamic theory yet research (cited in the test manual) makes it clear that the scales are temperamental rather than dynamic variables, the correlations with other personality tests, such as the 16PF, being incontrovertible evidence. We must now consider, then, how we can ensure that that we are dealing with dynamic rather than temperamental factors.

Traits and states

Traits are stable characteristics of individuals, relatively unchanging over time. States, on the other hand, are transient and may last for quite short durations. Anger is usually of this kind. This is an important distinction which has been stressed by Cattell (1973) and by Cattell and Kline (1977) and which is directly relevant to the distinction between temperament and dynamics. Anxiety is a good example.

Anxiety is a personality trait, one of the most important as was discussed in Chapter 15, both in ratings of personality and in questionnaires. Trait anxiety is an individual's general or usual anxiety level. This varies considerably, some people being stolid and unflappable, others being in almost perpetual acute anxiety. State anxiety is the anxiety caused by some particular set of events, for example an examination. Thus at any one time an individual's level of anxiety has two components: the state and the trait anxiety. State anxiety should fluctuate while trait anxiety should remain the same, if the two could be separately measured. In fact they can be and Spielberger *et al.* (1970) have produced an excellent measure of both types of anxiety, the State Trait–Anxiety Inventory (see Chapter 25).

This example of anxiety, which everyone can recognise from their own experience as being both a trait and a state, illustrates the importance of states in motivation. Thus a highly state-anxious individual will do things, on account of that anxiety, that she or he might well not do in other circumstances and the same is true of other states such as anger, fear, or jealousy. Even the law, which for the most part is profoundly innocent of psychology, recognises the force of jealousy as a motivational determinant, the *crime passionel* being more sympathetically treated than other cold-blooded murders, although not sufficiently to save the life of Ruth Ellis.

It should be noted, at this juncture, that this use of the word 'states' includes what are often referred to as 'moods' in the vernacular. It is simply a matter of English usage to call such feelings as boredom, anger or cheerfulness moods rather than states. Thus, from all this discussion, it is clear that the psychometrics of motivation must attempt to measure the most important states. Before I go on to set out the main state factors which have been discovered, a further point needs to be stressed. In understanding long term behaviour such as marital satisfaction or job success it is likely that stable aspects of individuals, i.e. traits, are more important than transient and fleeting states, although obviously that a person had frequent violent outbursts of anger could profoundly affect her or his life. States on the other hand are clearly important if we are trying to predict what a person will do at a given point of time.

Problems in the factor analysis of states and moods

Cattell is one of the few factor analysts to have tackled the problem of establishing state structure because there are some formidable logical and practical difficulties in its elucidation. These must be briefly mentioned or the table of factors set out later in this chapter will not be fully appreciated or understood.

1. States change over time

This is a difficulty which, Cattell (1973) argues, has been ignored by most researchers in this field and which, as a result, renders their work of little value. Since states, by definition, change over time and since this transience is what distinguishes them from traits, any factor analysis which will reliably reveal states, differentiated from traits, must also involve time. This means that factor analysis, designed to reveal states, must involve re-testing. However, as was seen in Chapter 8, R technique, regular factor analysis, takes the correlations between tests as its starting point. This means that R technique produces factors which could be states but may equally well be traits. This problem that R technique produces factors which may be states or traits renders dubious much of the work carried out with mood scales, such as that by Clyde (1963), Nowlis (Nowlis and Green, 1957) and Howarth (1980) who use only R technique.

The Howarth mood adjective checklist, for example, which was based upon a study of all previous mood scales and R factor analysis, claims to have isolated the following moods: aggression, scepticism, egotism, out-goingness, control, anxiety, cooperation, fatigue, concentration and sadness. However their validity as states, because of their reliance on R technique, is dubious although Howarth has shown (Howarth, 1980) that they are affected by weather, in accord to some extent with common sense.

Most workers in the field of moods who use R technique attempt to differentiate states from traits by stressing the present in phrasing the items. Thus I feel happy now is a state item while I generally feel happy measures the trait. However, this simple technique may not be as convincing as it appears because Watson (1988) found little difference in results when he used six different time periods: at this moment, today, past few days, past few weeks, and this year, in measures of mood. Thus state scales may be only face valid. In addition it must be pointed out that this approach is not satisfactory since the person who is generally happy or anxious will be in that state when tested. That is partly why Cattell insists that R technique is unsatisfactory.

2. Alternatives to R technique

In Chapter 8 of this handbook, it was pointed out that where repeated testing was necessary, as in moods and states, the correlations between occasions, on a variety of tests for each individual, were factor analysed – a procedure referred to by Cattell (1978) as P technique. Thus these factors account for the variance over time and must be, in terms of simple logic, states. It would be literally nonsensical to think of P factors as traits.

There are practical problems in executing P factor analysis which account for the rarity of its use.

a. First it requires that each subject is tested many times on each variable, for the factors are unique to each subject. This requires a huge dedi-cation on the part of subjects which, even if payment is available, is hard to guarantee.

b. Constant re-testing is likely to affect the validity of the tests, which are not usually intended to be thus used. For example, subjects simply get bored with answering the same items, they remember what they put on the previous occasion and, after a time, semantic satiation sets in – it becomes impossible to answer the items.

c. The time interval. This for some moods and states would have to be impossibly short, thus P technique, depending on the time interval between testings, is likely to miss out some states.

d. Samples. On account of the rigours, for the subject, of taking part in a P technique study, it is usually a far from representative sample which completes the testing sessions.

P technique involves work with a single subject. A large scale P technique investigation consists of many individual case studies. To overcome all these difficulties Cattell (1973) and Cattell and Kline (1977) suggested two other possible, compromise methods.

a. dR technique   This is an R analysis of the differences in scores of subjects on two occasions. Resulting factors must, therefore, account for the variance in scores across the two occasions and must, necessarily, be moods or states. With this method large and representative samples can be used.

Cronbach (1976) objects to difference scores as a basis for statistical analysis because of their large standard errors. Furthermore this weakness would be particularly exacerbated in factor analysis. However one method to overcome this problem is to split the sample, as is done in multiple regression where beta weights are notoriously volatile. Only replicated factors are interpreted.

b. Chain P technique   This is an attempt to combine the advantages of dR and P analysis. Here if twenty subjects are tested on five occasions, the results can be so arranged that effectively we have 100 occasions. However as Cattell (1973) argues, this is a compromise and the best approach is P technique with a large number of subjects.

Conclusions concerning the methodological problems in the factor analysis of states

I have reviewed many of the difficulties in studying moods and states because the majority of workers in this field simply ignore them, although their logic, as Cattell has made clear, is devastating. In considering tests of mood and state such problems must be borne in mind, for those tests produced by R analysis may be traits or simply collections of semantically similar items. This is an especial risk with mood scales with simple, face-valid items, all in the present tense.

The factor structure of states (Cattell, 1973; Cattell and Kline, 1977)

The factors set out in Table 17.1 have been isolated.

Table 17.1 State factors, according to Cattell

state exvia, state anxiety, state cortertia (alertness), state independence, depression, psychoticism, discreetness, subjectivity, good upbringing, fatigue, stress, guilt, general depression, low energy, anxious depression, strong superego

These, therefore, should form the basis of our mood and state tests. However, at first glance, they do not appear promising candidates for testing and some comments are required. These will be as brief as possible and for more detailed discussion readers are referred to Kline (1979).

Many of the factors listed in Table 17.1 seem to make little sense as state factors. Thus intelligence seems most odd since this is a variable which appears to fluctuate but little. I can never imagine that Aristotle or Plato were sometimes stupid or that people vary much on independence. This difficulty lies in our previous definition of state and trait where the former were seen as transient and the latter as stable. These terms must now be examined more closely.

Stability and transience

Some states are very brief. For example, if I am annoyed at being unable to find a pen and a colleague walks in and lends me one, this state is abruptly altered. Indeed some states may be so short that they are shorter than a testing session and thus highly difficult to measure. One the other hand, some states such as grief at the death of a spouse may be ended only by death. However if a state such as grief lasts for several years, it is in fact stable, and thus by definition becomes a state. In other words, how long must a state endure to become a trait? Obviously there is no absolute distinction between states and traits, at least in terms of transience and stability. However if this is so, how can the state factors, described above, be justified?

Differences in variance

Cattell (1973, 1985) and Cattell and Kline (1977) have attempted to improve the distinction between traits and states by distinguishing them in terms of variance. If one measures people on several occasions for traits the variance between people is greater than the variance between occasions. For states the position is reversed.

Some distinctions between states and traits can also be made in terms of the factor analyses from which the factors were derived.

1. Traits can appear only in R analysis.
2. States can appear in R, dR and P analysis.
3. Change factors can appear in dR and P technique.

Thus, by studying where factors appear in the three techniques, their true status can be determined.

Distinction between state, trait and trait-change factors

It was pointed out above that there was, in terms of factor analytic designs, a distinction between state and trait-change factors, and this makes it necessary to draw a final discriminating definition of each of these types of factor.

Trait-change factors   As is evident from the list of factors in Table 17.1, a number of them are simply states based upon the major second order personality factors found by Cattell and discussed in Chapter 15. Since it makes no sense to think of some of them as states, these factors were called by Cattell trait-change factors – a new concept in personality theorising, a concept which had arisen from dR factor analyses.

Such trait-change factors psychologically represent, not states, but the growth and decline of traits. Thus they are not necessarily motivational factors at all. They have been discussed here because they arose in the study of states and they resemble them. However, in the final list of Cattell's moods and states only some of these will have a place.

State factors   Anxiety is an interesting state factor in that there is presumably a trait-change anxiety factor. However there can be no question that anxiety is a state along with all the other factors which have been discovered through P and dR techniques that are not trait-change factors. Exvia is a highly interesting trait-change factor which, like anxiety, may also be a state as well as a trait. Thus as we all know, sometimes we do feel extraverted and outgoing and ready to be sociable, while on other occasions we can't face people at all. Thus this trait-change factor may well be, like anxiety, a genuine state. Examination of Table 17.1 shows that these state factors make good sense – arousal, fatigue, stress, aggression, guilt, anxiety, and the three depression factors. Most people have experienced these and clinicians use them in their theories.

Factors derived from objective tests, T factors

In Chapter 16 we discussed objective tests, described in the compendium by Cattell and Warburton (1967). It will be recalled that these tests, whose validity is difficult to establish, yield T factors as distinct from the Q factors of questionnaires. Whereas the factors which we have so far discussed have arisen from questionnaires sampling the personality sphere of traits, Cattell and his colleagues (e.g. Cattell and Scheier, 1961) have attempted to sample the state sphere by means of objective tests.

In this handbook, which is devoted to psychological testing, I cannot describe this work since it has led, unfortunately, to no practicable psychological tests. However, it is mentioned because some further third order state factors were extracted although these were not properly identified. These objective factors will be discussed in a later section of this chapter when the measure of drives and the strength of motivation are examined.

Conclusions from Cattell's work on moods and states

Cattell has distinguished trait-change factors, representing fluctuations in traits over time, from state and mood factors. Traits tend to be stable while states are transient, some states being brief while others may be relatively long lasting. Since the distinction between transience and stability is arbitrary, further distinctions, in factor analytic terms, are drawn between these factors. Traits can emerge only from R technique while states can arise from R technique, dR and P technique. Trait-change factors can be derived only from dR and P technique.

As a result of this the status of mood and state factors which have emerged only from R analyses is dubious – they could be but are not necessarily states, which is Cattell's objection to much other work in this area.

Given that state-change factors are not really moods or states and thus are not essentially motivational Cattell finally draws up a list of what he regards (Cattell, 1973) as well substantiated state factors and these are set out in Table 17.2. These factors are, as we have demonstrated throughout this handbook, those that tests of mood and state should measure, being the most salient dimensions in the field.

Table 17.2 Well-substantiated Cattell state factors

anxiety	independence	stress	regression
exvia	depression (general)	fatigue	depression (guilt)
cortertia	psychoticism	arousal	depression

Source: Cattell (1973)

These state or mood factors are, of course, motivational factors because clearly they are implicated in the dynamics of behaviour. These factors, therefore, should be the basis of state tests.

Cattell and his colleagues, indeed, have developed two tests of these factors. One of these, the Eight State Questionnaire (Curran and Cattell, 1974), not unsurprisingly, measures eight of the states in Table 17.2: exvia, anxiety, depression, arousal, fatigue, guilt, stress and regression. The other test is the the Central Trait-State Kit (Barton and Cattell, 1981). This measures the five largest second order trait and state factors: exvia, anxiety, cortertia, independence and conscientiousness, which is the superego trait and state factor (not included in the original list).

Both these tests reflect the view adopted in this handbook, that the variables to measure are those which have emerged from factor analysis. However, where I disagree (not in principle but in the application of the principle) with Cattell concerns the identification of these particular factors. As has been seen in Chapter 15 on temperament it is now generally accepted that the best description of the temperamental domain is not given by the Cattell primary factors although the second order factors are in some agreement with what appear to be the best and replicable solutions. In the sphere of states, however, there is far less support for the Cattell list which must be regarded as tentative rather than definitive. However there is no doubt that attempts should be made to measure these factors as a basis for good state tests. Only with further experimental and criterion oriented research can the status of this list of factors be evaluated accurately.

Other views of states and moods

Since there is no particularly sound evidence for the validity of any other set of mood scales and since there is the problem that R technique factors are not necessarily states, I shall not say much about other approaches to the measurement of moods and states.

However the work of Tellegen and colleagues deserves mention. Watson and Tellegen (1985) surveyed all studies of mood and reported some of their own factor analyses. They concluded that two orthogonal (Varimax) factors would account for a good proportion of the variance in mood scales. These two factors were named positive affect and negative affect. All moods and states which are thought of as pleasant load the first factor, while the second accounts for all the unpleasant moods and states.

Cooper and McConnille (1989) in a study of the Eight State Questionnaire and the Tellegen scales showed that effectively the positive scale was equivalent to the exvia state scale and that the negative scale was equivalent to state anxiety. This finding was essentially replicated by Boyle and Katz (1991) in their study of the Eight State Questionnaire where two factors emerged, extraversion being identified with arousal. Meyer and Shack (1989) went further than this, claiming in a study of the EPQR, the revised version of the EPQ (Eysenck and Eysenck 1975) and the Tellegen scales that there was a convergence of extraversion and positive affect and neuroticism and negative affect, holding whether the assessment was of state or trait.

Despite this confusion, the Tellegen dimensions should be measured in any investigation of moods together with the Cattell factors, although as we have seen, these sets of factors are not independent.

Further points about mood scales

In a further study of moods, Cooper and McConnille (1990) investigated variability of moods. They found individual differences in mood variability. Thus on the Eight State Questionnaire (Curran and Cattell, 1974) subjects who varied a lot on one of the scales tended to vary a lot on all of them and vice versa. Thus there are considerable individual differences in mood variability.

Such variability may be accounted for by the fact that there are common factors underlying the Eight State scales, and the Tellegen factors are obvious candidates for this explanation. However there are certain other conclusions which affect all measures of mood.

1. Norms Norms of the usual kind (as described in Chapter 4 of this handbook) are inappropriate not only because there are individual variations in mood variability but because there is variability at all. This point is stressed by Cooper and McConnille (1990). Certainly this makes good sense and it is interesting to note that the Eight State Questionnaire does provide norms and that norms were being collected (according to Barton, 1986) for the Central State–Trait Kit (Barton and Cattell, 1981).

2. Meaning of single measurements In variables which fluctuate considerably, the value of a measurement at any one time as a general indicator of a subject's level is limited. Thus mood scales are only useful when measurement at a particular time is valuable, as in measuring the effects of a variable on mood or state. In many applied settings this is important, especially in the study of the effects of drugs, or violence and pornography in television, for example.

3. Need for repeated measurements If a general indication of a subject's mood level is required, then repeated measurement is necessary, as is the case with blood pressure, for example. If this were done norms could be set up, norms which indicated both variability and mean level. This would then deal with the problem of individual differences in variability. Indeed it could be the case that norms of variability on their own were sufficient. This would depend on the data and on mean differences between individuals after repeated measurements. It is interesting to note, in this regard, that Larsen (1987) attempted to analyse mood variability by spectral analysis. However the value of such an approach remains to be worked out.

Conclusions concerning the measurement of moods and states

1. The factorial structure of moods and states is not well established and it requires other forms of factor analysis than the most common form – R technique. P and dR techniques are necessary.

2. Cattell has used these methods and has isolated states and trait-change factors which account for fluctuations in traits but which are not truly motivational states.
3. Cattell has developed two state tests, the Eight State Questionnaire and the Central Trait–State Kit, and these eight factors are clearly important in the sphere of moods and states.
4. Tellegen and colleagues have argued for two factors accounting for mood variance – positive affect and negative affect and these certainly overlap the factors described by Cattell.
5. There is considerable variability in mood (virtually by definition), and considerable individual differences in this variability.
6. Norms are not therefore useful for mood scales unless they indicate variability of the population. Repeated measurement is essential unless the point of interest is the score at the time of testing and no wider generalisations will be made.

Items in mood and state scales   There is little to say about items in mood and state questionnaires which has not been said in Chapter 15, where the problems in writing personality questionnaire items were described. Indeed the only difference between state and trait questionnaire items is one of tense. State items apply to the moment of completing the item, trait items refer to general tendencies, the present versus the past, but the work of Watson (1988) who found little difference in results when different periods of time were used should not be forgotten.

DRIVES

I shall now leave the topic of moods and states, which is only one aspect of motivation, and turn to what earlier theorists describe as drives. Just as with abilities and temperament, the selection of variables to measure with psychometric tests in a field without theoretical clarity must be made through factor analysis. (The lack of clarity was shown in the introduction to this chapter.)

The only factorist who has made a concerted attempt to define the factor analytic structure of drives is Cattell. Clear accounts of this may be found in Cattell and Child (1975) and Cattell and Kline (1977), although more recent and complex developments are described in Cattell (1981; 1985) and Cattell and Johnson (1986). What follows is a summary of the main points in these books.

Motivational structure

As we have proceeded, in this section of the handbook, from abilities through personality to states and moods it is evident that the problems of delineating the structure through factor analysis have become increasingly difficult. In abilities it was relatively simple to define the sphere of cognitive tasks and traits could be defined semantically. As for moods and states, we had to rely, in part, on P and dR techniques. Drives are even more difficult, which explains the paucity of factor analyses in the field.

The motivational sphere: drives and attitudes

Cattell (Cattell and Child, 1975) conceptualises drives as did McDougall (1932) (indeed Cattell's work in motivation can be seen as a brilliant blend of Burt and McDougall), arguing that there are three aspects to drives.

1. There is a tendency to attend to certain stimuli rather than others.
2. Each drive has its own characteristic emotion, e.g. sexual arousal.
3. There is an impulse to a particular course of action.

Of course, with this conceptualisation of drives the number of drives has to be specified since, without this, the emotions and goals particular to them cannot be studied. The question, therefore, arises as to how we can sample driven behaviour so as to extract the underlying factors (drives).

It is assumed by Cattell (e.g. Cattell, 1957) that drives underlie attitudes because the strength of an attitude reflects the strength of an impulse to action in response to a stimulus. Cattell and Child (1975) define attitudes thus: 'In these circumstances (stimulus) I (organism) want (need) so much (of a certain intensity) to do this (specific goal, response) with that (relevant object).' This definition of stimulus fits precisely the conceptualisation of drives, as discussed above, and is the rationale for using attitudes as the data for extracting factors as drives.

It should be noticed that this definition of attitudes implicates interests. Now there are many interest tests, because they are considered to be useful in vocational guidance and selection. However most of these have not been developed through factor analysis but by criterion-keying (as discussed in Chapter 9 of this handbook). These tests will be considered separately in a later section of this chapter.

The meaning of interest

Kline (1975) argued that the term interest is, scientifically, redundant. Thus interest is an explanatory construct inferred from observations of a subject's behaviour. For example if she or he spends a long time at a particular task, knows a lot about it and spends a good deal of money on it, we say she or he is interested in it.

However, the term interest is not useless because it summarises a large number of observations and, from the viewpoint of this chapter what is far more important, it suggests how interests may be measured or at least gives us a set of criteria to validate the test. Thus a measure of interest in x should load up, in a factor analysis, on: time spent on x; money spent on x; and so on. Thus if a test could be constructed which loaded on these objective and by definition valid indices of interest, this would be a good basis for the analysis of drives as well as a useful measure in vocational guidance and selection.

Objective tests, interests and ipsatisation

In Chapter 16 we discussed and described objective tests. It is quite clear from this analysis of interests that measures such as time spent on x, money spent on x, knowledge of x, are essentially objective, T, tests of interests and could well be a part of the study of drives.

However, there is one obvious problem with this type of test. A rich man, not forced to seek employment (the kind who curse the idleness of the working classes), may well spend more time and money on his interests than a less fortunate subject, without necessarily being more interested. To obviate this difficulty scores have to be ipsatised, that is a subject's scores are expressed as a deviation from his or her own mean. Thus rich and poor are rendered equal. This ipsatisation has to take place not only in respect of measures involving money and time but even of information, as was discussed in Chapter 16.

Thus what is important is the relative level of information within a subject not the absolute level. A clever individual, such is the effect of g, may well know more than a stupid one about everything. Ipsatisation reveals what a subject knows most about and this is what is important for the measurement of interests. This ipsatisation removes the effects of g from factor analyses, which is useful for it tends to be pervasive.

Strength of interest

From the arguments in the previous paragraphs it is clear that on a priori grounds we would expect, from ipsatised measures of time and money spent on a task and knowledge of it, that strength of interest factors would emerge. In fact, Cattell and his colleagues (Cattell, 1957) searched the literature of motivation and interests for indices of interest and ended up with sixty-eight different expressions which are set out in Cattell and Child (1975). High levels of information, perceptual skills, better memory for preferred material, and physiological indices are examples of these. The latter are interesting and it is said that experienced salesmen note the dilated pupil of the client who will buy.

Cattell (1957) factored a battery of such motivational T tests and similar studies replicating the findings are reported in Cattell and Child (1975). From these, seven factors of motivational strength have been extracted and the most important of these are the factors which tests of motivation should aim to measure. Table 17.3 sets out these strength of interest factors.

Table 17.3 Motivational strength factors

Alpha	'Conscious id.' The component related to the satisfaction of personal desires, even when this is unwise.
Beta	Realised, integrated interest. The component implicated in responding to standard attitude questionnaires, the ego component.
Gamma	'Superego.' This is the moral component of interest. This is the component that gives rise to the pretended aesthetic preferences of the middle classes.
Delta	A physiological factor, reflecting autonomic responses, the thrilling sensations to sights and sounds.
Epsilon	This is a conflict factor, loading on PGR, poor memory for material and poor reminiscence, probably related to repression.
Zeta	Not identified.
Eta	Not yet identified.

There are three second order strength of motivation factors:

Integrated component This loads on beta and gamma, reflecting reality oriented, information-based experience.
Unintegrated component This loads on alpha, delta and epsilon, reflecting interests below the level of awareness.
An unidentified component

Source: Kline (1979)

Discussion of Table 17.3 It is noteworthy that these factors fit, as has been argued by Kline (1981), a broadly psychoanalytic model, in that it becomes clear that strength of interest is multidimensional and to some extent (alpha, gamma, delta) below the level of awareness.

This analysis by Cattell and and his colleagues has profound implications for measurement. Thus the standard attitude questionnaire which simply asks face-valid questions related to the attitude cannot be a satisfactory measure because at best it deals only with the beta component. It also accounts for the frequent inaccuracy of market research and Gallup polls which, again, measure only the beta component. This is a factor analysis which takes into account the complexity of attitudes. Clearly any test of motivation must measure at least the first three factors and preferably the second orders. Cattell has developed one test, the Motivational Analysis Test (Cattell *et al.*, 1970) which measures the main drives and these two second order factors (see Chapter 26 for an evaluation of the MAT).

Finally it must not be forgotten that these factors are not well established and agreed by all workers in the field. Unfortunately, this is so far from the case that there is still a dearth of evidence against which they may be evaluated. In brief this work opens up a field of measurement which has yet to be explored.

The structure of drives

As was discussed earlier in this chapter, in addition to the strength of interest as a field of measurement, there is a further question which has been the centre of considerable theoretical speculation and controversy, namely, the number and nature of human drives. This is a question which factor analysis is ideally suited to answer, although Cattell and his colleagues are virtually alone in using this technique. I shall now examine this work.

Before the factors can be set out a few comments are necessary so that the results can be properly understood.

1. Choice of variables   As was mentioned in our preliminary discussion of the research on the motivational strength factors, Cattell and Child (1975) argued that these could be measured from interests and the same arguments hold for drives.

Thus both the work of McDougall (1932) and Murray (1938), as well as the psychoanalytic model (Freud, 1933), imply that drives are reflected in our interests, and that ultimately various behaviours can be traced back to certain goals, and conversely one piece of behaviour may relate to several goals. Consumer behaviour (forgive the hideous jargon of economic psychology) exemplifies the point perfectly. Take an interest in cars. One may buy an expensive car for a variety of reasons: to impress colleagues at work; to arouse envy among one's neighbours; to feel powerful; to show off wealth; to show aesthetic sensibility; to attract women or men; clearly the list is virtually endless. Interest in cars is a multidimensional variable, with many of the dimensions being beyond awareness.

In working out the goals of any behaviour it is usual to find that the goals are ordered: each may be regarded as a subgoal to a more remote goal until, at last, we arrive at a goal beyond which it seems impossible to go. These final or ultimate goals, examples of which are to get food, to get water, to enjoy sexual activity, to keep warm, are considered by Cattell to be our basic drives, which we share with other mammals. These basic drives are labelled ergs. However, in addition to these ergs, Cattell postulates another type of drive, one learned in the culture, which he labels sentiments. These are, almost certainly, uniquely human.

2. Definition of erg (Cattell, 1957)   'An innate reactive tendency, the behaviours of which are directed towards and cease at a particular consummatory goal activity.'

3. Definition of sentiment (Cattell and Child, 1975) 'Dynamic structures visible as common reaction patterns to persons, objects or social institutions and upon which all persons seem to have some degree of endowment.' Thus sentiments are culturally moulded drives.

Cattell and his colleagues (as summarised in Cattell and Child, 1975 and Cattell and Kline, 1977) have factored interests, using mainly objective T tests, as described in Chapter 16, with the aim of establishing the main ergs and sentiments in the motivational sphere.

Table 17.4 sets out the most recent list of ergs and sentiments emerging from these factor analytic studies of objective tests. The ergs are to be found in Sweney *et al.* (1986) while the sentiments are described in Gorsuch (1986).

Table 17.4 Ergs and sentiments

---

1. Replicated factors with tests

Food-seeking	Escape to security
Mating	Self-assertion
Gregariousness	Narcissistic sex
Parental pity	Pugnacity
Exploration	Acquisitiveness

2. Factors where proper identification requires more evidence

Appeal	Constructiveness
Rest seeking	Self-abasement
Laughter and Disgust (these factors are not well defined)	

3. Clearly defined sentiments

Career	Self-sentiment
Home-parental	Sports and games
Mechanical	Sweetheart-spouse
Religious	Superego

---

4. Discussion of Table 17.4 The ten ergs, or basic drives, which have emerged from the factor analysis of T tests, tend to show that the pre-measurement speculations of the theorists were incorrect. There are more drives than postulated by Freud and less than suggested by McDougall or Murray. Clearly, in the study of these basic human drives these are the factors which our tests should aim to measure. Finally it must be stressed that these factors are still in the tentative stage. Far more research than is reported in Cattell and Child (1975) or Cattell and Johnson (1986) is required to validate and explicate these ergs.

The sentiments in section 3 are admitted by Gorsuch (1986) to be an incomplete list. However, these have reasonable support from the objective test research of Cattell and his colleagues. There are clearly many other interests than these, as human experience tells us – the list of hobbies is surprising and endless, although many of them may be subsumed under these sentiment factors. Indeed these sentiments may really be second order factors if all the smaller narrower interests were included in the analyses. Some of these narrower interests are measured by other less theoretically but more practically oriented researchers and these tests will be discussed later in this chapter.

Cattell and his colleagues have developed tests to measure these factors. The Motivation Analysis Test (Cattell *et al.*, 1970) measures 10 factors – the best established ergs and sentiments, as well as the second order strength of motivation factors, as mentioned above. In addition there is an experimental test, the VIM (Sweney and Cattell, 1980), the Vocational Interest Measure. Both these tests are discussed and described in Chapter 26 of this handbook.

As has been stated, the factors in these tests are derived from objective T tests. These, by definition (see Chapter 16) are not face valid. Hence it is not useful to list typical items in this section. Rather readers must be referred to Chapters 16 and 26 of this handbook, and for more details to Cattell and Warburton (1967). However in discussing the principles behind motivation testing in an earlier section of this chapter it was pointed out that amount of information on a subject, misperception, and resistance to distraction, were typical objective T tests used in these tests.

Other work on motivation

In occupational psychology (see Chapter 22 of this handbook) in job selection there is considerable use made of measurement of interests. However, most of this work does not involve the Cattell tests mainly because their theoretical complexity is not attractive to those whose job is practical – efficient selection which costs as little as possible. Instead they tend to use face-valid interest tests and these must now be briefly discussed because they must be classified as motivational tests.

In the introductory section of this chapter it was pointed out that there were three approaches that might be adopted in developing psychological tests of motivation, factoring the field, as adopted by Cattell and his colleagues, attempting to test directly a motivational theory, and creating tests through criterion-keying. This last is the most usual approach but I shall first discuss attempts to produce psychological tests based upon motivational theories.

Theoretically derived tests

As was mentioned earlier in the chapter, two researchers of note, Edwards (1959; 1967) and Jackson (1974), have produced tests measuring the needs postulated by Murray (1938). The main tests of these workers, the Personal Preference Schedule (Edwards, 1959) and the Personality Research Form (Jackson, 1974) are fully described and discussed in Chapter 25 of this handbook.

This Chapter 25 is concerned with personality tests rather than motivation tests, it should be noted. This is because the research into the validity of these tests, especially the PRF (e.g. Nesselroade and Baltes, 1975) strongly suggests that these are tests of temperament rather than motivation, and they should be thus regarded. All this research is fully examined in Chapter 25 where each test is described.

Test items

These are typical personality test items as discussed in Chapter 15 and the EPPS was specifically devised by Edwards to obviate the problem of social desirability (Edwards, 1957).

Mention of the work of Murray on needs brings to mind one particular need which has been extensively studied – need achievement, especially by McClelland (e.g. 1961). This has been claimed to be important in driving entrepreneurs but again it seems to be a personality rather than a temperamental variable (Kline and Lapham, 1991c). Items in the Kline and Lapham scale, the Motivational Analysis Questionnaire, are typical trait items, as discussed in Chapter 15.

The fact that these scales seem to measure temperamental rather than motivational variables simply emphasises what was said earlier in this chapter about types of factors. Thus R technique factor analysis can produce state factors but does not necessarily do so, unlike P and dR techniques. Where possible these should be used in the elucidation of motivational factors.

Criterion-keyed tests

As was described in Chapter 9 of this handbook, criterion-keyed tests are developed by constructing items which will discriminate relevant groups. In the case of interest tests this means groups held to be interested in certain topics. Their items are of the kind discussed in Chapter 15, although the content is somewhat different. Usually they refer to job activities or simply consist of job titles to which subjects have to indicate 'like' or 'dislike'. Crowley (1981), incidentally, showed that these types of item were equivalent.

There are many problems with this type of test, of which the most severe are the difficulty of establishing clear criterion groups and the fact that such tests are only unifactorial, or univariate by chance, thus rendering such tests of dubious psychological meaning. Indeed it could be argued (Kline, 1975) that such tests hinder the development of psychological knowledge because even if they discriminate one group from another they can give no indication of why this should be so, whereas discrimination by a factored test of known validity is psychologically meaningful.

Despite these problems two interest tests of this type are widely used, especially in America: the Strong Vocational Interest Blank (Strong *et al.*, 1971) and various versions of the Kuder Preference tests (Kuder, 1970a and b). These are described and evaluated in Chapter 27 of this handbook.

Other methods of test construction

Some test constructors have attempted to develop tests based upon every-day notions of interest in which face-valid items are written and subjected to some form of item analysis. Of course if this done, items with similar meanings and content tend to form scales. However the validity of such face-valid tests still has to be demonstrated. Generally this is not done and many of these authors make ipsative tests in which interests are ranked which means that norms should not be used and investigation of their factorial nature is rendered impossible, as is discussed in Chapter 4 of this handbook. Such tests can be useful as a basis for discussion in vocational guidance where the rank order of interests is discussed with each individual but as psychometric tests for the study of individual differences they are not recommended. For discussion purposes one of the best is the Rothwell-Miller test which is fully described in Chapter 27.

The work of Holland

Finally, the theory of vocational choice and its concomitant test which has been developed by Holland must be mentioned. The test, the Vocational Preference Inventory (Holland, 1965) is fully described in Chapter 26 of this handbook. However it is sufficient for the purposes of discussion in this chapter to note that it measures eleven variables of which the first six are specifically concerned with interests. The scales are: realistic, intellectual, social, conventional, enterprising, and artistic interests. The five other scales are self-control, masculinity, status, infrequency and acquiescence.

Holland (1966) claims that there are six personality types, the realistic type, the intellectual type, the social type, the conventional type, the enterprising type and the artistic type which are distinguished in terms, *inter alia*, of their interests which reflect, in Holland's theory, personality. Subjects are classified into these types by the first six scales of the VPI, the items of which consist of job titles which subjects have to indicate 'like' or 'dislike'. A part of this theory claims that people of a given type are attracted into jobs which suit them, hence the emphasis on job preference for measurement.

I shall say no more about this theory, which is partly speculative and partly theoretical but I have said enough, I hope, for readers to understand the basis of the VPI, whose validity and reliability is fully discussed in Chapter 27.

CONCLUSIONS

In this chapter I have been forced to discuss the theoretical basis of the tests to a far greater extent than was necessary with other types of tests since there is no clear agreement in this area of testing as to what this theoretical basis should be. Nevertheless it is clear that the most rational and psycho-metrically sophisticated approach – that of Cattell and his colleagues – is not widely used or appreciated and it true to say that the findings need repli-cation and further explication. The other approaches which are far more simple are more commonly used but have severe problems while the work of Holland is particular to his theoretical approach which, while interesting, is not widely supported. This is a field of testing still urgently requiring further research.

Chapter 18

Other Types of Psychological Tests

In this chapter, as the title suggests, I shall discuss various types of psychological test which fall outside the boundaries of the groups of tests which have been the subjects of earlier chapters in this section of the handbook.

The tests described in this chapter are disparate in nature and their only coherence lies in the fact that that they do not fit the earlier categories. Perhaps, however, there is a faint, common theme, namely that they have been devised for specific purposes, often clinical or psychiatric.

1. PERCEPT-GENETIC METHODS

Percept-genetic methods have been developed mainly in Scandinavia, especially by Kragh and Smith at the University of Lund. Indeed a collection of papers by Kragh and Smith (1970) remains an excellent account of both the theory and methods of percept-genetics. Smith and Westerlundh (1980) brings in some further research.

Percept-genetics or perceptgenesis is concerned, as the name suggests, with the development of percepts. Thus underlying these methods is the assumption that perception is a constructive process which reflects the totality of our experience. For example, if we perceive a girl stepping out of an entrance to a university, our conscious percept is coloured by our life experience of girls and universities. This perceptual process is, of course, instantaneous and, normally, quite inaccessible to consciousness. Percept-genetic methods, however, seek, to quote Westerlundh (1976), to expose these processes to the searchlight of consciousness and thus to reveal critical life experiences and unconscious conflicts which affect perception. Such a description of course, resembles what in psychoanalysis are called defence mechanisms (Freud, 1946) so that it should come as no surprise that the best-known percept-genetic tests, in fact, purport to measure, *inter alia*, defence mechanisms.

Percept-genetic methods expose these unconscious processes of perception by the serial presentation of a stimulus, first below the threshold of perception and then at gradually decreasing speeds in a tachistoscope. At each presentation subjects are required to draw and describe what they see. Distortions and changes in the descriptions of the stimuli through the series of presentations are held to reflect the inner conflicts and experiences of the individual which affect perception. The instantaneous process of perception is broken up and exposed for inspection by this subliminal, serial presentation of percept-genetic methods.

There are two tests which are most commonly used in percept-genetic research, the defence mechanism test, the DMT, (Kragh, 1985 – the latest edition) and the Meta-Contrast Technique, the MCT (Kragh and Smith, 1970), both of which are described and evaluated in Chapter 29 of this handbook. In this chapter, however, although it will be necessary briefly to describe at least the DMT, I want to discuss the rationale of percept-genetics and to discuss whether it is possible, in principle, that tests of this kind could be valid measures of unconscious processes. Clearly, if they could, these would be about the best scientific tools psychology has developed since, prima facie, they appear to bear upon what is normally entirely inaccessible, even by definition, namely unconscious processes. Indeed, if it could be shown that percept-genetics could lay open to public inspection the private processes of perception, a real, human science could begin. The fundamental paradox that besets scientific psychology (that we know that our mental processes are important yet private and unobservable) would be, perhaps, resolved.

The DMT

In the DMT there are two stimulus cards which differ only in detail. These are adaptations of TAT stimuli, a test described in Chapter 26 of this handbook. In each card there is a hero figure, an attribute of the hero and a threat figure, a hideous face in the periphery of the picture. It is this peripheral threat which implicates the test in the measurement of defences because in the distortions to the percept during the series of presentations we can see how the subjects deal with threats. Sjoback (1967), in his description of this test, claims that at the early exposures in the series when subjects can see little the responses reflect primary, unconscious processes, while at later stages they become more stimulus bound. Certainly, in the scoring schemes for percept-genetic tests the point in the series at which the responses emerge is regarded as highly important.

There are several features concerning the scoring and interpretation of percept-genetic tests (of which the DMT is a typical example) which deserve comment. First, Kragh and Smith (1970) argue that the transformations of meanings, within the development of a percept, as revealed in the series of presentations, makes possible the representation of historical personality in present time. The past, it is claimed, becomes directly available to experimental investigation. New formations and meanings emerge which can only be understood by reference to the life history of the subject. Indeed experiences are actualised (to use their term) in the same order as they appeared in life. This, indeed, is parallelism, and it is claimed that the precise year of some traumatic event can be worked out from the percept-genetic series.

This somewhat fantastic claim has caused many empirically minded psychologists to reject the technique as being yet another example of wild, clinical assertions and its links with psychoanalytic theory have not helped in this regard. Indeed, in the UK apart from myself and my colleagues only Dixon (e.g. 1981) and his group have investigated the rationale of these methods. However, as has been pointed out by Kline (1987), the notion of parallelism can be dropped without abandoning the claim that important life experiences could be revealed by these techniques. In fact, it was demonstrated in that paper that parallelism had almost no meaning. Thus unless it is asserted that every aspect of a DMT response is in a strict time sequence (and it is not so asserted) and unless there is a clear demarcation of what constitutes a parallel response (and there is not) then parallelism means no more than that on some occasions responses early in the percept-genetic sequence reflect early life events and later ones later events. This is not, as is obvious, highly controversial or particularly striking. In brief parallelism can be dropped, without any loss in interpretative power. I shall now turn to an examination of the other, more important claims concerning what percept-genetic methods measure.

The validity of percept-genetic methods

I shall not consider the evidence for the validity of these methods in detail but I shall scrutinise the principles which underlie the methods. Again, I shall deal with the DMT because there is so much more research with this test than with the others, as Sjoback (1988) has shown. To clarify the discussion it is necessary to describe briefly how the DMT is scored. It should be pointed out at this juncture that scoring this test is a highly skilled procedure, and although the most recent manual (Kragh, 1985) contains improved information, much supervised practice is necessary. However with this it does appear that that the test can be reliably scored (Westerlundh, 1990).

The DMT scores

Repression. The hero or the threat figure is living or not human; or both are objects.

Isolation. The hero or threat figure are separated or isolated; one may not be seen.

Denial. The threat is emphatically denied.

Reaction-formation. The threat is turned into its opposite.

Identification with the aggressor. The hero becomes the aggressor.

Turning against self. The hero or his attribute is damaged or worthless; the attribute becomes a threat to the hero.

A study of the published work with this test, as set out in Sjoback (1988), fails to provide any definitive evidence for the validity of the DMT. This is partly because most of those who use the test simply assume that it is valid and make clinical statements about their clients which are accepted as true. Cooper and Kline (1982a) tried to remedy this deficit by carrying out an intensive study of the DMT and the Cattell 16PF Test (Cattell *et al.*, 1970a) and a variety of other measures. They concluded that the DMT was certainly measuring variance different from that in the 16PF. A further study in which the DMT was objectively scored using G analysis (Holley, 1973) which was fully described in Chapter 16 of this handbook, yielded a DMT factor which correlated positively with success in pilot selection and which was related to perceptual defence (Dixon, 1981) measures of repression. This study was reported in Cooper and Kline (1989). It should be noted that Kragh (1985) claims the utility of the DMT in pilot selection, the rationale being that those who defend too much will be slower in responding to threat and thus more likely to be involved in accidents.

The conclusions from these two studies are, however, far from definitive. They certainly show that the DMT could be valid but this is a long way from showing that it is. The best approach to demonstrating the validity of this test would be to combine with psychoanalysts and to work with patients whose unconscious was apparently known. If there was good agreement with clinical judgements it would be good evidence for the validity of the DMT. This appears to be an impeccable argument yet a few points deserve comment.

a. It should be clear from the rationale of percept-genetic methods, and from the argument that we should use patients to validate the DMT, that in principle any stimuli which offered threats could be used. Thus one of the difficulties with the DMT might be that the threat figure was simply not threatening enough, at least for some subjects. Westerlundh (1976) in his studies of schizophrenic aggression used different stimuli as did Kline and Cooper (1977) who studied oral threats by using pictures of a suckling pig (taken from the PN test by Corman, 1969, which is also described in Chapter 26 of this handbook). Here defences were seen to the oral stimuli but not to a control picture of a pig from an advertisement for bacon.

b. The phrase 'defences were seen' leads on to a more important point. When the DMT is scored for a defence, e.g. reaction formation if the threat figure is described as smiling and full of love, this is taken as some kind of objective support for Freudian theory. Yet interpreting it as a defence is doing nothing different from the analyst who construes a patient's complimentary remarks about her or his mother as reaction formation. In other words in scoring the DMT the same interpretative act as that of the analyst is made in labelling the response as a defence. In this sense the DMT is not an objective measure of defences.

c. However these percept-genetic measures do bring under public scrutiny the data from which inferences are made and they are data collected under precise conditions. For these reasons alone percept-genetic methods are useful since they give access to processes which are normally inaccessible.

Nevertheless, similar as these inferences are to those made by analysts in describing defences, it still remains necessary to show that these responses do indicate defences or other important unconscious conflicts. To fail to do this would be to rely solely on the face validity of these tests and that cannot be recommended.

Conclusions

This discussion of percept-genetic methods, as exemplified by the DMT, indicates that they may well allow access to material which is normally unconscious. The clinical studies to be found in Kragh and Smith (1970) and Sjoback (1988) support this conclusion. This being the case, it would appear useful to investigate the validity of the current percept-genetic tests and to test the efficacy of new stimuli. Congruence with clinical, psychoanalytic hypotheses would constitute evidence that at least the test protocols sampled salient material.

There is little doubt that percept-genetic methods deserve far more research into their validity than they have so far been accorded. If only half the Scandinavian claims about them turned out to be supportable, then these would be highly useful tests because they attempt to assay the unconscious.

2. SPECIAL TESTS FOR USE WITH BRAIN DAMAGED PATIENTS

Patients with brain damage or suspected brain damage after accident or stroke, and patients suffering from dementia, are frequently given cognitive tests to assess the degree of their impairment. This is often useful not only for diagnosis, as in discriminating between the effects of ageing and brain damage (Goldstein and Shelley, 1975) but for rehabilitation and treatment programmes. Many clinicians also use tests of cognitive ability to discriminate among psychiatric groups who are not normally thought of as brain damaged, even though their cognitive abilities are impaired. Schizophrenics would clearly fall into this category.

The use of such tests in clinical psychology is discussed in Chapter 20 of this handbook, while some of the best-known tests are described in Chapter 29. In this chapter I shall not repeat that material but shall examine the rationale and nature of these special tests of cognitive deficit.

a. The use of standard ability tests

One common approach is to measure cognitive deficits using standard tests of ability, of the kind discussed in Chapter 12 of this handbook. The WAIS (Wechsler, 1958), fully described in Chapter 23, is peculiarly suited for this purpose since the subscales, despite their suspect reliability, allow various aspects of ability to be assessed and particular deficits can be noted. As Howard (1989b) points out, different configurations of subscores are used by clinicians to denote organically caused cognitive deficits as well as those due to psychiatric problems. Maloney and Ward (1976) discuss this use of the WAIS in some detail.

This use of the WAIS in investigating cognitive deficits is hampered by the fact that, although it will function in this way on account of its subscales, these are really too short. Cognitive deficits are best assessed not by a global measure of cognitive ability but by tests which are far more specific, aimed at narrow abilities. Special measures of cognitive deficits fulfil exactly this purpose.

b. Special tests

Kay (1989) argues that IQ tests such as the WAIS are simply not designed to discriminate among abnormal groups, although, as was shown above, they will do so, but that specially designed tests which are more discriminating and sensitive are required. These tests, Kay argues, should concentrate upon measuring cognitive processes and functions. Furthermore it would be valuable if the tests were tied in to cognitive psychological theory, as has been advocated by Sternberg (1981) and long before this by Cattell (1971).

Goldberg (1989) has a clear discussion of the rationale of the development of these tests for use in diagnosis and treatment in clinical psychology. Ideally it would be good if, in the design of neuropsychological tests, they could be made as cognitive function-specific as possible. However most neuropsychological tests are not thus specific usually because they were designed to describe the cognitive status of patients without reference to the brain. Goldberg (1989) argues that even when attempts are made to design factor-pure tests of specific cognitive function this is rarely if ever successful. In the end, traits, skills or behaviours are factorially complex.

Although, from the psychometric viewpoint, as is made clear throughout this handbook, this is normally disastrous, this may not be the case with this group of special tests. If a particular cognitive deficit is measured, whether it is factor-pure or not is not important, certainly in the context of clinical work where the deficit may be diagnostic or where attempts are made to remedy it in rehabilitation.

However, as Goldberg (1989) argues, there are some important consequences from the fact that no one test is neuroanatomically precise. One of these is that neuropsychological diagnosis is bound to require the administration of a battery of tests. Indeed Goldberg (1989) states unequivocally that there is no such thing as a factor-pure, neuropsychological test and deficient performance on any single test cannot be necessarily regarded as evidence of dysfunction of a single neuroanatomical locus or simple cognitive dimension. In brief a battery of neuropsychological tests is required.

In the context of this discussion it would appear that to measure cognitive deficits usefully for clinical psychology, tests are required which measure a variety of functions especially those information processes which have been identified as important in cognitive psychology. Such measures might then allow sound inferences concerning the locus and extent of brain damage.

In Great Britain Warrington has long been associated with just such an endeavour; her efforts have been aimed at elucidating the deficits in various pathologies rather than the production of tests, although obviously the former often implies the latter. Warrington (1982, 1975) has carried out experimental cognitive psychological studies of the impairment of semantic memory and object recognition, just for example, and from this work (and other research) has sprung a highly useful measure – the Recognition Memory Test (Warrington, 1984). This test requires subjects to identify stimuli, both objects and words, which have been previously presented. Verbal and visual recognition scores may be obtained and the results are claimed to indicate the locus of brain damage and can be used both for diagnosis and as a basis for treatment. This test is, as has been indicated, embedded in psychological cognitive theory but it is but one measure and not part of a battery.

A typical battery for neuropsychological assessment is the Luria Nebraska Battery (Golden *et al.*, 1980) which evaluates a wide range of neuropsychological functions. The whole test takes 3½ hours to complete and fits well the prescription of Goldberg (1989). This measures motor, rhythm, tactile and visual functions, receptive and expressive speech, writing, reading, memory and intellectual processes. All these tests should enable users, with the help of norms, to build up a full picture of a subject's cognitive deficits and thus possible neuropsychological impairment.

Conclusions

Sufficient has been said about the nature of these tests of cognitive deficits. Their rationale and use is one of the more straightforward aspects of psychometrics. In essence these tests try to assess basic cognitive functions and are, at best, based on cognitive psychological theory. Norms are essential to see how typical brain damaged and other groups perform. Their clinical use is discussed in Chapter 20 and some of the commonly used tests are described and evaluated in Chapter 29 of this handbook.

3. SPECIAL TESTS AND CHECKLISTS

In this section of this chapter I shall briefly comment on the construction and use of tests which are virtually checklists, for example, of symptoms or of features of a therapeutic session. These are often used in the evaluation and study of psychotherapy, where they can be valuable in assessing the progress and outcome of therapy and how clients feel about their treatments. In the Sheffield studies of psychotherapy (Shapiro *et al.*, 1990) several tests of this kind featured in their research and I want to scrutinise this group of tests. I shall do this under a number of headings.

a. Test content

Although these tests are clinical in nature, similar tests could be constructed for use in almost any context. In educational psychology it is possible to construct checklists for the evaluation of teacher performance, and for the behaviour of problem children in the classroom. Stott (1957) indeed constructed a much used set of tests for just this purpose – the Bristol Social Adjustment Guides – which assess classroom and home behaviour. In occupational psychology again checklists for assessing the behaviour of employees are simple to construct and valuable in assessing what characteristics are desirable and necessary for particular jobs. The Positions Analysis Questionnaire (McCormick *et al.*, 1972) is a popular example of this genre, and its use is discussed in Chapter 21 of this handbook.

My point in mentioning these tests from educational and occupational psychology is to stress the fact that all the arguments which I shall use concerning the clinical tests apply with equal force to all tests of this kind.

b. The reliability and factor analysis of tests

SCL-90 Rating Scale (Derogatis *et al.*, 1973) exemplifies well this type of test. It consists of a list of ninety symptoms to each of which subjects have to say how much they they have been bothered by them in the last two weeks. Typical items are: feeling critical of others; feeling everything is an effort; overeating. It is obvious that if the symptoms are well chosen it may be useful, for diagnosis, in finding clusters of symptoms which go together and in the evaluation and monitoring of psychotherapy, in which, presumably, if things are going well symptoms would be expected to become less in intensity and number. A similar list could be envisaged for maladjusted children, just for example.

The use of this type of test, which is completely atheoretical and empirical, is harmless provided that it does not become, in this instance, the sole criterion for therapeutic success or failure. I do not want to discuss here the use of such tests in clinical psychology (see Chapter 20 of this handbook), but I shall make a few psychometric points.

Such scales are usually claimed to be reliable and to have been shown to have one or a number of factors in them. Now these demonstrations are essentially meaningless. Patients, assuming they are reporting accurately, either have or have not these symptoms. Thus the fact of the internal consistency of the scale is neither here nor there. Its internal consistency and thus reliability simply reflects the degree to which the symptoms happen to be, in real life, associated with each other. This, it should be noted, is far different from the case where one is striving to demonstrate that a set of personality test items are sampled from a common domain of items, where the test exercise is to show that these items are related. Thus to quote internal consistency reliabilities for checklists of this type is simply to make obeisance to psychometric ritual. The coefficients are not important.

The same applies to factor analyses. The information that there are x factors means nothing more than that x groups of symptoms tend to cluster together. Now this may confirm diagnostic categories and thus be of clinical interest, in this particular checklist. However, in many cases such factors simply reflect semantic similarities of items. An example of such a test is the client–therapist relationship scale which was used in the study by Shapiro *et al.* (1990) to which reference has been made. One cluster of items refers to what the client feels about the therapist and another to descriptions of the therapist. Such factors reflect the semantic similarities of the items. They do not refer to any variable beyond the test itself. The universe of items from which they are drawn is a set of items describing therapists. This is in sharp contrast to a set of extraversion items, which if the test is valid, reflect a wider set of behaviours, beyond the test items. Thus the fact that there may be more than one factor means only that one score should not be used based on simple addition of checked items. However these checklists are rarely used in such a way, interest often being in item by item analysis. Indeed, even if there were several factors in a symptom checklist, the absolute number of symptoms, before and after treatment, might still be of interest.

From this argument it can be seen that in checklists where it is not claimed that a variable is being measured but where interest is centred on the actual items, reliability and factorial construction are of less importance than in the psychometric tests described in the main categories of this handbook, where the variables are more than collections of similar items. These tests are essentially quantified interviews which is why they appeal so strongly to those in applied psychology.

c. Checklists and common sense

These lists are usually constructed on intuitive and common sense grounds. As a result it is difficult to discover anything new. Common sense may be refuted if the hypotheses are not confirmed but if they are, common sense is simply backed up. This is because these tests, from the nature of their construction, cannot yield new variables. This, again, is in sharp contrast to psychometric personality tests where the main factored variables, extra-version, anxiety, tough-mindedness and obsessionality (see Chapter 15 of this handbook) enable psychologists to develop new models of personality in which these variables are critical and not, say, the death instinct, the shadow, cerebrotonia, and need abasement, to name a few variables held to be important before psychometric quantification.

d. Conclusion: checklists and the nature of factors

The essence of this problem lies in the nature of factors. This topic was fully discussed in Chapters 7 and 8 of this handbook, and I want here to em-phasise a few critical issues. Throughout this handbook I have stressed the importance of working with factored tests. However, the factored tests which I have advocated have been tests measuring factors for which there was some kind of external, non-test, validity. Intelligence is the clearest example of this. The intelligence factor, as measured by intelligence tests, predicts academic and occupational success. Furthermore it has a high heritability index (see Kline, 1990, for details).

Unfortunately some tests measure simply bloated specifics (Cattell, 1978). Such tests are highly reliable and the items load well on their factor. How-ever bloated specific factors can be distinguished from factors of substantive importance by the fact that they do not correlate with other variables. In essence many checklists and similar tests are of this kind. Items form factors because they are obviously similar. In these cases the only psychological information which can be obtained from them resides in the items themselves.

One example will clarify this important point. In the client–therapist relation-ship scale there is an item: 'My therapist's professional skills are impressive.' It may be that that item and the set of similar items in which it is embedded distinguishes those who enjoy their therapy, who feel better as a result of it. However nothing more than that statement can be inferred – namely that those who get better and enjoy their therapy find their therapist impressive. If the results were the opposite, namely that those who did not get better found the skills of their therapist impressive, that is all that could be said.

Sometimes such information may be valuable but it is clear that nothing is added by factoring such tests. These tests seem to be quantifying responses in such a way as to be able to compare groups statistically. However it seems that little more than what was previously known, which led to the con-struction of the test in the first place, can emerge from them. Their main use is in fact-gathering. If this is used to attempt to develop theories, this is good. However as an end in itself it would appear to be of limited psychological and scientific value. As a psychometrist I should like to see such tests used as little as possible.

4. TESTS OF EMOTION BASED ON THE CIRCUMPLEX AND OTHER SIMILAR MODELS

In this handbook, the main emphasis has been placed on the classical model of error (discussed in Chapter 3) and on factor analysis and its implications for test construction and validation. In Chapter 11 a few other models of test construction were discussed, including Guttman scales. For reasons of space, and because there are few tests constructed on this rationale, another of the many contributions to statistical theory of Guttman was not scrutinised in that chapter and this deficiency will be made good here. It is a fitting place because there is a small group of tests constructed on a model proposed by Guttman – the circumplex – which is only one of a family of such models, the radex and simplex being the best known of the others.

Description of the circumplex

The circumplex is a particular model which arises from facet analysis which should be briefly discussed. A facet is a system of classification and within each facet there can be a number of classificatory levels. In facet analysis, as Nunnally (1978) points out, there are a number of stages. Let us suppose that we have a collection of tests. First a facet structure must be suggested, which is a specific combination of all the categories. This proposed structure should lead to a hypothesised matrix of test intercorrelations. Then the hypothesised correlations are compared with the actual, observed correlations, statistical tests of fit being possible. If the facet account is good, then test scoring must be computed such as to measure the underlying facets.

As Nunnally (1978) argues this facet analysis is frequently referred to as molar correlational analysis because it is concerned with the hypothesised structure of whole matrices rather than individual factors. Facets may be seen as explaining, in terms of their combinations, the underlying factors of a matrix. Although it is possible to derive facets from correlations among tests it is usual in facet analysis to begin with hypotheses concerning the facets and the combination of facets in each test.

In the circumplex the facet structure is circular. Each variable can be regarded as a cluster because it is a mixture of facet components. Starting with variable 1 (out of 8 variables) each variable has more in common with its neighbouring variable than those distant from it (e.g. 1 with 2 and 7 with 8). However they are arranged in a circle in that variables in the middle, 4, 5, 6, have less in common with the extremes than with one another, while variables at the extremes overlap in terms of facet composition (1 and 8). In a circumplex as one departs from the diagonal parts of the matrix, the numbers of facets in common decline to zero but then increase indicating the circular nature of the shared variance.

Nunnally (1978) has an excellent illustration of a circumplex based upon common facets, which clarifies the nature of the circular ordering of the circumplex. It should be pointed out that it is possible to convert a matrix of common facets to a hypothetical matrix of correlations: the number of common facets can be related to percentage of common variance of which the square root is the correlation. We reproduce this illustration of the circumplex as Figure 18.1.

Before I examine some tests made to conform to the circumplex, a few points about the model should be made. First, as Nunnally (1978) argues, the point of the circumplex is that it is an elegant summary of the data in a correlation matrix. Of course that is also the raison d'être of factor analysis but factor analysis, particularly at the primary level as was seen in Chapter 13 on abilities, can become unwieldy, with no obvious end to the number of factors, and a further summarising principle would be useful. This, the advocates of molar correlational analysis would argue, the circumplex does. McCrae and Costa (1989c), indeed, have argued that the circumplex fits personality ratings well and can be regarded as a complementary model to their factor analytic description.

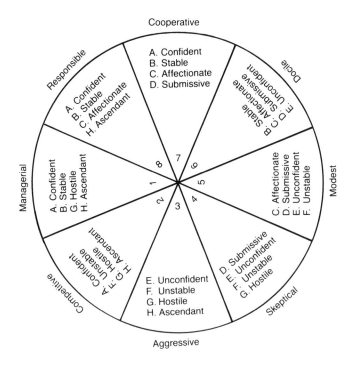

Figure 18.1 A circumplex

Source: Nunnally (1978)

However, neat as the results might be, the methods of molar analysis are statistically and logically complex and this difficulty is confounded by the fact that there is no clear differentiation between the notions of facet and variable.

There is a further problem pointed out by Nunnally (1978). Facet analysis, unlike factor analysis, is not a method of discovery. Rather it is a method of testing hypotheses. However the circumplex, as our description has made clear, is an exceedingly complex hypothesis and it is only rarely that one could hypothesise a structure of such complexity given current knowledge of the main psychometric fields of personality, motivation and ability.

In the simplified description of the circumplex which was constructed for illustrative purposes it is to be noted that facets were either present or absent. However in the realistic application of psychological tests such a simple metric would be highly unlikely. In addition different weights for the facets would have to be used. This makes the circumplex even more complicated.

There is a possibly more important point, which Nunnally (1978) makes concerning facet analysis, namely that there is no method built into the analysis for discovering the underlying facets. This, of course, distinguishes it completely from factor analysis.

There is a final point which I have always found difficult with the circumplex and other facet models. Even if it can be shown that these are neat, summary models of complex correlational matrices, the description has never seemed to me to be particularly meaningful. However, this is a subjective view; others may find such circular descriptions valuable or insightful. Sometimes they remind me of unrotated factor matrices, which, as was seen in Chapter 8 of this handbook, are mathematically as good accounts of the data as simple structure solutions but are not usually psychologically meaningful.

Conclusions

From this description and discussion of the circumplex it is clear that it is an ingenious method of summarising a matrix of test scores. Readers who require more information on these facet models are referred to Foa (1965) and to Wiggins (1980).

5. THE WORK OF PLUTCHIK

Plutchik has studied the emotions over a long period. His psychoevolutionary approach (Plutchik, 1980) to emotions binds them closely to traits and states. Traits he regards as affect states (emotions) which persist or frequently occur in a variety of situations. Into the theory, in addition, are brought defences, unconscious mechanisms to deal with conflicted emotions and coping mechanisms, the conscious techniques for solving these conflicts.

This is the theoretical background to Plutchik's tests of emotions which are made to fit the circumplex model, on the following grounds. As has been stated, personality traits, in this theory, are derivatives of emotions. Traits result from persisting situations which produce mixed emotions. For example, a person who is always in fearful situations but who wants to please is likely to develop the trait of docility (Plutchik and Conte, 1989). This fact that the inherent characteristics of emotions are reflected in personality traits implies, according to Plutchik and Conte (1989), the circumplex model, as a good fit to the measurement of traits and emotions. In terms of our example of the circumplex emotions can be thought of as facets of various personality traits.

a. The emotional profile index

This measures eight basic emotions as described by Plutchik (1980). It assumes that all personality traits result from the mixture of two or more primary emotions. Shyness implies fear, for example, gloominess sadness.

The index is a forced-choice test in which twelve trait terms are paired in every possible combination (excluding four which are virtually identical) and subjects have to choose which of each pair best describes them. Each time a word is chosen the score on one or more of the eight basic emotional dimensions is increased. These dimensions are: joy, acceptance, surprise, fear, sadness, disgust, expectation and anger. Thus the test measures all these dimensions which are arranged as a circumplex in terms of similarities and bipolarities.

Subjects receive a score on each of the eight dimensions in the test. This is then converted into a percentile score based upon a sample of 500 males and 500 females. These percentiles are plotted onto a circle divided into eight segments, where zero is at the centre and the 100th percentile on the circumference. Reliabilities of the scales are said to be high (Plutchik and Conte, 1989). According to these authors, the major value of the EPI is that it is based directly on a theory of emotions, which determined the choice of the dimensions to be measured, decided on the circumplex, provided the basis for identifying the emotional components of traits, and finally provided a basis for measuring the conflict of mixed emotions and traits.

Conclusions

My interest here is not to debate the virtues of the Emotions Profile Index but to use it as an illustration of the circumplex model as a basis for tests. From the description of the theory and the test it is clear how the circumplex may be used in test construction. However before I scrutinise the value of the circumplex model I shall describe, briefly, a further instrument developed by Plutchik – the Personality Profile Index, the PPI.

b. The personality profile index

This test, as with the EPI, is based upon the claim that the circumplex model is the best description of trait terms. The traits used in this test were those shown to form a circumplex by Conte (1975) and Conte and Plutchik (1981), who investigated the structure of 171 terms.

In the final version of the PPI there are eighty-nine items (trait terms) to which subjects respond on a five-point scale of 'never' to 'very often'. The dimensions of the circumplex are: acceptance, submission, passivity, assertion, sociability, rejection, aggression and suppression.

The question that needs to be asked about the PPI concerns the nature of these eight traits. Although they fit the circumplex, what does this tell us about them? In my view the fact that traits fit a circumplex is of little psychological interest. It contains less information than a simple structure factor analysis which informs us of the size of the factors, their intercorrelations and the fact that these are the main factors in the field. The circumplex simply states that they can be arranged logically around a circle. This leaves out the question of other factors that might not fit the pattern so well.

Furthermore there is the difficulty of the validity of these dimensions. Thus Plutchik and Conte (1989) state that an inspection of the way these terms were grouped around the circumplex indicated that they had an explicit similarity structure. For example 'One grouping was clearly related to aggression (e.g. "argumentative" and "belligerent") and a contiguous group of words such as "outspoken", "forceful" and "candid" reflected assertiveness and not aggression' (p. 249). This claim deserves careful scrutiny from the viewpoint of the psychometric arguments which we have asserted throughout this handbook.

Note the word 'clearly', in the clause 'one grouping was clearly related to aggression'. What does this actually mean? Nothing more than this is what the authors believe to be true. Now to say that terms are related to aggression is not a matter of opinion but is an empirical issue which needs evidence for support. Simple assertion is insufficient. It means that the aggression trait has nothing more than face validity. This is even more important in the second assertion, namely that similar words measure assertiveness rather than aggression. Thus the labelling of the dimensions is simply face validity. This is important because part of the argument for accepting the circumplex in the first place was the fact that the dimensions had the circumplical qualities of similarity and polarity.

In brief the dimensions of the PPI are identified only in terms of their items and such face validity is not satisfactory. In addition the fact that they are arranged as a circumplex tells us little about their structure. What is needed is a factor analysis of these scales with the main factors of personality. It is highly likely then there would be little unexplained variance in the PPI and the need for a circumplical description would be removed.

Conclusions

These two examples of tests by Plutchik and his colleagues which are based on the circumplex model do not seem strongly to support its use or value in test construction. There seems little advantage in the circumplex description and it would only appear useful if it were shown that variables in the circumplex could fit no other structure. This is manifestly not the case with the PPI. Thus all its scales correlate significantly with the Tennessee Self Esteem scale (Fitts, 1965). This means that they cannot be independent and thus the case for the circumplex structure disappears. As was suggested above a factor analysis of these scales would show little unexplained variance. All that has been achieved is that Plutchik has shown that a circumplex structure will fit the scales. However that it should do so appears to be of little psychological significance and it is clear, from the correlations with the self-esteem scale, that a more parsimonious account of the variance in these items is possible.

The same arguments apply to the earlier emotional scale. Thus the twelve trait terms which were used to construct the emotions were selected only on the grounds that there was good agreement among judges concerning their emotional consistency. However this amounts to no more than face validity. As was the case with the EPI a factor analysis of these scales with the main marker factors of personality would reveal the nature of their variance. At present their labelling is simply in terms of face validity and Plutchik's theory of emotion.

In brief these two examples of tests constructed around the circumplex model do not appear to give it strong support as a basis of test construction. The main problem with the model arises from the fact that even where it is the neatest description of the data, as it is not in the PPI, it is not an informative description. There is little information conveyed by the fact that the scales fit a circumplex.

The circumplex model would only appear useful when it is clear that normal psychometric models, such as simple structure factors, do not fit the complexity of the data.

6. REPERTORY GRIDS

Repertory grids were developed by Kelly (1955) as a method of collecting data relevant to his Personal Construct Theory. Although he always stressed that repertory grids were not tests (indeed it is intrinsic to the theory that they are not), they are often so regarded by many psychologists and I want to describe and discuss them in this chapter. I shall do so as briefly as possible, since, as shall be seen, they are so riddled with difficulties that I think they should be eschewed as any form of measurement, although they may well be useful in obtaining personal information.

The essence of construct theory which underlies the repertory grid is that human beings may be seen as archetypal scientists always attempting to make sense of the world. They do this by forming constructs which are dependent on their experience, and thus wholly specific and particular to the person who holds them. Thus Kelly and construct theorists, such as Bannister (Bannister and Mair, 1968) regard standard psychological tests as valueless because the meaning of the items is different for every individual. Repertory grids are aimed at elucidating the meaning of the important constructs in an individual's life. To take a simplified example: a good man to a convinced Christian would possess very different qualities from a good man in the eyes of Hitler.

Description of a repertory grid

A grid consists of elements and constructs. 'Elements can be anything in the world', to quote Bannister (1973), 'films, chess openings . . . , types of roses, coital positions and so on'. Constructs are the discriminations which a person makes among his or her elements. A repertory grid is aimed at elucidating these constructs, usually among elements which are relevant to the purpose of using the repertory grid in the first place.

An example of a grid

Suppose that we are interested in the constructs a woman has about people. We would have her name say fifteen important individuals in her life, e.g. mother, lover, brother, boss at work, and so on; these would be the elements. The constructs could be elicited from the subject by grouping the elements into three and asking her to say in what way two are alike and different from the third. Thus we might get that A and B are intelligent while C is dim. This is a construct: intelligent–dim. Similarly we might find that D and E are gentle while F is cruel and so on. In this way a grid can be constructed of elements and constructs. Note that it is essential that the constructs are elicited from the subject, because they are particular to her. There are other methods of eliciting constructs but these are essentially equivalent to the method which I have described. Fransella (1981) has further details of the precise techniques of repertory grid methods. Here it might be mentioned that there are rather different types of grids described by Kelly (1955), most of which have been rarely used. One, however, which explores the relationships between constructs, particularly which constructs imply others, is the implication grid (Hinkle, 1965) but this takes us far away from the realms of psychometrics and readers must refer to Fransella (1981) or to the work of Hinkle (1965) for further information.

Analysis of the grid

Subjects can be asked to rank each element on each construct or to rate each element on each construct. Both of these methods yield correlations between constructs. It is then possible to see what constructs go together and of course how similar individuals are on these constructs. Thus we might find that intelligence and cruelty are highly correlated, just for example and that, turning to elements, a hated school teacher was seen as similar to her mother and so on.

Now clearly this may yield information which is useful for understanding that particular individual and for such clinical use the grid seems well suited. However what further may be done with this information, especially since grids of different individuals are not comparable, is difficult.

Some workers factor analyse grids (e.g. Slater (1964; 1976) who has developed a statistically sophisticated set of computer programs for this purpose). However given the small number of observations in any grid, the statistical error of such factor analyses is likely to be so large as to render this approach highly dubious. Again even if factors were to emerge, they would be particular to that individual and hence of limited scientific interest. I agree with Fransella (1981) who has argued that much of the complex statistical analysis of grids appears to be done for its own sake rather than for any useful psychological information which might be obtained.

A number of important points arise from this claim that the constructs of each individual are distinct and particular to her or him. In one sense it is so obviously true as to be banal. We all recognise that our private experience may not be similar to that of anybody else. However that it is so different as to render tests worthless may well not be true. If this was the case conversation and understanding between people would be impossible. The fact that words can be understood suggests that they have a common core of meaning, even if this meaning is not identical.

However, there is a more severe difficulty. If the constructs individuals use are so different that they must be separately elucidated then it follows that the information about an individual from a repertory grid is particular to that individual and cannot be combined with the results of any other subject, nor can inferences be made from the results of one subject about any other individual. This effectively destroys the normal scientific aim of discovering general laws, applicable to all or large sections of humanity. If the basic premises of the repertory grid are accepted, we are saying that a scientific psychology is impossible and that only separate individuals can be understood.

Notice that it cannot even be argued that it would be useful to measure one individual well with a grid and then relate the scores to some environmental variables. Even if it were possible to establish such a relationship it would not be useful since the constructs that were so related are a priori different from any others in the world and no inference or extrapolation is allowable. Thus only in clinical work with individuals could the information yielded by a grid be useful.

Let me exemplify these points. The grid might be used in marital therapy. It might turn out that the husband saw his wife as a mother while the wife saw the husband as a father. Such incompatibility can create problems. Now discussion of this difficulty might lead to improvement. Suppose that this was a frequent finding. Strictly, since the constructs of individuals are different no generalisations can be made. However, common sense would suggest that it is a reasonable hypothesis to suppose that where men wanted mothers and women fathers there would be marital disharmony. However if this inference is made the whole point of using the grid as distinct from interview and questionnaire, with common constructs, disappears. Thus even in clinical usage there are logical inconsistencies and absurdities in the use of repertory grids.

For all these reasons I do not consider that the repertory grid is a useful tool of measurement. The Grid Test (Bannister and Fransella, 1966) is used in the study of thought disorders but, as is pointed out below, despite its name and provenance it is not essentially a repertory grid technique. If the results are used, in understanding a patient in clinical work, it would seem a harmless procedure, which could yield interesting information.

The grid test of thought disorder (Bannister and Fransella, 1966)

Despite Bannister's objections to thinking of the grid as a test, which have been discussed, Bannister and Fransella (1966) in fact developed the grid test as a measure of thought disorder. This is a repertory grid with fixed elements and constructs. These are rank ordered and normative data have been collected on the test. However, although this test has the form of a repertory grid, in that the constructs are given and not elicited, it is not truly a repertory grid. In fact it is no more than a set of rating scales. This is by no means to denigrate this instrument, but the fact that the constructs are common for subjects means that it is open to the same criticism, from the viewpoint of construct theory, as any other test.

7. ATTITUDE SCALES

The last group of tests which I shall discuss are attitude scales. I shall say little about them in this chapter because they are relatively simple and because each is best considered separately, as is done in Chapter 28. Furthermore their nature was explicated in Chapter 11 when scaling procedures were examined.

Most attitude tests, as was clear in Chapter 11, consist of relevant statements to which subjects have to agree or disagree, although the selection of statements depends upon the type of attitude scale which is being constructed.

Attitudes usually require an object so that the potential number of attitude scales is extremely large. In practice, however, most attitude scales which are at all widely used are concerned with broad, socially relevant attitudes, such as attitudes to society and to self-variables which shade off into personality measurement. As was discussed in Chapter 17, the problem with these standard attitude scales is that they load only on the beta component of attitudes, although they may be homogeneous, and thus are unlikely to be highly valid.

In Chapter 28 I examine and scrutinise the most important attitude scales – self esteem, locus of control, authoritarian personality (which I regard as the social emanation of obsessionality) and masculinity–femininity, together with certain other well-known attitude scales. In Chapter 28 items are discussed and for further information readers should turn to those pages.

FINAL COMMENTS

In this chapter I have reviewed a number of disparate tests which do not fit the major categories of tests which have been used in this handbook. As has become obvious from the discussion, most of these tests do not stand critical scrutiny, although attitude tests are accepted in social psychology despite the problems over their validity. The percept-genetic methods were the most interesting but even these demand far more research before they can be used with any confidence. The only other category of tests which appeared to be of substantive psychological value were the neuropsychological tests, designed to detect organic brain damage. The other tests may well be useful in certain specific experiments but in general their value was questionable.

Section III

The Use and Interpretation of Tests

The first two sections of this handbook have been concerned with psychometric theory and the tests which have been developed from its basis. In this third section the use and interpretation of tests in applied psychology is discussed.

The natural sciences, especially physics and chemistry, have been singularly impressive and exciting as the application of their findings has impinged upon and, indeed, more recently, profoundly influenced every aspect of society. Psychology has not been influential to any comparable extent but psychometrics is the one branch of psychology which is widely used in the real world, as distinct from that of psychological research. In education, medicine and industry psychological tests are widely used. In fact, their use in education has brought them into considerable disrepute in some political circles. As is the case with any science psychometrics can be misused.

For all these reasons Section III of the handbook deals with the use of tests in education, industry and medicine. In all these spheres of application the value of using psychometric tests is discussed. All the difficulties and problems with tests are freely and frankly examined. Much of their misuse and the resulting public opprobrium arises from impossible expectations of tests on the part of testers, who in many cases are not well versed in psychometrics. In Great Britain, at least, psychometric tests can be used with little training.

Finally, in every application of tests where the results affect an individual, his or her qualifications, career or treatment, there are ethical problems. These are discussed since there can be little doubt that in the past (see Kamin, 1974) psychological tests, especially intelligence tests, have been used with some impropriety.

Chapter 19

Tests in Educational Psychology

In this chapter the term 'educational psychology' is used to embrace all the psychological factors which affect the educational progress and achievement of children and young adults, in school and further education. Of course this means that there might be some overlap with vocational, counselling and clinical psychology since the distinction between these categories is somewhat arbitrary. However, for clarity, and because it is a distinction that is hallowed by usage, I shall discuss educational psychology separately, in this chapter.

In fact I shall restrict my discussion of testing in educational psychology to three topics. Two are related issues: the diagnosis and treatment of educational difficulties and the allocation of children and students to a suitable educational level – selection. The use of tests in vocational guidance and counselling (which is undoubtedly an aspect of educational psychology) is discussed in Chapter 21. The third issue is educational theory, to which psychometric testing can make a considerable contribution.

1. THE DIAGNOSIS AND TREATMENT OF EDUCATIONAL DIFFICULTIES

a. Diagnosis

By diagnosis I mean here the identification of the source of the problem. In many cases it might more accurately be called description and labelling. This can be seen in the most common referrals to educational psychologists: children who are not progressing well at school for reasons which the teacher cannot understand and children who behave badly, disrupting classes and who are a menace to pupils and staff (of course children may be in both these categories).

In the past educational psychologists working on the model developed by Burt for the London educational authority made extensive use of tests, especially intelligence tests. Educational psychologists were often referred to as Binet-Bashers and could be seen entering schools carrying the little cases in which these tests were packed – the psychological version of the doctor's bag.

More recently, however, there has been a change of emphasis in educational psychology. When I was trained in educational psychology, part of the course consisted of seeing children and subjecting them to the whole range of psychological tests which have been discussed in this handbook. The results of this testing had to be carefully written up and interpretations were assessed. Today the majority of educational psychological training courses have relatively little on psychological testing. Instead there is an emphasis on behaviour modification, and the organisation of education along sound psychological principles, although some educational psychologists do still see children (if this is unavoidable).

I do not intend in this chapter to enter this debate on what educational psychology should be about. Instead I shall ignore fashion and state as simply as possible how psychometric testing can contribute to the diagnosis of educational difficulties. I shall do this by discussing some hypothetical cases which will illustrate not only how tests can be used for diagnosis but also the problems and difficulties involved in the process.

Since this chapter is not intended to be a practical guide to educational testing the details of exactly which test should be used and precisely how it should be administered will not be described. Instead I shall concentrate upon the rationale of tests in diagnosis. Furthermore I shall make little reference to the other things which any competent educational psychologist might do.

The factual basis of the arguments used in this section of the chapter

The arguments used in this chapter have a factual basis, much of which cannot be described in any detail in a handbook of psychological testing. There are two sources of evidence. One is the factor structure of ability, personality and motivation, as it has emerged from psychometric testing. This has resulted in the identification of the most important dimensions in these areas of testing. This part of the evidence has been discussed in the first two sections of this handbook and I am assuming (without further discussion of the evidence) in this chapter that there are available reasonably valid measures of the variables which I shall discuss.

The second source of evidence which I shall discuss comes from the huge body of research into the prediction of academic success. I summarised much of this in Kline (1979) and the correlation of intelligence with academic success has been summarised more recently by Jensen (1980) and Kline (1990). Cattell and Johnson (1986) also contains useful summaries of recent work in this field.

Indeed it is simple to give a brief account of what has been found. Intelligence tests tend to correlate with academic success in all fields and personality and motivational variables have low but significant correlations with educational achievement. Table 19.1 contains a set of typical findings which form a basis for the subsequent discussion in this chapter both as regards diagnosis and treatment but also selection. Table 19.1 sets out correlations of variables with academic success.

In interpreting this table it should be noted that in any kind of selective education correlations are probably attenuated through homogeneity of variance. Thus across the whole population they are likely to rise.

The rationale of testing in diagnosis

From Table 19.1 it is possible to develop a rationale for the use of tests in diagnosis. What is required is the maximum amount of psychological knowledge from the minimum of testing. This is achieved by measuring the main ability, personality and motivational factors. This is the implication of the psychometric model, proposed by Cattell (1957), that behaviour can be predicted from a multiple correlation of the factors in the three fields of motivation, personality and ability.

Thus ideally every client referred should be tested on the most important factored variables in these three fields. The actual tests which would be used for this are described in Section IV of this handbook. However, it should be pointed out that this is rather an idealised procedure since such overall testing would require more time than could be available for every referral, with the result that, in practice, a psychologist may give only a selection of these tests.

I shall now consider what can be learned from each type of test, taking a particular, typical case as a starting point for the discussion.

Case 1

A 14-year-old girl, referred for poor academic performance at school. Obviously the task here, for the educational psychologist, is to discover the causes of this failure.

The use of tests

i. Intelligence tests In educational failure it is essential to know what the capabilities of the subject are. The cause of academic failure may be relatively straightforward – low intelligence. Thus a first step is the intelligence test. Until the intelligence of a subject is known, it is impossible to decide how she ought to be performing at school. Thus in cases of educational difficulty an intelligence test is a good first test. An individual test is always preferable if time allows. Seeing the way the subject does the test may provide a useful clue to the source of the difficulties. For example if she

Table 19.1 Relation of academic success to psychometric test variables

Variable		Primary school	Correlations and/or beta weights Secondary school						Higher education	Source of research and comments
			Language		Maths		Stanford			
			r	β	r	β	r	β		
Ability sphere	gc (including g)		0.40	0.09	0.45	0.13	0.43	0.08	235	Secondary school: 278 children in Cattell and Butcher's study (1968).
	gf		0.37	0.11	0.45	0.19	0.44	0.14	181 (estimated)	
	V		0.54	0.30	0.46	0.14	0.64	0.44		
	N		0.35	0.08	0.50	0.30	0.39	0.10		
	Fluency		0.46	0.19	0.38	0.05	0.41	0.06		
	K		0.26	0.03	0.33	0.08	0.34	0.08		
	Multiple correlation		0.60		0.64		0.68			

School achievement

Variable		Pass/Fail	r	β	β	Source of research and comments
Personality sphere	Anxiety Q$_1$ or N	−147 (U.S.A.)	−0.25	−0.25		Secondary school: 310 children. From HSPQ manual. Only largest correlations shown. N.B. The high multiple r. Beta weights in the second column are from Cattell (1971). Results for E and N: These are averages from a large number of studies reported by Entwistle (1972) and Cattell (1973).
	Exvia Q$_2$ E	138	0.3			
Cattell's tests 16 PF HSPQ CPQ	G		0.35	0.24	0.25	
	A	132	0.15	0.15	0.15	
	1					
	Q$_2$		0.30	0.21	0.20	
	Multiple correlation		0.53	(without B)		

Higher education

Variable		Higher education	Source of research and comments
Personality sphere Other tests	As	0.185	DPI results from Hamilton (1970).
	Om	0.173	
	H	−159	

Variable		Maths		Reading		Source of research and comments
		I^a	T^b	I	T	
Motivational sphere MAT	Self-sentiment	32	24	41	24	Secondary school: 13-year-old students. Figures from Cattell et al. (1972a); a decimal point should be inserted before all these figures.
	Superego	23	04	42	25	
	Self-assertion	27	23	27	15	
	Fear	13	22	16	32	
	Pugnacity	28	19	28	00	
	Sex	42	30	43	22	
	Narcissism	24	18	31	22	

I^a is integrated. T^b is total.

always sticks at every problem and refuses to continue until it is solved or if there is an obvious lack of concentration, then these may be the causes, in part, of the problem.

If a child is in the top 2 per cent of her age group for intelligence then there is no reason why she should not be highly successful at all school subjects in terms of ability, unless there is some specific weak ability, which can also be tested. Thus the sources of failure must lie elsewhere. Knowing she is of high intelligence eliminates a major possible determinant of the problem. It makes sense to search for personal problems or failure of the child to get on with the teachers. It should also be noted that, as Burt maintained (Burt, 1940) many extremely bright children do badly at school because they are bored. This is not to be confused with the gifted child syndrome of the pushy middle classes afraid that their darlings may not become accountants.

However, if it turns out that the child is slightly below average intelligence and is in a school where there is great emphasis on academic attainment and excellence little further explanation is required. Such children, if they are well behaved and well spoken, are often regarded as bright by teachers and their frustration and failure at work that is simply too difficult for them often leads to bad behaviour as well as failure. Here the intelligence test scores can suggest a change of curriculum which may well do the trick.

In summary the intelligence test score indicates the level of academic performance which we should expect from the child.

Let us suppose, in this first case, that the child is bright, and has an IQ of 120. This is more than sufficient for good school performance so that the cause of the educational difficulties lies elsewhere. I shall now consider what further tests should be given.

ii. Other ability tests If the educational performance is about the same in all subjects across the arts and sciences, there is little reason to test for the other main ability factors which were described in Chapter 13. However if performance is uneven it may well be worth assessing the main ability factors. It is possible if it were found, for example, that she was weak in verbal ability that this the consequent poorer performance in arts subjects was leading to dissatisfaction that was spreading more generally to other subjects. This, however, while a possibility, is not common.

The main use of the narrower ability factors is to investigate a more specific weakness. For example if a child were referred who was doing badly in languages it would make sense to investigate verbal ability. If this were consonant with her other abilities then it would be more likely that the problem lay with the teaching, and her failure to get on with those particular teachers.

A special mention must be made here of the diagnostic tests, described in Chapter 14, of the type designed by Schonell (Schonell and Schonell, 1950).

For children at primary school who are progressing badly in English and arithmetic these diagnostic tests are extremely useful since they pinpoint the actual failure, e.g. carrying zeros or mixing up p and q, thus enabling remedial teaching to concentrate on the actual difficulties. Of course these should always be used together with the other psychometric tests suggested in this chapter. Intelligence tests are particularly important because they can indicate the likelihood of plain low intelligence being influential in the problem.

iii. Personality tests and motivation tests Table 19.1 indicates that personality and motivation tests have correlations with academic success. Furthermore, these are more important than their absolute size might suggest simply because being uncorrelated with ability tests they account for a different part of the educational variance, as was shown by Cattell and Butcher (1968) and Cattell and Kline (1977).

However, despite the fact that there are significant correlations with these personality and motivational variables it is necessary to be cautious in their use with individual cases. From Table 19.1 it is clear that intraverted subjects do best at academic work at the secondary school. Suppose that we test our case and find that she is extraverted. The sceptic of testing, the experienced and embittered teacher, may well consider the finding useless. Certainly it must be said that teachers have sent aggressive and violent children to the educational psychologist only to be told after extensive testing that the child is aggressive and tends to be violent and needs careful handling. This, therefore, leads us beyond diagnosis or description, to what might be called treatment or interpretation.

b. Treatment or interpretation

When the problem has been diagnosed, we come to the other aspect of the testing, the treatment or interpretation on which treatment will be based.

As I must stress testing is not the only thing that an educational psychologist should do, and before treatment can be discussed I must briefly mention some non-test factors which have to be investigated, and which clearly must enter into any consideration of what needs to be done. These will simply be mentioned since this is a handbook of psychological testing: problems with family, including physical or sexual abuse; drink or drug problems; sexual problems; school difficulties, such as bullying; simple home problems – no room for working; financial difficulties – working outside school; medical problems. All of these can be influential in educational failure. Thus testing is only one, but an important aspect of diagnosis.

However if there are no obvious causes of educational failure in the types of problem listed above it makes sense to consider the psychological test results, in relation to our attempts to treat the problem. How this can be done is, perhaps, best explained by answering a number of objections which can be ranged against the use of psychological tests, objections which, as shall be seen, are not well founded.

Objection 1

Psychological testing is labelling an individual which not only serves no good purpose but is actually harmful. This argument runs as follows: if a child is labelled as of low intelligence (or in an academic school of average intelligence) some teachers give up and regard the task of teaching her as impossible. This, indeed, lies at the heart of the opposition to the selective grammar school (Pedley, 1955) together with the bad effect on the self-esteem of the child. Similarly if a child is described as extraverted, this seems to signify, again, that nothing can be done since, as is the case with intelligence, extraversion is a largely heritable variable (Cattell, 1982).

In both these instances, although it is true that extraversion and intelligence are considered to be stable variables, the inference that nothing can be done does not follow. If intelligence has been shown to be lower than required for the courses the child is following, then change the course. Similarly if the child seems too intelligent, and is therefore creating trouble, change the courses. Indeed this prescription is central to the notion of psychometric testing in educational psychology. Obtain a good psychological profile of the child's abilities and personality and then select the requisite curriculum.

In the case of personality it is likely that the correlation between intraversion and success at the secondary school can be attributed to teaching methods: examination oriented lessons favour the intravert who prefers a quiet and bookish environment. The extravert, on the other hand, is stimulus hungry (Eysenck, 1967) and likes a lively noisy environment – hence the relation of extraversion with academic success at the primary school where the type of teaching is more suitable for extraverts.

Thus if psychological testing and our knowledge of other relevant aspects of the child's life suggested that being extraverted was the source of difficulty, it would be sensible to see whether it was possible to move the child into classes with a more extraverted atmosphere. Again we change the environment to suit the child rather than attempt the much more difficult feat of changing the child.

Suppose that our testing revealed that a child was anxious and it was this anxiety that seemed to be hindering progress at school. This is clearly a more difficult case and it is wishful thinking that anxiety may be easily reduced by some simple therapy. There are two points here.

First, psychological testing is not a panacea. It may well turn out on some occasions that the testing reveals little can be done. It has to be faced, for example, that at present autistic children are unlikely to develop their full potential. However with anxiety, since this is a variable that is unlikely to change (I refer to trait anxiety rather than state anxiety) all that can be done is to mimimise the problem by attempting to keep the anxiety level of the individual as low as possible. Thus, contrary to the sceptical view, psychometric testing can have practical consequences. It is wrong, therefore, to argue that psychometric testing simply describes an individual. It may do so but there are practical consequences of the description.

I now want to discuss another possible set of personality results. Suppose that we have given the 16PF test (Cattell *et al.*, 1970a) to our subject, as the measure of personality factors. Our interest is in the extreme scores on the variables. Suppose that all her extreme scores are on variables that research shows are not associated with academic success. This indicates that it is unlikely that personality variables play a part in the problems of this subject. If however we have a subject whose extreme scores are on these variables, then it makes sense to examine this possibility in more detail. As has been indicated the aim would not be to change the subject but to change, if at all possible, the educational environment.

I shall now attempt to answer the objection that labelling individuals is harmful. There is no doubt that if children are simply told that they are too stupid to continue their courses or to attempt those they would like to try, this might be harmful to their self-esteem and cause them to give up. Similarly if teachers are informed that certain children are of low intelligence they may well give up on them. This is generally known as the self-fulfilling prophecy. However, this is not to accept the findings from the famous study which attracted so much popular attention – *Pygmalion in the Classroom* (Rosenthal and Jacobson, 1968) – where it was claimed that the progress of groups of children, matched for IQ, was determined by their teachers' view of their intelligence which had been manipulated by the researchers. The test used to measure intelligence initially was almost certainly invalid. Nevertheless, as Vernon (1960) long ago argued, to tell children and their teachers that they are of low intelligence is likely to do little good to either.

However, as has been argued, the knowledge can be useful, if it is used sensibly, to inhibit unrealistic expectations. All depends on how it is presented, especially to the child. This is one of the reasons that great care must be taken with automated forms of testing where subjects receive their results direct from the computer, as described in Chapter 6 of this handbook.

At this point, brief mention should be made of the use of automated and computer testing in educational psychology. If a validated computerised version of the relevant educational test has been produced it is probably sensible to use this simply because the psychologist has then an immediate print-out of the results which is highly useful in practice (rather than having to score the normal test and collate the result against the norms). If, further, there are relevant diagnostic profiles or scores in the computerised version of the test this is also valuable, although care must be taken that these are based on adequate numbers, just as would be the case with a standardisation sample.

I think this discussion is sufficient to show that, properly used, tests do not simply label children or necessarily harm them. Sound inferences which can lead to rational changes can be drawn from the results and provided that the results are sensitively relayed to the subjects there need be no bad effects. However, it has to be said, all depends on their proper use. Objection 1 has been refuted.

Objection 2

Psychometric tests are not sufficiently reliable or valid to be used to make individual decisions. The discussion of this objection to the use of tests can be answered briefly since it is in the main a matter of fact. As was demonstrated in Chapter 3 on the classical account of error variance, high reliability, at least greater than .7, is essential if decisions about individuals are to be made. This alone is not enough since it is possible to construct reliable but invalid tests. As the discussion of tests and testing throughout this book has shown, this objection can be sustained in some cases but not in others.

i. Tests of intelligence and ability   The evidence here is unequivocal. There is a variety of well validated tests of intelligence and the major ability factors. Details of the best tests can be found in Section IV of the handbook. There should be no problem in interpreting the results of such tests unequivocally.

ii. Personality tests   Here the objection has more force. Some well-known personality inventories such as the 16PF Test (Cattell *et al.*, 1970a) and the MMPI even in its latest form the MMPI-2 (Graham, 1990) do not reach the requisite standards of reliability for use with individuals. Furthermore there is some doubt as to the validity of the Cattell scales (Kline and Barrett, 1983) and of the old MMPI (Cattell, 1973) which the new version does not remedy. Jackson's Personality Research Form (Jackson, 1970) is certainly reliable but its validity is far from proven. A full discussion of these tests may be found in Section IV.

Thus in the case of personality questionnaires there is some strength in the argument although it should be pointed out that the Eysencks' EPQ (Eysenck and Eysenck, 1975) cannot be impugned on these grounds.

As must be clear from Chapter 16, the objection is well made in respect of both projective and objective personality tests. Few objective tests have any clear evidence of validity and the same is true of projective tests when they are scored in the orthodox fashion.

Given that this is the case, how can the use of personality questionnaires for diagnostic purposes be justified? The answer to this question is relatively simple. The results can be used but with caution. Thus, for example if we had a subject who scored high on Cattell's factor G, conscientiousness, then we might hypothesise that perhaps this was a cause of her problems. We would only act on this if further evidence that this was the case could be brought to light. This is in contradistinction to an intelligence test score which can be used as a benchmark index of ability in most circumstances.

Thus in the case of personality questionnaires, it can be argued that they are suitable for diagnostic use, provided that the results are not taken literally, like physical measurements, but are used with caution and treated as hypotheses which must be confirmed from other sources.

Although objective and projective tests might be used in this manner their reliability and validity is so poor, in many cases, that it does not seem useful to use them for diagnostic purposes.

There are certain other problems in the use of psychometric tests for diagnosis and treatment for educational difficulties which require discussion. To do this I want to describe two other typical referrals. First let us suppose that a child, a 12-year-old boy, has been referred as violent, frightening other children and defying the control of teachers. Our second case is an immigrant girl, about the same age, who knows little English and the psychologist is required to recommend a suitable education.

Case 1, the aggressive boy

I have chosen this case because it is particularly intractable. At the outset I shall admit that there is no simple solution but, nevertheless, psychometric testing of such an individual is not useless.

The first problem with aggression is that it is a complex phenomenon and is unlikely to have a single cause, ranging, as it does, from physical violence to verbal abuse or even what is referred to as mental cruelty. Furthermore psychology itself has no agreed theoretical account. Thus there is the frustration hypothesis (Dollard *et al.*, 1939); a function of modelling, i.e. a form of social learning (Bandura and Walters, 1963); the response to imperfect mothering (Bowlby, 1944); virtually biologically determined (Lorenz, 1966); while sociobiologists would argue that it results from the attempt to preserve our genes (Wilson, 1978).

As was argued at the beginning of this discussion, the whole battery of psychometric tests would be given, covering the main factors of ability, personality and motivation. The intelligence test score could be revealing in this case. A very high score suggests the possibility that the child was totally bored at school. Similarly a very low score suggests that frustration at the inability to do anything properly might be the cause – following Dollard's work. Of course, such scores only suggest these hypotheses which would have to be confirmed by talking to teachers and examining his school work. Another test of this hypothesis would be to examine the personality test scores. An aggressive child, of the kind described above, would be acting out his frustration and would be expected to be extraverted, rather than intraverted. If a mismatch of ability and curriculum appeared to be important the remedy is clear.

The personality and motivational tests could be revealing. For example, suppose that our subject scored high on N, anxiety, and P, psychoticism, the factors in the EPQ (Eysenck and Eysenck, 1975). Let us suppose, further, that on the Cattell 16PF test he scored low on G, superego, and high on E, dominance. On the Cattell motivation test, the SMAT (Cattell, Sweney and Radcliffe, 1960) the child scored high on pugnacity and self-assertion. All these tests are described in the appropriate chapters of Section IV of this handbook. The high N score suggests a highly anxious individual, with volatile moods, difficult to control. The high P score which is often seen in criminals (Eysenck and Eysenck, 1976) typifies a person who enjoys cruelty and violence for its own sake. The high dominance and self-assertion scores are self explanatory and the pugnacity score again suggests that this is a child who fights his way out, rather than talks.

It must be stressed that this psychometric description is not just saying, in other words, that the child is aggressive. These tests show that the problem lies in the nature of the child – that he is easily aroused and likes to be dominant and enjoys the resulting mayhem. This therefore means that the psychologist can make some suggestions: efforts must be made to try to avoid arousing aggression and efforts must also be made to teach the child to control it better. This is not to say that an intelligent teacher would not have attempted this without the test findings. However the psychometric results give a rational basis to the work.

This case illustrates how, even though the psychometric tests cannot give clear diagnoses or suggest clear treatments, they can be used as a basis for attempting some treatment of the difficulties. Furthermore these results rule out the previous hypothesis that the problem was attributable to a mismatch of curriculum and child. Thus even in these intractable and difficult cases psychometric tests may be able to provide valuable information.

Case 2, the immigrant girl

This case was selected because it raises an important problem – testing subjects from a culture different from that for which the test was designed. This is a subject which arouses strong passions which is hardly surprising given that ethnocentrism and prejudice are implicated in many of the worst difficulties faced by modern society.

The difficulties of making cross-cultural comparisons with psychometric tests have been extensively discussed (e.g. Irvine and Berry, 1983). It is generally accepted by specialists in the field that a test cannot be meaning-fully compared across cultures unless its equivalence has been demonstrated in those cultures. As I have argued (e.g. Kline, 1983), it is not easy to demonstrate such equivalence. This has to be done at the item level with similar factor structures of items and at the test level where it has to be shown that correlations with the test in the different cultures are the same. In the case of personality tests the meaning of items in different cultures changes and these are problems which have not been satisfactorily solved, although as Cattell (1957) argues, objective tests may ultimately be useful in cross-cultural comparisons. At present, unequivocally valid psychometric com-parisons across cultures are not possible, although if used with caution, tests can yield some interesting results.

As might be expected, the difficulties are greater with tests of personality than with abilities. Vernon (1979) argues that a comparison between cultures might be possible if, in the groups, there is equal access to education, equal freedom from physical disabilities, equal familiarity with the tests and free-dom from test anxiety and equal valuation of the skills involved in the test. There is, of course, the problem of language.

The immigrant girl in our example, who knows little English, may well suffer from all the disadvantages which make cross-cultural comparison difficult. Cattell has tried to overcome these difficulties with the development of the Culture-Fair Test (Cattell and Cattell, 1959). This is a largely non-verbal intelligence test which uses the type of items discussed in Chapter 12. However, although this test will give some indication of an individual's ability, even if their English is very poor, it would be difficult to rely on the results. If the child did well one could be confident that she was intelligent. A bad score, however, might be due to a variety of causes – failure to understand the task, nervousness of the test situation. If the examiner is male this can cause difficulties. Even at the postgraduate level this can be a problem. I supervised a student who told me, at the end of her course, that at the beginning she was terrified of supervisions because she had never been alone with a man before.

Thus in interpreting the results of an intelligence test with such a subject the score should be used as an indication that she is at least at this level and may be far superior.

Other ability tests are even more difficult to use with a subject who knows little English and it would not appear to be a useful exercise. Similarly personality tests are unlikely to be useful although the EPQ has been used cross-culturally and, if the results are treated with even greater caution than the intelligence test, some indication of personality might be obtained. However my own studies with personality questionnaires in Uganda and Ghana, just for example (Kline, 1967; Honess and Kline, 1973) indicate that cultural factors affecting the place of women in society and their general demeanour must affect scores on intraversion and probably anxiety. Thus item analysis and even factor analysis may show that the scales are homogeneous but there is a possibility that their psychological meaning has changed.

Thus I think that it is fair to say that psychological testing with subjects of this type is not likely to yield a great harvest for the psychologist. All results have to be treated with great caution although a good performance on an intelligence test certainly means that the child is intelligent, such a score being a lower bound to the estimate of her ability.

Norms   Although this case indicates the weakness of psychometric tests if we are forced to use them with subjects from a culture for which they were not designed, it also implicates another difficulty in using tests for diagnosis and treatment in educational psychology. This is the problem of inappropriate norms. Test norms and standardisation have been fully discussed in Chapter 4 of this handbook so I shall say little more here than that it is essential that these norms are appropriate for the individual who is being tested. This is a weakness of many tests, often because the cost involved in test standardisation is too great, which may not be important for research or working with groups. However for use with individuals poor norms can contraindicate the use of even the most valid test.

I shall now leave the first topic of our chapter and turn to the second – the use of psychometric tests in selection.

2. PSYCHOMETRIC TESTS IN SELECTION

This is the province of educational psychology, in which psychometric tests are most often used and are at their most effective. As was pointed out by Vernon and Parry (1949), for variables for which tests have been developed, these tests are always the best measures, and for selection in education most of the relevant variables can be measured by well-accepted and good tests. This, therefore, is one argument for the use of tests in educational selection, as distinct from, say, interviews or the recommendation of teachers.

The second argument in favour of tests is simple and rational. It claims that for any task, and education can be seen as the performance of academic tasks, there must be some ideal psychological configuration. This, indeed, is a statement of the psychometric model which underlies this handbook. Thus, for example, a librarian might be expected to be highly intraverted, verbal and orderly, while a steeple-jack would have to be high on risk-taking and have good spatial ability. Neither of these claims is necessarily true in practice but they illustrate the argument, that, in principle, it is likely that there is some ideal configuration for academic achievement in various fields. This leads on to the third argument for the use of tests in educational selection.

This is the empirical evidence showing the correlations between ability, personality and motivation at various levels of academic achievement. A summary of some of these findings is set out in Table 19.1. The proper use of psychometrics in selection should result in a battery of tests optimally weighted to produce the maximum multiple correlation with academic success, the weightings being derived from previous empirical work.

Table 19.1 (p. 314) requires some discussion and this will clarify a number of important issues concerning the use of psychometric tests in selection. First the results summarised in the table are typical results, as judged by myself. No attempt has been made to average the results across all studies or to apply any other kind of meta-analysis. This is because for a variety of reasons many published studies are vitiated by problems which render the work dubious.

Much of this work consists of correlations or multiple correlations with psychometric variables and academic success. For many years both in this country and especially in America this was a favourite field for research students in education. It was, in many cases, empiricism run mad. Any test would be correlated with academic success and, with a large enough sample some significant correlations were bound to turn up. These would then be reported. No attempt was usually made to interpret these findings which were, in fact, uninterpretable. Rushton (1966) found, for example, that Cattell's factor H (adventurousness) was correlated (.21) with French but not German O level results.

I shall list the reasons why much of this research is not worth consideration.

a. If a large number of variables is included in the study some correlations will be significant by chance. Thus only replicated correlations are useful.

b. If large samples are used very small correlations become significant. Thus a correlation of .16 may be significant. However it means that only 2.5 per cent of the variance is in common between the variables. In other words 97.5 per cent of the variance remains unexplained. This highlights the difference between statistical and psychological significance.

c. Many of the published correlations are reduced in size on account of attenuation due to homogeneity of variance and the unreliability of the measures of academic achievement. Thus simple averaging is bound to be an underestimate.

d. Some studies use pass rates as evidence for validity. However, before such figures can be evaluated the pass rate for the population as whole should be known. If this is very low the selection system has to be highly accurate and where it is low, selection methods can make matters worse.

e. In many studies the choice of variables is atheoretical and arbitrary. In one dissertation, which I examined, urban/rural residence was correlated with a variety of academic achievement targets. This makes interpretation of a mass of results extremely difficult.

f. Some workers attempt to correct correlations for attenuation due to unreliability and homogeneity of variance. However even though one may know that correlations are smaller than they would have been in the population or with perfectly reliable tests, such corrections yield only estimates of what the correlations might have been. I think it is misleading to quote such figures.

For all these reasons much of this type of research has little psychological value. However, as was argued in Chapters 7 and 8 of this handbook, in fields of huge complexity the best method of selecting variables is to choose those that encompass the most variance and these variables are selected by factor analysis. Hence in Table 19.1 I have included studies where the main factors in the field of ability, personality and motivation have been used. Although there is some doubt about the factor structure of the 16PF test, this has been included in the table because of the mass of research which has been carried out with it. As was discussed earlier in this section, the figures in the table are typical figures and have been selected, in the sense of not being attenuated through homogeneity or artificially boosted by correcting factors or the choice of unusual samples.

In this handbook I shall not scrutinize the results in this table in any detail. Its purpose is simply to present the evidence to show that factored psychometric tests are substantially correlated with academic success. The highest correlations are with the g factors and verbal ability but both personality and motivational variables account for a small but separate proportion of the variance such that a multiple correlation of around .6, with all variables included, was obtained (Cattell and Butcher, 1968).

This indicates that highly effective selection, or prediction, for academic success could be carried out using a battery of these variables. Even without the personality and motivation tests efficient (and in my view as socially just as is practical to obtain) selection for grammar school education was achieved after the war in Great Britain, using intelligence tests and measures of verbal ability, as has been fully described by Vernon (1960). It is to be noted that the weightings for some of the variables would vary for different subjects and at different levels of education.

I shall write no more about the use of tests in selection. I have presented sufficient evidence to demonstrate that psychometric tests can be most effectively used for this purpose.

3. EDUCATIONAL THEORY

I shall now examine the third contribution of psychometric testing to educational psychology – its bearing upon educational theory. Gillis (1986) in a discussion of the use of the Cattell variables in educational psychology attempts to demonstrate how these tests can contribute to educational psychological theory. His arguments are, of course, applicable to the results of any factored tests with good evidence of validity. I shall scrutinise his claims, as an introduction to the discussion.

He takes, essentially, the same data as those in Table 19.1 as a starting point although, in fact, he uses the regression weights for predicting educational achievement from the 16PF and its high school equivalent, the HSPQ (Cattell and Cattell, 1969a), both fully described in Chapter 25 of this handbook. We find, at the adult level, that intelligence, superego, and self sentiment are the best predictors of achievement. These two latter factors are also dynamic factors in the Cattell system, and when measured as dynamic factors similar beta weights are found, as Gillis (1986) argues.

Given that these are the most important variables in their respective fields of personality and motivation (being derived by factor analysis) we have to consider what theoretical account could be woven from these findings. Actually, in this case it is not hard to find since these results strongly support the armchair theorising of McDougall (1932) who always claimed that superego and the self sentiment were the two main energisers of human action, that most individuals strove not to feel guilty and to act in accordance with how they saw themselves.

I do not intend to discuss this claim further in this handbook, which is devoted to psychological testing rather than to the findings from such tests. I have used these findings to illustrate how the results from factored tests, because they are the fundamental variables in their fields, can be used to construct theories, theories which have, by their provenance, empirical support and operationally defined variables. Such theories, of course, must be tested in the same manner as other psychological theories.

In fact both Cattell (1981) and Eysenck (1967) have used their factor analytic findings to develop a grand theory of behaviour tying the psychometric results into other aspects of psychology. Eysenck, for example, relates his work to classical conditioning. This goes far beyond mere educational psychology, although it does include it. Broadly he would expect academic achievement to be related to intraversion and neuroticism, to a small degree and this, in general, is what emerges. Extraverts, hungry for stimulation, tend to be bored by academic work, while highly stable individuals do not worry enough about poor performance at academic work to make the necessary effort.

Cattell's (1981) structured learning theory attempts to fit everything into his theoretical framework of factored variables. However, it is so complex, goes so far beyond any evidence, and invokes mathematics which he admits has not yet been worked out, that I shall not describe it here. Furthermore it must be pointed out that there is no agreement among factor analysts that the Cattell factors are the best description of personality, so to describe the ramifications of the theory further would not be sensible.

Nevertheless the work of both these researchers underlines the point that when factored, psychometric tests are used which are measuring the most salient variables in their fields, the results are necessarily of theoretical interest and should be wrought into a theory. That is why, in principle, the correlations between such tests and educational success are capable of advancing educational theory, regardless of what those results actually are.

CONCLUSIONS

From the discussion in this chapter the place that psychometric tests can play in educational psychology is clear. In the diagnosis and treatment of educational problems in children a psychometric profile is always useful. This is particularly valuable since many problems stem, in part, from the mismatch of ability and curriculum. Furthermore the psychological profile is useful in helping to adjust teaching methods to children where this is possible in busy schools.

In selection for education the use of tests is more straightforward and involves multiple regression of variables on to the various educational objectives. There is little doubt that such use of factored tests would lead to more efficient selection.

Finally it was shown how research with factored tests can lead to a greater understanding of the determinants of educational success and failure and on such an empirical basis theories could and should be constructed.

Chapter 20

Psychometric Tests in Clinical Psychology

INTRODUCTION

In this chapter clinical psychology will refer to that branch of psychology which is involved with the treatment of mental disorders. It will, therefore, involve diagnosis, the assessment of treatment, and clinical theory.

First I need to make some general points about the use of tests in clinical psychology which must be understood before we examine the application of psychometrics to the three main branches of the subject. In clinical psychology tests of every type are used and it is important to distinguish the five categories of test, mainly in terms of test construction, which are set out below. These distinctions will permeate much of our discussion on the use of tests in clinical psychology, later in this chapter.

1. Factor analytic tests, derived from simple structure analyses of the field In this handbook I have stressed the importance of utilising, where possible, factor analytic tests, where these have been derived from a simple structure factor analysis of the field. This is because, as we have seen in our discussion of factor analysis in Chapters 7 and 8, such factors represent the fundamental variables in the field and, in the case of such complex aspects of psychology as personality and motivation, it is vital to deal with what are, empirically, in terms of variance accounted for, the most important variables. In both these fields, as we have seen in Chapters 15, 16 and 17 of this handbook, there is little guidance for testers from psychological theories.

In addition, there is the further advantage to unifactorial tests that the meaning of their scores is unequivocal, as can be seen from the classical test theory which was discussed in Chapter 3 of this handbook.

Both these arguments, in the tradition of the London School of Psychology (Spearman, Burt, Cattell and Eysenck, to cite its most distinguished members) underlie the psychometric model of behaviour which has been most explicitly stated by Cattell (1957 and 1981 for example) and which is assumed in much of the applied work with factored variables. This model states that any behaviour is a function, essentially, of a subject's ability, personality, motivation, state, mood and situation. Hence the model can be instantiated in terms of a multiple regression to the criterion using the main factors in all these spheres, factors which were described in Section II of this handbook. The best psychological measures of these factors are described in Section IV of this handbook.

Thus on all these grounds the use of factored tests in clinical psychology would appear to be essential, not only because they are likely to be the most effective predictors but because they are psychologically meaningful variables and any results are likely to be useful in the development of clinical theory.

2. Criterion-keyed tests Despite our arguments in favour of factor analytic tests they are not widely used in clinical psychology, perhaps because to the clinical psychologist, concerned with the individual, the mathematical and nomothetic nature of factor analytic tests seems repellent and irrelevant. Furthermore their statistical complexity may appear daunting despite the work of Meehl (1954) showing that statistical prediction was superior to that of the clinician.

Furthermore the most widely used personality questionnaire, with more than 10,000 references, the MMPI (Hathaway and McKinley, 1951), and its recent offspring MMPI-2 (Graham, 1990) are both specifically clinical tests developed through criterion-keying. Thus the value of these tests in clinical psychology will have to be discussed. A full description and evaluation of the MMPIs can be found in Chapter 25 of this handbook.

Indeed it is clear that for clinicians, working with diagnostic or noso-logical groups, criterion-keyed tests that can distinguish such groups would seem a useful type of measure. Such a viewpoint would be reinforced by the fact that other tests might not be able to discriminate as well as a criterion-keyed test developed precisely for that purpose.

3. Tests developed by other methods In Chapter 10 we saw how tests may be constructed using factor analysis or item analysis, which if the items are measuring only one variable, gives much the same results. Factor analytically constructed tests, where items are written and those loading their expected factor are selected for the final test, must be distinguished from tests in the first category in this chapter, in which the factors have been shown to account for the most important variance in the field.

Tests which have been developed simply through a factor analysis of their items have the virtue only of being homogeneous. Such tests can measure trivial variables and frequently do since it is a simple matter to write items which are essentially paraphrases of each other and these will load a factor most clearly. As was discussed in Chapter 10 factor analytic and item analytic tests are necessarily reliable but validity must be demonstrated.

In clinical psychology, rather specific tests, not falling into the broad fields of ability, personality, motivation, mood or state are often required, as in, for example, the evaluation of psychotherapy or the process of psychotherapy, and some clinicians have used factor analytic tests, of high face validity, to measure such variables. Thus the value of such tests as these in clinical psychology will have to be discussed.

4. Projective tests   In clinical psychology, unless a behavioural approach is taken, in which tests would play no part, clinicians find themselves having to deal with the inner conflicts and only partly articulated problems of their clients. Of course, the tests which claim to be concerned with and throw light upon these idiodynamics are projective tests, which have been fully described and discussed in Chapter 16 of this handbook. Here we will also discuss the application of percept-genetic techniques, on account of their similarity to projective tests, although for reasons of space it was necessary to describe them in Chapter 18 on special tests.

Despite the difficulties of establishing the validity of these tests, their clinical relevance has made them popular and the value of projective tests in clinical psychology will have to be examined in this chapter.

5. Other tests   In addition to all the tests mentioned above, in clinical psychology there are highly specialised tests in use to reveal cognitive deficits after brain damage or other specific neurological problems although, presumably, with the development of brain scanning such tests will gradually fall into disuse.

6. Computerised tests and expert systems   In addition we shall have to discuss the use of computerised tests although this is not a separate category of tests as are the first five groups.

CLINICAL DIAGNOSIS

Although diagnosis is considered by some psychiatrists to be a malevolent activity in which patients are labelled and written off (e.g. Laing, 1960), in fact diagnosis is an important aspect of the scientific study of mental disorders. Such obviously important topics as the causes of schizophrenia, depression, and other neuroses depend on an accurate diagnosis, as do evaluations of different treatments. Notice that diagnosis, as such, does not presuppose any particular type of answers to these questions. It could be that determining, environmental factors for all these disorders are the same and that they do not require different psychotherapeutic measures. If this is the case good diagnosis is still essential. Furthermore the evaluation of any genetic factors in the development of these disorders also necessitates clear diagnosis so that it is quite clear that if psychological tests were able to diagnose well, clinical psychologists would have valuable aids to the scientific study of mental disorders.

1. The use of the main factored tests in diagnosis

If the psychometric model is a useful approach to understanding human behaviour and if, as is maintained throughout this handbook, it is correct that simple structure (and confirmatory) factor analysis has isolated the main variables in the various fields of psychological measurement, then the study of the different psychiatric and abnormal groups ought to provide important insights into the psychological nature of these disorders.

Since it is probable that cognitive abilities are not of any great importance in the diagnosis of psychiatric orders, since mental defect can be seen amongst the psychiatrically normal and the abnormal, this discussion will be restricted to personality and motivation factors and will ignore ability factors.

In writing this section there are several severe difficulties. The first concerns the fact, discussed in Chapter 15 of this handbook, that until recently there was little agreement as to what the main personality factors were. This means that there is little clinical evidence concerning the 'big five' factors, which appear to be the best description at the second order level.

However at the primary level there is a huge amount of research conducted by Cattell and his colleagues into the Cattell factors, and despite the difficulties in replicating them, the clinical findings illustrate well the use of factored tests in clinical diagnosis. Hence I shall attempt to summarise the main implications of this research. As was mentioned at the beginning of this paragraph, there is a considerable body of research findings, set out in Cattell *et al.* (1970a), Cattell (1973), Cattell and Kline (1977), Kline (1979), Bolton (1986), Karson and O'Dell (1976), Schuerger and Watterson (1977), Krug (1981) and H. Cattell (1986) and it is on these books and papers that this account rests. In addition I shall also examine the extensive work carried out with the Eysenck tests which measure two of the main second order personality factors, extraversion and anxiety, as well as psychoticism.

The Cattell factors in clinical diagnosis

Cattell identifies sixteen primary factors among normal subjects and twelve abnormal factors. These factors are measured in one test, the Clinical Analysis Questionnaire (Krug, 1980a), which is fully described and evaluated in Chapter 25 of this handbook, although, of course, the normal factors are measured by the 16PF Test (Cattell *et al.*, 1970).

In the clinical application of Cattell's work both the normal and the abnormal factors are used and it will be convenient, here, to set these out in Table 20.1.

It should be pointed out that for the realisation of the full potential of factored tests in clinical psychology, factors from the other spheres should be used, as described in Chapters 12 and 13 on ability factors and Chapter 17 on motivation factors. However the Cattell personality factors have been set

Table 20.1 The Cattell normal and abnormal factors

Normal factors		Abnormal factors	
A reserved	B intelligence	D1 hypochondriasis	D2 zestful
C emotional	E submissive	D3 discontent	
F sober	G conscientious	D4 anxious depression	
H timid	I tough-minded	D5 euphoric	D6 guilty
L trusting	M conventional	D7 bored depression	Pa paranoid
N Naive	O untroubled	Pp psychopathic deviation	
Q1 conservative	Q2 dependent	Sc schizophrenia	
Q3 self sentiment	Q4 relaxed	As psychasthenia	Ps psychosis

out because it is with these that most of the research has been carried out. With the underlying psychometric model of human behaviour, using these factors there are two approaches to clinical diagnosis.

a. The specification equation Here the weights on the factors are computed in a multiple regression. In fact various diagnostic categories have such specification equations, as well as other clinical groups such as potential suicides (Bolton, 1986). In practical use the scores of a client are weighted according to the specification equations of the various categories and the one yielding the highest score suggests the diagnosis.

b. Pattern similarity matching Here we can use the pattern similarity coefficient, r_p, to match the profile of an individual's scores with the profiles of the various diagnostic categories. The category yielding the highest coefficient suggests the diagnosis. Formula 20.1 shows how the pattern similarity coefficient is calculated.

$$\textbf{20.1} \quad r_p = \frac{(4k + \Sigma D^2) - \Sigma d^2}{(4k + \Sigma D^2) + \Sigma d^2}$$

where k = the median chi-square with degrees of freedom equal to the number of variables; d = the difference of the individual's score from the designated group score on a variable; and D = the difference of that group's score on a variable from the population mean.

There are several points to be noted about this approach to clinical diagnosis, which is also viable in educational and occupational psychology, including vocational guidance. The use of the specification equation and profile matching in these spheres is discussed in chapters 21 and 22 of this section of the handbook.

a. Sampling. Both these methods depend upon adequate sampling of the diagnostic categories. If poor samples are used the results could be worse than useless. They could be actually misleading. This is particularly true of the specification equation method which makes use of the beta weights, which have large standard errors. This means that the sample must be large, as well as representative.

b. Meaning of variables. Part of the power of this approach to diagnosis springs from the fact that factor analytic variables, derived from simple structure analyses of the main fields of psychology, are psychologically meaningful (if simple structure truly has been reached, see c below). Thus what distinguishes one clinical group from another can be used in understanding the nature of the category. This distinguishes the method from a possible similar use (statistically) of criterion-keyed tests.

c. Choice of variables. In Chapter 15 it was pointed out that there was disagreement concerning the best primary factors in the personality sphere. However, the method can obviously be used with any set of variables. We have discussed the Cattell work, simply because so much research has been carried out with the factors and the specification equations and category scores actually exist. The methods used by Cattell and colleagues are those that should be used with factored variables.

d. Depth psychometry. This is a notion which has been much used by Cattell and his colleagues (e.g. Karson and O'Dell, 1976). This refers to the fact that the syndromes, as observed by psychiatrists and clinical psychologists, are composed of surface traits whereas the factors in Table 20.1 are source traits. As Bolton (1986) argues, it is claimed in depth psychometry that the same general neurotic syndrome can result from different configurations of the source traits which constitute neurosis.

e. As Krug (1986) has described, much of the research with the 16PF has been automated so that a computerised version of the test can be given and diagnoses can be worked out by the computer, an example of the use of expert systems in diagnosis. These illustrate the use of such computerised tests, even if the validity of the factors is not admitted.

f. As was mentioned above Cattell and his colleagues have collected data with the 16PF and the CAQ abnormal factors such that specification equations and diagnostic group scores exist for a variety of clinical groups, many of which are set out in the 16PF Handbook (Cattell *et al.*, 1970). However work has been carried out both with ergs and sentiments (discussed in Chapter 17), but on a far smaller scale, and with T tests (also discussed in Chapter 16). This work will be briefly considered.

g. Work with ergs and sentiments using the MAT test (Cattell, Horn and Sweney, 1970). Although the ergs and sentiments can be used as were the temperamental factors in the sections above, there is a more distinctive place for them in clinical diagnosis. This is to work out the underlying dynamics of patients in the various categories. This is done by computing from the P technique factors (see Chapter 17) for each individual, the dynamic calculus, which indicates how drives are expressed in behaviour, an approach likened by Cattell (1981) to quantified psychoanalysis. This is a highly complex technique which is described in Cattell and Kline (1977), Cattell and Child (1975) and Cattell (1985). However this is an approach which is only accepted by Cattell and his colleagues and goes well beyond the empirical evidence available and will not, therefore, be described in this handbook.

h. T tests in diagnosis. T tests, as was shown in Chapter 17 of this handbook, are potentially superior to questionnaires as measures of personality and motivation because of their resistance to faking and the objectivity of their scores. However, it was also shown in that chapter that the evidence for the validity of these tests was not high, mainly because there was simply insufficient research into these tests. In principle, however, they may be used just as the 16PF and CAQ, as soon as there is good evidence that they can discriminate among clinical groups.

Bolton (1986) strongly advocates the use, in clinical diagnosis, of one of the few published batteries of objective tests – the Objective–Analytic Battery (Cattell and Schuerger, 1976a) which measures ten source traits – ego standards, independence, evasiveness, exuberance, mobilisation, anxiety, realism, asthenia, exvia and discouragement. This test is fully evaluated and described in Chapter 26 of this handbook. According to the manual to the test (Cattell and Schuerger, 1978), which also deals with the clinical utility of the test, it is highly reliable and can make, by means of discriminant functions, remarkably accurate diagnoses – with about 65 per cent agreement with psychiatric diagnoses. Thus the O-A Battery would appear to be ideal for use in clinical diagnosis.

The work discussed by Cattell and Schuerger (1978) was actually a study of 114 subjects, who were tested on two occasions (thus enabling dR as well as R analyses to be carried out), by Cattell, Schmidt and Bjerstedt (1972). The clinical groups had been specially selected so that there was full psychiatric agreement about the diagnoses and if state-change factors from the dR analyses (see Chapter 17) were included in the discriminant functions, correct clinical diagnosis rose to 98 per cent.

However I think caution must be shown concerning these findings, which should be replicated before full acceptance. Given the unreliability of psychiatric diagnosis and the imperfect reliability of the O-A Battery such accurate placement seems beyond what could be rationally expected. Furthermore Kline and Cooper (1984b), in a factor analytic study of the O-A Battery with the main ability and personality factors, were unable to support the validity of the test. Not only was it impossible to extract the ten factors, the factors which were in the test were mixed – some measuring ability rather than personality. These findings will be discussed in Chapter 26 but they do not support the use of this battery without much more research, even if it will discriminate these clinical groups.

Conclusions concerning Cattell's factors in clinical diagnosis

There is no doubt that, in principle, diagnosis by the most important factors is a scientifically sound approach to understanding the psychology of these clinical diagnostic categories. However, despite the technical brilliance of Cattell's work the problem of the validity of all his factors, T factors, Q factors and the ergs and sentiments, means that the tests cannot simply be used as clinical tools for diagnosis. However the overall approach is a good example of how psychometrics should be applied in clinical psychology.

The work of other factorists

Of the other factor analytic researchers into personality I shall say little. This is a handbook of psychological testing, so the emphasis must be on how tests are to be used in diagnosis rather than on the substantive findings. This is why I chose to discuss the work of Cattell which, as has been argued, represents a model of how psychometrics should be applied in clinical psychology.

In fact, few other factor analysts have carried out much clinical research, the obvious exception being Eysenck and his colleagues at the Maudsley who have worked with the second order personality factors, P, psychoticism, E, extraversion and N, neuroticism, which are far more stable than the primary factors in the Cattell system.

Although their work, as summarised, for example, in Eysenck and Eysenck (1976), reveals interesting and psychologically meaningful differences between psychiatric groups, from the viewpoint of the use of tests in clinical diagnosis it simply backs up what has been argued in the previous section – namely that the use of factored tests in diagnosis can be valuable both in practice and theory. Indeed the theoretical implications of this work will be discussed later in this chapter.

From this discussion it may be concluded that the work of other factorists in clinical diagnosis, especially the work of Eysenck, confirms the value of the approach. What is truly required is the application of the factors which best describe the various domains of ability, personality and motivation (including moods). However, as yet there is insufficient research in some of these areas to be able to assert just what these factors are.

2. Criterion-keyed tests in clinical diagnosis

Even more than was the case with the work of Cattell, in attempting to discuss the use of criterion-keyed tests in clinical diagnosis, we are faced with a mountain of research, the MMPI (Hathaway and McKinley, 1951) being the most widely used personality test in the world. The MMPI and its modern sibling the MMPI-2, described by Graham (1990), which is as similar as possible to the original test, are described and evaluated in Chapter 25 of this handbook.

The original MMPI was developed by choosing items which could discriminate one clinical group from another, and the test was conceived by Hathaway and McKinley (1951) as a pool of items from which by similar procedures but with different clinical groups new scales could be developed. Dahlstrom and Welsh (1960), even by that date, were able to list more than 200 such scales.

However I hope that it is clear from the discussion of testing throughout this handbook and especially from the chapters on factor analysis and the different methods of test construction that the value of criterion-keyed tests in clinical diagnosis is not regarded as high, for the following reasons.

a. Problems in psychiatric diagnosis (e.g. Beck, 1962) mean that replication of discriminations among diagnostic groups, chosen by different psychiatrists, is likely to be less good than the original discrimination.
b. Criterion-keyed scales have no necessary psychological meaning. They are the result of pure empiricism – that the items will discriminate groups. Their use adds little or nothing to psychological knowledge. Indeed it detracts from it since such tests could be replaced by factored scales, as discussed above.
c. Criterion-keyed scales not only have no necessary psychological meaning but they are not necessarily univariate. Since, in the clinical case, psychiatric groups are likely to vary on many variables, clinical criterion-keyed clinical scales are almost certainly multivariate. Thus identical scores on such scales may have different psychological meanings.

Finally, it should be pointed out that computerised versions of the MMPI have been developed which will give immediate diagnoses based upon the normative and profile information in the computer, another example of the use of expert systems in diagnosis. However, given the difficulties with criterion-keyed tests it is difficult to recommend these procedures.

For all these reasons it seems difficult to support the use of these tests in diagnosis. Their only value is for mass screening. Thus if it becomes essential to screen out neurotics and psychotics, for example in the selection of soldiers on guard in the underground bunkers of nuclear missiles, then an effectively developed criterion-keyed test would be as useful as a factored test of similar discriminating power. If the need is simply to screen and not to understand then criterion-keyed tests have some value. However, if factored tests are as effective and as brief, there is no reason to give the criterion-keyed tests since they yield less information.

3. Tests specially designed for clinical diagnosis

We have already mentioned the problems of the unreliability of clinical diagnosis, which render the criterion-keyed approach to diagnostic test construction somewhat dubious. However, in American psychiatry and clinical psychology great efforts have been made to improve the accuracy of diagnosis by the introduction of highly detailed and precise diagnostic procedures and these are encapsulated into the *Diagnostic and Statistical Manual of Mental Disorders Revised*, the DSM-R-3 (American Psychiatric Association, 1987). This diagnostic system seems to be widely accepted in America (e.g. Friedman, 1989).

In a handbook of psychological testing a discussion of the DSM-R-3 would be out of place. However one point must be made. As Millon (1990) argues, the DSM-R-3 classifications are deliberately atheoretical and non-quantitative. This raises the question of their psychological meaning. The fact that they may be reliable is only reliability and thus classification by fiat. Such classification may be quite absurd. It would be possible to agree that, whenever a sigh of wind was heard in a chimney, a unicorn had passed overhead. With good training the judgement between wind and unicorn could be perfect. That is why scientific research has preferred the statistical, objective delineation of classes by such means as factor analysis to subjective classifications, however reliable. In the natural world, for example, we might classify organisms by the spots on their bodies or the length of their legs – meaningful and accurate categories, yet almost without biological sense.

These are fundamental doubts as to the DSM-R-3 classifications which seem to encapsulate clinical observations, as if these were objective and independent of theory which no philosopher of science would accept as possible: behind all observations are explicit or tacit theories (e.g. Clark and Wright, 1988). They do not necessarily rule out the practical utility of the system but they do make it dubious as a foundation for tests. This is important since, as might be expected, there is a variety of diagnostic techniques from interview to tests aimed at the DSM-R-3 diagnostic categories.

Thus psychological tests have been developed explicitly for diagnosis in terms of DSM-R-3 categories. Of these the best-known are those of Millon who has been concerned with development of the DSM-R-3 and its earlier versions (e.g. Millon, 1983a). His main test is the Millon Clinical Multiaxial Inventory (MCMI) (Millon, 1983b). The twenty scales were designed to fit the diagnostic and syndromal categories of the DSM-3 and in addition information can be derived on clinical syndromes, personality patterns, course of the disorder, psychosocial stressors and therapeutic implications, as well as other clinical inferences. Recently a new version, the MCMI-2, has been developed to fit the DCM-R-3.

I shall not comment here on the MCMI, except to say that on simple psychometric grounds (as discussed in Chapter 3 on the classical model of error variance) it would appear unlikely that so much could be measured by 175 items.

Of course tests have also been developed to classify patients according to other diagnostic systems. One of the most widely used of these is the SCL-90 (Derogatis *et al.*, 1973) which is essentially a self-report symptom checklist which enables patients to be classified into the commonly used Kraepelin diagnostic groups.

It is not difficult to construct symptom checklists, administer them to abnormal groups and then discover which symptoms cluster together, and the SCL-90 is a good example of this kind of test. Another much used example is the Beck Depression Inventory (Beck *et al.*, 1961) which is almost standard in the study of depression. Some readers may consider that this type of test is little different from the MMPI, which was also a symptom list, from which items were chosen because they discriminate one nosological group from another. However the MMPI has been developed far beyond the classification of subjects into clinical groups to become a personality test in its own right and thus it merits treatment as a particular kind of personality test.

Conclusions concerning personality tests specially developed for clinical diagnosis

It is clear that clinicians find it useful to use tests as diagnostic devices as tests enter into training programmes of clinical practitioners (Atkins, 1989) and are also used in research projects into the effectiveness of psychotherapy (Shapiro *et al.*, 1990). However as has been made clear from our discussion, there are severe limitations with this type of test. Thus if the classification scheme at which the tests are aimed is not good the tests are inevitably weak. Furthermore, as is the case with symptom checklists, the results do not add much to knowledge or understanding, although it is useful to confirm psychiatric observation.

Such tests are not useless since they ensure that the basis of diagnosis is known and they at least allow the study of similar groups if results from different researches are pooled. However they are unable to contribute to any kind of fundamental insight into the nature of these diagnostic categories, unlike the application of factored tests, described in the first section of this chapter. However, they might be useful if used in conjunction with factored tests since they probably improve the accuracy of diagnosis, compared with that based on psychiatric classification.

4. Projective tests and percept-genetic methods in clinical diagnosis

As was clear from Chapters 16 and 18 of this handbook the reliability and validity of both projective tests and percept-genetic methods is a matter of considerable dispute. There is little doubt that the conventionally scored projective test, except in the hand of a gifted user, is not a reliable source of information. However, as was discussed in Chapter 16 objectively scored projective tests may be more useful.

Despite these powerful standard psychometric arguments against projective tests, it should be noted that Vardy (1989) still suggests that the Rorschach is useful in the diagnosis of thought disorder and Howard (1989a) in describing Exner's system (Exner, 1986) of scoring the Rorschach cites a number of indices which are claimed to distinguish suicides, depressives and schizophrenics. Scoring the Rorschach is discussed in some detail in Chapter 26 of this handbook, and it is shown there that there is no rationale in the scoring system, and for this reason, among others, Exner (1986) has attempted to put it on a more empirical basis. However even if it turns out that these indices will discriminate these groups, it would still be necessary to demonstrate the meaning of these scores.

However this discussion of empirical discrimination with the Rorschach test leads us on to the discussion of objectively scored projective tests analysed by G analysis. G analysis (Holley, 1973), which was described in Chapter 20, in many ways is ideal for diagnostic studies because it is designed to discriminate among groups which is precisely what is required in diagnosis. Thus I would argue that projective tests, objectively scored and subjected to G analysis, or any other multivariate technique such as discriminant functions, could be useful research tools in clinical diagnosis and might also be useful for screening. I shall examine these two issues separately.

a. Research I think that it might prove useful to attempt to discriminate among clinical groups using projective tests, objectively scored and analysed, for the following reasons. As was argued in Chapter 16, projective tests yield data which are quite different from those that might be obtained from more conventional personality questionnaires and ability tests. Thus if it turns out that some tests can discriminate certain groups a study of the discriminating variables may, and the may needs to be emphasised, yield psychological information of considerable value. Certainly if there is anything in the claims of projective testers that these tests tap what is below the level of awareness, this should be the case.

Hampson and Kline (1977), for example, working with the House Tree Person (HTP) test (Buck, 1970) found through G analysis of offenders that a discriminating variable was age of the tree. Our offenders always put it as low. This response, however, is held by Buck (1970) to reflect emotional immaturity. This may well have been true in the case of this sample whose offences were impulsive, ill planned and almost certain of detection. This study is not regarded as evidence for the fact that offenders are immature but simply as an illustration of how the approach can yield insightful results although, before it did so, all results would need to be replicated on new samples.

In summary it is argued that the G analysis of projective tests might yield valuable diagnostic information in the clinical setting. Even if it did not, if there were reliable discrimination it could be useful for classification as is described in (b).

b. Classification If it turned out that the G analysis of certain projective tests (based on the research studies discussed above) reliably discriminated certain diagnostic groups, these could be used as diagnostic devices. For example Holley (1973) showed that certain Rorschach signs discriminated schizophrenics from depressives and normals. It should be noted that this separation was complete, every schizophrenic being differentiated from every depressive. This is not necessarily or usually the case, of course, if there is simply a significant mean difference on a test between two groups. Thus it would not matter if the projective test responses involved in the discrimination appeared to make sense, provided that they could reliably discriminate, much as criterion-keyed tests are used. At present, however, it must be said that I know of no findings which allow such a use of projective tests. All depends on the research being carried out to establish the discriminating variables.

If it could be shown that certain objectively scored tests could discriminate various clinical groups this would be a convenient method of diagnosis although, unless the variables made psychological sense, which is possible but of course is not guaranteed by the G analytic approach, the method would suffer from this defect, as does the use of criterion-keyed tests in diagnosis.

Percept-genetic methods in clinical diagnosis

Percept-genetic methods were described in Chapter 20 of this handbook. It will be remembered that these involve the serial presentation, through a tachistoscope of threatening stimuli at gradually increasing levels of illumination starting off so that subjects can see nothing and ending with veridical perception. After each exposure subjects are required to draw what they see and to label it. These responses are scored for the presence of defences. For example if the threatening face in the periphery of one of these tests, the Defence Mechanism Test (DMT) (Kragh, 1984), is blocked off by barriers, isolation is scored and if it is described as happy, reaction-formation. These tests have been developed in Scandinavia, where they are almost exclusively used, and much of the work and theory has been summarised in Kragh and Smith (1970).

There is even less general acceptance of percept-genetic findings than there is of projective test findings. Therefore all that is suggested in this section must be regarded as for research purposes only.

Of all the percept-genetic measures the best known is the DMT which has recently been given a new handbook (Kragh, 1984). This test alone of all the percept-genetic techniques has received some attention outside Scandinavia and I shall concentrate this discussion on this test for this reason. The other methods are not so well explicated, with the exception of the Meta Contrast Technique (MCT) which I shall briefly discuss.

The DMT, which is fully described in Chapter 29 of this handbook, seeks to measure the main psychoanalytic defences, repression, denial, reaction-formation, isolation, turning against self and identification with the aggressor. Careful use of the DMT handbook (and preferably consultation with Kragh or his experienced colleagues in Lund) enables the test to be scored with some reliability. Cooper and Kline (1986), in a factor analytic study of the validity of the DMT, showed that the scales were largely independent of the main personality factors, described in Chapter 15 of this handbook, and that a general defensive, repression factor accounted for much of the variance and was useful in pilot selection. A further study by Cooper and Kline (1989) where the responses were objectively scored and subjected to G analysis again yielded a factor replicable in pilots and in students. All this was some support for the validity of the test although it was argued by Kline (1987) that in scoring the DMT the same inferences had to be made as were made by analysts in imputing defences to their patients and to this extent the DMT could not be said to demonstrate, independently, the existence of defence mechanisms. It could not be said unequivocally that the DMT was a valid measure of defences although there is some evidence in its favour. The DMT is a highly interesting test which deserves far more clinical research than it gets, at least outside Scandinavia.

As I discussed above, the MCT deserves some mention here although this test is fully described in Chapter 29 of this handbook. In this test pairs of stimuli are presented by a tachistoscope separately, in immediate succession. The last stimulus, B, of a pair, represents a constant frame of reference to which subjects are accustomed. In the forms of the MCT this is a car or a living room. Then A is introduced which is either threatening or incongruent with B. As with the DMT these successive presentations of the stimuli are at gradually increasing levels of illumination. Subjects report what they see at each exposure.

This test is not sensitive among normals but is normally used with psychiatric groups and is thus of special relevance to this chapter. The incongruence of the MCT stimuli is held by Kragh and Smith (1970) to be valuable in the detection of projection and psychotic tendencies, while changes to the B stimulus which should be stable are pathognomic.

For more details of the nature of MCT variables and how these are scored readers are referred to Chapter 29 of this handbook. Repression. Isolation. Sensitivity (A absorbed into B). Stereotype. Depression. Instability. Discontinuity. Psychosis and abnormality are scored from the overall impression of the protocol. Scoring is reliable (Kragh and Smith, 1970).

Value of DMT and MCT in diagnosis

There are two useful and important sets of results that could be obtained from the use of these tests. The first is theoretical. As has been pointed out by Kline (1981, 1984) these tests, if valid, are about the only way of obtaining experimental access to defence mechanisms and other normally unconscious processes. Thus these tests enable researchers to put to the test various psychoanalytic notions concerning the nature of neurosis and psychosis. Thus there is some theoretical potential in these tests.

If the tests discriminate clearly among psychiatric groups they are useful for diagnosis at the purely practical level for psychiatrists and psychologists who remain unconvinced by the percept-genetic rationale of these tests (see Chapter 18).

As can be seen from the two paragraphs above, all depends, for our evaluation of the these percept-genetic tests, on their validity as measures of defences and on their ability to discriminate among diagnostic groups.

The validity of the DMT has already been discussed above and it was concluded that it could not be regarded as more than a promising test. As so often more research was necessary. This is even more true of the MCT, the use of which has been restricted to Scandinavia. This is not to denigrate the Scandinavian research but simply to indicate that the test is used in its own country as if were valid, i.e. results are reported with no attempt to demonstrate that the test does measure defences.

This means that at present all studies with these percept-genetic tests among psychiatric groups have to be examined in the tradition of construct validity (see Chapter 2 of this handbook), looking to see whether the results fit the psychoanalytic theory of defences and thus confirm the test validity.

Although this means that the theoretical contribution of percept-genetic methods is muted, this is not true of the empirical work with diagnostic groups where all that matters is whether the test will discriminate the groups reliably or not. If it can it is useful for diagnosis.

It would be out of place in a handbook of psychological testing to examine the considerable clinical evidence concerning these two tests, some of which is summarised in Kragh and Smith (1970) and also in Westerlundh (1976). In general the case for the discriminatory power of these tests is not clear cut. Useful differences can be found in clinical groups but none is large enough to use the methods as diagnostic instruments. However this does not mean to say that they could not be so used because no attempts have been made to use multivariate statistical methods to aid differentiation.

In conclusion, I should like to see considerable further efforts made to use these percept-genetic methods with psychiatric groups because I think some valuable psychological insights could be gained. I would hazard a guess that this is the more valuable aspect of the DMT and MCT for diagnosis, rather than simple differential power.

5. Other tests in clinical diagnosis

Obviously with several thousands of tests in existence, it would be surprising if the categories of test which we have so far discussed, although of great importance, covered all tests. In this section I want to discuss briefly the use of tests which fall outside these categories.

Testing for impairment due to brain damage

There is a group of tests which is widely used in clinical diagnosis, yet which fits none of our categories. These are the tests which are designed to tap cognitive deficits. They are usually used in the assessment of the cognitive deficits cases of brain damage due to accident, or in physical illness such as strokes or other vascular disease as well as Alzheimer's and other degenerative conditions.

The rationale and construction of such tests have been described in Chapter 18 of this handbook and the best-known examples of the genre are listed in Chapter 29. There is little to say about the use of these tests for the diagnosis of brain damage which is not obvious from the nature of the tests.

The Recognition Memory Test (Warrington, 1984) exemplifies the case. This test detects deficits in visual and verbal memory by presenting the subject with fifty verbal stimuli, one every three seconds. These are then presented together with distractors and subjects are required to recognise the original set. There is a similar procedure for visual stimuli.

Norms for approximately 300 patients with various types of brain damage are provided in the manual to the test. The fact that there are measures of both visual and verbal memory allows clinicians to determine the locus of brain damage and whether it is left and/or right hemisphere. Its diagnostic quality for location of brain damage depends much upon the quality of the norms and, of course, whether such localisation has such specific effects. Nevertheless if discriminating norms for brain damage can be produced in terms of memory deficits then such tests as the Warrington memory test are obviously useful. Whether such localisation can be done better by brain scan is beyond the scope of this handbook to answer but if psychological tests are used in the diagnosis of brain damage this is their rationale.

One further example will clarify the use of these neuropsychological tests for clinical diagnosis – the Kendrick Cognitive Test for the Elderly (Kendrick, 1985). There are two tests in this scale. One of them, object learning, consists of cards, depicting everyday objects, which subjects have to recall. The other measures a subject's speed in copying numbers. This test is for elderly subjects (over 55 years), I hope a curious extension forwards of the term 'elderly', and the norms enable differential diagnoses to be made, in terms of cognitive deficits, between normals, depressed and dementing patients, among others.

Again, as was the case with the Warrington test, all depends upon the quality of the norms. If the normative differences are clear and replicable the test will be efficient. In so far as they depart from a rigorous standard of discrimination so will the test fail in diagnosis. This is, of course, true of all clinical tests of this type which are attempting to diagnose by means of typical cognitive deficits.

It should be noted here that these tests are also useful for the assessment of treatment, since changes for the better can be monitored, and this will be discussed in the second section of this chapter.

I do not intend to discuss further any other of these special clinical tests, for their use in diagnosis is exactly the same as in our two examples. Some of them, as is clear from Chapter 29 of this handbook, offer a wide variety of variables for the assessment of deficit. Thus the Luria-Nebraska Neuro-psychological Battery (Golden *et al.*, 1980) takes more than two hours to administer and includes the following measures: rhythm; tactile, visual and motor functions; receptive and expressive speech; writing, reading and arithmetic; memory and intellectual processes.

Obviously this does more than attempt to assess brain damage and cognitive functioning, for it includes attainments such as reading and writing. Results on these scales would have to be compared with those of people having similar backgrounds and education and it is arguable that for abilities such as these, full-length, carefully standardised attainment tests would be better. Nevertheless it is obviously useful to be able to assess functional deficits as well as more purely cognitive deficits with one test.

I shall say no more about the use of this test for diagnosis since, despite its greater complexity, in principle it is no different from our earlier examples. Diagnostic power depends upon the quality of the norms.

One further point should be noted about the use of these special tests for diagnosis. Although all depends on their norms, they are more than simple empirical diagnostic devices, in contradistinction to criterion-keyed tests. With these latter there is little psychological insight to be gained from the fact that they discriminate. With these special tests the fact that they discriminate is psychologically meaningful because the type of deficit that typifies each category tells us something about the location of the brain damage and, as shall be seen, is obviously useful in the assessment of therapy and treatment. Goldberg (1989) contains a useful discussion of the use of such tests both for diagnosis and for general psychological assessment in psychopathology. This is clearly a specialised topic and in a general handbook of psychological testing I can mention only the principles and rationale of psychological testing in this field.

The use of standard ability tests in diagnosis

Brief mention should be made of the fact that cognitive deficits can be measured by standard ability tests such as the WAIS (Wechsler, 1974), which is fully described in Chapter 23 of this handbook. The subscale scores are used to differentiate different clinical groups from one another, not only brain damaged patients but also psychiatric groups such as schizophrenics and obsessionals, as is fully described in Howard (1989b and Maloney and Ward, 1976). However the problem here is that the WAIS scales are not sufficiently reliable for this type of differential work. Furthermore the scales were not designed to measure specific deficits, as is often required, and it would seem better to use special cognitive tests for this purpose. The work of Crawford and Parker (e.g. Crawford, 1991) with the WAIS in the assessment of neuropsychological damage should also be mentioned. These find the vocabulary scale a useful indicant of premorbid intelligence.

Conclusions concerning the use of tests in diagnosis

It can be seen that all the types of test discussed in this section have their uses in clinical diagnosis. For brain damaged patients the neuropsychological tests are certainly valuable diagnostic tools but of a highly specialised kind. Of the other types of tests, factored tests can probably yield the most psychologically useful information, although objectively scored projective tests and percept-genetic methods might turn out to be valuable. Criterion-keyed tests and specially constructed tests, such as symptom checklists, seem to be of less psychological value in diagnosis than the other tests but may prove useful as simple diagnostic measures.

PSYCHOLOGICAL TESTS IN THE ASSESSMENT OF TREATMENT

In this section of the chapter I shall examine the contribution to treatment that can be made by the five categories of tests which have been discussed in relation to diagnosis. First I shall make some general points about the use of tests in the context of treatment which will apply to virtually all of our categories.

The meaning of improvement In clinical psychology in almost all instances treatment is aimed to improve the client. Thus it is important to be able to specify what improvement might consist of, to be able to define improvement. In medical, as distinct from psychological, disorders this is relatively simple. A broken leg may be regarded as cured if former function is restored and the same is true of recovery from infection. However in the case of psychological disorders this is by no means the case. One of the problems bedevilling the scientific study of psychotherapy is precisely the measurement and meaning of recovery. Kline (1991) has discussed nineteen severe methodological problems in the assessment of psychotherapy and the measurement and definition of improvement was a major difficulty.

This is partly because in some psychotherapies recovery would be regarded as remission of symptoms, as in behaviour therapy, while in psychodynamic therapies a far more profound, albeit ill-defined, personality change is thought to be required if the therapy is successful. Thus while it may be difficult to specify what the improvement may be it is evident that, from the viewpoint of the psychological tester, in the assessment of treatment we must be able to measure changes in the treated groups.

The measurement of change   As Cronbach (1976) has argued the measurement of change is made difficult by the fact that change scores are unreliable, a function of the unreliability of the tests from which they were derived. In the study of the effectiveness of clinical treatment, where changes in score are the focus of treatment, high reliability is therefore essential. However, as the paragraph on the meaning of recovery implied, to develop valid measures of psychotherapeutic recovery is exceedingly difficult. This is brilliantly illustrated in a series of cases studies by Yalom (1991) where the qualitative difference in the outlook on life of the patients and its existential meaning were in some cases profound, albeit almost impossible to capture in a checklist. Thus the validity of tests used in the assessment of recovery needs carefully to be considered.

With all these obvious, but often neglected, points in mind, I shall examine the value of our five categories of test in the assessment of treatment in clinical psychology. However before I do this one important point should be noted. I argued in the introductory discussion to this section that there are considerable problems in the evaluation of psychotherapy. Amongst the most important are differences among patients with the same diagnosis, the unreliability of diagnosis, differences among psychotherapists of the same school, the need for control groups, both untreated and those receiving placebo treatment, the possible interaction of therapist and patients, the problem of spontaneous recovery, the influence, in therapy, of life events, the interaction between types of therapy and therapist, and the interaction of types of therapy and diagnosis; and this ignores the difficulty that much psychiatric or neurotic behaviour may be, as argued by Smail (1984), a perfectly sensible reaction to dreadful circumstances. My reason for raising these difficulties at this juncture is that I do not want readers to obtain the impression that all the problems in evaluating treatments can be dissolved away by using the right tests. This is not so. Certainly without the right tests even the most ingenious research designs to overcome these problems will be worthless; but proper research designs are necessary and, as was argued by Kline (1991) these are rarely employed, partly on account of the practical problems in sampling sufficient patients and therapists. With this warning I shall discuss the various categories of tests.

1. Factor analytic tests, derived from simple structure analyses of the field

The argument for the use of these factored tests in the evaluation and monitoring of treatments is of great simplicity and clarity. It can be shown, as we have discussed in our section on diagnosis, that various neurotic and psychiatric groups differ from normals on certain of the factors in the 16PF and CAQ, which measures the Cattell abnormal factors. Now if psychotherapy, or any other treatment, such as drugs, has in any way produced real personality change then we would expect subjects or clients to return to normal levels on these factors. Thus by the use of factored tests which measure the fundamental dimensions of personality real change can be monitored. Cattell (e.g. Cattell and Kline, 1977) would certainly argue that this approach overcomes many of the difficulties which have been mentioned above concerning measures of recovery.

It should be noted that this claim is a matter of scientific principle. Although Cattell (e.g. 1973) and Bolton (1986) would contend that such measurement should be done by their tests, the 16PF and the CAQ, this is simply because, in their view, these measure the fundamental personality factors. The point is that to return patients to normal on the factors that discriminate patients from normal must, almost by definition, indicate true personality change and in the desired direction.

In my view this constitutes the most powerful argument for using these factored personality tests in the monitoring and evaluation of therapy. Changes to normality must be unequivocal evidence of recovery, whether this is due to the psychotherapy or not.

The use of P factor analysis

In Chapter 8 of this handbook, on factor analysis, it will be remembered that we mentioned a number of varieties of factor analysis. Normal or regular factor analysis, R analysis, factors the correlations between tests. P analysis, however, factors the correlations between a set of scores taken from one person on many occasions. This P analysis is ideal for the study of psychotherapy provided that the patient is able to take the large number of testing sessions required. If, for example, in long-term psychotherapy, we tested the patient after every session and included in the analysis records of life events and even some details of what went on in the session, the P factor analysis would reveal all those aspects of the treatment and the things that happened to the patient which were relevant to his or her outcome.

Such a design answers clinical criticism that pooling patients may obscure important individual differences in the way subjects respond to psychotherapy and to life events. Furthermore by collecting together a series of P factor analyses it would quickly become obvious if there were common factors (in the ordinary sense of the word) involved in recovery.

It may be wondered why there are so few examples of P technique studies, given its apparently powerful qualities. As is so often the case with research into real life rather than laboratory phenomena there are considerable practical difficulties. Thus the patient would have to be tested at least 100 times, for this constitutes the statistical basis of the correlations, on a large number of variables, the more the better (provided they did not, in this example, exceed 100). Bolton (1986) cites studies where two hours' testing was involved. Apart from the fact that most patients could not afford the time or be willing to complete the tests on this scale there is the technical difficulty of dealing with the effects on test validity of repeated testing. This is a severe problem as I discovered in a study of ergs and sentiments in which the MAT (see Chapter 26 of this handbook) was administered to a subject every day of February (Kline and Grindley, 1974). Although this is an objective test (and thus not amenable to deliberate distortion by subjects, as is discussed in Chapter 17), by the end of the period the subject found it aversive in the extreme to complete the test. Indeed, although the results made sound psychological sense, it is still a matter of some doubt as to whether the later tests were valid.

Conclusions

The conclusions concerning the use of factored tests in the evaluation and monitoring of clinical treatment are clear. These tests are highly useful because, from the nature of factored variables, we can see the effects of the treatment on personality traits, and thus have a true measure of the return to normality. This is a very different criterion which would apply to many different schools of psychotherapy, as distinct from evaluations based upon remission of symptoms, a phenomenon which may be ephemeral and is regarded in psychoanalysis as a flight into health (Fenichel, 1945).

2. Criterion-keyed tests

As was mentioned in our introduction to criterion-keyed tests in this chapter, the most widely used personality questionnaire is a criterion-keyed test designed originally for clinical use and one with more than 12,000 references, mainly to clinical studies. This is the MMPI (Hathaway and

McKinley, 1951) and its updated version the MMPI-2 (Graham, 1990), tests both fully described and evaluated in Chapter 25. Most of the discussion of the value of criterion-keyed tests will be concentrated upon this test although it will be applicable to all tests constructed by this method.

With so huge a number of studies with the MMPI it would appear to be an impossible task in one section of one chapter to evaluate the value of the MMPI and this type of test. In fact, this is probably the case. However the task has been considerably lightened by the recent publication of a book which deals directly with this subject – *MMPI-2 in Psychological Treatment* (Butcher, 1990). Although I by no means agree with the conclusions of this book it forms an excellent basis for discussion. Since Butcher also argues that the MMPI-2 is useful as a basis for guiding treatment this will also be discussed since it is clearly an important aspect of clinical work. Finally, before the detailed discussion I must stress that the arguments which I shall use are all applicable to criterion-keyed tests in general and are not specific to the MMPI.

The use of the MMPI-2 as a guide to treatment

According to Butcher (1990) the various validity indices of the MMPI give an indication of whether the patient is being honest and cooperating with the therapist and thus ready for treatment. This may well be so but this is a rather trivial aspect of clinical work and I shall say little about this. However I would be surprised if such scales told any competent therapist or clinician anything he or she had not already inferred from the patient. It would be a poor psychologist who could not tell whether a patient was cooperative or honest.

However, the second issue raised by Butcher (1990) is of more fundamental importance since it deals with a point which is relevant to all criterion-keyed tests. Butcher argues that elevated scores on the clinical scales of the MMPI-2 reflect a need for treatment. I shall cite some of his examples which clarify the point. Thus the Pa scale, paranoia, is held to be a very important scale in the planning of treatment because 'it assesses the client's trust in interpersonal relationships, flexibility towards personality change, and attitudes towards personality figures' (p.57).

In my view this inference from the Pa scale of the MMPI-2 has no logical or empirical basis. In Chapter 9 of this handbook we discussed and evaluated the criterion-keyed method of test construction. There it was demonstrated that such tests had no necessary psychological meaning. Thus the paranoia scale of the MMPI is a paranoia scale by virtue only of the fact that it discriminates paranoids from other clinical groups. Since these groups may differ in a variety of variables it is impossible to infer the meaning of a test that so discriminates them from the fact that it does so. This, as was stressed in Chapter 9, is the weakness of the criterion-keyed method of test construction, its lack of necessary psychological meaning, an argument which Nunnally (1978) regards as contraindicating its use.

Butcher's claims about the value of the paranoia scale are based upon the meaning of the items in the scale. However this is simply face validity, discussed in Chapter 2 of this handbook; face validity is not necessarily a good guide as to what a test measures. If it were personality testing would not still be at its present stage where there is little agreement as to the best test or the most salient variables.

Of course, as was argued in our chapter on the factor analysis of tests, the best approach to establishing what tests measure is to factor them together with the best marker scales in the relevant area. In fact this has been done with the MMPI and the validity of the clinical scales is not supported. Indeed the abnormal factors of Cattell which were set out in Table 20.1 were derived from just such factorings of the MMPI and other items. Although there was a paranoid factor it was not identical with the MMPI scale. However even if it had been it would not have affected the principle of the argument, namely that psychological inferences from the MMPI factors are not really permissible.

Similar arguments apply to all the inferences about patients made from the nature of the scales. One approach that might be mentioned is simply to use the empirical nature of criterion-keyed tests to find out what scores or profiles of scores (as designated by the MMPI codes) tend to do well in therapy and use such scores as indicators for therapy. This would be a viable method providing that large samples of therapists were used so that the effects of individual therapists could be disregarded. Some studies of this kind have been done, which, indeed, Butcher (1990) cites and this is a viable approach. However as was the case with diagnosis by criterion-keyed tests such an empirical method, even if it were successful, suffers from the fact that it gives no psychological insight into the reasons why patients were successful in treatment.

Finally it should be mentioned that Butcher (1990) cites a number of MMPI-2 scales which are thought to be useful in evaluating the likely success of a patient in therapy. One such is the ego strength scale first developed by Barron (1953). However all the arguments that can be applied to criterion-keyed scales apply with force to this scale which was originally derived from a study of items that would discriminate seventeen patients who improved from sixteen who did not. Interpretation of the meaning of the scale depends on the face validity of the items.

Indeed Butcher (1990) suggests that individual items can be used to decide whether patients might benefit from therapy. Similarly the Harris and Lingoes (1968) scales of the original MMPI were derived by rational grouping of the items according to content. All these approaches ignore the psychometric analysis of test variance and assume that the meaning of an item is an accurate guide to what it measures.

Even if it turns out that these scales are effective in selecting patients who will do well in therapy the lack of psychological meaning of these scales means that they are inferior to factored scales whose meaning is known.

There is one further point which should be raised about this MMPI research into the evaluation of a patient's suitability for psychotherapy. This is the ethical point of whether there can be justification on the basis of a test score for regarding a patient as unsuitable and thus rejecting her or him for treatment. This is particularly important in the case of criterion-keyed tests since their value lies in their screening ability rather than the psychological insight or knowledge that can be gained from them. The only reason, therefore, for using these scales would be to reject a patient for treatment. Although there is a long tradition, perhaps stemming from psychoanalysis, of selecting patients for psychotherapy, it provides a strong contrast to orthodox, organic medicine where patients are simply patients and all receive treatment.

The use of criterion-keyed tests in the evaluation and monitoring of treatment

Butcher (1990) cites no studies with the MMPI or MMPI-2 in which scales have been developed which discriminate patients who have improved from those who have not, and I know of no other scales of this kind. Thus as such there are no criterion-keyed tests which could be used where the criterion is improvement. However it is possible, although not ideal as I shall argue, to use criterion-keyed tests to evaluate and monitor psychotherapy.

1. Using scales which discriminate abnormal groups One obvious possibility is to use the scales on which patients were elevated as an index of improvement. Presumably if, for example, a depressed patient, after treatment, no longer had high scores on the depression scale, this must be regarded as recovery. It would certainly be difficult to argue against this criterion of recovery – that they could no longer be discriminated by a criterion-keyed scale. In this case the fact that the psychological meaning of the scales is unknown is not a severe disadvantage. The low scores simply index recovery – a return to normality, as defined by the test.

2. Using item content or scales rationally grouped by items As was discussed above, Butcher (1990) considered the possibility, in the evaluation of patients' suitability for treatment, of using items or scales of apparently relevant items. Obviously we would do the same thing for judging whether subjects are recovered or not. However, all this assumes that items are face valid and that subjects are answering honestly and without typical item distortions such as social desirability or acquiescence.

Of course, using items or scales in this way is not really using criterion-keyed tests at all, even if the items are obtained from such tests. These are really tests which fall into our next category. However unless such tests have sound evidence of validity, although numbers can be obtained from them they do little more than does asking a patient how she or he feels.

Conclusions

From this discussion it is clear that for evaluating patients for psychotherapy criterion-keyed tests suffer from the problem of their lack of psychological meaning. The use of rational scales or individual items is difficult to recommend because all depends on their face validity. The same arguments apply to the monitoring and evaluation of psychotherapy or treatment, except that here the use of criterion-keyed scales, which distinguish clinical groups from normals, does make sense. If patients return to normal on these scales it is sound evidence that they are improved, even if the meaning of the scales is obscure.

3. Tests developed by other methods

This can be a brief section for in principle the use of such tests is a simple matter. Here all depends upon the reliability and validity of the test. The test needs to be reliable since change scores or comparison with norms will be used and validity is essential or the results will be meaningless.

One good illustration of the use of these tests in the study of the effectiveness of psychotherapy, and this will exemplify all the important points about the use of these tests, can be found in the work of Shapiro *et al.* (1990). These authors studied the effectiveness of four kinds of therapy and used a variety of outcome and process measures to achieve this end.

Shapiro *et al.* (1990) gave a variety of tests on five occasions – on intake, during the sessions and on follow ups. I shall not list all the tests but some of those which they used show the value of tests developed to be homogeneous, valid measures for specific purposes such as this study required. Thus anxiety and depression are a feature of many psychiatric patients and measures of these were administered – the Beck Depression Inventory (Beck *et al.*, 1961) and the Spielberger State–Trait Anxiety Inventory (Spielberger *et al.*, 1970), tests both discussed in Section IV of this handbook. It is obviously a sensible measure of recovery if depression and anxiety are both lowered. Thus if these are valid tests (and the evidence suggests that they are) then this is a demonstration that special tests can be useful in the evaluation of treatment, although as it happens the Spielberger trait scale is effectively a factored test, measuring the anxiety factor (see Chapter 25 of this handbook).

In addition Shapiro *et al.* (1990) used a well known symptom scale, the SCL-90R (Derogatis *et al.*, 1973), and again the rationale is obvious:

recovered patients should show less symptomatology. This further illustrates the utility of this class of tests in the assessment of psychotherapy.

However, some of the tests which were used in this investigation were of more dubious validity, i.e. their validity was attested by little more than the fact that they were consistent and the item content seemed to reflect the needs of the investigator. For example one scale of self-esteem had but eight items. Now given the relationship between reliability and length (see Chapter 3 of this handbook) it is difficult to see how this could be highly reliable. However, if it were, it is unlikely to be valid since it must be a remarkably small universe of items if eight items can reliably sample it. Similarly in our section on criterion-keyed tests, above, the problems of regarding the face validity of items as evidence for the validity of the test was discussed and all that was said there applies equally here.

Conclusions

This example of using a variety of tests from our third category in the evaluation of psychotherapy clearly illustrates what needs to be said. If the tests are valid and reliable then they can be useful. Where this is not the case the results can be highly misleading.

4. Projective tests in the evaluation and monitoring of treatment

In Chapter 16 the problems concerning the reliability and validity of projective tests were fully discussed. It was argued that objective scoring, using G analysis (Holley, 1973), might restore some scientific credibility to projective tests. However it is to be noted that such analyses are ideal for studying and discriminating between groups but application to the evaluation and monitoring of treatment is less obvious.

The only approach which seems possible would be to study the salient discriminating indices, as revealed by G analysis, in the treated subjects. An example will clarify this point. Suppose that four variables had been shown in the G analysis of a projective test to discriminate depressives from normal controls. In the evaluation of depressives who had received treatment these variables would be scrutinised and we would expect that they would be less apparent in the treated group.

However it has to be said that, as yet, no such variables on any projective test have been found, and that even if they had, their psychological meaning would have to be demonstrated before this approach would make much sense. To use it without understanding the meaning of the variables would be blind empiricism, of the kind which rarely leads to any useful psychological knowledge.

Thus G analysis of projective tests, while it seems promising for diagnosis, does not appear likely to be so useful for the study of the effectiveness of treatment. This judgement might well change if convincing and psychologically meaningful discriminations of diagnostic groups were to be made from the G analysis of these tests. The salient variables might then be valuable in the assessment of treatment.

The reliability and validity of projective tests scored in the orthodox fashion is such, as has been discussed in both Chapters 16 and 26 of this handbook, as to make them unsuitable for use in evaluating treatment. There is one possible exception to this general rejection of the projective test. In Chapter 26 it was shown that the Holtzman Inkblot Test (Holtzman *et al.*, 1968) was at least reliable but there is still no convincing evidence that the HIT variables are useful for evaluation.

Percept-genetic techniques in the evaluation of treatment

Percept-genetic methods and techniques (Kragh and Smith, 1970) were discussed in Chapter 18 and the DMT and MCT are described in Chapter 29 of this handbook. Although there is no firm agreement as to the validity of these tests, if they were accepted as valid they would be highly useful in the monitoring and evaluation of treatment, especially psychoanalytically oriented treatment. This is because percept-genetic methods are designed to measure defence mechanisms and, as Fenichel (1945) argues, these are in excessive use among neurotics and overwhelmed in psychotics. Thus we would expect considerable changes in those who had been treated. Indeed these tests, if valid, would be ideal for measuring the effectiveness of psychotherapy since the use of defences is fundamental to the psychoanalytic notion of cure, summarised as 'where id was there shall ego be' (Freud, 1933).

That is why, in Chapter 18, we called for more research into percept-genetic methods because potentially these are tests of great value in clinical psychology, being aimed at unconscious conflicts.

Conclusions

From this it may be concluded that in the monitoring and evaluation of treatment it would be valuable to use percept-genetic methods experimentally, for findings in accord with theory would all go towards establishing the construct validity of the methods. At present the use of projective tests does not seem helpful, although if G analyses turn out well that position could change.

5. Other tests in the evaluation of treatment

The first set of tests which I shall examine are those tests of cognitive deficit which have been specifically designed for the evaluation of patients with brain damage or stroke. In our section on the use of these tests for diagnosis we mentioned some of the best-known of these, the Luria-Nebraska Neuropsychological Battery (Golden *et al.*, 1980) and the Recognition Memory Test (Warrington, 1984).

In the evaluation and monitoring of treatment the use of measures of cognitive deficit is obvious. They can be given during and after treatment and improvement should be reflected in improved scores. In stroke patients, for example, where there may be considerable time invested in attempting to restore lost linguistic abilities, the use of such tests is valuable also in assessing these training procedures and in enabling those involved in the programme to concentrate their efforts where the patient has failed to improve.

In the evaluation of psychotherapy, special tests are often devised to measure patient improvement. Shapiro *et al.*, (1990) in their study of psychotherapy, to which I have already referred in this chapter, used several such measures. One such example is the inventory of Interpersonal Problems (Horowitz *et al.*, 1988) or a symptom checklist, such as the SCL-90R (Derogatis *et al.*, 1973).

Again, as was the case with the neuropsychological tests, the use of these tests in the evaluation and monitoring of treatment is obvious. Given that the tests are reliable and are filled in honestly, there should be changes in scores with few problems and symptoms being recorded. However, as the case studies of psychotherapy by Yalom (1991) show, to evaluate treatment in these simplistic terms may do gross injustice to highly subtle therapy – in which the client's feelings about herself may have changed or she may be able to accept herself or her death more honestly. Such important outcomes are not captured by simplistic measures of this type or by brief measures of self-esteem.

Nevertheless, despite these vital caveats a decrease in problems and symptoms would have to be thought of as good rather than bad, and such tests could be useful as one aspect of assessing the value and progress of therapy.

The use of standard ability tests

It should be pointed out, at this juncture, that standard ability tests can be used to evaluate treatment although they are less sensitive than the special tests of cognitive deficit which we have described in this section. The WAIS (Wechsler, 1974) is frequently used in this connection and its subscales enable one to see how different aspects of ability have been improved or not, as the case may be. However the problem with the WAIS is that it is really a test of global ability rather than specific abilities and it was constructed before the factor analysis of abilities, discussed in Chapter 12 of this handbook, had made it clear what were the most important specific abilities.

Despite the brevity of its subscales it is used in the clinical context apparently with some success as can be seen in Howard (1989b), Maloney and Ward (1976) and Crawford *et al.* (1988).

Conclusions

From this it can be seen that special tests have a part to play in the evaluation of treatment. Neuropsychological tests are clearly valuable where they are applicable at all and other special tests used to evaluate psychotherapy have a limited use in assessing some aspects of improvement.

PSYCHOLOGICAL TESTS AND CLINICAL THEORY

In the final section of this chapter I shall consider the theoretical contribution of psychological testing to the clinical field.

First I shall consider one highly specialised area of psychometric testing – that of neuropsychology. As has been discussed in the previous sections of this chapter on diagnosis and treatment, the use of special measures of cognitive functioning has proved valuable after vascular accidents and head injuries. However, as Goldberg (1989) makes clear in his study of neuro-psychology and psychopathology, the results of this type of testing have proved valuable in theorising about cerebral functioning. For example from the results of studying the cognitive deficits of those exhibiting 'asymbolias' – where specific objects cannot be recognised as members of a class – he concludes that left hemisphere functioning is not limited to processing in terms of linguistic codes.

There can be little doubt that these results from these neuropsychological tests are useful in forming hypotheses and ultimately theories about cognitive functioning in general and not only in subjects with some pathology.

Apart from this highly specialised field there are really two main areas where tests are useful. The first concerns the quantitative testing of clinical theory. The example of psychoanalytic theory illustrates this point. It is a commonplace that a major weakness of Freudian theory is the lack of quantitative evidence, as opponents of psychoanalysis never tire of reiterating (e.g. Eysenck, 1985; Gruenbaum, 1988), although in fact, as Kline (1981) and Fisher and Greenberg (1977) have shown, there is some quantitative evidence in its support. Furthermore, this same objection applies to most clinical theorising. This is because clinical observations are not sufficient data to construct a scientific theory. For this clear hypotheses must be formulated which can be refuted, to use the useful criterion of Popper (1959), and quantification is an essential for this purpose.

In our section on projective tests above, we discussed percept-genetic methods. The DMT (Kragh, 1984), the most widely used of these tests, assesses defence mechanisms. Here, then, is a technique, assuming that the test is valid, for the purposes of the argument, that can put to the test Freudian hypotheses concerning the defences in neuroses. For example, paranoid schizophrenics are considered to use two defences: reaction-formation and projection (Freud, 1911). The defences of paranoid schizophrenics and non-paranoid controls can be compared.

This is simply one example and Kline (1981) and Fisher and Greenberg (1977) were able to cite many hundreds of such quantified tests of Freudian hypotheses. In the same way other clinical theories can be examined, provided that valid and reliable tests have been constructed relevant to the theoretical variables.

This approach can constitute a useful contribution to clinical psychology although it has to be said that many of the salient variables of clinical psychology are hard to measure, and at present there is no large body of knowledge that has accumulated in this way.

The second contribution which psychometric testing can make to clinical theory arises from the test results themselves and may be regarded as genuine psychometric psychology. In other words the psychometric test findings are used to construct a new theory. Such a theory would have the advantage of using only quantified variables and would, therefore, more closely resemble the theories used in the natural sciences.

With so many psychological tests available, it might be thought impossible not only to construct a theory but even to know where to start. However, in fact this is far from the case. Tests derived from simple structure factor analyses of the relevant fields are ideal for theory construction and the rationale for psychometric theories on this basis, which has been implicit throughout this handbook, will be briefly set out below.

Factor analytic tests and psychological theory

In Chapters 7 and 8 of this handbook it was demonstrated that simple structure factors could be regarded as the fundamental dimensions or constructs underlying the variance in the correlation matrices from which they had been computed. Thus, if the whole field has been sampled, the resulting factors were bound to be the most salient in that field and hence the element of any proper theory. Such simple structure factors, embracing a whole field, have to be distinguished from factors derived from variables which represent no particular population, as is the case with many factored tests, which are little more than tautologous factors or bloated specifics.

The fact that simple structure factors are the salient elements in the field contributes to (in this instance clinical) theory in two ways. Examples will best clarify these points.

In the first case the simple structure factors may be compared with current theories. Thus as we saw at the beginning of this chapter Cattell (1973) has provided a set of normal and abnormal factors. That there are seven depression factors can be compared with clinical theories of depression. In fact, this is a novel notion and thus it fits no clinical account. Similarly the other abnormal factors do not confirm any of the common clinical concepts of abnormal personality.

Another, easier, example is from the field of motivation. Here Cattell (1985) has isolated through factor analysis a number of ergs and sentiments. These can be compared with the findings of clinically oriented psychologists and it is immediately obvious that many theories are not supported by these findings. Thus Freud (1933) has a two-factor theory of motivation, sex and aggression being the all-important variables, while Murray (1938) hypothesised far more.

In brief, simple structure factors can be used in a comparison with existing theories, not as a specific test of them, but to see whether there is a basic agreement with the clinical work. Confirmatory analysis is also useful here. However, useful as this is, the second contribution that factor analysis can make to clinical theory is potentially of far greater importance, although the only factorist who has attempted this is Cattell (1981 and 1985, especially). This is to use the factors to construct a new theory.

Cattell (1981; 1985) on the basis of his extensive factorings of the three fields of ability, personality and motivation has presented a complete theory of human psychology, including many clinical components.

To describe the structured learning theory, the dynamic calculus, which purports to explain human motivation, certainly of the utmost clinical relevance, and the Vidas systems model of personality, would go far beyond the scope of this handbook. Nevertheless they indicate how the findings from psychometric tests, where simple structure has been obtained, can be used to construct powerful theories.

The dynamic calculus is of real clinical relevance since it traces behaviour back to its roots. Indeed in Cattell (1985) thirty-seven basic dynamic equations can be found, e.g. anxiety level from ego control threat. Nevertheless I cite this work only to illustrate that theories can be made from psychometric tests. I do not want to go further into the details since, as is clear from our chapter on motivation and mood, Chapter 17, it is highly likely that these Cattell factors are not the best account of the field. Nevertheless despite these problems the work of Cattell indicates that from psychometric testing a considerable contribution to clinical theory could be obtained.

On a more simple level, if reliable differences can be found between diagnostic groups on simple structure factors, then these can be used to construct an explanation of these differences and abnormal, clinical theory can be built up. Eysenck (1967), in *The Biological Basis of Personality*, uses his factors in an account of personality and the development of neurosis, another example of the contribution of factor analytic tests to clinical theory.

Conclusions

At the beginning of this section we showed how tests of cognitive deficit were useful in theorising about brain function. However apart from this highly specialised form of testing our examples illustrated that factor analytic, simple structure variables can be used to develop psychological theory both generally and in the clinical sphere, as well as to test and compare with existing theories. Potentially such theories have the scientific advantage, compared with standard clinical theories, that they are constructed from quantified variables that are the most salient in the field. Despite these advantages, however, there are, at present, no adequate factor analytic clinical theories, despite the heroic efforts of Cattell and Eysenck. This is because, in the case of Cattell, there is some doubt as to whether his factors are the best and most simple account of the fields. Nevertheless, as more research is carried out and reliable, simple structure factors in all the main fields are established, the psychometric contribution to clinical theory should become more powerful.

Chapter 21

Tests in Counselling and Guidance

In this chapter I shall discuss the use and value of psychological tests in counselling and guidance. Of course counselling and guidance involves far more than psychological testing, and most modern texts (e.g. Nelson-Jones, 1982) devote only a tiny proportion of space to it. Many counsellors, indeed, especially those who use behaviouristic or psychoanalytic theories and methods, regard psychological testing as no part of their work.

In this chapter I do not intend to argue how great an emphasis should be placed on psychological testing. Instead I shall simply indicate how it can be effectively used and this should make its value obvious.

The main thrust of psychological testing in counselling and guidance is in the area of vocational counselling and career choice, and this chapter will be concerned with this aspect of the work. It should be noted at this point, therefore, that this chapter might have been incorporated into either that on educational psychology or the one on occupational psychology. However it is convenient to treat the topic separately, although there are no compelling logical reasons so to do.

ASSUMPTIONS

The approach adopted in this handbook to the use of psychological tests makes one assumption that should be stated at the outset. It is assumed that each occupation has an optimal requirement in terms of the aptitudes, abilities, personality characteristics and interests of the workers involved in it. The task, therefore, of vocational guidance and counselling becomes obvious: to find the job, by whatever means, formal or informal, which best fits the client. This, equally obviously, involves two things: person assessment and job assessment. In this chapter I shall deal chiefly with the assessment of individuals by psychological tests. This assumption seems logically impeccable although, as yet, there are insufficient empirical data to make the task as simple as it ought to be. In fact this approach to vocational guidance has been extensively developed in a previous book (Kline, 1975) and readers should be referred there for greater elaboration of the arguments in this chapter.

To argue that vocational guidance necessitates fitting individuals to the jobs best suited to them is to propound what is, essentially, the rationale of the work of Rodger (1962) and to follow the psychometric model which underlies the work of Cattell (e.g. 1981) and which is implicit throughout this handbook.

The two tasks of vocational guidance are, as has been argued, person assessment and job assessment. The finest person assessment in the world would be useless without good job assessment and vice versa. However, I shall not discuss how jobs can be evaluated in this chapter for such job description and analysis is a complex matter which is better left to Chapter 25, on the use of tests in occupational psychology, of which it is an integral part. For the purposes of discussing the value of psychological tests in vocational guidance I shall assume where it is necessary (only one of the four different approaches to the use of tests in vocational guidance and counselling demand this assumption), that there is some reasonable job specification or description at which to aim the testing.

ASSESSING PEOPLE FOR VOCATIONAL GUIDANCE

As is evident from the psychometric model the best description of an individual arises from measurements on the most important factors which have been discovered in the various fields of testing discussed in Section II of this handbook. Therefore, in general, I would advocate that all subjects be tested on these main factors, the five second order ability factors (see Chapter 12), the five personality factors which have emerged from ratings and questionnaires (see Chapter 15) and the motivational factors and tests discussed in Chapter 17. In addition where special abilities are necessary tests for these should be administered. This general picture will be clarified by some specific examples.

There are a variety of approaches to the use of the test results which will now be examined.

1. Comparison of test results with job profiles

Here the test results of our subject are compared to the psychological profiles of the occupants of a large sample of different jobs. Those jobs which closely fit the subject's profile of scores on the main factored variables are then considered as the most likely to appeal to her or him. There are several points which can be made about this method of using tests in vocational guidance.

a. First it will be noticed that a similar method was actually used to construct certain tests, of which the best-known is the Strong Interest Blank, discussed in Chapter 17. Here items were chosen if they discriminated among occupational groups. Those that discriminated accountants, for example, formed the accountants scale.

However, although there is a similarity in this method of test construction to matching job profiles in vocational guidance, there is an important and significant difference. The test construction was blind empiricism. The matching of job profiles is not, provided that the main factored variables are used which, because they account for the largest component of variance in their respective fields, are psychologically meaningful, as was discussed in the chapters on factor analysis in this handbook.

b. Holders of the jobs may not necessarily be suited to them It is possible that the occupant of a job might be better suited to other jobs. This is more likely to be the case at a time of economic recession, when jobs are difficult to obtain. In such circumstances people tend to stay in a job, even though it is not suited to them. In such instances the job profiles are not a good template to which to match subjects.

Although this is a problem, it is more likely that a group of accountants will contain more people suited to it than a similar-sized other occupational group. Unsuited individuals increase the variance in the test scores.

c. A more serious problem arises from the fact that jobs change About ten years ago when micro and mini computers were introduced into a variety of jobs their nature changed to a considerable extent. Thus many banking and accountancy positions required radically different skills and in the case of computing these were more than some people could cope with. Word processing and dictation machines have changed many aspects of secretarial work. Thus profiles of members of these jobs may be a poor guide to what is necessary for new jobs.

These are particular instances of a general point that this method of vocational guidance can be misleading in times of rapid technological and social change.

d. This method is, clearly, useless for new jobs For example, recruiting for workers in the new Japanese car factories where lean production is the norm could make no use of the psychological profiles of car production workers using mass production methods.

However where new jobs resemble old ones or where no data for a job exist it may be possible to extrapolate from the data from similar occupations provided that factored tests which are psychologically meaningful have been used, as is advocated here.

e. Job profiles may reflect aspects of a job which are better changed For example to work in the textile industry may demand an ability to withstand great noise. However it might be better to silence the machinery than select individuals who were able to work in such dreadful conditions.

There is one further point that should be noted concerning vocational guidance based upon the matching of psychological profiles. It is essential to use factored variables, as is advocated here, because they are psychologically meaningful. This allows a certain flexibility in interpreting the results. If non-factored tests are used of unknown psychological meaning, then the only fitting of profile to individual that can be used is statistical. If there is a fit then the individual resembles that group of workers. This does not provide a good basis for guidance, for it provides no psychological insight into the nature of the occupation.

Cattell *et al.* (1970), in the handbook to the 16PF Test, refer to this approach as the adjustment method and some further difficulties become clear from their discussion.

f. Sampling of occupational groups   In Cattell *et al.* (1970) may be found a most impressive table of the scores of a large number of occupational groups. As is discussed in Chapter 25 of this handbook this is one of the outstanding features of the 16PF test which gives a richness of psychological meaning to the scales which other personality tests are hard put to match. Nevertheless scrutiny of this table shows that many of these occupational groups consist of small numbers such that the adequacy of the sample as a reflection of the population must be dubious. Furthermore the statistical standard error, even if the sampling were adequate, would still be large giving rather broad confidence limits around the means. This, of course, makes profile matching difficult and of dubious worth.

This raises another obvious difficulty. The Cattell occupational groups are American. Thus there is no guarantee that there will be a good fit to British jobs. Certainly, for example, lawyers in the two countries are quite different. This is a simple practical problem, not a logical difficulty, since British data could be obtained. Nevertheless it means that matching must be done with caution and with common sense. Statistical rigour is quite out of place but this topic will be discussed later in this chapter.

g. The value of a profile   In some cases the profile may be misleading. Thus if we were to take horn playing as an example, perfect pitch is a *sine qua non* for high performance. A weakness here could not be made up by a high similarity on other components of the profile. This suggests that better than profile matching might be a method which concentrated upon the salient aspects of a job. Such an approach is, in fact, discussed in (2).

Conclusions concerning the matching method   The matching method can be useful in vocational guidance and counselling provided that the problems of sampling are not forgotten and that its limitations with respect to new or changing occupations are taken into account. Flexibility in interpreting the results is necessary and is possible only with psychologically meaningful, factored tests. Rigorous use of the procedure with precise statistical limits is not recommended for all the reasons of sampling problems and the fact that on some occasions profile analysis can be misleading, as when one particular variable is especially important.

2. Correlations with occupational success

Another approach to the use of tests in vocational guidance is to use as a basis the correlations of psychological tests with occupational success. Again it is important to use factored variables with psychological meaning (those which account for the most variance in the different spheres of measurement). As was the case with the profile matching method this allows extrapolation to new and similar jobs.

As should be obvious, the subject is tested and the variables on which she or he has scored high and low are noted. If any of these correlate highly with success in a particular job, then this becomes a possibility for this subject. There are certain problems with this method and these must now be scrutinised. Some of these can be treated with extreme brevity since they have been discussed in the previous section. The advantages of this method will also be examined.

a. Sampling error   It is important that a substantial number of subjects are used in the sample from whom the correlation is obtained. With small samples a few outliers in the distribution can drastically affect the results. With small samples the confidence limits of the correlations are large and it is difficult to use any results with much confidence.

b. The difficulties with changing jobs, new jobs, and occupational data that are from a different country have all been discussed and apply equally to this method.

c. Reduction of correlations due to homogeneity of variance   Correlations between variables are reduced if the range of any of them is reduced. Since there is restriction of range for any occupational group, especially for the salient variables, correlations between these and occupational success are smaller than they would be if the correlations were computed in a random sample. Despite this, correlations corrected for attenuation due to homogeneity of variance should be treated with caution.

d. Criteria of job success   Using correlations with job success has one huge advantage over the profile matching method. It overcomes the problem that some of the occupants of jobs may not be suited to them and that aspects of a psychological profile may be irrelevant to the job. This method points out the salient variables. However, as Ghiselli (1966) argued in his study of the predictive power of intelligence tests and their value in job selection, the evaluation of job success is no easy matter.

Ghiselli (1966) surveyed 10,000 researches in which job success was measured. The most common criterion was rating by a supervisor and the unreliability of ratings has been fully discussed. Other criteria were output, wastage, sales volume, and number of new accounts. It is quite clear that there are considerable difficulties with all these methods. First, some methods suit only certain jobs. None of these, for example, is suited to teaching or being a judge. Sales volume is restricted to salespeople. This makes comparison difficult between different occupations. Furthermore many of these indices are unreliable which limits the correlations which could be obtained with them.

There is a further problem which was noted by Ghiselli and this concerns the fact that many studies used criteria obtained during training and these may well be poor indices of actual success in the post. Skill acquisition may demand different psychological characteristics from its maintenance. Dixon (1976), indeed, showed that the qualities needed for success at the junior officer level were actually antithetical to those required for senior military posts. With all these difficulties it is not surprising that there is room for considerable error in correlations of psychological variables with occupational success. In general the more indices that can be obtained the better.

Conclusions

As was indicated at the beginning of this section, a subject is given a battery of tests and those variables on which she or he has extreme scores are examined. If these correlated with job performance, it is these occupations which have to be considered.

The correlational approach has the advantage over the profile matching method that the variables which correlate with success are salient to the jobs, given that these have not changed and that proper samples were used. On the other hand the value of these correlations is lessened by the problems of adequate criteria for success. One result of this which affects the practice of vocational guidance and counselling and which is easily overlooked in a theoretical discussion, as in this chapter, is that the correlations, even if they are significant, tend to be small. This makes it difficult to put much reliance on them in the individual case. This means that test scores have to be treated with considerable caution when using this method; but see section 5 in this chapter where the way in which the scores are used, in the various methods, is discussed.

3. Regression on to occupational success

This is a variant of the correlational approach where instead of the correlations of a battery of variables with occupational success, the beta weights from a multiple regression are used. The main proponent of this approach is Cattell (Cattell *et al.*, 1970) who refers to it as the effectiveness (fitness by performance) approach.

This method suffers from all the difficulties of the correlational approach (sampling and the adequacy of the criterion) plus a further statistical problem. Beta weights, because they arise from the maximisation of the multiple correlation, are highly sample bound. Thus in practice beta weights tend to fluctuate from sample to sample unless very large and representative samples are used, which are difficult to obtain. This means that unless there is replication of the weights in new samples, the results must be treated with considerable caution.

4. Job analysis

The fourth method of using psychological tests in vocational guidance and counselling is to match individuals to jobs based upon a description of the required psychological characteristics which has been derived from job description and analysis. As was indicated at the beginning of this chapter, how such analysis is carried out is described in Chapter 25 of this handbook. Nevertheless there is little doubt that a careful study of jobs can indicate what psychological characteristics are likely to be necessary.

Problems with the method

Even without a detailed description of how job analyses are performed, it is obvious that there are difficulties with the procedure, in principle, and these must be briefly discussed.

Job samples　Essentially job analysis and description consist of detailed observations of what people in the post actually do. This observation is time consuming and it is difficult to build up a large sample of subjects doing a particular job. We have discussed in Chapter 4 of the handbook the problems of obtaining good norms. The problems of sampling for job analysis are exactly the same but made more difficult to overcome on account of the time involved.

Subjective judgements　Although the description of a job can be accurate and objective, the judgement concerning the necessary skills is subjective. For example, having observed precisely what accountants do it is possible to argue that there is little requirement for mathematics. However there is no proof that this is so. All one can point to is the fact that little mathematics is actually used.

Teaching is a good example of the problems of job description and analysis. You could observe precisely what a teacher did each day and decide on the strength of it that certain characteristics were and were not required. However if one takes a lofty view of teaching, as a task that involves the full development of pupils, then the personal characteristics of a teacher become highly important. It could be argued that it is not what a teacher does but what she or he is that is important, thus allowing transference to occur. In this instance job analysis would appear to be inadequate.

Testing the judgements It is essential that the psychological characteristics that are deemed to be important for an occupation as the result of job analysis are shown to be so before too much credence is given to the findings. Such claims would be supported if there were high correlations between measures of the variables and success at the occupations, and if members of the occupational group scored higher on these psychological characteristics than comparable, occupational control groups.

Conclusions If the psychological characteristics derived from job analyses are supported by other evidence and if they are based upon reasonable samples then the results may be used as a basis for vocational guidance and counselling.

5. How psychological tests are used in vocational guidance and counselling

The first method which was described above compared test results with job profiles. It is possible to do this on a statistical basis using r_p, the pattern matching coefficient, which is described in Cattell and Coulter (1966) and which was there used to form types (empirically defined). However this correlational technique demands a computer program. A simpler form which can be easily computed is given in the handbook to the 16PF test. This computes the correlation of an individual profile of scores with a group profile.

21.1 $r_p = \dfrac{(4k + \Sigma D^2) - \Sigma d^2}{(4k + \Sigma D^2) + \Sigma d^2}$

where k = the median chi-square with degrees of freedom equal to the number of variables; D refers to the differences of the group means in the comparison from the population group means, on each variable; d refers to the difference of the individual's score from the group profile, on each variable.

From Formula 21.1 the correlation between the score of any individual and any group for whom the data exist can be calculated. The group with the highest correlation is that which she or he most resembles.

The second method, in which the correlations of variables with job success are used as a basis for vocational guidance, contains no special statistical procedures and I shall comment on this later in this section. The variant of this method, based on the regression weights, simply demands that the score of a subject on each variable be multiplied by the beta weight for that variable and added or subtracted according to the regression equation for that occupation. The higher the score the better that individual fits the job. Of course such specification equations of regression weights to job success are hard to obtain from sufficiently large samples and Cattell *et al.* (1970) in the handbook to the 16PF test contains a set of such weights derived from the occupational profiles. However the validity of such weights despite their computational ingenuity is unknown. In my conservative view there is no way that such statistical manipulation could replace actual data.

The final method in which the important requirements of jobs are derived from job analysis demands no special statistical procedures although it would be possible to use the first profile matching method.

Statistical procedures in vocational guidance   The group profiling method and the regression method both quantify the suitability of a subject for jobs. Indeed Cattell *et al.* (1970) suggest that in an ideal setting for vocational guidance practitioners would store on computer a data base of group results on the 16PF test and regression weights together with a set of programs that would give the pattern matching correlations and other relevant indices as soon as a subject's results were fed into the computer.

As should be clear from Chapter 6 of this handbook, this, in fact, is the province of computerised tests and expert systems. Krug (1986) demonstrates how such a system could be used for job selection and with some modification for guidance.

An encyclopedia of job specifications   Kline (1979) extended this notion of Cattell by proposing that an encyclopedia of job specifications be developed. This would consist of the regression weights for all the major variables isolated by factor analysis in the fields of ability, personality, temperament and motivation, for job success. These regression weights would be derived for a variety of criteria of job success and from large samples so that the weights would be reliable. In addition the mean scores of occupational groups could be used. This would enable the practitioner to match any profile with any job, and to obtain a fitness for the job index from the regression weights. As tests and data improve, ultimately the multiple correlations would approach unity and a rational basis for vocational guidance would have emerged. Match an individual to the encyclopedia and there is the ideal job. In practice, of course, this encyclopedia would be part of the data base of a computer system which could be immediately accessed by a test user, although for those without computing facilities a text form would be possible.

There is one severe objection to this encyclopedia. At present multiple correlations with occupational success are far from unity, even where they exist at all. Correlations are small. Furthermore there are few studies with large and representative samples, so that beta weights are unreliable. The consequences for this are clear. With the current state of knowledge it would be quite wrong to use any mechanical procedure for vocational guidance. Test results must be used with skill and discretion, i.e. they must be used as a basis for discussion with the subject.

This is not only because the relevant information about the relation of job success and test scores is sparse, but also because, with the exception of intelligence tests, the reliability and validity of most psychological tests are far from perfect, as is made clear in our discussion of what are generally regarded as the best tests in the various fields of individual differences, in Section IV of this handbook. In brief, it is argued that the mechanical use of test scores for vocational guidance cannot be supported through the imprecision of current tests and the paucity of data about different occupations.

The fact that test results have to be tempered by the other psychological skills and judgements of the practitioner implies clearly that this same rational but non-mechanical use of tests is required for the two other methods of vocational guidance discussed above – using correlations with job success and information derived from job analysis.

Conclusions

The conclusions from this discussion of the use of psychological tests in vocational guidance are obvious. There does exist, in the manuals to the best tests, a certain amount of information relating test scores to job success and showing the psychological characteristics of members of various occupations. All this begins to put vocational guidance onto a rational basis. However, the tests are far from perfect and the data are scarce and also imperfect, so that it is quite irrational to attempt to base vocational guidance simply on test results. Indices of similarity and regression equations demand far greater precision of measurement than is as yet possible. Thus test results must be tempered by discussion. They are a basis for discussion not the sole determinant of decisions. The practical use of tests in vocational guidance is the subject of the final section of this chapter.

What tests should be given in vocational guidance? The answer to this question, which applies equally to all the applied fields of psychology is that, where no specific variables can be shown to be important (and this is the case in vocational guidance) then the most important variables in the main spheres of testing should be used. What these are has been discussed in Section II of this handbook and the actual tests are described in Section IV. In brief we give the best tests of the most important factors in the main areas of psychological testing. On these results and a knowledge of what is entailed in jobs our discussion of occupational possibilities will be based.

As was mentioned at the beginning of the chapter, it is realised that there is more to counselling than vocational guidance. Furthermore it is also freely admitted that there is more to job satisfaction than having the psychological characteristics to do the job effectively. Work (see Jewell and Siegall, 1990) is intimately bound to a person's feeling of worth and to their mental health. Furthermore, this whole testing approach is naturally actuarial. A person may be an ideal schoolteacher, for example, yet in any particular school she or he may be a failure and not prosper on account of a particular headteacher or other staff members. Furthermore, questions of status and money, together with the social milieu offered by a job, are all important in job satisfaction.

All these matters are aspects of vocational guidance which must not be neglected but they are beyond the scope of psychometric tests. The part that psychological tests can play is in the assessment of individuals and here, in as much as tests have any validity, and it is clear from this handbook that they have, they are likely to be effective, for human judgement cannot compete with tests. However the tests are not yet good enough to be used mechanically by statistical matching of individual to job and there is still scope, and, indeed, necessity for human interpretation.

PRACTICAL USE OF PSYCHOLOGICAL TESTS IN VOCATIONAL GUIDANCE

So far in this chapter I have discussed the theoretical rationale underlying the use of tests in vocational guidance. Nevertheless, the last sentence of the previous paragraph noting that the mechanical application of test scores in vocational guidance, because of their imperfections, is impossible opens up the question of the interpretation of tests and how they should be used in counselling and guidance. These are the practical aspects of the use of tests and in the last section of this chapter I want to discuss a number of problems and principles in the use of tests in the context of vocational guidance.

1. Discussing the test results One of the main distinctions between the use of tests for vocational guidance and in personnel selection in occupational psychology (discussed in Chapter 22) is in the discussion of results. In vocational guidance, even if the predictions of job success and satisfaction were close to unity, discussion would play an essential part in the process. Vocational guidance is not telling people what they should do. It is helping them to make choices but on the basis of good information about themselves and the nature of jobs. Hence in vocational guidance, thus conceived, test results form a basis of discussion.

For example, if we have a child for vocational guidance whose profile of scores resembles that of a scientist we would ask if she or he had ever thought of that as a possible job and discuss the academic requirements for the profession. We could further discuss the fact that the child seemed to have characteristics that resembled those of successful practitioners and ensure that she or he knew what the job entailed. This would allow the child to make her or his own informed decision.

2. Quantification   Although we want the tests to be as accurate as possible and to yield high correlations with occupational choice and success, as is evident from the previous section, the emphasis is not on the statistics for their own sake. The better they are the better the basis for discussion. This means that in vocational guidance the use of ipsative test scores is not ruled out.

3. Ipsative test scores   Ipsative test scores, it will be remembered from Chapter 4 of the handbook, provide rankings of scores for each individual. Thus, for example, the Kuder interests test (described in Chapter 27) rank the interests of an individual. Since such rankings cannot be compared meaningfully across individuals, these ipsative test scores are suited only for discussion and amplification with each person. However this is ideal for vocational guidance where the aim is to extend the horizons of the client's knowledge and thinking about jobs.

4. Deliberate distortion and faking of test scores   Since vocational guidance is aimed at helping the clients, provided that they believe this and do not regard themselves as being examined, deliberate distortion or faking should be trivial, compared to, for example, the same people taking the same tests in job selection.

If the subjects have been seen before and there is a good rapport and trust between them and the counsellor, they will only fake good on those items, usually of personality or interest tests, which touch on aspects of their personality which they cannot accept. However, if there is truly a good counselling relationship even this degree of distortion might be removed. In brief, deliberate faking and lying should not be a problem in vocational guidance.

Confidentiality   In general confidentiality would seem to be essential for vocational guidance, especially in the school setting where discussion may involve teachers in the school and parents. Only if children feel confident that any criticisms of the school will not get back to the authorities will sufficient trust and rapport be established for effective guidance to be possible. Only then will psychological tests be completed without dishonesty.

Conclusions

How guidance should be carried out, how the psychometric scores should be best discussed in vocational guidance, and the important details of the practice, are beyond the scope of this chapter and readers must be referred to specialist books in this field, such as Nelson-Jones (1982). My intention in this final, brief section on the practical use of tests in vocational guidance has been to point out some of the most important problems and principles. In general psychological tests are used as an information base for discussion. Thus they should be as valid and reliable as possible; the emphasis is not on quantification but on the discussion of the results in an atmosphere of trust such that children can be unafraid to be open and honest.

Chapter 22

Psychological Tests in Occupational and Industrial Psychology

In this chapter I shall scrutinise the contribution that psychological testing can make to industrial and occupational psychology. These two terms, industrial and occupational psychology, refer to the psychology practised in the work place. It involves selection and placement of workers, the organisation of work so as to produce a psychologically pleasant environment, and the design of plant, factories and offices for efficiency and safety (where psychology becomes indistinguishable from ergonomics). In this chapter I shall deal only with personnel selection since this is the main area of industrial psychology to which psychometrics can contribute.

Personnel selection involves psychological assessment and hence depends on psychological testing. In Europe and America psychological testing for selection is big business, and as more testing is carried out commercially, the data base of results grows and problems proliferate. Herriot (1989) has recently edited a book entitled *Assessment and Selection in Organisations*. Its size, 802 pages, indicates the huge flowering of this field. However, to extend this metaphor, closer examination indicates that many of these flowers are weeds or, at least, far from ideal specimens of the psychometric art.

In one chapter it would not appear easy to summarise so much material. However I shall adopt the plan of indicating how, on theoretical grounds, psychological testing should be best employed, in the various areas of occupational psychology. This approach allows us to deal briefly with large amounts of detailed material. This theoretical section will be followed by another dealing with some important practical problems in the use of tests in occupational selection. I shall also deal briefly with utility theory, assessment centres and the qualifications necessary to use psychological tests.

1. THEORETICAL ISSUES

a. The psychometric model

The psychometric model underlies this whole handbook. However it is at its most explicit in personnel selection and I want to explicate the model as precisely as possible, at this point. This model assumes that there is an optimal set (or sets, for it is conceivable, although unlikely, that two different sets could be equally effective) of psychological characteristics for success at any human activity (in this instance, success at a particular job).

This may seem so obvious as to be banal. However the aim of psychometrics, and it has been partly achieved, in as much as there are any correlations of tests with external criteria, has been to measure psychological variables with sufficient precision to enable the model to be instantiated.

An obvious problem inherent in the model is that there is an infinity of psychological variables such that it is impossible to measure them, thus rendering it vacuous. However, as should be apparent from the first two sections of this handbook, this has been answered. Factor analysis has enabled the psychometrist to concentrate upon the variables which embrace the most variance. Thus, as has been argued throughout this handbook, using the main factored variables from the most important areas of psychology, themselves shown to be independent in factor analytic research, it should be possible to predict many aspects of human behaviour.

Thus the psychometric model, applied to any occupation, takes on the form of a regression equation, with the main factored variables, as described in sections II and IV of the handbook, and the criterion. The variables with the highest beta weights would be used in any selection procedure. It could be the case in certain occupations that some trait was useful which was highly specific to that occupation and this might not appear in any other specification equation. This could be accommodated in a special test.

From this it is clear what is required in industrial psychology. A huge research programme should be set up in which multiple regressions are run between success in jobs and the main factor analytic variables. In addition special variables should be added where these raise the multiple correlation. As was suggested in Chapter 21 these results should be stored in an encyclopedia of job specifications.

b. The use of the encyclopedia of job specifications

These specifications, the regression weights on the main factored variables plus any more specific variables, would be stored on computer. In addition, as was discussed in Chapter 21, the mean scores on these variables of occupational groups could be stored. Before discussing the use of this encyclopedia for selection, which is somewhat different from its use in vocational guidance, I want to emphasise certain aspects of this encyclopedia, which will clarify the proper use of tests in occupational selection.

i. The use of factored variables

It is essential that the specification equations use factored variables. This is because, as has been argued in our chapters on test construction, only factored variables (or those made up by analogous methods and which are factor pure) have psychological meaning. This psychological meaning is important in industrial psychology because it gives us insight into the nature of job success, and this in itself can improve selection. For example it has been shown that high C, ego strength, is important for airline pilots. This means that in selection we try to ensure that the chosen pilots possess this characteristic. No test being perfect, we would want to confirm that high C scores for a candidate were in accord with other information which we had about her or him. In addition understanding what psychological characteristics relate to success in certain jobs enables the selector to make a rational guess if the specification equation for that job has not been computed. Obviously, in reality, the encyclopedia of job specifications will take many years to complete (and completion is always notional as new jobs are created and old ones change).

This necessity of using specification equations based upon the main factored variables is particularly important to bear in mind because it is relatively easy to obtain correlations with job success with criterion-keyed tests. Thus, as was pointed out in our chapter on motivational and interest tests, one of the most famous such tests, the Strong Vocational Interest Blank (Strong *et al.*, 1971), was developed by selecting items which would discriminate members of one occupation from another. This type of test gives no information about the psychology of the occupants and all one knows is the fact that they are differentiated by the scale. Such criterion-keyed scales are almost always multifactorial which further obscures any possible psychological meaning.

For all these reasons, therefore, it is essential that the specification equations and the occupational profiles are based upon factor analytic, psychologically meaningful variables. It makes sense to use those factors which account for the most variance since with these it is most likely that correlations with job success and good differentiation between groups will be obtained.

ii. Use of specific, less general tests

Despite the fact that the main factors are the ones that should be included in any attempt to develop an encyclopedia of job specifications, it is obvious that in certain jobs some quite specific characteristics may be required. For example music and drawing demand clear specific skills. Thus it is useful to attempt to include such specific tests in developing the specification equation for any job. Job-specific factors will undoubtedly add to the multiple correlation and thus improve selection. Of course such variables are specific, by definition, to particular occupations and thus would only be used in selection where relevant.

iii. The encyclopedia in selection

Selection for a particular position If the requirement is to select a person for a particular post, the job encyclopedia is consulted and the applicants are tested on the salient variables in the specification equation. It is to be noted that, in a large organisation, where there is a variety of different jobs to be filled, an in-house encyclopedia can be developed.

Selection for a variety of positions Here all the specification equations would be consulted and a battery of tests would be given which included the most salient variables common to all the positions. This is obviously less effective than selecting for a specific post. If necessary some further, more specific testing can be done on a long list of candidates who have passed the first testing.

Matching results to the equations and the occupational profiles It is possible to scrutinise the equation or profile and select the candidates scoring high and low on the relevant tests. However it is possible to match the encyclopedia statistically.

Profiles The profile of mean scores for an individual can be matched to that of a group. To do this Cattell *et al.* (1970a) utilise the the pattern matching correlation r_p. The formula for this was given in Chapter 21 but is repeated here.

$$22.1 \quad r_p = \frac{(4k + \Sigma D^2) - \Sigma d^2}{(4k + \Sigma D^2) + \Sigma d^2}$$

where k = the median chi-square with degrees of freedom equal to the number of variables; d = the difference of the individual's score from the designated group score on a variable and D equals the difference of that group's score on a variable from the population mean.

The individual with the highest r_p is the best suited to the job.

Specification equation of regression weights Here the standardised scores are multiplied by the weights for the variables in the regression equation. The subject with the highest resulting score is the best fitted to the job.

In practice, subjects' scores on the test are put into the computer and these matching coefficients are produced for the relevant jobs. As was argued in Chapter 21, on the use of tests in vocational guidance and counselling, the profile of mean scores for an occupation is less valuable than the regression weights on success at the job, since this latter is what selection is aimed at. Job profiles are a second best where no specification equations exist.

Accuracy of the job specification equations If the multiple correlations are high, say greater than .8, it would be possible to use the statistical procedure alone to select candidates and it would be likely that interviews, which are notoriously unreliable and of little validity (Vernon and Parry, 1949) would make selection worse. However, at present, tests alone are not so precise that it is sensible to ignore other methods of selection and the test results must always be an element, albeit a most important element, in the selection procedure.

c. The present use of tests in occupational selection

In the previous sections I have discussed how tests could be used in selection for jobs in an ideal world where specification equations existed. This demonstrated the potential strength of factored psychometric tests in selection, given a good data base. Such a data base could easily be developed and there can be no doubt that this would greatly increase the quality of occupational selection.

However, no such encyclopedia exists or appears likely to come into being in the next few years. All this is the future of computerised tests and expert systems in personnel selection. Thus I must discuss how tests can be used in selection without such an aid.

i. Selection of tests

Without knowledge (beta weights and correlations) of what tests correlate with success at the job, the selection of tests must be based on job analysis and description. However such analyses may not be available and this is why it is argued that the best approach is to use the factored tests which have been shown to account for the most variance in the main fields of ability, personality, and motivation. Sometimes, as in the previous examples of music and art, the specific tests which are important are obvious.

Sometimes it is possible to make an informed guess, based upon the mean scores of the group on tests and on knowledge of the job as to what psychological characteristics are important, and to put these measures into the selection battery. Provided it is realised that such judgements are not proven so that results are treated with caution, this procedure can be useful although it is essential to check upon its efficiency, as far as that is ever possible.

ii. Job analysis and description

As was discussed in the previous paragraph, where no beta weights or correlations with job success exist, it is rational in job selection to attempt to estimate what psychological characteristics are required for any particular occupation. For these purposes industrial psychologists have evolved methods of job description and analysis and these must now be described. I shall summarise what is a considerable body of results and for more detailed information readers are referred to Jewell and Siegall (1990) and Greuter and Algera (1989). First a few definitions will be useful to the discussion.

Task This is a piece of work which has to be completed properly within a set time. Jobs essentially, therefore, can be broken down into a set of tasks.

Position The tasks performed by any individual define a position. There is one position for each individual in an organisation.

Job All identical positions make up one job in an organisation. This is a confusing use of the word job, in my opinion. Thus any individual, by this definition, has a position rather than a job. For example, my position at Exeter is a professor of psychology, of which at present there are three. This means that the job of professor of psychology includes three positions.

Job families This refers to groups of jobs similar in the demands which they make on employees.

From this description it is clear that the tasks performed in an organisation define what that organisation is.

Job analysis This is the procedure of data collection and analysis by which information about job tasks and requirements is obtained.

Job description This is the statement of the tasks, responsibilities and working conditions of a job.

Job specification This states the characteristics necessary for carrying out the job.

Job analysis is concerned with more aspects of a job than elucidating the psychological characteristics required by its occupants. However from the viewpoint of this chapter, this is what is important. Thus I shall describe some of the methods of job analysis as they bear on this problem.

Procedures of job analysis Data can be obtained from interviews, observations, and questionnaires. Jewell and Siegall (1990) argue that if the purpose of a job analysis is the development of better selection methods, then what is necessary is a precise knowledge of what tasks employees have to perform; in Jewell and Siegall's view this is best ascertained from the employees themselves.

Assessing the tasks Interviewing employees is an obvious and efficient method of gathering information, although it demands skilled interviewers who may not be readily available and in unskilled hands interviews can be unreliable.

Task analysis can be conceived of in terms of systems theory as it is by Gagne (1965) and Miller (1965; 1966), who seem to use task analysis and job description somewhat interchangeably. Both authors see task analysis as a minutely detailed description of what has to be done in a job. Both Gagne (1965) and Miller (1966) agree that conceiving of a job in terms of a system has several advantages over a general job description derived from common sense, and probably over information obtained from interviewing the occupants of a job. I shall discuss these since it will illuminate job analysis and the advantages of systems theory.

A good example of systematic thinking can be can be found in a pen. A pen is not simply, in these terms, an instrument for writing. It is part of a communication system since the writing has to be easily written and read. A fault with many old-fashioned copying systems was that, although the copies were clear, the smell and feel of the paper made them unpleasant to read, a fault, in my opinion, with some Xerox machines. Similarly a pen, even if it wrote superbly but only on newspaper or with ink that stains the hands, would not be a good pen in system-analytic terms.

Task analysis, in system-analytic terms, entails drawing up a highly detailed set of instructions for performing a job. The precision of such task analysis emphasises the weaknesses of job descriptions based upon common sense and intuition and even leads one to question the value of descriptions obtained from those who do the job, who may not be able to see their work in a broader context. Some examples will clarify these points.

First, general job descriptions may lead to insistence on skills which are not used. For example, psychiatrists must have a sound knowledge of anatomy and *materia medica*. At present this is demanded by the job description for psychiatrist. However, detailed analysis of what psychiatrists do might well show such knowledge to be unnecessary, if it is never used.

The detailed descriptions of jobs, which are required by task analysis, have another advantage over generalised job descriptions. They show clearly what is not done. For example, to take up the case of psychiatry, task analysis might show that psychiatrists spent almost no time keeping numerical records suitable for statistical analysis. If it were considered that research was an important aspect of a psychiatrist's work then this could be written into the job description and statistics and computer programming could be exchanged for anatomy and *materia medica* in training programmes.

Miller demonstrates that common sense job descriptions tend to underestimate what is required for a job. For example where sequences of operations may vary it is not sufficient simply to know the operations. A further problem in job description is concerned with emergency procedures. It is often the case that general job descriptions fail to note the crisis points in any procedure and thus take no note of emergency procedures but identify false crises. There was an excellent example of this in the M1 plane crash. When an engine caught fire, there was no emergency procedure for the cabin crew to report the incident to the flight deck. Not unnaturally (but incorrectly) they assumed the pilots would be able to see their engines. This was an important contributory factor to the disaster.

Miller's less spectacular example is important. A lorry driver should be able to diagnose and correct minor faults on the lorry, such as lights, hydraulic problems and starting difficulties, so as not to waste time immobilised. On the other hand, a professional flute or oboe player who learned sets of alternative fingerings of diabolical difficulty and faulty intonation, in case a key failed, would be wasting her or his time. Such failure is a rare event and, should it occur, it is better to stop and replace the instrument.

Detailed task analysis, Miller argues, reveals what has to be done and thus overcomes these problems. Such task analysis is then combined with task description which is a similarly minutely detailed statement of what is required for a job for which an algorithm can be developed. In this the function of a job, the context and other concomitant skills must be stated. The professional flautist again clearly illustrates these points. Thus an orchestral player must be able to play in a large orchestra, be familiar with the eighteenth, nineteenth and twentieth-century repertoire, be able to play with little rehearsal and to double up on the piccolo. The contextual aspect of the description indicates that she or he must be able to get on easily with colleagues, be prepared to be away from home and able to stand the strain of travel. These demands are clearly different from those on a jazz flautist or a specialist in small group playing.

From this it is clear that the combination of task description and analysis, in system-analytic terms, enables one to estimate the psychological characteristics that are necessary to perform the job. It must be pointed out here that our examples are not rendered in the fine detail of normal descriptions of this kind, and it is this minute detailing which is crucial to the identification of the psychological characteristics. Readers must refer to Miller (1965; 1966) and to Gagne (1965), to see precisely how it is done. Of course all such psychological profiles are only hypotheses and these must be validated against the criteria of job success and by a study of differences among the occupants of different jobs.

In conclusion, task analysis and description virtually compel an accurate and detailed job analysis, whereas general job descriptions arising from intuitive knowledge may be accurate but there is far more opportunity for error. It should also be pointed out that these methods can be applied to the design of new jobs, thus helping to tailor them to the psychological abilities of those who will do them. There is one further important point. In some jobs some special skill may be a necessity but task analysis can show that this is fortuitous and can easily be eliminated. Thus a particular machine may demand high finger dexterity which a minor redesign could change. Of course many characteristics are intrinsic to the task and cannot be thus altered. Finally, as has been argued, the psychological characteristics which are necessary for a job, as revealed by task and job analysis, must be validated empirically.

d. Other methods of job assessment

Job analysis and description, as carried out in terms of systems analysis, is time consuming and hence costly. Other methods have been developed and these must now be briefly described.

Structured questionnaires

As has been stated, descriptions of jobs can be obtained from interviews of those who carry them out. However the reliability and validity of interviews is always problematic and there are considerable individual differences in the skills of even trained interviewers, as was shown by Vernon and Parry (1949). For this reason questionnaires are often favoured.

The Job Analysis Questionnaire

The JAQ was developed by Krzystofiak et al. (1979). It consists of 754 items and employees have to rate on a 5-point scale of 'never' to 'frequently' how often they perform 600 or so tasks. Factor analysis of a sample of power station workers revealed sixty factors, indicating common aspects of certain jobs. Cluster analysis was also used to indicate which employees did similar jobs (regardless of job title). As Cook (1988) points out, this is a useful method of comparing jobs and thus developing selection methods for groups of jobs. However, doubt about whether these factors would be common to posts beyond the power industry, the large number of factors required to describe even a limited sample of jobs, and the difficulty of developing adequate measures of the ten factors, mean the JAQ may be somewhat impractical. For these reasons a more analytic approach has been attempted in what is probably the most widely used measure in job analysis, the PAQ.

The Position Analysis Questionnaire (PAQ) (McCormick et al., 1972)

The PAQ has 194 questions and covers six areas: job context, work output, mental processes, information input, relationship with other people, and other characteristics. Each of these items is rated on the most appropriate of six scales (five points): possibility of occurrence, importance to the job, extent of use, degree of detail, amount of time, and applicability.

Mecham (1977) factored the questionnaire and claimed that twelve factors emerged, which reflect the important aspects of jobs. These are:

1. Engaging in physical activity
2. Operating machines
3. Contacts with customers
4. Awareness of the work environment
5. Performing service/related activities
6. Performing clerical/related activities
7. Performing technical related activities
8. Performing routine/repetitive activities
9. Supervising and coordinating
10. Working regular day schedules
11. Working in bad environments
12. Having decision-making/communicating/general activities

This factor analysis suggests that any job should be describable in terms of these dimensions and a job profile could be produced, although Jewell and Siegall (1990) argue that some jobs cannot be evaluated by this questionnaire because the questions are not relevant.

Although this is one of the best-researched job questionnaires, two points should be noticed. It is disappointing that the dimensions are little more than common sense. The factor analysis has certainly failed to reveal any surprising and thus interesting underlying dimensions. The fact that it is not appropriate for all jobs is a further disappointment. Nevertheless it indicates how a job analysis questionnaire can be used to elicit information about jobs in order to yield a job description which will enable us to infer what are the required psychological characteristics for its execution, and thus help to determine the tests to be used in selection. In connection with this point it should be noted that Sparrow (1989) showed that PAQ attributes were positively correlated with the relevant abilities as measured by the Differential Aptitude Test (see Chapter 14).

All this may sound reasonable but its simplicity hides a plethora of problems which in a single chapter can only be mentioned, and it is doubtful whether they have been anywhere solved at whatever length. For example, the somewhat simplistic approach of the PAQ, where the items are common sense and face valid, as are the resulting factors, can be challenged. Thus Fleishman and Quaintance (1984) have argued that the study of performance is irrational when one has no means of classifying the huge number of 'performance behaviours' involved in jobs. They discuss various approaches to the classification of performance at work. These include:

1. Behaviour description. This is derived from observation of actual behaviour while the job is being done.
2. Behaviour requirement. This, on the other hand, is derived from what occupants should do in order to do the job well.
3. Ability requirement. Here tasks are described in terms of the abilities required to do them.

4. Task characteristics. Here work is described in terms of conditions that elicit performance and the emphasis is on the triggering events such as instructions.

As Greuter and Algera (1989) argue, not all these approaches to job description converge although the first three categories, especially the third, are likely to be the most useful in personnel selection, for obvious reasons. Indeed from the viewpoint of the psychometric model underlying this handbook, as was made clear at the beginning of this chapter, this third category is the one that should be adopted. However, as Greuter and Algera (1989) point out, the description is likely to be riddled with error, due to problems of judgement and faulty attribution, unless some objective assessment is used. Thus it is obvious that actuaries need to be good at maths, but they argue that it is not so clear what are the relevant traits for computer programmers or managers. These errors of attribution and even stereotyping affect actual observations of jobs not simply armchair theorising. Thus good training is essential for job analysts if they are to avoid these errors. Indeed in that there is quite a high correlation between scores on the PAQ for jobs experts and students who know little about them (Cornelius *et al.*, 1984) it could be argued that job stereotypes do influence the scores on the PAQ. However this agreement is artificial, in that there are a number of items which are inapplicable to some jobs, thus increasing agreement between raters. If these are excluded the correlations fall (De Nisi *et al.*, 1987). Nevertheless it is clear from this work that job analysts must be well trained and vigilant to avoid stereotyping.

There seem to be two ways of overcoming these difficulties, one of which has already been mentioned. This is to support the observations of the required psychological characteristics by studies of the actual job occupants. If some particular ability is thought to be important holders of the job should score higher than controls on this variable. The second approach was utilised by Fleishman and Quaintance (1984) where the job analyst indicates, for the Fleishman physical ability factors and other ability factors, described in Chapter 13, the degree to which a job demands them. The scales are anchored at various points by actual behaviour of which the relevance was supported empirically. Fleishman labels these as ability analysis scales. This approach can be adopted for any ability factors including personality and motivational factors, as described in Section II of this handbook.

Job description and specification

Based upon either observations or a questionnaire, of which the PAQ is a typical example, a job description and specification is drawn up. The specification sets out the qualities and characteristics to be demanded of the employee and thus around this specification the psychological tests to be used in the selection process are chosen.

Conclusions

It is possible to draw some conclusions from this discussion of the use of psychological tests in occupational selection. It is in essence a simple task to select individuals for a particular job. All that is required is to ascertain the characteristics necessary for the post and then put these to the test with valid and reliable measures. However, as has been discussed, it is not in practice an easy matter to evaluate jobs. However all methods, despite the difficulties, stress the importance of detailed observation whether this be done from interviews, observations or questionnaires such as the PAQ. Clearly all methods, other than the questionnaire, demand careful training of the assessors to avoid attributional and stereotypical biases. Specifications drawn up by these methods should enable psychologists to select the most relevant set of tests, and thus maximise the efficiency of selection.

2. PRACTICAL ISSUES

a. Importance of face validity In personnel selection it is important to use face-valid tests because it is essential to keep the cooperation of those who are tested. If tests appear to be absurd or wasting the time of the subjects, some individuals will lose interest and not take the selection procedures seriously. It could be argued, indeed, that those applicants who are prepared to complete apparently ridiculous entrance procedures may be unsuitable for selection anyway, except for jobs where authoritarian and unthinking submission is a desired attribute.

b. Ethics and confidentiality Under the Data Protection Act if test scores are kept on computer subjects have a right to see them. If they are not so stored there is clearly the problem of whether the results should be given back to the subject. This is a matter of personal judgement. I shall state my views briefly here.

I can see no reason to withhold scores from a subject. It can infringe no personal freedom of the subject to know her or his own scores. Indeed it seems so obvious that a subject should know how she or he has performed that it is difficult to see why subjects are not always so informed.

One counter-argument that I have heard from practitioners is that subjects would misunderstand the meanings of the scores, and feedback could become, therefore, a source of problems. This is the old expert argument used by doctors who may refrain from telling patients what is wrong with them. In psychological testing there is no excuse for such prevarication. If as psychologists we think that a score may be misunderstood it must be explicated. Thus I argue that subjects should receive feedback that informs them meaningfully about their performance on the tests.

A second argument concerns the time involved. Clearly with a large number of candidates personal verbal feedback is difficult to give. I remember, in one research project, I gave feedback, lasting half an hour, to 250 subjects. This was an exhausting experience and I realise that a commercial organisation might not be able to do this. However with the availability of computers a computer report is always possible. Some tests are computer scored and a printed account of the results suitable for subjects is a part of the test package. Even where this is not the case it is a simple matter to program a computer to print out a description of the meaning of any score on a test suitable for subjects and this is what is suggested as the best thing to do for subjects if verbal feedback is impossible.

The main difficulty with feedback (which is not avoided when feedback is denied) is when a score or combination of scores is regarded as pathological or otherwise dangerous. In such cases all that one can do is attempt to put the interest of the subject first. Psychological tests are actuarial in nature so that a set of scores with poor prognosis for heart disease, for example, may well not apply to any particular case. In general, therefore, it is probably better to stay silent but the only general principle seems to be to consult the interests of the candidate. This principle must also be entailed in the feedback of scores which a candidate might find upsetting such as low intelligence or lack of conscientiousness. The computer reports can always be worded appropriately without dishonesty.

It should be made clear to candidates that all scores, and information and reports derived from the scores, will remain confidential to those who see them.

Need for high test reliability As has been stressed throughout this handbook, high reliability of tests is essential where decisions have to be made about individuals, as distinct from groups. This is because the standard error of a score is dependent on the reliability of the test. A reliability of .7 is regarded as about the minimum for the use of tests in individual decision making. It must also be remembered that in comparing test scores the reliabilities of scores must also be high. The theoretical basis of these assertions has been discussed in Chapters 1 and 3 of this handbook.

Deliberate distortion of scores It is quite obvious that in personnel selection, beyond all other fields of applied psychology, deliberate distortion is likely to be a severe problem. All candidates want to appear in the best possible light. In clinical psychology, on the other hand, there is no need for subjects to cover up their problems and difficulties. Indeed clients may feel that they should be as honest as possible. Similar arguments apply in vocational guidance where, again the emphasis is on helping rather than rejecting, and helping is best done with as much knowledge as possible.

In tests of intelligence and ability deliberate faking is hardly a problem since subjects cannot pretend to be able to complete items which they are unable to complete. The opposite is possible but is obviously rare in personnel selection.

In tests of personality and interest, however (discussed in Chapters 15 and 17 of this handbook together with particular tests in Chapters 25–27), where items are concerned with behaviour which may appear to be unfitting for some if not all jobs, deliberate distortion is likely to occur.

Some tests such as the EPQ (Eysenck and Eysenck, 1975) and the MMPI (Hathaway and McKinley, 1951) contain scales to detect deliberate distortion. The L scale of the EPQ contains items which most people, if telling the truth, would certainly deny: a typical item might be 'I have never told even a little lie.' It is suggested in the test manual that beyond a certain cut-off point on the L scale, scores on the personality scales should be discounted. This is the safest approach but it means that candidates who are caught attempting to fake good are rejected. Some may think that this is a good thing. Eysenck (personal communication) claims that test instructions to the effect that there are means within the test for spotting dissimulators considerably increase the mean score on the EPQ Neuroticism scale, which is a scale clearly open to distortion by those who seek to create a good impression.

If only a few candidates are being tested and it is clear that a small number have attempted to fake good it is possible to call them in and to tell them that you have evidence of their misdeeds and to get them to complete the test again. Now this is a testing context similar to that where the instructions on the test warn candidates that distortions will be noted. Although this will probably reduce the L scores the effects on the validity of the test are unknown.

In the MMPI, on the other hand, it is possible to adjust the personality test scores in the light of particular scores on the validity scales. However, I agree with Cronbach (1984) who argues that distorted data are distorted no matter how they may be modified and that such alterations should be discouraged.

It is on account of these difficulties in dealing with deliberate distortion in tests, which is particularly pertinent to personality questionnaires, that Cattell (Cattell and Warburton, 1967) has advocated objective personality tests, which have been fully discussed in Chapter 16 of this handbook. However, unfortunately, as was there pointed out, objective tests require considerably more research before they are ready to be used for personnel selection, or, indeed, for any other applied purpose. Thus personnel selectors will have to make do with questionnaires for some time to come.

Finally it should be pointed out at this juncture that in a recent study of the validity scale of the PPQ (Kline and Lapham, 1990a), a personality questionnaire designed for occupational psychology, it was shown that individuals with low scores on the validity scale received significantly different scores on four of the five personality scales from high scorers on the validity scale (Kline and Lapham, 1991b). This indicates that it is sensible to ignore the scores of those subjects who score highly on the low or validity scales of personality or interest questionnaires.

In summary it would appear best to screen out those who have high faking scores. Certainly it would not seem sensible to attempt to adjust obtained scores in any way on the basis of validity scales. Probably if it is pointed out to candidates that deliberate distortion can be spotted, as part of the general instructions before testing begins, faking will be reduced as far as it is ever possible to do so.

Norms If scores are to be used with reference to norms it is essential to ensure that the norms are satisfactory. The criteria for good norms have been fully described in Chapter 4 of this handbook. The samples should be large and representative and the group should be identical or closely similar to the post for which the applicants are being selected. In a large organisation it is useful to build up in-house norms, if the organisation appears to be thriving.

Ipsative scores Ipsative scores have been discussed in Chapter 4 of this handbook. These are only useful for making comparisons of scores obtained from any one individual. They are, therefore, best used as a basis for discussion and hence are of some value in counselling and clinical psychology. Although ipsative tests do sometimes have norms (as in the Edwards Personal Preference Schedule, fully described in Chapter 25) these are entirely inappropriate and may be quite misleading. Ipsative tests, in my view, should not be used in personnel selection, other than as a basis for discussion at an interview.

Conclusions

From this brief discussion of the practical problems involved in occupational selection it is clear that the most severe is that of deliberate distortion. Until objective tests are better developed the best procedure is to reduce distortion by telling candidates that it is likely to be detected and by ignoring the scores of those who are detected. It seems reasonable to inform candidates of their performance on the tests and it was suggested that this is best done personally or if impossible by a properly prepared computer printed analysis of the scores. Subjects should always be assured of the confidentiality of the scores. Ipsative scores are not recommended, except as a basis for discussion, but tests with high reliability and good norms (and of course high validity) are valuable in occupational and industrial psychology.

3. SPECIAL ISSUES IN THE USE OF TESTS IN OCCUPATIONAL SELECTION

Before concluding this chapter certain topics relevant to the use of tests in occupational selection need to be discussed although these are highly specialised and more part of occupational psychology than psychometrics.

Utility theory

In our discussion of test validity, throughout this book, the emphasis has lain on the demonstration that a test measures what it claims to measure. However for industrial test users who may not be interested in psychometric minutiae, another criterion may be invoked: what is the financial value of using tests in selection? This is obviously related to validity since a valid test must increase the efficiency of selection and thus jobs will be better done, and an invalid test may actually make selection procedures less efficient. However if there are many good candidates for a post it is possible that elaborate selection procedures are unnecessary.

All these arguments are really concerned with the cost benefits attached to selection. Thus, for example it might be possible to design a selection procedure of superb efficiency but at so high a cost that even after forty years of work the added profitability of the candidates thus selected still did not pay for the selection. On the other hand, for air crew selection in air forces where accidents mean that planes costing millions of pounds are written off any selection procedure which reduced accident rate would be useful.

Utility theory or utility analysis aims to quantify the cost benefits of selection procedures and this must now be described.

Brogden (1949) developed and set out a utility equation which is regarded as a landmark in work on utility analysis and forms the basis of important later research by Cronbach and Gleser (1965):

$$\text{Savings per employee per year} = (r \times SD_y \times Z) - (C/P)$$

where r is the validity of the test or selection procedure (r being a correlation); SD_y is the standard deviation of employee productivity in pounds or any other currency; Z is the quality of the employee – the standard score on the test or selection procedure; C is the cost of selection per applicant and P is the proportion of applicants selected.

A number of points need to be made about this utility index.

1. The measurement of employee productivity is not a simple matter and clearly the efficiency of this equation turns on its accuracy. Cook (1988) has an interesting discussion of these problems. Using the method of rational estimates it is possible to quantify the value of employees as Schmidt *et al.*

(1979) have demonstrated with their Global Estimation Model. In this technique supervisors are asked to judge the cash value of an employee's worth, the assumption being that supervisors knew best what a person does. In this technique supervisors are asked to calculate the cash value of a worker at the 85th percentile and the 15th percentile, the approximate boundaries of one standard deviation above and below the mean. This allows an estimate of the necessary SD_y. Obviously such estimates must be rough at best, since as has been discussed, it is no simple matter in many jobs to establish a good criterion of success, but their accuracy can be improved by sampling as many supervisors as possible and averaging the results.

One implication of this approach to the measurement of employee productivity stands out. If the SD_y is small it means that the difference in productivity between good and bad employees is small. Where this is the case there is little point in attempting expensive selection procedures.

It is possible that differences in productivity are not normally distributed so that, for example, differences between average and good employees were different from those between average and bad employees. If bad employees were not much less productive than average but good ones were very much more productive then clearly selection procedures should be aimed at high calibre candidates.

Nevertheless despite deviations from normal distributions rational estimates allow calculation of SD_y, thus making the Brogden formula a workable proposition.

Cook (1988) makes two other important points about rational estimates.

a. As might be expected, there have been many variations introduced into the estimates of employee productivity, often necessary to suit the demands of different jobs. One well known variant is that of Cascio (1982) – the CREPID technique, an acronym in which the D represents dollars. In this method a job is divided into different components and the employee's contribution to each one is estimated. However these estimates are weighted according to the importance of the components. For complex multidimensional occupations this method appears to be advantageous.

b. Based upon research with a large variety of jobs, a simple rule for working out SD_y can be used. SD_y is between 40 per cent and 70 per cent of salary.

As was mentioned in the introduction to utility theory, these estimates indicate clearly that where expensive equipment is at risk, as in the armed forces or in many engineering contexts, good selection is economically essential.

2. Note the use of r, the validity coefficient of the test or selection battery, in this equation. Two points deserve discussion. First, as was shown earlier in this chapter, there is a considerable problem in establishing the validity of a test in occupational work, because the criterion of success is difficult, as was made clear in the discussion of productivity estimates above.

The second point, however, is particularly important. Examination of the equation makes it clear that even with a test of moderate validity, the savings per employee are considerable.

3. The use of Z   The implication of Z in this equation merely instantiates the point that has already been made that the higher the calibre of the workers (hence other than in the academic professions the higher the salaries) the more important it is to have effective selection procedures, at least in terms of costs.

4.   As is obvious, the more expensive the selection procedures the less the gain. However, as is clear from the calculation of SD_y, the most salient figure in the equation, this is so much greater than any selection costs, even for one year, that these may be virtually disregarded.

5. The use of P   P is the proportion of applicants selected, usually known as the selection ratio, and this is an important aspect in considering the efficiency of all selection procedures even if the elaborations of utility theory are not considered. Clearly if all applicants are taken selection is pointless, whereas if only one has to be chosen from a large pool methods should be as efficient as possible. Smith (1986) has an informative table where savings per £1000 salary for tests of different validities and with different selection ratios are set out. For example with a test of validity .1 where the selection ratio is 1 in 10 the savings are 1; where the ratio is 1 in 3 it is 9. Comparable figures for a test with validity of .7 are 29 and 70. From this it is clear that as the selection ratio rises so efficient testing becomes more important.

6. Other derivations from the formula   As Cook (1988) discusses it is possible to compute very clear conclusions from the Brogden formula and the arguments derived from it. For example Schmidt and Hunter (1981), using rational estimates, showed that an employer with 5000 workers might save annually $18 million by using psychological tests. Large employers such as the US government could save up to $16 billion. Of course since not every company by definition can employ the best workers gains for companies are unlikely to be as large as this. However it is clear that by using valid tests there are considerable savings.

The advantages of utility theory are that it allows psychologists to demonstrate the clear commercial gains to be obtained from their tests. These formulae allow precise calculations for particular firms and with particular test batteries to be computed. Utility theory places the decision to use psychological tests in selection on a clear economic and thus rational basis.

Concluding comments on utility theory

I have discussed the main principles of utility theory in order that readers can see its value in estimating the worth of a selection procedure. However, because this is a text on psychometrics I have ignored more recent modifications and extensions. These are the province of more specialised books on occupational selection. However a few general comments can be made. It is clear that in the Global Estimation Method and, indeed, in the CREPID method, much depends on the ability of the raters to estimate the value of the employees. It is obviously important that this should become as accurate as possible.

Furthermore because there is far from perfect agreement between these two methods, as Schuler and Guldin (1991) point out, workers have attempted to clarify the models and a new model has been developed by Raju *et al.* (1990) which appears to be a general equation of which the CREPID and GEM are simply special forms. Readers are referred to Raju *et al.* (1990) for a detailed exposition of this model. However if it is the case that it is simply a more general expression of the other models it is hard to see what advantages it has over these more simple forms, although Schuler and Guldin (1991) argue that it is more easily adaptable to a variety of occupations.

Finally it should be pointed out that more elaborate models where the shapes of distributions and non-linearity are taken into account appear to perform no better than those making assumptions of linearity, as Cronbach and Gleser (1965) demonstrated. Hunter and Schmidt (1982) have an excellent discussion of this issue and many others in the application of utility theory.

In conclusion it can be seen that utility models are valuable because they can clearly show the financial advantages of using a battery of tests or any other selection procedure. However, even with the most sophisticated models, it must be realised that all depends on the somewhat dubious validity of the ratings on which SD_y are based.

Test fairness and bias

This has long been a problem in America in the practical application of tests where legislation has been more effective than in Great Britain despite the efforts of the Race Relations Act and the Equal Opportunities Commission. I shall not discuss any of this legislation in detail as it affects test users but rather I shall make some general points about test fairness and bias.

As Jensen (1980) pointed out in his huge study *Bias in Mental Tests*, and as was fully discussed in Chapter 11 of the handbook, it is not evidence of bias if one group scores lower than another on a test, since it could be the case that the groups were different. To demonstrate bias it is necessary, therefore, to show that a test yields lower scores in one group for reasons other than that of ability at the test.

In America, ability and intelligence tests have been accused of bias mainly in respect to Blacks whose scores are about one standard deviation lower than those of Whites. As Jensen (1980) argues, critics of intelligence tests have put this down to such factors as: differential motivation between Blacks and Whites concerning tests; bias in the testers; adverse reactions by Blacks to being tested by Whites; inferior schooling; test items being selected by Whites and thus favouring them, and fear of being tested.

However, as was shown in Chapter 11 of this handbook, if the correlations with external criteria are the same for different groups, regardless of their mean scores, it is not possible to argue that tests are biased, and this has been done with tests of intelligence verbal and non-verbal.

Now, in the case of occupational selection, the necessary relevant criteria for demonstrating the fairness of tests are correlations with success at jobs in different groups. As Cook (1988) argues, this has been done and in a meta-analysis of a large number of studies it was shown that among racial groups bias was not evidenced. Thus tests appear to be fair for selection (Schmidt *et al.*, 1973).

In America, the use of selection tests, despite the fact that no bias can be demonstrated, has fallen considerably as a result of the legislation, although as Drenth (1989) points out this may mean that less able workers are employed. If this occurs, this only defers the problem from the time of selection to the time of promotion.

One possible solution is to take a predetermined 'fair' proportion of each group, affirmative action, for posts. This, however, may lead to loss of efficiency.

Conclusions

As Cook (1988) points out, the interpretation of fairness and bias by courts, especially in America, is often different from that of psychologists and is sometimes based upon erroneous interpretations of test scores. Thus it is important that the professional associations concerned with psychological testing produce clear guidelines on the use of tests with respect to bias and fairness having regard to the particular legislation of their countries. If the legislation appears to lag behind scientific knowledge appropriate pressure must be brought to bear on it.

Assessment centres

This chapter is concerned with the use of psychometric tests in selection procedures. However, as is well known, there are other selection methods, such as interviews, rating scales, or observations of job samples. Given this it is fair and relevant to this chapter to discuss briefly the place of tests in the totality of selection procedures.

In general it is true to say that psychometric tests are the most valid methods of assessment. Where valid test exists, such as in the fields of ability, motivation and personality, there is no point in trying to use other methods of assessment. Interviews frequently add in errors to selection procedures, as was shown, long ago, by Vernon and Parry (1949). As was argued earlier in this chapter, the weight attached to psychological tests in the selection process should be determined empirically by their correlations with job success or their ability to discriminate the relevant occupational groups. Sometimes, however, no battery of psychological tests has been developed for particular jobs or occupations and in these instances testing is only a part of the selection procedure. Indeed, in practice, this is almost always true, since for most jobs no perfectly valid ($r = 1$) battery of tests exists and for obvious reasons most personnel workers and managers with whom the candidates must work like to interview candidates.

One approach to combining a set of different selection methods is that of the assessment centre. Feltham (1989), who has investigated the efficiency of the assessment centre, defines it thus: a selection process in which a team of judges assesses one or more candidates with a variety of methods of which one should be a work sample or an exercise in which elements of the job are performed. From this emerge a qualitative and a quantitative report of the candidates concluding with decisions to select, promote or not as the case may be. The quantitative report is usually based upon tests such as have been described throughout this handbook.

Feltham (1989) shows that well-designed assessment centres have reasonable correlations with job success. However the meaning of well-designed must be explicated. A well-designed assessment centre involves extensive training of the raters, in interviewing techniques, for example, good selection of psychometric tests, and good samples of or exercises in job performance. These may be difficult to produce and depend, as does the selection of tests, in many cases, on adequate job analyses, which, as has been seen, are themselves no easy matter to execute. Good assessment centres are costly and time consuming. However as was clear from the section on utility analysis, valid selection procedures quickly repay selection costs.

However, what was equally clear from the review by Feltham (1989) was that assessment centres run by untrained personnel with poor job samples and tests were worse than useless. From this description of assessment centres it is also clear that their efficiency is likely to vary for different jobs. Thus for military selection they may be less useful because it is difficult to simulate the effects of working under threat of death.

Thus it may be concluded that where good simulations or performance exercises have been devised, and where the raters are skilled, assessment centres are useful and may add in information beyond what may be gained from psychometric tests. Where this is not the case, however, assessment centre procedures add in error to the selection process.

It may be argued, therefore, that the main assessment methods should be psychometric tests but that if there are resources to develop and validate simulations or job exercises these may be valuable. However, as is the case with tests, these methods must be validated and the validity studies must show that they are concerned with variance different from that of the psychometric tests. If these criteria are met assessment centres can be useful. Nevertheless, it should be noted, much of their efficiency is derived from the psychometric tests.

Training

A few paragraphs need to be devoted to training in the use of psychometric tests for selection, since unlike educational and clinical psychology where practitioners of any kind have to be at least trained psychologists, this is not the case in occupational work. Many personnel managers are not psychologists although they may use or be responsible for the use of tests. What is said here applies to Great Britain. It is difficult to be precise about what training is necessary for what tests because at the present time, as the use of tests for selection increases, there are many changes in constraints on their use.

There are different types of training and these are set out below.

a. First degree in psychology or its equivalent (as judged by the British Psychological Society) plus a degree in occupational psychology; or one of the few first degrees in occupational psychology, at present offered by Wales and Aston Universities. This allows the holders to use all psychological tests likely to be of value in selection or the occupational and industrial fields.

It is to be noted that a first degree in psychology does not *per se* entitle holders to use psychological tests. This is because with rare exceptions psychometrics is taught to only an elementary level and there is almost no practice in the interpretation of tests. Nevertheless some tests may be permitted to holders of these degrees. The situation on this point is fluid at the time of writing because of the recent introduction of the certificate in test competence, which is discussed below.

b. The British Psychological Society's certificate in test competence. For those needing to use tests the British Psychological Society issue a certificate in test competence in which knowledge of many of the concepts discussed in this book is tested. Topics have been selected to be useful for the practical test user.

Test users who hold the qualifications listed under (a) and (b) are entitled to use and purchase virtually all psychological tests useful for occupational selection. It should be pointed out that tests are classified into different groups, each group requiring a different amount of training. This training is discussed below.

c. Test publishers and selection agencies offer courses in testing which enable individuals to purchase and use their particular tests. These courses are at various levels. The first level, for example, allows the use of relatively simple tests of ability. The next level allows more complex personality tests. Publishers may or may not recognise the courses of other publishers as sufficient to use their tests. Usually they do, in part, but demand a briefer course for those who have completed other training. Publishers' courses are usually of a few days' duration.

Certain tests which need clinical interpretation (and which would be most unlikely to be used in occupational work) are only available to those who have special qualifications in clinical or educational psychology.

d. Other qualifications   Holders of other qualifications such as those of the Institute of Personnel Management, or certain degrees with an element of psychological testing, or certificates in counselling from certain institutions, may (dependent upon exactly what has been taught) be eligible to use certain tests. Before taking such courses it is sensible to enquire what the position is relative to psychological testing.

My view is that the more training and knowledge of psychological tests which a test user has, the more effectively they are likely to be applied. The brief courses offered by publishers are better than nothing, provided that caution is shown in the interpretation of results. Of course, as with many practical skills, experience combined with intelligent reflection is highly valuable and should, ultimately, outweigh initial deficiencies in training.

Some of the restrictions on tests seem unnecessarily rigid. For example, some years ago a personality test which I had constructed was classified as a clinical test and I discovered that, having no clinical qualifications, I was unable to use it.

In brief, generally the more training in testing the more likely it is that psychometric testing will be treated properly, as is implicit in this handbook: that scores are regarded with due scepticism but with the realisation that they are far more valid and reliable than assessments by any other methods.

Section IV

Psychological Tests
Lists, Descriptions and Evaluations

In this final section of the handbook I scrutinise some of the best-known tests within the various categories which have been discussed throughout this book. I describe them, without destroying test confidentiality, and discuss how they were constructed, which has considerable bearing on their utility. I examine them against the criteria of psychometric efficiency – reliability, validity and quality of standardisation – and conclude by discussing where each may be best used in applied psychology and research or whether it should be used at all, since many famous tests turn out to be quite inadequate. Where relevant these considerations embrace critical research findings with the tests.

In a book of this length I have had to be selective in my discussion of tests. I have chosen those tests which are generally regarded as the best within their fields and other tests which are of the highest technical standards or are of particular interest either on account of their method of construction or because they attempt to measure variables of psychological importance.

However that this section does not include every published test rests on more than convenience. This is a handbook of psychological testing and I hope that it will enable readers to make their own informed judgements about tests, both in respect of their technical qualities and their use and value in applied psychology. Furthermore, as examination of the Mental Measurement Yearbooks has always shown, most psychological tests are neither reliable nor valid.

Nevertheless, this scrutiny of tests in the final section of this handbook concludes what is essentially a scrutiny of psychometrics itself. How it withstands this examination readers must judge for themselves.

Chapter 23

Intelligence Tests

As was made clear from Chapter 12, intelligence testing is the longest established field of psychological testing. I shall not describe a large number of intelligence tests simply because there are a few tests which are regarded as valid measures by almost all workers in the field and which, in terms of convenience and length, are suited to a wide variety of applications.

INDIVIDUAL INTELLIGENCE TESTS

Two individual intelligence tests have dominated the measurement of intelligence, especially in the clinical and developmental fields, the Wechsler Tests (Wechsler, 1958) and the Stanford-Binet (Terman and Merrill, 1960). Both these tests were developed before the modern elaborations of the factor analytic account of intelligence, and more recently a new test, the British Ability Scale (Elliot, 1983) has been constructed to take these into account. These three tests will now be described and evaluated.

The Wechsler Scales

The first of Wechsler's scales was the Wechsler Bellevue Scale of 1938. Since then, a new adult scale, the Wechsler Adult Intelligence Scale (Wechsler, 1958), the WAIS, and two children's scales, the WISC and the WPSSI, for pre-school and primary school children, have been produced. I have not given exact dates and references for these tests, since they are constantly under revision, but the latest editions and manuals are available from the Psychological Corporation, New York. These are, *inter alia*, the WISC-R[s], for Scottish children, the WISC-R[uk] for use in other parts of the UK, the WPSSI-R[uk], the WAIS-R[uk] and a computerised form of both tests, the WAIS-R Micro and the WISC-R Micro. Wechsler (1944, 1958, 1974) has clear accounts of the rationale of these tests, as do the test manuals. These tests together allow intelligence testing from the ages of 4 years to beyond 70.

The WAIS

I shall describe the adult scale, the WAIS, since the other scales follow this format as far as is possible, their items simply being suited for children and thus of less difficulty.

Variables Verbal intelligence, performance intelligence and an overall intelligence score. In addition subscale scores and profiles of scores can be used.

Subscales There are eleven subscales, divided into verbal and performance scales. The verbal scales are: information, comprehension, arithmetic, similarities, digit span, and vocabulary. The performance tests are: digit symbol, picture completion, block design, picture arrangement and object assembly.

Description of subscales I shall describe the items in these scales. However, in this chapter and the others describing ability tests I shall not discuss the actual items in the test as this would destroy the confidentiality of the items. Instead I shall describe similar types of items.

1. The verbal subtests

a. Information: 29 items This is basically a test of general knowledge, involving the authorship of books, parts of the Bible and geographic locations. Such a test is clearly a test of g_c, crystallised ability, rather than the basic reasoning ability of the brain, fluid ability, g_f. Although scores on this scale are likely to be affected by social class and education, the rationale for its inclusion in an intelligence test is that, other things being equal, the intelligent person will be more knowledgeable since she or he learns more easily and can make more connections between new and old material, than the less intelligent.

It should also be realised that the efficiency of the WAIS in predicting educational success is augmented by such scales where the investment of g_f in skills valued by the culture, to use the terminology of Cattell (1971), is tested, which is a basic demand of educational success.

b. Comprehension: 14 items This test requires the subject to explain the meaning of proverbs, e.g. 'it's no good crying over spilt milk', and to solve practical problems. Some of the questions involve perhaps slightly more than general knowledge, for example, of taxes and the price of land but, in general, this is a good test of reasoning where subjects are required to get to the heart of a problem and, as such, it would be expected to load highly on crystallised ability.

c. Arithmetic: 14 items These items involve traditional arithmetic problem solving: if water flows into a bath at 2 gallons a minute and the bath holds 200 pints how long will it take to fill? Obviously such a test depends on knowledge of simple arithmetic but such knowledge does depend on g_c at least in part.

d. Similarities: 13 items In this test subjects are required to point out what is similar about two things, for example a sonnet and a sonata. The correct answer involves hitting on the essential similarity, in this case that they are both creations, rather than the superficial, that they have a similar first syllable. Again this is likely to be a test of g_c rather than g_f.

e. Digit span: 17 items Subjects are required to repeat strings of digits after they have been read to them at a steady rate. One set of items is repeated as heard, another is repeated backwards. Clearly this is not a test of crystallised ability since few cultures value such an ability. However the fact that it loads on fluid ability is of considerable theoretical interest from the viewpoint of the nature of intelligence. It is noteworthy that, as Jensen (1980) points out, the backward digit span loads more highly on g_f than does the forward span, presumably because the task requires more, and more complex, mental processing, a feature of all g_f loaded tasks. Jensen (1980) argues that the digit span loading on g supports the notion that intelligence reflects the speed and integrity of information processing in the brain, a view, however, which is perhaps too simple in the light of EEG findings and work with reaction times (as is fully argued in Kline, 1990).

f. Vocabulary: 40 items This is a straightforward vocabulary test and one which many practical psychologists would use if they were forced to estimate intelligence with a brief test, since it loads highly on both g factors. As was the case with information this is because the intelligent person learns better because she or he can connect new information to what is already possessed. It is this process which leads to the ever-widening disparity between the highly intelligent and those of low intelligence, as life proceeds.

Indeed as Cattell (1971) demonstrates, vocabulary loads highly on g_f in early life but gradually shifts over to crystallised ability for obvious reasons. Jensen (1980) has argued that in adulthood vocabulary scores reflect childhood rather than present fluid ability since subjects with a high vocabulary score may be poor at dealing with novel problems. This is a possible explanation of this finding but it should be pointed out that this disparity in performance may arise from the fact that some subjects whose work is closely involved with words may simply develop a good vocabulary for this reason alone, intelligence not being much implicated. This scale is also useful in the assessment of premorbid intelligence in brain damaged patients (Crawford *et al.*, 1988).

Conclusions concerning the verbal subtests These descriptions make it clear that the verbal intelligence score of the WAIS is essentially a measure of crystallised ability. The only exception to this is the digit span test. All these tests are concerned with intelligence as it is evinced in Western culture. It is clear, further, that these scales are to some extent influenced by social class and education, although to a lesser extent than is the case with school attainment tests. It is for all these reasons that the verbal intelligence score of the WAIS and WISC correlated well with academic and occupational success (e.g. Vernon, 1961; Ghiselli, 1966) since these criteria are also examples of the investment of intelligence in culturally valued activities.

2. The performance subtests

That the WAIS has performance tests as well as the verbal measures is, undoubtedly, one of the great assets of the test. These tests are far less likely than the verbal measures to be influenced by social class or education. Indeed, as shall be seen below, these tests exemplify the definition of Cattell (1971) of how to test fluid ability – namely with items that are so familiar in a culture that social factors are of no importance or with items so unfamiliar that no subject will have encountered anything like them before taking the test.

g. Digit symbol: 90 items in 90 seconds In this speeded test symbols are paired with digits. With the examples before them subjects have to place the correct digit to the symbols. The mental processing required for this task is within the capacity of most subjects so that the emphasis of the test is on speed. This test is likely to load highest on the cognitive speed factor, as well as g_f, but it is entirely sensible that it should correlate with real life success.

h. Picture completion: 21 items in 20 seconds Subjects are presented with pictures each with an element missing which has to be recognised within a second of presentation. This is a scale which demands familiarity with pictorial representation so that it could not be used in cross-cultural studies without first demonstrating that subjects could recognise the pictures (Deregowski, 1980). Such a test would be expected to load on fluid ability and perceptual speed. In Great Britain only highly deprived subjects would be obviously at a disadvantage.

i. Block design: 10 items with bonuses for rapid completion In this test subjects are presented with blocks and some designs which have to be made from the blocks. Bonus points can be scored for rapid completion. This is a skill that is largely unpractised so the test should load on fluid ability as well as on spatial and perceptual factors. There is an element of specific variance in this test since I have seen some subjects divide the pictures of the designs into rectangles, thus greatly simplifying the task.

j. Picture arrangement: 8 items with time bonuses for rapid completion Each item consists of a set of pictures which have to be arranged into a sequence such that they tell a story. Again for most subjects this is a novel task so that it should load on g_f.

k. Object assembly: 4 items with bonuses for rapid completion This test requires subjects to assemble pieces into a whole object, like a jigsaw. Such a test should load on spatial ability and g_f.

Conclusions concerning performance subtests These performance tests are the type of tests that load on fluid ability, and which are unlikely to yield scores inflated by good educational and familial factors. Indeed the differences between the verbal and performance scores are often considered to be important but this will be discussed in a later section on the WAIS.

Norms

The 1955 version of the test contained norms based upon a sample of 1700 American adults. British norms have been provided for the test.

Reliability

The corrected split-half reliabilities of the performance and the verbal IQ are both beyond .9 and the full scale IQ has a reliability of .97. This is exceedingly high. However, the reliability of the subscales varies from .65 to .94. It should be noted that the speeded digit symbol test reliability is not split half which would be inappropriate (see Chapters 1 and 3 of this handbook) but a parallel form coefficient.

In general it can be concluded that the reliabilities are sufficient but caution must be shown in interpreting difference between some of the subtest scores where the standard error of score may be high.

Test administration

The test takes about one hour to administer, each subtest being given separately. However the experienced tester can shorten the testing time in two ways. It is not necessary to administer all the items. The tester can gauge where to start and if there are no failures in the first three items the subject can be credited with the items which have not been given. The second approach is not to give all the subtests. This, however, leads to a greater unreliability of score.

Validity of the WAIS and conclusions

I shall not say much about the validity of the WAIS. This is because it is still, more than half a century after its development, regarded as a criterion test of intelligence and widely used in clinical assessment (e.g. Howard, 1989b). Other intelligence tests are validated against it despite the fact that it was developed before the modern factor analysis of human abilities.

Nevertheless, despite its formidable reputation some important points need to be made about the WAIS and all its related scales.

1. Caution should be used in interpreting the differences in subtest scores on account of their imperfect reliabilities. Differences have to be quite large before confident conclusions can be drawn justifiably about them.
2. Social class and educational factors must influence the verbal score. Furthermore the arithmetic test is highly dependent on adults having some formal mathematical background. This is even more important in the children's versions.
3. This objection is not quite so devastating as it appears, since disadvantaged subjects should show relatively better scores on the performance than the verbal tests just as, conversely, middle class subjects do better on the verbal scales (Jensen, 1980).
4. Factor analyses of the WAIS and the other versions of the test show that, as expected, the verbal scales load on the crystallised ability factor while the performance tests load on fluid ability (Woliver and Saeks, 1986); although, as these authors show, there is other ability variance in these scales, notably in the digit span tests which load on the Cattell memory factor. These loadings on the two main ability factors, g_f and g_c, demonstrate the insight of Wechsler into the nature of intelligence given that the WAIS was not constructed through factor analytic principles. Crawford *et al.* (1989; 1990) also demonstrated that the WAIS has substantial g loadings although it should be noted that, in the later study, Crawford relied on the first general principal component as evidence, which is not entirely satisfactory, as was shown in Chapter 7.
5. However, good as the loadings are, a modern psychometrist might well be able to construct a more precise measure of these factors and in fact, as Woliver and Saeks (1986) point out, Cattell and colleagues are engaged in such an endeavour, attempting to calibrate the WAIS such that it will provide more precise measures of the Cattell factors than the simple performance and verbal IQs. At the time of writing this test has not yet appeared. Even if it does, to abandon the vast amount of clinical data obtained with the standard WAIS and WISC scales would not seem sensible and it is doubtful whether it would be much used despite its factorial improvements.

In summary, despite some imperfections the WAIS does provide the opportunity to measure the two main intelligence factors, fluid and crystallised ability, and there is no reason to question its validity as a measure of intelligence.

In Section III of this handbook, the use of intelligence tests in the applied fields of educational, clinical and occupational psychology was discussed and I shall not repeat those arguments here. It is clear the Wechsler scales have proved valuable especially in educational and clinical psychology.

One point needs to be made here about the Wechsler scales in educational applications. The fact that the verbal scales are biased in favour of the middle classes and educated subjects improves, in the Western world, their educational predictive power since these biases affect their education systems. However, it should be noted that the performance scales indicate clearly disadvantaged subjects so that the tests as a whole are not grossly unfair and a prop of the bourgeoisie. However, the content of the information, arithmetic and comprehension scales probably needs regular revision since it appears outdated and may thus be less valid than it was. This is a perennial problem with all ability tests. However, as was indicated, modern revised versions of the WAIS and WISC have been produced.

Final conclusions

The Wechsler scales have shown themselves over a long period excellent and sensitive tests of ability in research and applied settings. They are valid tests of intelligence as it is conceived of as fluid and crystallised ability. Although it is possible that more highly loading tests might be produced, to throw away all the data obtained with these scales for a relatively small increase in factorial validity would not seem sensible. With plenty of testing time available, the Wechsler scales are still excellent tests. Nevertheless despite their quality it is still arguable that it is better to test the main ability factors separately and from these obtain measures of fluid and crystallised ability.

The Stanford-Binet Test (Terman and Merrill, 1960)

This is the second of the individual intelligence tests which, until the most recent factor analyses of intelligence, was accepted as a benchmark test of intelligence.

Variable measured Intelligence, almost certainly, as will be seen, g_c.

Age range 4–17 years with a supplement down to 2½ years. Although to have a single test covering so large an age range is highly convenient, there is the difficulty that for high level adults there are insufficient difficult items.

Items and scales Unlike the WAIS and WISC the items in the Stanford-Binet test are grouped by level of difficulty. There are items of many different types: vocabulary, recognition of absurdities, ability to name the days of a week, copying a chain of beads from memory, abstract word definition, paper cutting, building a sentence from a set of words, digit repetition, and explanation of proverbs, to name only some of the immense variety.

Reliability At most age groups and levels of IQ reliabilities are high, in excess of .9. This is partly a function of the length of the test.

Norms Over 3000 native-born, white subjects. The norms are divided into 6-month age intervals – 100 per group at ages up to 5½ years and from 15 to 18 years, 200 in the other groups.

It should be noted that although 3000 subjects constitutes a large normative sample, in fact numbers such as 100 and 200 for the age groups are still exceedingly small to be truly representative; but see Chapter 4 of this handbook for a full discussion of the problems of standardisation.

Administering the test Older children, about 12 years and beyond, take between 60 and 90 minutes to complete the test, younger children about half this time.

Validity of the test Woliver and Saeks (1986), in their useful summary of research with the Stanford-Binet, point out two telling findings. The first is that the vocabulary items of the S-B correlate .71 and .86 with the mental ages derived from the entire test. Secondly there is a correlation between the S-B and the WAIS of .78. Since vocabulary, as has been argued, is the best single measure of g_c, and since the WAIS loads primarily on this factor there can be little doubt that the Stanford-Binet is measuring crystallised ability. Such a conclusion is supported, of course, by the description of the types of item in the test which are all of the kind normally thought of as measuring this factor.

Discussion

There are a number of points which should be made about this test.

1. The fact that there are so many different types of item in this test is a great advantage given the nature of intelligence and its consequent universe of items. It is highly unlikely, for example, that a Stanford-Binet IQ could be some sort of bloated specific.
2. However, this has the disadvantage that comparison of the scores of a 4-year-old child on this test and those of a 16-year-old may be a problem. Thus in the Stanford-Binet, at the lower age level items are concerned with building a tower of blocks, identifying parts of the body on a doll,

and naming simple objects. At the older level subjects are required to complete sentences, memorise abstract designs, and make inferences to answer questions about a passage of English.

While it is possible for different tests to have identical loadings on a factor, these are so different that there must be a question of whether the intelligence measured by the Stanford-Binet is identical at all ages. This is, of course, a problem with all tests of intelligence and accounts for the fact that in general the earlier the IQ test the worse its correlations with later IQ.

3. The fact that there is only a global IQ score from the test limits its utility compared with the WAIS and WISC, even though, as has been argued, we have to be careful about interpreting differences between subtest scores.

4. The discussion of the meaning of the scale, in our section on validity, leaves no doubt that this test is measuring crystallised ability. This is well supported by the long-term studies of gifted individuals (e.g. Terman and Oden, 1959) which showed that children selected on this test as gifted at the age of 5, had, compared with controls, brilliant success in adult life.

Conclusions

The Stanford-Binet is an excellent test, especially for children between the ages of 5 and 12, of crystallised ability and one which is likely to predict educational achievement. For adults and older children of superior ability the WAIS and WISC would seem more useful because they are more discriminating at this level. However, as was the case with the WISC and WAIS, given the modern factor analysis of abilities it may be more sensible to test the individual factors separately.

Stanford-Binet Scale (Fourth Edition) (Thorndike et al., 1985)

I have described, above, the Stanford-Binet (S-B) scale, a classic measure of intelligence. Recently, however, Thorndike *et al.* (1985) have modified the test into a new fourth edition. These modifications improve the test in certain ways and bring it far closer to the WAIS or WISC, without, however, radically changing the nature of the test which still measures crystallised ability. These changes are briefly described.

Norms The norms are improved: 6000 subjects from 100 communities in the USA constitute the norms. Although this is by most standards a large sample, in fact, because there are so many age groups, there are still insufficient subjects for truly adequate norms. Obviously, however, they are better than the previous edition.

Scales The items have now been grouped into fifteen subtests so that they can be administered separately and four variables can be measured.

Variables Verbal reasoning, quantitative reasoning, abstract/visual reasoning and short-term memory.

Comments

Norms are provided for all these four scores so that some sort of diagnostic information is now yielded by the test, as is the case with the WISC and WAIS. However, the meaning of these differences or profiles in the clinical and educational context remains to be explored.

It is certain from the nature of the scales that the verbal and quantitative scores are measures of crystallised ability and it is likely that the abstract/visual score is the equivalent of the WAIS performance score and that it loads on fluid ability, at least to some extent. However the items in the new test are not different from those in the original edition and since that clearly measured crystallised ability it is difficult to see how any new arrangement of these items into scales can change this.

In brief the new S-B is a more convenient and better standardised form of the old test but essentially it must be regarded as a measure of crystallised ability, although some measure of fluid ability is possible. However if such a measure is required it is surely better to start from the beginning than group together the tests in an old scale which happen to load on this factor.

Conclusions concerning the Wechsler and Stanford-Binet Scales

There are two clear conclusions about these excellent group intelligence tests.

1. Both measure crystallised intelligence and are, therefore, valuable for work in the educational setting.
2. However, it is arguable that on psychometric grounds, both these tests should be retired. It is simply more efficient to measure the primary factors separately and derive from them overall IQ measures of both crystallised and fluid intelligence.

The British Ability Scales (BAS) (Elliot, 1983)

The BAS was developed to overcome some of the defects, discussed above, of the Stanford-Binet and the Wechsler scales. It was originally conceived in the late 1960s by Professor Warburton and his colleagues at Manchester. Its final production was delayed by his unfortunate early death. I mention this date of conception because it is probably true to say that if a new test were to be developed today it would be different from the BAS.

Original basis of the BAS

I was a research associate with Warburton at the time of the development of this scale. It was decided to incorporate the latest factorial findings and the work of cognitive psychology into the test. In fact this meant that the Guilford model of intelligence (Guilford, 1967) was used, which at that time postulated 120 factors and minimised the importance of g. Unfortunately, the factor model of Guilford has been shown to be technically flawed, since the Procrustes rotations, which appeared to support its validity, were shown by Horn and Knapp (1973) to be capable of fitting target matrices from random data, as has been discussed in Chapter 8 of this handbook.

The BAS was also developed to provide a variety of ability scores (thus strictly it was not an intelligence test) to make it more useful for teachers and educational psychologists, although an intelligence measure is available. The work of Piaget was highly influential in educational psychology (e.g. Piaget, 1947) and it is possible with the BAS to assess the level of thinking which a child has reached. Cognitive processes are also measured with this test.

The background to the development of the BAS is described in Manual 1 to the test (Elliot *et al.*, 1983) and despite the length of the labour pangs there has emerged a highly useful test of abilities which I shall describe below. I depart from the usual format of test descriptions in this handbook, simply for reasons of length. The whole test is extremely long and packs a large suitcase. Indeed it should be pointed out that the scales are available separately.

Variables measured   There are twenty-three scales, each of which yields a separate score with norms. These will be described below. In addition scores can be obtained in six major areas:

1. Speed of information processing (scale 1);
2. Reasoning (scales 2–5);
3. Spatial imagery (scales 6–8);
4. Perceptual matching (scales 9–11);
5. Short-term memory scales (12–16);
6. Retrieval and application of knowledge (scales 17–23).

In addition an intelligence score can be obtained.

BAS scales

1. Speed of information processing
2. Formal operational reasoning
3. Matrices
4. Similarities
5. Social reasoning

    6. Block design
    7. Rotation of letter-like forms
    8. Visualisation of cubes
    9. Copying
  10. Matching letter-like forms
  11. Verbal tactile matching
12/13. Immediate/delayed visual recall
  14. Recall of designs
  15. Recall of digits
  16. Visual recognition
  17. Basic number skills
  18. Naming vocabulary
  19. Verbal comprehension
  20. Verbal fluency
  21. Word definition
  22. Word reading
  23. Conservation

Reliabilities   The reliabilities for these scales are high (.8 or better) and the test is satisfactory from this viewpoint.

Age range   2½ – 17½ years.

Norms   A large representative sample from all areas of Great Britain. These norms were collected over many years by educational psychologists. Percentiles, T scores and sample-free ability scores are provided for most scales. For the IQ a standardised score of mean 100 and standard deviation 15 is supplied. Confidence limits for scores are also provided and the significance of differences between T scores on a subject's profile is indicated.

Validity of the test and discussion

As was argued earlier, the BAS is strictly not an intelligence test but a collection of ability scales. It could, therefore, have been reviewed in the next chapter of this book but as an individual test which does measure intelligence it fits here best.

    There are a number of points which need to be made about this test.

  1. Most of the BAS scales are standard fare for intelligence and ability tests. There is, therefore, every likelihood that they are valid tests. The authors chose the types of item that were known to load most highly on ability factors. This is not so in the case of the Piaget tasks, such as formal reasoning or conservation, but here the nature of the items is highly specified by the theory.

2. The IQ is measured by the following tests (short form): speed of information processing, matrices, similarities, recall of digits, visual recognition, naming vocabulary, verbal comprehension. These tests indicate clearly that the BAS IQ is little different from that of the WISC and S-B tests. It would, as in those tests, be a mixture of g_f, fluid ability (matrices and speed of information processing) and g_c, crystallised ability.
3. The provision of other ability scales is certainly useful, especially in the applied setting, and it is a good feature of the test that careful consideration is given to the meaning of differences between scale scores in which the standard errors of the scores are taken into account.
4. Another useful feature of the test is the provision of scales of school achievement, number and reading, since, as is discussed in Section III of this handbook, school achievement can only be properly understood in the context of the ability of the individual.

Conclusions

As a measure of IQ the BAS is remarkably similar to the two standard individual intelligence tests. However the items are naturally more modern than in these earlier tests and the British norms are extensive and up to date. For these reasons, in Great Britain at least, it is probably a better measure to use than the older tests, although for obvious reasons the meaning of BAS scores is not underpinned by so large a body of research, as is the case with older tests.

The fact that other abilities and achievement can be measured by this test is also an advantage compared with the older tests although it is a theoretical issue, which I cannot discuss in a handbook of testing, as to whether one might want to assess Piagetian variables. However, if this seems desirable, the BAS tests are clearly useful.

It will be remembered that in our discussion of the S-B and the Wechsler scales it was concluded that it was a pity that they were developed before the modern factor analysis of abilities. In the case of the BAS I feel that a great chance was lost. Here an individual test could have been constructed which measured the most important factors as set out by Hakstian and Cattell (1974) and Ekstrom et al. (1976) which could well have supplied an excellent picture of the cognitive abilities of the child and provided measures of both crystallised and fluid ability. This would not have precluded the Piagetian measures which teachers and educators appear to find useful.

In brief, the BAS is a psychometrically highly refined individual test which measures crystallised intelligence and some other abilities and which with its modern norms and items is a good test in the UK. Nevertheless it still fails to provide a set of tests for the major ability factors and on account of this it still falls short of an ideal test.

Unorthodox individual tests of intelligence

I shall briefly describe two unusual intelligence tests which deserve mention and might be useful occasionally, in clinical practice for example, when the standard tests, as described above, are inappropriate.

1. Porteus Maze Test (Porteus, 1965)

This test was designed in 1914 and is often used in cross-cultural studies, for reasons that will become obvious from its description.

Age range   3 years to adults.

Items   Mazes, graded in difficulty. A line has to be traced from entrance to finish, without a break and without touching the sides.

Number of items   28.

Comments

There is no information concerning the reliability of the PMT, and the mental age and IQ conversion tables to be found in Porteus (1965) are not to be trusted, being based on inadequate standardisation (Jensen, 1980).

Since the PMT requires virtually no language, although the subject must be made to understand what needs to be done, it has been popular in cross-cultural studies of intelligence (e.g. Lynn, 1978).

Porteus (1965) claims that the PMT also measures adaptive competence, which is valuable in the clinical measurement of the retarded or subnormal. As a measure of g the PMT is probably quite good given that the maze test of the WISC scales (an alternative to digit symbol) loads the g factor, as Jensen (1980) argues, although not as highly as some of the other subtests.

Conclusions

The PMT is a useful g measure where the utmost simplicity of instructions is necessary; however, it can never be as accurate as an orthodox intelligence test.

2. Draw a Man Test (DMT) (Goodenough, 1926) and revised version, the Goodenough Harris Drawing Test (GHDT) (Harris, 1963)

Age range   3–17. However these tests are best below the ages of 12 or 13 (Jensen, 1980).

The task and scoring   In the original DMT, the child is simply asked to draw a man. The score does not depend on artistic skill but reflects accurate observation and the development of concepts of the human figure and its clothing. The presence or absence of 51 specific points is noted, e.g. head present, coat non-transparent. In the revised GHDT, the child has to draw a picture of a man, a woman, and her or himself. As with the earlier test the scoring reflects developmental features of the drawings: proportions of body parts; attachment of limbs and details of clothing, just for example. Since the GHDT is an improved version of the original I shall restrict my comments to this more recent test.

Reliability Inter-scorer reliability is around .9 and test-retest reliability is about .7.

Norms Extensive norms have been collected by Harris (1963).

Validity Jensen (1980) summarises the evidence succinctly for validity. The correlations with the Stanford-Binet Test and the Wechsler scales are highly similar to those of the subscales of the Wechsler with the full scale IQ. Thus it is a reasonable measure of g. Beyond the age of 12 increase of scores is not highly correlated with age and variance is restricted. That is why the test is best for children below the age of 12.

Conclusions

This is a test simple to administer, reliable, enjoyed by children and loading substantially on g. Its intelligence scores are not related to artistic ability and thus it might be thought of as a useful test when a conventional test is not suitable. Its cross-cultural use is dubious since clothing scores are obviously culturally influenced.

GROUP INTELLIGENCE TESTS

As was discussed in Chapter 12, for reasons of convenience group tests of intelligence have been developed although such group testing loses considerable useful information about a subject's ability, over and beyond the actual intelligence test score. Although there are a large number of group intelligence tests I shall list here a few examples whose validity is well attested, so well attested indeed that they can be used as marker variables for the g factors.

Raven's Progressive Matrices (Raven, 1965a)

There are three versions of the Raven's Matrices: 1. Standard Matrices; 2. Coloured Matrices; 3. Advanced Matrices.

1. Standard Matrices Age range: 6½– 65 years.
Subjects: average ability.
Time for completion: 45 mins. This is a power test; the time given is what is

usually sufficient for most subjects. The same is true of the other versions of the matrices.

2. Coloured Matrices Age range: 6–85 years.
Subjects: young children and older adults who are mentally impaired.
Time for completion: 15–30 mins.

3. Advanced Matrices Age range: 11 years to adult.
Subjects: above average ability.
Time for completion: 40–60 mins.

Variable measured: fluid ability Raven (1938) devised his matrices test from first principles, considering carefully the nature of reasoning. Although this test was constructed before fluid ability had been unequivocally identified, in fact Raven's Matrices can be regarded as a marker variable for g_f. Indeed Cattell (1971) makes it clear that his only objection to matrices being used as the only type of item in tests of fluid ability is that it means that the final score is confounded with the factor specific to matrices. Thus he argues for tests with several kinds of item which minimises the effect of specific factors.

Type of item: matrices These were described in Chapter 12 of this handbook and consist of sequences of related patterns. Subjects have to select the next one in the sequence. For a successful choice subjects have to work out the relationship between the patterns and apply the rule to the new cases (the correct response is one from a multiple-choice array). Figures can increase or decrease in size, elements can be rotated, shaded, flipped over, or shown in the form of a mirror image, just for example, and these items can be made of varying degrees of difficulty. The final items of the Advanced Matrices are exceedingly difficult.

Number of items
Standard: 60 in five sets, each set involving different principles of variation and at all levels of difficulty.
Coloured: 36 items in three sets, arranged as the Standard Matrices.
Advanced: 36 items.

Norms British norms are supplied but these are now old and clearly defective in terms of sampling and numbers in the sample, although in 1982 supplementary norms, which are some improvement, were supplied. This problem means that where norms are important, as in the applied setting, Raven's Matrices are far from ideal, although in-house norms might be built up in a large organisation. For research into the nature of intelligence this lack of norms is irrelevant.

Reliability The internal consistency of these scales is high – >.9. This is hardly surprising, given the homogeneity of the items.

Validity and discussion

As Jensen (1980) points out, the validity of the Raven's Matrices is highly attested. It is virtually that ideal of test construction, a unifactorial test. Almost all its reliable variance is accounted for by one factor, fluid ability. A study by McArthur and Elley (1963), who factored a variety of ability and achievement tests, typifies the factorial findings. Raven's Matrices loaded .73 on the fluid ability factor.

As befits a marker test of fluid ability the Matrices correlates with almost all other intelligence tests to a substantial degree, more highly with measures of fluid ability and less with tests of crystallised ability such as verbal intelligence tests.

As might also be expected the predictive validity of Raven's Matrices for scholastic achievement is lower for the general population than is the case for measures of crystallised ability since these are affected by the cultural factors which influence educational success. However, for disadvantaged pupils, whose attainments may not reflect their real ability, the Raven's Matrices is a highly useful test.

Indeed, as Jensen (1980) argues, this is the main value in applied psychology of the Raven's Matrices for assessing the potential of those with deprived linguistic backgrounds. However, it should not be assumed that the Matrices are therefore able to test fluid intelligence across cultures. As Vernon (1979) points out, the same tests may load different factors in different cultures and even the Raven's Matrices requires subjects to have some experience of testing before it performs adequately (Ortar, 1963). Indeed even with immigrant children in Great Britain who have been subjected to considerable environmental deprivation and who know little English, it may underestimate their ability although certainly not to the same extent as a traditional intelligence test, loading g_c.

There is one further criticism of the Raven's Matrices, which was made by Jensen (1980) and with which I am in full agreement. This concerns the rather small number of items in each test given the huge age range which the test covers. This means that there are relatively few items particularly suited to each age group and that items tend to increase in difficulty by rather large steps. It also follows that a difference of one or two items correct makes a substantial difference to the score. This clearly leads to inaccuracy. What are required, therefore, are more items of more finely graded difficulty. If these were written (and matrices are relatively easy to write) and if the norms were further improved (beyond the 1982 supplementation), the Matrices could become a truly excellent test.

Conclusions

The Raven's Matrices is an excellent measure of fluid ability. Its only disadvantage is that the items are of one kind. I have certainly found children who scored abnormally high on this test who did so because of an ability at this type of item, although such subjects are rare. As a marker for fluid ability in studies of intelligence it is a valuable test.

In applied psychology I would use this test where a subject knew little English or had other severe disadvantages likely to lower her or his score on a crystallised ability test. Although it is about the best test for such subjects it may well still underestimate their ability and due caution must be shown in interpreting the results of such testing. As was mentioned the norms are not satisfactory and this means that even more care must be shown in interpreting the scores from the Matrices.

The Mill Hill and the Crichton Vocabulary Scales (Raven, 1965b; 1965a)

The Mill Hill is designed for use with the Standard Matrices and the Crichton with the Coloured version. As has been mentioned, the correlations between the Raven's Matrices and educational criteria are reduced simply because of the factorial purity of the test and its relative imperviousness to cultural bias. To improve educational prediction Raven has provided two vocabulary tests, which, it will be remembered from Chapter 12, are the best individual measures of g_c.

These tests, as might be expected, load highly on the crystallised ability factor and are useful to give together with the Raven's, if a measure of both intelligence factors is required. As with the Matrices, the norms for these tests are far from ideal although the Mill Hill Scale norms were improved in 1982.

Conclusions

As a quick measure of crystallised ability to administer along with the Matrices, the Mill Hill and the Crichton tests are useful. Of course, for a truly adequate measure of g_c, a test with more varied items is to be preferred.

The Culture Fair Tests (Cattell and Cattell, 1959)

There are three versions of the Culture Fair Test which was designed to measure fluid ability. Since fluid ability is a concept introduced by Cattell it should be the case that his tests should best define it, especially since the development of the test and the emergence of the factor were closely intertwined, as is made clear in Cattell (1971) and in the Technical Supplement to the tests (IPAT, 1973).

Test 1 Age-range: 4–8 years and retarded adults. I shall say little about this test since it it is awkward to administer, (parts of it have to be given individually) and lengthy, taking about an hour, although it can be given in two shorter sessions. Part of the problem lies in the fact that the Scale 1 consists of 8 subtests which vary in length from two to four minutes and which have complex and precise instructions. As Jensen (1980) argues this is particularly unfortunate for a culture fair test in which the effects of familiarity with language and the habits of listening and attending should be set at a minimum. For these reasons this test could not be recommended.

Test 2 Age range: 8–13 years and unselected adults.

Test 3 Age range: High school, college and superior adults.

Culture Fair Tests 2 and 3 are identical except that, as is clear from the populations for which they were designed, Test 3 is more difficult. Each has two forms, A and B, which ideally would be used together, but which, in practice, are regarded as convenient alternative forms for retesting. Actually, for unsophisticated subjects, subjects indeed with whom the Culture Fair Test is likely to be used, Cattell suggests that Form A be used as practice.

Variable measured Fluid ability.

Items: number of items and timings Items are abstract and non-verbal, falling into four scales.

1. Series. 12 items in 3 mins (2). 13 items in 3 mins (3).
2. Classifications. 14 items in 4 mins (both scales).
3. Matrices. 12 items in 3 mins (2). 13 items in 3 mins (3).
4. Conditions (topology). 8 items in 2½ mins (2). 10 items in 2½ mins (3).

Total items. 46 items in 12½ mins (2). 50 items in 12½ mins (3). However it should be noted that it takes about 30 mins to administer these tests.

These item types have been fully described in Chapter 12 of this handbook, with the exception of topological conditions. These items are peculiar to Cattell and I shall describe one of his example, unscored items. Five boxes are drawn in which are circles and squares in various configurations. Subjects are required to indicate into which of these five boxes a dot could be placed so that it is inside a circle but outside a square.

Reliability Krug (1973) reports internal consistency reliabilities of both scales (alpha coefficients) of approximately .8. Test-retest reliabilities are also high, beyond .7. It can be said that the reliability of these scales is satisfactory although the reliability of the subtests with so few items is lower.

Norms Norms are given for age groups at six-month intervals with a total sample of more than 4000, from the USA and the UK in the case of scale 2 and more than 3000, just from the USA for scale 3. These are certainly reasonable, if rough guides for the practical application of the test.

Validity of the scales   Barton (1973) cites several studies in which the validity of the Culture Fair Scales as a measure of fluid ability is left in no doubt. The test correlates highly with other intelligence tests and, as just one example, in a study by Cattell (1967b) there is a clear, high loading on the gf factor.

Discussion and conclusions

It is clear from my description of this test that it is an excellent, reliable measure of fluid ability with reasonable norms. However as a culture fair test which is suitable for cross-cultural comparison or for use with immigrant populations who have little formal education, a poor knowledge of English and no experience of testing, it is by no means certain that this is a suitable test.

As was argued in the case of Raven's Matrices, it cannot be assumed that the test can be used in different cultures without clear evidence that it works efficiently in those cultures, as has been discussed by Kline (1977) in respect of personality inventories. However as was exemplified by Jensen (1980) it cannot be assumed that this test works efficiently with severely disadvantaged children in the American or British context. This was because the instructions of the test are so formal and require concentration that many children failed to grasp them and clearly disliked the test and gave up the attempt to complete it. However the Raven's Matrices provided no such problems.

For these reasons, ironically in view of their title, the Culture Fair tests are probably best with subjects who are not particularly disadvantaged. Then as a pure measure of g_f it really comes into its own. Certainly compared with more verbal intelligence tests, loading g_c, it yields a score less affected by education and social class.

In summary this is an excellent test of fluid ability but one which, on account of its complex instructions, is not ideal for severely disadvantaged subjects.

OTHER TESTS OF INTELLIGENCE

So far in this chapter I have listed and and discussed the best measures of fluid and crystallised ability, both individual and group tests. It will be noted that in the group testing there has been emphasis on fluid ability rather than crystallised ability. This is for two reasons. In the applied field fluid ability is often the critical variable. Thus if a child is failing at school we want to measure fluid ability to see whether this reflects low ability or not. If fluid ability is higher than suggested by the child's performance, then investigations must be begun as to why this should be. If a child is performing well at school her or his score on crystallised ability is of little interest.

Similarly if we are engaged in the selection of adults for jobs, crystallised ability is of little interest because this will be reflected in the educational and occupational achievement of the subjects. Thus where it is important to know the intelligence of a subject, fluid ability is the important one.

A further reason why we have not concentrated upon crystallised ability tests is that they are relatively easy to construct from the types of item which were described and discussed in Chapter 12 of this handbook. In addition to this, crystallised intelligence can be measured using the scores from tests of other abilities such as verbal and mathematical ability, tests which are discussed in Chapter 26 of this handbook. Indeed since vocabulary loads so highly on crystallised intelligence it is often sufficient to give the Raven's and the Mill Hill tests to obtain a good overall measure of intelligence which includes both fluid and crystallised ability.

Consequently, I shall conclude this section of the chapter by listing and briefly describing some of the best tests of crystallised ability. I shall not go into the details of these tests as I did with the major tests of intelligence. Some of these are useful tests because they have been developed for special populations.

The AH series of tests (Heim *et al.*, 1970; 1974)

Over the years, Alice Heim and her colleagues at Cambridge have developed a series of group intelligence tests which are excellent quick tests of crystallised and fluid ability, for both normal and above average subjects.

The most recent versions are AH2 and AH3 (Heim *et al.*, 1974), parallel versions for average subjects of 11 years of age and above, and AH6 (Heim *et al.*, 1970) of which there are two versions, one for scientists and engineers and another for arts and general students, both tests designed for potential students, actual students and entrants to the professions.

AH2/3

Each test has three sets of 40 items, yielding three scores, verbal intelligence, numerical intelligence and perceptual intelligence, together with a total score.

The verbal reasoning test includes four kinds of items, all of which are typical of verbal reasoning tests and would be expected to load on g_c. These are: analogies, which have been described in Chapter 12 of this handbook; problems, which include following instructions (as in the S-B test); the odd-man-out type of item (also described in Chapter 12); and family relationships – of the 'Y is the second cousin of X whose brother married Z . . .' type.

The numerical reasoning test also uses four types of item: series; problems; analogies, and the four basic rules. These items are self evident except, perhaps, for problems which embrace topics such as the speed of vehicles, football averages, timetables and laying tiles of different colours.

The perceptual test includes items which are diagrammatic and pictorial. The four types of item are similar to those in previous parts of the test: features in common (resemblances); analogies; features in common (differences); and series.

This description of the tests makes it clear that the N and V scores are typical measures of crystallised intelligence while the P score should measure fluid ability.

Reliability The reliability of these scales, test-retest, parallel form and internal consistency, is excellent. Even for the individual scales coefficients are mostly in the high 80s and the full scale reliabilities are greater than .9.

Norms The norms are far short of what is usual in the best American tests but are useful if treated with care. For example 600 11-year-old children and similar numbers, in year groups up to 14 years; 224 technical college students (mostly male); 648 health visitors in training. Sex differences are not clearly dealt with in these norms, but this lack represents the problems British test constructors have in collecting large numbers of subjects.

Validity of the test and discussion

It is clear that the AH2/3 tests are valid measures of crystallised ability and that the overall score is a good measure of intelligence, conceived as a mixture of fluid and crystallised ability. There is a substantial correlation with Raven's Matrices and a surprisingly high correlation with the English and arithmetic scores in two Public School entrance examinations. There are high correlations between the subtests and between the subtests and the total score.

As has been discussed in Chapter 12 of this handbook, Alice Heim is one of the few constructors of intelligence tests to eschew factor analysis (no doubt influenced by Bartlett, who regarded factor analysis as a technical cul-de-sac of psychology). Thus what is really needed to demonstrate beyond doubt the validity of these tests is a factor analysis of the scales with other marker intelligence tests. As it is we have to make do with the correlations. However, these are sufficient and there can be little doubt that AH2/3 are excellent group intelligence tests for the general population which yield scores closely equivalent to the WISC and WAIS.

AH6

This is a similar test to AH2/3 but is a high level test really suited to those capable of success in higher education. The two versions, essentially for arts or science graduates, differ in their mix of items.

AG version   30 items are verbal, 15 numerical and 15 diagrammatic. In this test there are two scores, V and N+D, but the total is regarded as the most important. This total score must be a mixture of crystallised and fluid ability.

SEM version   24 verbal, 24 numerical and 24 diagrammatic items.

The two subtests of these tests correlate between .5 and .7, as would be expected of crystallised and fluid ability tests, but no test-retest reliabilities are given.

Validity of the tests

Although the nature of the items in these tests appears highly similar to that of the easier versions, which are clearly valid, the evidence of validity of AH6 in the manual to the test is somewhat disappointing. Ag correlates .4 with the Raven's matrices but SEM only .193. However this is probably because there was little variance in the sample of 68 Cambridge scientists. Indeed it is likely that all the criterion correlations are reduced through homogeneity of variance, since this a test for high level subjects.

However the correlations of this test with GCE O-level results fits in well with this writer's prejudices about the intellectual content of many school subjects. Thus physics and chemistry are correlated beyond .5 while cookery is actually negative at − .162 (but not significantly) and history has a correlation of .066.

In all the evidence for the validity of the AH6 is insufficient to be confident that it is a valid test. What is presented suggests that it is not as good a test as AH2/3 although high level tests of this kind are hard to validate on account of the restriction of variance. This test should be factored with a wide variety of other tests on a large sample of students. If this were done I think it would load well on both g factors. More research is necessary to establish its validity and to obtain better norms for these are unduly weighted by Oxbridge students who comprise some of the brightest in the country as well as others who have obtained places through advantages of education open only to the rich.

Nevertheless if a test for high level subjects is required AH6 would be a good choice despite the quibbles over validity and norms.

Miller Analogies test (Miller, 1970)

This is a test widely used in America for selection to Graduate School. It consists simply of verbal analogies. Analogies are, of course, one of the best available measures of crystallised ability which is important in graduate work. The test suffers from the disadvantage as a pure test of g that many of the items require knowledge, as well as the necessary analogical reasoning, to solve them. For graduate selection this is reasonable enough but for any other purposes a less culturally loaded test would be more useful.

Watson–Glaser Critical Thinking Appraisal (Watson and Glaser, 1964)

This is another test of crystallised ability (verbal reasoning), designed for graduate recruitment and management selection. It consists of five subtests: drawing inferences from facts; recognising assumptions implicit in statements; drawing deductions from facts; interpretations of statements; and evaluation of arguments.

I do not want to say much about this test, which would appear from the nature of the items to be a good measure of crystallised ability, of which verbal reasoning is an important component. The total score is reliable and it correlates highly with the AH tests (e.g. AH6, .51 and, in one study, .71 with AH4, an earlier version in the AH series of tests). All this suggests strongly that the Watson–Glaser is a valid measure of crystallised intelligence and verbal reasoning.

Because more reading is required to complete this test than is usual for an intelligence test, and because as a result the items do not resemble those of conventional measures of intelligence, the Watson–Glaser is useful where there might be hostility towards psychological testing, as in some selection contexts.

CONCLUSIONS

As was discussed at the beginning of this chapter the measurement of intelligence is one of the oldest branches of psychometric research. Benchmark individual tests have been produced and certain group tests are generally accepted as valid by virtually all psychologists.

The WAIS or WISC scales, Raven's Matrices, the Culture Fair tests plus their vocabulary scales and the AH scales would all adequately measure intelligence. For fluid ability the Cattell Culture Fair and the Raven's Matrices would have to be recommended. For crystallised ability the WAIS and the WISC are still excellent measures, while among the group measures the AH tests, the Watson-Glaser or even the Mill Hill scales would all be more than adequate measures.

However, as was pointed out in Chapter 12 of this handbook, the factor analysis of abilities has revealed more than twenty ability factors and some psychometrists would prefer to measure these abilities separately and thus obtain measures of the higher order factors, especially crystallised ability. It is to the measurement of these primary factors that we now turn.

Chapter 24

Ability, Aptitude and Attainment Tests

As was made clear in Section II of this handbook, although the two intelligence factors account for a considerable proportion of the ability variance, a large number of primary ability factors have been identified and a variety of tests have been developed to measure them. These are, in part, the subject of this chapter. However, it should be recalled that in our chapter on aptitude and attainment tests it was pointed out that the term 'aptitude test' applied to tests of two different kinds of variable: pure ability factors and collections of abilities and skills which happen to be valued in our culture. Some aptitude tests contain both types of variable and such tests are also included in this chapter. Tests of this kind, such as computing ability or clerical aptitude, could well be called attainment tests.

Thurstone Test of Primary Mental Ability (PMA) (Thurstone, 1938; Thurstone and Thurstone, 1962)

This test was based upon Thurstone's original factor analysis of abilities. There is a modern version produced by the test publisher Science Research Associates and this deserves brief description although more recent tests are probably more efficient.

Variables measured Verbal meaning; perceptual speed; number facility; spatial relations; for older children reasoning replaces perceptual speed.

Age range Kindergarten to 12th grade.

Testing time for most ages around one hour, although this can be split into two sessions.

I shall not go into further detail about this test which has been mentioned in honour of its brilliant originator, whose multiple factor analysis lies at the heart of modern psychometrics. However, as Cronbach (1976) and Woliver and Saeks (1986) argue, this test has a number of problematic features, although it measures its factors with reasonable validity. Thus, there is little evidence concerning the validity of the profiles of different factor scores particularly with younger children and for many practical purposes, as in educational and occupational selection, it is these profiles which are most useful and which distinguish tests of separate abilities from those of general intelligence. In addition, the PMA does not measure many of the factors which are generally agreed upon by modern factorists to be the largest and most stable.

The Comprehensive Ability Battery (CAB) (Hakstian and Cattell, 1978a)

Variables measured

1. Verbal ability (V)
2. Numerical ability (N)
3. Spatial ability (S)
4. Speed of closure (Cs)
5. Perceptual speed and accuracy (P)
6. Inductive reasoning (I)
7. Flexibility of closure (Cf)
8. Rote memory (Ma)
9. Mechanical ability (Mk)
10. Memory span (Ms)
11. Meaningful memory (Mm)
12. Spelling (Sp)
13. Aesthetic judgement (E)
14. Spontaneous flexibility (Fs)
15. Ideational fluency (Fi)
16. Word fluency (W)
17. Originality (O)
18. Auditory ability
19. Aiming
20. Representational drawing

The meaning of these factors is mostly obvious and they have been described in Chapter 12 of this handbook. However, the more obscure are described below, together with other relevant comments.

Speed of closure is the ability quickly to perceive a whole stimulus when parts are missing.
Flexibility of closure is the ability to ignore material in a perceptual field and to find key stimuli within it.
Mechanical ability depends upon some acquired knowledge as well as understanding mechanical principles.
Auditory ability is the ability to detect differences in pitch and the ability to remember a sequence of tones.
Aesthetic judgement is the ability to detect adherence to basic principles of good art and design.
Aiming is eye-hand coordination.

Time taken The CAB is divided into five forms. CAB 1: 30 mins; CAB 2: 35 mins; CAB 3/4: 25–30 mins; CAB 5: 40 mins.

Age range 15 years and older.

Reliability This is satisfactory for all scales.

Norms Norms are supplied for American adolescents and adults.

Validity

Hakstian and Cattell (1976b) claim that the validity of the test is high because it was constructed to measure the main ability factors emerging from simple structure factor analyses, as found by Hakstian and Cattell (1974) and Horn (1976), a factor structure which does, indeed, emerge from the CAB. Furthermore correlations with the WAIS are high, beyond .8. All this suggests that the CAB is a valid test.

However, despite the fact that it would appear to be advantageous to measure the most important primary ability factors as well as the broader intelligence factors, and despite the fact that many intelligence tests confound fluid and crystallised ability, the CAB is rarely used outside Cattell's laboratories.

Kline and Cooper (1984c) examined the factor structure of seventeen of the CAB scales (leaving out 18–20 in the list above). They found that the resulting factor structure, six factors obliquely rotated by Direct Oblimin (Jennrich and Sampson, 1966), essentially second orders, fitted the Cattell model of abilities well. Thus all the main factors emerged marked by their hypothesised tests: retrieval, cognitive speed, fluid ability, crystallised ability, memory and visualisation.

One further study deserves brief mention. Cooper *et al.* (1986) correlated the CAB with a measure of inspection time which has been regarded as an objective measure of intelligence. Inspection time is the time required to discriminate reliably two lines of similar length exposed in a tachistoscope or on a computer screen. Brand and Deary (e.g. 1982) have claimed that this is an excellent measure of intelligence, although the samples they used were small and highly skewed. However Nettelbeck (1982) who was one of the first to publish results with this technique (Nettelbeck and Lally, 1976) showed that with a more balanced sample correlations with intelligence tests were small, certainly not sufficient to allow inspection time to be used as a test of intelligence. Cooper *et al.* (1986) showed, not unexpectedly, that inspection time correlated with the speed and visualisation factors of the CAB.

Conclusions

The CAB must be regarded as the best test of the main primary factors and is certainly the one to be used in the exploration of the factor structure of abilities.

The Differential Aptitude Test (DAT) (Bennet *et al.*, 1962)

The DAT is one of the most widely used aptitude tests in the USA measuring a number of aptitudes. As has been pointed out, aptitude refers to pure factors, as is the case with verbal aptitude, for example, and to a culturally valued set of abilities and even personality traits. Clerical or computing aptitude tests would be of this kind. The DAT contains variables of both types.

Variables measured Verbal reasoning, numerical ability, abstract reasoning, clerical speed and aptitude, mechanical reasoning, space relations, spelling and grammar.

Time taken Verbal (30 mins); numerical (30 mins); clerical (6 mins); abstract (25 mins); mechanical (30 mins); language usage (35 mins); space (30 mins).

Age range 12–17 years.

Norms Approximately 50,000 American children were included in the normative sample. However, as Quereshi (1972) has argued, despite this enormous sample, it is not truly representative, although how much this distorts the norms is not clear. What is, perhaps, less satisfactory is the fact the norms are for whole year groups. Thus a child tested just after the relevant birthday may well obtain significantly lower scores than one tested just before.

For users of the DAT in Great Britain, it should be noted that the American norms are obviously not applicable, as is the case in all tests where the influence of the school curriculum is likely to be important. Indeed in respect of all ability tests even British norms are likely to be outdated on account of recent changes in the curriculum and teaching methods. In fact the current (1991) national curriculum changes will mean that many tests will have to be renormed. In a study with the DAT in Devon (Kline, 1971c) I found that the norms, especially at the top end of the spectrum of ability, were misleading. The DAT was too easy, especially the test of mechanical aptitude.

Reliability Both test-retest reliability and internal consistency reliability are high. Most scales have reliabilities beyond .9 and almost all beyond .8.

Validity and discussion of the DAT

It is fair to say that the DAT is a highly reliable test with extensive American norms. However the validity of this test remains a difficulty and this must now be scrutinised. Quereshi (1972) has an excellent discussion of this topic and Kline (1975) has examined the validity of the DAT for vocational guidance in considerable detail.

There can be no doubt that the DAT measures ability. The manual to the test (Bennet *et al.*, 1962) quotes substantial correlations with course grades and with other aptitude tests such as the PMA (Thurstone and Thurstone, 1962), which we discussed above, and with the General Aptitude Test Battery (USA Government Printing Office, 1970) which is scrutinised later in this section of the chapter. However as Quereshi (1972) has argued what is necessary for establishing the validity of a differential aptitude test is evidence of *differential* power. This is where the DAT seems to fail.

Thus, 1700 subjects were followed up eight years after testing and placed in occupational groups. The DAT scores (percentiles) of these groups were then compared. Engineers were the highest scorers on *all* the tests. On the clerical aptitude test they were on the 74th percentile. The clerks on this test were on the 45th percentile. Thus if we were to use the DAT as a differential test we would not have recommended the clerks to be clerks. Furthermore the clerical score was not the best score of the clerks. This means that neither on absolute score level nor profile could the clerks have been predicted to be clerks on the basis of their DAT scores.

As Quereshi (1972) argues, what is needed to demonstrate the differential validity of the DAT are the combinations of scores which differentiate each group and the weights of these scores in the classifications. The fact that the engineers are best at all these tests strongly supports the theoretical position, argued in Chapter 12 of this handbook, that the two g factors are pervasive in abilities. Indeed the positive manifold among human abilities makes the development of a differential test extremely difficult. If the g factors were partialed out of the DAT how much variance would be left? This is the critical question.

Two lines of evidence bear on this point. Quereshi (1972) factored some of the correlations reported in the manual to the DAT. He found that four factors accounted for most of the variance in the test and that some DAT scales were superfluous. He used an orthogonal rotation and, as we have shown in our chapter on rotation, an oblique rotation would have been more likely to reach simple structure and an even more parsimonious solution. However, as it stands, these findings suggest that the DAT is largely measuring a few common factors.

Yet more impressive in support of the claim that the variance in the DAT is largely composed of a mixture of fluid and crystallised ability, are Tables 34 and 35 in the manual to the test. With the Otis intelligence test, a group test of general intelligence, among the male sample the correlations with the DAT scales were: .81 (vr), .69(num), .65 (abstract), .58 (space), .61 (mech), .31 (clerical), .48 (lang). This means that only the clerical speed and accuracy test is relatively free of the influence of crystallised ability. These correlations make it clear that the DAT is essentially an intelligence test and is not differential.

Conclusions concerning the DAT

The DAT is a carefully constructed, reliable, and valid measure of the variables it claims to measure. It is a test, furthermore, with impressive American norms. However, it is difficult to recommend it for use because, as we have shown, despite its name it is not differential. It is essentially a good measure of g, mainly g_c, but also g_f if we consider its abstract reasoning and spatial scales.

It is the fact that it measures the g factors that accounts for its correlations with school grades and the fact that high level occupations contain more high scorers on the scales than low scorers. However, as we have seen, these high g individuals do better at all the scales and even the profiles are affected by the pervasiveness of g.

In brief the DAT is flawed not because of any failures in psychometric methods but rather because human abilities are not differential. Except, possibly, in rare and special cases of artists, composers and other highly gifted individuals, general intelligence, a mixture of fluid and crystallised ability, accounts for much of the variance in human abilities. For this reason general tests of intelligence are to be preferred to differential aptitude tests which are essentially inefficient (because they are long and cumbrous) measures of intelligence.

Other differential aptitude tests

As we have pointed out, the flaws in the DAT do not lie in any psychometric failures of test construction, unless the fact that the authors of the test did not attempt to measure the factors accounting for the test variance is regarded as failure. This means that it is highly likely that other aptitude tests will suffer from this same defect. This is indeed the case. The DAT was examined in some detail so that the problem could be clearly seen.

It would be senseless, therefore, to scrutinise in any detail any other differential ability tests unless, in these cases, there was some particular reason for so doing. One test, however, should certainly receive at least a brief mention. This is the General Aptitude Test Battery, which is the test used by the Department of Employment in the USA for vocational counselling.

The General Aptitude Test Battery (GATB) (USA Government Printing Office, 1970)

Variables measured Nine factors are measured by eight pencil and paper tests and four tests which use apparatus. The factors and their tests are set out below.

G – general intelligence (vocabulary, three-dimensional space and
    arithmetic reasoning)
V – verbal (vocabulary)
N – numerical (arithmetic reasoning and computation)
S – spatial (three-dimensional space)

Note that the general factor is accepted by the authors of the GATB because it consists of measures of these first three primary factors. This G must, therefore, be a mixture of the two g factors with an emphasis on g_c.

P – form perception (tool matching and form matching)
Q – clerical perception (name comparison)
K – motor coordination (mark making)
F – finger dexterity (assemble, dissemble)
M – manual dexterity (place turn)

Items in the tests The items in these tests are similar to those discussed in our chapter on ability tests, at least as regards V, S, N and Q. Some of the other tests are worthy of a brief note.

Tool matching requires subjects to compare pictures of tools; form matching is a pencil and paper form board in which subjects match the shapes in one diagram to the shapes in another; in mark making subjects have to put a special mark into a set of squares, doing as many as possible in a minute; the place test requires subjects to put pegs into holes as quickly as possible while in the turn test the peg has to be inverted; in the assembly test subjects put a rivet and washer into each of fifty holes while in the dissemble test they put the rivets in a bin and the washers on a pole.

Time taken The whole battery takes about 2½ hours. As Cronbach (1976) argues the test is superbly efficient given that it is administered to more than 1,000,000 subjects every year by testers with relatively little training. The pencil and paper tests take only six minutes and the psychomotor tests are so designed that each subject leaves them ready for the next subject to use.

Norms There is a representative sample of 4000 adults in the USA. These are clearly reliable norms. In addition there are norms for a huge variety of occupations (385).

Reliabilities Test-retest reliabilities over varying periods are all high, many beyond .9 and virtually all beyond .8.

Validity and discussion of the GATB

There is a huge amount of data concerning the ability of the GATB to predict success in occupations, mostly as rated by supervisors. There is little doubt that the test scores will correlate positively and significantly with success in many different jobs.

However, the correlations between the subtests of the GATB and with corresponding GATB variables make it clear that there is a large g_c factor accounting for much of the variance in this test. Cronbach (1976), examining the relation of spatial ability to occupational success, notes that the correlations are small and that there is improvement if all scales of the GATB are taken into account. This is tantamount to saying that it is as a measure of g_c that the GATB works best. However it should be noted that the motor tests, which load only to a small extent on the crystallised ability factor, are useful in the prediction of certain jobs where such motor skills are obviously relevant.

Hammond (1984) administered the GATB to 1084 workers in Ireland and subjected a maximum likelihood factor analysis of the correlations to a Direct Oblimin rotation. He found that four factors accounted for the variance: g_c, a perceptual factor, and two correlated motor factors – manual dexterity and finger dexterity. This supports the claim that the motor tests of the GATB are separate from the intelligence factor. We shall say something about tests of such motor skills later in this chapter.

Conclusions

This test is a brilliant example of a test which measures the main ability factors and a number of motor factors simply and efficiently. Nevertheless the extensive occupational data in the manual to the test all suggest that it is at its best as a measure of crystallised ability. This is clearly the case at college level where, regardless of course, all the predictions are non-differential. Thus a composite score – crystallised ability – yields the best predictions. The motor factors are quite useless here, even in engineering. These factors are useful for some jobs but the GATB tests are quick and simple and if these factors need to be measured then longer and more specialised tests are likely to be needed.

Tests of creativity

Creativity tests load on the fluency factor, g_r, discussed in Chapter 13. These tests have been extensively studied by Guilford and colleagues (e.g. Guilford and Hoepfner, 1971) and some of them are available as separate published tests. I shall list them and discuss them together.

1. Consequences (Christensen, Merrifield and Guilford, 1980)

Variables measured   Ideational fluency, originality and flexibility.

Age range   9 years to adult.

Items   Subjects have to write out the consequences of unusual situations, which are then scored for the three variables.

Number of items Two forms of this test with five items per form.

Time taken 20 mins for both forms together.

2. Fluency (Christensen and Guilford, 1980)

Variables measured Word fluency; expressional fluency; ideational fluency; associational fluency. In addition originality and flexibility can also be measured.

Age range 14 years upwards.

Time taken 12 mins for c, 8 mins for a, b and d.

Items Word fluency: subjects have to produce a list of words with specified letter requirements; expressional fluency: subjects have to produce as many words as possible with a given first letter; ideational fluency: subjects have to produce ideas relevant to specified situations; associational fluency: synonyms have to be given to adjectives (form A) and to verbs (form B).

3 Alternate Uses (Christensen, Guilford, Merrifield and Wilson, 1980)

Variable measured Flexibility, but originality and fluency can also be measured.

Age range 12 years upwards.

Items Alternate uses for common objects have to be produced.

Time taken 8 mins for each of two forms.

Comments on all these tests

The origin of all these tests lies in the research into human abilities carried out over many years by Guilford and his colleagues and summarised under the name of the structure of intellect model (Guilford, 1967). However, it has been convincingly shown that this model was vitiated by the Procrustes methods of rotation (Horn and Knapp, 1973). Nevertheless these tests clearly load a second order fluency factor as set out in Cattell (1971) and as is evident from Ekstrom et al. (1976).

If a wide variety of measures of this fluency factor are required then these are the tests to use. They are designed and developed by the researchers who developed the concepts and they have a wealth of research underpinning their validity. This validity, it should be noted, is concept validity, in the sense used by Cattell for many of his tests, for example the 8SQ (Curran and Cattell, 1976), that is there is no doubt that these tests load what is generally agreed upon as a fluency factor. However, the extent to which this factor is associated with real life creativity is far from proven.

The reliability of these tests is generally good, but the short forms are not recommended unless there is no time for both versions. Norms are American so other users must be careful.

Conclusions

As measures of the fluency factor, one of the main second order ability factors, these tests are essentially marker variables. Thus they are ideal for research into the nature of this factor. However their title 'creativity tests' could be misleading and they should not be used as substantive measures of creativity, although they are useful for research in this field.

MUSICAL ABILITY

I shall deal briefly with these tests because they are highly specialised, useful for research into the nature of musical ability rather than as an individual measure *per se*, where most people would like to see actual attainment and performance.

Seashore Measures of Musical Talent (Seashore *et al.*, 1960)

This is the oldest test of musical ability originating from Seashore's (1919) work on musical talent.

Variables measured Pitch discrimination; loudness discrimination; rhythm; sense of time; timbre discrimination and tonal memory.

Items These are presented on a long-playing record.

Pitch Fifty pairs of tones. Subjects have to say whether the second is higher or lower.
Loudness Fifty pairs of tones. Subjects indicate whether the second is louder or softer.
Rhythm Thirty pairs of rhythmic patterns. Subjects have to indicate whether the patterns in the pair are the same or different.
Time Fifty pairs of tones of different durations. Subjects determine whether the second tone is longer or shorter.
Timbre Fifty pairs of tones of different timbre. Subject has to decide whether the tones are the same or different in timbre.
Tonal memory Thirty pairs of tonal sequences. Subjects have to indicate whether these are the same or different in each pair.

Time for the test One hour.

Age range 11 years upwards.

Norms   Norms are based for some tests on large samples (4000) and for others on samples of less than 400. There are norms for two age groups of children and students.

Reliabilities   Most of the KR20 reliabilities are in the region of .7 and .8 but a few are as low as .55. Some caution in interpretation needs to be shown.

Validity

There is little doubt that the test measures the variables it purports to measure. However the extent to which it is a measure of musical talent is still open to doubt, as has been argued by Shuter (1968). Thus, it is clear that these abilities are amenable to training so that to reject a person for musical education on the grounds of low score would be unfair. In addition it is obvious that musical ability demands far more than the skills measured by this test, even though it is difficult to specify exactly what this is. Empirically there is not much support for the validity of this test in that in studies with musically talented groups correlations are sometimes positive and sometimes not.

Conclusions

This test is mentioned because it must be one of the oldest in use. Yet, despite its face validity, it is difficult to recommend it as a measure of musical ability. A problem with this test, for many musicians, is the fact that it makes use of tones and is essentially unmusical.

Gordon Musical Aptitude Profile (Gordon, 1965)

Variables   Eleven: tonal imagery (memory, harmony and total), rhythm imagery (tempo, metre, total), musical sensitivity (phrasing, balance, style and total), total.

Time taken   Around two hours in three sessions. In the tonal imagery and rhythm imagery tests the items consist of pairs of phrases and subjects have to say whether members of the pair are the same or different.

Items   These are on three tapes. In the three other tests of sensitivity, the pairs of phrases differ in terms of musical expression (phrasing), endings (balance) and tempo (style) and subjects have to say which is the better.

Age range   10–18 years.

Reliabilities   The reliabilities are high: about .7 for the subscores; .8 for the subtotals and beyond .9 for the total score. These are high enough for profiles to be used, although with some caution.

Validity

Gordon (1967) followed up pupils over a three-year period. Performance tests and achievement tests were given after each year. Correlations were around the .6 to .7 mark and suggest strongly that this test can predict who will learn an instrument to some effect.

Conclusions

As Thorndike and Hagen (1977) argue this appears to be a reliable and probably valid test of musical aptitude. Its advantages over the Seashore Test probably arise from the fact that it uses musical material as distinct from tones. It would appear to be a promising test, although I would be loath to refuse training to a child who wanted to learn music on the grounds of a low score. The correlations are not that high. In sum this is a test that will predict musical success, at least at the school level.

Wing Test (Wing, 1962)

This is another musical ability test which originated from Wing's (1936) studies of musical aptitude. Although restricted to the UK it deserves a brief mention.

Variables Chord analysis, pitch change, memory, rhythm, harmony, intensity and phrasing. All pieces are played on a piano.

Time taken One hour but the first three subtests can be used as a short form.

Age range 8 years upwards.

Norms In all the norms are based on 10,000 subjects.

Reliability Beyond .9 for the whole test and virtually as high for the first three tests. The individual tests have reliabilities around .7.

Validity

Shuter (1968) has summarised studies of the validity of the Wing Tests. Scores are positively correlated with perseverance in continuing to play instruments, with those successful in training at the Marines' School of Music and members of the National Youth Orchestra, all scoring grade A.

Conclusions

As a straightforward measure of musical ability the Wing Test is probably useful. However, as has been argued previously, the practical utility of such tests is low. They are better suited to the study of musical ability and its development.

TESTS OF MOTOR ABILITIES

In Chapter 13 we discussed the motor abilities and their tests, isolated by Fleishman (e.g. Fleishman and Quaintance, 1984). However as Dunnette (1976b) has shown, the correlations of these tests with real life criteria and even with other purportedly similar tests are low. Thus the motor skill factors are highly specific. For this reason we shall describe tests extremely briefly. We shall ignore the laboratory based measures such as reaction time and pursuit rotor which can hardly be regarded as psychological tests, although they are valuable where specialised measurement is required.

Purdue Pegboard (Tiffin, 1965)

Variables measured Dexterity of two types: finger dexterity and gross hand finger and arm dexterity. Five variables: right hand, left hand, both hands, right plus left plus both hands, and assembly.

Description The pegboard has two columns of holes down its centre. Across the top are four cups: the extreme left and right hand cups contain 25 pins. The cup right of centre contains 20 collars and that left of centre, 40 washers. Pins have to be placed as rapidly as possible in the holes first with the preferred hand then the other. The number inserted within 30 secs is the score. This is repeated for both hands using the two pin cups. The sum of these three scores constitutes the fourth score. The assembly score requires subjects to assemble pins, collars and washers.

Reliability Test-retest reliability is around .7.

Norms There are normative data for various groups of workers of which sample sizes vary considerably.

Validity

As was discussed in Chapter 13 the Purdue Pegboard is a marker factor for the measurement of finger dexterity in the Fleishman list of factors. Thus it must be regarded as a valid test. However, in general, correlations with real life performance are small although in the test manual (Tiffin, 1965) assembly correlates .61 with the production records of proof-machine operators and .47 with supervisors' ratings for packers.

Conclusions

For a measure of finger dexterity this test is about the best there is. Tiffin (1965) suggests that local norms be built up and it may prove useful for selection for certain specific and specialised jobs.

Crawford Small Parts Dexterity Test (Crawford and Crawford, 1956)

Description This consists of a board with three wells for pins, collars and screws. There is a metal plate insert with seven rows of holes for pins and another seven for screws. In Part 1 tweezers are used to insert pins into holes and to put collars over them. In Part 2 screws have to be threaded into holes with a screwdriver.

Scores Two scores: times to complete each task.

Norms Norms are supplied for a variety of occupations.

Reliability Split-half reliabilities for both scores are beyond .9.

Validity

There is not much evidence in the test manual that this test measures much more than a specific factor. However the Part 2 score has moderate correlations with supervisors' ratings of female assemblers in an electronics plant. This test might be useful in selection for some specific tasks but as a general measure of dexterity it is weak, as is the case with most of these tests.

Hand Tool Dexterity (Bennet, 1965)

Description Two vertical boards with holes are attached to the ends of a horizontal board. On one of the vertical boards is a set of nuts and bolts. These have to be dismantled with a spanner and replaced in corresponding holes on the other vertical part of the apparatus.

Score Time taken to complete the task.

Norms Norms are supplied for eight groups – e.g. job applicants, airline mechanics, but numbers vary from 1123 to 50.

Reliability Around .85 (test-retest).

Validity

There are moderate correlations with ratings for a number of jobs, the highest being .51 for female riveters in aircraft construction. As with the other tests, reviewed above, this may be useful for some particular job, although the utility of all these tests of dexterity may have been overtaken by modern automation.

ATTAINMENT TESTS

As was made clear in Section II attainment tests are measures of how much skill or information individuals have acquired, as distinct (but not entirely) from ability tests, which attempt to tap potential. Attainment tests are most widely used, for obvious reasons, in education and sometimes in selection, although here attainment is measured by qualifications. Most university and professional examinations are attainment tests.

As is the case with tests of attitudes (see Chapter 28) a problem with attainment tests is that there are virtually as many attainments as there are activities, with the result that potentially a list of attainment tests might be lengthy in the extreme. However there is a further difficulty which limits the value of attainment tests, namely that in most attainments, especially the important ones which become part of the education system, what can be expected of children and, indeed adults, varies with what is taught. Even in Great Britain it is difficult to devise an attainment test in mathematics which would be fair to pupils taught by various different methods and following different schemes. These problems certainly make it difficult to use American tests in Great Britain and vice versa. Perhaps the only common knowledge, thus allowing attainment testing, is that required for reading and for mastery of a language.

For all these reasons it is difficult to set out a list of attainment tests which would be of much value to a tester, in most fields. Instead I shall set out the demands of a good attainment test, some of which, being so familiar to readers of this handbook, demand no comment.

Requirements for good attainment tests

1. General requirements

High reliability, validity, discriminatory power and well established norms. Of course, if the test has been developed using item response theory it is essential that the item characteristic curves were derived from large samples. All these points have been carefully discussed in Section I of this handbook and no more will be said here.

2. Special requirements

1. Proper coverage of the subject matter. Little needs to be said about this. Clearly the test must cover what the subject should be expected to know and not include material which she or he has had no chance of acquiring.
2. Criterion reference. Some attainment tests may be better as criterion referenced rather than normalised tests. These tests simply require that

certain skills or information have been acquired. To get the item correct is sufficient. Norms are not necessary for these tests although they may be useful. Thus in a criterion referenced mathematics test it might be useful to know at what age most children acquired particular mathematical skills, e.g. being able to solve simultaneous equations.

3. Tests should be recent. Because syllabuses, methods of teaching and the types of materials used to teach various subjects tend to change, even the best attainment tests begin to look old fashioned and may become unsuitable, especially for children. If norms exist these can quickly become out of date.

CONCLUSIONS

In this chapter I have described the best known and most efficient tests of special abilities and aptitudes. From these tests some suitable measures for most purposes should be found. In the case of attainment tests such listing is not possible but the criteria for good tests have been set out instead. In all cases it is important to consider whether intelligence tests, described in Chapter 23, might not be more effective.

Chapter 25

Personality Questionnaires

In this chapter I shall describe the most widely used personality questionnaires which also meet the technical criteria which have been discussed in this handbook. I shall use the same categories, for description, as for the other types of tests.

1. Ai3Q (Kline, 1971a)

Age range 16 years upwards.
Sex differences None.
Norms 2000 sixth-formers and 350 students.
Variable measured Obsessional traits.
Reliability .67.
Validity Evidence for construct validity (see Comments).
Item type Yes–no.
Number of items 30.
Completion time 10 mins.

Comments

This test was originally developed in an investigation of the Freudian anal character (Freud, 1908) in which it was correlated and factored with a number of other personality tests. The method of test construction was initial item analysis followed by factor analysis and location of the factor in personality factor space. It was there shown that this scale was independent of the main personality factors, as measured by Cattell and Eysenck, and was distinct from measures of obsessional symptoms (Kline, 1968a). More recent studies (Kline and Cooper, 1984a) showed that this scale was the highest loading scale on a clear obsessional trait factor, which included the F scale of the authoritarian personality (Adorno *et al.*, 1950) and the dogmatism scale (Rokeach, 1960). Indeed, Kline and Barrett (1983) concluded, from a survey of all the technically sound factor analytic studies, that there were four clear factors in personality questionnaires among normal subjects of which authoritarian personality was one. Ai3Q is a salient variable on this factor.

Ongoing research into this factor, based upon a different test, the PPQ (Kline and Lapham, 1990a) also showed the independence of the obsessional factor from extraversion and neuroticism and at the second order only two factors could be found – obsessionality and neuroticism (Kline and Lapham, 1991a).

Ai3Q discriminates arts from science students (Kline, 1971b) and art students score lowest of all the student groups, which fits the construct validity of the scale. This test seems to be a simple valid measure of obsessional traits.

2. The Californian Psychological Inventory (CPI) (Gough, 1975)

Age range   13 years and above.

Norms   Means and standard deviations of a variety of groups.

Variables measured   Eighteen variables are measured by the CPI.

Do – dominance.	Py – psychological mindedness.
Sy – sociability.	Cs – capacity for status.
Sa – social acceptance.	Sp – social pressure.
Re – responsibility.	Wb – sense of well being.
Sc – self control.	So – socialisation.
Gi – good impression.	To – tolerance.
Ac – achievement via conformance.	Cm – communality.
Ai – achievement via independence.	Fx – flexibility.
Ie – intellectual efficiency.	Fe – femininity.

Reliability   Test-retest reliability varies from .55 to .75, after 1 year. This suggests a reasonable stability.

Validity   Essentially construct validity, arising from the large numbers of studies conducted with this test, but see discussion under Comments.

Item type   Statements to be answered true or false.

Number of items   480.

Comments

The CPI is a widely used personality test and by 1972 there were more than 1000 references to it. Yet I shall not say much about it for a number of reasons.

First, as has been made clear throughout this handbook the factor analytic or any analogous method (such as item analysis followed by factor analysis) of test construction is far superior to any other. This is because if the variables in the field have been properly sampled, factors are psychologically meaningful. This is not the case with the CPI, which was constructed largely through the method of criterion-keying, as described in Chapter 9 of this handbook.

Indeed, the CPI has been called the sane man's MMPI because it is an adaptation and extension of the MMPI (see 9, in this chapter) which was designed for abnormal subjects. Gough decided to construct a test suited for work with normals, using 178 MMPI items and adapting 35 others, while the remainder are original to the test. The aim of the test was to measure traits which were most important in social life and which were likely to arise in any culture.

As has been indicated most of the scales were developed by criterion-keying, items being selected if they could discriminate groups. A few of the scales were developed through item analysis. In fact there are some severe problems with this test.

a. Lack of psychological meaning of the scales   This difficulty has been fully discussed in Chapter 9. However, in the case of the CPI it is particularly acute because, as Cronbach (1959) pointed out, some of the criterion groups were not adequate for their task, a good example being the sociability scale where items were selected which correlated with number of extracurricular activities.

b. Validity of the scales   Cronbach (1959) again points out a statistical weakness in the evidence for scale validity. To establish validity biserial correlations between the scale scores and membership of extreme groups was used. However without the intermediate group such indices can be misleading. Furthermore, if the extreme groups had represented the top and bottom 3 per cent of the sample these biserial correlations would have dropped from around .6 to .2.

c. Redundancy of the scales   Thorndike criticised the fact that the scales of the CPI are far from independent. Thus only four of the eighteen scales do not correlate at least .5 with some other scale. Indeed as S.J. Goldberg (1972) argues factoring the CPI usually yields but four factors and Gough himself (1957) in the test manual argues that the test measures four areas of personality – poise and self assurance, achievement potential, maturity and responsibility, and interests. However, there is little evidence for the validity of these four variables and, given the methods of test construction, it would be pure accident if the scales happened so conveniently to overlap. Nevertheless, it should be pointed out that McCrae and John (in press) claim that the big five can be found in the CPI.

For all these psychometric reasons it is difficult to regard the CPI as a valuable psychological test, measuring the most important personality factors: its use could not be advocated. Indeed that it is so popular pays tribute to the effects of naming scales. The scale titles appeal to intuitive notions of personality, as was intended by Gough, and this outweighs the lack of evidence for their validity.

3. Clinical Analysis Questionnaire (CAQ) (Krug, 1980a)

Age range   16 years upwards.

Sex differences   Yes, but separate norms.

Norms   The CAQ is essentially a test for use with clinical patients. It contains norms for normals and for 'clinical adults and adolescents' which consist of a mixture of patients with various psychiatric diagnoses. These will be discussed in Comments.

Variables measured   Two sets of variables are measured by the CAQ.

Firstly, the sixteen factors of the Cattell 16PF test. These are described and discussed below in our discussion of the 16PF. They will be simply set out here:

A. Warmth.	B. Intelligence.	C. Emotional stability.
E. Dominance.	F. Impulsivity.	G. Conformity.
H. Boldness.	I. Sensitivity.	L. Suspiciousness.
M. Imagination.	N. Shrewdness.	O. Insecurity.
Q. Radicalism.	Q2. Self sufficiency.	Q3. Self-discipline.
Q4. Tension.		

Secondly, these twelve clinical factors:

D1. Hypochondriasis.	D2. Suicidal depression.
D3. Agitation.	D4. Anxious depression.
D5. Low energy depression.	D6. Guilt and resentment.
D7. Boredom and withdrawal.	Pa. Paranoia.
Pp. Psychopathic deviation.	Sc. Schizophrenia.
As. Psychasthenia.	Ps. Psychological inadequacy.

Reliability   The median internal consistency reliability (alpha) of the scales is .6 although it is claimed that the reliability of the factors in Part 2 is higher than this. Test-retest reliability is generally also higher than this. These reliabilities are lower than is desirable but are just about adequate for use of the CAQ with individuals rather than groups.

Validity   See Comments.

Item types   The items, except for scale B, intelligence, consist of statements to which subjects can respond on a three-point scale: yes, sometimes, no; true, uncertain, false; and three choices based on the stem of the question – I prefer friends who are (a) quiet, (b) . . . ; always, sometimes, never.

Number of items   Part 1 has 120 items plus 8 intelligence items in factor B. Part 2 has 144 items.

Time taken   Two hours but longer with depressed patients.

Comments

The CAQ is essentially two tests. The first half measures the Cattell 16PF factors, claimed by Cattell (1973) to account for the variance of normal personality, and the second half measures the main abnormal factors.

Part 1

The 16PF test is discussed later in this chapter. As is there pointed out, there are problems with the factor structure which makes the use of these factors dubious. However, even if it is decided that these factors are psychometrically useful, the measures of them in the CAQ are inadequate, since there are only eight items per factor. The CAQ scales are simply not reliable enough for individual use. This is admitted in part by Krug (1980b) who suggests that, if time allows, the 16PF should be administered rather than the CAQ Part 1.

Part 2

This, of course, is the most interesting part of the questionnaire since it measures the twelve abnormal personality factors, which were fully described by Cattell (1973) and for which there is no other test. These twelve factors are derived from three sources. Psychiatric texts were searched for descriptions of abnormal behaviour – an abnormal semantic personality sphere; items were written to tap factors as they appeared in ongoing clinical research and the MMPI item pool (discussed in a later section of this chapter) was subjected to a joint factor analysis with the 16PF, although item parcels rather than items were used (Cattell and Bolton, 1969). Kameoka (1986) investigated the factorial structure of the CAQ in a sample of 214 students using fifty-six item parcels and some items from another depression scale. Rotating factors by Maxplane and Rotoplot, as advocated by Cattell (1978), he confirmed the factor structure but found that the seven depression factors were more highly intercorrelated than in the original studies.

The reliabilities of the clinical scales are, perhaps, just high enough for individual work, although caution would have to be shown. However the evidence for the validity of these factors is far from convincing. The scores of a small number of clinical groups are presented in the test manual and in general these make sense. Nevertheless, compared with the 16PF test there is a dearth of information about the psychological meaning of these abnormal factors, and it is the richness of meaning which makes the 16PF attractive.

This problem with meaning is not helped by the fact that the term 'clinical' is used for some of the norms when more precise nosological groups are necessary.

Conclusions

There seems little reason to use the first part of the CAQ, except for convenience at the expense of reliability. The second part of the test containing the abnormal factors is certainly worthy of research on abnormal and psychiatric groups but there is insufficient evidence concerning the validity and meaning of these factors to permit the CAQ to be used sensibly in substantive studies.

4. Comrey Personality Scales (Comrey, 1970)

Age range   16–60 years.

Sex differences   Yes.

Norms   365 males and 362 females, all volunteers. No other information in manual.

Variables measured   Eight personality dimensions and two validity scales:

Trust vs. defensiveness.   Orderliness vs. lack of compulsion.
Social conformity vs. rebelliousness.   Activity vs. lack of energy.
Emotional stability vs. neuroticism.   Masculinity vs. femininity.
Empathy vs. egocentrism.   Extraversion vs. intraversion.

In addition there is the V scale, measuring consistency of response, and a measure of social desirability response bias.

Reliability   Split-half reliabilities (corrected by the Spearman-Brown formula, as described in Chapter 1 of this handbook) for the personality scales were all beyond .9 except for the masculinity scale (.87). These reliabilities are highly satisfactory.

Validity   Comrey has made considerable efforts to demonstrate the validity of these scales, but see Comments.

Item types   Statements to be answered on seven-point rating scales: Always–Never and Definitely–Definitely not.

Number of items   180.

Comments

The Comrey scales are particularly interesting for a number of reasons. First, as the manual to the test makes clear, Comrey developed the scales because he felt that the then current factor analytic tests must be at fault in that they all yielded different sets of factors. He cited the work of Cattell, Guilford and Eysenck, all of whose scales are discussed in this chapter. There is no doubt that he identified a serious problem, and as readers of this handbook must be aware, this central problem has not been entirely resolved (see Chapter 15). Furthermore, Howarth (1978) regards this test as one of the best factored personality tests. The use of seven-point rating scales for items, rather than the simple yes–no response certainly increases the reliability of the items.

However there are more important psychometric reasons for examining the Comrey scales which have certain original features.

a. Factored homogeneous item dimensions, FHIDs

In Chapter 10 of this handbook we discussed the problem in factoring items that the reliability of individual items was low thus adversely affecting the precision of factor analyses. To obviate this Comrey put items which were factorially and semantically similar into groups – the FHIDs. These were the variables, rather than items, which were subjected to factor analysis. Generally, there were four items per HID and five FHIDs per scale.

There can be no doubt that the use of FHIDs increases the reliability of the correlation matrix compared with the matrix of inter-item correlations. However it has to be recognised that resulting factors are secondary rather than primary factors because effectively the FHIDs are short scales. Thus I would argue that Comrey's factors are second order rather than primaries. Comrey (1970) tries to counter this by arguing that item factors are pre-primary, being little more than specifics, sets of almost identical items.

b. The rotational procedures

Comrey rotated the factors emerging from the analysis of the FHIDs by his own method – the Tandem criteria. I have not the space to describe this idiosyncratic and interesting approach to rotation but I agree with Cattell (1978) who argued that it was unlikely to reach simple structure.

Nevertheless, interesting or not, all turns on the validity of these scales and their location in factor space. Comrey and Duffy (1968) studied the FHIDs and the 16PF and EPI factors (E and N in the precursor of the EPQ, see Test 7 in this section). Unfortunately they hand-rotated the results so that the reliability and generality of the findings is dubious. However one result was clear cut. The Comrey extraversion and anxiety factors are closely aligned to those of Eysenck and Cattell.

Barton (1973) in research cited by Cattell (1973) carried out an analysis of the Comrey, 16PF and EPI, using the techniques recommended by Cattell, including oblique rotation, for obtaining replicable, simple structure, methods discussed in Chapter 9 of this handbook. Extraversion and neuroticism or anxiety again emerged and Cattell (1973) argued that there was a strong agreement between the Comrey factors and the second orders in Cattell but that the Comrey factors were misaligned because of the failings of the Tandem Criteria as a rotational method. However, since the second orders of Cattell are themselves difficult to replicate clearly yet more factorial study is required. Noller *et al.* (1987) factored the Comrey, the Cattell factors and the EPI using the minimum residual method and the Tandem Criteria for rotation. They found seven factors and supported the validity of the big five factors, which appear to underlie much of the variance in questionnaires and ratings. This was in a sample of 669 Australian adults. Boyle (1989) reanalysed these data and found much the same result, using more orthodox simple structure rotations, although he extracted only six factors, the sixth being a response distortion factor.

In the manual to the test Comrey (1970) claims that there is good agreement between his scales and those of Guilford. However, where this leaves us as regards the validity of the Comrey scales is unclear since, as can be seen in section 8 of this chapter, the validity of the Guilford scales is itself uncertain.

Conclusions

I think it is clear that the Comrey scales, by virtue of their scale construction, are reliable and as second order factors they clearly measure the two largest personality dimensions – extraversion and anxiety. Furthermore some of the other scales, orderliness, trust and rebelliousness, resemble the big five factors that have emerged from ratings (McCrae and Costa, 1987). However the lack of normative data and the fact that it is probable that the factors have not been rotated to the simple structure position suggests that this test should be used for research purposes only and not as a substantive measure. It should be noted, however, that the Comrey factors are stable. Thus Noller *et al.* (1988) working with a large Australian sample found the eight expected factors. Nevertheless, what is required is to factor this test along with the other major personality questionnaires. If this were done it is possible that it would turn out to be a useful measure of the most important second order factors.

5. The Dynamic Personality Inventory (DPI) (Grygier and Grygier, 1976)

Age range   16 years and upwards.

Sex differences   Yes.

Norms Norms for general population, males, females, old and young subjects and a sample of neurotics. Generally numbers rather small and samples unrepresentative.

Variables measured The DPI measures thirty-three variables derived from psychoanalytic theory. These are:

H. Hypocrisy – satisfaction with one's own moral standards, lack of insight.

Wp. Passivity – liking for comfort, warmth and mild sensual impressions.

Ws. Seclusion and introspection as a defence against social anxiety.

O. Orality – interest in food, liking for sweet, creamy food.

Oa. Oral aggression – pleasure in biting and crunching, liking for bitter and strong-tasting food, suggestions of free-floating aggression.

Od. Oral dependence, especially on parents and parental substitutes.

Om. Need for freedom of movement and emotional independence, a reaction formation against oral dependence.

Ov. Verbal aggression.

Oi. Impulsiveness, spontaneity, reactive speed, changeability, emotional expressiveness.

Ou. Unconventionality of outlook.

Ah. Hoarding behaviour – anxious possessiveness, stubborn persistence.

Ad. Attention to details – orderliness, conscientiousness and perfectionism.

Ac. Conservatism – rigidity and tendency to stick to routine.

Aa. Submissiveness to authority and order.

As. Anal sadism – emphasis on strong authority, cruel laws and discipline.

Ai. Insularity – reserve and mistrust, social and racial prejudice.

P. Interest in objects of phallic symbol significance.

Pn. Narcissism – concern with clothes and appearance, sensuous enjoyment of luxury.

Pe. Exhibitionism – conscious enjoyment of attention and admiration.

Pa. Active Icarus complex – the drive for achievement.

Ph. Fascination by height, space and distance, aspirations at the fantasy level.

Pf. Fascination by fire, winds, storms and explosives: vivid imagination.

Pi. Icarian exploits – interests in active exploration, a love of adventure.

S. Sexuality – conscious acceptance of sexuality.

Ti. Enjoyment of tactile impressions, interest in crafts and the creative manipulation of objects.

Ci. Creative, intellectual and artistic interests.

M. Masculine sexual identification in terms of interests, attitudes and roles; or

F. Feminine sexual identification in terms of interests, attitudes and roles.

MF. Tendency to seek roles regardless of their sexual identification.

Sa. Interest in social activities.

C. Interest in children, need to give affection.

EP. Ego defensive persistence – tendency to act with renewed effort in the face of difficulties.

Ei. Initiative, self reliance, the tendency to plan, manage and organise.

Reliability The test manual (Grygier and Grygier, 1976) is difficult to follow. Thus it claims that the mean Kuder-Richardson coefficient of all the scales is .85. However the scale split-half reliabilities are almost all lower than this. In the largest and thus the most reliable sample, only twelve of the DPI scales have reliabilities beyond .7 and two are lower than .4. Test-retest reliabilities are reasonable, around .5 with a delinquent sample.

Validity There is no clear evidence for the validity of the DPI (but see Comments).

Item type Words and phrases to which subjects have to indicate 'like' or 'dislike'.

Number of items 325.

Completion time 45 mins.

Comments

This test is interesting for a number of reasons which make it worthy of note, despite some obvious difficulties. It was developed from another test, the Krout Personal Preference Questionnaire (Krout and Krout, 1954), which purported to measure psychosexual variables but which was almost certainly not valid (Kline, 1981).

Validity of the DPI scales

Kline (1981), in his study of the evidence bearing on the validity of psychoanalytic theory in general, carried out a minute scrutiny of the research bearing on the factor structure of the DPI, together with the other evidence for the validity of its scales, the main findings of which are summarised below.

Although, in the manual to the test (Grygier and Grygier, 1976), some effort has been made to validate some of the scales against external criteria, in this instance this information is not helpful in answering the question as to what these scales measure. This is because even if the scales were validated there is no guarantee that the scales would be unifactorial. Furthermore psychoanalytic theory is sufficiently flexible to allow the possibility of most results.

What are required, therefore, are construct validity studies in which the DPI scales are factored and located in factor space. Stringer (1976) cites a number of factor analytic studies in the test manual but these are woefully short of the standards of adequate analysis, as set out in Chapters 7 and 8 in this handbook.

Indeed, the only study that came near meeting the criteria which we laid down was that of Kline and Storey (1978a). These authors administered the DPI together with the EPQ and the 16PF test (both discussed in this chapter) in order to locate these factors alongside those of Eysenck and Cattell. In addition since, as has been seen, the DPI attempts to measure factors that would not be expected in these scales certain other tests were also put into the factor analysis – Ai3Q, which is also described in this chapter, and the scales of Gottheil (1965) and Lazare *et al.* (1966).

With a study of this size, to factor items would have involved at least 2000 subjects, so we were forced to use factor scales. Fifteen factors were rotated to an oblique position and the emergence of E and N, the usual Cattell factors and the similarity of the DPI factors to a previous small scale study (Kline, 1968b) indicated that simple structure had been found.

There is little doubt that the DPI has little overlap with the main factors, in most questionnaires. Of the fifteen factors three were of interest. One loaded on all the anal and obsessional scales in the battery and Kline and Barrett (1983) argued that this was the obsessional factor which is the third of the questionnaire factors which they were able to identify, in their survey. The other two factors were one of feminine interest and one of masculine interests and attitudes, each loading on DPI scales alone. It is curious that the 16PF test has no such measures, given its basis in ratings of behaviour.

Conclusions

The DPI measures variables separate from those in most personality questionnaires. However there is no good factorial evidence (or evidence of any other type) that the scales are valid. The A scales certainly measure an obsessional factor but this is better measured with a more specialised test. There is some evidence that masculine and feminine interest and attitudes can be measured but whether these are genuine personality factors as distinct from culturally determined attitudinal factors is not clear. Thus there would be little reason to include the DPI in any test battery unless one had unlimited resources of time for testing and computing. If that were the case, then the DPI might be considered as a possible personality test, simply because it does measure variables different from those in more orthodox questionnaires.

6. Edwards Personal Preference Schedule (Edwards, 1953, first edition)

Age range 18 years upwards.

Sex differences See Comments.

Norms There are norms, but see Comments.

Variables measured Fifteen variables are measured, based upon Murray's (1938) needs: achievement, deference, order, exhibition, autonomy, affiliation, intraception, succorance, dominance, abasement, nurturance, change, endurance, heterosexuality, aggression.

Reliability Satisfactory but see Comments.

Validity   Little evidence for validity but see Comments.

Item type   Forced choice (2) items. Subjects have to say which of two statements is the more characteristic of them or which they enjoy the more.

Number of items   225.

Time for completion   One hour.

Comments

This test has been chosen because it has been widely used, for example, by 1979 there were over 1600 references to the test; and because it illustrates the problems of test construction which have been discussed throughout this handbook.

Edwards is best known for his work on the response set of social desirability (Edwards, 1957) which was fully discussed in Chapter 15 of this handbook. Thus the driving force behind this test was the elimination of social desirability, as was pointed out by McKee (1972). To do this items were constructed of pairs of statements, each statement having been equated for social desirability. Subjects had to choose from the 225 pairs.

Unfortunately as McKee (1972) argues, when statements, equated for social desirability, are presented together, small differences in social desirability which inevitably remain become exacerbated, and the problem returns.

Furthermore a more severe problem ensues – namely that by using forced choices between items, the scoring becomes ipsative. Thus each score reflects the relative strength of the needs within each individual. However while this may make the test valuable for counselling and guidance it makes comparison between individuals impossible and the meaning of norms (which are presented in the manual to the test) is dubious. In addition it makes correlations between the scales and with any other tests and, of course, factor analyses, inappropriate. Again reliabilities are boosted in ipsative tests where the scales are not independent.

For all these reasons the EPPS cannot be recommended as a psychometric test despite the ingenuity of the test construction. Even as a test to discuss in counselling and guidance it is difficult to recommend, because there is little evidence of validity, either in the manual or in the huge range of published articles where the validity of the scales is assumed, as Heilbrun (1972) has argued. Indeed that the test has been so widely used bears tribute to the reputation of its author and the psychometric ignorance of its users.

7. Eysenck Personality Questionnaire (EPQ) (Eysenck and Eysenck, 1975)

It should be noted that I shall discuss this version of the test, although there is a more recent one, the EPQR. This is because so much research has been carried out with the EPQ (and there are extensive normative data) that the meaning of the scales and scores is particularly clear. Furthermore the psychological meaning of the EPQ variables should be identical to those of the new version, if it is equivalent. If it is not, then new studies with the test will have to be carried out. The one major claimed point of difference between the two tests will be discussed where relevant.

Age range   16 years upwards. There is a version of the test suitable for children, the JEPQ, which can be used with children of 11 and upwards.

Sex differences   Yes, but separate norms.

Norms   Large number of occupational and abnormal groups, age norms and a general sample of more than 5000 subjects. These will be discussed below in Comments.

Variables measured   Three variables are measured, those claimed by Eysenck to be the most important personality dimensions (e.g. Eysenck, 1967): E. Extraversion; N. Neuroticism; P. Psychoticism. There is also an L scale to screen out those giving socially desirable responses.

Reliability   Internal consistencies are all above .7, many above .8 with the exception of P for normal females, which is just below this. With this exception the reliabilities are highly satisfactory. Test-retest reliabilities, for various groups with the exception of P are all beyond .7, many beyond .9 and thus are highly satisfactory.

Validity   The validity of these scales is the best supported of any personality measure. This support comes from the extensive experimental work, carried out over the years by Eysenck and colleagues, into the nature of these variables and from numerous factor analytic studies. This evidence will be discussed under Comments.

Item type   Simple questions to be answered 'Yes' or 'No'.

Number of items   90.

Time for completion   15 mins.

Comments

a. Norms

The general population norms are based on a large sample of all classes, except the down-and-outs, which probably, as the authors claim, represents the typical urban population. However, the occupational norms are not so satisfactory, although, perhaps, better than nothing. For example, there are only 21 accountants, 29 actors, 19 butchers, bakers, cooks, 9 shop assistants, and 9 physiotherapists. Clearly such samples are not satisfactory for personnel selection or vocational guidance.

The abnormal norms are useful although, again, some of the categories are clearly too small, for example there are only 8 drug addicts and 19 alcoholics.

b. Reliabilities

As was indicated above, these were all satisfactory except for P. However this is due to the fact that the mean score of normal individuals on this scale is low. The mean for females is only 2.63, which means that three or less items are endorsed by more than half the subjects. Since the standard deviation is 2.36, a large number of female subjects must score zero on the P scale. This lack of discrimination of P among normal subjects (men score little higher) has been corrected in the EPQR and this is the main difference between the tests.

Validity

This is the great strength of the EPQ. The factor analytic validity of the EPQ is impeccable. As Barrett and Kline (1980) showed, simple structure rotation of the inter-item correlations revealed virtually complete separation of the items. E, N and P almost perfectly loaded their factors. Furthermore Kline and Barrett (1983) showed that these factors were common to most of the well-known personality questionnaires and that, together with ob-sessionality, these factors accounted for much of the variance in personality questionnaires. Helmes (1989), who has specialised in the structure of the EPQ, demonstrated in an intensive study of the items that only the P scale items were at all weak in a study in which the factors were rotated to a target matrix set out according to the marking keys. However this failing is partly due to the low endorsement rate of some of the P items and has been remedied in the new version of the test. There is little doubt that the factor structure of the EPQ is as it should be.

Powerful as it is, this is not the only evidence in support of the validity of these factors. In fact, there is a vast amount of experimental and other criterion-related evidence supporting the identification of these factors, much of it set out in *The Biological Basis of Personality* (Eysenck, 1967). It is not possible to summarise it in a section of this length and it would not be appropriate in this handbook. Nevertheless the main findings supporting the validity of these factors can be stated.

These factors are not simply groups of intercorrelated items. Extraversion has been related to the arousability of the central nervous system, neuroticism to the lability of the autonomic nervous system and psychoticism to androgen level. Thus the extravert is low on arousal, hence his or her

454   Lists, Descriptions and Evaluations

stimulus hunger, his or her craving for noise and excitement, his or her low threshold for monotony and boredom. The intravert, on the other hand, is highly aroused. Thus he or she likes to be quiet. Almost any stimulation is over-stimulation and is painful. The lability of the nervous system is clearly implicated in anxiety or neuroticism. The rapid mood swings, the sweating, pallor, breathlessness, contractions of stomach, the dryness of mouth, all bear witness to the claim. The fact that males are higher scorers than females on the P scale fits the androgen hypothesis for psychotism but, of course, the evidence here is primarily physiological.

In addition to this the implication of these factors in clinical syndromes, in such behaviour as smoking, learning, political choice and criminality, all point to their theoretical importance. Finally, as befits such physiologically based variables, it has been shown that they have a high heritability index, with around 60 to 70 per cent of the variance determined by genetic factors (Eaves, Eysenck and Martin, 1989). Indeed Heath *et al.* (1989) examined the genetic components in the items of the EPQ and showed interesting item differences in dominance, just for example, and interactions with sex. The results, however, confirmed the importance of genetic factors in the determination of these variables.

Although these factors emerge with striking clarity, it should be mentioned that they do support the claims of McCrae and Costa (e.g. 1985) concerning the importance of their big five factors since extraversion and neuroticism are clearly identical to two of the big five factors and psychoticism would appear to be a mixture. Certainly McCrae and Costa (1985) argue that there is an overlap of the EPI (an early form of the EPQ, without the P factor) and their factors, and Amelang and Borkenau (1982) argue that the big five factors can be found in the Eysenck scales.

Conclusions

The conclusions are clear. If we want a reliable and valid measure of these three basic personality factors the EPQ is about as good as can be desired. It represents a clear marker in personality factor space. Its only flaw, and this mainly affects personnel selection, is that the factors are broad, and that more detail is required for the discriminations that have to be made in job selection. In brief it is a benchmark personality test, and one that supports the ubiquity of three of the big five.

8. The Guilford Zimmerman Temperament Survey (GZTS) (Guilford *et al.*, 1976)

Age range   16 years upwards.

Sex differences   Yes, but separate norms are supplied.

Norms   Profiles or means and standard deviations for seventy-two groups.

Variables measured

G – general activity: energetic, quick vs. slow and deliberate.
R – restraint: serious minded vs. impulsive.
A – ascendance: assertive, confident vs. submissive, hesitant.
S – sociability: friendly, talkative vs. shy, withdrawn.
E – emotional stability: cheerful, composed vs. gloomy, excitable.
O – objectivity: tough vs. tender-minded.
F – friendliness: respect for others vs. hostility, contempt.
T – thoughtfulness, reflectiveness vs. interest in the outer world.
P – personal relations: tolerance of people vs. fault-finding.
M – masculinity: hardboiled, emotionally inexpressive vs. sympathetic, emotional.

Reliability   Table 25.1 sets out the internal consistency reliabilities, the standard errors of the obtained scores and the test-retest reliability (one year) of the GZTS scales (as set out in Guilford *et al.*, 1976).

Table 25.1 Reliability of the GZTS scales

Scale	Internal consistency	SE of score	Test-retest reliability
G	.79	2.5	.67
R	.80	2.2	.74
A	.82	2.5	.53
S	.87	2.4	.71
E	.84	2.4	.71
O	.75	2.6	.64
F	.75	2.5	.65
T	.80	2.2	.58
P	.80	2.2	.64
M	.85	2.3	.80

Source: Guildford *et al.* (1976)

Validity   Considerable evidence for the construct validity of the GZTS is presented in Guilford *et al.* (1976) and this will be discussed in the comments on the test.

Item type   Affirmative statement with a yes–no answer format.

Number of items   300–30 per scale.

Completion time   50–60 mins.

Comments

The GZTS is the final form of a test which had its origins in the 1930s when Guilford was one of the first psychologists to apply factor analysis to personality questionnaire items.

As Table 25.1 indicates, the test is highly reliable and the test-retest reliability over a one-year period is also impressive, given that it is reasonable to suppose that individuals will vary to some extent over time on these variables. The standard errors of scores are certainly small enough to make the test suitable for use with individuals.

There are sufficient occupational norms which are, in the main, based upon reasonably sized samples, although these are American, to make the test useful in vocational guidance and counselling and in industrial psychology. It discriminates well among these groups.

As is usual with personality questionnaires the validity of these scales is the most controversial issue. The handbook to the test (Guilford *et al.*, 1976) presents a large number of factor analyses with other tests as well as more simple correlational studies. The problem here is that correlations tend, naturally, to be small as do factor loadings so that a wide variety of interpretation of results is possible. Furthermore, as was pointed out by Kline and Barrett (1983), many of the samples were too small for reliable factors to emerge. All this means that the mass of data presented in the handbook to the test still fails to illuminate the psychological meaning and thus the validity of the scales.

What is required is to identify these factors in personality space, and to investigate whether the orthogonal structure of these factors is, in fact, the simplest solution. It will be recalled that in Chapters 7 and 8 of this handbook it was demonstrated, following the approach of Cattell, that simple structure was a necessity for meaningful and replicable factors.

There have been a small number of critical investigations of the problem of the meaning of the Guilford factors. Eysenck and Eysenck (1969) investigated this question in a joint study of items in the Guilford scales, the Cattell scales (see 13, below) and Eysencks' EPI (Eysenck and Eysenck, 1965) an early form of the EPQ, but without the P scale. In this study the primary Guilford factors did not emerge although it has to be said that only eight items per Guilford scale were used and, given the problem of item unreliability, this might account for the failure of the factors to load. In addition it is possible that the Promax oblique rotation did not reach simple structure. Thus keen advocates of the Guilford factors might be able to assert that it was these somewhat minor deficiencies which led to failure to find the Guilford factors.

Cattell and Gibbons (1968) administered 424 items from the Guilford and Cattell scales to 300 student subjects. These items were grouped into 68 parcels and rotated to simple structure following the procedures advocated by Cattell – a hand-adjusted Rotoplot (Cattell and Foster, 1963), Maxplane (Cattell and Muerle, 1960), oblique solution, and, in fairness to Guilford, an orthogonal solution.

In this study the Guilford factors did not emerge in the orthogonal solution but aligned themselves with the Cattell factors in the oblique case. Some of the Guilford factors appeared to be identical to those of Cattell; others were a mix of factors. Thus Cattell and Gibbons (1968) claimed that essentially the Guilford factors were similar to those of Cattell but had an apparent separation because they had been rotated orthogonally.

This argument is, however, complicated by the fact that, as shall be seen in section 13 of this chapter, the Cattell factors do not themselves emerge clearly from factor analyses. All that can be concluded from this study is that the Guilford factors are not clear homogeneous factors and on account of this it is difficult to recommend this test for use in the applied context.

A further study, that of Perry (1952) deserves mention. He clustered the scales together, using a graphical procedure, so that essentially he was dealing with crude second order factors. These were neuroticism, social adaptation, energy, intraversion and masculinity. These clusters are interesting because they resemble, to some extent, the big five traits which have been discussed in Chapter 15 of this handbook.

Mention of the big five leads us on to a study by Amelang and Borkenau (1982) who identify these factors within the Guilford system, as they did within the Cattell and Eysenck personality tests.

Conclusions

The Guilford scales are among the earliest personality tests developed through factor analysis. Despite their distinguished lineage and the not inconsiderable body of research into the nature of these factors, it would not seem sensible to use this test as a factorial account of personality. The factors are simply not sufficiently clear.

9. Minnesota Multiphasic Personality Inventory (MMPI) (Hathaway and McKinley, 1967, the original edition)

We shall evaluate this test and its recent offshoot MMPI-2 (Graham, 1990).

Age range 16 years upwards. Although used with normals, there is little variance with such a sample and this test is best used with clinical or psychiatric, abnormal samples.

Sex differences Yes, but separate norms.

Norms Normative groups in test manual and extensive normative data in published literature, especially (Dahlstrom and Welsh, 1960).

Variables measured The standard MMPI measures fourteen variables but more than 200 scales have been developed from the item pool. The standard scales are four validity scales (question, lie, validity and test taking attitudes) plus ten clinical scales:

Hs. Hypochondriasis.	D. Depression.	Hy. Hysteria.
Pd. Psychopathic deviate.	Mf. Masculinity Femininity.	Sc. Schizophrenia.
Pa. Paranoia.	Pt. Psychasthenia.	Si. Social intraversion.
Ma. Hypomania.		

Reliability The reliability of some scales is low, but see discussion in Comments.

Validity See Comments.

Item types Statements to be answered as true or false.

Number of items 566 but various short forms have been developed.

Time for completion 90 mins.

Comments

Eysenck (1989) in the preface to a recent book on the MMPI points out that the MMPI is undoubtedly the most widely used and researched personality test with more than 10,000 published articles, books and chapters about it. In a brief section on the test, all that can be done is to pick out what appear to me to be critical features of the MMPI and to refer readers to further sources of information. Friedman *et al.* (1989a) is certainly a useful reference in this respect. In addition I shall discuss the MMPI-2, which has been developed to overcome many of the difficulties and problems with the original test. These difficulties despite the popularity of the test are considerable and I shall list them briefly.

a. Criterion-keyed construction In Chapter 9 of this handbook this method of test construction, of which the MMPI is the finest illustration, was described and evaluated. It was pointed out that the fact that a set of items discriminated one group from another gave no necessary psychological meaning to the items. Groups might differ on a number of quite different dimensions, and this meant that criterion-keyed scales were empty of psychological meaning. This is a severe problem if we wish to obtain psychological knowledge from testing, as distinct from having an efficient screening procedure.

b. Establishing clear criterion groups This is always a difficulty in developing criterion-keyed tests, particularly so in the clinical field where diagnosis is notoriously unreliable.

c. Overlapping items Scales developed from an item pool can always have overlapping items, unless this is deliberately prevented. Where this is the case it makes correlational analyses and factorial analyses of the scales difficult.

d. Low internal consistency of the scales Some of the best-known scales, developed from the MMPI item pool, are the Harris Lingoes scales (e.g. Harris and Lingoes, 1968). Yet as Graham (1990) shows many of these have alphas which are not acceptable, several being .2 and others around .3. Of the twenty-eight scales only two were beyond .7. With the classical model of test error, discussed in Chapter 3 of this handbook, these alphas call seriously into question what these scales must be measuring.

e. Factors in the MMPI item pool The obvious solution to the problem of the psychological meaning of the MMPI is to factor the items or even the scales, although the scale solution is less satisfactory since one must ask which scales – the basic clinical scales or a selection of those to be found in Dahlstrom and Welsh (1960). In addition there is the problem of item overlap.

In general, it can be said that there are two clear factors in the MMPI (Friedman *et al.*, 1989a), anxiety and ego strength or repression. This is at the scale factor level. These are essentially second order factors. The anxiety factor should surprise no reader of this handbook.

At the item level, the results of factor analyses have been somewhat inconclusive mainly because in many cases no attempt to reach simple structure was made. In terms of the Cattell (1973) criteria for technically adequate factor analyses they were defective. One study, however, deserves note – the research by Johnson *et al.* (1984) who factored the responses to the MMPI of 11,000 subjects. Here the factors were at least statistically reliable. Twenty-one factors emerged which corresponded to the content categories of the items, that is the factors were loaded by items of similar content. This is hardly surprising and the psychological significance and meaning of these twenty-one factors remains unknown. They may be little more than bloated specifics and their validity and meaning would have to be evidenced in factor studies with other tests and by correlations with external criteria. In my view these are the scales which should be investigated rather than the empirically derived scales.

Johnson *et al.* (1984) named these factors (based on the content of the items loading them) and the results are not unexpected: thus there was an anxiety factor (found also at the scale level), a psychoticism factor, extraversion, paranoia, psychopathic deviation, and psychasthenia. These have been picked out because they include three of the main personality questionnaire factors, anxiety, extraversion and psychoticism, while the remaining three factors are found in the other study of the MMPI items, which must be mentioned because it formed the basis of a new test, the CAQ, which was discussed in section 3 of this chapter.

In the CAQ (Krug, 1980a), factors derived by Cattell and Bolton (1969) from a parcel factoring of the MMPI items were set out. These were: paranoia, psychopathic deviation, schizophrenia, psychological inadequacy and psychasthenia. These are different from those usually found in factor analysis of the scales, but the CAQ factors are first orders. Here there was a clear anxiety factor and one of the other factors was tentatively lined up with the repression factor.

From this it is clear that the factor structure of the MMPI items is not well defined. The study by Johnson *et al.* (1984) shows a large number of factors but their psychological meaning is not known. It does appear, however, that, as from the scales, anxiety and extraversion can be extracted.

A study by Costa *et al.* (1985) has gone some way to remedy this factor analytic confusion. They carried out an item factor analysis on 1567 coronary patients. Nine factors emerged: neuroticism, psychoticism, masculinity, extraversion, religious orthodoxy, somatic complaints, inadequacy, cynicism, and intellectual interests. All these factors were highly reliable. Popham and Holden (1991) studied these factors in a sample of forty pairs who knew each other well. Although these factors were again internally consistent there were only modest correlations with ratings by each member of the pairs and test-retest reliability was not good.

These more recent studies have clarified the factor structure of the MMPI to some extent although the validity of these factors against external criteria remains unknown. Costa *et al.* (1986) have claimed that these factors are essentially the big five and if this is so they could certainly be measured more economically.

Conclusions concerning the MMPI

There are very severe problems with the original MMPI and I find it difficult to recommend its use other than as an experimental measure whose meaning has to be discovered, surely a strange argument for a test with more than 10,000 references.

I do not think that this judgement is idiosyncratic, in the light of its vast usage. The fact is, as Cattell (e.g. 1981) has stressed, psychology in general, and clinical psychology in particular, has attracted into it refugees from the hard, numerical sciences. Such researchers have never come to grips with the theory of psychometrics. If they had, as the arguments of this handbook demonstrate, the MMPI with its poor reliabilities, uncertain factor structure and dubious psychological meaning would never have been used. The MMPI was developed before factor analysis was easily computed on a large item pool. In its day it was no doubt splendid but almost half a century later with little evidence for validity, other than a screening ability, it is surely time to turn to personality tests devised on a better psychometric rationale.

Of course, a number of workers with the MMPI have been psychometrically skilled and over the years a new version of the test, the MMP1-2, has been developed. I shall now, briefly, consider this test.

MMPI-2 (Butcher, 1990)

Graham (1990) contains a detailed description of the development and rationale of the MMPI-2 and readers who wish for more information should consult this text. Graham (1990) lists a number of reasons for the development of the new test.

a. Concerns about the original sample on which the clinical scales were based. This was not a representative clinical or normal sample.
b. Problems with item content. Some of the language in the items was obsolete or referred to unknown aspects of the past. For example, the game 'Drop the Handkerchief' is unknown in the USA and was in Great Britain in the late 1950s when I used the test. In addition there was sexist language and references to the Christian religion, bowel and bladder control and to sexuality which were considered inappropriate.
c. The item pool was considered to be too narrow. For example there were no items referring to drugs other than alcohol.

In constructing the new test every effort was made to overcome the four problems listed above and to develop a test which was sufficiently similar to the original to make the huge mass of research done with it applicable, in terms of meaning, to the new test.

The MMPI-2 sample A normative sample of 2600 subjects was tested.

The MMPI-2 items The basis were the 550 unique items of the MMPI. Eighty-two were rewritten to overcome the faults mentioned above and tested to ensure that they were still viable. In addition 154 new items were written to extend the pool. These 704 items formed the new item pool from which, as in the original scale, 567 items were selected on the following criteria. All items in the standard clinical and validity scales were included, as were items needed to form the most important supplementary and new scales. Items were eliminated, as discussed above, if they could be called sexist, or referred to sexual preferences, religious beliefs or bowel and bladder control.

In brief, Graham (1990) argues that there is little change in the new form. On account of attempting to make the MMPI-2 scales as similar as possible to the originals there is still a degree of overlap in the items of the basic clinical scales.

Reliability of the scales The new clinical scales are more internally consistent than the originals but, including the validity scales, only five scales have reliabilities higher than .7. One of them, Pa, is as low as .34 for males. Clearly these scales are still far from being internally consistent.

Factor structure As yet, there have been no factorisations of the new test. However Graham (1990) considers that the factors would be highly similar to those found by Johnson *et al.* (1984).

Conclusions

Almost all the arguments against the original MMPI apply to the new version which is simply a better phrased and better standardised MMPI. The fundamental psychometric objections which have been raised against that scale still apply to the new test. It is a valuable research tool for use in abnormal psychology but an entirely new factored questionnaire might have been very much superior.

10. Myers-Briggs Type Indicator (Myers and McCauley, 1985)

Age range 15 years and above.

Sex differences Yes, but separate norms.

Norms Many different educational groups, of which some are based on huge samples – more than 3000. The manual has more information than almost all other texts.

Variables measured This is not simple and will be discussed under Comments. However it is possible to categorise individuals into the eight Jungian types:

1. extraverted thinking.	2. intraverted thinking.
3. extraverted feeling.	4. intraverted feeling.
5. extraverted sensing.	6. intraverted sensing.
7. extraverted intuition.	8. intraverted intuition.

Reliability Most split-half reliabilities of scale scores are beyond .7 and attempts to provide a split-half reliability for types are around this same figure, although the statistical procedure is dubious.

Validity For a test of this type, to establish validity is difficult. Construct validity is attested by correlations with a variety of other personality tests including some which attempt to produce a similar typology – such as the Gray-Wheelwright (1946), where the correlations in some cases, when corrected for reliability, were greater than 1.0.

Item types 1. forced-choice items (two choices); 2. two words are presented of which subjects choose the more appealing. Thus some scores are ipsative.

Number of items 126 (form G).

Time for completion 30 – 40 mins.

Comments

In addition to the typology, continuous scores, useful for parametric statistical analysis, can be obtained from this test. However I shall not discuss these at any length, because the interest of this measure stems from the fact that it claims to be able to classify individuals into their Jungian typology. Indeed this is the main reason this test is scrutinised in this chapter since, as is evident from the bulk of this handbook, generally only factor analytic tests are worthy of consideration. The other reason for discussing this test is that, in Great Britain at least, it is a popular measure for personnel selection.

Before discussing the ability of the MBTI as a typological instrument it should be noted that the ubiquitous big five factors are claimed to account for the variance in this test by McCrae and Costa (1989a).

Thus the critical question is whether the MBTI does classify individuals into types or not. If it does we might still ask to what extent these types resemble those suggested by Jung. Even if they did not, however, it might still be the case that the typology was valuable for selection or vocational guidance.

Mendelsohn (1965), Sundberg (1965) and Carlyn (1977) have all surveyed the evidence for the validity of this test and have been forced to conclude that it has not been proved, at least as regards the continuous scores. Certainly the most extensive study (Stricker and Ross, 1964) in which the MBTI was correlated with a number of other tests, notably the MMPI, the CPI (both discussed in this chapter) and the Strong Interest Blank (discussed in Chapter 27), produced no convincing support for the validity of the scales. This is a position which is taken by Coan (1979). However, there are problems with the ipsative scales.

However Coan (1979) argues that the differences in scores between the different educational groups are supportive of the validity of the scales in a somewhat general way and this is what has made the test appealing to the industrial user.

Stricker and Ross (1964) also investigated the validity of the typologies in the MBTI, by examining the distributions. They could find no convincing evidence for true typologies. However a study by Broadway (1964), which can be found in Vetter and Smith (1971) used a different approach to validity. He had twenty-eight Jungian analysts classify themselves into types. The result was full agreement between self classification and the MBTI scores for intraversion–extraversion and for sensation–intuition there was a better than chance result. However, impressive as this may seem, this is not really support for the validity of the MBTI. It is quite possible to classify oneself as an extravert or intravert without there being a typology. The classification could simply represent one's position above or below the mean of a continuous distribution.

Conclusions

Without clear evidence that the MBTI can really classify individuals into the eight Jungian groups, the reason for using the MBTI, which is not measuring clear factored variables, becomes hard to justify. That the continuous scales make interesting discriminations among occupational groups is not doubted but this is not sufficient to make the test valuable except for further research into what these scales actually do measure. Certainly there is little other evidence for Jungian personality theory such that its theoretical rationale makes the test attractive. In brief it is an interesting and original personality test, like the Dynamic Personality Inventory, which needs factorial explication. Finally it might be interesting to submit the MBTI to a modern multivariate configural frequency analysis (von Eye, 1990) which is specially designed to detect types.

11. The NEO Personality Inventory (Costa and McCrae, 1988a)

This is fully described in Costa and McCrae (in press) and by McCrae and John (in press).

Age range Adults.

Variables Neuroticism, extraversion, openness, agreeableness and conscientiousness – the big five (see Chapter 15).

Items 180 items, balanced for acquiescence: 48 items in each of N,E and O scales, 18 in A and C scales, which have been recently revised (Costa *et al.*, in press).

NEO Personality Inventory – R. There is a special form of the NEO, the R form, in which the items are phrased in the third person, thus making it an observer, rather than a self-report, inventory. This can be used for validation studies, although even if self and observer reports agree, this demonstrates reliability rather than validity. The factor structure and reliabilities of this R form are highly similar to the standard form.

Norms A large adult sample.

Reliability Internal consistency: .76 to .93; test-retest reliability (N, E and O) over a six-year period: .82 to .83.

Time for completion 30 mins.

Validity See under Comments.

Comments

a. Rationale of the test As was pointed out in Chapter 15, studies of ratings and results from the simple-structure factoring of personality questionnaires all point towards a five-factor description of personality traits. As Digman (1979; 1990) makes clear the main protagonists of this position are McCrae and Costa and the NEO Personality Inventory is one of the results of their research – an inventory designed to measure the 'big five'. This is an inventory which, straight from the horse's mouth, should be taken seriously.

b. Construct validity The evidence for the validity of this test comes from a series of papers in which, effectively, these factors were located relative to the factors in a wide variety of personality tests. Thus Piedmont *et al.* (1991) factoring the Gough Adjective Check List and including the marker scales for the NEO developed by John (1990) in large samples of students (N=414) and adults (N=445) were able to recover the five factors, thus supporting the claim that these underlie much personality variance. Costa *et al.* (1985) carried out an item factor analysis of the MMPI on 1567 normal (coronary) patients. Nine internally consistent factors were extracted which, in a further study (Costa *et al.*, 1986) correlated as predicted with the NEO. From this Costa *et al.* argued that the NEO five-factor structure accounted for much of the variance in the MMPI (see test 9). It should be pointed out that these MMPI factors were investigated by Popham and Holden (1991), in a study which was discussed in our comments on that test above. They found that these scales were reasonably reliable but self ratings did not agree with ratings by others who knew them well, in a small sample of forty pairs. McCrae and Costa (1985) showed that the five factors of the NEO could be found in the EPI (Eysenck and Eysenck, 1965) and a measure of P, thus effectively demonstrating that the EPQ variance was similar to that of the NEO. Costa and McCrae (1988b) showed that the NEO factors accounted for much of the variance on the PRF (see test 13) as they did with the Myers-Briggs Type Indicator (see test 10) (McCrae and Costa, 1989a). There were similar results with the Californian Psychological Inventory (Costa and McCrae, in press). All these studies therefore support the claim that the five factors of the NEO are indeed ubiquitous among some of the best-known questionnaires. Indeed only the study by Livneh and Livneh (1989) with the Adjective Check List failed to confirm the big five.

c. Are these factors the big five factors? To some readers the studies of the NEO, cited in the previous paragraph, might appear to be overwhelming proof of the validity of the test. However this is not so. It could be the case that the five factors of the NEO did account for variance in all these other personality tests, yet they were not the factors claimed by their authors. Similarly the fact that self and other ratings on the NEO agree does not support the validity of the test. It is evidence for nothing more surprising than that self report and observations of others on almost identical items agree. It still does not demonstrate what these items measure and, given that social desirability was ruled out, there is little reason why there should be differences.

For this reason the study by Costa and McCrae (1988b) is of considerable interest. In this study an attempt was made to rotate factors to maximise convergent and discriminant validity – validimax rotation. In this technique all depends on the external criteria employed. If these are not good the process *ipso facto* fails.

In validimax rotation the aim is not simple structure but to obtain factors with a satisfactory pattern of external correlations. In this particular study the aim was to maximise the correlations of the NEO factors with the NEO R factors, completed by peers and spouses, with adjective check list measures completed by peers and self report, with self Q sorts and biographical factors. In a sample of nearly 1000 subjects the construct validity of the NEO scales was supported.

However, ingenious as this method is, a few caveats should be made. In the first place, as has been argued previously, Procrustes rotations are able to hit target matrices even where there is no support in the data. Furthermore there is no real evidence of validity from correlations with the R form of the NEO since the same errors could affect both scales and to some extent the same applies to the other external criteria, which had been developed, in any case, to correlate with the NEO.

Conclusions

The NEO is by far the best-developed measure of the big five and there seems little doubt that these are the main factors among traits. Nevertheless there still is a need for construct validity beyond correlations with other highly similar measures. However this is as yet the best test of the big five (but see the next scale).

12. The Professional Personality Questionnaire (PPQ) (Kline and Lapham, 1990a)

Age range   18 years upwards. The test was designed for graduate personnel selection.

Sex differences   Eliminated in test construction.

Norms   Large sample undergraduate norms and some small professional groups.

Variables measured   This test attempts to measure the big five variables, discovered in ratings of personality (McCrae and Costa, 1987). These are: conscientiousness, conformity, extraversion, anxiety and tough-mindedness. In addition there is a validity scale (V).

Reliability Alphas, for the five scales, range from .70 to .78. These are satisfactory reliabilities.

Validity The test manual (Kline and Lapham, 1990b) attempts to demonstrate construct validity by an examination of occupational and educational differences on the scales and by a factor analytic study with the EPQ (Kline and Lapham, 1991a), but see Comments.

Item type All items have the following format: 'Ideally I would like to work in a job setting where . . . ' Each item portrays a situation to which subjects have to respond 'Yes' or 'No'.

Number of items 68.

Time for completion 15–20 mins.

Comments

a. Rationale of the test As was pointed out in Chapter 15 of this handbook, in personality questionnaires there are generally four higher order factors, extraversion, tough-mindedness, anxiety and obsessionality, factors which have a remarkable resemblance to the five factors usually found in ratings. Indeed the similarity is even more striking when it is realised that conformity and conscientiousness are both aspects of obsessionality. This is the theoretical background to the choice of variables in the PPQ. These would appear to be the factors which would account for the most variance.

b. There was one further aspect to the development of the PPQ. This concerned the form of the items which was deliberately selected to appeal to the graduate entrants to jobs for whom the test was designed. Many personality test items are unsuited to this purpose and subjects object to being asked to respond to items such as 'My heart is beating when I wake up' or 'I would like to drink blood'.

c. Validity of the test In the manual to the test Kline and Lapham (1990b) show that the PPQ items load their respective five factors in a rotated Direct Oblimin (Jennrich and Sampson, 1966) simple structure factor analysis. However, to support the validity of the factors the PPQ and the EPQ (Eysenck and Eysenck, 1975) were subjected to a rotated factor analysis (Kline and Lapham, 1991a). The results of this study were unexpected. Thus one factor emerged which loaded the anxiety scales of both tests at one pole and the anxiety scales of both tests at the other. While this supports the validity of these PPQ scales, it is quite contrary to Eysenck's theory where these two factors are supposed to be independent. As a further check, Paul Barrett rotated the original EPQ standardisation data and obtained the same result.

These are strange findings whose replication ensures that they are not the results of chance or artifact. While their import for psychological theory is beyond the scope of this chapter, the similarity of loadings for the EPQ and PPQ extraversion and neuroticism variables supports the validity of these scales.

In the manual to the test it was shown that various occupational groups and educational groups (members of different faculties) scored significantly differently on some of the PPQ scales. Some of these differences supported, to a modest extent, the validity of the scales. For example social workers and therapists were the most tender-minded group while engineers were the most tough-minded, findings which are in accord with the occupational profiles in the handbook to the 16PF test.

d. The V scale   The V scale is based on inconsistency of response to items which are identical other than in being positively or negatively worded. A high score is considered to be evidence that the test has not been properly completed for whatever reason. A study of the validity of the V scale (Kline and Lapham, 1991b) showed that the scores on four of the five personality scales of those with different scores on the V scale were significantly different.

Conclusions

Far more research is needed with the PPQ but there is some evidence for its validity, and in terms of items, it is more suited to personnel selection than are many questionnaires.

13. Jackson Personality Research Form (PRF) (Jackson, 1974)

Age range   13 years and upwards.

Sex differences   Yes, but separate norms.

Norms   Adults, students, adolescents, military samples and psychiatric patients. For the shorter Form E the psychiatric norms are not available in the manual.

Variables measured   The PRF is based on the theory of needs and presses, described by Murray (1938). There are various forms of the PRF but this discussion concerns Form E, which contains all the scales developed by Jackson, but in the shortest possible form and with language simplified to make the test more generally applicable. The twenty-two variables are:

Abasement. Meek, self-accusing, subservient.

Achievement. Striving, purpose- ful, aspiring.

Affiliation. Loyal, warm, friendly.

Aggression. Irritable, threatening, antagonistic.

Autonomy. Free, independent, unconstrained.

Change. Inconsistent, fickle, wavering.

Cognitive structure. Precise, exacting, meticulous.

Defendence. Self-protective, justifying, suspicious.

Dominance. Controlling, domineering, forceful.

Endurance. Persistent, steadfast, persevering.

Exhibition. Colourful, ostentatious, flashy.

Harm-avoidance. Fearful, careful, timorous.

Impulsivity. Rash, spontaneous, reckless.

Nurturance. Sympathetic, helpful, benevolent.

Order. Neat, systematic, disciplined.

Play. Playful, jolly, frivolous.

Sentience. Aesthetic, responsive, enjoys physical sensations.

Social recognition. Approval seeking, courteous, proper.

Succorance. Trusting, ingratiating, seeks support.

Understanding. Reflective, curious, analytical.

Desirability. Presents a favourable self-picture on test.

Infrequency. Responds in implausible or pseudo-random manner on test.

Reliability Split-half reliabilities are satisfactory. Ten of the scales are lower than .7 and two of these are lower than .6. This is impressive given the brief length of the scales.

Validity See Comments.

Item type Self-descriptive statement of the true–false format.

Number of items 352.

Time for completion 45 mins – one hour.

Comments

In the manual to the Personality Research Form (Jackson, 1974) Jackson argues that Form E is the version of the test that should be most widely used since it has been made easier to understand and it is briefer than the earlier forms – which is the reason that it is discussed here.

The items in Form E were selected from the 880 items which comprised Forms AA and BB of the original PRF. Thus to understand the Form E items it is necessary to discuss, briefly, the construction of the original scales. In fact there are a number of interesting points about the construction and validity of this test which are set out below.

a. Choice of variables The variables used were the needs of Murray

(1938). However no rationale for choosing this set of variables other than that they were comprehensive and not abnormal were given. Since there is little independent evidence in support of this analysis this was a strange choice, which could only be justified by strong evidence of validity.

b. Item analysis Item analysis, biserial correlations of items with their purported scales, was used. However, the biserial correlations with certain other scales, including social desirability measures, were also computed and items had to have higher correlations with their own scales than with these if they were to be included in the final test. These procedures should reduce inter-scale correlations, and the influence of social desirability.

These methods of item analysis make the test about as effective as it could be. Nevertheless it is clear that factor analysis would be a yet more efficient method and it is curious that it was not used in the original test construction.

The 880 items thus selected for the original forms of the PRF formed the item pool for Form E.

c. Construction of form E Item analysis was used to reduce the item pool but certain improvements were put into practice. If a scale was sufficiently reliable it was retained, and items on it had to have p values between .2 and .8, as advocated in Chapter 10 of this handbook. In addition items had to show higher correlations with their own scales than with a number of other related scales. Since the majority of items met these hurdles a differential reliability index was developed which subtracts the variance associated with social desirability from scale variance of the item.

d. Further refinements To improve further the efficiency of the scales special efforts were made to reduce scale intercorrelations. An item efficiency index was developed which took account of the biserial correl-ations of an item with its own and all other scales, and the correlations between these scales.

Statistically ingenious as these procedures are, it is difficult to see what they gain over a factor analysis of these items.

e. Validity of the scales It is clear from the comments up to this point that the PRF has been constructed with considerable psychometric skill. Hogan (1978), indeed, regards it as a marvellous example of test construction. Yet, as Kline and Barrett (1983) argued, it is difficult to justify the attempt to measure the Murray variables and the item analytic methods are indisputably clumsy.

What is needed is good evidence for the validity of these scales. Yet search the test manual how you will there is almost no evidence of validity presented, other than correlations with ratings for the original forms of the PRF. Although these are high it reflects little other than that the items of the PRF are face valid and thus, providing subjects are honest, correlations with ratings are not surprising. The PRF scales are psychometrically refined and reliable scales but measuring what?

To this question the factor structure might provide the answer and the relation of the factors to those in other tests would also be informative. Nesselroade and Baltes (1975) factored the PRF and the HSPQ (see 13 below) in a large sample of adolescents, using technically adequate methods of factor analysis, although they factored scales rather than items. This study could not be said to confirm the validity of the PRF in that eight factors were found, which are of course second orders. These are conscientiousness, ascendance, independence, aggression, aesthetic-intellectual social contact and one factor which could not be named.

Furthermore of the HSPQ scales only those related to the anxiety factor and intelligence, which is not included in the PRF, did not correlate significantly with the PRF factors, while, conversely, only five of the PRF scales failed to correlate with the HSPQ.

It is not easy to draw any simple conclusions from this study, despite its large sample size and its technical proficiency. There are many reasons for this, of which the most important will be discussed. First there is the problem of the meaning of the Cattell factors. Although Cattell (e.g. Cattell, 1957) regarded them as a reference set of personality factors, as is clear from our discussion of the Cattell tests in this chapter, this claim cannot be supported. This makes identification of the factors in this study difficult. The second major difficulty concerns the factoring of scales rather than items. The latter would have been more valuable, at least for answering our question.

Nevertheless some conclusions can be drawn. The first is that there is considerable overlap between the Cattell and the Jackson tests. Secondly it is clear that extraversion and conscientiousness, two of the most ubiquitous personality factors in questionnaires, again emerge. Anxiety, however, seems to be absent from the PRF and this seems to be an important omission. In brief, it would appear that, as is the case with so many personality questionnaires, the second order factors are more robust than the primaries, although as a test of these second orders the PRF is lacking because there appears to be no anxiety factor.

Digman (1979) supports this conclusion. He argued that the four second order factors in the HSPQ were highly similar to four of the big five and showed that these correlated significantly and positively with the PRF scales.

Another study which reports a factoring of the PRF is that of Guthrie et al. (1981) in a sample of Filipino students. Six factors accounted for the variance – impulsivity, endurance, abasement exhibitionism, nurturance, succorance and avoidance of harm – factors which were also found among comparable American and French samples. Of these impulsivity usually emerges in questionnaires but little more can be said about these factors given the problems of cross-cultural testing, although it is encouraging to note that these factors were stable in the three groups.

Costa and McCrae (1988b) in their endless search for the big five found them, as they always do, among the scales of the PRF. This indicates, as might be expected, that the variance in this test is not much different from that of the other leading personality inventories, reviewed in this chapter.

Conclusions

The PRF is a cleverly constructed test. However its lack of factorial clarity, its idiosyncratic theoretical base, and the fact that the scales have something in common with the Cattell set do not provide, despite its popularity, strong grounds for its use.

14. The 16 Personality Factor Test (Cattell, Eber and Tatsuoka, 1970)

Age range   16 years upwards.   However, it must be noted that this test has several variants, designed for younger age groups. These are:

The High School Personality Questionnaire (Cattell and Cattell, 1969a) – 12 to 15 years.

The Child's Personality Questionnaire (Porter and Cattell, 1963) – 8 to 11 years.

The Early School Personality Questionnaire (Coan and Cattell, 1966) – 6 to 7 years.

The Pre-school Personality Quiz (Cattell, 1957) – 4 to 6 years.

My description and discussion will deal mainly with the adult version.

Sex differences Yes, but see norms below.

Norms The 16PF test has separate norms for males and females. The American edition has general population norms for men and women of around 2000 subjects and the British importers of the test, NFER, have British norms. In addition there are norms for a very large number of occupational and clinical groups, although in some cases the numbers in these samples are smaller than is desirable.

Variables measured The 16PF test, as is fully described in Cattell (1957), measures the factors shown by Cattell to account for the most variance in the personality sphere. These factors are all bipolar and although Cattell gives them technical names I shall give their descriptive titles here. The primary factors are:

A. Reserved, detached vs. outgoing, warmhearted (high score on the right).
B. Low crystallised intelligence vs. high crystallised intelligence.
C. Emotionally unstable vs. emotionally stable.
E. Humble, mild vs. assertive, dominant.
F. Sober, taciturn vs. happy-go-lucky, enthusiastic.

G. Expedient, disregards rules vs. conscientious, persistent.
H. Shy, timid vs. venturesome, uninhibited.
I. Tough-minded, self-reliant vs. tender-minded, sensitive.
L. Trusting vs. suspicious.
M. Practical, down-to-earth vs. imaginative, bohemian.
N. Forthright, artless vs. shrewd, acute.
O. Self-assured, secure vs. guilt prone, apprehensive.
Q1. Conservative vs. radical.
Q2. Group dependent vs. self-sufficient.
Q3. Undisciplined, lax vs. self-sufficient, resourceful.
Q4. Relaxed, tranquil vs. tense, frustrated.

These primary factors are correlated and a number of second order factors can be measured:

1. Intraversion vs. extraversion.
2. Low anxiety vs. high anxiety.
3. Sensitivity, emotionalism vs. tough poise.
4. Dependence vs. independence.

Most of these variables are measured in the other tests for younger subjects together with factors such as D, excitability and J, active vs. passive, which are only reliably found in children.

Table 25.2 Test-retest reliabilities and the parallel form reliabilities of the 16PF Test

Test-retest reliability		Parallel form (a with b)
A.	80	57
B.	43	49
C.	66	54
E.	65	52
F.	74	61
G.	49	47
H.	80	71
I.	85	47
L.	75	16
M.	67	35
N.	35	21
O.	70	51
Q1.	50	26
Q2.	37	40
Q3.	36	33
Q4.	66	37

Source: These figures are taken from the handbook to the 16PF Test (Cattell *et al.*, 1970)

Reliability   The manual to the test (Cattell *et al.*, 1970) includes a number of different studies of reliability. Two points need to be made. Cattell, alone among the leading psychometrists, does not believe that internal consistency reliability should be high and as a result he quotes no figures. I shall give in Table 25.2 typical test-retest reliabilities for the 16PF and also parallel form reliabilities.

Validity   Evidence for construct validity (see discussion).

Item type   Items are trichotomous, with a warning to use the middle category as little as possible. Some items offer a choice of three responses, others are of the yes, uncertain/in-between/occasionally, no/never type.

Number of items   187.

Completion time   35–45 mins.

Comments

The 16PF test represents the result, in questionnaire form, of Cattell's prodigious factor analytic researches into personality and motivation over virtually half a century. This work has been superlative in the breadth of its conception and in the development of sophisticated statistical, especially factor analytic, methods.

Furthermore the 16PF test has been extensively used in both research and occupational and clinical psychology with the result that there is a huge body of empirical, factual knowledge about all the scales in this test. Thus the scales are especially meaningful in a way that tests without such a body of research never can be. The meaning of the 16PF variables has been fully described and explicated in the handbook to the test (Cattell *et al.*, 1970) and in Cattell (1973) and Cattell and Kline (1977).

This depth of psychological meaning makes the 16PF test particularly useful for research into personality and the test can be valuable as a factorial framework into which other tests can be located as evidence of their construct validity.

Nevertheless despite the impeccable psychological provenance of the 16PF test, and the family of tests which it has spawned for the needs of younger subjects, a number of warnings need to be given about its use.

a. Low reliability

Despite the claim by Cattell *et al.* (1970) in the handbook to the test that low reliability is inevitable when one is measuring a broad variable, there is no escaping the deleterious consequences, for the psychological tester, of low reliability, as set out in the classical theory of measurement, which was discussed in Chapter 3 of this handbook. The psychometric answer to Cattell's argument is that if the universe of items is so broad that it is impossible to produce one homogeneous scale it is better to split it into two correlated but reliable scales.

This being the case it must be said that the reliability of many of the 16PF scales is too low, certainly for individual use, as can be seen from Table 25.2. If we take .7 as the minimum reliability to use a test with individuals, as distinct from research on groups, it is clear from the table that ten scales fail to meet this criterion. N and Q3 are extremely low and it would hardly seem safe to use them at all.

b. Low parallel form reliability

We saw in Chapters 1 and 3 of this handbook that increasing the number of items should increase the reliability of a test. Thus one way round the problem of low reliability is to use two forms of the test. However, as is clear from Table 25.2, in the case of the 16PF this will not do. Thus the fact is that the forms are not truly parallel. I would be unhappy using a composite score of two scales which correlated less than .7. It makes little sense. Even on this modest criterion only one scale, H, venturesomeness, could be used. Some of the other correlations are so small that one is forced to conclude that the forms are measuring different variables. If this is so one or both forms of the 16PF must be invalid.

c. Validity of the test

There has always been controversy over the factor structure of the 16PF test. Eysenck and Eysenck (1969) failed to find the factor structure in a study involving the Eysenck, Cattell and Guilford factors. However, as was pointed out by Kline (1979), the number of items used in the research was such as made the emergence of the primary factors somewhat unlikely. Indeed, Cattell (e.g. 1973) argued that failure to obtain his factor structure both from the items from the 16PF test and from other item sets used by Guilford and Comrey, just for example, was due to poor factor analytic methodology. In essence, the failure to reach simple structure, due to the inefficient rotation of the wrong number of factors, was the main cause of error. The factor analytic methods advocated by Cattell (1973; 1978) have been fully described in this handbook.

I was convinced by this argument until I undertook a series of studies of the 16PF and EPQ tests with Paul Barrett (Barrett and Kline, 1980; 1982c), the results of which together with many other researches were summarised in Kline and Barrett (1983). They found that simple structure analyses of the Cattell items yielded seven factors which were each composed of items from several putative factors and were thus difficult to interpret. In addition many items loaded more than one factor. At the second order level extraversion and anxiety were clear cut. From their study of other factored questionnaires Kline and Barrett (1983) concluded that four second order factors might be found in questionnaires among normal subjects, the two factors in the Cattell questionnaires, obsessionality and tough-mindedness. Before, however, concluding that the 16PF is a useless test a few points need to be made about this research.

First, it is important to note that this work was not susceptible to the normal criticism of Cattell, that is it did not reach the technical standards necessary for obtaining simple structure. In fact we were careful to follow all the important rules, defined by Cattell, for adequate factor analyses, a good ratio of subjects to variables, the Scree test for the number of factors, oblique rotation with hyperplane count. Indeed we even attempted to find the sixteen factors through confirmatory analysis. Our results forced us to conclude that the primary factor structure of the 16PF test did not consist of sixteen factors, as was claimed in the test manual.

Incidentally it should be pointed out that Barrett and Kline (1980) used a precisely similar methodology with Eysencks' EPQ (Eysenck and Eysenck, 1975) and extracted three factors from the items which loaded almost exactly as designed, thus demonstrating that the factor analytic techniques were appropriate.

All this raises two further questions concerning the utility of the 16PF test. The first was discussed by Howarth (1976). He argued that perhaps the weakness of the factor structure of the 16PF arose from the fact that in the initial studies of ratings of personality the wrong number of factors were identified. If this were so, this would account for the failure to obtain the factors since the 16PF questionnaire was designed to measure these rating (L) factors (Cattell, 1957). There is some good support for this claim, in that, as has been discussed through this chapter, recent, carefully conducted studies of ratings have converged on the big five (McCrae and Costa, 1987) – tough-mindedness, openness to experience, conventionality, extraversion and anxiety. It should not escape notice that these factors are highly similar to the second orders which emerged from most questionnaires in the study by Kline and Barrett (1983). Indeed Noller *et al.* (1987) and Boyle (1989), who reanalysed the same data, argued from factoring the Comrey scales, the 16PF and the EPI that the reliable variance in the Cattell test was that of the big five factors, a conclusion also argued by Amelang and Borkenau (1982).

Thus it appears that it may well be the case that the original twelve life factors, the basis of Cattell's personality sphere, were wrong in the first place. Indeed this is hardly surprising since this preliminary work was carried out before the advent of rapid computers allowed accurate factor analysis and for some of this pioneering work more simple cluster analysis had to be used.

The second point is a more diffuse issue. If these sixteen factors are not a good factorial description of the items in the 16PF test it is strange that practical users of the test continue to find the scales useful and there is no doubt that it is still widely used in occupational selection. One argument might be that the peculiar mix of factors in the 16PF scales just happened to be useful in practice. This is unlikely statistically and the analysis of the scales, referred to above, did not support this hypothesis.

I think, as I have previously argued (Kline, 1990) that the power of the 16PF to make impressive discriminations among occupational groups is more apparent than real. Thus, although it is easy to make psychological sense of the profiles equal sense can be made of their reversals since there are no good theories of occupational choice. The arguments are simply *ad hoc.*

Even if this were the case, advocates of the 16PF might still argue that obviously the test worked in selection or it would not be so widely used, so that whatever its psychometric shortcomings it was still an effective tool. Actually examination of much practice in occupational selection reveals that this is not necessarily so. This is because there is no follow up of those whom the test rejects. Thus it may well be the case that the vast majority of applicants could do the jobs well (especially true in times of high unemployment) so that a short list based upon education and experience would be a perfectly adequate selection method. The fact that employers are satisfied with the results does not, therefore, necessarily mean that the 16PF is a useful test.

Finally it should be noted that the modest correlations, reported in the manual to the 16PF test, between occupational success and primary scales may well be the result of the influence of the second order factors.

Conclusions

Despite all these problems and difficulties it is a fact that the 16PF will discriminate among occupational and clinical groups, and in this sense the meaning of these scales, despite their factorial unclarity, is known. Furthermore it does measure the two largest second order factors, extraversion and anxiety with high validity and has measures of tough-mindedness and conventionality (G). This suggests, as was argued above, that the big five factors underlie the variance in the 16PF test, as seems to be the case with most personality tests. For all these reasons as a personality test in the applied setting and as a test with which to compare a new set of personality scales it is useful. However, it should not be interpreted too literally, as if the scales were unquestionably valid, and caution must be shown because of the low reliability of the scales. If the test is used with common sense, as is described in Section III of this handbook, valuable results can be obtained from it.

15. State–Trait Anxiety Inventory (STAI) (Spielberger *et al.*, 1970)

Age range   16 years and upwards.

Sex differences   Yes, but separate norms.

Norms   High school and college students, psychiatric and medical patients, prisoners.

Variables measured   Two variables: state anxiety and trait anxiety.

Reliability   Test-retest reliability for state anxiety is around .75 and is highly satisfactory. For state anxiety it is about .3 but this is an inappropriate measure since state anxiety fluctuates, by definition. Internal consistency reliability for both scales is about .9, which is as high as can be expected.

Validity The trait scale has correlations with two other anxiety scales, the IPAT Anxiety Scale (Cattell and Scheier, 1963) and the Manifest Anxiety Scale (Taylor, 1953) of between .75 and .85. Given the reliabilities of all these scales, it appears that the STAI is essentially measuring the same variable which supports the concurrent validity of the scale.

Spielberger *et al.* (1970) present evidence for the validity of the state scale by showing how scores increase under 'stressful' conditions among samples of students. However, it is obvious that for ethical reasons no true stress could have been induced and in one condition students were asked to respond as they would feel if they were about to take a stressful exam. Not only is this experiment entirely unconvincing (although the scores duly increased) but the fact that the scores increased shows that the test can be easily faked. Hence all these student results are somewhat suspect since there is a strong demand characteristic built into such experiments. Thus this evidence for the validity of the STAI state scale is not regarded as unequivocal.

Item types Statements to which subjects reply on a four-point scale: Almost never, sometimes, often, almost always. The state test requires subjects to indicate how they feel now, while the trait test asks how they generally feel. All items are direct and face valid.

Number of items 20 in each scale.

Time for completion 15 mins.

Comments

There is little doubt, as has been made clear throughout this handbook, that anxiety is one of the main factors that account for the variance in personality questionnaires. Similarly, there is little doubt that the IPAT anxiety scale (which consists of the relevant items from the 16PF test) measures this anxiety factor. It follows, therefore, that the trait test of the STAI is valid because, as has been discussed, this correlates very highly with this factor. This leaves the state test. All the evidence, the face validity of the items and their similarity to those in the valid trait scale, the fact that the experimental manipulations reported in the manual all work (despite the reservations which were discussed under the section on the validity of the test) supports the validity of this test as a state measure, although it is all too easy to fake.

Conclusion

As a quick and easy measure of state and trait anxiety, the STAI would appear to be about as good as you can get.

Chapter 26

Projective and Objective Tests

In the first part of this chapter I shall describe and evaluate those projective tests which are sufficiently well validated to deserve some use, even if with caution, in applied and experimental psychology. In the second part I shall describe the two objective tests, one of personality, the other motivational, which have been published from the Compendium (Cattell and Warburton, 1967).

PART I: PROJECTIVE TESTS

1. The Rorschach Test (Rorschach 1921)

Form

Ten symmetrical inkblots, each on a separate card. Half are monochrome, shades of grey, half are coloured or with grey plus colours.

Administration

Individual. As Brown (1976) points out, in an admirably succinct account of a subject of almost mystical complexity, there are essentially two stages of administration: 1. the cards are presented one at a time in order and subjects have to describe the cards – what they look like and suggest. These responses are recorded together with response latencies to each card, time spent on each card and its orientation. 2. the subject goes through the cards again, explicating his responses and answering questions about them.

Scoring

There are various systems of scoring and interpretation – those of Beck (1944) and Klopfer (Klopfer and Kelley, 1942) being the most well known. Recently Exner (1974; 1978) has introduced an empirically based scoring system. In addition to this there are other well known books on Rorschach interpretation, Piotrowski (1957), Rapaport *et al.* (1945) and Schafer (1954) coming immediately to mind. A good account of the administration, scoring and interpretation of the Rorschach may be found in Allison *et al.* (1988) which is reasonably eclectic but typifies the modern Yale approach. Howard (1989a) contains an excellent summary of the Exner system. I shall attempt to describe the essence of modern Rorschach scoring, although any brief account is difficult.

The Exner system

The Exner system consists of eight coding categories.

1. Location. How the subject approaches her or his environment and with what amount of cognitive energy. This follows the traditional Beck scheme and is similar to that used by Allison *et al.* (1988), which is described below.
2. Developmental quality. This gauges the subject's interest in synthesis and analysis of information.
3. Determinants. The aspects of the blot used in formulating the response. There are nine categories of determinants, listed later in this section.
4. Form quality. This yields information about the perceptual and reality testing capacities of the subject.
5. Content analysis. Each response is coded for its contents, which fall into twenty-seven categories.
6. Populars. These are the common responses of which Exner (1978) recognises thirteen. They indicate the willingness of a subject to respond in an obvious way.
7. Organisational activity (Z score). This assesses the response to the complexity of the stimuli and is claimed to be useful in the diagnosis of psychopathology.
8. Special scores. Twelve special scores classify qualitative aspects of the responses: unusual verbalisations, personalised responses, just for example.

As Howard (1989a) points out, these eight categories form the data base of Rorschach interpretation. Various ratios, percentages and other derivations are calculated from them and form the structural summary of the structural analysis. Interpretation then consists of assessing the values in the structural summary against norms and examining combinations to reveal patterns of functioning.

Determinants The Exner determinants, which are vital aspects of the structural analysis, are set out below. As will become obvious these are difficult to score (Howard, 1989a).

1. Form. Scored if this is the basis of response. Claimed to be related to control or delay.
2. Movement. This differentiates human, animal and inanimate movement and is said to be related to high level conceptualisation fantasy and delay, stress and tension and problems over immediate gratification.
3. Chromatic colour. Four colour categories are used: pure colour, where colour is more important than form, where form is more important than colour, and colour naming. These responses are held to indicate effect and its expression.
4. Achromatic colour. Three categories: achromatic, where achromatic colour is more important than form, and the converse. Achromatic responses are thought to show inhibition of emotions.
5. Shading texture. Scored where texture is perceived through shading. Three categories as in determinant 4, above, which indicate needs for affection and contact.
6. Shading dimension. Scored where dimensionality depends on shading. Again three categories, reflecting negative self appraisal.
7. Shading-diffuse. Again scored in three categories where responses are based on light–dark features. This is related to anxiety and feeling out of control.
8. Form dimension. Scored when response depends only on form. This is related to introspection.
9. Pairs and reflections. Scored where two identical objects are mentioned, a distinction being drawn where form demands are vague and where a mirror image depends on form. These relate to egocentricity and to self absorption.

Howard (1989a) gives a good indication of how these various scores are used although for full details readers must be referred to Exner (1986). However two examples will indicate the style of interpretation in the Exner system.

1. The EB ratio. This is the ratio of human movement responses to the sum of the weighted chromatic colour responses. It is said to indicate coping style. For example if the ratio is weighted to the movement side, the subject is said to be deliberate and considered. The other side indicates the use of affect in a trial and error fashion (Howard, 1989a).
2. EA. This is the sum of both sides of the EB ratio and is regarded as a measure of a subject's resources.

In my discussion of the basic variables in the Exner system, I briefly mentioned the interpretations which were placed upon them. These are manipulated – sums, ratios and subtractions – to form indices of cognition, ideation, conventionality and affect. Furthermore the resulting figures are used normatively and there are constellations of scores which are claimed to identify suicides, schizophrenics, and depressives, just for example.

I hope that this description gives some idea of the Exner system which has attempted to combine the best of previous scoring systems with empirical findings. Before I comment on this I shall discuss another approach to the Rorschach, that summarised by Allison *et al.* (1988) and utilised by the Rorschach workers at Yale.

Allison *et al.*

They usually extract the following scores:

1. Location of the responses.
2. Level of accuracy of the percept.
3. Determinants used in forming the response.
4. Content, which includes the extent of the conventionality of the response.
5. Qualitative features of the verbalisation.
6. Number of responses.
7. Reaction times of each response.
8. Total amount of time on each card.
9. Cards to which no response is given.

Location, accuracy and determinants are considered to reflect the formal characteristics of a Rorschach record (Allison *et al.*, 1988). They indicate the organisation of the psychological functions and are, according to these authors, not affected by situational factors, such as the sex or personality of the tester or even the sex of the subject.

The number of responses is held to reflect ideational productivity and its quality indicates the quality of intellectual performance. Reaction time is a function of the characteristics of each card and the personal characteristics of the subject. Fast reaction times are held to indicate quick, unreflecting people. The total time spent on each card shows how much energy and time a subject is prepared to spend on the task but observations of the subject's behaviour (e.g. not attempting to speak) have to mediate the interpretation of this index.

Failure to respond to a card may be due to inhibition, guardedness or blocking. It is common in depressives and paranoids, just for example.

The variables indicating perceptual organisation must now be briefly described. Allison *et al.* (1988) supply an excellent summary of this complex topic.

Location   The area chosen for the response is held to reflect the perceptual organisation of the subject, whether and to what extent it is concerned with details, with complexity and whether impressions are global and amorphous or well articulated and defined. Location is an index of how much the subject integrates her or his perceptual world.

Location scores
W.   Response to the whole blot.
D.   Response to a prominent part of the blot.
Dd. Response to a very small part of the blot.
Dr. Response to an unusual part of the blot.
S.   Response to the white space.
DW. Response to the whole blot but arising from a detail.
Do. Response to an isolated aspect of a usually more complete response.
Po. Response by position regardless of the form of the blot.

As Allison *et al.* (1988) point out, there are almost endless combinations of these responses and well organised and integrated Rorschach protocols show a balance of these responses. D is the most frequent. Scoring and interpreting the Rorschach requires extensive training so I shall not go into detail concerning the alleged meaning of the responses. This is especially true since their interpretation depends, to some extent, on to which card the response was given. However I shall give some examples of interpretation, from the first three location scores.

A high proportion of W in a record depends, for its meaning, on the context. Thus, in a brief record, it may indicate a simpleminded world view, as in mental defectives, whereas in a long record it may reflect a striving for unification, and/or oceanic feelings. To exemplify the problems of Rorschach interpretation, in their next paragraph, Allison *et al.* (1988) argue that W responses are typically said to represent integrative abilities and the capacity for abstraction and generalisation. To overcome the obvious contradiction with the first claims they argue, further, that the quality of the W responses must be taken into account.

There are usually about 50 per cent of D responses in a Rorschach record. If there are many more than this it is held to reflect thought processes which are conventional, undifferentiated and unintegrated and possibly a practical and conservative approach to life. However the level of complexity and the accuracy of D must be taken into account in the interpretation.

As might be expected, Dd responses, being concerned with details, are considered to reflect obsessionality.

Determinants Determinant scores, concerned with form, colour and shading, have been discussed as part of the Exner system. As described by Allison *et al.* (1988) the scoring of determinants is essentially similar to that of Exner (1986) but it is quite clear that considerable judgement and skill are required (thus leading to low reliability) and that interpretations are in some cases different from that of Exner.

A few examples will illustrate these points. Firstly, F (form response). This is a response based solely on the outline of the percept. However in addition there are subtle variants of F.

F+   indicates an accurate and well articulated response.
F+−   is almost an F+ response.
F−   is scored where the formal attributes of the blot are distorted.
F+−   is not quite as bad as F−.

These form responses are held to represent objective, defensive responses, formal reasoning uninfluenced by anxiety or emotion. It is noteworthy that these subtle variants must be difficult to score and that the interpretation of the form response is different from that of Exner where it was related to introspection.

Secondly, M (movement response). As Allison *et al.* (1988) point out, even Rorschach admitted that there were problems of variability in scoring this response. Some interpret movement broadly, others restrict it to human movement. Thus no one definition is accurate for all scorers. Allison *et al.* (1988), as one example of a scoring system of high repute in the Rorschach world, define the categories thus:

M.   Complete or almost complete humans in actual movement.
FM.   Weak, non-active human movement; large, active, part-human figures; human-like animals in human activity.

Again, M reveals the subjectivity of the standard Rorschach scoring and interpretation since it is held to represent an individual's intellectual endowment and potential and intraversion. In addition it represents richness and flexibility of thinking.

In the light of our analyses of test and true score variance in the first section of this handbook, it is difficult to see how one score could measure all these different factors. Even if it could they must be inextricably mixed such that intuitive separation must be impossible. It is precisely the nature of such a score as the M score which forces so many psychometrists to be sceptical of the Rorschach. Such scepticism must remain until there is indubitable evidence of validity, evidence which is not yet forthcoming. However, it should be noted that the objectively scored and analysed Rorschach, as described in Chapter 16, where G analysis (Holley, 1973) was discussed, is not psychometrically flawed in this way. However this does not mean that it is necessarily valid, simply that it is not necessarily invalid.

Finally it should be noted that the interpretation of these movement determinants are quite different from those suggested by Exner (1986) and discussed above.

Another set of determinants are used to tap the emotional and affective life of the subjects. These are the colours − chromatic and achromatic. However the influence of the form on these colours must also be evaluated so that where form is the predominant determinant and where colour is predominant is recorded. Interpretively when C is predominant affects are very strongly experienced. This, of course, agrees with the Exner system.

However, there are differences. Thus according to Howard (1989a), as was shown above achromatic colour was related to inhibition. Allison *et al.* (1988) claim that they indicate depressive feelings, lifelessness, coldness, desolation and loneliness. Black connotes death, white coldness.

Discussion of the scoring systems

Although I have described only certain aspects of these two scoring systems, and many details have had to be left out, I think there is sufficient material to form a sound basis for discussion.

Lack of theory   The objection raised by Eysenck (1959) to the Rorschach scoring system, namely that it lacked any coherent theory, is surely supported here. In some cases the same score implies a variety of characteristics, some of them contradictory. However the theory is simply intuitive, the association between blackness and depression and between whiteness and desolation. If this meant that these scores were valid there would be no requirement for special stimuli, such as the Rorschach blots. The responses to anything would do.

Reliability of judgements   As is obvious, many of the scoring categories demand fine judgements. Wherever human judgement is required there is bound to be a degree of unreliability, however hard the training. Nevertheless it should be pointed out that inter-rater reliabilities of not less than .85 are claimed for each scoring category in the Exner system (Wiener-Levy and Exner, 1981) and that the test-retest reliability of many of the variables is also high. This might be so for some scorers but such scoring may well be beyond the reach of most users of the test.

Psychometric improbability   It seems unlikely that any one response could measure so diverse a set of variables as is claimed for some of these Rorschach scores, which span ability and personality. Even should they load on these diverse factors, unpacking the meaning of multivariate or multi-factorial variables is extremely difficult.

Validity of the test   All these problems mean that there must be exceptional evidence for the validity of the test, before it could be recommended for any purpose, since on good a priori grounds we would not expect it to be valid. Exner (1986), at least attempts to validate the interpretations in his system empirically but the evidence is far from strong. In fact, despite the enormous output of research into the Rorschach, it still has to be said that there is no firm evidence for the validity of the Rorschach test. It is noteworthy how different were the interpretations offered by Howard (1989a) and Allison *et al.* (1988). However, it may well be the case that gifted individuals can use the test to gather useful information about their clients which they would not have been able to obtain from other sources. However that some few Rorschach testers are able to do this is not a recommendation for the test for general use.

In Chapter 16 G analysis of projective tests was described and it is suggested here that this is a useful, experimental technique to use with the Rorschach and with other projective tests. However this is a long way from arguing that they should be used for substantive research, where the findings are taken as valid.

Conclusions

This has been a long discussion of the Rorschach because it is, in all probability, the most famous, if not notorious, psychological test. Nevertheless, I have described it and evaluated it in some detail because I believe it is wrong to write it off as useless as has been done by Eysenck (1959), just as it is equally dubious to interpret the protocols as if they were valid, as to a large extent is done by Allison *et al.* (1988) and by adherents of the Exner system. Because it can be used by some testers, because the data are unusual such that they are unlikely to be derived from other tests and because objective scoring methods are available which enable powerful multivariate analyses to be used, it is concluded that the Rorschach still deserves experimental use, if objectively scored, in those cases where personality questionnaires would seem unable to capture the richness and subtlety of the psychological material. Used in that way some reliable findings both in clinical and even occupational psychology might gradually be built up.

Over the years there have been a number of variants of the Rorschach test but only one of these is sufficiently different to deserve inclusion as a separate test. This is the Holtzman Inkblot Test, the HIT, which was designed in an attempt to overcome the psychometric deficiencies of the original test.

2. The Holtzman Inkblot Test (Holtzman *et al.*, 1961)

Form

There are two parallel forms of the HIT, A and B, each consisting of forty-five cards portraying an inkblot. There are two practice blots which are not usually scored and the other blots are either black and grey, monochromatic, black with a bright colour or multicoloured.

Administration

There are standard administrative procedures: the subject is asked to give only one response to each card; the brief enquiry is given after each response; the questions in the enquiry are limited and almost always asked.

There are three kinds of question in the enquiry: L clarifies location; C examines the nature of the percept; and E encourages elaboration of the response.

Scoring

Twenty-two variables are scored: reaction time, rejection, location, space, form definiteness, form appropriateness, colour, shading, movement, pathognomic verbalisation, integration, human, animal, anatomy, abstract, anxiety, hostility, barrier, penetration, balance, popular. The scores on these variables are derived from the sum across cards.

Holtzman (1981) in an excellent summary of qualities of the HIT points out that these quantitative variables were developed in an attempt to cover the most important scoring categories of the original Rorschach Test. It is claimed that experienced testers can score the test in approximately half an hour, although it is admitted that it is far more time consuming for the less practised.

Reliability of the scoring system

As was made clear in our discussion of the original Rorschach, there was a severe objection concerning the reliability of the test. Our description of the scoring categories showed that high reliability would be unlikely. The HIT was deliberately designed to overcome these psychometric difficulties.

Inter-scorer reliability Highly trained scorers have a median value for agreement on the twenty-two variables of .98, while those with less training have a median value of .84, and that was for the nine most difficult variables. Inter-scorer reliability can, therefore, be said to be high.

Intra-scorer reliability This is similar with a median r of .93.

Interaction of tester and subject An objection to projective tests is that there is a strong possibility, absent in inventories, that examiners influence the subject. Analysis of variance, with examiners as a source, indicated that this was rarely the case and that, where this was so, only one examiner was at fault and this was an untrained examiner, a secretary who had been asked to score the test as best she could from the manual. Thus interaction may be ruled out as a source of unreliability.

Split-half reliability Split-half reliabilities were almost all beyond .7 and the only low coefficient was for the popular response. The HIT is certainly by this measure a reliable test, suitable for use with individuals.

Test-retest reliability Holtzman (1981) cites a number of studies of the temporal stability of the HIT, some with a year between testing. Most of the reliabilities were again high, certainly sufficient to justify the use of the HIT to study changes in perception and personality, although caution would have to be shown with certain of the HIT scores.

Conclusions concerning reliability From all these findings it can be concluded that the HIT is sufficiently reliable to make it a useful test for individual use – an important improvement over most projective tests.

Validity of the HIT

From the nature of the variables in the HIT it is clear that any test of their validity must be concerned with their meaning. For example, the variable, shading, is of no interest *per se*. All depends upon its psychological meaning and correlates.

Holtzman (1981) reports the results of factor analyses of the HIT variables, carried out separately on the samples in the reliability studies. Six factors were found in all studies:

1. Perceptual maturity, integrated ideational activity. This loads on movement, integration, human barrier and popular. The high end of the dimension is held to reflect well organised ideational activity, good imagination and well differentiated ego boundaries.
2. Perceptual sensitivity. This bipolar factor loads positively on colour and shading and negatively on form definiteness. The positive pole indicates a strong reaction to the colour shading or symmetrical balance of the blot while at the negative pole form is the sole determinant.
3. Psychopathology of thought. Pathognomic verbalisation is the most salient variable on this factor which also loads anxiety and hostility. High scores are claimed by Holtzman (1981) to indicate disordered thought processes and fantasy life.
4. Perceptual differentiation. This is not as clear a factor as the first three but among children especially, form appropriateness and location are the defining variables.
5. This is difficult to name although three loadings define the factor – reaction time, rejection and animal (negatively). Holtzman (1981) argues that a high score may reflect strong inhibition or an inability to perceive concepts in the blots.
6. In about half the samples this factor loaded on penetration, anatomy and sex and is thought by Holtzman to reflect bodily preoccupation.

Although these six factors account for a good proportion of the variance in the twenty-two scores there is still sufficient reliable variance in many of the scores to make it sensible to use them. Thus for most purposes Holtzman recommends the use of the individual variables rather than six factor scores. However if a few broad scores are required from the HIT it is suggested that the first three factor scores be used.

It should be noted that the identification of these factors was made from their loadings. To do this assumptions had to be made concerning the meaning of these scores. For example the variable pathognomic verbalisation is assumed to reflect thought disorder. Thus while it is interesting and important to demonstrate that three factors underlie much of the HIT variance, it is insufficient from the viewpoint of establishing the validity of the HIT since assumptions are still made about the meaning of these variables. What is necessary is to locate these factors in personality factor space or show a convincing pattern of correlations with other tests and external criteria.

Comparability with the Rorschach

There seems to be a good comparability with the Rorschach test although the results are difficult to evaluate since correlations between comparable HIT and Rorschach scores had to be corrected for attenuation due to unreliability (see Chapter 1 of this handbook). Nevertheless if this is so the greater reliability of the HIT and the fact that it is standardised and has parallel forms makes it preferable to the original.

However, since the Rorschach is, itself, of unknown validity, this comparability, although interesting, is not important in establishing the validity of the HIT. As has been argued, external correlations and factor analyses with other variables are required for this purpose.

External correlations with the HIT

Holtzman (1981) has a good discussion of some of the external correlations of the HIT and I shall summarise the main conclusions.

Firstly, ability tests. There tend to be small but significant correlations with intelligence tests and a number of the HIT variables. These are mostly around .2. This is hardly surprising given the requirements of the response to the HIT. There are more rejection responses among low-intelligence subjects, for example, and this is presumably because such people simply cannot see anything in the blots. Such findings do not invalidate the test but suggest that it is not entirely suitable for those of low intelligence and that new norms for this group should be produced.

As regards other tests of ability, Clark et al. (1965) found that tests of divergent ability were correlated to certain HIT variables partly because divergent subjects gave more responses and seem to produce more imaginative responses. Again this is hardly surprising. This is a problem with all tests, and especially projective tests, which require free responses, that divergent subjects produce more and thus are enabled to score more. Ipsatised scores, as used with objective tests (see Chapter 16 of this handbook) might overcome the difficulty.

Secondly, personality questionnaires. Holtzman reports that generally there have been few reliable correlations found between the HIT variables and personality questionnaires. Since this failure cannot be attributed to the low reliability of the HIT variables it suggests that they are tapping different variance from that in questionnaires, which is psychometrically useful since if two measures are highly correlated one must be redundant.

Among children there was a low but significant negative correlation between the Cattell neuroticism factor in the Junior Personality Quiz (see Chapter 25 for a description and evaluation of this test) and the Human response, which is at least sensible. Further, the factor three variables of the HIT are correlated with the N factor of the Maudsley Personality Inventory (a precursor of the EPQ – Eysenck and Eysenck, 1975), a test also described in Chapter 25 of this handbook. This again is a psychologically sensible finding.

While attempts to relate HIT hostility and anxiety to questionnaire measures have been equivocal, Holtzman *et al.* (1975) in their well known cross-cultural study of Mexican children found that high colour scores on the HIT were correlated with high scores on the exhibitionism, impulsiveness and nurturance scales of the PRF (Jackson, 1974) which is described in Chapter 25 of this handbook. Furthermore, HIT integration was correlated with the understanding scale of the PRF, all findings supporting the Rorschach interpretation of these scores.

Conclusions   These results point to the fact that the HIT measures variables somewhat different from those in personality questionnaires. They do little either to confirm or deny the validity of the HIT.

Differential diagnosis

The HIT appears to be able to distinguish between diagnostic clinical groups – schizophrenics and normals and schizophrenics and depressives. Other investigators have found differences between emotionally disturbed children and normal controls. The barrier score differentiated between arthritic patients and those with ulcers. In summary Holtzman (1981) claims that the HIT is a good diagnostic instrument.

As regards differential diagnosis, but of a different kind, between cultures, the HIT is powerful and Gorham (1967) has developed a computer scoring system for seventeen of the HIT variables, which Moseley (1967) showed was effective in predicting cultural identity. While interesting, this kind of differential diagnosis is difficult to use as evidence for the validity of the HIT variables. However it indicates that the HIT variance is not simply specific variance.

Nevertheless, with the exception of the Barrier score where the discrimination makes good sense, given the work on body image and experience (Fisher, 1970), the fact that these discriminations are made is difficult to interpret in respect of the validity of the HIT variables. After all it would be a curious thing if responses of schizophrenics and normals were not different.

Conclusions

There is no doubt that the HIT is a reliable measure and that it is able to make interesting discriminations among clinical and national groups. Nevertheless this is not the same as demonstrating that the test scores can bear their Rorschach interpretations. However the HIT variables must be measuring useful variance and this deserves to be further investigated in factor analytic studies with the best-established personality and ability factors. If this were done it might prove possible to identify the HIT factors.

3. The House-Tree-Person Test (HTP) (Buck, 1948; 1970)

Unlike the inkblots of the first two tests, there are no stimuli in the HTP. Instead the subject is requested to draw a house, a person and a tree. There are two phases to this test. In the first of these, subjects have to draw a house, tree and person in pencil and answer questions about them. This procedure is repeated in the second phase but with crayons.

Materials and administration

There are special forms on which the subjects make their drawings, one for each of the objects. As each drawing is finished the examiner asks the subject to complete the next. On commencement of drawing details of how each object is drawn are recorded, including spontaneous comments and how long it takes. Full details may be found in the test manuals.

The interrogation comprises sixty questions concerning these drawings, although others may be asked in addition if this seems useful. Typical questions might be:

a. person. Who is he, what is he thinking about and how does he feel?
b. tree. How old is that tree, is the tree alive and is the tree by itself?
c. house. What is the house, is it a happy house and what is the house made of?

Phase two, with the coloured drawings, is highly similar.

Scoring the HTP

In the manual to the HTP (Buck, 1970), there is a detailed objective scoring scheme for these drawings which is based upon the often minute details of them. Associated with the quantitative scoring scheme there are norms for interpretation. This quantitative scoring scheme allows for a rather broad assessment of intelligence which according to these tables yielded correlations as high as .75 with the full scale WAIS on 100 disturbed subjects of low intelligence. Given the reliability of the tests this is a remarkably high figure but it may well be restricted to such disturbed and abnormal groups.

However, despite this quantitative approach to the assessment of intelligence, the main value of the HTP lies in its qualitative, subjective scoring scheme, which is aimed at personality.

The revised manual (Buck, 1970) goes into great detail concerning the scoring of both the enquiry and the drawings themselves and all I can do here is to give some typical illustration so that readers can catch the flavour of the scoring system.

Tree. Groundline.   Note is taken as to whether a groundline is drawn. An arc-like groundline implies maternal dependence with feelings of isolation and helplessness, if the tree is small. If it is big, however, then the S has strong needs for dominance and exhibitionism.

Tree.   A tree with a slender or tiny trunk but a large structure of branches implies a precarious personality balance because of satisfaction seeking.

Person. Head.   The head represents the area of intelligence (control) and fantasy. Emphasis on the face represents the conscious effort to maintain an acceptable social front.

Person.   An overly large mouth implies oral eroticism or oral aggression, while shoulder size is an index of basic strength or power.

House. The roof.   Sound empirical evidence exists, Buck (1970) claims, that the roof represents the area of thinking and fantasy when the house is considered a psychological self-portrait of the person who drew it. Thus, for example, emphasis on the eaves implies an over-defensive and suspicious attitude.

House. Chimney.   This is not necessarily a sexual symbol but sexually maladjusted subjects tend to view it as a phallus and to react accordingly.

Comments on the scoring system

In Chapter 16 of this handbook, I quoted the objections of Eysenck (1959) to projective tests among which were the facts that there was little evidence for validity, that there was no rationale to their interpretation and that, in general, they were little more than vehicles for the riotous imaginations of clinicians. I have inserted these points here because it must be said that the manual to the HTP (Buck, 1970) confirms them all to perfection, as the scoring excerpts illustrate.

Thus although the manual runs to 350 pages nowhere can be found any evidence for the validity of the interpretations of the scores. Even where, as in the illustration from scoring the roof, empirical evidence is cited, there are no indications of what such evidence might be, and there are no references to any studies where the nature of this evidence could be scrutinised. I am not saying that there is no evidence, merely that it has to be taken on trust. This is clearly not satisfactory.

As regards the rationale for scoring or interpreting these drawings, again the illustrations in the paragraphs above, which are not atypical, in any way, of the HTP scoring system, demonstrate that there is no rationale, or not one based in psychological theory. Clearly psychoanalysis is used interpretively, as can be seen in the instance of the chimney as phallic symbol and the mouth being regarded as an index of orality. However the interpretation of the face as a social front and eaves as defensive, is not psychoanalysis. It is a literal-minded analogy or simile, which is not self evident and would need sound empirical support to be taken seriously. On what psychological theory, it must be asked, should house eaves reflect defence or the roof the head? Why should subjects identify with the house at all?

An objective scoring scheme for the HTP   Hampson and Kline (1977) and Kline and Svasti-Xuto (1981) utilised G analysis (see Chapter 16) with the HTP test. Hampson and Kline (1977), for example, found that a discriminating variable among criminal youths was regarding the tree as extremely young, as trees go. Buck (1970) regards this as a sign of immaturity, an interpretation which seemed to fit in well with this particular group. However, regardless of fit, the point of G analysis of the HTP is to discover variables that will discriminate criterion groups. Their interpretation may be worked out later experimentally although it is interesting to see whether the interpretations in the manual make psychological sense, as sometimes, as in our example, they appear to do.

Comments and conclusions

As was mentioned earlier in this discussion of the HTP tests, despite the size of the manual there is no reference to or discussion of its validity. In fact there seems nowhere to be any clear evidence. It is used, almost exclusively, by those who believe its worth.

I think that there is sufficient case material in the manual to warrant investigation using objective, reliable scoring procedures and G analysis. This is so not only on account of this case material but also because the HTP, by virtue of its nature, allows considerable freedom of response, a quality that should be nurtured in tests of personality where, very often, the demands of reliability produce narrow and constrained tests.

4. The Thematic Apperception Test (Murray, 1938)

The Thematic Apperception Test, TAT, was developed by Morgan and Murray (1936), although it came to prominence through its use in *Explorations in Personality* (Murray, 1938).

As Karon (1981) makes clear, TAT was not designed to discriminate clinical, diagnostic groups, either the then current Kraepelinian categories or those of DSM-3R. Rather, Karon (1981) asserts it is aimed at elucidating aspects of human personality which are closed to other methods. To quote her phrase, 'the TAT is an extraordinary tool'.

Materials and administration

The TAT consists in total of thirty-one stimuli on cards, of which one is a blank. Subjects are required to say, using their imagination, what they think the people in the cards are feeling and thinking and to explain their actions. The pictures are designed to provoke fantasy and to elicit stories without being so structured that all subjects produce highly similar responses.

As Swartz (1978) points out, the original TAT consisted of ten cards which were given to all subjects followed by a further ten selected on grounds of age and sex. Two separate administrations were thought to be desirable.

For research or for other special purposes different stimuli may be used as has been done by cross-cultural psychologists. Henry (1956) exemplifies this trend and Lee (1953) developed a special African version of the TAT. However such applications are not the true TAT and I shall restrict my comments to the original cards.

There has arisen, over the years, considerable variation in the administration, scoring and interpretation, not to say what subset of TAT cards is used, as is illustrated in the excellent papers by Allison *et al.* (1988) and Karon (1981). This is partly due to the claim by Murray (1938) that, in a sense, what particular stimuli were used was unimportant, provided that they were sufficiently ambiguous to elicit imaginative stories. Nevertheless I shall briefly describe the cards.

TAT Cards

1. A young boy contemplates a violin on a table.
2. Country scene: In the foreground a young woman with books; in the background a man works the field under the gaze of an older woman.
3. A boy huddles on the floor against a couch, beside him a revolver.
4. A young woman stands with her face in her hands, her left arm against a door.
5. A woman clutches at the shoulders of a man with face and body averted.
6. A middle-aged woman stands looking through an open door into a room.

7. A short elderly woman stands, back turned to a tall young and perplexed man.
8. A young woman on a sofa looks back at an older man, with a pipe, apparently addressing her.
9. A grey-haired man looks at a younger man staring sullenly into space.
10. An older woman sits on a sofa reading or speaking to a girl who has a doll on her lap and is looking away.
11. An adolescent boy stares out of the picture, on one side a rifle barrel, in the background a surgical operation.
12. A young woman sits looking into space, chin in hand.
13. Four men rest on grass.
14. A young woman behind a tree gazes upon another young woman running on a beach.
15. A young woman rests her head on the shoulder of a man.

The above are the pictures of the first series, of which 10 are given.

16. On a road between high cliffs are two obscure figures. On the cliffside a dragon can be seen.
17. On a couch a young man reclines, eyes closed. Over him with hands outstretched stands an elderly man.
18. Portrait of a young woman. In the background an old woman with a shawl and a strange expression.
19. A rowing boat beside the banks of a woodland stream.
20. A young man stands miserably, head in arms. Behind him a woman lies in bed.
21. A small boy sits on the doorstep of a log cabin.
22. A small girl climbs a winding staircase.
23. A human silhouette against a bright window. All the rest of the card is black.
24. A gaunt man stands, hands clenched, in a graveyard.
25. The blank card.
26. A naked man clinging to a rope.
27. A female figure leans over the railings of a bridge against a background of tall buildings and the small figures of men.
28. A man is clutched from behind by invisible assailants. Three hands can be seen.
29. A woman is strangling another woman and pushing her backwards over the banisters of a stairway.
30. Strange clouds overhang a snow-covered cabin in the country.
31. Night and a dimly lit human figure leans against a lamp post.

As was intended by the authors of the TAT these cards are not highly ambiguous although they are sufficiently unstructured to allow a variety of interpretations. In my experience of this test, today, about half a century after the test was published, the cards appear old fashioned and subjects frequently suggest that they are portraits of old black and white films.

Scoring and interpreting the test

Murray (1938) regarded the TAT as an instrument for the exploration of personality. He coded stories for needs and presses, the pressures individuals felt their environment was exerting on them. In the manual to the test nineteen needs are set out: abasement, achievement, aggression, dominance, intraggression, nurturance, passivity, sex, succorance, acquisition, affiliation, autonomy, blamavoidance, cognizance, creation, deference, excitance, exposition, and harmavoidance.

Emotions can be investigated by the TAT: conflict, emotional change, dejection, anxiety, exaltation, distrust and anxiety. As regards presses the following are listed although it is claimed that others can be assessed: affiliation, aggression, dominance, nurturance, rejection, loss, physical danger, physical injury.

From a combination of these needs and presses motivational trends can also be worked out.

However, as Swartz (1978) points out, many users of the TAT do not score the test in terms of needs and presses. Indeed almost any dynamic theory of personality can be used to interpret the TAT stories and Murray (1971) even goes so far as to claim that a layman with a refined psychological intuition can make valid psychological inferences from the stories. Psychoanalytic theories are particularly easy to apply to the interpretation of TAT protocols.

This discussion can be summarised briefly. The TAT can be used and (as the large number of research studies shows) is used to measure almost any dynamic variable in which the investigator was interested. However, the question arises as to whether it is a valid and reliable test.

Reliability and validity of the TAT

Swartz (1978) found that there was relatively little evidence for the validity of the TAT and almost none for its reliability. It is fair to say that this position has not radically changed in the succeeding thirteen years. This is partly because, as the large number of publications indicates, clinicians simply find it useful. Thus Allison et al. (1988) cite clinical examples as if it were valid. In addition it is fair to say that a completely traditional approach to reliability (especially) and validity may not do justice to the TAT. This is claimed by Karon (1981) and a discussion of these arguments will be useful.

Inter-scorer reliability Karon (1981) argues that inter-scorer reliability may be low because the scorers are looking for different things. While this may be so it is still a real issue as to whether what each is looking for may be scored reliably. However Karon claims that by drawing up a good scoring key, reliability may be made as high as .9.

This is interesting in the light of the claims that I have made concerning projective tests, in Chapter 16 of this handbook, where G analysis was recommended. The detailed scoring keys are not dissimilar to the careful content analyses required in G analysis, where no judgement is needed. Thus we may argue that, given a clear guide for scoring, inter-rater reliability may be satisfactory, at least.

Actually it is interesting to note that Karon (1981) argues that reliability is usually only an issue in research studies. This is a surprising claim but it may explain why clinicians are not worried by using scores of unknown reliability.

Test-retest reliability For some of the TAT variables test-retest reliability may not be appropriate because, as even the list of the original variables showed, some of these are states rather than traits which would be expected to fluctuate. This is also true of the myriad variables which might be derived from the TAT on the basis of dynamic theory.

However, this is not true for all the needs and presses, and it would seem reasonable to investigate the temporal stability of the TAT to measure these. Here it should be noted that temporal stability refers not to the production of an identical story but to the production of a story which yields the same assessment as on the first occasion. Karon (1981) cites studies by Tomkins (1947) which show that reliabilities for some of the variables were quite high: .8 after two months and .5 for ten-month intervals. These are old investigations and may be exceptional but if these figures can be regularly attained it is clear that on grounds of reliability the TAT is not altogether useless, although there is a paucity of data.

Validity of the TAT

Karon argues that the reliability of the TAT is really not important, given that it can be shown to be valid. As we have seen from our first three chapters in this handbook, this is indeed the case and we shall now examine the evidence for the validity of this test.

First, Karon (1981) argues that the clinical validity of the TAT has to be established for each user since the instrument is not the test but the test plus interpreter. This is a very important point, because it implies that the test is not necessarily valid but that in the hands of a highly skilled tester it may be so. Indeed, that is how she reconciles the fact that studies of the validity of the TAT give such disparate results – all depends upon the skill and training of the researcher. It is interesting to recall that this is the conclusion that was reached in this chapter concerning the Rorschach and I would argue that this is true of all projective tests. Thus the TAT, in the hands of a gifted 'intuitive' tester to quote the manual to the test (Murray, 1971) can yield useful information concerning personality. However who those testers are is difficult to recognise and this makes the test highly unsatisfactory as a general measurement device.

Vernon and Parry (1949) in their study of interviews found that, in general, interviews made selection worse rather than better and that it was not a valid selection method. However they did find a small number of individuals whose ability to interview was exceptional and these people could sometimes equal or prove themselves superior to psychometric tests. Here the problem was in recognising the good interviewer. It should be noted that there was no correlation between confidence in one's interview skills and ability to interview.

Conclusions concerning the TAT

From this discussion some clear conclusions may be drawn.

1. The TAT may well yield in the hands of gifted and intuitive testers some useful information concerning drives and conflicts which are relevant to personality.
2. There is no reason to use the needs and presses of Murray as the variables. It does appear that many other dynamic interpretations are possible, although those based on poor theories would be of little value.
3. Given this there would appear little reason to use the TAT in practical, applied psychology unless the test user had clear and unequivocal evidence that it was efficient in the precise context in which it was used, for example in the selection of managers in a particular firm.
4. Since the cards are, themselves, somewhat old fashioned, and since, in theory at least, other stimuli which could excite the imagination could be substituted, there again seems no reason to use the TAT.

In sum, it would be difficult to advocate the use of the TAT except to investigate what it does measure (perhaps by G analysis) but this seems hardly worth while. Perhaps the time has come to bury what in its heyday was an exciting and interesting test which, no doubt, Murray could use well. However there are few Murrays. That there is still much research with this test indicates that this is a still a minority opinion but projective testing was never based on reason.

Variants on the TAT. A number of other tests have been devised, which owe much to the TAT since they consist of stimuli, usually portraying humans or animals in somewhat ambiguous but structured situations. None of these tests has anything like the weight of research behind it of the TAT, and virtually all of the objections to the TAT apply also to these tests. I shall restrict myself, therefore, to a brief description and discussion of these tests, which should be used only for research purposes into their own validity. None is of sufficiently demonstrated validity that scores from it could be regarded as substantive measures of any variable.

5. Children's Apperception Test (CAT) (Bellak and Bellak, 1949)

The CAT was overtly designed to provide a TAT for children between the ages of 3 and 10 years. The stimuli were chosen to elicit fantasy and to bear upon aspects of personality and child rearing which are considered to be important in psychoanalytic theory. In fact there are two series of cards: an animal version, because it was thought that children would identify with animals more readily, and a human set.

Materials

a. Original animal cards

1. Chicks seated around a table on which there is a bowl of food. An adult chicken looms faintly in the background.
2. A tug of war, one bear against another bear and a baby bear.
3. A huge lion sits on a throne, with a pipe and a walking stick. A mouse peers at him from a mousehole.
4. A mother kangaroo with bonnet and basket strides along with a baby in her pouch and an older kangaroo child on a bicycle.
5. A darkened room with a large double bed, with two bulges, in the foreground of which is a cot with two baby bears.
6. A dim cave in which two bears lie side by side. In the foreground a baby bear.
7. A ferocious tiger is leaping at a monkey which is jumping for the safety of a tree.
8. Two adult monkeys are taking tea on a sofa while another adult monkey, sitting on a cushion, talks to a child monkey.
9. Through an open door a dim room can be seen in which a rabbit sits looking out from a child's bed.
10. A puppy is being spanked across the knees of an adult dog. In the foreground is a lavatory.

b. The human cards

1. Three children sit round a table on which there is a bowl of food. An adult is standing in the background.
2. A tug of war, one adult human vs. one adult and a child.
3. A man with pipe and cane sits on a large chair. A small child sits against a wall in the background.

4. A lady with bonnet and basket is walking carrying a baby while an older child follows on a bicycle.
5. A double bed, with two bulges, in a dim bedroom. In the foreground of the room is a cot with two small children.
6. Two adults sleep side by side in a tent. In the foreground lies a child.
7. A ferocious cannibal-like man pursues a small boy who is attempting to escape.
8. Two ladies sit on a settee, taking tea, as a third on a cushion talks to a child.
9. Through a door can be seen a dark room in which a baby looks out from a cot.
10. A child is being spanked across an adult's knees. A lavatory can be seen in the foreground.

It is clear from these descriptions of the two series of CAT cards that they are as equivalent as is possible, although the ambiguity of sex which is possible with animals is difficult to produce in the human figures.

In the manual to the human form of the test it is argued that there is little difference between the two versions but that some children feel insulted by the childishness of the animal form and for these the human version should be used. In my experience of administering both forms of the CAT I find that the animal form of the test goes down better with most children, although that may be because I prefer the stimuli. However, given that these CAT cards are intended simply to provoke phantasy on certain themes it appears to me that elaborate comparison of the two versions is irrelevant. If a child is not getting on well with one form, try the other.

Variables measured by the CAT

As with the TAT it is possible to interpret the CAT protocols with great freedom, in accord with any dynamic theory of personality. However the manual to the test suggests that variables to be assessed should include: the main themes of the series; the main heroine (or hero) of the stories, who she is and her attributes; the main needs of the heroine; how the subject sees her personal environment – peers, parents, family; conflicts; anxieties; defences; severity of the superego and the integration of the ego.

It will have been noticed, of course, that the cards have been designed to tap into conflicts and anxieties, indeed to the concepts, held to be important in psychoanalytic, developmental theory. For example, card 10 bears upon toilet training and masturbation, card 7 castration fears, card 6 the primal scene.

Discussion and conclusions

As was the case with the TAT, it has to be said that there is no unequivocal evidence in support of the validity of the CAT as being able to assess conflicts, needs, anxieties or any of the more clearly defined Freudian variables. As was the case with the other projective techniques discussed in this chapter it is possible that gifted and insightful researchers are able to use this test to gain useful information about personality. However as a routine test which any trained psychologist can use it is difficult to recommend it, certainly scored in its normal way.

Again, in accord with previous tests in this chapter it is possible to investigate the validity of the test using G analysis. Thus, for example, if mention of the tail of the monkey being cut off with awful blood and screaming turned out to be correlated with castration anxiety as evinced in analysis then this would be good evidence for the validity of that interpretation of the response. However, careful and laborious investigation of this kind is required together with the construct validation of factors in the CAT with other marker factors in personality such as E and N in the JEPQ, the child's version of the EPQ (Eysenck and Eysenck, 1975). Until such studies of the CAT are carried out, the CAT could not be recommended for anything other than exploratory use, although it remains a fact that the animal form appears to be an attractive test with children.

6. The Blacky Pictures (Blum, 1949)

The Blacky Pictures is a projective technique specifically designed to test psychoanalytic hypotheses. It consists of eleven cartoons portraying a family of dogs in situations which are relevant to Freudian psychosexual personality theory (Freud, 1905). There are four in the family: two parents, Blacky, the eponymous hero, whose sex is that of the subject of the test, and Tippy, a sibling. To each card, subjects have to tell a story about what they think is going on and how each of the characters is feeling. In addition after each story there are some multiple-choice questions about each story.

Description of the Blacky picture and variables

1.	Blacky being suckled.	Oral erotism.
2.	Blacky tearing his mother's collar.	Oral sadism.
3.	Blacky defecating between his parents' kennels.	Anal sadism and anal expulsion (Separate scoring schemes).
4.	Blacky watching his parents making love.	Oedipal intensity.
5.	Blacky licking his genitals.	Masturbation guilt.
6.	Blacky watching Tippy whose tail is about to be lopped.	Castration anxiety or penis envy.
7.	Blacky playing with a toy dog.	Positive identification.
8.	Blacky watching parents fondle Tippy.	Sibling rivalry.

9. Blacky having a vision of an angel.	Guilt feelings.
10. Vision of an ideal female dog.	Positive ego ideal and love-object, derived from 10 and 11 by different scores for each sex.
11. Vision of an ideal male dog.	

Principles of scoring

As is obvious from this description of the cards, the Blacky pictures are designed to test psychoanalytic theory. They are thus far more specific than the CAT or TAT which can be interpreted in accord with any theory of personality. The manual to the test (Blum, 1949) sets out the criteria for scoring the stories, which are tied in closely to standard psychoanalytic theory and are claimed to indicate the presence or absence of disturbance in the level of psychosexual development to which the card is relevant. The multiple-choice questions are used for this purpose as is the task of choosing the most liked and least liked of the cartoons.

One example of the scoring will make the scoring system plain. Thus if, as has occurred to me, in response to card 1, a subject claims that Blacky is not drinking but is playing hide and seek, then this would be scored as fixated at this level since this response involves the defence of denial.

Incidentally, at this juncture it should be pointed out that there is a special set of questions which can be used with the Blacky Pictures and which are designed to elicit defences. This variant of the test is known as the DPI, the Defence Preference Inquiry (e.g. Blum, 1956). No studies of the validity of this use of the Blacky Pictures has ever been carried out and it will not be further discussed. Kline (1981) examines this test in some detail.

Test-retest reliability of the Blacky Pictures

Some studies find a low test-retest reliability while others have reached more acceptable figures. This variation in results, despite the presence of the more reliable multiple-choice questions, suggests that, as is usual with projective tests, much depends on the skill of the tester. However, even a good (from the viewpoint of reliability) study, such as that by Berger and Everstine (1962) yielded a range of coefficients from .3 to .54. This is just about sufficient to use the test with groups, where gross affects might be picked up, but must cast doubt on the utility of this test for many purposes, especially with individual cases where, as was shown in Chapter 1 of this handbook, reliabilities must be at least .7.

Internal consistency of the Blacky Pictures

In a study by Granick and Scheflin (1958) involving forty children it was found that there was reasonably good inter-judge agreement, between 68 and 95 per cent with ten judges on all but two dimensions in scoring the spontaneous stories. Some judges could match test-retest protocols with high accuracy, again confirming the admittedly rather banal claim that marking skill is a critical variable in projective testing.

It may be concluded that the reliability of the Blacky Pictures is not as high as is desirable but that for research use with large groups there is probably sufficient true variance to make the test useful.

Validity of the Blacky Pictures

Kline (1981) has examined the validity of these Blacky Pictures in some detail. As should be obvious the problem with establishing the validity of this test lies in the difficulty of setting up clear criteria. Psychoanalytic variables are notoriously difficult to measure. Thus if the Blacky oral pictures, for example, fail to predict gastric ulceration, this may mean that the test is invalid. However it could well be that the theory is wrong, or, more likely, both theory and test are invalid.

Sappenfield (1965) reviewing all studies up to that date of the Blacky Pictures tried to argue that validity was supported in that usually some theoretical predictions were supported and only rarely have results contradicted hypotheses. However, regrettably, this will not do since psychoanalysis is so flexible a theory that many findings can be made to fit.

Indeed Kline (1981) concluded that there is some evidence for the validity of the Blacky Pictures, despite the low reliability. This arises from the fact that some psychoanalytic hypotheses have been confirmed which are difficult to explain by other theories even of the ad hoc variety. However this evidence is far from definitive. It means that, for experimental purposes, the Blacky Pictures might be used to test certain psychoanalytic hypotheses. If these were confirmed and there was no alternative explanation, the findings might be said to support both test and theory. If the theory was not confirmed it is not possible to say whether this failure is due to weakness of the theory or lack of validity of the test.

Conclusions

In conclusion it is argued that these Blacky Pictures are suited to experimental use where cautious interpretations are made. Similarly, as with all projective tests, G analysis and a comparison of those factors with other more reliable and valid factors might prove useful. A test for research rather than applied psychology, at least for the moment.

7. The Test PN (Corman, 1969)

Corman (1969) further developed the Blacky Pictures especially for use with children and produced what is essentially a new test. This is the Le Patte-Noire, the PN test. This consists of seventeen cards, plus a frontispiece, portraying PN, a black legged pig, in situations which are claimed to be important in psychoanalytic theory. It differs from the Blacky Pictures in a number of ways which will be discussed below. These differences, it is claimed by Corman (1969), render the PN far superior to the Blacky Pictures.

Variables measured	*Cards*
Urethral sadism.	PN is urinating into a trough of food.
Oral sadism.	PN is biting a pig.
Orality.	Several cards: PN being suckled; PN suckling a goat.
Orality and fear of exclusion.	Mother suckling a pig and feeding watched by three piglets.
Orality and sibling rivalry.	PN watching a piglet being suckled and a piglet feeding from a trough; PN being suckled watched by two piglets.
Anal sadism.	PN jumping in dung and mud and splashing an adult pig.
Leaving home.	PN heads out along a road.
Castration fears.	PN with his tail in the bill of a goose.
Oedipal conflicts.	PN, at night, peers at two adult pigs; PN watches two pigs making love.
Self ideal.	PN dreams of a beautiful pig.

There are several other cards where the variable tapped is more general: PN dreams that he is being loaded onto a wagon; PN sees a celestial pig with a wand; PN trapped in a hole at night.

Comments on the cards   It is obvious from this description of the cards in the PN that there are considerable similarities with the Blacky Pictures. On account of the way the test is administered, which is described below, there are duplicates, in terms of the variables tapped, and it seems to me that the PN pictures are more pleasant than the somewhat coarse Blacky cartoons.

Administration

The critical characteristic of the administration of the PN test is its freedom. When the child is shown the frontispiece of the pig family, its members are not described. The age and sex of the pigs are ordained by the child. Furthermore the order in which the cards are administered is chosen by the child who can reject a card and say nothing about it if he or she so wishes. Indeed all that the child is required to do is to tell a story about the picture.

Corman (1969) argues that it is in this freedom that the superiority of the PN over the Blacky Pictures lies. In the Blacky Pictures, as has been seen, the family consists of parents and two children. In the PN this is not so. Sometimes the piglets are not seen as siblings; sometimes the parents are seen as outsiders. Occasionally the female sow (whose gender is obvious) is described as a father. In all these cases Corman stresses the fact that the tester must appear unsurprised.

Once the family is sorted out from the frontispiece, the child is presented with the cards and asked to tell a story about those which interest her or him. After these attention is paid to the reject card but there is no insistence on telling a story against the child's wishes.

However after the stories there is another procedure – preference identification. The cards are collected together and the child sorts them into two piles – liked and disliked. The child then selects the picture she or he likes best of all and gives reasons why and says which of the characters she would like to be. The process is then repeated for all the pictures in the favoured pile, and, at any stage, the child can deny identification with the characters. This same process is carried out with the disliked pile although here the child selects the most disliked and so on.

After the preference identification the tester can ask any other questions which she or he may feel are likely to be useful and then the third part of the test is begun.

This section consists of questions aimed at elucidating the general impression of the test which the child has. The child is asked to name the happiest and the unhappiest character, the most and least gentle and the pig which she or he likes the most. The reasons for all these choices are also obtained. The test is concluded by ascertaining from the wishes card of the test the three wishes of the child.

Comments and conclusions

I have described this test in some detail because it is an attempt to provide a projective measure of psychoanalytic, psychodynamic variables which, if successful, would be highly useful for the study of personality. For the sake of brevity I shall make my comments under a number of heads.

1. The use of this test is virtually restricted to France. I can find no recent references to it in British or American journals.
2. As can be guessed from the description, this is a long test to administer. It takes about ninety minutes and there must be clear evidence that a test of this length measures variables that are useful and cannot be measured more easily before it could be expected to be used.
3. The manual to the test is disappointing in providing the necessary evidence of reliability and validity. However, there are good examples

in the manual of the responses representative of the scoring categories and there are norms based on a small sample of 100 boys and 100 girls. What is lacking, however, are important indices of the worth of a projective test – the inter-scorer reliability, the test-retest reliability and correlations with other external criteria and tests. Without this the clinical material is merely suggestive. Its interpretation assumes validity.

4. In the manual to the test it is claimed by Corman (1969) that the preference identification is a unique feature of the PN test. It was designed to allow the measurement of defences. It must be noted at this point that defences can be measured by the Defence Preference Inquiry of the Blacky Pictures which has already been described. However the Blacky version can be reliably scored since it consists of multiple-choice questions. Corman's preference identification requires the interpretative skill of the tester and thus is likely to be unreliable. I use the term 'likely' here because there are no data in the manual relevant to the reliability or validity of the scores. The case material appears to indicate defences but this measure could not be used except in studies whose aim was to establish the validity of the measures.

It must be concluded that the PN test is a promising test which, if the manual is to be believed, yields rich data relevant to psychodynamic psychology. Clearly it could not be used as a substantive measure of these variables. It is suited only to research and it would appear to be an ideal candidate for G analysis. Its freedom and its more elegant cards do make it more attractive than the earlier Blacky Pictures, from which it was derived, but against this it is inherently less reliable (if used in the traditional manner) because it makes no use of objective questions.

8. The Object Relations Technique (ORT) (Phillipson, 1955)

The ORT is yet another variant of the TAT (the book describing the technique being dedicated to Murray) but one deliberately based on post-Freudian, British analytic theory, the object relations theory of Klein (1948) and Fairbairn (1952). I shall briefly describe and scrutinise this test since, if valid, it would be a highly valuable clinical instrument, at least for those who espouse object relations theory. In that this is a more modern form of psychoanalysis than the traditional theory underlying the Blacky Pictures and the Test PN, the ORT can be seen as a fourth step in the evolution of projective measures from the TAT.

ORT Cards

There are three series of four cards, A, B, C, and a blank card. In all cards there is a considerable degree of ambiguity, especially in respect of the age and sex of the individuals portrayed in the cards, details of the face being sparse or missing.

The A series cards are in light charcoal shading, with no definite setting in terms of objects in the physical world.

The B series of cards are in much darker, charcoal shading to provide depth. Here the figures are in conventional but ambiguous environments, two outdoors, two inside.

The C series cards present figures which are more mature and lifelike, although still ambiguous. The environments are drawn with considerable detail and colour is used.

The blank card is used as in the TAT.

A1. In the centre a faint silhouette, on the left of which a grey shape, possibly human.

A2. Silhouettes of two figures facing each other.

A3. Two silhouette figures on the left, almost touching. On the right another grey figure.

A4. Highly ambiguous but three possible figures in the foreground watching another three in the background.

B1. A bedroom can be seen through the open door of which is a half-hidden human figure.

B2. Two figures stand beneath a tree, in front of a house.

B3. Two merged silhouettes of human figures in a light area. In the dark foreground a third figure.

B4. A structure with two arches, five silhouette figures in one, one in the other arch.

C1. Interior of a cottage showing a chair and table and in the window the faint outline of a human figure.

C2. A figure stands outside the open door of a bedroom.

C3. Interior of a room in which two figures are seated at a table while one stands at the mantelpiece, on which there is a conspicuous coloured object.

C4. A stairway, with dark figures at the bottom and the shadow of a figure at the top.

The blank card.

Administration

There is an arbitrary order of presentation of these cards of which subjects are expected to give some account, indicating what they think is going on.

Scoring and interpreting the test

Some normative data are supplied in the handbook to the test (Phillipson, 1955). These detail the responses to the pictures of two samples: fifty clinical cases, out-patients, and forty adolescent girls. However, these samples are not only far too small to be representative but the information supplied is purely of a factual nature – e.g. x girls thought the coloured object was a lamp. If these samples were bigger such data might have been useful to pick out the statistically abnormal response or a response typical of a certain kind of patient. As it stands, however, these data are of little interest.

Far more important would have been to know the reliability of the interpretations of the meaning of the responses to the pictures, both between different testers and on different occasions. Some indication of the validity of the scores would have been useful, but on these topics the manual is, alas, silent.

This is not to say that the problem of the validity of the ORT is ignored. On the contrary, an attempt is made to demonstrate validity through case studies. These are highly interesting, but as is usual with impressionistic material of this kind, they cannot be convincing to the sceptic.

Conclusions

The ORT is worthy of consideration because it has been devised to help in the elucidation of object relations theory, a branch of psychology which would appear ill suited to measurement. The choice of cards and their rationale appear to be sound and in accord with theory. However until there is some convincing evidence that the ORT can enable the tester to assess the object relations of her or his subjects (and there is little beyond case studies, presumably because psychometrics and object relations theory are uneasy bedfellows) the ORT is again, as with so many projective techniques, suitable only for the investigation of its own reliability and validity. Until this is done, deductions from it are of little more weight than the clinical deductions it was supposed to buttress. However they are a little more weighty because at least other psychologists can inspect the ORT protocols from which they were derived.

In conclusion, the ORT is an interesting and ingenious test but it requires considerable psychometric attention before it could be used for any substantive, psychological purposes.

Other projective tests

As Semeonoff (1981) points out, there are other projective tests where the subject is required to manipulate materials rather than describe ambiguous stimuli. The use of sand as a method for understanding children has been extensively used by Lowenfeld (1939) and Bowyer (1970) has discussed this approach in considerable detail. However none of these techniques is sufficiently reliable or valid to be recommended as a test, although as a technique for improving the rapport between therapist and child they are probably useful. Lowenfeld (1954) also developed the Mosaic test where materials have to be manipulated by the child but again this seems more suited to improving the patient – therapist relationship than to precise measurement.

Conclusions concerning projective tests

From this discussion of the best-validated projective tests it is clear that none of them can be used with confidence, as demonstrably reliable and valid measures. The G analysis which has been suggested throughout this chapter as a psychometrically sound method may improve this gloomy situation and it would appear to be a useful research objective to investigate its value for projective tests.

An obvious question arises as to why I have devoted so much space in this handbook to tests which are neither reliable nor valid. As was argued at the beginning of this chapter, projective tests have been widely used in psychology and certain gifted individuals appear to obtain impressive results with them. Projective tests seem to measure aspects of personality which inventories are unable to tap and the task of psychometrics is to evolve methods which can utilise this reliable variance. Semeonoff (1981) concluded his chapter on projective tests by arguing that psychology would be the worse if projective tests were abandoned because they yield data which are unobtainable elsewhere. This is my view and I feel that it is essential that research continues in how these tests may be used with proper psychometric precision.

PART II: OBJECTIVE TESTS

Cattell and Warburton (1967) list virtually all the objective tests which had been devised up to that date and this is still a complete catalogue. However, as was discussed in Chapter 16, few of these objective tests, defined as tests of which the purpose was hidden from subjects taking the tests and which could be objectively scored, had any evidence of validity.

In fact only two objective tests have any serious claims to validity and these will be described in this section. For descriptions of other objective tests readers should turn to the compendium by Cattell and Warburton (1967).

1. The Objective-Analytic Battery (OAB) (Cattell and Schuerger, 1978)

The OAB consists of the best-validated set of objective personality factors.

Variables measured

The OAB measures ten source trait factors. The universal index number indicates their position in the overall set of source trait factors isolated by Cattell and his colleagues.

1. U.I.16. Ego standards – self assertion and achievement.
2. U.I.19. Independence vs. subduedness.
3. U.I.20. Evasiveness.
4. U.I.21. Exuberance.
5. U.I.23. Capacity to mobilise vs. regression – emotional balance.
6. U.I.24. Anxiety.
7. U.I.25. Realism vs. tense inflexibility.
8. U.I.28. Negative asthenia vs. self assurance.
9. U.I.32. Exvia vs. invia.
10. U.I.33. Discouragement vs. sanguineness.

Test materials. All tests are timed

U.I. 16 has eight tests:
1. Attitudes. This is a typical attitude test but objectively scored – the number of extreme responses.
2. Coding. Vowels have to be selected from letter strings.
3. Letter and number comparison. Pairs of letters and numbers have to be marked as same or different.
4. Goodness of work. Estimates have to be made of how good certain performances are.
5. Modernistic drawings. Subjects have to say what they can see in certain modern drawings.
6. Assumptions. This a test of logic: deductions from sentences.
7. Rapid calculation. Simple, rapid arithmetic.
8. My interests. Subjects tick off from a list things in which they are interested.

U.I.19 has seven tests:
1. Problems. Simple mathematical problems.
2. Hidden shapes. Geometrical figures are hidden in other figures and have to be discovered.
3. Reading comprehension. A memory and comprehension test of English prose.
4. What is the right design? This is a test where sequences of patterns have to be completed.
5. Searching. Pictures in which subjects have to discover details.
6. Picture memory. Pictures have to be remembered.
7. Observation. Types of figures have to be rapidly coded, according to a key.

U.I.20 has seven tests:
1. Opinions 1. Subjects have to indicate the extent of their agreement with certain opinions.
2. Opinions 2. Similar to 1.
3. Opinions 3. Similar to 1.

4. Memory. Subjects have to say whether sentences were found in test 3 or not.
5. Opinions 4. This is test 1 with the response scale reversed.
6. Common annoyances. Subjects have to say to what extent certain things annoy them.
7. Human nature 1. Subjects have to indicate the extent of their agreement with certain common beliefs about people.

U.I.23 has eight tests:
1. Annoyances. Similar to test 6 of U.I.20.
2. Comparing letters. Pairs of letter strings have to be compared.
3. Where do the lines cross? Imaginary lines between points have to be drawn and their point of crossing indicated.
4. Which would you rather do? Subjects have to choose between pairs of occupations.
5. Assumptions 2. A logic test similar to assumptions 1.
6. What do you see? Two drawings and subjects have to indicate whether they can see certain objects in them.
7. Matching words. Subjects have to indicate which word goes best with other words.
8. How fast can you write? Subjects have to write a word as many times as possible and then a phrase.

U.I.24 has eight tests:
1. Humour test. Subjects have to say how funny they think a number of jokes.
2. How much do you like? Subjects have to indicate how much they like or dislike doing certain things.
3. Do you sometimes? Subjects have to say how often they have done certain things which are somewhat undesirable.
4. What's your comment? Subjects have to choose from one of three comments made about a set of statements.
5. Jokes and tricks. Subjects have to say if they would have considered, when younger, certain practical jokes to be funny.
6. Putting up with things. Subjects have to say if they are prepared to do certain unpleasant tasks.
7. What bothers me. Subjects have to indicate how much they are bothered by certain common events, some similar to common annoyances.
8. Favourite titles. Subjects have to indicate which book titles, with brief synopses, they would prefer to read.

U.I.25. This factor has seven tests:
1. Human nature 2. Subjects are required to indicate the extent of their agreement with statements about human beings. Highly similar to human nature 1.

2. Memory. Phrases from test 1 have to be discriminated from other phrases.
3. Memory for numbers. Strings of digits are read out. Subjects have to say whether certain strings were read out or not.
4. Wise statements. Subjects have to indicate the wisdom or stupidity of a set of statements.
5. Best words to fit. Words have to be matched to other words. Different principles can be used.
6. Memory. Words are learned. They have to be recognised embedded among other words.
7. Counting letters and numbers. Target letters and digits have to be counted in strings of digits and letters.

U.I.28. This factor has seven tests:
1. Opinions 5. Statements about human behaviour to which subjects have to indicate the extent of their agreement.
2. Human nature 3. A similar test to opinions 5.
3. How long would it take you? Subjects are asked to select from two possibilities how long they would take to do certain things.
4. What will happen? Brief stories with two possible endings, one of which subjects select.
5. What does it take? Two identical lists of jobs: to one subjects have to say how important are intelligence and hard work; for the other the importance of the right friends and cheating.
6. Opinions 6. More statements to which subjects have to indicate the extent of their agreement.
7. Longer or shorter. Subjects are given rest periods which they have to judge as relatively shorter or longer than the one before.

U.I.32. This factor has seven tests:
1. Judging lines. Sets of lines of different lengths are given and subjects have to choose which is the bigger within each pair.
2. Which is more? Pairs of circles contain a number of numbers. Which circle contains the greater number of numbers has to be selected.
3. Qualities. Figures have to be compared for size, or other qualities, with an exemplar.
4. Crime and punishment. A series of crimes is described and to each subjects have to indicate their seriousness by means of a fitting punishment.
5. Can you hear the word? Muffled words are played on a tape recorder and subjects have to write down what they hear.
6. Obstacles. There is an obstacle course with lines and slanted lines and rules for passing them. Subjects have to work as quickly as possible in completing four courses.
7. Writing signatures. Subjects write their signature as quickly as possible. They then write it backwards as quickly as possible.

U.I.33. This factor has seven tests:

1. Performance estimates. Subjects have to judge whether a particular performance is good or poor on a five-point scale.
2. How many friends? Situations are presented to subjects who have to say whether none, one or more friends would help them.
3. What is fun? A number of events are listed and subjects have to say whether they would enjoy them or not.
4. My feelings. Subjects have to indicate on a five-point scale how happy or unhappy they felt to a list of events.
5. Chances of success. This is a list of desirable activities and subjects have to estimate on a three-point scale their chances of doing each one.
6. Opinions 7. In this test subjects have to indicate the extent of their agreement or disagreement on a five-point scale to a number of statements.
7. How would events affect you? This is a list of events and subjects have to indicate the effects on them on a five-point scale, very bad to very good.

Reliability

Cattell and Schuerger (1978) cite test-retest reliability over three to six weeks. These range from .58 to .85 for the ten factors and are generally satisfactory. As is usual with the tests of Cattell, despite the classical theory of test error, Cattell and Schuerger (1978) do not report internal consistency reliabilities on the grounds that reduced homogeneity increases validity (the argument being that the multiple correlation of the items with the criterion must be increased by the lower intercorrelations). There is some force in this point and the test-retest reliabilities are satisfactory.

Validity

Cattell and Schuerger cite, as evidence for validity, the multiple correlation of the subtests with the pure factor, an example of concept or construct validity. These are impressively high, ranging from .64 to .92. However it must be pointed out that statistically brilliant as this validity coefficient is, it begs the essential question as to just what these factors are. Furthermore, as Nunnally (1978) argues, with seven or eight variables multiple correlations are likely to be high. These coefficients are more like internal consistency measures although they are boosted by the fact that multiple correlations make the most of random sampling factors.

Cattell and Schuerger (1978) offer further evidence of validity by quoting correlations between the O-A factors and occupational, clinical and occupational criteria. However two points should be noted about these claims. First, the correlations, although significant, are small, in the range of

.2 to .3. This means that less than 10 per cent of variance is explained, or put another way 90 per cent is unexplained. This is not, therefore, particularly impressive. The second point concerns the tests used. Over the years different subtests were used in the O-A Battery, which was modified in the light of results obtained with them. This means that the correlations in the manual are in most cases not actually with the O-A Battery.

It may be concluded from the results presented in the manual to the test that the O-A Battery might be valid but there is no unequivocal evidence. For these reasons Kline and Cooper (1984a) carried out a study of the construct validity of the O-ATB by factoring its subtests together with a range of the best-established factors in the personality and ability spheres. Thus the factors emerging would not simply be identified by their factor loadings but by their location in factor space.

To this end, the EPQ (Eysenck and Eysenck, 1975), the 16PF test (Cattell et al., 1970) and Ai3Q (Kline, 1971a), all tests fully described in Chapter 25 of this handbook, were selected to cover the field of personality. The major attitude factors were measured by the following scales: for authoritarian personality, Kohn's (1972) F Scale, Ray's (1970) Balanced Dogmatism Scale, the Conservatism Scale of Wilson and Patterson (1970); for machiavellianism, the Christie and Geis (1970) measure. All these variables are discussed in Chapter 28 of this handbook. For ability the Comprehensive Ability Battery (Hakstian and Cattell, 1976a) was used, a test which is fully described in Chapter 24 of this handbook.

This battery of tests was administered to 154 students and the scales were subjected to a rotated simple structure factor analysis in which significant factors, selected by the Scree test (Cattell, 1966) were rotated by the Direct Oblimin procedure (Jennrich and Sampson, 1966) to the position where the hyperplane count was maximised. In fact two analyses were carried out. The first used the O-ATB factor scores as scored by Cattell and Schuerger (1978). Nine factors emerged in this study but none corresponded to the expected factors in the O-ATB. Indeed most of the O-ATB scales were loading on both personality and ability factors. This study casts considerable doubt on the validity of the O-ATB.

In the second analysis we located the ten factors that had been shown to underlie the O-ATB, when analysed separately, in the same factor space as the first study. Here thirteen factors were extracted but these again showed that the O-ATB was far from unifactorial, most factors being loaded on both ability and personality, although two possible O-A factors emerged, of authoritarianism and machiavellianism, which Cooper et al. (1986) did cross-validate on a small sample.

Despite these two factors Kline and Cooper (1984b) were forced to conclude that in Great Britain at least, the O-ATB was not a valid measure and that its tests of extraversion and anxiety were not measuring the questionnaire factors. As might be expected from their form, many of the O-ATB scales measured, somewhat inefficiently, ability factors. This test, alas, cannot be recommended.

2. The Motivation Analysis Test (MAT) (Cattell *et al.*, 1970b)

Variables measured a. Ergs (basic drives): mating, assertiveness, fear, narcissism (comfort seeking) and pugnacity; b. sentiments (culturally moulded drives: self-sentiment, superego or conscience, career, sweetheart and parental home). Within these factors there are two components, unintegrated and integrated, corresponding roughly to unconscious and conscious aspects (Cattell and Child, 1975).

Number of items 208.

Type of items There are four subtests in the MAT each with a different type of item. All are questionnaire-type objective tests, i.e. it is not possible for subjects to guess what the items are measuring. The four item types are:

1. Forty-eight forced-choice items where subjects have to indicate what is the better use for a given amount of time or money or some other commodity.
2. Estimates. Fifty-six questions involving estimates have to be answered on a four-point scale, for example 'What percent of adults are happy to give money to . . . ?'

These two tests measure the unintegrated components of these drives.

3. Paired words. In this test a key word is printed with a pair of words. Subjects have to choose which of the pair goes better with the key word. There are forty-eight items.
4. Information. Forty-eight items testing everyday knowledge.

These two tests measure the integrated component of the drives on the argument advanced by Cattell and Child (1975) that subjects know more about the subjects in which they are interested and thus will have more knowledge (information) and will be likely to associate words to their interest (paired words).

Reliability

Cattell *et al.* (1970b) in the handbook to the MAT quote alpha coefficients ranging from .33 to .71. The median alpha was only .45 and this suggests that the MAT scales are not sufficiently reliable to be valid although, as has been discussed, Cattell is virtually alone among leading psychometricians in believing that high reliabilities lead to low validity because the test becomes too homogeneous and thus too specific. While there is some force in this argument, the reliabilities of these scales seem too low. However, if there is evidence that they are valid, such low reliability is unimportant.

Norms

American norms are provided but these are somewhat small samples.

Validity

Cattell *et al.* (1970b) claim validity coefficients for these MAT variables beyond .9. However these are correlations with the true factors, coefficients which, as Alker (1972) pointed out, are necessarily highly inflated. Cattell and Child (1975) demonstrate clearly that the MAT variables are independent of the personality factors (temperamental rather than motivational) in the 16PF test but the study by Burdsall (1975) produced six factors which did not fit well with those claimed to be in this test.

Non-factorial attempts to demonstrate the validity of the MAT have included studies where the fear erg and the sex erg were aroused and scores on the relevant ergs before and after were compared. These two studies (Kawash *et al.*, 1972 and Cattell, Kawash and De Yong, 1972) did provide evidence of the validity of the test. Kline and Grindley (1974) also showed the test to fit diary reports of behaviour and feelings. In this research one subject completed the MAT every day for twenty-eight days. She also kept a confidential diary over this period. Fluctuations in ergs and sentiments related clearly to diary reports.

However, a study by Cooper and Kline (1982b) casts considerable doubt on the validity of the MAT on simple psychometric grounds. The test clearly needs considerable revision before it can be used with any confidence. A Direct Oblimin, rotated simple structure factor analysis of the MAT and 16PF scales was carried out on a sample of 109 male subjects. Eight factors emerged from this study but none fitted the postulated structure of the MAT and the validity of the test is called into considerable doubt by these findings.

As a further check a classical item analysis of the twenty scales was carried out and it was shown that these scales are not homogeneous. The items simply do not fit the scales to which they are claimed to belong.

Conclusions

The MAT is a highly interesting test because it is one of the few objective tests which has been standardised and published. However it must be concluded that in Great Britain, at least, it is not a valid test and it could not be recommended except for further exploratory research.

Final conclusions concerning objective tests

The two published batteries of objective tests do not stand close psychometric scrutiny. Their factor structures are not as their authors intended them to be. I have examined them carefully, however, rather than ignoring or rejecting them because, as was pointed out in Chapter 16, these tests have great potential with obvious advantages over questionnaires. For this reason the two published tests deserve careful scrutiny. That they have failed this searching examination must not lead us to despair of objective tests. What is required is systematic study of the a priori best tests in the compendium of Cattell and Warburton (1967), in which these T factors are located in the factor space both of ability and personality. If this is carefully executed and simple structure is reached with the appropriate marker factors, a useful and valid battery of objective, T, tests could be constructed.

Chapter 27

Motivation and Interest Tests

Tests of interest and motivation have largely been the concern of occupational and vocational psychologists rather than theorists of motivation, and for this reason the majority of tests are empirical and atheoretical. Exceptions are the Motivation Analysis Test (Cattell, Horn and Sweney, 1970) which was discussed in the previous chapter and the newer Vocational Interest Measure (Sweney and Cattell, 1980), both based on factor analysis. I shall begin with the latter test.

Vocational Interest Measure (VIM) (Sweney and Cattell, 1980)

This is an objective test, as defined in the previous chapter. However I discuss it here because it is a test designed for occupational and vocational application, measuring the same variables as the majority of non-factored empirical tests, which form the bulk of this chapter.

Variables measured Ten variables: Two ergs and eight sentiments.

1. protectiveness erg
2. rest-seeking erg

Sentiments:

1. career
2. mechanical interests
3. clerical work interests
4. scientific interests
5. aesthetic–dramatic interests
6. business–economic interests
7. sports interests
8. nature–outdoor interests

Type of tests Four objective devices (as described in Chapter 16): (a) word association; (b) autistic distortion; (c) information; (d) projection. All these tests, although objective, are in questionnaire format so that the VIM is a group test.

Time 70 mins.

Comments

I shall not say much about this VIM simply because, as was shown with the other objective tests, the MAT and the OAB (discussed in the previous chapter), there is a problem concerning validity. However the VIM is worthy of research investigation because it is the only factored motivation test designed for applied work. The test needs validation against empirical criteria of work success, as has been done with the 16PF test. Such work is in progress under the direction of Sweney at Wichita University.

As is made clear by Sweney *et al.* (1986) this test is complementary to the MAT. It is tied in to Cattell's factor analytic descriptions of personality and to his complex theories of motivation, subsumed under the notion of the Dynamic Calculus (1985).

In brief a test worthy of research and should it prove valid, because it is rooted in the factor analytic exploration of motivation, a far more powerful test than any so far developed.

The Strong Vocational Interest Blank (SVIB) (Strong *et al.*, 1971) and the Strong-Campbell Interest Inventory (SCII) (Strong and Campbell, 1974)

The SVIB was introduced in 1927 (Strong, 1927) and there have been regular modifications and developments to the scale of which the most recent edition was that of Strong *et al.* (1971). Since that date it has been further revised and renamed as the Campbell-Strong Interest Inventory although it is still recognisably an edition of the old test.

I am including this test because it is one of the outstanding examples of a criterion-keyed test (see Chapter 9) and because it has been so widely used as a test of interest. Buros (1972), indeed, cited almost 1100 references. However the extensive revisions have virtually made a new test and, although the handbook to the new version claims high similarity between the tests, Williams *et al.* (1968) have cast some doubt on this assertion.

Variables measured   Occupational interests. Scores are compared with the scores of fifty-seven female and sixty-seven male occupational groups. In addition the SCII contains six general occupational scales: realistic, investigative, artistic, social, enterprising and conventional. These categories were derived from the work of Holland (1966), discussed in Chapter 17 of this handbook.

Furthermore there are twenty-three basic interest scales based upon correlated items: agriculture, nature, adventure, military, mechanical, science, mathematics, medical science, medical service, music/drama, art, writing, teaching, social service, athletics, domestic arts, religious, public speaking, law/politics, merchandising, sales, business management, office practice.

Item type   Activities, occupations, amusements, school subjects and the like are set out. Subjects have to indicate like, dislike or indifference.

Item numbers   399 SVIB; 325 SCII.

Time taken   One hour for the longer test, about 40 mins for the shorter – for subjects who are good readers.

Reliability   Test-retest reliabilities for these scales are high over a short period (beyond .9) and around .6 and .7 after several years.

Validity of the test and conclusions

My discussion is equally applicable to both versions of the test which will be referred to as the Strong test. There are several points to be made which are dealt with separately.

1. The Strong test is a criterion-keyed test. This means that the scales have no psychological meaning. Thus a high score on the accountants scale means only that a subject scored highly on the set of items which discriminates accountants. She or he resembles accountants on those items.
2. This means that as jobs change and need different requirements (for example, computers have altered the nature of many occupations) these scales may be inadequate.
3. The norms are based on American occupations. In so far as these are different from jobs of a similar name in other countries the Strong test will be inadequate. Lawyers are a good case in point.
4. Even if good discriminations among the holders of various jobs can be made the meaning of these discriminations is unknown. Hence there is no gradual build up of psychological knowledge about occupations which could be useful in occupational psychology. Nor is it possible to extrapolate any results to new jobs.

All these points strongly suggest that the Strong test is not a good test to use in the applied field, even if it discriminates well among occupational groups. Blind empiricism can only be advocated where more rational, theoretical methods have failed.

5. The discriminatory and predictive power of the Strong tests. Katz (1972) reviewing the validity of the SVIB argues that, while it is clear from the manual to the test that the Strong will discriminate among occupations, it does so no better than asking a simple question of whether the subject is interested in an occupation, a point first made by Dolliver (1969). There is no more recent work to refute this point, and it suggests that the Strong tests are not useful in prediction.
6. The occupational scales and the basic interest scales share common items. This makes correlational analysis and factor analysis difficult to interpret, techniques which might help to give psychological meaning to the scales.
7. Conclusions. All these points make it difficult to recommend the Strong

scales. Their lack of psychological meaning, the fact that knowledge about vocational interests cannot be built up on the basis of the results, the difficulty of applying the test to new or changing jobs and the fact that it discriminates no better than expressed interest, support this claim. As Sweney *et al.* (1986) argue, it may still be useful as a basis for discussion in vocational guidance or counselling but far more simple and less time consuming tests would be equally valuable. However, such a use is a far cry from what should be expected of a good psychometric test – a valid score – and this the Strong scales are unlikely to yield.

The Kuder Tests

Kuder has produced a number of tests which are essentially rivals to the Strong scales and which have been extensively used especially in America.

Kuder General Interest Survey (KGIS) (Kuder, 1970a)

This is a revised version of the Kuder Preference Record – Vocational.

Variables measured Areas of interest – outdoor, mechanical, computational, scientific, persuasive, artistic, literary, musical, social service and clerical.

Kuder Occupational Interest Survey (KOIS) (Kuder, 1970b)

This is the revised version of the Kuder Preference Record – Occupational.

Variables measured Seventy-seven male occupational scales and fifty-seven female occupational scales, together with a number of academic interest scales.

Items In both tests triads of activities are given of which subjects have to choose the most liked and the most disliked.

Number of items 168 (KGIS); 100 (KOIS).

Scoring the items

As should be obvious, there is a major problem with this type of item. Since items require subjects to rank choices the scores are interlinked. If a subject chooses the artistic item in the triad she or he cannot choose the other two interests. This is ipsative scoring. As was discussed in Chapter 4 ipsative scoring has a number of severe disadvantages which will be briefly listed here.

1. The correlations derived from ipsative tests are artefacts of the scoring system. The mean correlation between scores must be negative and is $-1/(n-1)$ where n = the number of scales.
2. This renders the scores unsuitable for factor analysis and thus it is difficult to estimate their construct validity.
3. Since ipsative scores are rankings made by subjects the establishment of meaningful norms is impossible. This is because identical rankings by subjects in no way indicate real equivalence, because they ignore differences in strength of interest.
4. This produces quite grotesque consequences for the KGIS as Stahmann (1971) has pointed out. Thus if a student has a percentile score of 90 on the Mechanical scale and a percentile score of 70 on the Artistic scale it does not mean that she or he is more interested in mechanical than artistic activities. All that can be said is that in responding to the triads of items the subject chose mechanical activities more frequently than 90 per cent of the norm group and artistic activities more frequently than 70 per cent of the group. As Husek (1965) argues a higher score can be obtained on scale A than B although the subject is more interested in B than A.
5. These absurdities arise from attempting to develop norms for ipsative tests. The absolute rank order of interest for an individual, however, still stands.
6. It follows that the numbers derived from the Kuder tests must be treated with considerable caution, although the results may be suitable for discussion with the individual by a vocational guidance counsellor. Here however all the problems of subjective interpretation come into play.
7. Conclusions. For all these reasons I shall not consider the KGIS further. Its only use would appear to be as a basis for discussion and it is far too complex and time consuming a test for such a purpose.

I shall now examine the KOIS, where the item format is not so disadvantageous.

Rationale of the KOIS test

The scores from the KOIS indicate the occupations to which the subject appears the most suited. Unlike the equivalent Strong test which included items in the scales if they differentiated one occupational group from another, items were chosen for an occupational scale by similarity. Thus if preference for an item was made by an engineer, it was weighted on the engineer scale. However this scoring system, as Thorndike and Hagen (1971) point out, means that many scales are highly similar and a subject may appear suited to a number of occupations. Again, as was the case with the Strong test, this test measures similarity to an occupational group and is a criterion-keyed inventory, with all the disadvantages which have been discussed in connection with the Strong.

Conclusions

I shall not repeat here the points which have been made about the SVIB and which are equally relevant to the KOIS – the lack of meaning of the scales, the problems when jobs change, the fact that the norms are American and the inability of the test to build up a base of psychological knowledge. Thus all depends on the validity of the test, its ability to predict job satisfaction or success.

Here, as the surveys by Cronbach (1976), Thorndike and Hagen (1971) and Brown (1976) indicate the KOIS is just about as good as the SVIB. However, since we have shown that stated interest performs as well as the Strong in job prediction, the same arguments apply and it would be difficult to support the use of the KOIS. Indeed, in connection with this point in Project Talent (Cooley and Lohnes, 1968) in which young people were followed up it was also found that expressed interest was the best predictor. In brief it is difficult to recommend the Kuder tests, although they have been widely used especially in America.

The Kuder and Strong are certainly the best known and most highly researched interest tests. However, as has been shown, they suffer from the disadvantage of their criterion-keying and in the case of the Kuder the ipsative scoring. I shall not consider any other interest test utilising this type of construction.

Vocational Preference Inventory (VPI) (Holland, 1985a)

This is the eighth revision of a test which was first developed in 1953 and which stems from a programme of research and a theory of vocational choice (Holland, 1966; 1985b). This is discussed in Chapter 17.

Variables measured Eleven scales: realistic, investigative, artistic, social, enterprising, conventional, self-control, masculinity–femininity, status, infrequency and acquiescence.

Time taken 15 – 30 mins.

Age range 14 years and upwards.

Item type 160 occupational titles to which subjects have to indicate 'like' or 'dislike'. Items can be left blank where subjects are undecided.

Reliability

KR20 reliabilities are all >.8 except for three scales which are greater than .5 (masc., status and infrequency). Test-retest reliabilities are moderate to high after 4 years – around .5.

Norms Huge student norms – 6000 males and 6000 females from thirty-one diverse institutions – together with various occupational groups.

Validity see Comments.

Comments

Holland (1985a) argues that the normative data in the manual to the test are not definitive, merely suggestive, and that ideally local norms should be built up by those who want to use the test in the applied field. High and low scores are the important ones for interpretation. Thus all depends upon the validity of the scales.

Holland (1985b) has shown in extensive studies that there is a relationship between personality types, as defined by the Holland scales, and choice of job. He has demonstrated, in more than 400 investigations, that subjects do tend to choose occupations which suit them, to a moderate extent. However the correlations are far from unity. The concurrent and predictive validity of the Holland scales relative to occupational membership is, however, equal or superior to that of similar interest tests.

In the original studies (Holland, 1966) the VPI variables were also regarded as indices of personality. In an attempt to demonstrate this point Holland (1985a) cites correlations with a wide variety of personality tests, all of which have been discussed in Chapter 25 of this handbook – the NEO scales, the Guilford-Zimmerman Temperament Survey, the Californian Psychological Inventory, the 16PF Test, the Edwards Personal Preference Schedule and the Kuder Preference Record, discussed in this chapter.

It is difficult to summarise so huge a number of correlations. Here, indeed, factor analysis of all these scales would have been valuable. Nevertheless in general the validity of these scales is supported. For example, the enterprising scale of the VPI correlates with Cattell's A, sociability, E, dominance, F, enthusiasm, and H, adventurousness. This clearly makes good sense. What is noticeable is that some VPI variables tend to correlate with a greater number of personality scales than do others. This suggests that the VPI may itself be measuring little more than the ubiquitous big five or even just extraversion and neuroticism (see Chapters 25 and 15). Correlations with the NEO scale (Costa *et al.*, 1984) support this claim since 1 scale correlates with the neuroticism scale, 2 with extraversion and 3 with openness (the two other more recent scales of the NEO were not administered). Unfortunately no adequate factor analyses of the VPI are reported in the manual, although Holland claims that the scales are independent.

Conclusions

The manual to the test contains less information than the books (Holland, 1966; 1985b). From the mass of studies which have been conducted with the VPI it does appear to measure interests and this would account for the correlations with personality variables. It is also moderately able to predict job choice and it is a reliable test. It should also be pointed out that a computer version of this test correlated well (between .6 and .8) with the original form (Hodgkinson, 1986). The VPI is probably about the best interest test available since it is not simply empirical although it has to be said that the vocational theory is less than remarkable – that people seek jobs that suit them. What is required is a study in which the Holland scales are located in factor space, not just of personality but also of interest and ability.

Rothwell-Miller Interest Blank (Miller, 1968a)

Variables measured   Twelve areas of interest: mechanical, computational, outdoor, scientific, persuasive, aesthetic, literary, musical, social service, clerical, practical and medical.

Items   Sets of jobs have to be ranked in order of preference, ignoring money and status.

Number of items   Nine sets of twelve jobs. Each job represents an interest area.

Scoring   Ranks across sets for each type of job are summed.

Time to complete   10 mins at most.

Comments

This description makes it clear that the Rothwell-Miller Test yields ipsative scores. The scores represent the ranked preferences of an individual for these twelve areas of interest. In the test manual (Miller, 1968b) no evidence is presented that it predicts job satisfaction or success better than a simple statement of interest, and I know of no such subsequent research. Furthermore despite the fact that the scores are ipsative, norms are set out in the manual which, as we have discussed in connection with the Kuder tests, are necessarily meaningless.

For all these reasons as a psychometric test this test has little to recommend it. However I have listed it in this chapter because it is so simple and quick to complete and so easy for subjects to understand that as a basis for discussion about jobs it is truly excellent. Since, as has been indicated, many interest tests are of low psychometric efficiency, despite great length and complexity, and are best used on a similar basis for practical vocational guidance, the Rothwell-Miller may be just as useful as these in practice but quick and cheap.

The Brook Reaction Test (Heim *et al.*, 1969)

This is an interest test developed by Alice Heim and her colleagues at Cambridge, of a very different kind from any others discussed in this chapter. It has never been much used and I mention it here because, as should be obvious, most of the best-known interest tests are not powerful psychometric tests. Possibly with research and considerable refinement a good measure might be developed from this test.

Variables measured Twenty-two interest areas: aesthetic, business, clothing and appearance, dancing and social functions, entertainment, food, agricultural, humanitarian, intellectual, practical, literary, legal, military, outdoor, people, political, religious, biological, science, physical science, secretarial, sport and travel.

Items Eighty stimulus words, presented by tape recorder, one every twelve seconds, to which subjects have to respond by giving their first association and then the one that follows and so on until the next stimulus. Subjects write down their responses.

Age range 13 years and upwards.

Scoring the Test

Each response to each stimulus is classified for interest, four points of interest being available for each stimulus. Since it is an oral test there are good possibilities for different interpretation, thus increasing variance. For each word there is a response book with most possible answers categorised, to ensure that scoring is reliable. An example will clarify the system, although this stimulus does not occur in the test.

Example of Brook scoring: Red or Read (the Brook is an oral test)

1. Politics, Gorbachev, Kennedy. Here all the responses are political and the subject would be scored 4 on political interest.
2. Green, whales, Melville. Here we would give 2 for aesthetic interest, as the first response, 1 for biological and 1 for literary interests.

These two imaginary but typical responses illustrate the rationale of the Brook Reaction Test: responses are held to indicate interest and this principle was invoked in the construction of the objective MAT (Cattell, Horn and Sweney, 1970) discussed in the previous chapter.

Scoring a complete Brook test takes about one hour even for a skilled marker.

Reliability

With such a long and complex scoring system reliability is obviously a problem. Kline (1969) computed the split-half reliability of the twenty-two scales in a sample of students and found that it was around .8 for most of the scales. This compares well with the reliability of interest inventories. If one marker can achieve this reliability presumably others can also do so.

Validity

This test has been little used and there is almost no evidence for validity. Heim *et al.* (1969) showed that scores on the test fitted in well with activities. For example members of the Cambridge University mountaineering society had high scores on outdoor interests. Indeed I am one of the few who has investigated this test. I showed that the Brook was largely independent of the Cattell 16PF test (Kline, 1970), and had low correlations with the Rothwell-Miller test in a sample of 13-year-old children but which was the more accurate could not be ascertained (Kline and Thomas, 1972). Finally Kline (1971c) found that the Brook scores were unrelated to aptitude as measured by the DAT (see Chapter 24).

Conclusions

It is obvious that the Brook test has virtually no evidence for validity. This combined with the complexity of the scoring system has caused it to fall into disuse. I have discussed it here and investigated it previously because it *could* be a good interest test. Its rationale makes sense, it is difficult to fake because suppression of responses shows up in missed responses as the relentless 12-second succession of stimuli are delivered. Furthermore it does not force respondents into making absurd choices such as saying whether they prefer to run a tea party for old age pensioners or organise a cricket match when they hate both with an equally bitter hatred.

In brief a test of great potential. Clearly the principle deserves further investigation to see whether it could be instantiated into a brief and easily scored measure which could predict occupational success or satisfaction.

The Eight-State Questionnaire (8SQ) (Curran and Cattell, 1976)

Two forms A and B.

Variables measured Eight moods or states: anxiety, stress, depression, regression, fatigue, guilt, extraversion, arousal.

Age range 16 years upwards.

Items Statements to be answered on four-point scales, usually true to false.

Number of items 96.

Reliability Test-retest reliabilities are low, around .3 and .4. However, as states or moods this does not mean the scales are useless. Internal consistency reliabilities are not stated in the manual. Parallel form reliabilities are high – about .8.

Norms Adult norms are given (N = 1701) and norms for prisoners. However since moods are variable, the status of norms is doubtful (see Chapter 17).

Validity

Concept validities are quoted – factor loadings of the scales with the pure factor. How this was measured is not stated and this is the weakness of the notion of concept validity. Otherwise in the test manual no other evidence for validity is cited.

Cattell and his colleagues have carried out little further research into the validity of this test and no new information concerning validity is to be found in Cattell and Johnson (1986). However a recent study by Boyle and Katz (1991) suggests that two factors account for the variance in the 8SQ – extraversion/arousal and negative state factors. This analysis, of course, resembles the positive and negative affect scales of Watson and Tellegen (1985). Indeed there is still considerable uncertainty concerning the structure of moods as is fully discussed in Chapter 17 of this handbook.

Conclusions

The 8SQ deserves experimental research to establish its validity, and to clarify the structure of moods and states. It is, clearly, a useful but experimental measure.

The Central State–Trait Kit (CTS Kit) (Barton and Cattell, 1981)

This test measures personality traits and states so that it might have been placed in Chapter 25. However its main interest is its state measurement and thus it is placed here.

Variables measured The five second order traits and states in the Cattell system (e.g. Cattell, 1973; Cattell and Kline, 1977): anxiety, extraversion, independence, conscientiousness, cortertia both as traits and states. Two forms, A and B.

Age range Normal adults.

Administration time One hour for all variables.

Items Statements to be answered on six-point scales. How you usually are (traits) and how you are now (states).

Number of items 250.

Comments

Barton (1986) described this test as experimental and said that data on reliability and validity, as well as norms were still being collected. Unfortunately, I have not seen the completed manual. However, the second order trait factors are based on those in the 16PF test, and although these are similar to the big five (McCrae and Costa, 1987), these are no longer considered the most satisfactory account of the variance in personality questionnaires. For the same reason the second order state factors, which were described in Cattell (1973) and which are far less supported by empirical work than the corresponding traits, are also suspect. For all these reasons it is clear that as with the 8SQ this test should be regarded only as a research instrument, albeit a useful one, in establishing the structure of states. No matter how reliable and valid measures of their factors these scales may turn out to be, the fact is that the Cattell personality factors in general are now generally regarded as less than adequate accounts of personality variance and the CTS Kit will be restricted by its adherence to this structure.

Conclusions

Nevertheless this is a test which should be used for experimental studies of the structure of states and their relationship to traits but preferably with other measures.

Chapter 28

Measures of Attitudes

In this chapter I shall list and evaluate measures of attitudes. In fact many of these tests are not published as tests but may be found in papers and monographs. This is often because they are of more interest to research than to commerce and does not reflect any kind of inferiority. Another reason is that, potentially, there are almost as many attitudes as there are objects in the world and it is difficult to know which attitudes to test. This has meant that generally researchers develop their own tests to suit their needs.

My task in this chapter was greatly aided by the work of Shaver *et al.* (1991) who list a huge number of social attitude scales, in a book running to nearly 750 pages, although I must stress that my evaluations of many of these measures differ greatly from theirs. However although they used statistical criteria of high reliability and validity in selecting their tests, there are still many scales which have no real validity. As was discussed in Chapter 18 of this handbook, there is an important distinction between simple structure factors with validity in terms of external criteria, which the best tests possess, and factors which are tautologous or bloated specifics, consisting of sets of highly similar items.

Nevertheless, there are a small number of attitude tests which meet at least some of the criteria for good tests, which have been discussed throughout this handbook, and these tests will be described and evaluated below. Occasionally I discuss tests which are shown to be of little value. Such tests are discussed only if they have been widely cited and used in the social psychological literature. As will become clear from this chapter social psychology has been hindered by the fact that many researchers ignore the psychometric rationale underlying test construction, and end up with tests of unknown validity.

Unlike the chapters listing the tests in clearly defined areas of measurement such as ability and personality, where there is good agreement as to the major variables and where there are a large number of well tried and accepted tests, it is necessary in this chapter to define the attitudinal variables and to locate them in their psychological context. Despite the problem of the huge proliferation of attitude scales, for the reasons mentioned in the first paragraph, certain variables or constructs turn up throughout the social psychological literature. One such is self esteem, which, as Blaskovich and Tomaka (1991) point out, is nearly as ubiquitous as intelligence. However, unlike intelligence, it has not been clearly defined either verbally or in terms of factors, but some tests can be found, which have been extensively used. For these reasons I shall begin with tests of self esteem.

MEASURES OF SELF ESTEEM

1. The Self Esteem Scale (the SES) (Rosenberg, 1965)

This is the most widely used measure of self esteem. Blaskovich and Tomaka (1991) found more than 1200 references to this scale.

Number of items Ten.

Type of item Statements to which subjects have to indicate degree of agreement on a four-point scale. Half positive, half negative.

Method of test construction Originally this was a Guttman scale, although it is generally used as a modified Likert scale (see Chapter 11 of this handbook for a discussion of these methods).

Reliability Internal consistency reliability is high, beyond .75, and after one week the test-retest reliability on more than 250 subjects is beyond .8. Factoring the scale produces one or two correlated factors, with loadings on the positive and negative items.

Validity Blaskovich and Tomaka (1991) cite a number of studies showing correlations with other similar tests and negative correlations with constructs which should be so correlated. Thus, Fleming and Courtney (1984) found a correlation of −.64 with anxiety and −.54 with depression, but .78 with self regard, .51 with social confidence, and .42 with physical appearance. They found no correlations with age, work experience or marital status, which could be regarded as discriminant validity for the SES.

These results appear to support the validity of the test and this scale is used as a bench mark measure when constructing other tests of self esteem.

Norms More than 5000 New York adolescents. This is certainly a statistically reliable sample even if it may not be fully representative of American adolescents.

Discussion of the Rosenberg SES

The fact that this scale is so widely used in social psychology demonstrates the unfortunate gap between psychometrics and that branch of the subject. There are a number of severe objections to this scale which are set out below.

a. The Guttman scale As has been discussed in Chapter 11, there are serious difficulties with Guttman scales. Nunnally (1978) succinctly summarised these difficulties: the deterministic model underlying the scale is illogical because almost no items fit the model; the triangular model is a necessary but not sufficient condition of item fit; the model is reached by having a few items that vary grossly in difficulty; the scale is only ordinal.

b. The use of the scale as a Likert scale In practice the scale is used as a Likert scale. However the items still must fit the Guttman model and are likely to yield peculiar distributions of scores. This is, indeed, the case, as Blaskovich and Tomaka (1991) argue, and distributions tend to be negatively skewed.

c. Only ten items This is a severe objection. As was made clear in Chapters 1 and 3 of this handbook, so small a number of items is likely to yield a test of low reliability because it is not possible to sample adequately the universe of items. Since the reliability of the test is not low, it suggests that the test is nothing more than a bloated specific, where the items are simply para- phrases of each other. Inspection of the items supports this case.

d. The evidence for validity The correlational evidence for the validity of the scale is not as impressive at it might appear. Thus the other scales of self esteem and self regard with which it was correlated were made up of similar items, and the high negative correlations with anxiety and depression suggest that it may be a measure of those factors.

What is required is a factor analysis in which this scale is factored with the marker factors in the area of personality in order to see what the variance in this test is. Much of the non-specific variance is probably anxiety.

All the evidence for validity that is put forward in the meticulous survey by Blaskovich and Tomaka (1991) amounts to little more than face validity. The attempt to demonstrate discriminant validity by showing no sex or age differences is feeble in the extreme. There must be dozens of variables which would not show such differences. Certainly a ten-item scale would not appear to be sufficient to measure a variable which is far from narrow. For all these reasons this scale despite its wide usage cannot be recommended as a measure of self esteem.

2. The Coopersmith Self Esteem Inventory (SEI) (Coopersmith, 1967)

Number of items The original full scale contained fifty-eight items. The items were selected in terms of their face validity to measure four aspects of self-esteem: peers, parents, school and personal interests.

Subsequently two twenty-five-item versions were produced both for children and adults which consisted of the items having the highest correl- ation with the total score (Coopersmith, 1981).

Type of item Statements in the first person to which subjects have to indicate 'like me' or 'not like me'.

Reliability For long and short versions alphas of beyond .8. Test-retest reliabilities are also high. Coopersmith (1981) in the latest manual reports reliabilities over three years of .64 which are not significantly different from earlier coefficients of .7 over three years (Coopersmith, 1967).

Norms The norms for the school version are impressive. Coopersmith (1981) has one study based upon the results of more than 7000 children. The adult norms are less satisfactory, being based on only 226 students.

Validity Although there are substantial correlations with other scales of self esteem, factor analyses of the SEI indicate that it is not unidimensional and that there are variable numbers of factors found by different researchers. For example, Gibbs and Norwich found ten factors in their twenty-five-item version, while Ahmed *et al.* (1985) found four. Kokenes (1978) claimed nine factors accounted for the long version of the test. This is less than six items per factor which is quite hopeless for valid measurement.

Two points should be noted about these factor analyses. First, the factors do not correspond to the four a priori scales built into the test. Second, no attempt has been made to identify these factors other than by the items loading on them. Such identification is nothing more than face validity. As has been stressed throughout this handbook, the fact that similar items load a factor and are internally consistent is neither a matter of surprise nor for psychometric congratulation. Such scales are manifestations of the obvious and of little psychological significance other than that words do have a similar meaning for normal individuals.

Conclusions

Although this is a widely used test of self esteem, the factor analyses suggest that it is not measuring either one variable or the variables intended by the author. Twenty-five items are insufficient to measure four factors and the fifty-item version is obviously superior. However it is difficult to recommend this scale as a valid measure of self esteem. It is consistent and reliable but it is probably measuring little more than variance specific to items of the type used in these scales.

3. Tennessee Self Concept Scale (the TSCS) (Roid and Fitts, 1988)

Number of items 100.

Type of item Self-descriptive statements to which subjects have to indicate the extent of their agreement or disagreement on a five-point scale.

Variables measured According to Roid and Fitts (1988), twenty-nine scores may be obtained from the TSCS, although, more usually, five scales are used: physical self; moral self; personal self; family self; social self. Within each of these categories three measures may be computed: identity; self-satisfaction; and behaviour.

In addition to this matrix of scores, among the twenty-nine scales mentioned above can be found: self-criticism; conflict; defensive posture; general maladjustment; psychosis; personality disorder; neurosis; personality integration.

From Chapter 3 of this handbook on the classical theory of error, it will be recalled that the true score was the score on the universe of items relevant to a particular variable. The items in tests are assumed to be a random sample from the universe. With even the selection of thirteen measures (ignoring the three subsets) listed in the previous paragraphs, it can be seen that each scale has less than ten items. It is hardly credible that so few items could sample adequately universes as broad as psychosis and personality disorder.

Furthermore since a total score, based on all items, is used to measure self concept, its psychological meaning, given that these items measure all these variables, must be bizarre.

This analysis of the TSCS, derived from classical test theory, suggests that it could not possibly be valid. A mere 100 items could not tap so many sources of variance. The only possibility is that the total scale score measures self concept. If it does the subscales could not be valid as well. Indeed if this scale is shown to yield valid subscores then there is something gravely wrong with psychometric theory. Marsh and Richards (1988) certainly found little support for the validity of the subscales of this test.

Reliability Internal consistency of the total score and test-retest reliability are both high, greater than .9. Subscale coefficients are, naturally, somewhat lower but are all satisfactory.

Validity I have argued that this test could not be valid, although the total scale score might be psychometrically viable. Roid and Fitts (1988) contains a number of correlations of the TSCS with other variables. It correlated .8 with another self concept scale, the Piers-Harris Scale (Piers, 1984). However this is hardly surprising since the items are highly similar. It correlates .75 with the Coopersmith scale, described above, and .62 with simple self ratings for self esteem. Finally Fitts (1965) working with the older version of the test found that it correlated −.7 with the Taylor Manifest Anxiety Scale, while Roid and Fitts (1988) cite a correlation of .53 with the EPQ extraversion scale (Eysenck and Eysenck, 1975), a scale which is discussed in Chapter 25 of this handbook.

Conclusions

These validity data are interesting not only for the light they cast on this scale but also because they are relevant to many of the self concept scales in use.

It correlates highly with the Coopersmith scale and with the Piers-Harris scale which itself correlates .85 with the Coopersmith scale. The Coopersmith scale correlates highly with the Rosenberg scale. In other words all these self concept scales correlate highly with each other.

Does this mean that they are valid scales as their authors would like us to believe? Alas it does not. This is because, in the main, validity has been attested by correlation with another self concept scale. Thus there is a circular argument with all measures taking validity from each other but none with strong independent evidence of validity. Self concept scales belong, on this evidence, not to the world of science but to hermeneutics. Only within a private world of self concept measurement could these data on validity be seriously regarded.

Some attempts have been made to break this chain and establish a different kind of external validity. However, it is precisely these attempts that actually destroy the validity of all these scales. Thus the TSCS correlates $-.71$ with the Taylor Manifest Anxiety Scale and .53 with the EPQ extraversion scale. As was discussed in Chapters 25 and 15 of this handbook, extraversion and anxiety are the two largest factors in the realm of personality questionnaires. It would appear, therefore, from these correlations that the items in the TSCS are heavily loaded on these two factors which account for much of the reliable variance in the scale.

Since it is clear from our discussion that the two other self concept scales which we have listed are measuring essentially the same variables as the Tennessee scale, these tests also are essentially compounds of extraversion and neuroticism or anxiety.

Conclusions concerning all self concept scales

I have listed the three most widely used self concept scales, which between them, according to Blaskovich and Tomaka (1991), have been used in nearly 3000 studies, and I have examined them in some detail. They are all highly similar and correlate highly with each other. It should be pointed out, at this juncture, that the other self concept scales described by Blaskovich and Tomaka (1991) are also similar and correlate with one or more of the scales which I have described. Thus the first conclusion may be drawn that self concept scales show a high degree of agreement as to what they measure. This, as has been pointed out, is hardly surprising, since they closely resemble each other in terms of item form and content.

However, this fact that the self concept scales are highly correlated should not be taken as evidence of validity. Correlations with the best-established personality questionnaires suggest that they are measuring a mixture of anxiety and extraversion. Thus although the items appear to deal with self concept in fact the variance they tap is simply that of extraversion and neuroticism. This is presumably because feelings about oneself are a function of these variables.

It must be concluded that what is necessary is a factor analysis, by items of self concept scales, not on their own but together with the items of the best-established personality factors. Then it will be possible to see whether there is any reliable variance in these scales that is not picked up by personality factors. If there is, a useful self concept measure might be constructed. However the current measures could not be recommended. Indeed, as the correlation with a self rating of self esteem showed, we might as well ask subjects how they feel about themselves. Of course, this is only what the tests do 100, fifty-eight or ten times.

In brief, these self concept tests are not powerful psychometric instruments. They measure a mixture of extraversion and anxiety and illustrate the futility of simple, intuitive measurement, where items are chosen because they are face valid and then factored. Not surprisingly items with the same content form a factor. These tests support the principles of factor analytic test construction, discussed in Chapter 10 of this handbook, where the necessity of identifying a factor in factor space and relating it to external criteria was stressed. The labelling of factors from the items loading on them is the clear road to self delusion and invalid tests.

MEASURES OF LOCUS OF CONTROL

Locus of control is a variable or construct which originated in Rotter's social learning theory (e.g. Rotter, 1966). External locus of control refers to the belief that outcomes are not determined by personal effort but by external environmental factors. Internal locus of control is the opposite, namely that outcomes are contingent on one's actions. Locus of control is regarded as a personal characteristic or trait which is broadly generalisable. However, as Lefcourt (1991) argues, the major workers in this field (Lefcourt, 1976; Phares, 1976; and Rotter, 1975) all suggest that measures should be tailored to particular populations and concerns, that these are more useful than a broad measure of locus of control. However if this is the case it suggests that locus of control is not a broad trait at all, but is rather a particular belief and thus of little psychological interest.

Certainly this approach has led to a proliferation of tests and research and in this section I shall discuss those scales with the highest validity. It should be noted, at this point, that Lefcourt (1991), who reviews a large number of scales, and who is highly influential in this area of research, takes up a profoundly anti-psychometric stance: he argues that a four-item special scale may be more useful than a more general measure of locus of control. A four-item scale could hardly be expected to be valid. If it were reliable it must be highly specific and if not reliable it could not be valid. I shall now list some general tests of locus of control.

1. Internal–External Locus of Control Scale (the I–E scale) (Rotter, 1966)

This is the original locus of control scale and is still the most widely used and cited scale of this variable.

Variable   In this scale the I–E variable is assumed to be unidimensional, low scorers being internal, high scorers external.

Number of items   23 plus 6 filler items.

Item type   Internal statements are paired with external statements – a forced choice format. The score is the number of external statements endorsed.

Norms   The original scale had norms based upon more than 4000 subjects. Lefcourt (1991) cites some more recent normative data in addition.

Reliability   Test and retest reliabilities are about .7.

Validity   Lefcourt (1991) argues that this scale, which has been used in more than 50 per cent of all studies of locus of control, seems to be sensitive to individual differences in the perception of control about one's destiny. However, he also shows that it correlates moderately with scales of social desirability, a finding which is discussed below.

Factor analysis and item analysis of the scale   The original item analysis of the scale, the correlation of each item with the total score not including that item is revealing. Five items are below .2, twelve are between .2 and .29, six are above .3 of which only one is above .4. These correlations do not suggest that the items are strongly loaded on a common factor, as was intended by Rotter (1966).

This inference is supported by factor analyses of the items, where there are usually two factors, although one is somewhat larger than the other, as well as a number of small factors, which given the number of items are useless. Ashkanasy (1985) has reviewed much of this factor analytic work and for further details readers are referred to that paper. The first factor loads on items phrased in the first person, and the second on items relevant to the influence of social and political institutions.

Conclusions

Given the item analyses and the factor analyses it is difficult to recommend this much-used scale as a good unidimensional measure of locus of control. Furthermore the fact that it is contaminated, to some extent, with social desirability, makes the use of this test even more dubious. Collins (1974) not only found four components in this scale but he also showed that there was poor equivalence between the members of each pair of statement which formed items. Thus if these were given as separate scales subjects could endorse both members of a pair. This means the forced-choice format must distort the scores on the Rotter scale.

However, even worse from a psychometric viewpoint than the fact that there is not one clear factor underlying these items, is the fact that identification of the factors is always in terms of the item content. As has been stressed throughout this handbook, this is not sufficient. The factor or factors of the I–E scale need to be identified with reference to clear external criteria and to be located in factor space. Unfortunately, this has not been done, despite the extensive use of this test, mainly because the authors, in the main, assume that the test is valid, and thus are not concerned to identify a factor which they believe correctly labelled.

In brief, this I–E scale cannot be recommended because it has too many psychometric deficiencies.

2. Internality, Powerful Others and Chance scales (Levenson, 1981)

This scale is an offshoot of the I–E scale and will thus be briefly described.

Provenance   This test was devised using items from the I–E scale together with some devised by the author.

Variables measured   Locus of control is broken into three components: internality, powerful others and chance. The meaning of these variables is obvious.

Number of items   8 per scale.

Type of item   Statement to which subjects have to indicate their extent of agreement or disagreement on a six-point Likert scale.

Reliability   Both internal consistency and test-retest reliabilities for these scales vary between .64 and .79.

Validity   Levenson (1981) has carried out studies of the construct validity of these scales by relating them to achievement, occupation, political involvement and interpersonal perception, as Lefcourt (1991) points out.

The scales correlate with the I–E scale which, since they share items, is of little interest. There are substantial positive correlations between the Power and Chance scales (indeed given the reliabilities of these scales they could hardly be higher). Social desirability which was eliminated in the test construction does not correlate with the variables in this test.

Norms   Scores of various normative groups are given for comparative purposes.

Comments and conclusions

The problem with this scale is similar to that which afflicts the original I–E scale. There is no satisfactory evidence concerning the nature of the variables. The construct validity studies with variables of this sort are far too vague to be convincing. Almost any result could be fitted with sufficient ingenuity and certainly to differentiate them from intraversion and neuroticism would be difficult. What is needed is a simple structure factor analysis so that the relation of these variables to the well established personality factors can be made. As they stand the identification of these factors is essentially by item content.

However even if it were considered that these were useful variables, eight-item tests for reasons that we have made clear throughout this handbook are unsatisfactory. If reliable such short tests are likely to be measuring rather specific variance.

For all these reasons it is difficult to recommend this test for use. It is too short and has no clear factorial evidence of what it measures. As with the measures of self esteem which were reviewed in this first section, its links with the original Rotter scale are liable to create a private world of locus of control measurement which bears little relation to reality.

Finally mention should be made of the three components which are allegedly independent. It looks from the correlations as if at the second order, factors highly similar to the I–E factors would emerge.

In summary this is not a scale which could be used with confidence to elucidate the nature of locus of control.

3. The Nowicki-Strickland I–E scale (Nowicki and Duke, 1974)

Variable measured Internal vs. external control, as in the I–E scale.

Number of items 40.

Type of item Questions to which subjects respond 'Yes' or 'No'. The language of these items was made to be easier than in the I–E scale, thus making the scale suitable for non-students.

Norms 156 students. More than 700 subjects have been used in further studies.

Reliabilities Internal consistency reliability is at least .75 and test-retest reliability varies, partly depending on the time interval, but is satisfactory being around .7.

Validity This scale correlates with the Rotter scale in various studies from .44 to .68, but unlike that scale there is a general factor accounting for some of the variance in this scale.

Conclusions

This scale is essentially similar to the I–E scale. Given that there is little sound evidence for the validity of that scale, there would seem little reason to be confident of this scale either.

Conclusions concerning the Locus of Control scales

These are the three main general scales of locus of control, in use with adults. As can be seen from the evaluation of these tests, they are beset by the single problem that the factor (or factors) which they measure has not been identified in factor space. It has been labelled simply from the meaning of the items. As was noted with the self esteem scales, there is a private world of locus of control for all these scales correlate with each other, a fact which is used as evidence for validity. Indeed, Lefcourt (1991) examines another scale, the Spheres of Control scale (Paulhus, 1983), which I have ignored because its three variables have a multiple correlation with the I–E scale of .75. Given the unreliability of measurement this means that essentially the scales are measuring the same variable. The construct validity studies, even where they show differences between groups are not nearly precise enough to establish the validity of these measures.

A recent paper by Coombs and Schroeder (1988) examines in detail published factor analyses of the Rotter scale, the children's version of the Nowicki-Strickland Scale and the Collins' scale (Collins, 1974) which separates the forced choices of the Rotter scale items into two scales. These authors failed to find a convincing general factor in these scales and were forced to conclude that it is better to study locus of control with reference to a particular object, than as a general variable. However, if this is the case it is a variable of little psychological interest, an issue which will be discussed later in this section.

Although there is no clear general factor in the Rotter I–E scale it is instructive to examine its correlates with the main personality factors. Although there have been a number of such studies, a particularly useful one is that of Layton (1985) who correlated the test with the EPQ (Eysenck and Eysenck, 1975). He found that the I–E scale correlated significantly with N, P and L (.24, .29 and .24 respectively). Given the lack of factorial clarity in the Rotter scale, this suggests that much of the reliable variance can be explained in terms of the major personality factors.

Other scales of locus of control

I do not intend to review here other scales of locus of control. Given the problems with the variable at the adult level it would not be sensible to review the children's scales which have been developed to aid study of the development of locus of control.

As was indicated at the beginning of this section Lefcourt (1991) argued that it was more useful to measure locus of control not as a general construct but in a specific context. Thus there have been developed locus of control measures relevant to health, drinking, weight, marital satisfaction and sexual behaviour. These, however, seem so specific and beset with conceptual problems over the meaning of 'locus of control' that I shall not discuss them here.

The problems with the specific scales

The interest in locus of control stems from the fact that it purports to be a generalised trait which will account for a variety of behaviours. As soon as it is admitted that it will not do so, then its psychological importance is questionable.

Specific locus of control scales are obviously of less interest because these must be virtually infinite in number. Furthermore if one examines the content of these scales one can see that that the items are asking questions about some highly specific behaviour.

The Multidimensional Health Locus of Control Scale (Wallston *et al.*, 1978) illustrates this point. It uses the three variables of the Levenson scale, which was discussed above, personal control, the effectiveness of powerful others and the role of chance, in determining one's health status. There are two forms of the scale, each having only six items per scale, statements which are answered on a six-point Likert scale. These scales are so short that it is hard to see how any universe of variables could be sampled. This indeed is one of my objections to these scales, that they do not sample a universe of items but simply ask specific questions.

Examples of items might be: 'When I get sick I am to blame', 'I am in control of my health' (externality); 'Health professionals control my health', 'Regarding my health I can only do what a doctor tells me to do' (powerful others); 'My good health is largely a matter of my good fortune', 'No matter what I do I'm likely to get sick' (chance).

Lefcourt (1991) regards this as a useful research test and it has been given to sufferers from a large number of different medical disorders. However even where differences between groups are found it is hard to see what psychological insights could emerge from the answers to these questions, which were not obvious.

For all these reasons I shall not list and evaluate these specific scales, because it is my hope that psychometrics can go beyond face-valid questions to the establishment of powerful variables which can account for a broad spectrum of behaviour.

I have written sufficient about locus of control. It is not a variable, as I have shown, despite the plethora of research, of great psychological interest and there is no scale of high psychometric quality.

MEASURES OF THE AUTHORITARIAN PERSONALITY

Adorno *et al.* (1950) introduced the concept of the authoritarian personality which was measured by their F scale. There have been many criticisms of the measures used in the authoritarian personality – namely that the scale was not balanced and that it was affected by the response set of acquiescence, that it was affected by the response set of social desirability, that it only tested right-wing authoritarian attitudes, and many attempts were made to overcome these problems with modifications of the original F scale and the other related scales which were used in the original investigation.

Kline and Cooper (1984a) carried out a factor analytic study of a number of authoritarian scales, in an attempt to locate the variable in factor space and thus demonstrate finally whether it was a useful variable or whether the variance could be accounted for by other factors. In the course of that research they showed that the authoritarian personality was highly similar to the personality factor of obsessional traits and to the Freudian anal character. They concluded that the authoritarian personality was the social emanation of the obsessional personality. Thus it did seem to be a useful attitudinal variable, even if one which was related to personality traits such that authoritarian characteristics were only likely to develop in individuals who were rigid and obsessional.

In Chapter 25 of this handbook I have described the highest loading measures of obsessionality, the factor which provides the seedbed for the development of the authoritarian personality, and in this chapter I shall describe the best measures of the authoritarian personality itself.

Christie (1991) has an excellent summary of the manifold variants of the F scale and his work has made the selection of the best scales a relatively simple task although any faults or problems with my choices cannot be laid at his door.

I shall not include here the original versions of the scales, the Anti-Semitism Scale, the Ethnocentrism Scale and the California F Scales, as used in *The Authoritarian Personality* (Adorno *et al.*, 1950). This is because there are undoubtedly contaminations from social desirability and acquiescence, although the item content still is useful in developing new scales as Christie (1991) argues.

Many of the attempts to produce F scales with counterbalanced items, as the review by Christie (1991) shows, have not been entirely successful. The G scale by Bass (1955), despite the reversal of its items, still had most of its variance explained by acquiescence rather than authoritarianism. This factor also influenced, but to a less extent, the counterbalanced F scale of Christie *et al.* (1958). Lee and Warr (1969) and Kohn (1972) both produced counterbalanced scales, including in the case of Kohn, left-wing items, but in both tests the correlation between the negative and the positive items was lower than desirable and the scale by Lee and Warr was not unifactorial. The Kohn (1972) scale however does make sensible discriminations between political groups. The scale by Ray (1971) appears to be defective in item content and that by Couch and Kenniston (1960) has only five items. For all these reasons none of these scales can be recommended. It should be pointed out that many of these scales are highly similar in content since their starting point was the original work by Adorno *et al.* (1950).

Christie (1991) argues that one scale is superior to all of these both in terms of item content and in its psychometric qualities and I am in full agreement with him on this point. This scale is described below.

The Right-Wing Authoritarianism Scale (RWA) (Altemeyer, 1981)

Variable measured   The traditional F scale, fascistic authoritarianism.

Number of items   24, 12 positive, 12 negative.

Item type   Statements to which subjects respond on a six-point scale – 'disagree strongly' to 'agree strongly'. The negative statements are not simple negatives of positive items. They are positive statements with which authoritarians would disagree.

Item construction methods   Altemeyer attempted to ensure that the negative items were truly psychometrically equivalent to the positive items. The means and variances of the reversed items had to be highly similar to their positive counterparts and a reversed item had to correlate at least .4 with a scale of positive items. All these statistics were computed on large samples from the University of Manitoba.

Reliabilities   Internal consistency reliability was found by Altemeyer to be .88 although other investigators have reported lower coefficients. Nevertheless the internal consistency of this scale is certainly in the region of .8.

Validity   In his 1981 book *Right-Wing Authoritarianism*, Altemeyer attempts to demonstrate the validity of the scale by relating it to hypothetical situations which would convince none but a social psychologist. However, in an experimental study in which subjects had to obey orders and apparently give electric shocks it correlated .44 with persistence at the task.

Altemeyer (1988) has a revised version of the 1981 scale with items changed to fit the differing political context. In a study in Russia by McFarland *et al.* (1990), using a Russian translation of this scale, as well as other scales, some convincing correlations were found between this scale and attitudes to the press and to ethnic minorities in the Russian states, just for example.

Conclusions

In terms of content and psychometrically this F scale appears to be about the best of the current measures of authoritarian personality. In addition since it appears that F scale items date rather quickly and since Altemeyer has revised his items over the years his scale seems to be the one to choose.

However it should be pointed out that the Kohn (1972) scale did load highly on the obsessional authoritarian factor in the study by Kline and Cooper (1984) which was discussed above. This and the somewhat similar scale by Lee and Warr (1969) are probably viable scales but there would seem little reason to use them rather than the RWA.

The Dogmatism Scale (Rokeach, 1956)

Variable measured This scale was designed to tap rigidity of belief, authoritarianism of both the left and right.

Number of items 40.

Type of items Statements to which the subject has to indicate degree of agreement on a seven-point scale, agreement indicating dogmatism.

Internal consistency reliability Studies indicate that the reliability of this scale is around .8.

Validity The meaning of this dogmatism scale is still not clear. If it were valid members of extreme parties of both the left and right would score higher than centre groups. This, however, is not the case, as is clear from Rokeach (1956). Furthermore although there are high correlations with the F scale, these to some extent may reflect acquiescence since, as Christie (1991) points out, correlations drop if counterbalanced F scales are used. Kline and Cooper (1984a) found a low correlation of only .23 between a counter-balanced F scale (Kohn, 1972) and a counterbalanced dogmatism scale (Ray, 1970), although the validity of this latter scale is uncertain.

Conclusions concerning the Dogmatism Scale

As Rokeach (1960) has shown dogmatism and rigidity of thinking as measured by his scale is an interesting variable. However the correlational and factorial work show that it is not measuring the same variable as the F scale. It would be useful, in further studies of the authoritarian personality, to include this scale together with the Altemeyer (1988) scale and personality measures such as Ai3Q (Kline, 1971a) and Cattell's factor G (Cattell *et al.*, 1970a), tests which loaded on the obsessional, authoritarian factor in the study by Kline and Cooper (1984a).

Final comments on dogmatism and authoritarian scales

Unlike the earlier variables in this chapter, self esteem and locus of control, we do seem to be dealing with important psychological variables in the notion of authoritarianism and dogmatism which have significant political and social implications. Testing has proved difficult on account of social desirability and acquiescence, social desirability because in educated society these views are undesirable and acquiescence simply because the early scales ignored this problem. However it should be noted that acquiescence, or agreeing with test items (presumably constructed by authorities) could be an aspect of the authoritarian personality.

Many of these difficulties could be resolved if good simple structure factor analyses of the items in the Altemeyer scale and the dogmatism scale were undertaken together with items from the best-established personality tests and measures of social desirability and acquiescence.

MASCULINITY AND FEMININITY: MEASURE OF SEX ROLE

An important attitudinal variable is the dimension or dimensions (it is a theoretical and empirical issue whether these variables are separate or constitute a dimension) of masculinity and femininity, embracing all the attitudes, experiences and behaviours which in most cultures distinguish males and females. Lenney (1991) points out that there are over 150 scales. However only a small number of these are frequently used. An examination of these tests shows that they are all highly correlated together. Thus the most popular of these scales, the Bem Sex Role Inventory (1981) correlates highly, sometimes beyond .7 and .8 with other frequently used scales which themselves correlate almost as highly with each other, as Lenney clearly demonstrates. It takes no great experience of factor analysis to show that some factor runs through all these scales, although what this might be cannot be assumed.

For all these reasons the only scale which I shall describe is the Bem SRI.

The Bem Sex Role Inventory (BSRI) (Bem, 1974)

Variables measured Independent measures of masculinity and femininity.

Number of items 60: 20 in each scale and 20 filler items which can measure social desirability.

Type of items Each item describes some personal characteristic and subjects have to indicate how true it is for them on a seven-point scale.

Scoring the scales The masculinity score is the average of the ratings on the masculinity scale items. The femininity scale is scored in the same way. Although there is some controversy on how subjects should be classified, having been measured on the scales, there is a general consensus that a median split method is usually appropriate. Thus a subject is masculine if the score is above the male median and below the female median. The converse rule classifies the individual as feminine. Scores above both medians classify a subject as androgynous and below both medians as undifferentiated. For a discussion of this and other scoring procedures readers must be referred to Handal and Salit (1985).

Selection of items   Items were selected for the scales on the judgements of only fifty male and fifty female students that traits were more desirable for a man than a woman (masculinity scale) and vice versa for the femininity scale. The mean social desirability of the items in the two scales was virtually the same.

It should be noted here that ratings by so few individuals and ones drawn from so limited a sample (Stanford undergraduates) are far from ideal, especially if the scale is to be administered to different groups.

Reliability   Internal consistency reliability is high – coefficients above .8. Test-retest reliabilities after four weeks are also high – around .9.

Validity of the SRI   Bem (1974) showed that there was a negligible correlation between the two scales so that they may be regarded as independent and the review of the evidence concerning the influence of social desirability on the scales by Lenney (1991) makes it clear that this is also negligible. However this is still a long way from demonstrating that the test is valid.

The problem with establishing the validity of the SRI is that it is not clear just what findings would constitute evidence for its validity. In a culture such as that of the USA or Europe where sex typing and stereotyping occurs I would argue that sex difference on these scales would be expected. It makes no sense to say that females are more masculine than males although possibly certain categories of women might be expected to be above the male mean. However this line of reasoning is denied by Lenney (1991) who argues that there is no necessary link between these items and biological sex. However this strains the meaning of socially desirable, masculine and feminine personality characteristics beyond sense. The only meaning of masculine is that it is related to the male sex. Without this connection the term is vacuous. In any case it is good to report that the expected sex differences are found. However this difference alone is not enough to support the validity of these scales.

One of the difficulties in evaluating the validity of this scale is that some of the studies do so within the context of Bem's theoretical approach to sex and gender (e.g. Bem, 1974). However if this theory is not adopted (and it is certainly contentious) much of the work appears not so relevant to the validity of the test. Thus, for example, androgyny is not correlated with measures of mental health although those who have developed both masculine and feminine traits are deemed in Bem's (1974) theorising to be superior to those trapped in their sex roles. However in a sex typed society surely this is unlikely to be so.

Conclusions

The fact that the SRI correlates highly with most other similar measures, the fact that it is reliable, and the fact that it has been used so extensively, so that there is considerable information concerning its correlates and relationships with other criteria, all suggest that is the sex role scale to use if these variables must be measured.

However, it is interesting to note how difficult it was to specify what findings would be regarded as evidence for the validity of the test. This difficulty implies that there is not much psychological significance in the variables. The fact that there are so many studies with this test indicates that, as so often in psychology, a private, hermeneutic world has been constructed in which this variable and others similar play a part. How such work may be extrapolated to a world outside this theorising is not clear. In brief the question raised in the evaluation of this scale is the psychological importance of the measurement of sex role.

THE MEASUREMENT OF VALUES

It would appear, on intuitive, a priori grounds, that the values which an individual holds should account, in some degree at least, for some of her or his actions. For example, a scientist who put the pursuit of truth beyond all else might be expected to have a different career from one who also values wealth and social acclaim. Thus the measurement of values seems a useful social, psychological tool, although it could well be that such values are mere rationalisations, defences against failure in the first instance, and the social explanation of greed and self interest in the second.

In fact, as might be expected, the measurement and definition of values has proven difficult but over recent years two tests have been more extensively used than the rest and these will be briefly described.

The Study of Values (Allport, Vernon and Lindzey, 1960)

This is the third edition of a test which was originally constructed in 1931. It was revised in 1951 and again in 1960 although the test items are unchanged since the second edition.

Variables measured   Six basic interests or motives: theoretical, economic, aesthetic, social, political, and religious. These six variables were taken from the typology of Spranger (1928).

Number of items   45 items, 30 in part 1, 15 in part 2.

Type of items   In part 1 each item consists of two alternatives and subjects indicate their strength of preference by distributing three points between them. In part 2 items have four possible responses which subjects rank in order of preference. The different responses represent different values thus allowing the six values to be scored.

Scoring This scoring is ipsative (see Chapter 27 of this handbook for a discussion of the problems of ipsative scoring). It thus measures the relative strength of values within each individual.

Norms Despite the fact that norms are not meaningful for ipsative scores since a value can be primary for two individuals but of quite different strength, norms are provided. These should not be used.

Reliability Both split-half and test-retest reliabilities are high, usually beyond .8.

Validity The manual to the test makes it clear that the scale will differentiate in the expected direction people in different jobs and students following different fields of study, as well as value changes in individuals over almost forty years (Hoge and Bender, 1974).

Braithwaite and Scott (1991) present factor analytic studies which are said to support the validity of these scales. However the factor analysis of ipsative scales makes little sense since there are artefactual correlations between the scales and the meaning of scores is different for different subjects. These results are best ignored.

Conclusions

The ipsative nature of the Study of Values makes it a test which is difficult to recommend except for use with individuals. For this purpose the scale is probably effective, given that the Spranger typology is acceptable. However statistical analyses and comparisons which involve the assumption that scores are equivalent for different subjects are dubious, as are all norms and factor analyses. Even comparison among groups if mean scores are used is of doubtful validity although the comparison of rank orders among the six values is quite legitimate. In brief, this is a scale which should be used mainly with individuals. If group statistical tests are to be computed, then rank-order data must be involved.

The Value Survey (Rokeach, 1967)

Variables Eighteen terminal values (goals) and eighteen instrumental values (modes of conduct). These values were based on a survey of the literature, but are essentially intuitive.

The eighteen terminal values are: comfortable life, exciting life, sense of accomplishment, world at peace, world of beauty, equality, family security, freedom, happiness, inner harmony, mature love, national security, pleasure, salvation, self respect, social recognition, true friendship, wisdom.

The eighteen instrumental values are: ambitious, broadminded, capable, cheerful, clean, courageous, forgiving, helpful, honest, imaginative, independent, intellectual, logical, loving, obedient, polite, responsible, self controlled.

Number of items 36.

Type of items Each item (which is the the title of a goal) has to be rank ordered.

Reliability Internal consistency reliability cannot be measured since there is only one item per scale. Test-retest reliability for individuals is about .6 to .8, although the computation, the median for the rank distribution of the eighteen items for each subject, is not the standard test-retest reliability coefficient.

Validity Braithwaite and Scott (1991) cite a host of studies in which the Value Survey discriminated between different religious groups, different occupational and different cultural and educational groups, as might be expected. In addition, they cite research where there are sensible be-havioural correlates such as returning lost property and honesty.

Furthermore, they discuss factor analyses of the Value Survey, although, as an ipsative test, such analyses make no sense, which is presumably why there is little firm agreement in the results.

Conclusions

This scale has been reviewed because it has been widely used and because Rokeach has been a major contributor to the study of values (e.g. 1973) and is not simply a test constructor. However it is difficult to recommend this test. The fact is that it is a collection of thirty-six one-item scales. The hopeless-ness of one-item scales has been demonstrated in our chapters on classical test theory. It seems inconceivable how one item could measure a value. Furthermore the fact that it is an ipsative test means that it should only be used as a test for individuals where no comparison of the scores is made.

CONCLUSIONS

As was indicated at the beginning of this chapter there are huge numbers of attitude measures because there can be attitudes towards anything. However I have covered the areas of research which appear to be of some psycho-logical importance and in which there is considerable current activity. I have selected the best known and most used measures in the fields and, as is now evident, many of them are sadly inadequate.

The reason for these problems is that social psychology and psycho-metrics have been divorced for a variety of reasons. Many of these test constructors have demonstrated reliability and factor structure but few have gone further to demonstrate what these factors are – an essential for a demonstration of real validity. In all these tests the identification of the construct has depended upon the meaning of the items and little more. This is far from satisfactory and until these scales are located in factor space their true meaning and value to psychology will remain problematic.

Chapter 29

Other Tests

In this chapter I shall discuss a number of tests which do not fall easily into any of the standard psychometric categories. These are tests which are designed for highly specialised purposes, as for example in clinical psychology, or are based upon different principles of testing, as with percept-genetic tests. I also include here a few specialised computer tests.

I shall not describe or discuss these in such great detail as the tests in the previous chapters in this section of the handbook simply because on account of their specialised use and rationale, this would be of less interest and value in a general handbook of testing. However I shall enable readers to decide whether these tests are likely to be valid and useful in their specific applications.

PERCEPT-GENETIC TESTS

I shall describe two measures, the DMT and the MCT.

The Defence Mechanism Test (DMT) (Kragh, 1985)

The DMT is the most widely used percept-genetic test, the rationale of which was discussed in Chapter 18.

Description The DMT consists of a small tachistoscope and two test slides which are TAT pictures with a threatening face introduced into the periphery. There are distractor slides and an eye test.

Administration The DMT slides are exposed in a series at gradually increasing levels of illumination, such that at the first exposure almost nothing can be seen. At each exposure the subject is required to draw and describe what she or he sees. The test is usually stopped before the subject is able fully to describe the stimulus.

Variables measured Ten defence mechanisms: repression, isolation, denial, reaction, formation, identification with the aggressor, introaggression, introjection of the opposite sex, introjection of another object, projection and regression.

Reliability Split-half and test-retest reliabilities are not sensible to compute for the test is supposed to be subliminal at the early exposures and thus cannot be used again except after a long gap. However parallel form reliability can be meaningfully computed and on small samples figures around .5 are cited in the manual. With careful training inter-rating reliability is satisfactory.

Validity This is a complex matter since defence mechanisms are constructs which many psychologists would not be willing to accept. However results are presented in the test manual showing some correlations in the order of .5 with performance in stressful military tasks.

Comments

Kragh and Smith (1970) contains a considerable amount of clinical data concerning the ability of the DMT to discriminate among clinical groups, and its power to aid pilot selection especially by discriminating the accident prone is attested in the manual. However, as has been pointed out by Kline (1987), even if these results are accepted, they are not *per se* evidence for the validity of the tests. Good pilots cannot differ from bad only on defence mechanisms. The inferences made from the descriptions and drawings of the subliminal stimuli are no different in kind from the inferences made by analysts from clinical material. Thus even clear agreement between these two sources of information would not demonstrate the validity of the test.

Cooper and Kline (1986) showed that DMT variables were largely independent of the main personality factors as measured by the 16PF (see Chapter 25), although the hypothesised moderate correlations were as expected. In a further study (Cooper and Kline, 1989) it was shown that the first factor extracted from a G analysis of the DMT loaded on a perceptual defence measure of repression (Wallace and Worthington, 1970) and in addition correlated with success in a jet flying course. This factor was replicated in a further investigation with students.

Conclusions

All this suggests that the DMT is possibly a valid measure of defences, although the evidence is far from perfect. However, as Kline (in press b) has argued this is a distinct advantage compared with questionnaire measures of defences which by their nature could never be valid. This is a promising test which demands rigorous further research.

The Meta Contrast Technique (MCT) (Kragh and Smith, 1970)

I shall briefly describe this test which has not been so widely used as the DMT but which may be valuable for clinical groups.

Presentation of stimuli Two stimuli are presented in serial, subliminal, tachistoscopic progression. One stimulus represents a constant frame of reference whereas the other is incongruent or threatening. This is introduced gradually until the series is concluded or it is perceived. Full details of the timings are found in Kragh and Smith (1970).

Stimuli At present there are two sets of stimuli in the MCT.
A1 is a drawing of a car;
B1 is a drawing of a living room, the car being flashed on the lower part of the room. These are the incongruent set.
A2 is an ugly threatening face of a man;
B2 is a boy sitting against the background of a dark wall with a window in the right top corner. The face is flashed into this. This is the threat set.

Scoring Subjects draw and describe the stimuli as in the DMT. Attention is paid to changes in B before and after A has appeared as an independent percept and changes in A as it develops as a correct percept. The scoring system for this test is complex and full details may be found in Eberhard *et al.* (1965).

Variables measured Repression, isolation, sensitivity, projection, stereotypy, depression, instability, discontinuity and psychosis.

Reliability and validity The inter-rater reliability of these dimensions is high (Kragh and Smith, 1970) as is the parallel form reliability if the two forms are given close together. As regards validity this MCT is useful in discriminating criterion clinical groups and changes due to psychotherapy, although how well this discriminatory power validates the test is still open to dispute.

Conclusions

There is little doubt that the research with the MCT, which is almost exclusively in Scandinavia, strongly suggests that this is a useful test in clinical psychology which may well be valuable in the study of unconscious processes. Even more than the DMT, however, it needs independent research to tie down, preferably by factor analysis, the nature of the variance in the test.

MEASURES OF NEUROPSYCHOLOGICAL FUNCTIONING

I shall describe and evaluate two well known examples.

Luria-Nebraska Neuropsychological Battery (LNNB)
(Golden *et al*, 1980)

This is a test designed to assess cognitive deficits in great detail. It is based upon, as the name suggests, the clinical approaches used by Luria (1973) and is effectively a standardised version of them.

Items and scales   269 items forming eleven content scales. Golden (1981) claims that each item is a test in itself, a notion which should be taken into account in interpreting the scale scores. The scales are:

1. Motor scale. This scale measures, *inter alia*, motor speed, unilateral and bilateral, motor control and the quality and speed of simple drawings.
2. Rhythm scale. This includes pitch discrimination and analysis of rhythms, as well as singing lines from songs.
3. Tactile scale. This includes (to both hands) location of touch, discrimination of hard, soft, blunt, sharp, direction of movement, tactile identification and recognition of objects.
4. Visual scale. Here visual perceptual skills and visual spatial abilities are measured, for example picture and object recognition, naming of objects, telling time with numberless clocks, two dimensional rotations and spatial integration.
5. Receptive speech scale. This tests all aspects of understanding language from phonemic discrimination to complex sentences.
6. Expressive speech scale. This is concerned with all aspects of speech production.
7. Reading scale.
8. Writing scale.
9. Arithmetic scale. (These are all standard tests of attainment in these skills.)
10. Memory scale. This scale includes assessment of verbal and non-verbal short term memory, for rhythms, hand positions and word–picture associations.
11. Intelligence scale. Here the items are similar to those in the WAIS (see Chapter 23) but deductive and inductive reasoning items are also included.

A number of other scales have been developed, on an experimental basis, from the item pool, of which three are commonly used:

a. The pathognomic scale. This is a thirty-four-item scale which reliably picks out the most damaged patients.
b. The left hemisphere scale. Twenty-one items which are highly sensitive to left hemisphere damage.
c. The right hemisphere scale. The obverse of the left scale above.

Administration time 150 mins on average, ranging from 80 mins for a normal intelligent adult to five hours for those with severe injuries.

Scoring Each item is scored 0 (performance resembles that of a control), 1 (probability is equal for a control or a neurological subject) or 2 (where the score resembles that of a neurological subject). Scale scores are then converted to T scores but on the basis of two small samples.

Reliability Inter-rater and split-half reliabilities are all high (well beyond .8) and test-retest reliability is good (.88 on average) (Golden, 1981).

Validity and conclusions

A discussion of the studies of the validity of this test, many of which are summarised in the test manual (Golden *et al.*, 1980) and in Golden (1981) is beyond the scope of this handbook, involving specialised discussion of clinical work. Nevertheless a few general conclusions can be drawn. There can be little doubt that the LNNB can differentiate diagnostic groups of brain damaged patients, and that it is useful in identifying cerebral dysfunction among schizophrenics and the localisation of brain damage.

Furthermore there are high multiple correlations with the other well known measure of neurological functioning, the Halstead-Reitan Battery (which is described below), and with the WAIS intelligence test. Factor analysis of these scale scores is being undertaken, but it is possible that the factors might be, in this instance, less sensitive than the subscales, since emerging factors would be necessarily broader than the individual scale scores.

In conclusion, this is a test which is clearly effective in clinical use as an index of neurological functioning.

Halstead-Reitan Battery (HRB) (Reitan and Davison, 1974)

There are eleven subtests in the HRB:

1. The Minnesota Multiphasic Personality Test (MMPI), fully discussed in Chapter 25 of this handbook. This is the measure of personality in the battery.
2. Seashore Rhythm Test. This part of one of the best-known tests of musical aptitude (see Chapter 24).
3. WAIS. This is fully described in Chapter 23 and is one of the best-known intelligence tests.
4. Reitan-Klove Sensory Perceptual Examination.
5. Halstead Finger Tapping Test.
6. Halstead Category Test.
7. Speech-Sounds Perception Tests.

8. Trail Making Tests.
9. Reitan Indiana Aphasia Examination.
10. Tactual Performance Test.
11. Lateral Dominance Examination.

Time for testing   Five hours.

Discussion and conclusions

I do not want to describe this test in any more detail here because, as is clear from the description of the scales, it is remarkably similar to the more recent Luria-Nebraska Battery. However, comparison of these two tests yields some important points.

1. The HRB contains a standard measure of personality – the MMPI – widely used in clinical psychology and a useful, although atheoretical, diagnostic tool. This may well be valuable in clinical diagnosis and there is no equivalent in the Luria test, although testers could give it separately.
2. The HRB contains a full test of intelligence – the WAIS. This must be superior to the briefer scale in the Luria test although again it could be given separately if required.
3. The HRB is inordinately long and in practice a shorter equivalent test is to be preferred, if it is truly equivalent and not less efficient.
4. The work discussed by Golden (1981) illustrates that within the margins of test reliability the scores and diagnoses offered by these two tests are highly similar. As was pointed out in our discussion of the Luria test the multiple correlations between these two tests are remarkably high. On these grounds I think little is lost in using the Luria test and extra personality scales could always be given if required.
5. The HRB is clearly an excellent test for the diagnosis of neuropsychological function but the newer scale is based on the work of Luria whose clinical work is renowned. Because of this more modern background it is perhaps to be preferred. On the other hand, because it is a newer test, there is more known about the meaning and implications of the HRB.
6. Conclusions. The Luria and the Halstead-Reitan are both excellent examples of neuropsychological tests. They are highly similar but because it is more brief I would be inclined to use the more recent test.

SOME TESTS USEFUL IN CLINICAL WORK

Beck Depression Inventory (Beck, 1967; Beck and Beck, 1972)

Variable measured   Intensity of depression.

Number of items   21; 13 items in the short form (Beck and Beck, 1972).

Item type Statements reflecting depressive feelings and attitudes. Subjects rank them on a four-point scale to indicate degree of severity.

Sample Original sample consisted of approximately 400 patients. Since its development the scale has been given to many hundreds of other samples.

Reliability Corrected split-half .93; test-retest is around .7 after one week but care must be taken to ensure that trait depression rather than state depression (present feelings) is measured.

Validity The test scores are significantly related to clinical diagnoses of depression – correlations ranging from .6 to .9 (Shaver and Brennan, 1991). Furthermore, as these authors point out, it is positively correlated to most other tests of depression simply because these were constructed and validated so to do. Factor analysis of the test reveals three oblique factors and one second order factor, thus supporting the validity of the scale.

Short form The thirteen items of the short form were selected on the basis of their correlations with the full test and with clinical diagnoses. The correlation with the full test is .96.

Conclusions

This is the most widely used depression scale. All the evidence suggests that it is a valid measure, which is hardly surprising, given the obvious nature of the items, which are essentially a checklist of depression symptoms. Langevin and Stance (1979) showed that the BDI correlated –.8 with the Edwards measure of social desirability (see Chapter 15). However it is likely that this latter scale measures self esteem to some extent and this would account for the negative correlation with depression. A claim that the BDI measures social undesirability would be difficult to sustain as an explanation of this result, because it would be incoherent with the high correlations with diagnosed depression. In brief, a useful measure of clinical depression.

General Health Questionnaire (GHQ) (Goldberg and Williams, 1988)

Variable measured Current psychiatric state.

Age range Adolescent to adult.

Item type Each item is a phrase referring to feelings or behaviour, preceded by 'Have you recently', recently being defined as within the last few weeks. Subjects respond on a four-point scale indicating the relevant extent of the feeling or behaviour.

Number of items Three versions: 60, 30 and 28 items.

Time taken   4 mins and 8 mins.

Reliability   Cronbach's alpha: .92 (GHQ60); .87 (GHQ30).

Differences between scales   GHQ30 was produced by removing those items which were endorsed by the physically ill and further selecting items with the highest correlations with the total score. GHQ28 was devised from a Varimax orthogonal analysis of GHQ60 which, after several analyses, finally yielded four seven-item factors, although, as was shown in Chapter 3, these scales are extremely short. The factors are: somatic symptoms, anxiety, social dysfunction and severe depression.

Q-28 is the test to use where subscales are required although the validity of these scales has relatively little evidence in its favour, as yet. GHQ60 and GHQ30 are highly similar, except for the physical symptoms, and the longer scale should be used where possible, simply on grounds of increased reliability and the extra information it contains.

Validity   Correlations between assessment by psychiatric interview and the GHQ in all its versions suggest that the GHQ is valid. These correlations were in the .7s except for GHQ30 which was somewhat lower. Using a sensitivity index (the proportion of true cases identified) and a specificity index (the proportion of normals correctly identified) all versions of the GHQ appear to be valid with median sensitivities around the .8 level and specificities even higher. All versions are satisfactory, even an experimental GHQ12 (useful with illiterate subjects where the items have to be read out), but the GHQ60 is the most efficient.

Conclusions

As a test of psychiatric disorder the GHQ seems to be a useful screening device. If for some reason subscores are required GHQ28 should be administered, despite the lack of clear evidence for the validity of the subscales. Otherwise it is sensible to use the longest version possible. Two notes of caution should be sounded. First, the test is limited to states of relatively short duration (within the last few weeks, referring to all the items). Thus long-standing problems may be missed. In addition it is not sensible to attempt to use the test in predictive work, since it measures states by definition, although some workers, including myself, have tried to do so (Goble *et al.*, 1978). In brief this is a useful screening device for general psychiatric disorder. One final point deserves mention. The fact that GHQ12 seems to work virtually as well as GHQ60 suggests that it may well be that one question such as 'Do you feel awful?' might be as effective as the test, as was the case with the Strong Interest Blank, discussed in Chapter 27.

Schizotypy Questionnaire (STQ) (Claridge and Broks, 1984)

This is a relatively new test, based on the distinction in DSM-111 (1980) between schizotypal and borderline personality disorder. The test uses typical clinical symptoms to define these personality dimensions. The interest of these scales is that they are rooted in a theoretical approach to the schizophrenias which has been articulated by Claridge (1985). Part of this theory states that some of the characteristics of schizophrenics are exaggerations of what may be found among non-psychiatric groups and the STQ attempts to assess these.

Variables measured Schizotypy, schizotypal symptoms (STA) and borderline personality (STB).

Number of items 37 in STA scale, 18 in STB.

Type of items Yes/no items, the content of which reflects the descriptions in DSM-11.

Discussion

The main reason for discussing this test, which is frankly experimental, does not lie in the uniqueness of the factors which it measures. Indeed, evidence presented in the paper by Claridge and Boks (1984) suggests that it loads on both N and P and the two scales, A and B, are highly correlated. Actually a study by Raine and Allbutt (1989) of seven schizotypy scales and P shows that the STQA and B both load highly on the schizotypy factor and are independent of the P factor. However there was no measure of N (which might be this first factor) and the sample were students. Despite these difficulties the high loadings on both STQ scales indicate that they are psychometrically efficient. Furthermore, a study by Hewitt and Claridge (1989) in which the STA was factored was encouraging since three factors emerged – magical thinking, unusual perceptual experience and paranoid thinking. These factors were identified from the items loading on them and make sense in terms of schizophrenic symptoms. Caution must be shown with this study, however, because tetrachoric correlations were used in the analysis and these have large standard errors, as was discussed in our chapters on test construction. A further study by Bentall *et al.* (1989) is relevant. These authors factored fourteen different scales of schizotypy together with the EPQ in a sample of 180 students. The analysis of the scales yielded four Varimax factors. Both the A and B scales loaded on the N factor, as defined by the EPQ, and on a factor which was labelled the positive aspects of schizotypy. In factorial terms it supports the claim that both the A and the B scales are related to P and N.

Rather than clarity of factorial structure, what is interesting about these scales is the pattern of results which have been found with them in studies with normals and schizophrenics. Thus, there is a considerable genetic component in the variance on the STA, in a study with normal twins (Claridge and Hewitt, 1985) and borderline patients are discriminated by the STB.

Beech and Claridge (1987) used the experimental technique of negative priming, where a response to a target stimulus is slowed down if preceded by a priming display containing target-relevant information and demanding a response. These effects are considered to reflect the action of an unconscious inhibitory mechanism in selective attention. Beech and Claridge (1985) found a highly significant correlation between negative priming and scores on the STA and this is what would be expected if schizophrenics show exaggerated schizotypy.

The STA has also been used in studies of hemisphere function. High scorers on the STA do resemble schizophrenics in showing either weakened or even reversed laterality with nonsense syllable (Broks, 1984) and single letters (Rawlings and Claridge, 1986). They were particularly efficient where the material was presented first to the right hemisphere. This finding was replicated in one experiment but not in another with the aural modality (Broks *et al.*, 1984).

Since these findings fit well with the theoretical position of Claridge concerning the relation of schizotypy and schizophrenia, they are powerful support for the construct validity of the STQ and they suggest that it is certainly useful in the study of schizophrenia.

Finally a study by Jackson and Claridge (1991) showed that both the A and B scales of the STQ had reasonable test-retest reliability over a four-year period and discriminated psychotic patients from controls. Again the conclusion must be that this test is most useful in the study of schizophrenia.

The Embedded Figures Tests (Witkin *et al.*, 1971)

There are three EFTs – the original EFT, individually administered and suitable for subjects 10 years old and upwards; the children's version, the CEFT, individually administered and suited to the 5–10 year range and the group test, the GEFT, which may be used over a broad age range. I shall describe the original version, the EFT.

Variable measured Psychological differentiation or field independence.

Age range See above.

Items Complex figures in which a simple figure has to be recognised.

Number of items Twelve cards per set; there are two parallel forms.

Scoring The average time in seconds to complete the set is the subject's score.

Completion time for test 3 mins.

Reliability Split-half reliabilities are around .8 and .85 for college students.

Norms The normative data by age are on small groups (Ns mainly in the .2s) and are clearly unsatisfactory. The number of college students used was 150 but this is a very small sample.

Validity of the test and conclusions

With a variable such as psychological differentiation, which is a psychological construct, not common in the real world, clear evidence for validity, in terms of correlations with external criteria, is impossible. Instead we have to rely on construct validity and this is to be found in the manual to the test.

Thus studies are cited indicating that the EFT measures field dependence in perception and, by extension, seems to refer to disembedding in intellectual functioning. It loads on the block design, object completion and picture assembly tests of the WAIS, with Piagetian tasks that would appear to require disembedding; and on a flexibility of closure factor. Further studies are cited which pertain more to the concept of psychological differentiation. This is a metaphorical use of the term, yet it seems to hold. Thus subjects high on EFT have a differentiated body concept and use more specific rather than general defences, although these measurements are suspect, being based on projective measures such as the Rorschach and TAT. Some of the studies try to relate EFT performance to pathology such as asthma or catatonic rather than paranoid schizophrenia, for example. Such results, however, although interesting, extend the concept so far that it includes almost all cognitive activity. This is particularly true when the EFT performance relates to physiological functioning such as specific vasoconstriction response to a tone.

Since psychological differentiation is a concept developed by Witkin mainly on the basis of the EFT it is difficult to attack the construct validity of these results. Psychological differentiation is what Witkin claims it to be. In this sense the test is valid. Its relationship to other psychological variables is well established. In my view its loading on the flexibility of closure factor, a well established ability factor, makes a good deal of sense in indicating the nature of the variable measured by the EFT. This test can certainly be recommended as a measure of psychological differentiation, although I would still argue that the nature of this variable needs clarification.

I shall say little more about the other versions of the EFT, the CEFT and the GEFT. The group version is highly correlated with the original – beyond .8, which given the reliabilities of the test indicates that they are essentially identical. Similarly the children's version also correlates highly with the original. These should be used where appropriate and, since the group test is easier to administer than the individual version, this is probably the best test.

COMPUTER TESTS

As was pointed out in Chapter 6 many standard tests have been computerised and since these are intended to be equivalent to the originals they will not be discussed here. Rather I shall discuss true computer tests where the special characteristics of the computer are utilised.

The Micropat (Bartram, 1987)

Micropat is an acronym standing for microcomputerised personnel aptitude tester. In fact Micropat is a fully automated selection system for pilot training. It runs on IBM microcomputers and those using the Z80S-100 bus, running under CP/M2.

Tests

Two tracking tests

1. Adaptive pursuit tracking. This has a fixed difficulty level or the level can be made adaptive to the subject's performance, difficulty being varied by changing the speed or the control law.
2. Compensatory tracking. Here varied tasks can be set up: two-dimensional displays requiring hand–foot coordination; two-dimensional, hand–hand coordination; four-dimensional, foot–foot, hand–hand.

Bartram (1987) points out that success on these tasks is related to ability at arcade video games. However there was no evidence that practice at games improved performance on the tests.

Tests of information management ability

1. Risk. A gambling task. In this one of eight keys to be used selected at random produces a penalty. After one set of trials the penalty key is present in only half the trials.
2. Two rectangles are displayed, one smaller than the other – the signal. Then a single rectangle is presented at each trial and subjects have to indicate whether this is the signal or not.
3. Dual task. Here the ability to allocate information processing resources to two tasks is measured, in this case a tracking task and mental arithmetic.
4. Landing. This test resembles a simulated plane landing. This test requires subjects to allocate attention to two sources of information – speed, fuel height – and visual cues on the screen.
5. Schedule. This is a dynamic task, in which five columns are displayed each containing a box with a target number and with five corresponding keys. When a key is pressed a line rises up the column. If it reaches the box the subject scores the number in the box. The task is complicated by a number of factors: the boxes are replaced from time to time and any

line in its column is erased; lines grow at different rates in different columns; box and line growth rate are affected by a random variable; in some boxes (specially marked) the score is doubled.

Validity and conclusions

The multiple correlation of Micropat variables with pass/fail on the advanced helicopter test in the Royal Air Force was .57 which was substantially higher than the standard procedures. Furthermore the Micropat variance was not accounted for by the traditional tests.

This is clearly a useful computerised selection battery for pilot selection. It should be noted that both the items and the scoring procedures require a computer. There could be no pencil and paper equivalent. It is still highly experimental and it would be interesting to know of its predictive powers for other comparable jobs. What should be noted about this test, however, is that both the software and the hardware are capable of withstanding use in the real testing context and that tests constructed from a task analysis of what pilots have to do can yield impressive multiple correlations. Certainly a test worthy of research with different groups and of further development and refinement.

The ABC Tests (Collis *et al.*, 1990)

The ABC tests are an attempt to develop a series of scales based upon the cognitive analysis of abilities and using items which can be generated (at any required level of difficulty) by a computer algorithm. This work is fully described in Irvine *et al.* (1990). It should be pointed out that these tests were administered in pencil and paper form although it is fair to say that, their items being generated by computer, they should be regarded as genuine computer tests.

Scales

1. Letter checking: semantic encoding and comparison, the cognitive speed factor.
2. Symbol rotation: spatial rotation, the visualisation factor.
3. Transitive inference: fluid ability.
4. Letter distance: reconstructive memory, the general memory factor. Subjects have to find which of two letters is further away from a third.
5. Number distance task. Similar to above but with numbers.
6. Alphabet forward and backward. This measures a similar factor and process to (3) but is in a slightly different form, e.g. B + 1 = C.
7. Odd man out. A typical intelligence test item, as discussed in Chapter 12.

Discussion of the ABC tests

These tests are clearly too new for a large body of evidence to have accumulated around them. Irvine *et al.* (1990) investigated five of these scales, all but (5) and (7), in a sample of army recruits. These scales were highly reliable at around .9 and items of a given difficulty level could be produced by the computer's algorithm. However, in a rotated Direct Oblimin factor analysis with other intelligence tests two factors emerged, one loading on the intelligence tests, the other on the ABC tests. Although these factors were correlated (.65) it is clear that the ABC tests cannot as yet be regarded as equivalent to intelligence tests although they are measuring cognitive abilities.

The ABC tests look promising as measures of simple cognitive processes where the items can be computer generated but more research is required before it can be claimed that these processes are the essence of intelligence.

OCCUPATIONAL PSYCHOLOGY

As was made clear from Chapter 22 the needs of occupational psychology can be well met by the best factored tests in the different fields of psychology. However since the analysis and description of jobs is so important one test, at least, which does this, deserves mention in this handbook, together with a test of occupational stress.

The Position Analysis Questionnaire (PAQ) (McCormick *et al.*, 1972)

Variables measured Twelve factors: engaging in physical activity; operating machines; contact with the public; being aware of the work environment; performing service activities; performing clerical activities; performing technical activities; performing routine activities; supervising other personnel; working regular day schedules; working in harsh environment; having responsibilities.

Number of items 194.

Type of item Each item refers to some aspect of a job and it has to be rated on one (the most appropriate) of six scales: possibility of occurrence; importance to the job; extent of use; degree of detail; amount of time; applicability.

Discussion and conclusions

This is a useful questionnaire for the objective description of jobs. The end result produces a description in terms of the twelve dimensions, thus enabling the occupational psychologist to decide the qualities necessary for its performance.

An obvious difficulty is that it cannot accurately reflect the level of activity in a job, for example the intellectual difference involved in inventing hardware for computers and working with them. In addition, despite its generality, for some jobs the items are inappropriate, although to remedy this a special version for use with professional and managerial positions has been produced – the PMPQ (Mitchell *et al.*, 1986). In brief this is a useful measure for job description.

The Occupational Stress Indicator (OSI) (Cooper *et al.*, 1988)

Variables measured There are six scales in the OSI together with a biographical questionnaire which I shall not discuss.

1. Job satisfaction. Here are five subscales: satisfaction with achievement; satisfaction with the job itself; satisfaction with organisational structure; satisfaction with organisational processes; satisfaction with personal relationships.
2. Mental and physical health. Two parts: mental health; physical health.
3. Type A personality. Three subscales: attitude to living; style of behaviour; ambition.
4. Control. Three subscales: organisational forces; management processes; individual influence.
5. Job pressure. Six scales: factors intrinsic to the job; managerial role; relationships with other people; career and achievement; organisational structure and climate; home/work interface.
6. Coping with stress. Six subscales: social support; task strategies; logic; home and work relationship; time; involvement.

Number of items Scale 1: 22. Scale 2: 30. Scale 3: 14. Scale 4: 12. Scale 5: 61. Scale 6: 28.

Type of items Statements to be answered on relevant six-point scales.

Scale construction Factor analysis was generally used although the samples were small (90, 156). Scale 5 was not factored or even item analysed but the items were used as written. This is a highly unusual and unsatisfactory procedure. It must be noted that many of the subscales are far shorter than desirable given our discussion of reliability in Chapters 1 and 3 of the handbook. One must question the validity of a three-item scale (subscale 5 of job satisfaction).

Reliability Split-half reliabilities are quoted for the scales. The reliability of many of the scales is low: all the control scales are below .22. All the Type A scales are below .45. The logic scale had a reliability of .7. Only seven of twenty-eight scales had a reliability greater than .7. This means that comparing scale scores is highly dubious.

Validity There is no evidence for validity cited in the manual.

Norms Norms for British managers are supplied but no N is quoted. Sixty-seven American bank workers form American norms.

Comments

The OSI is an instrument designed by one of the leading workers in the field of occupational stress. It is a new test and, as it is used, it is to be hoped evidence for its validity will become available. Psychometrically it needs to be improved. Further items should be written for the brief scales so that their reliability becomes acceptable. No inferences can be made about scales where most of the variance is error. The location of the factors in factor space needs to be computed so that their construct validity can be assessed. Finally the scores on the scales of different occupational groups need to be collected as a further index of the validity of the scales. As it stands the OSI should not be used for substantive work. As a basis for scale development it is useful.

Chapter 30

Finale

I hope that this handbook contains much of what any user of psychological tests needs to know to select the most suitable test and to interpret it correctly. In addition I hope it provides a basis for the critical evaluation of tests and their uses so that much error can be avoided.

In the first section can be found the theoretical and statistical basis underlying psychological tests. If this is understood the dreadful and misleading practices in testing both of practitioners in the applied fields and experimental psychologists who may want to classify their subjects can be spotted: brief tests; tests of unknown validity; claims that intelligence tests measure specific variance; the use of unrotated factors; the use of Procrustes rotations; the failure to locate factors in factor space – all examples of psychometric error which no rational reader of the first section of this handbook could make.

In the second section I discuss, describe and outline the rationale of different types of psychological test, explicating where possible the different kinds of items or materials. This indicates to readers the boundaries and limits of current psychometric testing and it makes clear where testing is on solid ground and where the tester must tread with caution. Again this section should allow a number of misconceptions to be laid to rest: that intelligence is not a useful concept; that there is no agreement concerning the variables in personality questionnaires; that projective tests are necessarily useless; that aptitude tests are vital to occupational testing; that unconscious processes are necessarily ever hidden.

Taken together the first two sections of the handbook provide a rational basis for psychological testing in its various fields. As far as is possible the arguments have been developed so that nothing is asserted and readers should be able easily to justify the use of any kind of test and admit it openly where the evidence for the validity of an approach is as yet uncertain.

The third section of the book indicates how psychological tests may be used in four typical, applied settings: educational, clinical, vocational and industrial psychology. Here the emphasis is not on the detail, which test is best used for what, but on principle. I attempt to show how psychometrics can contribute to these areas of psychology. This is important because in many cases the full potential of tests is not realised and sometimes a greater burden is placed upon them than they can bear. Current tests, even the best of them, are not perfect and results must be interpreted accordingly. Yet, well constructed and validated psychological tests are superior to interviews and the plethora of unusual tests which appear to be so popular such as colour preference or graphology.

The fourth section of this handbook sets out some of the best-known tests of each of the major categories. In most cases a clear description and evaluation of its qualities, especially its validity, is provided. Where tests are so invalid or otherwise flawed with error I have not discussed them although some famous tests such as the Rorschach for example, which it is difficult to recommend, are discussed in some detail. This, again, is so that readers can come to a rational conclusion and do not have to accept dogmatic assertion. A final chapter examines some interesting tests which do not fall easily into any group.

The aim of this final section is to put readers in the position of being able to select a good test for any purpose and to understand the strengths and weaknesses of most of the best-known and widely used measures. For obvious reasons of space this section cannot be comprehensive but I do not believe this to be a serious defect since I hope that readers of this handbook will be able to evaluate for themselves any test which they come across. Indeed, if all the tests in this section had been superseded, I hope that readers would unerringly select the best.

Finally I hope that this handbook can bring about a change. Some critics of psychometrics have described it as a pseudoscience. Perhaps, as it is prac- tised by psychologists who seem to ignore its statistical and theoretical basis and accordingly misinterpret their findings, this epithet is accurate. Yet, as the handbook makes clear, there is a sound basis to psychometrics and used properly it can contribute to psychological theory and be highly valuable in practical application. This, then, is the change: that psychologists who use tests will understand psychometrics and pseudoscience will become science.

Appendices

Appendix 1: Statistical Formulae

Attenuation due to the unreliability of measures The correlation between two tests is limited by the reliability of the tests. The correcting formula, estimating the correlation if the reliabilities are perfect, is:

$$r(\text{corrected}) = \frac{r_{12}}{\sqrt{r_{11}}\sqrt{r_{22}}}$$

where r_{12} is the obtained correlation; r_{11} is the reliability of the test 1 and r_{22} the reliability of test 2.

Chi-Squared test The formula for chi-square is:

$$X^2 = \Sigma \frac{(o-e)^2}{e}$$

where o = observed frequencies in a contingency table and e = expected frequencies.

Correlations The formulae for the different kinds of correlations are set out below.

Biserial correlation. $r_{\text{bis}} = \dfrac{M_s - M_u}{\sigma} \dfrac{pq}{z}$

where M_s = the mean score on the continuous variable of the successful group on the dichotomous variable; M_u = the mean score of the unsuccessful group; σ = the standard deviation on the continuous variable of the total group; p = proportion falling in successful group on the dichotomous variable; q = 1 – p and z = ordinate of normal curve corresponding to p.

Intra-class correlation. (B–W)/(B+W) where B = the between pairs variance and W the within pairs variance in the analysis of variance of the scores of pairs of twins.

Point-biserial correlation. $r_{\text{pb}} = \dfrac{M_s - M_u}{\sigma} \sqrt{pq}$

where M_s = the mean score on continuous variable of successful group on dichotomous variable; M_u = the mean score on the continuous variable of unsuccessful group on dichotomous variable; σ = the standard deviation on continuous variable of the total group; p = proportion of subjects in successful group on the dichotomous variable and q = 1– p.

Pearson product-moment correlation. The standard correlation coefficient.

$$r = \frac{N\Sigma XY - \Sigma X\Sigma Y}{\sqrt{N\Sigma X^2 - (\Sigma X)^2} \sqrt{N\Sigma Y^2 - (\Sigma Y)^2}}$$

where X and Y are the variables and N is the number in the sample.

Phi coefficient. $\text{Phi} = \dfrac{ac - bd}{\sqrt{(a + b)\,(c + d)\,(b + c)\,(a + d)}}$

where a, b, c, d, are the frequencies in a contingency table for items:
a = the number who passed both items; c = the number who failed both items;
b = the number who passed item two but failed one and d = the converse number.

Rank-order correlation. $\text{Rho} = 1 - \dfrac{6\Sigma d^2}{N(N^2 - 1)}$

where N = the number of subjects ranked; d = the algebraic difference in ranks for each subject in the two distributions.

Partial correlation. $r_{12.3} = \dfrac{r_{12} - r_{13}r_{23}}{\sqrt{1 - r^2_{13}} \sqrt{1 - r^2_{23}}}$

where $r_{12.3}$ is the correlation between variable 1 and 2 with the effects of variable 3 partialed out.

Semipartial correlation. $r_{1(2.3)} = \dfrac{r_{12} - r_{13}r_{23}}{\sqrt{1 - r^2_{23}}}$

where $r_{1(2.3)}$ = the correlation between variable 1 and 2 when the effects of variable 3 are partialed from variable 1 but not from 2.

Multiple correlation. $R^2_{y.123} = r^2_{y1} + r^2_{y(2.1)} + r^2_{y(3.12)}$

where r_{y1} = the correlation between variables y and 1; $r_{y(2.1)}$ = the semipartial correlation between y and 2 with 1 partialed from 2; and $r_{y(3.12)}$ = the semipartial correlation between y and 3 with 1 and 2 partialed from 3.

Shrinkage correction. $R^2 \text{ (Est)} = 1 - (1 - R^2)\,((N - 1)/(N - k))$ where R (est) = unbiased estimate of multiple correlation; R = multiple correlation found in sample of size N; k = number of independent variables.

Covariance $\sigma_{12} = \dfrac{\Sigma x_1 x_2}{N}$

where x_1 = deviation scores on variable 1; x_2 = deviation scores on variable 2; N = number of subjects and σ_{12} = the covariance.

Covariance and correlation $r_{12} = \sigma_{12}/\sigma_1\sigma_2$ where r_{12} = the correlation between variables 1 and 2; σ_{12} = the covariance; σ_1 = the standard deviation of variable 1 and σ_2 = the standard deviation of variable 2.

Delta $\delta = \dfrac{(n + 1)\,(N^2 - \Sigma f^2_i)}{nN^2}$

where N = number of subjects; n = number of items and f_i = the frequency at each score.

Factor analytic model of test variance

$\sigma^2 t = \sigma^2 a + \sigma^2 b + \ldots \sigma^2 n + \sigma^2 s + \sigma^2 e$ where $\sigma^2 t$ = test variance, $\sigma^2 a$ to $\sigma^2 n$ are common factor variances, $\sigma^2 s$ is specific factor variance and $\sigma^2 e$ is error variance. This equation can be divided by $\sigma^2 t$ and rewritten thus: $1 = a^2 x + b^2 x + \ldots n^2 x + s^2 x + e^2 x$ where $a^2 x$ = the proportion of test variance contributed by factor a and so on.

G index $G = 2P_c - 1$ where P_c = the sum of a + d in a normal fourfold contingency table.

Mean Mean = $\Sigma X/N$ where X is a score on a test and N = the number of subjects.

Regression equation To predict y from x the regression equation is:
y (predicted) = a + bx where y is the predicted score, a the intercept constant and b is the slope or regression constant.
The slope. b = $r_{xy}\,(\sigma_y/\sigma_x)$ where r_{xy} is the correlation between x and y and σ_y and σ_x are the standard deviations of y and x.
The intercept. a = mean of y – b(mean of x).

Reliability

The alpha coefficient. $r_{kk} = k/k{-}1\,(1 - \Sigma\sigma^2_i/\sigma^2_y)$ where r_{kk} = the reliability, coefficient alpha, of a test of k items; k = the number of items; σ^2_i = the item variance and σ^2_y = the variance of the test.
KR–20. $r_{kk} = k/k{-}1\,(1 - \Sigma pq/\sigma^2_y)$ where r_{kk} = the KR–20 reliability for a test with k items and all other symbols are as in the coefficient alpha; p = the proportion getting an item right and q = 1 – p.

Spearman-Brown prophecy formula. $r_{kk} = \dfrac{k(av)\ r_{ij}}{1 + (k-1)\ (av)\ r_{ij}}$

where r_{kk} = the reliability of a test with k items; $(av)\ r_{ij}$ = the average correlation among items and k = the number of items.

Standard deviation See variance.

Standard error of measurement $\sigma_{meas} = \sigma_x\ \sqrt{1 - r_{xx}}$ where σ_{meas} = the standard error of measurement; σ_x = standard deviation of test x and r_{xx} = the reliability of test x.

Transformed scores $X_t = \sigma_t/\sigma_o\ (X_o - M_o) + M_t$ where X_t = scores on transformed scale; X_o = scores on original scale; M_o and M_t = means of X_o and X_t; σ_o and σ_t = standard deviations of X_o and X_t.

Variance $\sigma^2 = \Sigma x^2/N$ where σ^2 = variance; Σx^2 = deviation scores on a test and N = the number of measurements. The standard deviation is:

Standard deviation. $\sigma = \sqrt{\text{variance}}$.

Appendix 2: Glossary

Alpha coefficient The most accurate index of internal consistency reliability.

Attenuation The reduction in size of a correlation coefficient, usually for one of two reasons: a. homogeneity of variance in one or both variables; b. low reliability of one or both measures.

Beta weights The weights used in multiple regression equations to maximise the correlation with the criterion.

Communality The proportion of variance of scores on a test or item, accounted for by a set of factors.

Concurrent validity The concurrent validity of a test is measured by its correlations with other similar tests taken at the same time.

Construct validity A test is said to have construct validity if the results of using the test fit hypotheses concerning the nature of the test variable. The better the fit, the higher the construct validity.

Content validity A test, usually an achievement test or a test of ability, has content validity if the items are judged by experts in the field to be suitable for their purpose.

Correlation An index of the degree of relationship between two variables. It runs from −1 to +1, a correlation of 0 showing no relationship, +1 perfect agreement. There are varieties of correlation coefficient which are set out below.

Biserial correlation. The coefficient suited to correlate a continuous variable with a dichotomised variable which is essentially continuous, e.g. pass/fail.

Intra-class correlation. The measure of similarity between pairs, as in the study of twins.

Phi coefficient. The correlation to be used where both variables are dichotomous, as in item analysis.

Point-biserial correlation. The coefficient suited to the case where one variable is continuous and the other is a genuine dichotomy, e.g. dead or alive.

Product-moment correlation. Also known as the Pearson product moment correlation, after the great statistician, this is the standard correlation coefficient ideal for normally distributed or at least symmetrically distributed variables.

Rank-order correlation.   This correlation, rho, is used where two rank orders are to be correlated.

The formulae for all these coefficients are set out in the statistical appendix (Part 1).

Covariance   The average cross product of two sets of deviation scores.

Criterion-keyed tests   Tests constructed on the principle of including items in scales if they will discriminate criterion groups.

Criterion validity   If a test is validated against some criterion, this is evidence of validity: a specific form of predictive validity.

Differential validity   The differential validity of a test indicates its ability to predict one criterion better than another criterion. Thus the differential ability of an intelligence test is low because it is a good general predictor.

Distributions   Bimodal distribution. A frequency distribution of scores where the scores are grouped at the two extremes of the continuum.

Normal distribution.   The bell shaped Gaussian curve with highly useful mathematical properties making it suitable for parametric statistics.

Rectangular distribution.   This is a straight line distribution of scores which maximises the discrimination of a test such that $\delta = 1$.

Error variance   The variance in test scores attributable to random error, measured by subtracting the squared reliability of the test from 1.

Face validity   A test is face valid if it appears to be measuring what it claims to measure. This may or may not be related to the actual validity of the test although some social psychologists appear to use this as their sole evidence for validity.

Facility value   In item analysis this refers to the proportion of the sample who respond correctly, or put the keyed response, to a test item.

Factor analysis   A statistical method useful for discovering the determinants of a correlation matrix and accounting for the variance with a small number of factors or dimensions. The various technical terms are defined below.

Factor.   Any linear combination of variables can constitute a factor. Such combinations are thought of as constructs, dimensions or vectors which can mathematically account for the correlations in a correlation matrix. There are three kinds of factors:

a. General factor. This is present in all tests in the correlation matrix.

b. Group factor. This is present in a group of tests in the correlation matrix.

c. Specific factor. This is specific to one test in the matrix.

Factor loadings.   These are the correlations of the variables with the factors. Factor loadings are used to identify factors.

Factor pattern.   In rotated analyses the factor pattern is the matrix of the beta weights of the variables, for predicting the factors. In orthogonal rotation the factor pattern and structure are identical.

Factor rotation. If factors are conceived as vectors then it is possible to rotate one factor relative to another. In so doing the loadings are changed but remain mathematically equivalent. There is thus an infinity of solutions but the simple structure solution is usually chosen. Rotations may be oblique or orthogonal.

Oblique rotation. These factors are oblique. They are correlated, their correlation being the cosine of the angle between them.

Orthogonal rotation. These factors are at right angles to each other and uncorrelated.

Simple-structure rotation. Rotating to simple structure aims to produce factors with a few high loadings and the rest zero. Such a solution is usually stable and easy to interpret.

Factor score. The scores for subjects based on the factors – the linear combinations of variables.

Factor structure. In rotated solutions the factor structure is the matrix of correlations of variables with factors. This is the matrix which should be interpreted in most psychological work.

Higher order factors. The factors emerging from a factor analysis are first order factors. Second order factors result from factoring the correlations between the first orders. Third order factors result from factoring the correlations between the second orders and so on.

Hyperplane. A plane in the spatial representation of factors, formed by all those variables with zero loadings on the factor perpendicular to the hyperplane.

Guttman Scale A scaling procedure used in attitude measurement, developed by Guttman, with items so ranked in order of difficulty that endorsement of any one implies endorsement of all those lower in rank.

Intercept See Regression.

Internal consistency reliability A measure of the homogeneity of the test and an index of true score variance.

Interval scale A scale in which the difference between scale points at all points of the scale is equal. Many statistical procedures assume an interval scale.

Item analysis One of the standard procedures of test construction in which each item is correlated with the total score. Those with the highest correlation are selected for further testing.

Item characteristic curve Shows the probability of correct response to an item by individuals at different levels of ability on the latent trait.

KR-20 reliability coefficient This is the alpha coefficient of reliability for the special case of dichotomous items.

Latent roots In factor analyses these indicate the size of the factors.

Likert scales Attitude tests in which responses are on five or seven-point scales such as 'strongly agree' to 'strongly disagree'.

Measures of central tendency There are three common measures:

Mean. The average score of a set of scores.

Median. The middle score of a set of scores.

Mode. The most popular score in a set of scores.

Multiple regression This is the technique in which a correlation is obtained between a number of variables and a criterion.

Nominal scale A scale in which subjects are classified, e.g. male /female.

Normalised scores A set of scores with a distribution transformed to a normal distribution.

Norms Sets of scores from different groups of subjects on a test – used to make the interpretation of test scores meaningful.

Objective test A test which can be objectively (no judgement required) scored and, in the terminology of Cattell, of which the meaning is hidden from subjects taking the test.

Ordinal scale In this scale subjects are ranked or ordered.

p values This is identical, in item analysis, to the facility value of the item (qv).

Partial correlation The correlation between two variables with the influence of a third variable partialed out.

Percentile The score below which a given proportion of a standardisation sample falls.

Power test In a power test there is no time limit. Items are so graded that only a few subjects could get all items correct, no matter how long they tried.

Predictive validity A test is said to have predictive validity if it can predict some criterion or criteria.

Principal axes or factors The factors of a true factor analysis: always a smaller number than the variables of the correlation matrix and excluding the error variance in the matrix.

Principal components The principal components of a correlation matrix differ from factors in that there are as many components as variables and because they include the error variance of the matrix.

Projective tests These are tests usually consisting of ambiguous stimuli which subjects have to describe and in so doing it is assumed that they project into their responses their own conflicts and feelings – hence the name.

Q analysis A factor analysis on which subjects rather than variables are correlated. The resulting factors reveal groups of people rather than tests.

R analysis This is regular factor analysis in which the correlations between tests are factored.

Rasch scaling An item scaling method developed by Rasch which assumes that the probability of a correct response depends upon two parameters which can be estimated independently: the extent to which the item elicits the latent trait and the status of the subject on the latent trait.

Ratio scale This is an interval scale but with a meaningful zero. This is a scale rarely found in psychometrics although some methods of test construction allow the production of such scales.

Regression With two sets of scores on variables Y and X, Y can be predicted from a regression line. This line is is described by a regression equation (see Part 1 of the appendix). In this there are two constants, a and b.

Intercept. The intercept constant, a, corrects for differences in the means of X and Y.

Slope. The slope constant, b, indicates the rate of change in Y as a function of changes in X. When X and Y are standard scores r, the correlation = b.

Reliability This has two meanings: a. refers to the internal consistency of a test; b. refers to the stability of the scores over time – measured by the correlation of scores on the same test on two occasions. The reliability squared indicates the proportion of true score variance in the test.

Response sets Patterns of responding to test items which tend to distort the validity of tests. Acquiescence, agreeing with items regardless of content, and social desirability, the tendency to endorse items because it is socially desirable so to do, are the most common.

Selection ratio The proportion of applicants accepted for a job. In personnel selection where there are many applicants the selection ratio can be low, in the reverse situation it tends to be high.

Shrinkage correction In multiple correlations, it is possible to correct for the fact that the calculations take advantage of sampling errors and are likely to yield a smaller correlation on cross validation. This is the shrinkage correction (see Part 1 of this appendix).

Spearman-Brown formula A formula for estimating the reliability of a test with different numbers of items (see Part 1 of this appendix).

Standard deviation This is the square root of the variance (qv) and is thus an index of the variability in a set of test scores.

Standard error of measurement The range of scores within which the true score (qv) falls, given the obtained score, at various degrees of probability.

Standard scores These are sets of scores transformed such that they have new means and standard deviations. There are several common types of standard score:

Stanines. A normally distributed standard nine-point score.

Stens. A normally distributed ten-point standard score, favoured by Cattell.

T Scores. A standard score with mean 50 and standard deviation 10.

Z scores. Standard scores with mean 0 and standard deviation 1.

Thurstone scales Attitude scales, developed by Thurstone, which involve judges rating statements.

True score A hypothetical score – the one a subject would have if she or he had taken the whole universe of items of which the test items are a random sample.

Unique variance In factor analysis the unique variance consists of specific + error variance.

Validity A test is valid if it measures what it claims to measure. The various indices of validity are described in this appendix: concurrent, construct, content, criterion, differential and predictive validity.

Variance An index of the variability around the mean of a set of measurements, the average of the squared deviations from the mean; the squared standard deviation.

References

Adler, A. (1927). *Understanding Human Nature*. New York, Chilton.

Adorno, T.W., Frenkel-Brunswick, E., Levinson, D.J. and Sandford, R.N. (1950). *The Authoritarian Personality*. New York, Harper & Row.

Ager, A. (Ed.) (In press). *Microcomputers in Clinical Psychology*. Chichester, Wiley.

Ahmed, S.M.S., Valliant, P.M. and Swindle, D. (1985). Psychometric properties of the Coopersmith Self-Esteem Inventory. *Perceptual and Motor Skills*, 61, 1235–1241.

Alker, H.A. (1972). Review of the MAT. In Buros, O.K. (1972).

Allison, J., Blatt, S.J. and Zimet, C.N. (Eds) (1988). *The Interpretation of Psychological Tests*. Washington, Hemisphere.

Allport, G.W. (1937). *Personality: A Psychological Interpretation*. New York, Holt, Rinehart & Winston.

Allport, G.W., Vernon, P.E. and Lindzey, G. (1960). *Study of Values. Manual and Test Booklet*. Boston, Houghton Mifflin.

Altemeyer, B. (1981). *Right-Wing Authoritarianism*. Winnipeg, University of Manitoba Press.

Altemeyer, B. (1988). *Enemies of Freedom*. San Francisco, Jossey-Bass.

Amelang, M. and Borkenau, P. (1982). On the factor structure and external validity of some questionnaire scales measuring dimensions of extraversion and neuroticism (trans). *Zeitschrift fur Differentiale Diagnostiche Psychologie*, 3, 119–146.

American Psychiatric Association (1987). *Diagnostic and Statistical Manual of Mental Disorders* (3rd Edition Revised). Washington, D.C., A.P.A.

Angleitner, A. and Wiggins, J.S. (Eds) (1988). *Personality Assessment Via Questionnaires*. Berlin, Springer-Verlag.

Angleitner, A., John, O.P. and Lohr, F.J. (1986). It's what you ask and how you ask it: an itemetric analysis of personality questionnaires. 61–107 in Angleitner, A. and Wiggins, J.S. (1986).

Anstey, E. (1966). *Psychological Tests*. London, Nelson.

Arrindel, W.A. and Ende, van der J. (1985). An empirical test of the utility of the observation-to-variables ratio in factor and components analysis. *Applied Psychological Measurement*, 9, 165–178.

Ashkanasy, N.M. (1985). Rotter's internal-external scale. Confirmatory factor analysis and correlations with social desirability for alternative scale formats. Cited in Robinson, J.P. *et al.* (1991).

Atkins, A.A. (1989). Contemporary training in psychological assessment. 325–334 in Wetzler, S. and Katz, M.M. (Eds) (1989).

Bandura, A. and Walters, R.H. (1963). *Social Learning and Personality Development*. New York, Holt, Rinehart & Winston.

Bannister, D. and Bott, M. (1973). Evaluating the person. 155–177 in Kline, P. (1973).

Bannister, D. and Fransella, F. (1966). A grid test of schizophrenic thought disorder. *British Journal of Social and Clinical Psychology*, 5, 95–101.

Bannister, D. and Mair, J.M.M. (1968). *The Evaluation of Personal Constructs*. London, Academic Press.

Barrett, P. and Kline, P. (1980). Personality factors in the Eysenck Personality Questionnaire. *Personality and Individual Differences*, 1, 317–333.

Barrett, P. and Kline, P. (1981a). A comparison between Rasch analysis and factor analysis of items in the EPQ. *Journal of Personality and Group Behaviour*, 1, 1–21.

Barrett, P. and Kline, P. (1981b). The observation to variable ratio in factor analyses. *Journal of Personality and Group Behaviour*, 1, 23–33.

Barrett, P. and Kline, P. (1982a). Factor extraction: an examination of three methods. *Journal of Personality and Group Behaviour*, 2, 94–98.

Barrett, P. and Kline, P. (1982b). The itemetric properties of the Eysenck Personality Questionnaire: a reply to Helmes. *Personality and Individual Differences*, 3, 73–80.

Barrett, P. and Kline, P. (1982c). An item and radial parcel analysis of the 16PF Test. *Personality and Individual Differences*, 3, 259–270.

Barron, F. (1953). An ego-strength scale which predicts response to psychotherapy. *Journal of Consulting Psychology*, 17, 327–353.

Barton, K. (1973). Recent data on the Culture Fair Scales. 13–20 in IPAT (1973).

Barton, K.S. (1986). Measuring emotional states and temporary role adoptions. In Cattell, R.B. and Johnson, R.C. (Eds) (1986), 344–377.

Barton, K. and Cattell, R.B. (1981). *The Central State–Trait Kit (CTS): experimental version*. Champaign, IPAT.

Bartram, D. (1987). The development of an automated testing system for pilot selection: the Micropat project. *Applied Psychology: An International Review*, 36, 279–298.

Bartram, D. and Bayliss, R. (1984). Automated testing: past, present and future. *Journal of Occupational Psychology*, 57, 221–237.

Bartram, D., Beaumont, J.G., Cornford, T., Dann, P.L. and Wilson, S.L. (1987). Recommendations for the design of software for computer based assessment – summary statement. *Bulletin British Psychological Society*, 40, 86–87.

Bass, B.M. (1955). Authoritarianism or acquiescence? *Journal of Abnormal and Social Psychology*, 51, 616–623.

Bayley, N. (1969). *Bayley Scales of Infant Development*. New York, Psychological Corporation.

Bean, K.L. (1965). The Sound-Apperception-Test: origin, purpose, standardisation, scoring and use. *Journal of Psychology*, 59, 371–412.

Beaumont, J.G. (In press). Expert systems and the clinical psychologist. In Ager, A. (In press).

Beck, A.T. (1962). Reliability of psychiatric diagnoses: a critique of systematic studies. *American Journal of Psychiatry*, 119, 210–215.

Beck, A.T. (1967). *Depression: Causes and Treatment*. Philadelphia, University of Pennsylvania.

Beck, A.T. and Beck, R.W. (1972). Screening depressed patients in family practice: a rapid technique. *Postgraduate Medicine*, 52, 81–85.

Beck, A.T., Ward, C.H., Mendelson, M., Mock, J. and Erbaugh, J. (1961). An inventory for measuring depression. *Archives of General Psychiatry*, 4, 561–571.

Beck, S.J. (1944). *Rorschach's Test. Vol.1: Basic Processes*. New York, Grune and Stratton.

Beech, A.R. and Claridge, G.S. (1987). Individual differences in negative priming: relationship with schizotypal personality traits. *British Journal of Psychology*, 78, 349–356.

Bellak, L. and Bellak, S. (1949). *The Children's Apperception Test.* New York, CPS.

Bellak, L., Bellak, S. and Haworth, M.R. (1974). *The Children's Apperception Test.* Larchmont, CPS.

Bem, S.L. (1974). The measurement of psychological androgyny. *Journal of Consulting and Clinical Psychology,* 42, 155–162.

Bem, S.L. (1981). *Bem Sex-Role Inventory: Professional Manual.* Palo Alto, Consulting Psychologists Press.

Bendig, A.W. (1959). Score reliability of dichotomous and trichotomous item responses in the MPI. *Journal of Consulting and Clinical Psychology,* 23, 181–185.

Bennet, G.K. (1965). *Hand-Tool Dexterity Test.* New York, Psychological Corporation.

Bennet, G.K., Seashore, H.G. and Wesman, A.G. (1962). *Differential Aptitude Tests* (2nd Edition). New York, Psychological Corporation.

Bentall, R.P., Claridge, G.S. and Slade, P.D. (1989). The multi-dimensional nature of schizotypal traits: a factor analytic study with normal subjects. *British Journal of Clinical Psychology,* 28, 363–375.

Berger, L. and Everstine, L. (1962). Test-retest reliability of the Blacky Pictures Test. *Journal of Projective Techniques,* 26, 225–226.

Bilodeau, A. (1960). *The Acquisition of Skill.* New York, Academic Press.

Binet, A. and Simon, T. (1905). Méthodes nouvelles pour le diagnostic du niveau intellectual des anormaux. *L'Année psychologique,* 11, 191–224.

Birnbaum, A. (1968). Some latent trait models and their use in inferring an examinee's ability. In Lord, F.M. and Novick, M.K. (1968).

Blascovich, J. and Tomaka, J. (1991). Measures of self-steem. 115–160 in Robinson, J.P. *et al.* (1991).

Bloom, B. (1950). *Taxonomy of Educational Objectives Handbook 1: Cognitive Domain.* New York, Longmans Green.

Blum, G.S. (1949). A study of psychoanalytic theory of psychosexual development. *Genetic Psychology Monograph,* 39, 3–99.

Blum, G.S. (1956). Defence preferences in four countries. *Journal of Projective Techniques,* 20, 33–41.

Bolton, B.F. (1986). Clinical diagnosis and psychotherapeutic monitoring. 348–376 in Cattell, R.B. and Johnson, R.C. (1986).

Boring, E.G. (1923). Intelligence as the tests test it. *New Republic,* 35, 35–37.

Bowlby, J. (1944). 44 juvenile thieves. *International Journal of Psychoanalysis,* 25, 1–57.

Bowyer, L.R. (1970). *The Lowenfeld World Technique.* Oxford, Pergamon.

Boyle, G.J. (1989). Re-examination of the personality type factors in the Cattell, Comrey and Eysenck scales: were the factor solutions by Noller *et al.* optimal? *Personality and Individual Differences,* 10, 1289–1299.

Boyle, G.J. and Katz, I. (1991). Multidimensional scaling of the Eight State Questionnaire and the Differential Emotions Scale. *Personality and Individual Differences,* 12, 565–574.

Bradway, K. (1964). Jung's psychological types: classification of test versus classification by self. *Journal of Analytic Psychology,* 9, 129–135.

Braithwaite, V.A. and Scott, W.A. (1991). Values. In Robinson, J.P. *et al.* (1991).

Brand, C.R. and Deary, I.J. (1982). Intelligence and inspection time. Chapter 5 in Eysenck, H.J. (1982).

Brierley, H. (1971). A fully automated intellectual test. *British Journal of Social and Clinical Psychology,* 10, 286–288.

Briggs, K.C. and Myers, I.B. (1962). *The Myers-Briggs Type Indicator.* Princeton, Educational Testing Service.

Briggs, S.R. and Cheek, R.R. (Eds) (In press). *Personality Measures (Vol 1).* Greenwich, JAI Press.

Brogden, H.E. (1949). A new coefficient: Application to biserial correlation and to estimation of selective efficiency. *Psychometrika*, 14, 169–182.

Broks, P. (1984). Schizotypy and hemisphere function – 2. Performance asymmetry on a verbal divided visual field task. *Personality and Individual Differences*, 5, 649–656.

Broks, P., Claridge, G.S., Mattison, J. and Hargreaves, J. (1984). Schizotypy and hemisphere function – 4. Story comprehension under binaural and monaural listening conditions. *Personality and Individual Differences*, 5, 665–670.

Brown, F.G. (1976). *Principles of Educational and Psychological Testing* (2nd Edition). New York, Holt, Rinehart & Winston.

Buck, J.N. (1948). Manual for the HTP. *Monograph Supplement 5, Journal of Clinical Psychology.*

Buck, J.N. (1970). *The House-Tree-Person Technique: Revised Manual.* Los Angeles, Western Psychological Services.

Burdsall, C. (1975). An examination of second-order motivational factors as found in adults. *Journal of Genetic Psychology*, 127, 83–89.

Buros, O.K. (Ed.) (1959). *The Vth Mental Measurement Yearbook.* Highland Park, Gryphon Press.

Buros, O.K. (Ed.) (1965). *The VIth Mental Measurement Yearbook.* Highland Park, Gryphon Press.

Buros, O.K. (Ed.) (1972). *The VIIth Mental Measurement Yearbook.* Highland Park, Gryphon Press.

Buros, O.K. (Ed.) (1978). *The VIIIth Mental Measurement Yearbook.* Highland Park, Gryphon Press.

Burt, C. (1940). *The Factors of the Mind.* London, University of London Press.

Buss, D.M. and Craik, K.H. (1983). The act frequency approach to personality. *Psychological Review*, 90, 105–126.

Butcher, H.J. (1973). Intelligence and creativity. 43–64 in Kline, P. (1973).

Butcher, J.N. (1990). *MMPI-2 in Psychological Treatment.* New York, Oxford University Press.

Campbell, D.P. (1971). *Handbook for the Strong Vocational Interest Blank.* Stanford, Stanford University Press.

Carlyn, M. (1977). An assessement of the Myers-Briggs Type Indicator. *Journal of Personality Assessment*, 41, 461–473.

Carroll, J.B. (1983). Individual differences in cognitive abilities. 213–235 in Irvine, S.H. and Berry, J.W. (1983).

Carstairs, G.M. (1957). *The Twice-Born: A Study of a Community of High Caste Hindus.* London, Hogarth Press.

Cascio, W.F. (1982). *Costing Human Resources: The Financial Impact of Behaviour in Organisations.* Boston, Kent.

Cattell, R.B. (1957). *Personality and Motivation Structure and Measurement.* Yonkers, World Book Company.

Cattell, R.B. (1966). The Scree test for the number of factors. *Multivariate Behavioural Research*, 1, 141–161.

Cattell, R.B. (1967a). The theory of fluid and crystallised intelligence. *British Journal of Educational Psychology*, 37, 209–224.

Cattell, R.B. (1967b). La théorie de l'intelligence fluide et crystallisée, sa relation avec le test 'Culture Fair' et sa verification chez les enfants de 9 à 12 ans. *Revue de psychologie appliquée*, 17, 135–154.

Cattell, R.B. (1971). *Abilities: Their Structure, Growth and Action.* New York,

Houghton Mifflin.

Cattell, R.B. (1973). *Personality and Mood by Questionnaire*. San Francisco, Jossey-Bass.

Cattell, R.B. (1978). *The Scientific Use of Factor Analysis*. New York, Plenum.

Cattell, R.B. (1981). *Personality and Learning Theory*. New York, Springer.

Cattell, R.B. (1982). *The Inheritance of Personality and Ability*. London, Academic Press.

Cattell, R.B. (1985). *Human Motivation and the Dynamic Calculus*. New York, Praeger.

Cattell, R.B. (1986). The art of clinical assessment by the 16PF, CAQ and MAT. 377-424 in Cattell, R.B. and Johnson, R.C. (1986).

Cattell, R.B. and Bolton, L.S. (1969). What pathological dimensions lie beyond the normal dimensions of the 16PF? A comparison of MMPI and 16PF factor domains. *Journal of Consulting and Clinical Psychology*, 33, 18–29.

Cattell, R.B. and Butcher, H.J. (1968). *The Prediction of Achievement and Creativity*. Indianapolis, Bobbs-Merrill.

Cattell, R.B. and Cattell, A.K.S. (1959). *The Culture Fair Test*. Champaign, IPAT.

Cattell, R.B. and Cattell, M.D. (1969a). *The High School Personality Questionnaire*. Champaign, IPAT.

Cattell, R.B. and Cattell, M.D. (1969b). *Handbook for The High School Personality Questionnaire*. Champaign, IPAT.

Cattell, R.B. and Child, D. (1975). *Motivation and Dynamic Structure*. London, Holt, Rinehart & Winston.

Cattell, R.B. and Coulter, M.A. (1966). Principles of behavioural taxonomy and the motivational basis of the Taxonome computer program. *British Journal of Mathematical and Statistical Psychology*, 19, 237–269.

Cattell, R.B. and Foster, M.J. (1963). The Rotoplot program for multiple, single-plane, visually guided rotation. *Behaviour Science*, 8, 156–165.

Cattell, R.B. and Gibbons, B.D. (1968). Personality structure of the combined Guilford and Cattell personality questionnaires. *Journal of Personality and Social Psychology*, 9, 107–120.

Cattell, R.B. and Johnson, R.C. (Eds) (1986). *Functional Psychological Testing*. New York, Brunner Mazel.

Cattell, R.B. and Kline, P. (1977). *The Scientific Analysis of Personality and Motivation*. London, Academic Press.

Cattell, R.B. and Muerle, L.J. (1960). The Maxplane program for factor rotation to oblique simple structure. *Educational and Psychological Measurement*, 20, 569–590.

Cattell, R.B. and Scheier, I.H. (1961). *The Meaning and Measurement of Neuroticism and Anxiety*. New York, Ronald Press.

Cattell, R.B. and Scheier, I.H. (1963). *Handbook for the IPAT Anxiety Scale*. Champaign, IPAT.

Cattell, R.B. and Schuerger, J. (1976). *The O-A (Objective-Analytic) Test Battery*. Champaign, IPAT.

Cattell, R.B. and Schuerger, J. (1978). *Personality Theory in Action: Handbook for the Objective-Analytic (O-A) Test Kit*. Champaign, IPAT.

Cattell, R.B. and Warburton, F.W. (1967). *Objective Personality and Motivation Tests*. Urbana, University of Illinois Press.

Cattell, R.B., Eber, H.W. and Tatsuoka, M.M. (1970). *The 16-Factor Personality Questionnaire*. Champaign, IPAT.

Cattell, R.B., Horn, J.L. and Sweney, A.B. (1970). *Motivation Analysis Test*. Champaign, Illinois.

Cattell, R.B., Kawash, G.F. and De Yong, G.E. (1972). Validation of objective measures of ergic tension; response of the sex erg to visual stimulation. *Journal of Experimental Research in Personality*, 6, 76–83.

Cattell, R.B., Schmidt, L.R. and Bjerstedt, A. (1972). Clinical diagnosis by the Objective-Analytic Batteries. *Clinical Psychology Monographs*, 34, 1–78.

Cattell, R.B., Sweney, A, B. and Radcliffe, J. (1960). The objective measurement of motivation structure in children. *Journal of Clinical Psychology*, 4, 39–51.

Chopin, B.H. (1976). Recent developments in item banking. In de Gruijter, D.N.M. and van der Kamp, L.J.T. (1976).

Christensen, P.R. and Guilford, J.P. (1980). *Fluency Tests*. Palo Alto, Sheridan.

Christensen, P.R., Merrifield, P.R., and Guilford, J.P. (1980). *Consequences Test*. Palo Alto, Sheridan.

Christensen, P.R., Guilford, J.P., Merrifield, P.R. and Wilson, R.C. (1980). *Alternate Uses*. Palo Alto, Sheridan.

Christie, R. (1991). Authoritarianism and related constructs. 501–571 in Robinson, J.P. *et al.* (1991).

Christie, R. and Geis, F.L. (1970). *Studies in Machiavellianism*. New York, Academic Press.

Christie, R., Havel, J. and Seidenberg, B. (1958). Is the F Scale irreversible? *Journal of Abnormal and Social Psychology*, 56, 143–159.

Claridge, G. (1985). *Origins of Mental Illness*. Oxford, Blackwell.

Claridge, G.S. (1987). 'The schizophrenias as nervous types' revisited. *British Journal of Psychiatry*, 151, 735–745.

Claridge, G.S., and Broks, P. (1984). Schizotypy and hemisphere function – 1. theoretical considerations and measurement of schizotypy. *Personality and Individual Differences*, 5, 633–648.

Clark, C.M., Veldman, D.J. and Thorpe, J.S. (1965). Convergent and divergent thinking of talented adolescents. *Journal of Educational Psychology*, 56, 157–163.

Clark, P. and Wright, C. (Eds) (1988). *Mind Psychoanalysis and Science*. Oxford, Blackwell.

Cliff, N (1988). The eigen value greater than one rule and the reliability of components. *Psychological Bulletin*, 103, 276–279.

Clyde, D. (1963). *Clyde Mood Scale*. Miami, University of Miami Press.

Coan, R.W. (1979). The Myers-Briggs Type Indicator. In Buros, O.K. (1979).

Coan, R.W. and Cattell, R.B. (1966). *The Early School Personality Questionnaire*. Champaign, IPAT.

Cohen, J. (1969). r_c a profile similarity coefficient invariant over variable reflection. *Proceedings 76th Annual Convention of the American Psychological Association*.

Collins, B.F. (1974). Four components of the Rotter Internal-External Scale: Belief in a difficult world, a just world, a predictable world and politically responsive world. *Journal of Personality and Social Psychology*, 29, 381–391.

Collis, J.M., Irvine, S.H. and Dann, P.L. (1990). *The ABC Tests. An Introduction*. London, HMSO.

Comrey, A.L. (1962). The minimum residual method of factor analysis. *Psychological Reports*, 11, 15–18.

Comrey, A.L. (1970). *The Comrey Personality Scales*. San Diego, Educational and Industrial Testing Service.

Comrey, A.L. and Duffy, K.E. (1968). Cattell and Eysenck factor scores related to Comrey personality factors. *Multivariate Behaviour Research*, 3, 379–392.

Conte, H.R. (1975). A circumplex model for personality traits. *Dissertation Abstracts International*, 36, 3569b. Cited by Plutchik, R. and Conte, H. (1989).

Conte, H.R. and Plutchik, R. (1981). A circumplex model for interpersonal personality traits. *Journal of Personality and Social Psychology*, 40, 701–711.

Cook, M. (1988). *Personnel Selection and Productivity*. Chichester, Wiley.

Cooley, W.W. and Lohnes, P.R. (1968). *Predicting Development of Young Adults*. Palo Alto, Project Talent Office.

Coombs, W.N. and Schroeder, H.E. (1988). Generalized locus of control: an analysis of factor analytic data. *Personality and Individual Differences*, 9, 79–85.

Cooper, C. and Kline, P. (1982a). A validation of the Defence Mechanism Inventory. *British Journal of Medical Psychology*, 55, 209–214.

Cooper, C. and Kline, P. (1982b). The internal structure of the Motivation Analysis Test. *British Journal of Educational Psychology*, 52, 228–233.

Cooper, C. and Kline, P. (1986). An evaluation of the Defence Mechanism Test. *British Journal of Psychology*, 77, 19–31.

Cooper, C. and Kline, P. (1989). A new objectively scored version of the Defence Mechanism Test. *Scandinavian Journal of Psychology*, 30, 228–238.

Cooper, C., Kline, P. and May, J. (1986). The measurement of authoritarian traits by objective tests; a cross-validation. *Personality and Individual Differences*, 7, 15–21.

Cooper, C. and McConnille, C. (1989). The factorial equivalence of the state-extraversion positive affect and state-anxiety negative affect. *Personality and Individual Differences*, 10, 919–920.

Cooper, C. and McConnille, C. (1990). Interpreting mood scores: clinical implications of individual defences in mood variability. *British Journal of Medical Psychology*, 63, 215–225.

Cooper, C., Kline, P. and MacLaurin-Jones, L. (1986). Inspection time and primary abilities. *British Journal of Educational Psychology*, 56, 304–308.

Cooper, C.L., Sloan, S.J. and Williams, S. (1988). *Occupational Stress Indicator*. Windsor, NFER-Nelson.

Coopersmith, S. (1967). *The Antecedents of Self-Esteem*. San Francisco, W.H. Freeman.

Coopersmith, S. (1981). *Self-Esteem Inventory*. Palo Alto, Consulting Psychologists Press.

Corah, N.L., Feldman, M.J., Cohen, I.S., Green, W., Meadow, A. and Ringwall, F.A. (1958). Social desirability as a variable in the Edwards Personal Preference Schedule. *Journal of Consulting Psychology* 22, 70–72.

Corman, L. (1969). *Le Test P.N. Manuel*. Paris, Presses Universitaires de France.

Cornelius III, E.T., Schmidt, F.L. and Carron, Th.J. (1984). Job classification approaches and the implementation of validity generalisation results. *Personnel Psychology*, 72, 247–261.

Costa, P.T. and McCrae, R.R. (1988a). *The NEO Personality Inventory Manual*. Odessa, Psychological Assessment Resources.

Costa, P.T. and McCrae, R.R. (1988b). From catalogue to classification: Murray's needs and the five factor model. *Journal of Personality and Social Psychology*, 55, 258–265.

Costa, P.T. and McCrae, R.R. (In press). The Neo Personality Inventory (NEO-PI). In Briggs, S.R. and Cheek, J. (In press).

Costa, P.T., McCrae, R.R. and Dye, D.A. (In press). Facet scales for agreeableness and conscientiousness: a revision of the NEO Personality Inventory. *Personality and Individual Differences*. (In press).

Costa, P.T., McCrae, R.R. and Holland, J.L. (1984). Personality and vocational interests in adulthood. *Journal of Applied Psychology*, 69, 390–400.

Costa, P.T., Zondeman, A.B., Williams, R.B. and McCrae, R.R. (1985). Content and comprehensiveness in the MMPI: an item factor analysis in a normal adult sample. *Journal of Personality and Social Psychology*, 48, 925–933.

Costa, P.T., Busch, C.M., Zondeman, A.B., Williams, R.B. and McCrae, R.R. (1986). Correlations of MMPI factor scales with measures of the five factor model of personality. *Journal of Personality Assessment*, 50, 640–650.

Couch, A. and Kenniston, K. (1960). Yeasayers and naysayers: agreeing response set as a personality variable. *Journal of Abnormal and Social Psychology*, 60, 151–174.

Crawford, J.E. and Crawford, D.M. (1956). *Small Parts Dexterity Test*. New York, Psychological Corporation.

Crawford, J.R. (1991). Current and premorbid intelligence measures in neuropsychological assessment. In Crawford, J.E. *et al.* (1991).

Crawford, J.R., Allan, K.M., Stephen, D.W., Parker, D.M. and Benson, J.A.O. (1989). The Wechsler Adult Intelligence Scale – Revised (WAIS-R): factor structure in a UK sample. *Personality and Individual Differences*, 10, 1209–1212.

Crawford, J.R., Jack, A.M., Morrison, F.M., Allan, K.M. and Nelson, H.E. (1990). The UK factor structure of the WAIS-R is robust and highly congruent with the USA standardisation sample. *Personality and Individual Differences*, 11, 643–644.

Crawford, J.R., Parker, D.M. and Benson, J.A.O. (1988). Estimation of premorbid intelligence in organic conditions. *British Journal of Psychiatry*, 153, 178–181.

Crawford, J.R., Parker, D.M. and MacKinlay, W.M. (Eds) (1991). *Practice of Neuropsychological Assessment*. London, Taylor & Francis.

Cronbach, L.J. (1946). Response sets and test validity. *Educational and Psychological Measurement*, 6, 475–494.

Cronbach, L.J. (1951). Coefficient alpha and the internal structure of tests. *Psychometrika*, 16, 297–334.

Cronbach, L.J. (1959). The Californian Psychological Inventory. 718–720 in Buros, O.K. (1959).

Cronbach, L.J. (1976). *Essentials of Psychological Testing* (3rd Edition). New York, Harper & Row.

Cronbach, L.J. (1984). *Essentials of Psychological Testing* (4th Edition). New York, Harper & Row.

Cronbach, L.J. and Gleser, G.C. (1965). *Psychological Tests and Personnel Decisions* (2nd Edition). Urbana, University of Illinois Press.

Cronbach, L.J. and Meehl, P.E. (1955). Construct validity in psychological tests. *Psychological Bulletin*, 52, 281–302.

Crowley, A.D. (1981). The content of interest inventories: job titles or job activities. *Journal of Occupational Psychology*, 54, 135–140.

Crowne, D.P. and Marlowe, D. (1964). *The Approval Motive*. New York, Wiley.

Curran, J.P. and Cattell, R.B. (1974). *The Eight-State Questionnaire*. Champaign, IPAT.

Curran, J.P. and Cattell, R.B. (1976). *Manual for the Eight-State Questionnaire*. Champaign, IPAT.

Dahlstrom, W.G. and Welsh, G.S. (1960). *An MMPI Handbook*. London, Oxford University Press.

Damarin, F. (1978). Bayley Scales of Infant Development. 206–207 in Buros, O.K. (1978).

Dan, P.L., Irvine, S.H. and Collis, J.M. (Eds) (In press). *Advances in Computer Based Human Assessment*. London, Plenum.

Deregowski, J.B. (1980). *Illusions, Patterns and Pictures: A Cross-Cultural Perspective*. London, Academic Press.

Derogatis, L.R., Lipman, R.S. and Covi, M.D. (1973). SCL-90, an outpatient rating scale: preliminary report. *Psychopharmacology Bulletin*, 9, 13–20.

Digman, J.N. (1979). The five major domains of personality variables: analysis of personality questionnaire data in the light of the five robust factors emerging from studies of rated characteristics. Los Angeles, Paper at Annual Meeting of the Society for Multivariate Experimental Psychology.

Digman, J.N. (1990). Personality structure: emergence of the five factor model. *Annual Review of Psychology*, 41, 417–440.

Dixon, N.F. (1976). *The Psychology of Military Incompetence*. London, McGraw-Hill.

Dixon, N.F. (1981). *Preconscious Processing*. Chichester, Wiley.

Dollard, J. and Miller, N.E. (1950). *Personality and Psychotherapy*. New York, McGraw-Hill.

Dollard, J., Doob, L.W., Miller, N.E., Mowrer, O.H. and Sears, R.R. (1939). *Frustration and Aggression*. New Haven, Yale University Press.

Dolliver, R.H. (1969). Strong Vocational Interest Blank versus expressed vocational interests: a review. *Psychological Bulletin*, 72, 95–107.

Drenth, P.J.D. (1989). Psychological testing and discrimination. 71–80 in Herriot, P. (1989).

Dryden, W. and Feltham, A. (Eds) (In press). *Psychotherapy and its Discontents*. Milton Keynes, Open University Press.

DSM-111. (1980). *Diagnostic and Statistical Manual of Mental Disorders* (3rd Edition). Washington, A.P.A.

Dunnette, M.D. (Ed) (1976a). *Handbook of Industrial and Organisational Psychology*. Chicago, Rand McNally.

Dunnette, M.D. (1976b). Basic attributes of individuals in relation to behaviour in organisations. 469–520 in Dunnette, M.D. (1976a).

Dunnette, M.D. and Fleishman, E.A. (Eds) (1982). *Human Capability Assessment*. Vol 1. Hillsdale, Erlbaum.

Eaves, L.W., Eysenck, H.J. and Martin, N.G. (1989). *Genes, Culture and Personality*. London, Academic Press.

Eberhard, G., Johnson, G., Nilsson, L. and Smith, G.W. (1965). Clinical and experimental approaches to the description of depression and anti-depressive therapy. *Acta Psychiatrica Scandinavica*, 41, Suppl. 186.

Educational Testing Service. (1963). *Multiple-Choice Questions: a New Look*. New Jersey, E.T.S.

Edwards, A.L. (1953). *The Edwards Personal Preference Schedule*. Chicago, Science Research Associates.

Edwards, A.L. (1957). *The Social Desirability Variable in Personality Research*. New York, Dryden Press.

Edwards, A.L. (1959). *The Edwards Personal Preference Schedule*. New York, Psychological Corporation.

Edwards, A.L. (1967). *Edwards Personality Inventory*. Chicago, Science Research Associates.

Edwards, A.L., Wright, C.E. and Lunneborg, C.E. (1959). A note on social desirability as a variable in the Edwards Personal Preference Schedule. *Journal of Consulting Psychology*, 23, 598.

Ekstrom, R.B., French, J.W. and Harman, H.H. (1976). *Manual for Kit of Factor-Referenced Cognitive Tests*. New Jersey, E.T.S.

Elliot, C. (1983). *The British Ability Scales*. Windsor, NFER.

Elliot, C., Murray, D.J. and Pearson, L.S. (1983). *British Ability Scales Revised*. Windsor, N.F.E.R.

Engelhard, G. (1984). Thorndike, Thurstone and Rasch: a comparison of their methods of scaling psychological traits. *Applied Psychological Measurement*, 8, 21–38.

Entwistle, N.J. (1972). Personality and academic attainment. *British Journal of Educational Psychology*, 42, 137–151.

Evan, W.M. and Miller, J.R. (1969). Differential effects on response bias of computer vs. conventional administration of a social science questionnaire: an exploratory, methodological experiment. *Behavioural Science*, 14, 216–227.

Exner, J. (1974). *The Rorschach: A Comprehensive System (Vol 1)*. New York, Wiley.

Exner, J. (1978). *The Rorschach: A Comprehensive System (Vol 2)*. New York, Wiley.

Exner, J. (1986). *The Rorschach: A Comprehensive System* (2nd Edition). New York, Wiley.

von Eye, A. (1990). *Introduction to Configural Frequency Analysis*. Cambridge, Cambridge University Press.

Eysenck, H.J. (1947). *The Maudsley Personality Inventory*. London, University of London Press.

Eysenck, H.J. (1957). *Sense and Nonsense in Psychology*. Harmondsworth; Penguin.

Eysenck, H.J. (1959). The Rorschach. In Buros, O.K. (1959).

Eysenck, H.J. (1967). *The Biological Basis of Personality*. Springfield, C.C. Thomas.

Eysenck, H.J. (Ed.) (1982). *A Model for Intelligence*. New York, Springer.

Eysenck, H.J. (1985). *The Decline and Fall of the Freudian Empire*. Harmondsworth, Penguin Books.

Eysenck, H.J. (1989). Preface. In Friedman, A.F. *et al.* (1989a).

Eysenck, H.J. and Eysenck, S.G.B. (1965). *The Eysenck Personality Inventory*. London, University of London Press.

Eysenck, H.J. and Eysenck, S.G.B. (1969). *Personality Structure and Measurement*. London, Routledge & Kegan Paul.

Eysenck, H.J. and Eysenck, S.G.B. (1975). *The Eysenck Personality Questionnaire*. Sevenoaks, Hodder & Stoughton.

Eysenck, H.J, and Eysenck, S.G.B. (1976). *Psychoticism as a Dimension of Personality*. London, Hodder & Stoughton.

Fairbairn, W.R.D. (1952). *Psychoanalytic Studies of Personality*. London, Tavistock Publications.

Fallstrom, K. and Vegelius, J. (1976). A discriminatory analysis based on dichotomised Rorschach scores of diabetic children. Unpublished Ms, University of Gothenburg.

Feltham, R.T. (1989). Assessment Centres. 401–420 in Herriot, P. (1989).

Fenichel, O. (1945). *The Psychoanalytic Theory of Neurosis*. New York, Norton.

Ferguson, G.A. (1949). On the theory of test development. *Psychometrika*, 14, 61–68.

Fisher, S. (1970). *Body Experience in Fantasy and Behaviour*. New York, Appleton-Century-Crofts.

Fisher, S. and Greenberg, R.P. (1977). *The Scientific Credibility of Freud's Theories and Therapy*. Hassocks, Harvester Press.

Fitts, W.H. (1965). *The Tennessee Self-Concept Scale*. Nashville, Counsellor Recordings and Tests.

Fleishman, E.A. (1964). *The Structure and Measurement of Physical Fitness*. Englewood Cliffs, Prentice Hall.

Fleishman, E.A. (1966). Human abilities and the acquisition of skill. In Bilodeau, A. (1960).

Fleishman, E.A. (1975). Towards a taxonomy of human performance. *American Psychologist*, 30, 1127–1149.

Fleishman, E.A. and Quaintance, M.A. (1984). *Taxonomies of Human Performance*. Academic Press, New York.

Fleming, J.S. and Courtney, B.E. (1984). The dimensionality of self esteem – 2.

Hierarchical facet model for revised measurement scales. *Journal of Personality and Social Psychology*, 39, 921–929.

Foa, V.G. (1965). New developments in facet design and analysis. *Psychological Review*, 72, 262–274.

Fransella, F. (Ed.) (1981). *Personality*. London, Methuen.

Freud, A. (1946). *The Ego and the Mechanisms of Defence*. London, Hogarth Press and the Institute of Psychoanalysis.

Freud, S. (1966). *The Standard Edition of the Complete Psychological Works of Sigmund Freud*. London, Hogarth Press and the Institute of Psychoanalysis.

Freud, S. (1905). Three essays on sexuality. *S.E.*, 7, 135–243.

Freud, S. (1908). Character and anal erotism. *S.E.*, 9, 169.

Freud, S. (1911). Psychoanalytic notes on an autobiographical account of a case of paranoia (dementia paranoides). *S.E.*, 12, 3.

Freud, S. (1933). New introductory lectures on psychoanalysis. *S.E.*, 22.

Freud, S. (1940). An outline of psychoanalysis. *S.E.*, 23, 141.

Friedman, A., Webb, J.T. and Lewak, R. (1989a). *Psychological Assessment with the MMPI*. Hillsdale, Erlbaum.

Friedman, A., Webb, J.T., Smeltzer, D.J. and Lewak, R. (1989b). *Workbook for Psychological Assessment with the MMPI*. Hillsdale, Erlbaum.

Friedman, J.M.H. (1989). Structured interviews: the experts' vantage. 83–87 in Wetzler, S. and Katz, M.M. (1989).

Gagne, R.M. (Ed.) (1965). *Psychological Principles in Systems Development*. New York, Holt, Rinehart & Winston.

Garmonsway, G.N. (1979). *The Penguin English Dictionary* (3rd Edition). Harmondsworth, Penguin.

Gesell, A. and Amatruda, C.S. (1947). *Developmental Diagnosis*. New York, Hoeber.

Ghiselli, E.E. (1966). *The Validity of Occupational Aptitude Tests*. New York, Wiley.

Gibbs, J. and Norwich, B. (1985). The validity of a short form of the Coopersmith Self-Esteem Inventory. *British Journal of Educational Psychology*, 55, 76–80.

Gillis, J.S. (1986). Classroom achievement and creativity. 447–465 in Cattell, R.B. and Johnson, R.C. (1986).

Gilmer, B.V.H. (1966). *Industrial Psychology*. New York, McGraw-Hill.

Gleser, G.C. and Ihelevich, D. (1969). An objective instrument for measuring defence mechanisms. *Journal of Consulting and Clinical Psychology*, 33, 51–60.

Goble, R.E.A., Gowers, J.I., Morgan, D.C. and Kline, P. (1978). Artificial pacemaker patients – treatment outcome and Goldberg's General Health Questionnaire. *Journal of Psychosomatic Research*, 23, 175–179.

Goldberg, D. and Williams, P. (1988). *A User's Guide to the General Health Questionnaire*. Windsor, NFER-Nelson.

Goldberg, E. (1989). Neuropsychology in the studies of psychopathology. 213–235 in Wetzler, S. and Katz, M.M. (1989).

Goldberg, L.R. (1971). A historical survey of personality scales and inventories. 293–336 in McReynolds, P. (1971).

Goldberg, P.A. (1965). A review of sentence completion methods in personality assessment. *Journal of Projective Techniques*, 29, 12–45.

Goldberg, S.J. (1972). The Californian Psychological Inventory. In Buros, O.K. (1972).

Goldberger, A.S. and Duncan, O.D. (Eds) (1973). *Structural Equation Models in the Social Sciences*. New York, Seminar Press.

Golden, C.J., Hammeke, T. and Purisch, A.D. (1980). *The Luria-Nebraska Neuropsychological Battery: Manual (Revised Edition)*. Los Angeles, Western Psychological Services.

Golden, C.J. (1981). The Luria-Nebraska Neuropsychological Battery. 191–235 in McReynolds, P. (1981).

Goldstein, G. and Shelley, C.H. (1975). Similarities and differences between psychological deficit in ageing and brain damage. *Journal of Gerontology*, 30, 448–455.

Goodenough, F.L. (1926). *Measurement of Intelligence by Drawings*. New York, Harcourt Brace.

Gordon, E. (1965). *Musical Aptitude Profile*. Boston, Houghton Mifflin.

Gordon, E. (1967). *A Three-Year Longitudinal Study of the Musical Aptitude Profile*. Iowa, University of Iowa Press.

Gorham, D.R. (1967). Validity and reliability studies of a computer-based scoring system for inkblot responses. *Journal of Consulting Psychology*, 31, 65–70.

Gorsuch, R.L. (1974). *Factor Analysis*. Philadelphia, Saunders.

Gorsuch, R.L. (1986). Measuring attitudes, interests, sentiments and values. 316–333 in Cattell, R.B. and Johnson, R.C. (1986).

Gottheil, E. (1965). An empirical study of orality and anality. *Journal of Nervous and Mental Diseases*, 141, 308–317.

Gough, H.G. (1957). *The Californian Psychological Inventory*. Palo Alto, Consulting Psychologists Press.

Gough, H.G. (1975). *The Californian Psychological Inventory*. Palo Alto, Consulting Psychologists Press.

Graham, J.R. (1990). *MMPI-2 Assessing Personality and Pathology*. New York, Oxford University Press.

Granick, S. and Scheflin, N.A. (1958). Approaches to the reliability of projective tests with special reference to the Blacky Pictures test. *Journal of Consulting Psychology*, 22, 137–141.

Gray, H. and Wheelwright, J.B. (1946). Jung's psychological types: their frequency and occurrence. *Journal of Genetic Psychology*, 34, 3–17.

Greuter, M.A. and Algera, J.A. (1989). Criterion development and job analysis. Chapter 22 in Herriot, P. (1989).

Gruenbaum, A. (1988). Precis of *The Foundations of Psychoanalysis: A Philosophical Critique*. 3–32 in Clark, P. and Wright, C. (1988).

de Gruijter, D.N.M. and van der Kamp, L.J.T. (Eds) (1976). *Advances in Psychological and Educational Measurement*. Chichester, Wiley.

de Gruijter, D.N.M. (1986). The use of item statistics in the calibration of an item bank. *Applied Psychological Measurement*, 10, 231–238.

Grygier, T.G. (1975). *The Dynamic Personality Inventory*. Windsor, NFER.

Grygier, T.G. and Grygier, P. (1976). *Manual to the Dynamic Personality Inventory*. Windsor, NFER.

Guilford, J.P. (1956). *Psychometric Methods*. New York, McGraw-Hill.

Guilford, J.P. (1959). *Personality*. New York, McGraw-Hill.

Guilford, J.P. (1967). *The Nature of Human Intelligence*. New York, McGraw-Hill.

Guilford, J.P. and Hoepfner, R. (1971). *The Analysis of Intelligence*. New York, McGraw-Hill.

Guilford, J.S., Zimmerman, W.S. and Guilford, J.P. (1976). *The Guilford-Zimmerman Temperament Survey Handbook*. San Diego, EDITS.

Gustaffson, J.E. (1988). Hierarchical models of individual differences in cognitive abilities. 35–71 in Sternberg, R.J. (1988).

Guthrie, G.M., Jackson, D.M., Astilla, P. and Elwood, B. (1981). Personality measurement: do scales have different meanings in another culture? Kingston (Ontario), Paper at Nato conference on Human Assessment and Cultural Factors.

Guttman, L. (1950). The basis for scalogram analysis. In Stoufer, S.A. (1950).

Guttman, L. (1956). Best possible systematic estimates of communalities. *Psychometrika*, 21, 273–285.

Hakstian, A.R. (1971). A comparative evaluation of several prominent factor transformation methods. *Psychometrika*, 36, 175–193.

Hakstian, A.R. and Cattell, R.B. (1974). The checking of primary ability structure on a broader basis of performance. *British Journal of Educational Psychology*, 44, 140–154.

Hakstian, A.R. and Cattell, R.B. (1976a). *Manual for the Comprehensive Ability Battery*. Champaign, IPAT.

Hakstian, A.R. and Cattell, R.B. (1976b). *The Comprehensive Ability Battery*. Champaign, IPAT.

Hakstian, A.R. and Cattell, R.B. (1978). Higher stratum ability structure on a basis of 20 primary abilities. *Journal of Educational Psychology*, 70, 657–659.

Hamilton, V.J. (1970). Non-cognitive factors in university students' examination performance. *British Journal of Psychology*, 61, 229–241.

Hammond, S.M. (1984). An investigation into the factor structure of the General Aptitude Test Battery. *Journal of Occupational Psychology*, 57, 43–48.

Hampson, S. and Kline, P. (1977). Personality dimensions differentiating certain groups of abnormal offenders from non-offenders. *British Journal of Criminology*, 17, 310–331.

Handal, P.S. and Salit, E.D. (1985). Gender role classification and demographic relationships: a function of type of scoring procedure. *Sex Roles*, 12, 411–419.

Harman, H.H. (1976). *Modern Factor Analysis*. Chicago, University of Chicago Press.

Harris, D.B. (1963). *Children's Drawings as Measures of Intellectual Maturity: A Revision and Extension of the Goodenough Draw-A-Man Test*. New York, Harcourt Brace.

Harris, R. and Lingoes, J. (1968). *Subscales for the Minnesota Multiphasic Personality Inventory*. Minnesota, the Langley Porter Clinic.

Hathaway, S.R. and McKinley, J.C. (1951). *The Minnesota Multiphasic Personality Inventory Manual (Revised)*. New York, Psychological Corporation. (Revised 1967).

Hattie, J. (1985). Methodology review: assessing unidimensionality of tests and items. *Applied Psychological Measurement*, 9, 139–164.

Heath, A.C., Jardine, R., Eaves, L.J. and Martin, N.G. (1989). The genetic structure of personality – 2: genetic item analysis of the EPQ. *Personality and Individual Differences*, 10, 615–624.

Hedl, J.J., O'Neil, H.F. and Hansen, D.N. (1973). Affective reactions to computer based intelligence testing. *Journal of Consulting and Clinical Psychology*, 40, 217–222.

Heilbrun, J.R. (1972). The Edwards Personal Preference Schedule. In Buros, O.K. (1972).

Heim, A.W. (1975). *Psychological Testing*. London, Oxford University Press.

Heim, A.W. and Watts, K.P. (1966). The Brook Reaction Test of Interests. *British Journal of Psychology*, 57, 171–185.

Heim, A.W., Watts, K.P. and Simmonds, V. (1969). *Brook Reaction Test*. Windsor, NFER.

Heim, A.W., Watts, K.P. and Simmonds, V. (1970). *AH4, AH5 and AH6 Tests*. Windsor, NFER.

Heim, A.W., Watts, K.P. and Simmonds, V. (1974). *AH2/3 Manual*. Windsor, NFER.

Helmes, E. (1989). Evaluating the internal structure of the Eysenck Personality Questionnaire – Objective criteria. *Multivariate Behavioural Research*, 24, 353–364.

Henry, W.E. (1956). *The Analysis of Fantasy*. New York, Wiley.

Herriot, P. (Ed) (1989). *Assessment and Selection in Organisations.* Chichester, Wiley.

Hewitt, J.K. and Claridge, G. (1989). The factor structure of schizotypy in a normal population. *Personality and Individual Differences,* 10, 323–330.

Hinkle, D.E. (1965). The change of personal constructs from the viewpoint of a theory of implications. Unpublished PhD thesis, Ohio, University of Ohio.

Hodgkinson, G.P. (1986). A note concerning the comparability of the standard and automated versions of the Vocational Preference Inventory. *Journal of Occupational Psychology,* 59, 337–340.

Hogan, R. (1978). The Personality Research Form. In Buros, O.K. (1978).

Hoge, D.R. and Bender, I.E. (1974). Factors influencing value change among college graduates in adult life. *Journal of Personality and Social Psychology,* 29, 572–585.

Holland, J.P. (1965). *The Vocational Preference Inventory.* Palo Alto, Consulting Psychologists Press.

Holland, J.P. (1966). *The Psychology of Vocational Choice.* Waltham, Blaisdell.

Holland, J.P. (1985a). *The Holland Vocational Preference Inventory (Revised).* Odessa, Psychological Assessment Resources.

Holland, J.P. (1985b). *Making Career Choices: A Theory of Personality Types and Work Environments.* Englewood Cliffs, Prentice Hall.

Holley, J.W. (1973). Rorschach Analysis. 119–155 in Kline, P. (1973).

Holley, J.W. and Guilford, J.P. (1964). A note on the G index of agreement. *Educational and Psychological Measurement,* 24, 749–753.

Holley, J.W. and Kline, P. (1976a). On the generalisation of the G index of agreement, g_o, for use with ordinal scores. *Scandinavian Journal of Psychology,* 17, 149–152.

Holley, J.W. and Kline, P. (1976b). On the use of the symmetrical square root in G analysis. *Scandinavian Journal of Psychology,* 17, 246–250.

Holtzman, W.H. (1981). Holtzman inkblot technique. 47–83 in Rabin, A.I. (1981).

Holtzman, W.H., Thorpe, J.S., Swartz, J.D. and Herron, E.W. (1968). *Inkblot Perception and Personality: Holtzman Inkblot Technique.* Austin, University of Texas Press.

Holtzman, W.H., Diaz-Guerrero, R. and Swartz, J.G. (1975). *Personality Development in Two Cultures: A Cross-Cultural Longitudinal Study of School Children in Mexico and the United States.* Austin, University of Texas Press.

Honess, T. and Kline, P. (1973). Extraversion, neuroticism and academic attainment in Uganda. *British Journal of Educational Psychology,* 44, 74–75.

Horn, J. (1976). Human abilities. *Annual Review of Psychology,* 27, 437–485.

Horn, J. and Cattell, R.B. (1966). Refinement and test of the theory of fluid and crystallised intelligence. *Journal of Educational Psychology,* 57, 253–270.

Horn, J. and Knapp, J.R. (1973). On the subjective character of the empirical base of Guilford's Structure of Intellect Model. *Psychological Bulletin,* 80, 33–43.

Horowitz, L., Rosenberg, A.E., Baer, B.A. Ureno, G. and Villasenor, V.S. (1988). Inventory of Interpersonal Problems: psychometric properties and clinical applications. *Journal of Clinical and Counsulting Psychology,* 56, 885–892.

Hotelling, H. (1933). Analysis of a complex of statistical variables into principal components. *Journal of Educational Psychology,* 24, 417–441, 498–520.

Howard, J.C. (1989a). The Rorschach test: standardisation and contemporary developments. 127–153 in Wetzler, S. and Katz, M.M. (1989).

Howard, J.C. (1989b). Clinical interpretation of intelligence assessment. 157–176 in Wetzler, S. and Katz, M.M. (1989).

Howarth, E. (1976). Were Cattell's personality sphere factors correctly identified in the first instance? *British Journal of Psychology,* 67, 213–230.

Howarth, E. (1978). Comrey Personality Scales. In Buros, O.K. (1978).

Howarth, E. (1980). *Technical Background and User Information for State and Trait Inventories.* Alberta, University of Alberta Press.

Howe, M.J.A. (1988). Intelligence as an explanation. *British Journal of Psychology,* 79, 349–360.

Hundleby, J.D. (1973). The measurement of personality by objective tests. 65–87 in Kline, P. (1973).

Hunt, E. (1978). Mechanics of verbal ability. *Psychological Review,* 85, 109–130.

Hunter, J.E. and Schmidt, F.L. (1982). Fitting people to jobs: the impact of personnel selection on national productivity. 233–284 in Dunnette, M.D. and Fleishman, E.A. (1982).

Husek, T.R. (1965). The Kuder General Interest Survey. *Journal of Educational Measurement,* 2, 231–233.

IPAT (1973). *Technical Supplement for the Culture Fair Intelligence Tests.* Champaign, IPAT.

Irvine, S.H. and Berry, J.W. (Eds) (1983). *Human Assessment and Cultural Factors.* London, Plenum.

Irvine, S.H. and Dan, P.L. (In press). Challenges of computer-based human assessment. Chapter 1 in Dan, P.L. *et al.* (In press).

Irvine, S.H., Dan, P.L. and Anderson, J.D. (1990). Towards a theory of algorithm-determined cognitive test construction. *British Journal of Psychology,* 81, 173–195.

Jackson, D.N. (1967). *Personality Research Form.* New York, Research Psychologists Press.

Jackson, D.N. (1970). A sequential system for personality scale development. 61–96 in Spielberger, C.D. (1970).

Jackson, D.N. (1974). *Personality Research Form.* New York, Research Psychologists Press.

Jackson, D.N. (1975). The relative validity of scales prepared by naive item writers and those based on empirical methods of personality scale construction. *Educational and Psychological Measurement,* 35, 361–370.

Jackson, D.N. and Messick, S. (Eds) (1967). *Problems in Human Assessment.* New York, McGraw-Hill.

Jackson, M. and Claridge, G.S. (1991). Reliability and validity of a psychotic traits questionnaire (STQ). *British Journal of Clinical Psychology,* 30, 45–56.

Jennrich, C.I. and Sampson, P.F. (1966). Rotation for simple loadings. *Psychometrika,* 31, 313–323.

Jensen, A. (1980). *Bias in Mental Testing.* New York, Free Press.

Jewell, L.N. and Siegall, M. (1990). *Contemporary Industrial/Organisational Psychology* (2nd Edition). New York, West Publishing Co.

John, O.P. (1990). The 'big five' factor taxonomy. Dimensions of personality in the natural language and in questionnaires. In Pervin, L. (1990).

Johnson, J.H., Giannetti, R.A. and Williams, T.A. (1979). Psychological systems questionnaire. An objective personality test designed for on-line computer presentation, scoring and interpretation. *Behaviour Research Methods and Instrumentation,* 257–260.

Johnson, J.R., Null, C., Butcher, J.N. and Johnson, K.N. (1984). Replicated item level factor analyses of the full MMPI. *Journal of Personality and Social Psychology,* 47, 105–114.

Joreskog, K.G. (1973). General methods for estimating a linear structural equation system. In Goldberger, A.S. and Duncan, O.D. (1973).

Jung, C.G. (1910). The association method. *American Journal of Psychology,* 21, 219–269.

Kaiser, H.F. (1958). The Varimax criterion for analytic rotation in factor analysis. *Psychometrika*, 23, 187–200.

Kameoka, V.A. (1986). The structure of the Clinical Analysis Questionnaire and depression symptomatology. *Multivariate Behavioural Research*, 21, 105–121.

Kamin, L.J. (1974). *The Science and Politics of IQ*. Harmondsworth, Penguin Books.

Karon, B.P. (1981). *The Thematic Apperception Test*. 85–120 in Rabin, A.I. (1981).

Karson, S. and O'Dell, J.W. (1976). *A Guide to the Clinical Use of the 16PF*. Champaign, IPAT.

Katz, M.R. (1972). The Strong Vocational Interest Blank. In Buros, O.K. (1972).

Kawash, D.F., Dielman, T.E. and Cattell, R.B. (1972). Changes in objective measures of fear motivation as a function of laboratory controlled manipulation. *Psychological Reports*, 30, 59–63.

Kay, S.R. (1989). Cognitive diagnostic assessment. 177–200 in Wetzler, S. and Katz, M.M. (1989).

Kelly, G.A. (1955). *The Psychology of Personal Constructs*. New York, Norton.

Kendrick, D. (1985). *The Kendrick Cognitive Test for the Elderly*. Windsor, NFER.

Kent, G.H. and Rosanoff, A.J. (1910). A study of association in insanity. *American Journal of Insanity*, 67, 37–96; 317–390.

Klein, M. (1948). *Contributions to Psychoanalysis 1912–1945*. London, Hogarth Press and Institute of Psychoanalysis.

Kline, P. (1967). The use of Cattell's 16PF Test and Eysenck's EPI with a literate population in Ghana. *British Journal of Social and Clinical Psychology*, 6, 97–107.

Kline, P. (1968a). Obsessional traits, obsessional symptoms and anal erotism. *British Journal of Medical Psychology*, 41, 299–304.

Kline, P. (1968b). The validity of the Dynamic Personality Inventory. *British Journal of Medical Psychology*, 41, 307–313.

Kline, P. (1969). The reliability of the Brook Reaction Test. *British Journal of Social and Clinical Psychology*, 8, 83–84.

Kline, P. (1970). The validity of the Brook Reaction Test. *British Journal of Social and Clinical Psychology*, 9, 42–45.

Kline, P. (1971a). *Ai3Q*. Windsor, NFER.

Kline, P. (1971b). Obsessional traits, and academic performance in the VIth form. *Educational Research*, 13, 230–232.

Kline, P. (1971c). The use of aptitude and interest tests for vocational guidance in a comprehensive school. York, Paper at the Annual Conference of the Education Section of the British Psychological Society.

Kline, P. (Ed.) (1973). *New Approaches in Psychological Measurement*. Chichester, Wiley.

Kline, P. (1975). *The Psychology of Vocational Guidance*. London, Batsford.

Kline, P. (1977). Cross-cultural personality testing. In Warren, N. (1977).

Kline, P. (1979). *Psychometrics and Psychology*. London, Academic Press.

Kline, P. (1981). *Fact and Fantasy in Freudian Theory* (2nd Edition). London, Methuen.

Kline, P. (1983). Cross-cultural personality testing. In Irvine, S.H. and Berry, J.W. (1983).

Kline, P. (1984). *Psychology and Freudian Theory*. London, Methuen.

Kline, P. (1986). *Handbook of Test Construction*. London, Methuen.

Kline, P. (1987). The scientific status of the DMT. *British Journal of Medical Psychology*, 60, 53–59.

Kline, P. (1990). *Intelligence: The Psychometric View*. London, Routledge.

Kline, P. (1991). *The Validity of the 16PF Test*. Maidenhead, ACE.

Kline, P. (in press a). Methodological problems in the assessment of psychotherapy. In Dryden, W. and Feltham, A. (In press).

Kline, P. (in press b). Defences: a critical overview. In Hofste, P. (ed.) *Defence Mechanisms and Personality*. Berlin, Springer-Verlag.

Kline, P. and Barrett, P. (1983). The factors in personality questionnaires among normal subjects. *Advances in Behaviour Research and Therapy*, 5, 141–202.

Kline, P. and Cooper, C. (1977). A percept-genetic study of some defence mechanisms in the test PN. *Scandinavian Journal of Psychology*, 18, 148–152.

Kline, P. and Cooper, C. (1984a). A factorial analysis of the authoritarian character. *British Journal of Psychology*, 75, 171–176.

Kline, P. and Cooper, C. (1984b). A construct validation of the Objective-Analytic Test Battery (OATB). *Personality and Individual Differences*, 5, 328–337.

Kline, P. and Cooper, C. (1984c). The factor structure of the Comprehensive Ability Battery. *British Journal of Educational Psychology*, 54, 106–110.

Kline, P. and Grindley, J. (1974). A 28 day case study with the MAT. *Journal of Multivariate Experimental Personality Clinical Psychology*, 1, 13–32.

Kline, P. and Lapham, S. (1990a). *The PPQ*. London, Psychometric Systems.

Kline, P. and Lapham, S. (1990b). *Manual to the PPQ*. London, Psychometric Systems.

Kline, P. and Lapham, S. (1991a). The validity of the PPQ: a study of its factor structure and its relationship to the EPQ. *Personality and Individual Differences*, 12, 631–635.

Kline, P. and Lapham, S. (1991b). The validity of the V scale of the PPQ. *Personality and Individual Differences*, 12, 636–641.

Kline, P. and Lapham, S. (1991c). *The Motivation Analysis Questionnaire*. London, Psychometric Systems.

Kline, P. and Storey, R. (1978a). The Dynamic Personality Inventory: what does it measure? *British Journal of Psychology*, 69, 375–383.

Kline, P. and Storey, R. (1978b). A factor analytic study of the oral character. *British Journal of Social and Clinical Psychology*, 16, 317–328.

Kline, P. and Storey, R. (1980). The aetiology of the oral character. *Journal of Genetic Psychology*, 65, 85–94.

Kline, P. and Svasti-Xuto, B. (1981). The HTP in Thailand with four and five-year old children: a comparison of Thai and British results. *British Journal of Projective Psychology*, 26, 1–11.

Kline, P. and Thomas, M. (1972). The Brook Reaction Test and the Rothwell-Miller Interest Blank. *Occupational Psychology*, 46, 31–34.

Klopfer, B. and Kelley, D.M. (1942). *The Rorschach Technique*. Tarrytown-on-Hudson, World Book Co.

Knowles, J.B. (1963). Acquiescence response set and the questionnaire measurement of personality. *British Journal of Social and Clinical Psychology*, 2, 131–137.

Kohn, P.M. (1972). The authoritarian-rebellion scale: a balanced F scale with left wing reversals. *Sociometry*, 35, 171–189.

Kokenes, B. (1978). A factor analytic study of the Coopersmith Self-Esteem Inventory. *Adolescence*, 13, 149–155.

Kragh, U. (1984). *The Defence Mechanism Test*. Persona, Stockholm.

Kragh, U. (1985). *Defence Mechanism Test Manual*. Persona, Stockholm.

Kragh, U. and Smith, G.S. (Eds) (1970). *Percept-Genetic Analysis*. Lund, Gleerups.

Krout, M.H. and Krout, T.J. (1954). Measuring personality in developmental terms. *Genetic Psychology Monographs*, 50, 289–235.

Krug, S.E. (1973). Psychometric properties of the Culture Fair Scales: reliability and validity. 9–12 in IPAT (1973).

Krug, S.E. (1980a). *Clinical Analysis Questionnaire*. Champaign, IPAT.

Krug, S.E. (1980b). *Clinical Analysis Questionnaire Manual.* Champaign, IPAT.

Krug, S.E. (1981). *Interpreting 16PF Profile Patterns.* Champaign, IPAT.

Krug, S.E. (1986). Solid-state psychology: the role of the computer in human assessment. 127–141 in Cattell, R.B. and Johnson, R.C. (1986).

Krzystofiak, F., Newman, J.M. and Anderson, G. (1979). A quantified approach to measurement of job content: procedures and payoffs. *Personnel Psychology*, 32, 341–357.

Kuder, G.F. (1970a). *Kuder General Interest Survey.* Chicago, Science Research Associates.

Kuder, G.F. (1970b). *Kuder Occupational Interests Survey.* Chicago, Science Research Associates.

Laing, R.D. (1960). *The Divided Self.* London, Tavistock.

Lang, V.K. and Krug, S.E. (1978). *Perspectives on the Executive Personality: A Manual for the Executive Profile Survey.* Champaign, IPAT.

Langevin, R. and Stance, H. (1979). Evidence that depression rating scales primarily measure a social undesirability response set. *Acta Psychiatrica Scandinavica*, 59, 70–79.

Larsen, R.J. (1987). The stability of mood variability: a spectral analytic approach to daily mood assessments. *Journal of Personality and Social Psychology*, 52, 1195–1204.

Last, C. and Hersen, M. (Eds) (1987). *Issues in Diagnostic Research.* New York, Plenum.

Layton, C. (1985). The relationship between externality and E, N, P and L: an experiment and review. *Personality and Individual Differences*, 6, 505–507.

Lazare, A., Klerman, G.L. and Armor, D.J. (1966). Oral, obsessive and hysterical personality patterns: an investigation of psychoanalytic concepts by means of factor analysis. *Archives of General Psychiatry*, 14, 624–630.

Lee, R.E. and Warr, P.B. (1969). The development and standardisation of a balanced F scale. *Journal of General Psychology*, 81, 109–129.

Lee, S.G. (1953). *TAT for African Subjects.* Pietermaritzberg, University of Natal Press.

Lefcourt, H.M. (1976). *Locus of Control: Current Trends in Theory and Research.* Hillsdale, Erlbaum.

Lefcourt, H.M. (Ed.) (1981). *Research with the Locus of Control Construct Vol.1.* New York, Academic Press.

Lefcourt, H.M. (1991). Locus of control. 413–419 in Robinson, J.P. *et al.* (1991).

Lenney, E. (1991). Sex Roles: the measurement of masculinity, femininity and androgyny. 573–560 in Robinson, J.P. *et al.* (1991).

Levenson, H. (1981). Differentiating among internality, powerful others and chance. 15–63 in Lefcourt, H.M. (1981).

Levy, P. (1966). Properties of the Holley-Guilford 'G index of agreement' in R and Q analyses. *Scandinavian Journal of Psychology*, 7, 239–243.

Levy, P. (1973). On the relation of test theory and psychology. In Kline, P. (1973).

Lewis, D.G. (1966). Commentary on 'the genetic determination of differences in intelligence: a study of monozygotic twins reared together and apart' by Cyril Burt. *British Journal of Psychology*, 57, 431–434.

Likert, R.A. (1932). A technique for the measurement of attitudes. *Archives of Psychology*, No. 140.

van der Linden, W.J. (1986). The changing conception of measurement in education and psychology. *Applied Psychological Measurement*, 10, 325–332.

Livneh, H. and Livneh, C. (1989). The five factor model of personality; is evidence of its cross-measure validity premature? *Personality and Individual Differences*, 10, 75–80.

Lord, F.M. (1952). A theory of test scores. *Psychometric Monograph*, No. 7.

Lord, F.M. (1974). *Individualised Testing and Item Characteristic Curve Theory*. Princeton, ETS.

Lord, F.M. (1980). *Applications of Item Response Theory to Practical Testing Problems*. Hillsdale, Erlbaum.

Lord, F.M. and Novick, M.K. (Eds) (1962). *Statistical Theories of Mental Test Scores*. New York, Addison Wesley.

Lorenz, K.Z. (1966). *On Aggression*. London, Methuen.

Lorge, I. and Thorndike, R.L. (1957). *Technical Manual, Thorndike Lorge Intelligence Tests*. Boston, Houghton Mifflin.

Lowenfeld, M. (1939). The world pictures of children: a method of recording and studying them. *British Journal of Medical Psychology*, 18, 65–101.

Lowenfeld, M. (1954). *The Lowenfeld Mosaic Test*. London, Newman Neame.

Luria, A.R. (1973). *The Working Brain*. New York, Basic Books.

Lynn, R.L. (1978). Ethnic and racial differences in intelligence: international comparisons. In Osborne, R.T. *et al.* (1978).

McArthur, R.T. and Elley, W.B. (1963). The reduction of socioeconomic bias in intelligence testing. *British Journal of Educational Psychology*, 33, 107–119.

McClelland, D.C. (1961). *Achieving Society*. Princeton, Van Nostrand.

McCormick, E.J., Jeanneret, P.R. and Mecham, R.C. (1972). A study of job characteristics and job dimensions as based on the Position Analysis Questionnaire (PAQ). *Journal of Applied Psychology*, 56, 347–368.

McCrae, R.R. and Costa, P.T. (1985). Comparison of EPI and psychoticism scales with measures of the five factor theory of personality. *Personality and Individual Differences*, 6, 587–597.

McCrae, R.R. and Costa, P.T. (1987). Validation of the five factor model of personality across instruments and observers. *Journal of Personality and Social Psychology*, 52, 81–90.

McCrae, R.R. and Costa, P.T. (1989a). Reinterpreting the Myers-Briggs Type Indicator from the perspective of the five factor model of personality. *Journal of Personality*, 57, 17–40.

McCrae, R.R. and Costa, P.T. (1989b). Rotation to maximise the construct validity of factors in the NEO Personality Inventory. *Multivariate Behavioural Research*, 24, 107–124.

McCrae, R.R. and Costa, P.T. (1989c). The structure of interpersonal traits: Wiggin's circumplex and the five factor model. *Journal of Personality and Social Psychology*, 56, 586–595.

McCrae, R.R. and John, O.P. (In press). An introduction to the five factor model and its implications. *Journal of Personality* (In press).

McDougall, W. (1932). *Energies of Men*. London, Methuen.

McFarland, S., Agayev, V. and Abalakina, M. (1990). Russian authoritarianism. In Stone, W.F. and Lederer, G. (1990).

McKee, M.G. (1972). Edwards Personal Preference Schedule. In Buros, O.K. (1972).

McReynolds, P. (Ed.) (1971). *Advances in Psychological Assessment Vol.2*. Palo Alto, Science and Behaviour.

McReynolds, P. (Ed.) (1981). *Advances in Psychological Assessment Vol.5*. Palo Alto, Science and Behaviour.

Maloney, P.M. and Ward, P.M. (1976). *Psychological Assessment*. New York, Oxford University Press.

Marsh, H.W. and Richards, G.E. (1988). Tennessee Self-Concept Scale: reliability, internal structure and construct validity. *Journal of Personality and Social Psychology*, 55, 612–614.

May, J., Kline, P. and Cooper, C. (1987). The construction and validation of a battery of tests to measure flexibility of thinking in army officers. Farnbororough, APRE Working Papers, WPIS/87.

Mayer-Gross, W., Slater, E. and Roth, M. (1961). *Clinical Psychiatry*. London, Cassell.

Mecham, R. C. (1977). Cited in Jewell, L.N. and Siegall, M. (1990).

Meehl, P.E. (1954). *Clinical versus Statistical Prediction*. Minnesota, University of Minnesota Press.

Meier, C. (1963). *The Meier Art Tests*. Iowa, Bureau of Education and Science.

Mellenbergh, G.J. (1983). Conditional item bias methods. In Irvine, S.H. and Berry, J.W. (1983).

Mendelsohn, G.A. (1965). The Myers-Briggs Type Indicator. In Buros, O.K. (1965).

Messick, S. (1962). Response style and content measures from personality inventories. *Educational and Psychological Measurement*, 22, 1–7.

Meyer, G.J. and Shack, J.R. (1989). Structural convergence of mood and personality: evidence for old and new directions. *Journal of Personality and Social Psychology*, 57, 670–691.

Meyer, L. and Kline, P. (1977). On the use of delegate scores in the G analysis of clinical data: a Q factor method for diagnostic classification. *Multivariate Behavioural Research*, 12, 479–486.

Miller, K.E. (1968a). *The Rothwell-Miller Interest Blank*. Windsor, NFER.

Miller, K.E. (1968b). *Manual to the Rothwell-Miller Interest Blank*. Windsor, NFER.

Miller, R.B. (1965). Task description and analysis. Chapter 6 in Gagne, R.M. (1965).

Miller, R.B. (1966). Human factors in systems. Chapter 14 in Gilmer, B.V.H. (1966).

Miller, W.S. (1970). *Miller Analogies Test*. New York, Psychological Corporation.

Millon, T. (1983a). The DSM-III: an insider's perspective. *American Psychologist*, 38, 804–814.

Millon, T. (1983b). *Millon Clinical Multiaxial Inventory*. Minneapolis, Interpretative Scoring Systems.

Millon, T. (1987). On the nature of taxonomy in psychopathology. In Last, C. and Hersen, M. (1987).

Millon, T. (1990). *Towards a New Personology*. New York, Wiley.

Mischel, W. (1968). *Personality and Assessment*. New York, Wiley.

Mitchell, J.L., McCormick, J., Jeanneret, P.R., McPhail, S.M. and Mecham, R.C. (1986). *The Professional and Managerial Position Questionnaire*. Purdue, Purdue Research Foundation.

Morgan, C.D. and Murray, H.A. (1936). A method of investigating phantasies: The Thematic Apperception Test. *Archives of Neurology and Psychiatry*, 34, 289–306.

Moseley, E.C. (1967). *Multivariate Comparison of Seven Cultures*. Cited by Holtzman, W.H. (1981).

Mulaik, S.A. (1972). *The Foundations of Factor Analysis*. New York, McGraw-Hill.

Murray, H.A. (1938). *Explorations in Personality*. New York, Oxford University Press.

Murray, H.A. (1971). *Manual to the Thematic Apperception Test*. Boston, Harvard University Press.

Murstein, B.I. (1963). *Theory and Research in Projective Techniques*. New York, Wiley.

Myers, I.B. and McCaulley, M.H. (1989) *Manual: A Guide to the Development and Use of the Myers-Briggs Type Indicator*. Palo Alto, CA, Consulting Psychologists Press.

Nelson-Jones, R. (1982). *The Theory and Practice of Counselling Psychology*. London, Holt, Rinehart & Winston.

Nesselroade, J.R. and Baltes, P.B. (1975). Higher-order convergence of two distinct personality systems: Cattell's HSPQ and Jackson's PRF. *Multivariate Behaviour Research*, 10, 387–408.

Nettelbeck, T. (1982). Inspection Time: an index for intelligence. *Quarterly Journal of Experimental Psychology*, 24a, 299–312.

Nettelbeck, T. and Lally, M. (1976). Inspection Time and measured intelligence. *British Journal of Psychology*, 67, 17–22.

de Nisi, A.S., Cornelius III, E.T. and Blencoe, A.G. (1987). Further investigation of common knowledge effects on job analysis ratings. *Journal of Applied Psychology*, 72, 161–168.

Noller, P., Law, H. and Comrey, A.L. (1987). Cattell, Comrey and Eysenck personality factors compared: more evidence for the five robust factors. *Journal of Personality and Social Psychology*, 53, 775–782.

Noller, P., Law, H. and Comrey, A.L. (1988). Factor analysis of the Comrey Personality Scales in an Australian Sample. *Multivariate Behavioural Research*, 23, 387–411.

Norman, W.T. (1963). Towards an adequate taxonomy of personality attributes. *Journal of Abnormal and Social Psychology*, 65, 574–583.

Nowicki, S. and Duke, M.P. (1974). The locus of control scale for college as well as non-college adults. *Journal of Personality Assessment*, 38, 36–137.

Nowlis, V. and Green, R.F. (1957). The experimental analysis of mood. Brussels, *Proceedings of the 15th International Congress of Psychology*.

Nunnally, J.O. (1978). *Psychometric Theory*. New York, McGraw-Hill.

O'Brien, T. and Dugdale, V. (1978). Questionnaire administration by computer. *Journal of the Market Research Society*, 20, 228–237.

Ortar, C.R. (1963). Is a verbal test cross-cultural? *Scripta Hierosolymitana*, 13, 219–235.

Osborne, R.T., Noble, C.E. and Weyl, N. (Eds) (1978). *Human Variation; The Biopsychology of Age, Race and Sex*. New York, Academic Press.

Paulhus, D. (1983). Sphere specific memories of perceived control. *Journal of Personality and Social Psychology*, 44, 1253–1265.

Pedley, R.R. (1955). *The Comprehensive School*. Harmondsworth, Penguin Books.

Perry, P.C. (1952). *GZ Temperament Map (R-gram)*. Beverly Hills, Sheridan.

Pervin, L. (Ed.) (1990). *Handbook of Personality Theory and Research*. New York, Guilford Press.

Peterson, N.G. and Bownas, D.A. (1982). Skill, task structure and performance acquisition. 49–105 in Dunnette, M.D. and Fleishman, E.A. (1982).

Phares, E.J. (1976). *Locus of Control in Personality*. Morristown, General Learning Press.

Phillipson, H. (1955). *The Object Relations Technique*. London, Tavistock.

Piaget, J. (1947). *The Psychology of Intelligence*. London, Routledge & Kegan Paul.

Pichot, P. and Perse, J. (1967). Analyse factorielle et structure de la personalité. *Paper in Honour of Prof. Essen-Muller*, Lund, University of Lund.

Piedmont, R.L., McCrae, R.R. and Costa, P.T. (1991). Adjective check list scales and the five factor model. *Journal of Personality and Social Psychology*, 60, 630–637.

Piers, E.V. (1984). *Piers-Harris Children's Self Concept Scale (Revised Edition)*. Los Angeles, Western Psychological Services.

Piotrowski, Z.A. (1957). *Perceptanalysis*. New York, Macmillan.

Plutchik, R. (1980). *Emotions: A Psychoevolutionary Synthesis*. New York, Harper & Row.

Plutchik, R. and Conte, H.R. (1989). Measuring emotions and their derivatives: personality traits, ego defences and coping styles. 239–269 in Wetzler, S. and Katz, M. (1989).

Popham, S.M. and Holden, R.R. (1991). Psychometric properties of the MMPI factor scales. *Personality and Individual Differences*, 12, 513–517.

Popper, K. (1959). *The Logic of Scientific Discovery*. New York, Basic Books.

Porter, R.B. and Cattell, R.B. (1963). *The Child's Personality Questionnaire.* Champaign, IPAT.

Porteus, S.D. (1965). *Porteus Maze Test: Fifty Years Application.* Palo Alto, Pacific Books.

Quereshi, M.Y. (1972). The Differential Aptitude Test. In Buros, O.K. (1972).

Rabin, A.E. (Ed.) (1981). *Assessment with Projective Techniques.* New York, Springer.

Raine, A. and Allbutt, J. (1989). Factors of schizoid personality. *British Journal of Clinical Psychology,* 28, 31–40.

Raju, M.S., Burke, M.J. and Normand, J. (1990). A new approach to utility analysis. *Journal of Applied Psychology,* 75, 3–12.

Rapaport, D., Gill, M. and Schafer, R. (1945). *Diagnostic Psychological Testing.* Chicago, Year Book Publishers.

Rasch, G. (1960). *Probabilistic Models for some Intelligence and Attainment Tests.* Copenhagen, Denmark Institute of Education.

Rasch, G. (1961). On general laws and the meaning of measurement in psychology. In *Proceedings of the Fourth Berkeley Symposium on Mathematical and Statistical Psychology,* Berkeley, University of California Press.

Rasch, G. (1966). An item analysis which takes individual differences into account. *British Journal of Mathematical and Statistical Psychology,* 19, 49–57.

Raven, J.C. (1938). *Progressive Matrices: A Perceptual Test of Intelligence.* London, H.K. Lewis.

Raven, J.C. (1965a). *Progressive Matrices.* London, H.K. Lewis.

Raven, J.C. (1965b). *The Crichton Vocabulary Scale.* London, H.K. Lewis.

Raven, J.C. (1965c). *The Mill-Hill Vocabulary Scale.* London, H.K. Lewis.

Rawlings, D. and Claridge, G.S. (1986). Schizotypy and hemisphere function – 3. Performance asymmetries on tasks of letter recognition and broad global processing. *Personality and Individual Differences,* 6, 657–663.

Ray, J.J. (1970). The development and validation of a balanced dogmatism scale. *Australian Journal of Psychology,* 22, 253–260.

Ray, J.J. (1971). An 'attitude towards authority' scale. *Australian Psychologist,* 6, 31–50.

Reitan, R.M. and Davison, C.A. (1974). *Clinical Neuropsychology: Current Status and Applications.* New York, Winston/Wiley.

Robinson, J.P, Shaver, P.R. and Wrightsman, L.S. (Eds) (1991). *Measures of Personality and Social Psychological Attitudes.* New York, Academic Press.

Rodger, A. (1962). *The Seven Point Plan.* London, Paper No. 1, NIIP.

Rogers, H.J. (1984). Fit statistics for latent trait models. Unpublished MSc thesis, University of New England, Armidale.

Roid, G.H. and Fitts, W.H. (1988). *Tennessee Self-Concept Scale (Revised Manual).* Los Angeles, Western Psychological Services.

Rokeach, M. (1956). Political and religious dogmatism: an alternative to the authoritarian personality. *Psychological Monographs,* 70, No. 425.

Rokeach, M. (1960). *The Open and Closed Mind.* New York, Basic Books.

Rokeach, M. (1967). *Value Survey.* Sunnyvale, Halgren Tests.

Rokeach, M. (1973). *The Nature of Human Values.* New York, Free Press.

Rorschach, H. (1921). *Psychodiagnostics.* Berne, Hans Huber.

Rosenberg, M. (1965). *Society and The Adolescent Self-Image.* Princeton, Princeton University Press.

Rosenthal, R. and Jacobson, L. (1968). *Pygmalion in the Classroom.* New York, Holt, Rinehart & Winston.

Roskam, E.E. (1985). Current issues in item-response theory: beyond psychometrics.

3–20 in Roskam, E.E. (Ed.) (1985), *Measurement and Personality Assessment*, Amsterdam, Elsevier.

Rotter, J.B. (1966). Generalised expectancies for internal versus external control of reinforcement. *Psychological Monographs*, 80, No. 609.

Rotter, J.B. (1975). Some problems and misconceptions related to the construct of internal versus external control of reinforcement. *Journal of Consulting and Clinical Psychology*, 43, 56–67.

Royce, J.R. (1963). Factors as theoretical constructs. Chapter 24 in Jackson, D.N. and Messick, S. (1967).

Rushton, J. (1966). The relationship between personality and scholastic success in 11 year old children. *British Journal of Educational Psychology*, 36, 178–184.

Rust, J. (1990). *The Rapid Personalty Questionnaire*. London, Psychometric Systems.

Sandler, J. (1948). A factor analysis of the Rorschach Test with adult mental patients. *Proceedings of the 12th Annual Congress of Psychology*.

Sandler, J. (1958). Some notes on delegate analysis. In Tacon, S.F., An investigation of some psychoneurotic symptoms in adult neurotic patients. Unpublished PhD thesis, University of London.

Sapinkopf, R.C. (1978). A computer adaptive testing approach to the measurement of personality variables. *Dissertation Abstracts International*, 38, 10b, 4993.

Sappenfield, B.R. (1965). The Blacky Pictures. In Buros, O.K. (1965).

Schafer, R. (1954). *Psychoanalytic Interpretation in Rorschach Testing*. New York, Grune & Stratton.

Schmidt, F.L. and Hunter, J.E. (1981). Employment Testing: old theories and new research findings. *American Psychologist*, 36, 1128–1137.

Schmidt, F.L., Berner, J.G. and Hunter, J.E. (1973). Racial differences in validity of employment tests: reality or illusion? *Journal of Applied Psychology*, 53, 5–9.

Schmidt, F.L., Hunter, J.E., Pearlman, K. and Shane, G.S. (1979). Further tests of the Schmidt-Hunter validity generalisation model. *Personnel Psychology*, 32, 257–258.

Schonell, F.J. (1951). *The Schonell Reading Tests*. Edinburgh, Oliver & Boyd.

Schonell, F.J. and Schonell, F.E. (1950). *Diagnostic and Attainment Testing*. Edinburgh, Oliver & Boyd.

Schuerger, J.M. and Watterson, D.G. (1977). *Using Tests and Other Information in Counselling: A Decision Model for Practitioners*. Champaign, IPAT.

Schuerger, J.M., Zarrela, K.L. and Katz, K.S. (1989). Factors that influence the temporal stability of personality by questionnaire. *Journal of Personality and Social Psychology*, 56, 777–783.

Schuler, H. and Guldin, A. (1991) Methodological issues in personnel selection research. 213–264 in Cooper, C.L. and Robertson, I.T. (1991).

Seashore, C.E. (1919). *The Psychology of Musical Talent*. New York, Silver Burdett.

Seashore, C.E., Lewis, D. and Saetveit, J.G. (1960). *Manual for the Seashore Measures of Musical Talents*. New York, Psychological Corporation.

Semeonoff, B. (1971). *Projective Tests*. Chichester, Wiley.

Semeonoff, B. (1981). *Projective Techniques*. 37–55 in Fransella, F. (1981).

Shapiro, D.A., Barkham, M., Hardy, G.E. and Morrison, L.A. (1990). The second Sheffield psychotherapy project: rationale, design and preliminary outcome data. *British Journal of Medical Psychology*, 63, 97–108.

Shaver, P.R. and Brennan, K.A. (1991). Measures of depression and loneliness. 195–289 in Robinson, J.P. *et al.* (1990).

Shuter, R. (1968). *The Psychology of Musical Ability*. London, Methuen.

Sjoback, H. (1967). *The Defence Mechanism Test*. Lund, The Colytographic Research Foundation.

Sjoback, H. (1988). *The Defence Mechanism Test: A Bibliography.* Lund, Dept of Psychology.

Skinner, B.F. (1953). *Science and Human Behaviour.* New York, Macmillan.

Slater, P. (1964). *The Principal Components of a Repertory Grid.* London, Vincent Andrews.

Slater, P. (Ed.) (1976). *The Measurement of Intrapersonal Space by Grid Technique (Vol. 1).* London, Wiley.

Smail, D. (1984). *Illusion and Reality.* London, Dent.

Smith, G.S. and Westerlundh, B. (1980). Perceptgenesis: a process perspective on perception and personality. *Review of Personality and Social Psychology,* 1, 94–124.

Smith, M. (1986). Selection: where are the best prophets? *Personnel Management,* December, 63.

Sparrow, J. (1989). The utility of the PAQ in relating job behaviour to traits. *Journal of Occupational Psychology,* 62, 151–162.

Spearman, C. (1904). 'General Intelligence': objectively determined and measured. *American Journal of Psychology,* 15, 201–292.

Spearman, C. (1927). *The Abilities of Man.* London, Macmillan.

Spielberger, C.D. (Ed.) (1970). *Current Topics in Clinical Community Psychology (Vol. 2).* New York, Academic Press.

Spielberger, C.D., Gorsuch, D.L. and Lushene, R.E. (1970). *Manual for the State-Trait Anxiety Inventory.* Palo Alto, Consulting Psychologists Press.

Spranger, E. (1928). *Types of Men.* New York, Steckhert-Hafner.

Stahmann, R.F. (1971). The Kuder General Interest Survey. *Journal of Counselling Psychology,* 18, 190–191.

Sternberg, R.J. (1977). *Intelligence, Information-Processing and Analogical Reasoning: The Componential Analysis of Human Abilities.* Hillsdale, Erlbaum.

Sternberg, R.J. (1981). Testing and cognitive psycholgy. *American Psychologist,* 36, 1181–1189.

Sternberg, R.J. (Ed.) (1988). *Advances in the Psychology of Human Intelligence (Vol. 4).* Hillsdale, Erlbaum.

Stone, W.F. and Lederer, G. (Eds) (1990). *Strength and Weakness: the Authoritarian Personality Today.* New York, Springer-Verlag.

Stott, L.H. (1957). *Bristol Social Adjustment Guides.* Windsor, N.F.E.R.

Stoufer, S.A. (Ed.) (1950). *Studies on Social Psychology in World War 2. Vol. 4 Measurement and Prediction.* Princeton, Princeton University Press.

Stricker, L.J. and Ross, R. (1964). An assessment of some structural properties of the Jungian personality typology. *Journal of Abnormal and Social Psychology,* 68, 62–71.

Stringer, P. (1976). Factor structure of the DPI. In Grygier, T. and Grygier, P. (1976).

Strong, E.K. (1927). A vocational interest test. *The Educational Record,* 8, 107–121.

Strong, E.K. and Campbell, D.P. (1974). *Strong-Campbell Interest Inventory (Revised Edition).* Stanford, Stanford University Press.

Strong, E.K., Campbell, D.P., Berdie, R.E. and Clerk, K.E. (1971). *Strong Vocational Interest Blank.* Stanford, Stanford University Press.

Sundberg, N.D. (1965). The Myers-Briggs Type Indicator. In Buros, O.K. (1965).

Swartz, J.D. (1978). The TAT. In Buros, O.K. (1978).

Sweney, A.B. and Cattell, R.B. (1980). *Manual for the Vocational Interest Measure.* Champaign, IPAT.

Sweney, A.B., Anton, M.T. and Cattell, R.B. (1986). Evaluating motivation structure, conflict and adjustment. 288–315 in Cattell, R.B. and Johnson, R.C. (1986).

Tatsuoka, M.M. (1971). *Multivariate Analysis.* New York, Wiley.

Taylor, J.A. (1953). A personality scale of manifest anxiety. *Journal of Abnormal and Social Psychology,* 48, 285–290.

Terman, L.M. and Merrill, M.A. (1960). *Stanford-Binet Intelligence Scale*. New York, Houghton Mifflin.

Terman, L.M. and Oden, M. (1959). *The Gifted Group at Mid-Life*. Stanford, California University Press.

Theunissen, T.J.J.M. (1986). Some applications of optimization algorithms in test design and adaptive testing. *Applied Psychological Measurement*, 10, 381–390.

Thorndike, E.L. (1919). *An introduction to the Theory of Mental and Social Measurements*. New York, Teachers' College, Columbia.

Thorndike, R.L. (1959). The Californian Psychological Inventory. In Buros, O.K. (1959).

Thorndike, R.L. and Hagen, E.P. (1977). *Measurement and Evaluation in Psychology and Education* (4th Edition). New York, Wiley.

Thorndike, R.L., Hagen, E.P., and Sattler, J. (1985). *Stanford-Binet Intelligence Scale: Fourth Edition*. New York, Houghton Mifflin.

Thurstone, L.L. (1925). A method of scaling psychological and educational tests. *Journal of Educational Psychology*, 16, 433–451.

Thurstone, L.L. (1938). *Primary Mental Abilities*. Chicago, University of Chicago Press.

Thurstone, L.L. (1947). *Multiple Factor Analysis. A Development and Expansion of Vectors of the Mind*. Chicago, University of Chicago Press.

Thurstone, L.L. and Thurstone, T.W. (1962). *SRA Primary Mental Abilities Test*. Chicago, Science Research Associates.

Thyssen, D. and Steinberg, L. (1988). Data analysis using item response theory. *Psychological Bulletin*, 104, 385–395.

Tiffin, J. (1965). *Purdue Pegboard: Examiner's Manual*. Chicago, Science Research Associates.

Tinbergen, N. (1951). *The Study of Instinct*. Oxford, Oxford University Press.

Tomkins, S.S. (1947). *The Thematic Apperception Test*. New York, Grune & Stratton.

Undheim, J.O. (1981). On Intelligence 2: a neo-Spearman model to replace Cattell's theory of fluid and crystallised intelligence. *Scandinavian Journal of Psychology*, 22, 181–187.

USA Government Printing Office (1970). *General Aptitude Test Battery Manual*. Washington, USA Government Printing.

Vale, C.D. (1981). Design and implementation of a micro-computer based adaptive testing system. *Behaviour Research Methods and Instrumentation*, 13, 399–406.

Vale, C.D. (1986). Linking item parameters on to a common scale. *Applied Psychological Measurement*, 10, 333–344.

Vardy, M.M. (1989). Scales for the assessment of formal thought disorder. 203–212 in Wetzler, S. and Katz, M. (1989).

Vegelius, J. (1973). Correlation coefficients as scalar products in Euclidean spaces. *Report 145*, Dept of Psychology, University of Uppsala.

Vegelius, J. (1974). On various G index generalisations and their applicability within the clinical domain. *Acta Universitatis Uppsaliensis*, 4, Uppsala.

Velicer, W.F. (1976). Determining the number of components from the matrix of partial correlations. *Multivariate Behavioural Research*, 12, 3–22.

Velicer, W.F. and Jackson, D.N. (1990). Component analysis versus common factor analysis: some issues in selecting an appropriate procedure. *Multivariate Behavioural Research*, 25, 1–28.

Vernon, P.E. (1950). *The Measurement of Abilities*. London, University of London Press.

Vernon, P.E. (1960). *Intelligence and Attainment Tests*. London, University of London Press.

Vernon, P.E. (1961). *The Measurement of Abilities*. London, University of London Press.

Vernon, P.E. (1963). *Personality Assessment*. London, Methuen.

Vernon, P.E. (1979). *Intelligence, Heredity and Environment*. New York, W.H. Freeman.

Vernon, P.E. and Parry, J.B. (1949). *Personnel Selection in the British Forces*. London, University of London Press.

Vetter, H.J. and Smith, B.D. (Eds) (1971). *Personality Theory: A Source Book*. New York, Appleton-Century-Crofts.

Wallace, G. and Worthington, A.G. (1970). The dark adaptation index of perceptual defence: a procedural improvement. *Australian Journal of Psychology*, 22, 41–46.

Waller, N.G. and Reise, S.P. (1989). Computerised adaptive personality assessment. *Journal of Personality and Social Psychology*, 57, 1051–1056.

Wallston, K.A., Wallston, B.S. and De Vellis, R. (1978). Development of the Multidimensional Health Locus of Control Scales. *Health Education Monographs*, 6, 161–170.

Warren, N. (Ed.) (1977). *Studies in Cross-Cultural Psychology*. London, Academic Press.

Warrington, E.K. (1975). The selected impairment of semantic memory. *Quarterly Journal of Experimental Psychology*, 27, 635–657.

Warrington, E.K. (1982). Neuropsychological studies of object recognition. *Philosophical Transactions of The Royal Society*, B298, 16–33.

Warrington, E.K. (1984). *Recognition Memory Test*. Windsor, NFER.

Watson, D. (1988). Vicissitudes of mood measurement: effects of varying descriptions, time frames and response formats on measures of positive and negative affect. *Journal of Personality and Social Psychology*, 55, 128–141.

Watson, D. and Tellegen, A. (1985). Towards a consensual structure of mood. *Psychological Bulletin*, 98, 219–235.

Watson, D., Clarke, L.A. and Tellegen, A. (1988). Development and validation of brief measures of positive and negative affect. *Journal of Personality and Social Psychology*, 54, 1063–1070.

Watson, G. and Glaser, E.M. (1964). *Critical Thinking Appraisal*. New York, Harcourt Brace Jovanovich.

Wechsler, D. (1944). *Measurement of Adult Intelligence* (3rd edition). Baltimore, Williams & Wilkins.

Wechsler, D. (1958). *The Measurement and Appraisal of Adult Intelligence* (4th edition). Baltimore, Williams and Wilkins.

Wechsler, D. (1974). *Manual for the Wechsler Intelligence Scale for Children (Revised)*. New York, Psychological Corporation.

Wechsler, D. (1975). Intelligence defined and undefined: a relativistic appraisal. *American Psychologist*, 30, 135–139.

Weizenbaum, J. (1965). ELIZA – a computer program for the study of natural language communication between man and machine. *Communications of the Association for Computing Machining*, 9, 30–45.

Wenig, P. (1952). The relative role of naive, artistic, cognitive and press compatibility, misperceptions and ego defence operations in tests of misperception. Unpublished MSc thesis, University of Illinois.

Werner, P.D. and Pervin, L.A. (1986). The content of personality test items. *Journal of Personality and Social Psychology*, 51, 622–628.

Westerlundh, B. (1976). *Aggression, Anxiety and Defence*. Lund, Gleerups.

Westerlundh, B. (1990). The reliability of scoring the DMT. Paper at DMT Conference, Copenhagen.

Wetzler, S. and Katz, M.M. (Eds) (1989). *Contemporary Approaches to Psychological Assessment*. New York, Brunner Mazel.

Wheeler, L. (Ed.) (1980). *Review of Personality and Social Psychology*, 1, Beverly Hills, Sage.

Wiener-Levy, D. and Exner, J.E. (1981). The Rorschach Comprehensive system: an overview. 236–293 in McReynolds, P. (1981).

Wiggins, J.S. (1980). Circumplex models of interpersonal behaviour. 265–294 in Wheeler, L. (1980).

Williams, P.A., Kirk, B.A. and Frank, A.C. (1968). New mens' SVIB: a comparison with the old. *Journal of Counselling Psychology*, 15, 187–214.

Wilmott, A.S. and Fowles, D.E. (1974). *The Objective Interpretation of Test Performance: The Rasch Model Applied*. Windsor, NFER.

Wilson, E.O. (1978). *On Human Nature*. Boston, Harvard University Press.

Wilson, G.D. (1975). *Manual for the Wilson-Patterson Attitude Inventory*. Windsor, NFER.

Wilson, G.D. and Patterson, J.R. (1970). *The Conservatism Scale*. Windsor, NFER.

Wilson, S.L., Thompson, J.A. and Wylie, G. (1982). Automated psychological testing for the severely physically handicapped. *International Journal of Man Machine Studies*, 17, 321–330.

Wing, H.D. (1936). Tests of musical ability in children. MA thesis, University of London.

Wing, H.D. (1962). A revision of the Wing Musical Aptitude Test. *Journal of Research in Musical Education*, 10, 39–46.

Witkin, H.A. (1962). *Psychological Differentiation*. New York, Wiley.

Witkin, A., Oltman, P.K., Raskin, E. and Karp, S.A. (1971). *Manual to the Embedded Figures Tests*. Palo Alto, Consulting Psychologists Press.

Woliver, R.E. and Saeks, S.D. (1986). Intelligence and primary aptitudes: test design and tests avaliable. 166–188 in Cattell, R.B. and Johnson, R.C. (1986).

Wood, R. (1976). Trait measurement and item banks. In de Gruijter, D.N.M. and van der Kamp, L.J.T. (1976).

Wood, R. (1978). Fitting the Rasch model: a heady tale. *British Journal of Mathematical and Statistical Psychology*, 31, 27–32.

Wright, B.D. (1968). Sample free calibration and person measurement. Paper in *Proceedings of International Conference on Testing problems*, Princeton, Educational Testing Service.

Yalom, I.D. (1991). *Love's Executioner and Other Tales of Psychotherapy*. Harmondsworth, Penguin Books.

Name Index

Subject Index

MECHANICS OF FLUIDS

Also published by Van Nostrand Reinhold:

B. S. Massey: *Units, Dimensional Analysis and Physical Similarity*